JOHN RAE'S ARCTIC CORRESPONDENCE, 1844–1855

TouchWood Editions
touchwoodeditions.com

LIBRARY AND ARCHIVES CANADA CATALOGUING IN PUBLICATION
Rae, John, 1813–1893
[Correspondence with the Hudson's Bay Company on Arctic exploration, 1844–1855]
John Rae's Arctic correspondence, 1844–1855 / with a foreword by Ken McGoogan.

(Classics West)
Reissue of: Correspondence with the Hudson's Bay Company on Arctic exploration, 1844–1855.
Issued in print and electronic formats.
ISBN 978-1-77151-084-4

1. Rae, John, 1813–1893—Correspondence. 2. Hudson's Bay Company—Employees—Correspondence. 3. Explorers—Scotland—Correspondence. 4. Arctic regions—Discovery and exploration—British. 5. Northwest Passage—Discovery and exploration—British. 6. Canada, Northern—Discovery and exploration—British. 7. Franklin, John, Sir, 1786–1847. I. McGoogan, Kenneth, 1947–, writer of supplementary textual content II. Title. III. Title: Arctic correspondence, 1844–1855. IV. Series: Classics West collection

FC3961.R337 2014 917.1904 C2014-902756-7

Proofreader: Holland Gidney
Cover image: *The Portrait of Dr. Rae, F.R.G.S., Chief Factor*, by Stephen Pearce, 1862, engraving by James Scott

Canadian Heritage Patrimoine canadien

Canada Council for the Arts Conseil des Arts du Canada

We gratefully acknowledge the financial support for our publishing activities from the Government of Canada through the Canada Book Fund and the Canada Council for the Arts, and from the Province of British Columbia through the British Columbia Arts Council and the Book Publishing Tax Credit.

The interior pages of this book have been printed on 100% post-consumer recycled paper, processed chlorine free, and printed with vegetable-based inks.

1 2 3 4 5 18 17 16 15 14

PRINTED IN CANADA

JOHN RAE'S ARCTIC CORRESPONDENCE, 1844–1855

With a Foreword by
KEN McGOOGAN

Fort Confidence, Winter View, 1850–51, by John Rae
FROM THE FIRST EDITION, 1953

CONTENTS

FOREWORD

Late in February 1852, having recently completed his third Arctic expedition, John Rae wrote a progress report to the London secretary of the Hudson's Bay Company (HBC). Rae was returning to England and had just reached Detroit. His search for Sir John Franklin had been "fruitless," he wrote. But he had found, and was bringing with him, "two pieces of wood—the one oak, the other pine." He described these in detail, noting that the first appeared to be a stanchion, while the other had certainly belonged to a Royal Navy vessel, "as there was a piece of line and two copper tacks attached to it, all of which bore the Govt. mark."

As you can read in this collection of correspondence, a few days later, from New York, Rae wrote to Sir George Simpson, governor of the HBC. He explained that "as even the little information I have to give may affect the movements of the Expedition about to leave England this spring in search of Sir J. Franklin, I consider it my duty to hurry home, without permitting my own feelings . . . to have any voice in the matter."

In their 1953 introduction to this volume, R.J. Cyriax and J.M. Wordie devote five pages to analyzing the two pieces of wood that Rae found at Parker Bay, on the south coast of Victoria Island. "That these pieces were derived from the Franklin expedition has not been proved," they write, "but that they were so derived is virtually beyond doubt." Three paragraphs later, they add that "Rae confined himself to stating the facts, and he left the authorities to draw their own conclusions."

What do we deduce from all this? John Rae could be excited by a discovery. A trained doctor, he would analyze what he found, paying close attention to detail. As a man of science and a self-effacing Orcadian, he would not advance any dramatic claims without convincing evidence. These aspects of Rae's character would have implications for the history of Arctic exploration, which I will return to later.

John Rae's Arctic Correspondence, 1844–1855 is the main source for information about Rae's 1851 expedition. In the introduction, we read that this expedition "saw Rae at the height of his powers." It comprised two journeys in a single season, one on snowshoes, the other by boat, and has "in the writers' opinion, never been equalled." During the spring, Rae trekked 1,080 miles (1,740 km) over Arctic ice. Then, in two small boats, he sailed 1,390 miles (2,240 km) while charting 630 miles (1,015 km) of unexplored coastline. Despite all this, as I note in *Fatal Passage*, "to call Rae's third expedition his most successful is to mistake subsequent mythologizing for history. It was but a prelude."

Now might be a good time to acknowledge that while *Rae's Arctic Correspondence* is extraordinarily valuable, and is indeed necessary to serious students of Arctic exploration history, it is not a book for beginners. It assumes a familiarity with the centuries-long quest for the Northwest Passage. But because it contains essentially unedited letters written in action, it gives us the clearest of all windows into the mind of John Rae. He comes to life in a letter of 1848, for example, where he interjected, while writing of earlier HBC explorers Peter Warren Dease and Thomas Simpson, "I forgot to mention that we found one of their boats on the banks of the Coppermine at the place where she had been left 9 years before."

As well, this book reveals worlds about Rae's complex relationship with Sir George Simpson, whose letters to Rae are included as an appendix. Simpson, famously expert at taking credit for the work of others, created a paper trail suggesting that Rae's first expedition was his idea. "An idea has entered my mind," he wrote in May 1844, "that you are one of the fittest men in the country to conduct an expedition for the purpose of completing the survey of the Northern Coast that remains untraced . . ." That this idea should have entered Simpson's mind is not surprising, since Rae had been discussing it with him since the previous summer and had spent Christmas of 1843 at Simpson's mansion in Lachine, near Montreal. The detail-oriented Rae had been keenly interested in exploration since at least the late 1830s, when at Moose Factory he shared living quarters with Alexander Simpson, the brother of Thomas Simpson, who was then charting the Arctic coastline for the HBC. Here, and in Rae's later exchanges with George Simpson, we read the truth between the lines.

The polemical introduction to *Arctic Correspondence*, which runs almost 100 pages, illustrates the way the British establishment framed, controlled, and projected an "authorized history" of Arctic exploration. Edwin Ernest Rich, general editor of the Hudson's Bay Record Society, the book's original publisher, studied and taught at Cambridge before assuming the Vere Harmsworth Chair of Imperial and Naval History. Sir James Wordie, identified as co-writer of the introduction, was a Scottish geologist (and master of a Cambridge college) who sailed on nine polar expeditions, and so added prestige and credibility by his presence.

But the real author of the introduction, as is obvious to anyone familiar with the relevant literature, was Richard Julius Cyriax, an English medical doctor and fellow of the Royal Geographical Society. Cyriax established his reputation with his 1939 book *Sir John Franklin's Last Arctic Expedition*, which takes its lead from Jane, Lady Franklin. Anyone who has read my book *Lady Franklin's Revenge* will appreciate that he might not have been the most sympathetic reader of John Rae's correspondence.

Criticism and indignation arose in England, Cyriax tells us, after John Rae returned from the Arctic with news of the fate of the 1845 Franklin expedition—specifically, that some of the final survivors had been driven by starvation to cannibalism. The public attacks, Cyriax adds, were directed "principally against [his Inuit informants] rather than against Rae." He summarizes those attacks and concludes that "the religion, courage, discipline, and sense of duty of Franklin's men would have prevented anything whatever of the kind described by the [Inuit]."

Remarkably, Cyriax neglects to mention that Charles Dickens—the most influential writer of the age—was the one who originally made those arguments. He may only have guessed that Dickens acted with the encouragement of Lady Franklin. But he certainly knew whose arguments he was paraphrasing, because his footnotes refer to the relevant issues of Dickens's magazine *Household Words*. Rather than incorporate Dickens in full-throated rant, fulminating about tattooed tribes and "barbarous, wide-mouthed, goggle-eyed gods" (the whole text is available in *The Arctic Journals of John Rae*) Cyriax opts for omission. But at what point does omission become deception?

To contextualize Rae's accomplishments, Cyriax summarizes a series of expeditions sponsored by the British Admiralty. Arriving at 1821 and Franklin's first Arctic expedition, Cyriax writes: "Extreme privations were endured during the return journey, for food supplies failed, and several members of the party perished." The food supplies failed because Franklin ignored the warnings of the native peoples that he should turn back. The "extreme privations" led to murder and cannibalism, and the "several members" who perished included eleven of twenty men—more than half the expedition.

But let us turn to the two great questions of nineteenth-century Arctic exploration. First, who discovered the fate of the 1845 Franklin expedition? Cyriax admits that "the relics recovered by Rae from the [Inuit] precluded any possible doubt concerning the identity of the white men who were said to have died near the estuary of the Great Fish River." But later he adds, "The private search expedition organized by Lady Franklin and commanded by [Leopold] McClintock succeeded in 1859 in ascertaining more fully the proceedings and ultimate fate of the missing officers and men. McClintock, not Rae, has ever since been acknowledged as the real discoverer of the fate of the Franklin expedition."

Here we have a fascinating spectacle. In the introduction to a collection of correspondence, we encounter a preemptive repudiation of the letter-writer—and, in fact, another unconscionable omission. Why does this collection end in 1855? If the editors were going to open the issue of the Fate of the Franklin Expedition, then surely they should have included several more pertinent letters, which can also be found in Cambridge (at the Scott Polar Research Institute).

In March 1860, William Arrowsmith, a member of the Arrowsmith family of mapmakers, informed McClintock, who was busily proclaiming "his" discovery of the Fate, that Rae had a prior claim. McClintock wrote to Rae complaining of Arrowsmith's tone. Rae defended Arrowsmith and, as I write in *Fatal Passage*, "entered into a protracted, somewhat testy correspondence, originating the argument . . . that McClintock merely confirmed and clarified Rae's findings and that, in future, other searchers would shed additional light on the fate of the Franklin expedition."

As Rae himself wrote, the relics he brought to London "were sufficient evidence that a large portion of [the men on] both Franklin's ships had died of disease and starvation in the neighbourhood of the Back River and King William's Land on, or previous to, 1850 and that these were the last survivors of the party . . . I write in perfect good feeling, as I hope people may do in a matter of opinion on a subject where there always will be *two* sides of the question, perhaps *three*, were another expedition to go out and find the journal of some of the latest survivors."

As he anticipated, many investigators have since added detail and nuance to Rae's original findings. Those who came after McClintock but before Cyriax include Charles Francis Hall, Frederick Schwatka, and Knud Rasmussen. Those who came after Cyriax include David Woodman, Owen Beattie, Margaret Bertulli, and Anne Keenleyside. Woodman, author of *Unravelling the Franklin Mystery*, correctly writes of McClintock that "the vague stories he collected . . . added detail to Rae's account, but presented little that was new." The list of those who have clarified the Fate of Franklin continues to grow. But as I say in *Fatal Passage*, "John Rae, not Leopold McClintock, deserves to be commemorated at Westminster Abbey as the discoverer of the fate of Franklin. Yet even that would right only half the historical wrong."

And so we come to the second great question: Who discovered the Northwest Passage? In the introduction to this collection of correspondence, paraphrasing the final paragraph of his 1939 book, Cyriax tells us, "The Franklin expedition is universally admitted to have been the first to find a North-west Passage." He explains that one of Franklin's men may have demonstrated the existence of a passage in 1847. If not, there is "no doubt that the officers and men who marched towards the Great Fish River [from Franklin's trapped ships] discovered a North-west Passage in 1848." In a footnote, he adds that "there are several North-west Passages." At one time, Cyriax continues, "priority of discovery" went to Sir Robert McClure (another Royal Navy man), but McClintock's 1859 voyage showed that "the honour of priority of discovery . . . belongs to the Franklin expedition which had found a Passage" two or three years before McClure.

In my two books mentioned above, I devote chapters to repudiating these claims and showing how they became authorized history. Today, because of climate change, mariners can cross the High Arctic along any number of routes. But in the mid-nineteenth century, both McClure and Franklin got trapped in perennially ice-blocked channels. McClure had to be rescued and transported across the ice in 1853, and Franklin and his men perished and so reported no discovery, or even any failure to discover.

Franklin had been dispatched to link two Arctic waterways, one navigable from the Atlantic, the other from the Pacific. In 1854, while travelling overland less than 100 miles (160 km) from where Franklin got trapped, John Rae discovered the last missing link between those two channels. He brought news of that discovery back to England. Mapmaker John Arrowsmith recorded it on a map published in 1857, identifying the final link as "Rae Strait," even before McClintock sailed. Half a century later, when Roald Amundsen became the first to navigate the Northwest Passage, he did it by sailing through Rae Strait, which even then was the only passable route.

But here we encounter yet another omission: the maps that accompany this volume fail to identify Rae Strait. Because of course to do so would acknowledge its significance. Why did Rae not claim that the strait he discovered represented the missing link in the only Passage navigable by ships of his time? For the same reason that, when he found those two pieces of wood in 1851, he did not claim that they derived from one of Franklin's ships: he could not prove it. And he would not advance claims for which he had no evidence.

He did, however, present one claim, based on the walk-a-passage logic employed by Robert McClure. While charting the east coast of Victoria Island, Rae had trekked north beyond the southernmost point attained by others, two years before McClure was rescued.

In his introduction to the present volume, in a section called "Rae's Later Life," Cyriax writes that in 1855, Rae spent his own money to build a small schooner in Canada, "his object being to complete the survey of the American arctic coastline." That modest objective would hardly justify such an expenditure. Rae intended to sail that ship, the *Iceberg*, through Rae Strait, and so prove that he had discovered the final link in the Northwest Passage. Unfortunately, the ship got lost in a storm on the Great Lakes, and the vindication of Rae's discovery had to await Roald Amundsen.

Today, the champions of authorized history produce increasingly strained arguments to deny Rae his rightful recognition. Some point to a tiny stretch of coastline that remained uncharted in 1854—an irrelevance, since Rae Strait is not part of a coastline but of a passage linking waterways. Others argue that Franklin's men must have found the strait first, as if discovery does not require communication. Or maybe Franklin's ships were too big to sail through Rae Strait? Nobody says finding the best way would have been easy, but the strait is twenty-two kilometres wide, and contemporary ships with far deeper draughts pass through it every season, as I have seen for myself half a dozen times.

The introduction to this volume, subtly hostile and wonderfully revealing, conveys us to the wellhead of specious arguments. The letters collected here bring to life the greatest Arctic explorer of the nineteenth century. And the inscription on the statue of John Rae at the Stromness pierhead in Orkney, Scotland, newly erected in September 2013, rightly identifies its subject as "discoverer of the final link in the first navigable Northwest Passage." In a better world, a truly post-colonial world, that would be the end of the matter.

Ken McGoogan
March 2014
Toronto, Ontario

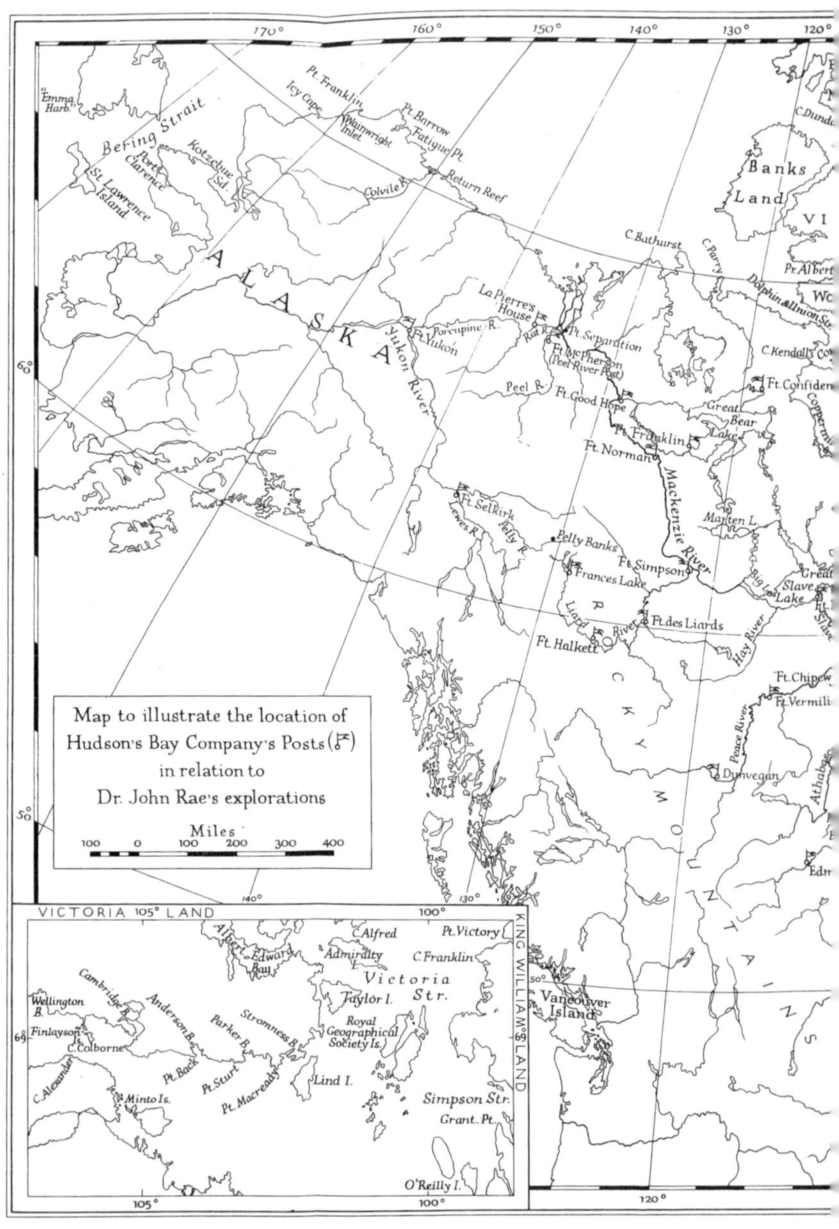

Map to illustrate the location of Hudson's Bay Company's posts in relation to Dr. John Rae's explorations, drawn by V. Nehring

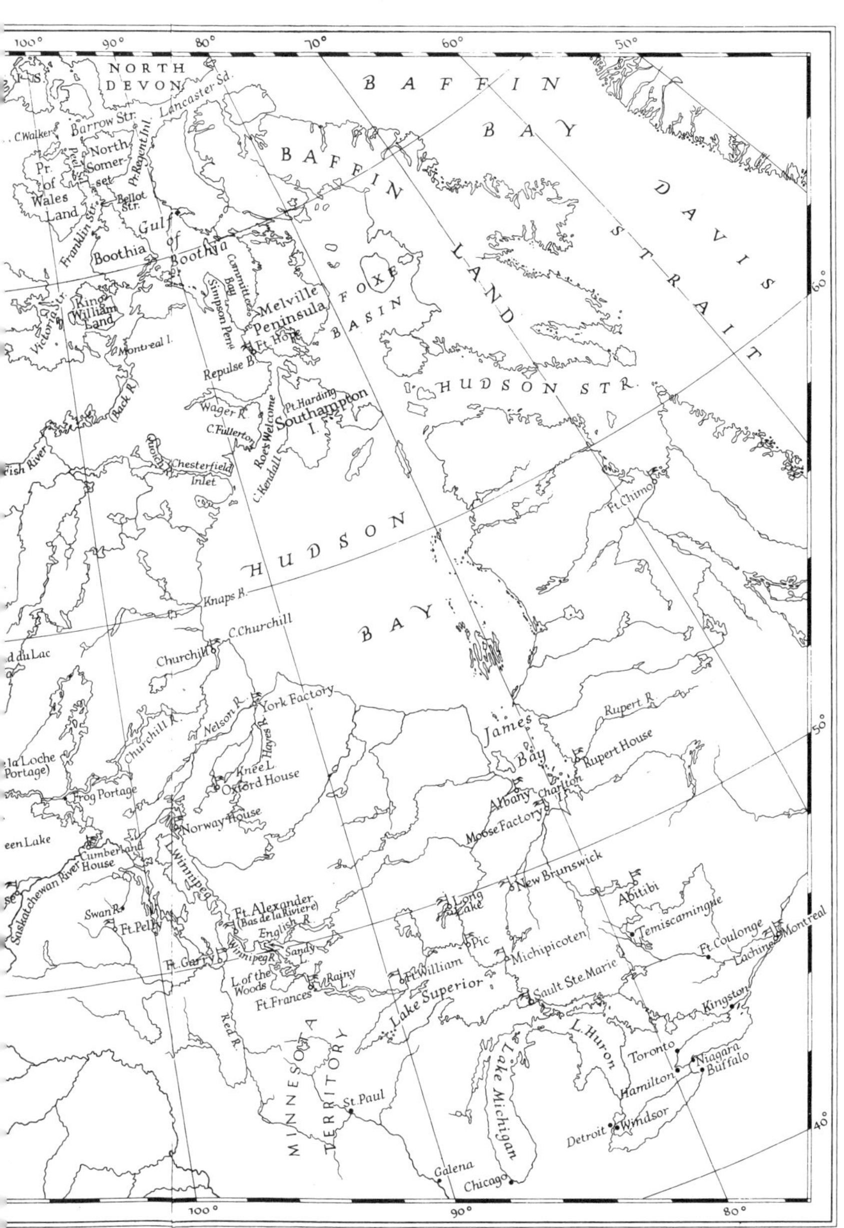

NORTH DEVON
Lancaster Sd.
BAFFIN BAY
DAVIS STRAIT
BAFFIN LAND
C. Walker
Barrow Str.
North Somerset
Pr. Regent Inl.
Pr. of Wales Land
Peel
Bellot Str.
Franklin Str.
Boothia
Gulf of Boothia
Committee Bay
Simpson Pena
King William Land
Victoria Str.
Melville Peninsula
FOXE BASIN
Ft. Hope
Montreal I.
Back R.
Repulse B.
HUDSON STR.
Wager R.
Pt. Harding
Southampton I.
C. Fullerton
Roe's Welcome
C. Kendall
Fish River
Chesterfield Inlet
Ft. Chimo
HUDSON BAY
Knaps R.
C. Churchill
Churchill
York Factory
Nelson R.
Churchill R.
Hayes R.
James Bay
Rupert R.
Rupert House
Knee L.
Oxford House
Frog Portage
Norway House
Albany
Charlton
Moose Factory
Cumberland House
Saskatchewan River
L. Winnipeg
Swan R.
Ft. Pelly
Ft. Alexander (Bas de la Riviere)
English R.
New Brunswick
Abitibi
Long Lake
Temiscamingue
Pic
Michipicoten
Ft. Coulonge
Montreal
Lachine
Winnipeg R.
Sandy L.
Ft. Garry
L. of the Woods
Rainy L.
Ft. Frances
Ft. William
Lake Superior
Sault Ste. Marie
Kingston
Red R.
MINNESOTA TERRITORY
L. Huron
Toronto
Niagara
Buffalo
Hamilton
Lake Michigan
St. Paul
Detroit
Windsor
Galena
Chicago

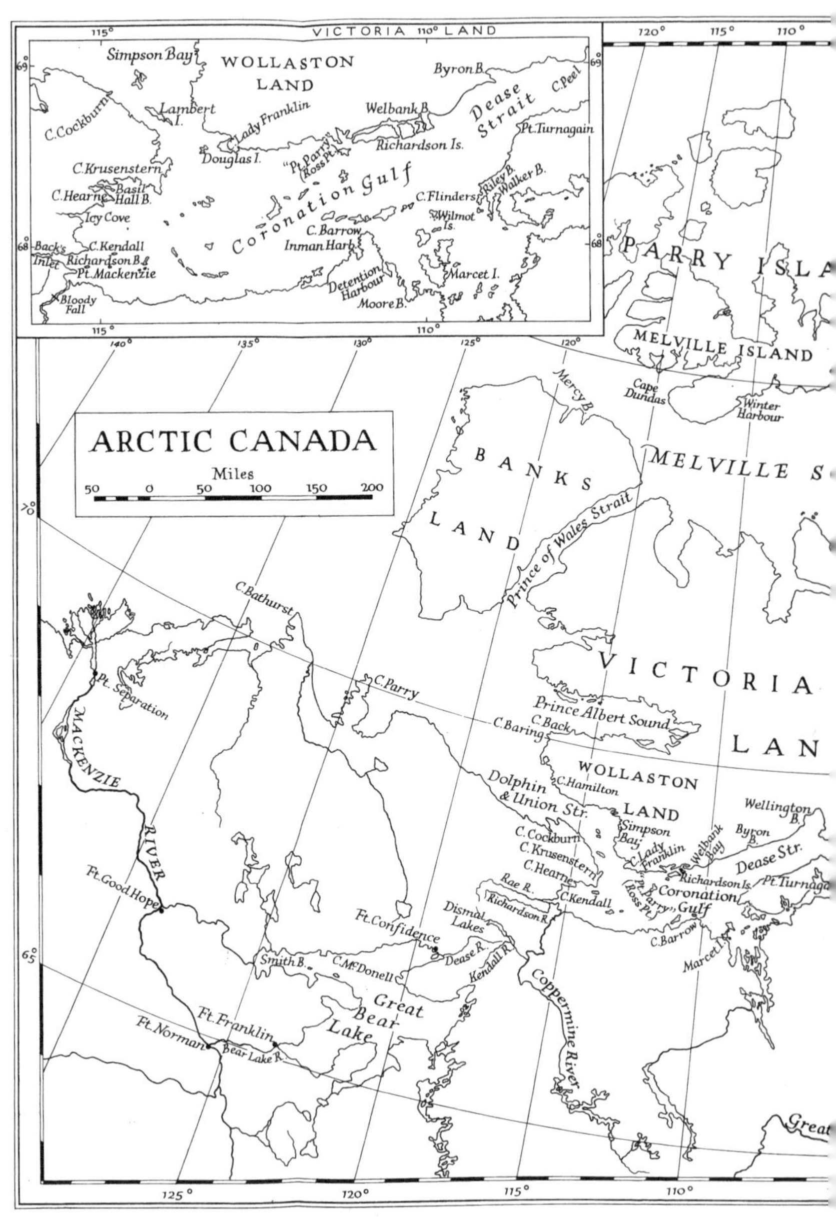

Arctic Canada, drawn by V. Nehring

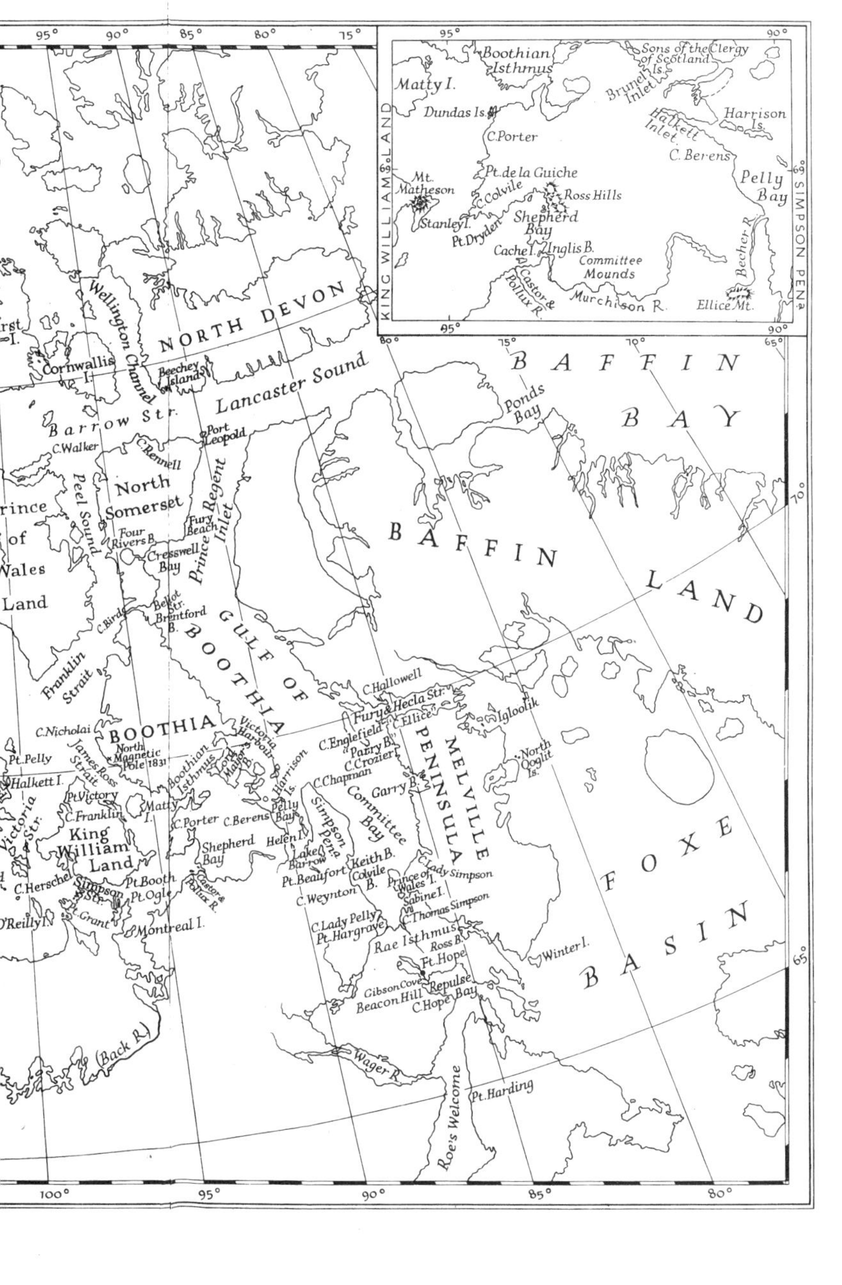
NORTH DEVON
Wellington Channel
Cornwallis I.
Beechey Island
Lancaster Sound
Barrow Str.
Port Leopold
C.Walker
C.Rennell
North Somerset
Peel Sound
Prince Regent Inlet
Fury Beach
Four Rivers B.
Cresswell Bay
Prince of Wales Land
Bellot Str.
Brentford B.
C.Bird
Franklin Strait
GULF OF BOOTHIA
BAFFIN BAY
Ponds Bay
BAFFIN LAND
C.Hallowell
Fury & Hecla Str.
C.Englefield
C.Ellice
Parry B.
C.Crozier
Igloolik
North Ooglit Is.
C.Chapman
Garry B.
MELVILLE PENINSULA
Committee Bay
C.Nicholai
BOOTHIA
North Magnetic Pole 1831
Victoria Harbour
Lord Mayor B.
Boothian Isthmus
Pt.Pelly
James Ross Strait
Halkett I.
Pt.Victory
C.Franklin
Matty I.
C.Porter
C.Berens
Pelly Bay
Harrison Is.
Simpson Pena.
King William Land
Victoria Str.
Shepherd Bay
Helen I.
Lake Barrow
Keith B.
Pt.Beaufort
Colvile B.
Prince of Wales I.
C.Lady Simpson
Sabine I.
C.Herschel
Simpson Str.
Pt.Booth
Pt.Ogle
Castor & Pollux R.
C.Weynton
C.Thomas Simpson
Pt.Grant
Montreal I.
C.Lady Pelly
Pt.Hargrave
Rae Isthmus
Ross B.
Ft.Hope
Winter I.
FOXE BASIN
Gibson Cove
Beacon Hill
Repulse Bay
C.Hope
Back R.
Wager R.
Pt.Harding
Roe's Welcome
Boothian Isthmus
Sons of the Clergy of Scotland Is.
Matty I.
Brunel Inlet
Dundas Is.
Harrison Is.
Halkett Inlet
C.Porter
C.Berens
KING WILLIAM LAND
Pt.de la Guiche
Mt. Matheson
C.Colvile
Ross Hills
Pelly Bay
SIMPSON PENa.
Shepherd Bay
Stanley I.
Pt.Dryden
Cache I.
Inglis B.
Committee Mounds
Becher R.
Castor & Pollux R.
Murchison R.
Ellice Mt.

JOHN RAE'S CORRESPONDENCE
WITH THE HUDSON'S BAY COMPANY ON ARCTIC EXPLORATION
1844–1855

EDITED BY

E.E. RICH, M.A.

ASSISTED BY

A.M. JOHNSON
ARCHIVIST, HUDSON'S BAY COMPANY

WITH AN INTRODUCTION BY

J.M. WORDIE, C.B.E.,
MASTER OF ST. JOHN'S COLLEGE, CAMBRIDGE,
PRESIDENT OF THE ROYAL GEOGRAPHICAL SOCIETY

and

R.J. CYRIAX

LONDON
THE HUDSON'S BAY RECORD SOCIETY
1953

PREFACE

In publishing the Arctic exploration letters of John Rae the Hudson's Bay Record Society is breaking fresh ground. For although the search for a North-west Passage, and Arctic exploration in general, have always been closely interwoven in the Company's history, these are problems which have not hitherto formed the subject of a volume of the Record Society's publications.

The natural interest of these matters, the participation of the Company, the personality of Rae and his great contribution to the technique of Arctic exploration, are all enhanced by his dramatic contribution to the solution of the mystery of Franklin's last expedition. But to produce a volume of Rae's letters bearing on these problems it has been necessary to discard many of the lengthy letters which Rae wrote in the course of his normal duties in the fur trade. The provenance of each letter here printed is given in the footnotes. They are all to fellow-participants in the fur trade, to the London Secretary or to the Governor and Committee in London, to the Governor or the Governor and Council of the Northern Department of Rupert's Land, or to some few Chief Factors. Despite a certain animosity which creeps into the later letters (perhaps caused by Rae's presumption in comparing the times of his journeys with those of the Governor, perhaps by his reflections on the Governor's choice of wines, or perhaps by the fact that Simpson became more testy after the death of his wife) it becomes clear from the letters that Sir George Simpson was Rae's firmest supporter, that he placed at his disposal for the purposes of exploration a generous share of the resources of the Company, and that he took a constant and active interest in Rae's projects and achievements.

Although the letters here printed, and the appendixes, are from the Company's archives, and the frontispiece* portrait of Rae is copied from an engraving in the possession of the Company, the Society owes its thanks to the Trustees of the National Maritime Museum, Greenwich, for permission to publish here information derived from the Franklin relics preserved there.

In dealing with such a problem as that presented by John Rae, the Society is particularly fortunate in that the Master of St. John's College and Dr. R.J. Cyriax, with their unrivalled knowledge of the subject, have consented to help in the publication. Their contribution is to be seen not only in the introduction and in the maps but also in the footnotes, many of which reveal a knowledge of the history of Arctic exploration which in itself proclaims their authorship.

E.E. Rich
St. Catharine's College
Cambridge

* The portrait that was reproduced as the frontispiece in the original 1953 edition of this book does not appear within the body of the text in this edition. Instead, the portrait has been used on the front cover.

INTRODUCTION

INTRODUCTION

1. *Preliminary*

In the introduction which follows, the writers have endeavoured to assess Rae's various polar journeys and to relate them to other arctic explorations taking place at the same time. Rae's journeys stand out from others of the period, such as the many Franklin search expeditions, not only by his speed of travel but also by his dependence on procuring fresh food with rifle and fishing net. Rae's success was due to his expert use of these methods and was in contrast with the experience of many travellers unaccustomed to them and often not prepared to learn.

Rae's first expedition of 1846–47 was made under orders from the Company to complete the discoveries of the American arctic coast undertaken some years earlier by Dease and Simpson. In 1845, however, the veteran Sir John Franklin, who had himself in his younger days explored so much of the coast, had sailed on a voyage in the *Erebus* and *Terror* to seek and navigate a North-west Passage. Both ships failed to return, world interest was aroused, the Hudson's Bay Company was swept into the search, and Rae's later expeditions were dominated by an entirely new motive.

On his second expedition he was under Admiralty orders and for the first of the two winters was under Sir John Richardson's command in the field. Both years proved unsuitable for extended travel and little new ground was covered.

The third expedition, again under Admiralty orders, saw Rae at the height of his powers. The two journeys to Wollaston Land and Victoria

Land, both made in one season, the first on foot and the second by boat, have, in the writers' opinion, never been equalled.

The fourth expedition, once more under the Company's orders, to extend exploration in the American Arctic, would probably have achieved its object had circumstances permitted. The journey, however, was broken off after the unexpected discovery of relics of Franklin and evidence of his probable fate, for Rae decided to return to England without delay.

Rae's travels are so interwoven with the activities of the Franklin relief expeditions that appreciation of the Rae letters is not possible without continuous reference to, and knowledge of, the details of the Franklin search.

2. *Rae's Early Life*

John Rae was the fourth son of John Rae and Margaret Glen of the Hall of Clestrain and was born there on September 30, 1813,[1] and baptised on October 14. The father, who was not himself an Orkney man, had gone there as Factor to Sir William Honeyman, Bt.[2]

Rae described his boyhood in an article in the *Volunteer Record*, which was reprinted in the *Orkney Herald* for February 16, 1887, with the title "Roughing it. Boy life in Orkney. By Private J. Rae, M.D., F.R.S., London Scottish". Rae describes how he and his brothers had a sailing boat 18–20 feet long. He also mentions how he learned to shoot from an early age and sums up his boyhood activities as follows: "By the time I was fifteen, I had become so seasoned as to care little about cold or wet, had acquired a fair knowledge of boating, was a moderately good climber among rocks, and not a bad walker for my age, sometimes carrying a pretty heavy load of game or fish (fishing both in fresh and salt water was a favourite pursuit) on my back. All of these acquirements, often though useless, were of great service to me in after life".[3]

Rae does not state where he went to school but he remarks on an excellent grouse moor, within five minutes of his home, which he often visited "after school hours in the evening". He was presumably educated at Stromness in Orkney, or possibly was taught by a private tutor at the Hall of Clestrain.

Rae commenced his medical studies at Edinburgh, and remarks that he began "before he was sixteen"; that is to say, before October 1829, and this suggests that he went to Edinburgh for the summer session of 1829. He states that he studied at the University, but there is a possibility that much of his work was done in extra-mural classes, as was the usual custom in Edinburgh in the nineteenth century. According to the records at Surgeons' Hall, Edinburgh, Rae is listed as having passed the necessary examination for the licence of the Royal College of Surgeons (L.R.C.S.) of Edinburgh on April 18, 1833.

His first appointment was made very soon afterwards when he sailed as surgeon for the summer voyage to Moose Factory in the Hudson's Bay Company's ship *Prince of Wales*. His father, who had been the Company's agent at Stromness, received a letter from William Smith, Secretary of the Company in London, dated June 7, 1833, as follows: ". . . the Governor and Committee have been pleased to appoint your Son Jock Surgeon of the *Prince of Wales* for the ensuing voyage".[4] Rae himself has described his experiences of that period, unfortunately very briefly, in the *Orkney Herald* for March 16, 1887, under the title "Roughing it on Board Ship".

Rae appears to have made a very favourable impression on Chief Factor McTavish who, writing from Moose Factory on September 18, 1833, to Governor George Simpson, stated: "There is a fine young man a Son of Mr. Rae's Surgeon to the Ship *Prince of Wales* here at present whom I should like to detain if I thought it would be approved of".[5] As events turned out, Rae was in the end detained whether he wanted to be or not, as the *Prince of Wales* was beset by ice and forced to winter at Charlton Island in James Bay at the south end of Hudson Bay.

George Simpson wrote to Rae on May 17, 1834, as follows: "Having heard from Mr. McTavish, in the course of the past winter, that you seemed to have no disinclination to remain in the country, I requested permission of the Governor and Committee to offer you an engagement in the service, feeling satisfied, from the report I had of your character, and from what I know of your family, that you would do honour to my recommendation. The board, in compliance with that request, have authorised me to offer you an engagement in the service, in the double capacity of Clerk and surgeon, for a term of five years, at £100 p. anm. salary, which I now do, and, with reference to Mr. McTavish for information as to the rules of the service, and as to the prospects of advancement therein."[6] Simpson also wrote to McTavish on May 28 saying: "If Mr. Rae declines to enter into a five years' engagement for the country, have the goodness to ask him to remain one year . . .",[7] to which McTavish replied on September 18, 1834: "Dr. Rae consented to remain . . . for two years at £100—but cannot be prevailed upon to become a Counting house Clerk, he is a very attentive pleasant young Man, hardy and well adapted to the Country, however he only wishes I presume to feel his way, and may in time take a notion of remaining, as to his medical capacity all I can say is, that he appears to wish to study his profession".[8]

Rae was stationed, according to Hudson's Bay Company records, at Moose Factory during outfits 1834–35 and 1835–36. This completed his two years' contract but he stayed on and remained in and about Moose Factory for about ten years in all. The Moose Factory journals frequently mention Rae's duties in the office and store, his attendance on the sick, and his work on his trap line and the results of his shooting excursions. He seems to have spent some of his leisure compiling a Swampy Cree Indian vocabulary.

The story of how Rae became an explorer can be pieced together from Hudson's Bay Company records and began in August 1843, when Sir George Simpson[9] visited Moose Factory and held a Council of the Southern Department of Rupert's Land. It would be about this time that Rae applied for and obtained permission to visit friends and relations in Canada. This permission must have been granted as a favour, as in the ordinary course only Chief Factors and Chief Traders were allowed furlough. Rae, however, was ordered to carry the duplicate letters for England from Rupert's Land to Canada, and on his return to

Moose he was to take charge of the "Winter packet" of letters.

He left on this journey on September 28, 1843, as the Moose Factory journal records: ". . . About 9 A.M. Mr. John Rae, accompanied by the following Indians for his crew Viz. Acouché of Abitibi and Uckanackeeshick and Sackiscumacoe of Moose, to Abitibi or Temiscamingue and from thence to Canada. Mr. James Watt takes a passage as far as Temiscamingue . . .".

The party arrived at Timiskaming on October 18, and Rae resumed his journey the following day by way of Fort Coulonge, and finally arrived at Kingston, Upper Canada, on December 15.

He subsequently went to Lachine, where Governor Simpson had his house, and was given instructions by Simpson for the return to Moose Factory. He was to be accompanied as far as Timiskaming by Wemyss M. Simpson, a brother of the Governor's wife, and from there by James S. Watt as far as Moose. The date on which Rae left Lachine has not been traced, but he and Wemyss Simpson reached Fort Coulonge on January 2, 1844, and were at Lac des Allumettes post on January 5. They reached Timiskaming on January 15, having travelled most of the way on snow-shoes. Rae, now accompanied by Watt, finally reached Moose on February 19, 1844, and resumed his duties at the Factory. In a letter to Sir George Simpson dated April 27, 1844, he mentions that his weight was one hundred and seventy-four lbs.

It became necessary at about this time for Robert Cowie, who had charge of Rupert River District, to be relieved of his duties on account of ill health, and Simpson arranged for Rae to take over the charge. The letter informing him of the appointment was dated May 11, 1844.[10]

Clearly Rae had attracted Simpson's attention in no ordinary way, and was a man who might be picked for exceptional duties. The chance came at once, for in a second letter, also dated May 11, 1844, Simpson wrote from Michipicoten: "An idea, has entered my mind that you are one of the fittest men in the country to conduct an Expedition for the purpose of completing the Survey of the Northern Coast that remains untraced . . . As regards the management of the people & endurance of toil, either in walking, boating or starving, I think you are better adapted for this work than most of the gentn. with whom I am acquainted in the country".[11]

Rae was instructed to be at Moose Factory from July 15–20. Simpson was at Moose from July 15–18, and during that time the appointment to Rupert River must have been cancelled. Simpson wrote Rae a letter on July 17 instructing him to carry out the exploratory work suggested. This was the beginning of explorations which lasted till 1854.

Preparations were begun for the journey to the Red River Settlement, where Rae was to qualify himself to conduct the surveying work of the expedition so as to be able to delineate the "Northern Shores . . . from the Straits of the Fury & Hecla to Dease & Simpsons farthest point".

The Moose Factory journal for August 20, 1844, states: ". . . About ½ past four this evenings tide, Dr. Jno. Rae took his departure for Red River Settlement to join Mr. C. F. Christie there agreeable to his instructions from Sir George Simpson. One Servant accompanies him the whole distance, viz. Jno. Corrigal besides whom he has one Servant of New Brunswick—a tripper from the Sault St. Maries Francoes Misère: and two Indians to return hither from New Brunswick, in all five hands, the Canoe being about ¾ths. the No[rth]. Canoe size".

Rae reached the New Brunswick post on August 30, left Michipocoten on September 6, and was at Fort Frances on Rainy Lake on September 27. He arrived at Red River on October 9, only to find that Mr. George Taylor, who was to help him with his scientific studies, was too ill to do so. Taylor died on November 15 and Rae decided to journey as far as Sault Ste. Marie on snow-shoes during the winter of 1844–45 to await further instructions from Sir George Simpson. This is the journey on snow-shoes, over a distance of about one thousand two hundred statute miles, which Rae in his "Achievement" letter[12] of February 1856, describes as occupying "two months of constant travelling, and at the end of it, the only man who had accompanied me the whole distance was found to have lost 26 lbs. in weight (he was certainly rather fat when he started), whilst I had gained 2 lbs.". Rae went on to Toronto, and with the help of Lieutenant John Lefroy, R.A., of the Observatory set about acquiring the training necessary for the proposed expedition.

We have two contemporary descriptions of how Rae appeared at that time. Mrs. Letitia Hargrave, whose husband was Chief Factor at York Factory, writing to her mother in Scotland on November 30, 1845, remarks: "... Dr. Rae is still here ... Dr. Rae came out with Dugald [Mactavish, Letitia's brother] to Moose & is now 32 years old. He had got his Diploma unusually early & has not been home since nor (he says) opened a medical book for 7 years. He is very good looking & can walk 100 miles easily in 2 days. He has got a small observatory where he works away ... ".[13]

Still more interesting is R. M. Ballantyne's description of a meeting with Rae on Winnipeg River on September 7, 1845.[14] Ballantyne writes as follows:—

> In the afternoon we met another canoe, in which we saw a gentleman sitting. This strange sight set us all speculating as to who it could be, for we knew that all the canoes accustomed annually to go through these wilds had long since passed. We were soon enlightened, however, on the subject. Both canoes made towards a flat rock that offered a convenient spot for landing on; and the stranger introduced himself as Dr. Rae. He was on his way to York Factory, for the purpose of fitting out at that post an expedition for the survey of the small part of the North American coast left unexplored by Messrs. Dease and Simpson, which will then prove beyond a doubt whether or not there is a communication by water between the Atlantic and Pacific oceans round the north of America. Dr. Rae appeared to be just the man for such an expedition. He was very muscular and active, full of animal spirits, and had a fine intellectual countenance. He was considered, by those who knew him well, to be one of the best snow-shoe walkers in the service, was also an excellent rifle-shot, and could stand an immense amount of fatigue ... He does not proceed as other expeditions have done—namely, with large supplies of provisions and men, but merely takes a very small supply of provisions, and ten or twelve

> men . . . The whole expedition is fitted out at the expense of the Hudson's Bay Company. The party are to depend almost entirely on their guns for provisions; and after proceeding in two open boats round the north-western shores of Hudson's Bay as far as they may find it expedient or practicable, are to land, place their boats in security for the winter, and then penetrate into these unexplored regions on foot. After having done as much as possible towards the forwarding of the object of his journey, Dr. Rae and his party are to spend the long dreary winter with the Esquimaux, and commence operations again early in the spring. He is of such a pushing, energetic character, however, that there is every probability he will endeavour to prosecute his discoveries during winter, if at all practicable.

3. *Progress of Discovery on the North Coast of America and among the Islands of the Arctic Archipelago, 1818–39*

Geographical knowledge of arctic North America down to 1818 was very scanty. Davis Strait, Hudson Strait, Hudson Bay and Repulse Bay were known; Bering Strait and the coast of Alaska extending northwards from that Strait to Icy Cape were also known. The Coppermine River and the Mackenzie River had both been found to enter the Polar Sea; but only the estuaries had been examined. That was all that was positively known, or rather was accepted as based upon fact.[15] Systematic exploration did not begin till 1818, when the initiative was taken by the British Government.

An Admiralty expedition sailed that year under the command of Commander (later Rear-Admiral Sir) John Ross (1777–1856) to seek a North-west Passage. Sir John Ross sailed in the *Isabella* and his second-in-command, Lieutenant (later Rear-Admiral Sir) William Edward Parry (1790–1855) in the *Alexander*. Ross established the general accuracy of William Baffin's observations made in 1616.[16] This had in effect, however, already been done in 1817, when the Leith whaler *Larkins* and the *Elizabeth* of Aberdeen made a circuit of Baffin Bay.[17] Considerable controversy arose after Ross's return as to whether Lancaster Sound was a closed bay or open towards the west.

Exploration on the Atlantic side of the North-west Passage by way of Lancaster Sound continued in 1819, when the Admiralty sent Lieutenant Parry to search for a North-west Passage. Parry sailed through Lancaster Sound and Barrow Strait, examined the upper part of Prince Regent Inlet and then continued westwards as far as Melville Island. All his attempts to sail still further westwards towards Bering Strait were frustrated by the close pack-ice which he encountered at Cape Dundas on the south-west coast of Melville Island, and Parry returned home in 1820.[18] His report of close pack-ice between the south-west coast of Melville Island and Banks Land was accepted as convincing evidence that there was no practicable passage in that direction.

Parry made two further expeditions in search of a North-west Passage. During his second expedition (1821–23) he examined Repulse Bay, which he finally proved to be a bay and not the opening of a Passage; he also explored the east coast of Melville Peninsula, and Fury and Hecla Strait.[19] During his third expedition (1824–25) he endeavoured to find a North-west Passage through Prince Regent Inlet. On this voyage H.M.S. *Fury* was lost and Parry returned home in the second ship, the *Hecla*, after landing the *Fury*'s stores at Fury Beach on the west coast of Prince Regent Inlet.[20]

In 1819, Lieutenant (later Captain Sir) John Franklin (1786–1847) was appointed to command an overland expedition which, starting from Hudson Bay, was to determine the latitudes and longitudes of the north coast of America[21] and to trace this coast to the eastward of the estuary of the Coppermine River, which had been reached by Samuel Hearne during his journey down that river in 1771. Dr. (later Sir) John Richardson (1787–1865), a surgeon in the Royal Navy, and two Admiralty Midshipmen, one of whom was Mr. (later Admiral Sir) George Back (1796–1878), accompanied Franklin. Voyageurs and guides were engaged in Athabaska. The party, after wintering at Fort Enterprise, descended the Coppermine River in 1821, travelled in boats eastwards along the coast and examined all its many indentations, including Coronation Gulf, as far as Point Turnagain. Franklin had hoped to reach Repulse Bay but could not proceed beyond Point Turnagain. Extreme privations were endured during the return journey, for food supplies failed, and several members of the party perished.[22] Franklin returned to England in October 1822.

Franklin left England in 1825 in command of a second overland expedition, the purpose of which was to descend the Mackenzie River (first explored by Alexander Mackenzie in 1789) and then to examine the coast both to the westward of the estuary as far as Icy Cape, and to the eastward as far as the estuary of the Coppermine River. Franklin was again accompanied by Richardson and George Back. The party spent the winter, 1825–26, at Fort Franklin, on Great Bear Lake, and in July reached the estuary of the Mackenzie, where the party divided. Franklin took command of the western detachment, and with Back travelled along the coast in boats as far as Return Reef, which they reached on August 16, 1826. H.M.S. *Blossom*, as the sequel will show, had been sent to Bering Strait, and Franklin had hoped to meet her or a party from her, but he decided to return the way he had come, and went back to the Mackenzie. Meanwhile, Richardson, commanding the eastern detachment, travelled in boats to the estuary of the Coppermine, and during this journey saw to the north but did not visit part of the south coast of Wollaston Land, separated from the mainland by Dolphin and Union Strait. The two parties came together again on September 21 at Fort Franklin, where they spent a second winter, and returned to England during the autumn of 1827.[23]

On the Pacific side of the continent, Captain Frederick William Beechey (1796–1856) went to Bering Strait in H.M.S. *Blossom* in 1826 and again in 1827, his instructions being to render any necessary assistance to Parry and Franklin, either of whom it was thought might reach the strait. In 1826 Beechey examined the coast to the north of Icy Cape as far as Point Franklin, and Thomas Elson, master of the *Blossom*, explored the coast lying still further to the northeast by "barge" as far as Point Barrow, where he arrived on August 22. Elson was then one hundred and sixty miles from Return Reef, reached by Franklin on August 16. The result of Beechey's explorations, in conjunction with those made previously, was the delineation of the whole of the west coast of Alaska. He returned to England in 1828.[24]

John Ross, commanding a private expedition in the *Victory*, left England in 1829 to seek a North-west Passage through Prince Regent Inlet, and spent three successive winters in his ship in harbours on the east coast of Boothia. His second-in-command was his nephew, Commander (later Rear-Admiral Sir) James Clark Ross (1800–62) who had already served in five Admiralty Arctic expeditions.[25] The best known achievement of this enterprise was James Ross's determination in 1831 of the position of the North Magnetic Pole, which he located on the west coast of Boothia. The coastline on the west side of Prince Regent Inlet and its southerly continuation the Gulf of Boothia, were charted from Cresswell Bay on the north to Lord Mayor's Bay on the south. In 1830 James Ross crossed the Boothian Isthmus and then the Strait named after him and reached the north coast of King William Land. He then marched southwards along the north-west coast to Point Victory;[26] the coast beyond that cape stretched towards the southwest, and James Ross gave the name Cape Franklin to the furthest headland visible in that direction. Ross was under the impression that King William Land was part of the mainland, and that the coast extended beyond Point Victory westwards past Cape Franklin as far as Point Turnagain. The *Victory* could not be extricated from the ice and was abandoned in Victoria Harbour on the east coast of Boothia in 1832. The party then proceeded in May and June 1832 to cover a distance of over two hundred miles to Fury Beach, where stores had been deposited by Parry in 1825. The party wintered at Fury Beach and next season John Ross and his men reached the *Isabella*, now a whaling ship, at the entrance to Lancaster Sound and arrived back in England in the autumn of 1833.[27]

The prolonged absence of John Ross caused great alarm in England, and George Back took command of a private overland relief expedition, the purpose of which was to travel down the Great Fish River towards Prince Regent Inlet, where it was thought that Ross would be found. Back left England in 1833, wintered at Great Slave Lake, and was about to start for the Polar Sea when he received a letter informing him of Ross's safe return to England, but requesting him to descend the Great Fish River and examine the coast to the westward in the direction of Point Turnagain. Back reached the estuary of the Great Fish River in boats but could not proceed further westwards owing to pack-ice and was forced to return. He arrived back in England in September 1835.[28]

At the conclusion of the explorations which have been briefly described, three portions of the north American coast still remained unexamined. The first lay between Point Barrow (Elson, 1826) and Return Reef (Franklin, 1826), the distance between them being about 160 geographical miles. The second portion lay between Point Turnagain (Franklin, 1821) and Cape Franklin (James Clark Ross, 1830), the distance between them, in a straight line, being 222 geographical miles. The third portion lay between the estuary of the Great Fish River (Back, 1834), and Fury and Hecla Strait (Parry, 1822), the distance between them, in a straight line, being about 220 geographical miles; the complicated geographical problems awaiting a solution in this third portion are discussed in detail on a later page. In particular the relatively small unexplored area between Cape Franklin, on the north-west coast of King William Land, and the, estuary of the Great Fish River, was a matter of conjecture.

In 1836 the Hudson's Bay Company entrusted to two of its officers, Peter Warren Dease (1788–1863) and Thomas Simpson (1808–40) the task of examining the unexplored parts of the North American coastline. In June 1837 they left Fort Chipewyan, descended the Mackenzie, and travelled westwards towards Point Barrow, which Simpson reached on August 4. This closed the gap between Point Barrow and Return Reef. Dease and Simpson returned up the Mackenzie, and wintered on the shore of Great Bear Lake in houses which they built and named Fort Confidence.

In 1838 Dease and Simpson went down the Coppermine River, and travelled in their boats towards the east. Simpson examined the coastline past Point Turnagain almost to the Minto Islands, and during this voyage saw extensive land lying to the northward which he named Victoria Land.

The third winter was also passed at Fort Confidence, and in 1839 Dease and Simpson again descended the Coppermine and travelled in boats eastwards towards the estuary of the Great Fish River. They expected to find the continental coastline extending to the north-west coast of King William Land, but found that it turned eastwards to form the south side of Simpson Strait, which separates the mainland from the south coast of King William Land. They passed through Simpson Strait, and on August 16 arrived at Montreal Island (reached by Back in 1834) at the estuary of the Great Fish River. They extended their discoveries still further to the eastward as far as Castor and Pollux River, south of Inglis Bay, and then returned. During their journey back to Fort Confidence they traced the south coast of King William Land for a distance of about sixty geographical miles, and part of the south coast of Victoria Land for a distance of one hundred and fifty-six geographical miles, from Point Back to Point Parry. They reached the Coppermine River on September 16, and Fort Confidence eight days later. They then abandoned the Fort, and travelled southwards.[29]

Their explorations, together with those of their predecessors, resulted in the delineation of the whole north American coastline from Point Barrow to Castor and Pollux River. They did not, however, settle two important details, namely, whether Boothia was an island or a peninsula, and (of equal importance) whether King William Land was an island or not. The fact that both these questions were still awaiting solution had a very important influence on Rae's journeys.

4. *Rae's First Expedition, 1846–47*

PURPOSE OF THE EXPEDITION

Thomas Simpson, at the conclusion of his third boat voyage with Dease, volunteered to survey the north American coast from Castor and Pollux River to Fury and Hecla Strait. He proposed, in a plan submitted to the Hudson's Bay Company, to descend the Great Fish River, and, after completing his explorations, to return either along that river or through Fury and Hecla Strait and Foxe Basin, to York Factory, Hudson Bay. The Directors of the Company in London accepted Simpson's offer on June 3, 1840. Simpson, however, died eleven days later on the 14th, and never knew that the Company had agreed with his suggestions.[30]

The question of another expedition to be led by an officer of the Hudson's Bay Company remained in abeyance for a few years, but ultimately in 1844, under circumstances which have already been described, the Company entrusted Rae with the duty of carrying out the explorations which Thomas Simpson had proposed.

Rae's first expedition was thus a successor to Dease and Simpson's explorations, but the plan which Rae was finally ordered to adopt differed in detail from that proposed by Thomas Simpson. Rae was to travel in boats from Churchill along the west coast of Hudson Bay to Repulse Bay or Fury and Hecla Strait. He was then to examine the coastline from that strait to Castor and Pollux River, or, if Boothia proved to be part of the mainland, to some point already reached by the officers of the *Victory* expedition (1829–33). At the conclusion of his explorations he was either to return to Churchill, or to proceed to Great Slave Lake by way of the Great Fish River.

This plan originated with Sir George Simpson,[31] who hoped, as no doubt Rae did, that the expedition would, firstly, find Boothia to be an island, separated from the continent by a strait running from the Gulf of Boothia to Castor and Pollux River; and, secondly, would discover a continuous coastline extending from the south side of Fury and Hecla Strait, round the south end of the Gulf of Boothia, to the land on the south side of this possible strait. If these hopes had been fulfilled, Rae would not only have completed the survey of the north American coastline but would also have discovered a North-west Passage, thereby solving a problem which had awaited a solution for centuries.

Part only of the locality to which Rae was directed had been examined by explorers, but additional particulars had been obtained from Eskimos. The information which he had at his disposal when he set forth on his first expedition may be briefly summarised as follows.

When Parry, during his second expedition (1821–23), discovered Fury and Hecla Strait, neither he nor any of his officers actually reached either Cape Hallowell or Cape Englefield, although some of them saw these capes on the north and south sides respectively of the western end of that strait. Parry, however, had no doubt that these two capes bounded the junction of Fury and Hecla Strait and Prince Regent Inlet. He did not explore any part of the west coast of Melville Peninsula, but, according to maps drawn by Eskimos, that coast extended approximately in a south-south-west direction from Cape Englefield to a point not far to the west of Repulse Bay, which thus appeared to be situated on the south side of a narrow isthmus uniting Melville Peninsula and the mainland. This information confirmed what Parry, partly from his own observations, partly from those of some of his officers, had already thought to be possible, and he was sufficiently convinced of its truth to warrant his indicating on his charts the probable position of the west coast of Melville Peninsula.[32]

During his expedition in the *Victory* (1829–33) Sir John Ross obtained from Boothian Eskimos some additional information. According to the map which they drew, no strait led from the Gulf of Boothia to the westward, and Boothia was part of the American continent.[33] Ross and his officers confirmed this information so far as it concerned the whole east coast of Boothia and of the Boothian Isthmus as far south as Lord Mayor's Bay.[34] Moreover, John Ross concluded from his own observations that the sea on the east side of Boothia was on a different level from that on the west side, and hence that no direct communication existed between these two seas. It should be noted that James Clark Ross did not accept his uncle's conclusions regarding the supposed difference in level.[35] Although the Hudson's Bay Company Directors may not have agreed, these considerations resulted in fairly general acceptance that the Gulf of Boothia had no outlets to the open sea other than by Fury and Hecla Strait on the east and by Prince Regent Inlet on the north.[36]

Thomas Simpson's narrative of his third boat voyage with Dease cast considerable doubt on the validity of John Ross's conclusions. Dease and Simpson, when they reached Castor and Pollux River, left their men to build a cairn while they themselves went to an eminence three miles distant. They thought that they saw the coast to the eastward turn off about five miles away to the southwards. "Far without", wrote Simpson, "lay several lofty islands; and in the north-east, more distant still, appeared some high blue land: this, which we designated Cape Sir John Ross, is in all probability one of the south-eastern promontories of Boothia. We could therefore hardly doubt being now arrived at that large gulph, uniformly described by the Esquimaux as containing many islands, and, with numerous indentations, running down to the southward, till it approaches within forty miles of Repulse and Wager bays".[37] Dease and Simpson thus thought that they had reached the Gulf of Boothia, and that the "lofty islands" which they believed that they saw in the distance and named the "Committee Islands", lay in that gulf.[38] Thus one of the principal problems which Rae was expected to solve was whether Dease and Simpson had been right in believing, contrary to the opinion of Sir John Ross, that the Gulf of Boothia was connected directly with the estuary of the Great Fish River and Simpson Strait.

RAE'S EXPLORATIONS, 1846–47

Sir George Simpson hoped that the expedition would start in 1845, but the preparations required longer time for their completion than had been expected. Rae, in his letter of February 25, 1845, stated that he had been unable to obtain adequate instruction in surveying in time to begin exploration during the 1845 open season. He ultimately arrived at York Factory on October 8, spent the winter at that place, and was ready to start his journey in June 1846.

Rae left York Factory with ten men and two boats on June 13, 1846, reached Churchill on the 27th, and on July 4 received his final orders from Sir George Simpson.[39]

Sir George Simpson's orders, particularly paragraph 5, with their insistence on shooting, hunting and fishing, are an important landmark in the history of Canadian arctic travel. They enforce the necessity of "living on the land", of which Rae, though not the originator, was to become the foremost practical exponent as an explorer.

Rae left Churchill on July 5, 1846, and reached Repulse Bay on the 25th. The Eskimos there confirmed, as Ross and Parry had already been told, that only a narrow isthmus separated Repulse Bay from the sea to the north. The isthmus is now called after Rae. He crossed it soon afterwards and reached the lower end of the Gulf of Boothia, naming this part Committee Bay. Rae first tried to travel westward but was hindered by ice. Returning, he met the same difficulty to the eastward. Finding it impossible to accomplish his task in the 1846 navigable season, Rae changed his plans, arrived back at Repulse Bay on August 10, and prepared for the winter. He explains that the unlikelihood of getting a winter supply of reindeer meat and other animal food was his main reason for having to turn back. At Repulse Bay a house named Fort Hope was built of stones; deer and birds were shot, and fish were caught in large numbers during the autumn.

On April 5, 1847, Rae left Fort Hope on foot, crossed the isthmus, and then travelled on his second attempt along the west side of Committee Bay, but found no strait leading to the westward. On April 18 he reached a position close to Brunel Inlet, in the south-east corner of Lord Mayor's Bay. This bay had already been charted by James Clark Ross, who after Rae's return stated that Rae's description left no room for doubt that Rae had been at the identical place that he himself had reached during the *Victory* expedition.[40] During Rae's outward and return journeys he completely examined the whole of the west coast of Committee Bay, with the single exception of the south end of Pelly Bay. He did not actually walk round Pelly Bay, but distinctly saw land there from the summit, seven hundred and thirty feet above sea level, of Helen Island. Since he did not traverse this part of the bay, some geographers were unwilling to admit that the possible existence of a channel leading westwards from Pelly Bay had been finally disproved,[41] but Rae himself was by now fully convinced that the land was continuous all round the south end of the bay. He arrived back at Fort Hope on May 5.

This journey had the important result of showing that Boothia was not an island but a peninsula.

Rae set out again from Fort Hope on May 13 and travelled along the east side of Committee Bay towards Fury and Hecla Strait. The supporting sledge with dogs was sent back three days later and the journey thereafter, one of Rae's hardest efforts, was carried out without sledges.

Owing to shortage of food Rae just failed to reach Fury and Hecla Strait, Cape Crozier being his furthest northern point. Rae gave the name of Cape Ellice[42] to the most distant point which he could see to the northward, and according to his calculations Parry's Cape Englefield at the western end of Fury and Hecla Strait was about twenty-five miles north of Cape Crozier and about ten miles beyond Cape Ellice. Rae arrived back at Fort Hope on June 9. He states in one of his letters "my journey to the Fury and Hecla Strait gave me harder work than any thing I had previously experienced".[43]

Rae had now examined the whole coastline (except the south end of Pelly Bay) from Lord Mayor's Bay to Cape Crozier, and had traced about six hundred and fifty-five statute miles of new land and coast.[44] He had thus virtually connected Ross's discoveries on Boothia with those effected by Parry on Melville Peninsula. Moreover, he had demonstrated, at least to his own satisfaction, that Boothia was not an island but part of the mainland, and that no channel connected the Gulf of Boothia directly with the sea near Dease and Simpson's turning point at Castor and Pollux River.

Leaving Fort Hope for the south on August 12, Rae reached Churchill on the 31st and York Factory on September 6. Before sailing for England, where he arrived on October 25, 1847, he met the sappers and miners who, as the sequel will show, had come out from England to York Factory to serve in Richardson's Franklin search expedition planned for 1848.[45]

Rae's letters describing his first expedition are, like all the later letters, written in a vigorous and buoyant style and the reader cannot fail to notice the enthusiasm which was one of Rae's characteristics. The first expedition was typical of Rae's methods. The conditions under which the party lived were strenuous and primitive, but everybody concerned appears to have been almost as hardened and tough as Rae himself. The journey to Fury and Hecla Strait called for as much endurance from his men no doubt as it did from the leader himself.

Rae wrote several accounts of his first expedition. None of his letters to Sir George Simpson, included in the present collection, appears to have been published before. His official report to the Hudson's Bay Company, dated September 21, 1847, also included in the present collection was, however, published, and furnishes a much more detailed account than his letters to Simpson. This official report, after undergoing a few alterations at the hands of the Secretary to the Company, was published in *The Times* on November 1, 1847, a few days after Rae's arrival in England.[46] The most complete account, however, of his first expedition is that contained in his book, *Narrative of an Expedition to the Shores of the Arctic Sea in 1846 and 1847.* The present letters contain details that are not included in the book and these two sources supplement each other and together form a complete picture of his journey.

The expedition established Rae's reputation as an Arctic traveller, and his name, as a result, probably became as familiar to English readers as the names of Franklin, Parry, John Ross, and James Clark Ross.

THE MAN SEEN BY KIA AND REPORTED BY KOOLOOA

Rae appears to have seen no Eskimos on the north-west part of Melville Peninsula, but at least one Eskimo saw him, and others found traces of his visit. These circumstances, together with others now to be enumerated, had a curious sequel about twenty years later. Briefly stated, it was as follows.

Sir Leopold M'Clintock, after his return to England in 1859 from King William Island, on which he had found definite proof of the fate of the Franklin expedition in the *Erebus* and *Terror*, declared that none of Franklin's officers or men could still be living. The principal authorities agreed with M'Clintock.

Nevertheless, Charles Francis Hall (1821–71), an American, believed that survivors might still be found and undertook two expeditions in search of them. The first of these in 1860–62 owing to the loss of his twenty-eight foot boat was limited to Baffin Land and no discoveries affecting Franklin were made. During his second expedition (1864–69) Hall wintered first on the west side of Roes Welcome and then for four further winters at Repulse Bay, and while there during the autumn of 1867 received from Eskimos some information which led him to believe that white men had been seen near Fury and Hecla Strait on some occasions between 1849 and 1865. Since Hall was not alive to the full significance of the results of the previous Franklin searches and knew of no arctic explorers who had been there during that period of time, he was convinced from this information that his long cherished belief was correct and that the white men of the Eskimo report must have been survivors of the Franklin expedition. He went in search of these white men in 1868, and at the North Ooglit Islands, on the east coast of Melville Peninsula, met an Eskimo named Koolooa, who told him that he and another Eskimo named Kia, no longer living, had once travelled with their families to the north-west part of Melville Peninsula in order to hunt deer, and that, while there, Kia saw a strange man.

The Appendix in the published narrative of Hall's second Arctic expedition contains two accounts, both in detail and written by Hall himself, of Koolooa's statements about the strange man seen by Kia. Both accounts are records of conversations between Koolooa and Hall's interpreters, and both appear to have been written down by Hall in the form in which they were given him by the interpreters. The first account runs as follows:

> . . . Koo-loo-a was with Kia on the deer-hunt when the latter saw the strange man, though not present at the time when Kia sighted and followed the strange man. A short time before Kia saw the stranger in black clothes Koo-loo-a felt thirsty and came to a lake. He had laid himself down to take a draught of water, and at the very instant he was placing his face down to

> it, he heard a loud crack, which he thought must be of a gun, for when small and living at Too-noo-nee (Pond's Bay) he had become familiar with the reports of the guns of white men that came there to kill whales. He was at the time so far from the sea that it could not have been the noise of ice cracking. Kia was very particular in telling him all about the strange man he had seen on Koo-loo-a and Kia meeting each other. The strange man was tall and carried some long thing on his shoulder and walked very fast. He had a cap on his head that was independent of his coat, but there was a hood to the long dark coat he had on. Kia kept himself hid behind the rocks and followed the strange man—for some time. Not long after Kia saw the strange man, that he (K.) thought must be an Indian; Kia heard a loud crack, which made him think of ice cracking, but the sea was too far off to hear so plain.[47]

The second account, after mentioning the noise heard by Koolooa and believed by him to be that of gun-fire, continues as follows:

> . . . Same day Koo-loo-a heard the crack . . . while walking around he came to fresh tracks on some grass and the tracks longer than his foot, the tracks so fresh that the blades of earth, grass had not all regained their upright position. Some of the grass was then gradually lifting up as it had been trod upon. The steps long and foot-marks 'turning out.'
>
> Next morning after hearing the crack and seeing tracks both Koo-loo-a and Kia moved their tents and families away from that place. The next morning after moving, Koo-loo-a went to work fixing the skin of the deer he had killed.
>
> As Koo-loo-a was late in getting ready, Ki-a started off deer-hunting alone. By and by Kia saw a man coming up the hill on which he (Kia) was, coming directly toward him. Kia thought at first the man to be Koo-loo-a, but on looking longer and more observingly Kia saw his mistake, for it was not Koo-loo-a, but a

> strange man having a cap on his head that was distinct from his coat. He saw that he (the stranger) had strange clothes on and carried something strange in a strange way on his shoulder. Kia could not, from his position behind the rock, see much of the stranger's face; the clothes not black nor white; coat on that came down to or almost to his knees; the make of clothes altogether different from Innuits. The stranger had something across his shoulder running diagonally; this something was long and wide at one end and narrow at the other end. He was walking rather fast and going directly toward the point on N.W. extremity of Melville Peninsula, as showed by Kia[48] on Parry's chart. Kia followed the stranger up for some time and looked sharp at him. Kia kept himself hid among the rocks all the time. Next morning Kia and Koo-loo-a moved their tents and families to the same place as when Kia saw the strange man, and then they all saw the stranger's tracks, which showed a long foot narrow in the middle.[49]

That same day Koolooa found a cairn built of stones, and some other stones which had apparently been used to form a cache. He told Hall that he did not think that Eskimos had built the cairn. Koolooa and the other natives present when Hall was given this information showed, after deliberations lasting a quarter of an hour, by the raising of thirteen fingers that the stranger had been seen in 1854.

Hall, guided by Koolooa, went to seek the cairn; and found it in Parry Bay,[50] immediately to the north of Cape Crozier, on the west coast of Melville Peninsula. The cairn, built of stones, stood on a plateau situated between two rivers running into the bay, and was about one hundred feet above sea-level. No clue to its origin could be found. Close to it were two places where tents had been pitched, and one of these places, in the opinion of Hall's Eskimo interpreters, had not been used by Eskimos.

According to Rae's track-chart, which Hall had with him, Rae had stopped at Cape Crozier and had not actually entered Parry Bay. This was an assumption on Hall's part, and he concluded that Rae could not have built the cairn. Being short of food, Hall did not visit Cape Crozier. His further search for traces of white men on Melville Peninsula yielded no result, but he continued to believe that survivors of the Franklin expedition had lived there for many years. Hall did not relinquish that belief until he at last succeeded in 1869 in reaching King William Island, the principal scene of the Franklin catastrophe. There he became convinced that he had been mistaken, and that none of Franklin's officers and men had survived.[51] Hall died in 1871 before he was able to write a detailed account of his second expedition, but a book was compiled some years later by Professor J.E. Nourse from journals and notebooks and published in 1879.[52] Unfortunately, this narrative gives no indication of what may have been Hall's final opinion, reached after his visit to King William Island, regarding the identity of the stranger seen by Kia and the origin of the cairn at Parry Bay.

In 1880 Rae sent to the *New York Herald* a long letter[53] containing several criticisms of and comments on the statements contained in Nourse's recently published narrative of Hall's second expedition. Rae stated that he himself had in all probability been the strange man seen by Kia, for during his journey to Cape Crozier in 1847 he had worn clothes exactly of the kind described by Kia. In a further letter, ultimately published in the *Journal of the American Geographical Society*, Rae wrote: "I reached and named Cape Crozier on the west side of Melville Peninsula, about 25 miles south of Cape Englefield. I had a cairn built there (according to my usual practice when stones could be found) not on the extreme point of the cape but some miles east of it, and a note deposited therein recording briefly the work done".[54] Rae's other remarks in this letter show quite clearly that he was confident that he had built the cairn found by Hall, and his account of its position agrees entirely with Hall's sketch-map, although this does not include a scale of miles.[55] Rae does not seem to have had a tent with him, but Hall's interpreters may have been mistaken in thinking that one of the tent-places had been used by white men. In any case, there can be no reasonable doubt that Rae was the strange man seen by Kia, not in 1854, but in 1847, and that the cairn was Rae's handiwork.[56]

5. *The Franklin Expedition, 1845–?48*

When Rae returned to England in October 1847 he found that widespread anxiety prevailed regarding the safety of Sir John Franklin's expedition, which, it was greatly feared, was probably beginning its third arctic winter. Franklin had sailed in 1845 and no news had been received for more than two years. The following account of the Franklin expedition includes only such particulars as are essential for a correct understanding of the part taken by Rae in the Franklin search.[57]

Early in 1845 the Admiralty decided to send an expedition to seek, and if possible to pass through, a North-west Passage. Only a small part still remained undiscovered. The whole north American coastline had been examined from Bering Strait to Castor and Pollux River and the coastal waters were supposed to be navigable during any ordinary summer season. At the eastern end of this coastline three masses of land had been seen to the north and partly charted. These were Wollaston Land, Victoria Land and King William Land. Some hundreds of miles further north lay Melville Sound and the principal discoveries of Parry, who in 1819 had sailed from Baffin Bay through Lancaster Sound and Barrow Strait to Melville Island. Parry noted but did not explore several openings leading from these channels still further to the north and the largest of these, which lay between North Devon and Cornwallis Island, was named by him Wellington Channel. On the south side of Barrow Strait Parry charted the whole north coast of North Somerset, and some forty miles further to the west saw but did not visit a prominent headland which he named Cape Walker. It appeared to be situated approximately in the centre of a line of coast about seventeen miles in length. Parry saw no land between North Somerset and this line of coast at Cape Walker. Parry, however, from Melville Island saw the north coast of Banks Land about two hundred miles to the west of Cape Walker, and since no land was seen between Cape Walker and Banks Land that cape appeared to be the most westerly land on the south side of Barrow Strait. These discoveries in the north stretched about three hundred miles further west than the eastern end, at Castor and Pollux River, of the known part of the North American coast-line ending at Bering Strait.

Between the extremities of the known lay an unexplored quadrilateral,[58] with its north-east corner formed by Cape Walker, its south-east by King William Land, its south-west by Wollaston Land, and its northwest by Banks Land. This unexplored quadrilateral was believed to be occupied either by an archipelago or by a landless sea; its total area was about seventy thousand square miles. It afforded the shortest stretch of unknown land or sea intervening between Barrow Strait and the mainland. If ships could sail southwards or south-westwards from the neighbourhood of Cape Walker, and reach the American coast-line anywhere between Castor and Pollux River and Bering Strait the problem of the North-west Passage would be solved. Attempts in this direction were therefore considered to be the most desirable.

It should be pointed out that Parry's observations made in 1819 and 1820 on the ice conditions between the south-west coast of Melville Island and Banks Land had convinced the Admiralty that this route was impracticable. Prince Regent Inlet was not considered as affording good prospects of completing a North-west Passage, for it was uncertain at the time of Franklin's sailing whether a channel existed from the Gulf of Boothia to the sea observed by Dease and Simpson at Castor and Pollux River.

The most likely route seemed to be south-westwards from Cape Walker, but, should there be no possible route in that direction, an alternative route appeared to be afforded by Wellington Channel. This route was not, however, considered as the one that should be tried first, for its adoption would necessitate an attempt to go round by the north of the Parry Islands and thereby lose all the advantages likely to accrue from utilizing to the fullest possible extent channels which were already partly known.

The Franklin expedition sailed in 1845 while these opinions were dominant. H.M. Ships *Erebus* and *Terror*, which had been in the Antarctic under the command of James Clark Ross, were equipped at Woolwich for Arctic service. Franklin himself sailed in the *Erebus* with

James Fitzjames as Commander. His second-in-command, Captain Francis Rawdon Moira Crozier, who had served in three Arctic expeditions under Parry and had been second-in-command of the Antarctic expedition under James Clark Ross, sailed as Captain of H.M.S. *Terror*. The expedition was equipped on a lavish scale and was provisioned for three years.

Franklin was directed to sail through Baffin Bay, and then through Lancaster Sound and Barrow Strait until he reached "the longitude of that portion of land on which Cape Walker is situated, or about 98° west". Thence he was to sail southwards and westwards towards Bering Strait, but if progress in that direction proved impracticable owing to "ice of a permanent appearance", he was authorised to seek a passage through Wellington Channel. He was expressly cautioned against repeating Parry's attempts to pass to the westward between Melville Island and Banks Land.[59] The other rather unpromising route down Prince Regent Inlet was not referred to.

The Hudson's Bay Company was requested to afford any necessary assistance to Franklin, and on March 11, 1845, the Governor and Committee in London issued the following instructions to the Governor and Council of Rupert's Land:—

> The subject of Arctic discovery again engages the attention not only of the Government, but of the public, and Sir John Franklin is about to proceed in command of an expedition, consisting of two vessels, with a view of effecting a passage by sea round the northern shore of the American Continent. To that end he proposes going up Davis's Straits, into Baffin's Bay, through Lancaster Sound, Barrow's Straits, and inside Melville Island, on to Point Barrow. As he will in all probability endeavour to approach the shore near the Mackenzie or Coppermine River, with a view of landing despatches, it may be well to give intimation to the natives to be on the look-out for the expedition, and to convey to the nearest establishment any papers or letters that may be entrusted to their charge, for which they will

> be liberally rewarded, such letters to be forwarded from post to post with the least possible delay.
>
> In order to guard against the difficulties of providing means of subsistence to the persons engaged in the expedition, in the event of their landing near the Mackenzie or Coppermine, you will direct that additional net-thread and fishing tackle be forwarded to Fort Good Hope on the Mackenzie, and to Fort Resolution on Great Slave Lake, there to remain in depot for the use of the expedition until it be ascertained that such supplies will not be required; and we have further to desire, that the persons in charge of our establishments near the Arctic Sea take such measures as may be within their power for the protection and maintenance of the party in the event of their landing, charging all expenses connected therewith to an account to be headed 'Sir John Franklin'.[60]

The Hudson's Bay Company's connection with the Franklin expedition and the Franklin search began with the issue of the above instructions; it was destined to be maintained at irregular intervals for eleven years.

Franklin sailed from the Thames on May 19, 1845, with one hundred and thirty-four officers and men.[61] At the end of the following July his ships were seen for the last time by a British whaling ship. Franklin had then reached the northern part of Baffin Bay and was awaiting a suitable opportunity to cross to Lancaster Sound.

Many years were to elapse before his subsequent proceedings and the fate of his expedition became known. It was, however, finally ascertained that he passed through Lancaster Sound and Barrow Strait, and then entered Wellington Channel, having no doubt failed for some reason to sail southwards and westwards from the neighbourhood of Cape Walker. He sailed up Wellington Channel to latitude 77°N., returned down the west side of Cornwallis Island, and then wintered at Beechey Island. In 1846 he sailed southwards, no doubt through Peel Sound and Franklin Strait, until his ships were beset in ice near the north extremity of King William Land on September 12, 1846. The winter was passed in the ice.

Franklin in 1846 had thus found navigable channels from Barrow Strait to King William Land, so that all that remained to complete the discovery of a North-west Passage was proof that the channel (Victoria Strait) in which his ships were beset was continuous with the water along the mainland; the distance from the ships to the western end of Simpson Strait was about ninety geographical miles, measured in a straight line.[62]

During the following spring (1847) a small party commanded by Lieutenant Graham Gore left the *Erebus* on May 24. The examination of the remaining ninety miles is believed[63] to have been Gore's principal purpose on this journey, but neither the full extent of his journey nor the date of his return to the *Erebus* is known.

Franklin died on June 11, 1847, and the command of the expedition devolved on Captain Crozier. The ships remained beset and must have drifted southwards down Victoria Strait. There is reason to believe that a severe outbreak of scurvy occurrred among the officers and men during the third winter.

Crozier, with only a few months' provisions left, abandoned the ships on April 22, 1848. The ships then lay fifteen miles north-north-west of Point Victory, and Crozier landed near there with 104 officers and men, 9 officers and 15 men having died. He intended to travel along the west and south coasts of King William Land to the estuary of the Great Fish River, and then to ascend the river. The attempt ended in complete disaster, and it is doubtful if any of the officers and men reached the estuary. Most of them died on King William Land, where skeletons and much abandoned equipment were found by Sir Leopold M'Clintock and his second-in-command, Lieutenant Hobson, in 1859, and since then by several other explorers. One of the ships apparently sank in Victoria Strait. The other was found by Eskimos either near O'Reilly Island or near Grant Point off the west coast of Adelaide Peninsula. Some of the officers and men presumably returned to the ships after these had been abandoned, and a few, according to Eskimo reports, lived on the one which was found near O'Reilly Island (or near Grant Point) where she sank apparently in the spring of 1849. These few men cannot have survived much longer and there is no reason to suppose that they were still living during the summer of 1849. The vast majority must already have died along the coast of King William Land within a few months of the abandonment of the ships in 1848.

The Franklin expedition is universally admitted to have been the first to find a North-west Passage. The existence of a passage may probably have been demonstrated by Gore in 1847. There is, however, no doubt that the officers and men who marched towards the Great Fish River and left behind them a terrible trail on the west and south coasts of King William Land, discovered a North-west Passage in 1848, even if Gore had not done so in 1847.[64]

6. *Rae's Second Expedition, 1848–49*

FRANKLIN RELIEF EXPEDITIONS, 1848

In February 1847 the Admiralty wrote to Sir Edward Parry regarding two communications received from Sir John Ross. In its letter to Parry, the Admiralty stated that, although it felt no apprehensions about the safety of the missing expedition, active measures for assisting Franklin would nevertheless have to be taken if no news of him arrived by the end of the year. The Admiralty asked Parry for his opinion and suggested his conferring with Sir James Clark Ross, with Colonel Sabine (an authority on gravity and on terrestrial magnetism who had served in several Arctic expeditions) and with Sir John Richardson, who had taken part in both of Franklin's overland expeditions to the North American coast.[65]

Richardson, in his written report to Parry, made several suggestions, one of which was the despatch of a search party in boats. This party was to go down the Mackenzie River in 1848; travel along the coast towards the Coppermine;[66] examine Wollaston Land, Victoria Land and the neighbouring islands; then return south up the Coppermine; and pass the winter at the north end of Great Bear Lake. If the whole plan could not be carried out in 1848 it was to be completed in 1849.

If the Admiralty approved of the plan, arrangements should at once be made with the Hudson's Bay Company for the despatch of boats and men from England in the summer of 1847, and for their conveyance as far as possible towards the Mackenzie before the onset of winter. The officers should leave England early in 1848, and by forced marches, and travelling as rapidly as possible, overtake the boats and men as soon as possible after the ice had broken up in "the rivers to the north". Richardson believed that these arrangements would enable both officers and men of the expedition to reach the Mackenzie River by the end of July and the estuary a few days later.

Richardson thought that Franklin had probably sailed southwest from Cape Walker and had found his progress to the westward impeded in the narrow channels of an archipelago lying between Victoria Land, Wollaston Land and Banks Land. He was further of opinion that Franklin, if compelled to abandon his ships, would try to reach either Lancaster Sound or the North American mainland, whichever happened to be the nearer, but would not attempt to ascend any river except the Mackenzie, which, Richardson said, "is navigable for boats of large draught, without a portage, for 1,300 miles from the sea, or within 40 miles of Fort Chepewyan, one of the Company's principal depots, and there are five other posts in that distance. Though these posts could not furnish provisions to such a party, they could, by providing them with nets, and distributing the men to various fishing stations, do much towards procuring food for them".[67] Richardson volunteered to conduct the party if the Admiralty approved of the plan.[68]

These proposals were submitted by the Admiralty to Sir George Simpson, who had arrived in England in March 1847. Simpson suggested no alterations;[69] the Admiralty accepted Richardson's suggestions, and preparations were at once made to put them into effect. Fifteen men of the Corps of Royal Sappers and Miners, and five experienced seamen of the Royal Navy were recruited in England; two boats were constructed at Portsmouth and two at Gosport; and the necessary stores, provisions and equipment were prepared. The men, the four boats and the stores left England on June 15, 1847, in two of the Hudson's Bay Company's ships, and reached York Factory in September. As has already been mentioned, Rae met these men when he himself reached York Factory from Repulse Bay on September 6. On arrival the men from England were placed under the orders of Chief Trader John Bell pending the arrival of Richardson in 1848. Bell himself was duly attached to the expedition by the Hudson's Bay Company.[70] He made immediate arrangements to leave for the interior. Bell and most of the members of the party wintered at Cumberland House.[71]

In the autumn of 1847 no news whatever had been received of Sir John Franklin, not even from whaling ships returning from Davis Strait in the late autumn. It was then certain that Richardson would be leaving England early in 1848 to join his men already in Canada. By now the manner in which Rae had conducted his expedition in 1846–47 had shown him to be an exceptionally capable explorer, in every way qualified for taking part in the enterprise which Richardson was to carry out. Richardson, not unnaturally, suggested to the Admiralty the appointment of Rae as his second in command. The Admiralty on December 16, 1847, approached the Hudson's Bay Company and asked if Rae could be spared, and on receiving an answer in the affirmative, the Admiralty directed Richardson to make all the necessary arrangements with Rae, then in England, who had, presumably, already agreed to serve if the several authorities consented to his being appointed.[72]

At much the same time Richardson's original plan underwent certain modifications. It had been adopted by the Admiralty at a time when no definite decision had been reached regarding the possible despatch of other relief expeditions. During the late autumn of 1847, the Admiralty decided to equip two further Franklin relief expeditions, both by sea. These, in conjunction with Richardson's party, were to carry out an extensive plan of operations in accordance with suggestions made principally by Sir James Clark Ross.[73] Each of the three expeditions was to be responsible for its allotted share in the successful accomplishment of what was virtually a single plan. This was as follows:

H.M.S. *Plover*, Commander (later Rear-Admiral) Thomas Edward Laws Moore (1819–72), was sent to Bering Strait. As soon as she had been secured in a suitable harbour in 1848, boat parties were to be sent to the eastward towards the Mackenzie along the North American coastline, and were to communicate if possible with Richardson. These measures were to be repeated if necessary in 1849, and the *Plover* was to be joined during the summer of 1848 by H.M.S. *Herald*, Captain (later Vice-Admiral Sir) Henry Kellett (1806–75). Moore sailed from England early in 1848 but did not reach Bering Strait in time for the despatch of boat parties in 1848. He reached St. Lawrence Island on October 13, 1848, and, unable to go farther northwards, wintered in Emma Harbour on the Siberian coast.[74] It was not until 1849 that his boat parties were able to start for the Mackenzie River.[75]

On the Atlantic side, H.M. Ships *Enterprise* and *Investigator*, under the command of Sir James Clark Ross, who had volunteered his services, were to proceed to Barrow Strait in the summer of 1848. A steam launch was attached to each ship. The *Investigator* under Captain Edward Joseph Bird was to winter near Cape Rennell on the north coast of North Somerset, while the *Enterprise* was to proceed further westwards, either to Melville Island or to Banks Land. It was planned that in the spring and early summer of 1849 a party from the *Enterprise* would examine the west coast of Banks Land, proceed either to Cape Bathurst or to Cape Parry, (both on the North American coast east of the Mackenzie) and then to Fort Good Hope on the Mackenzie River. A second party from the *Enterprise* was to explore the east coast of Banks Land, proceed to Cape Krusenstern or Cape Hearne (both on the mainland near the estuary of the Coppermine River), communicate with Richardson, and under his orders either help him to examine the shores of Wollaston Land and Victoria Land, or return to England by the route which he thought best.[76]

Ross and Richardson reached complete agreement regarding these proposals. Richardson promised also to leave depots of provisions for the use of Ross's detached parties at Cape Bathurst, Cape Parry, and either at Cape Krusenstern or at Cape Hearne. The Hudson's Bay Company undertook to provide boats and provisions to assist Ross's men to travel from Fort Good Hope to England.[77]

In the event no men from Ross's expedition ever approached the mainland or came into contact with either Richardson or Rae.

Richardson's final orders did not mention the possibility that boat-parties from H.M.S. *Plover* might reach the Mackenzie, but he was fully aware that this might be the case.[78] His orders were as follows:

> *Instructions to Sir John Richardson, M.D., 16th March 1848. By the Commissioners for executing the office of Lord High Admiral, &c.*
>
> Whereas we think fit that you should be employed on an overland expedition in search of Her Majesty's ships 'Erebus' and 'Terror,' under the command of Captain Sir John Franklin, which ships are engaged in a voyage of discovery in the Arctic seas, you are hereby required and directed to take under your orders Mr. Rae, who has been selected to accompany you, and to leave England on the 25th instant by the mail steamer for Halifax in Nova Scotia, and New York; and on your arrival at the latter place, you are to proceed immediately to Montreal, for the purpose of conferring with Sir George Simpson, Governor of the Hudson's Bay Company's Settlements, and making arrangements with him for your future supplies and communications.
>
> You should next travel to Penetanguishene, on Lake Huron, and from thence, by a steamer, which sails on the 1st and 15th of every month of open water, to Saut Ste. Marie, at the foot of Lake Superior, and there embark in a canoe, which, with its crew, will have been provided for you, by that time, by Sir George Simpson.
>
> Following the usual canoe route by Fort William, Rainy Lake, the Lake of the Woods, Lake Winipeg, and the Saskatchewan River, it is hoped that you will overtake the boats now under charge of Mr. Bell, in July 1848, somewhere near Isle a la Crosse, or perhaps the Methy Portage.
>
> You will then send the canoe with its crew back to Canada, and having stowed the four boats for their sea voyage, you will

go on as rapidly as you can to the mouth of the Mackenzie; leaving Mr. Bell to follow with the heavier laden barge, to turn off at Great Bear Lake, and erect your winter residence at Fort Confidence, establish fisheries, and send out hunters.

Making a moderate allowance for unavoidable detention by ice, thick fogs, and storms, the examination of the coast between the Mackenzie and the Coppermine Rivers will probably occupy 30 days; but you cannot calculate to be able to keep the sea later than the 15th of September, for, from the beginning of that month, the young ice covers the sea almost every night, and very greatly impedes the boats, until the day is well advanced.

If you reach the sea in the first week of August, it is hoped you will be able to make the complete voyage to the Coppermine River, and also to coast a considerable part of the western and southern shores of Wollaston Land, and to ascend the Coppermine to some convenient point, where the boats can be left with the provisions ready for the next year's voyage; and you will instruct Mr. Bell to send two hunters to the banks of the river to provide food for the party on the route to Fort Confidence, and thus spare you any further consumption of the pemican reserved for the following summer.

As it may happen, however, from your late arrival on the coast, or subsequent unexpected detentions, that you cannot with safety attempt to reach the Coppermine, you have our full permission in such a case to return to Fort Good Hope, on the Mackenzie, there to deposit two of the boats, with all the sea stores, and to proceed with the other two boats, and the whole of the crews, to winter quarters on Great Bear Lake.

And you have also our permission to deviate from the line of route along the coast, should you receive accounts from the Eskimos, which may appear credible, of the crews of the 'Erebus' and 'Terror,' or some part of them, being in some other direction.

For the purpose of more widely extending your search, you are at liberty to leave Mr. Rae and a party of volunteers to winter on the coast, if, by the establishment of a sufficient fishery, or by killing a number of deer or musk oxen, you may be able to lay up provisions enough for them until you can rejoin them next summer.

As you have been informed by Captain Sir James Ross, of Her Majesty's ship 'Enterprize,' who is about to be employed on a similar search in another direction, of the probable directions in which the parties he will send out towards the continent will travel, you are to leave a deposit of pemican for their use at the following points—namely, Point Separation, Cape Bathurst, Cape Parry, and Cape Krusenstern; and as Sir James Ross is desirous that some pemican should be stored at Fort Good Hope, for the use of a party which he purposes sending thither in the spring of 1849, you are to make the necessary arrangements with Sir George Simpson for that purpose, as his directions to that effect must be sent early enough to meet the Company's brigade of Mackenzie River boats at Methy Portage, in July 1848.

Should it appear necessary to continue the search a second summer (1849), and should the boats have been housed on the Coppermine, you are to descend that river on the breaking up of the ice in June 1849, and to examine the passages between Wollaston and Banks's and Victoria Lands, so as to cross the routes of some of Sir James C. Ross's detached parties, and to return to Great Bear Lake in September 1849, and withdraw the whole party from thence to winter on Great Slave Lake, which would be as far south as you will have a prospect of travelling before the close of the river navigation.

Should you have found it necessary to return to the Mackenzie (September 1848), instead of pushing on to the Coppermine, the search in the summer of 1849 would, of course, have to be commenced from the former river again; but should circumstances render it practicable and desirable to send some of the party down the Coppermine with one or two boats, you are at liberty to do so.

A passage for yourself and Mr. Rae will be provided in the 'America,' British and North American mail-steamer, which sails from Liverpool on the 25th of March, and you will receive a letter of credit on Her Majesty's Consul at New York for the amount of the expense of your journey from New York to Saut Ste. Marie, and the carriage of the instruments, &c.

And in the event of intelligence of the 'Erebus' and 'Terror' reaching England after your departure, a communication will be made to the Hudson's Bay Company to ascertain the most expeditious route to forward your recal.

We consider it scarcely necessary to furnish you with any instructions contingent on a successful search after the abovementioned expedition, or any parties belonging to it. The circumstances of the case, and your own local knowledge and experience, will best point out the means to be adopted for the speedy transmission to this country of intelligence to the above effect, as well as of aiding and directing in the return of any such parties to England.

We are only anxious that the search so laudably undertaken by you and your colleagues should not be unnecessarily or hazardously prolonged; and whilst we are confident that no pains or labour will be spared in the execution of this service, we fear lest the zeal and anxiety of the party so employed may carry them further than would be otherwise prudent.

It is on this account you are to understand that your search is not to be prolonged after the winter of 1849, and which will be past on the Great Slave Lake; but that, at the earliest practicable moment after the breaking up of the weather in the spring of 1850, you will take such steps for the return of the party under your orders to England as circumstances may render expedient.

It must be supposed that the instructions now afforded you

can scarcely meet every contingency that may arise out of a service of the above description; but reposing, as we do, the utmost confidence in your discretion and judgment, you are not only at liberty to deviate from any point of them that may seem at variance with the objects of the expedition, but you are further empowered to take such other steps as shall be desirable at the time, and which are not provided for in these orders.

Given under our hands, 16th March 1848.

(Signed) AUCKLAND,
J.W.D. DUNDAS.

To Sir John Richardson, M.D., &c.

By command, &c.
(Signed) W.A.B. Hamilton.[79]

RICHARDSON AND RAE, 1848

Richardson and Rae left Liverpool on March 25, 1848, by the mail-steamer *Hibernia*, and reached New York on April 10. On April 11 they embarked on the *Empire* for Albany and Troy, and travelled by way of Lake Champlain to Montreal, where they arrived on April 15. They stayed with Sir George Simpson at his residence at Lachine until April 19, and then travelled via Buffalo and Detroit to Sault Ste. Marie, which they reached on April 29. At Sault Ste. Marie they embarked in two fully manned canoes, which had been ordered by Sir George Simpson, and then travelled via Fort William (reached on May 12), Lake Winnipeg, Norway House (June 5), Saskatchewan River, Cumberland House (June 13), Frog Portage, Churchill River, Sandy Lake, Primeau Lake (June 23), and Ile-à-la-Crosse (June 24) to Methy Portage (Portage la Loche), which they reached on June 28. There they overtook John Bell with the enlisted men from England and additional men recruited in Rupert's Land.

On July 6 the canoe-men who had brought Richardson and Rae from Sault Ste. Marie left Methy Portage on their return journey, and on the same day Richardson, Rae, and John Bell left the Portage for the north. They reached Fort Chipewyan five days later, and on July 15, when on the Slave River not far from Fort Resolution, separated into two parties. Richardson and Rae, with three boats and eighteen men, reached Fort Resolution two days later, crossed Great Slave Lake, and then descended the Mackenzie to the sea. Bell, with two boats and his men, went on to Great Bear Lake to construct suitable winter quarters.[80]

Richardson and Rae landed pemmican for the use of parties from the *Enterprise* or *Plover* at Fort Good Hope and Point Separation and reached the sea on August 3. They then travelled in the boats along the coast towards the estuary of the Coppermine, left pemmican near Cape Bathurst and at Cape Parry, and marked the sites, as had been agreed with James Clark Ross. The voyage progressed well until they neared Cape Cockburn on August 22. Dolphin and Union Strait was packed with ice, and the weather became very cold. As Richardson stated, "By keeping close to the beach in places where the shallowness of the water kept off the larger pieces of ice, by cutting passages for the boats where the packs abutted against the rocks, by dragging the boats over the smoother floes, and by making portages along the shore, according to circumstances, with the aid of occasional spaces of open water, we succeeded, with much labour, in making our way to a bay between Capes Hearne and Kendall by the end of the month".[81] One of the boats and some stores and pemmican were left at a rocky point twelve miles to the north of Cape Krusenstern; the two other boats, which had become scarcely seaworthy owing to the damage they had sustained from ice, were left with pemmican and stores at Icy Cove, about eight miles from Cape Kendall. The condition of the ice was such that the party could not reach either Wollaston or Victoria Land.

The last stage of the journey up the Coppermine and across to Great Bear Lake was completed on foot and Fort Confidence reached on September 15. At Fort Confidence they found that Bell and his men had already built several houses to replace the original station, which, built for Dease and Simpson, had been burnt down owing to the carelessness of some Indians. Richardson sent thirteen of the enlisted men, and three of Bell's men, to winter on Big Island, Great Slave Lake, as the resources at Fort Confidence were insufficient for the entire party. Two of Bell's men were sent to Ile-à-la-Crosse with dispatches.

Richardson, when serving on Franklin's second overland expedition had himself, in 1826, already examined the coastline between the estuary of the Mackenzie and that of the Coppermine, so that his journey with Rae in 1848 added very little to geographical knowledge. The only new discovery of interest was a river falling into Back Inlet, which Richardson named Rae River in honour of his companion. Nothing was heard of the Franklin expedition.

Soon after they had reached Fort Confidence, if not before, Richardson and Rae apparently agreed that Richardson would return to England at the first opportunity, and that Rae in 1849 was to complete the explorations left unfinished. Rae had volunteered to do this. Wollaston and Victoria Lands had not been visited, and a party from H.M.S. *Enterprise* (under Sir James Clark Ross's command) was expected to reach the estuary of the Coppermine, or Cape Krusenstern, in the summer of 1849.

Richardson's book[82] describing the expedition contains the most complete account which has hitherto appeared of the boat voyage, but Rae's letters to Sir George Simpson mention many interesting particulars, such as his criticisms of Richardson and his methods, which naturally do not appear either in Richardson's book or in the official report to the Admiralty.[83] There is no doubt that Rae was irritated by Richardson, and still more by the men recruited from England, whom he describes as the "most awkward, lazy, and careless set I ever had any thing to do with".[84]

RAE'S ATTEMPTED JOURNEY TO WOLLASTON LAND, 1849

Richardson had several reasons for leaving further exploration to be carried out under Rae's sole command. Only one boat was available; two of the three boats left on the coast were barely seaworthy, and all three were within reach of Eskimos, who, as soon as they found the boats, would almost certainly break them up. The single remaining boat which had been brought by John Bell could not hold more than a few men, and only one officer was needed. Richardson consequently had to determine whether he or Rae should be that officer. As he himself said, "Setting all personal considerations aside, and looking solely to the means of providing for the examination of as large a portion of the Arctic Sea as could be accomplished, I had no hesitation in deciding in favour of Mr. Rae. His ability and zeal were unquestionable; he was in the prime of life[85] and his personal activity and his skill as a hunter fitted him peculiarly for such an enterprise. The arrangement I made for withdrawing the European party, and employing volunteers from the men engaged in the country, was a considerable pecuniary saving,[86] which I was bound to consider, as far as I could, without cramping the means of search".[87]

On April 12, Richardson and Rae received letters from England containing news up to June 22, 1848. These letters must have mentioned that James Clark Ross had sailed from England in H.M. Ships *Enterprise* and *Investigator* on May 12, 1848.

Richardson, Bell, and the men whose services Rae did not need, left Fort Confidence on May 7, 1849; two of Rae's men, Thomas Hope and Neil McLeod, accompanied them for a few days on their way so as to fetch some articles from Fort Norman, and then returned to Fort Confidence.[88]

Richardson's orders to Rae were as follows:[89]

> Fort Confidence, Great Bear Lake,
> May 1. 1849.
>
> (Memorandum.)
>
> As in the prosecution of the search for traces of the Discovery Ships under command of Sir John Franklin, the continental coast line between the Mackenzie and Coppermine Rivers has been carefully examined, the only part of my instructions not yet complied with, is the examination of the adjoining shores of Wollaston and Victoria Lands, which the state of the ice in Dolphin and Union Straits rendered inaccessible last autumn. That these two islands are separated from each other by a strait

lying between the 111th and 113th meridians,[90] is rendered almost certain by a consideration of the direction of the flood tide, which, on the west side of these parallels, sets to the westward through Dolphin and Union Straits, and to the eastward of them, sets to the eastward towards Cape Alexander; coming, we must conclude, from the northward between the lands in question: for the survey by Messrs. Dease and Simpson has shown that the coast of Victoria Land is continuous up to the 111th parallel; and the latter gentleman records his opinion, that much of the heavy drift ice that encumbers Coronation Gulf descends between these lands from the north.[91]

The exploration of the shores of this strait is of much importance in the search for the Discovery Ships, for the following reasons:—Sir John Franklin having been directed to steer to the south-west after he had passed Barrow's Straits, would be led directly into it, and he would be deterred from attempting a more westerly course by the circumstance of Sir Edward Parry having found that route impracticable for two successive seasons. Should there be several islands between Wollaston and Banks's Lands, and the channels between them be intricate, it is not unlikely that the ships may have been shut up therein by ice. It was the intention of Sir James Ross, in the event of his reaching Winter Harbour[92] last year, to send a party across the ice this spring to pass between Victoria and Wollaston Lands towards Cape Krusenstern and the Coppermine River. To co-operate with that party and to aid it with provisions, or to supply its place, should circumstances have prevented its being sent, it is expedient that a party should go from hence, and as you and a sufficient number of men have volunteered for this service, I hereby, in virtue of the clause of my instructions which authorises me to detach you and a party of volunteers under your command, appoint you to this duty. You are therefore to descend the Coppermine River; and as soon as the sea opens in July, are to proceed to explore the strait in question, endeavouring to communicate with any parties of

Eskimos you may meet with on Wollaston or the neighbouring islands. Should you reach the northern coast of Banks's Land, you are there to erect a pile of stones, and deposit a memorandum of your object and proceedings at the distance of 10 feet from its base, marking that side of the pile with a broad arrow in red or white paint. You are also to erect similar piles, and deposit in the same manner on conspicuous headlands, memoranda for the guidance of the party detached by Sir James Ross, when you can do so without materially delaying your progress. Should you discover any signal posts erected by that party, and learn from the memoranda deposited near them that the strait has been sufficiently explored down to that place, you are to proceed no further in that direction; and you are at liberty to use you own judgment in deviating from this route, if, from information given by the Eskimos, or obtained from other sources, you are of opinion that the ships, or part of their crews, may be found in another quarter.

Having the fullest confidence in your judgment, experience and prudence, I shall not name a period to your advance, further than by requesting you not to hazard the safety of the party entrusted to your care, by delaying your return too long. The last season furnishes a strong instance of the early date at which the winter occasionally commences in these seas*.

Having performed this service, or prosecuted it as far as practicable, with a due regard to the safety of your party, you are to return with all speed to Fort Confidence, and, embarking without delay the instruments and stores remaining at that post, to proceed forthwith to Fort Simpson. Such of the stores as are useful to the Company are to be valued and handed over to them, and the instruments are to be forwarded to England, addressed to the Secretary of the Admiralty. The men are to be sent to winter at some fishing station sufficiently to the southward to ensure their

* "The 25th of August was the date at which I considered it prudent that Mr. Rae should endeavour to be on the south side of Dolphin and Union Straits, and I expressed this opinion in a private note to him."

early arrival at Norway House next spring; and you are to direct them to be furnished with nets, that they may provide for their own sustenance during the winter, with as little expense to the Government as possible.

Immediately on your return from the coast, you are to communicate an account of your proceedings to the Secretary of the Admiralty, for the information of their Lordships; and you are also to transmit to him a chart of any hitherto unexplored coasts or straits you may discover, as soon as you have had leisure to construct it.

Given under my hand, at Fort Confidence, 1st May, 1849.

(Signed) JOHN RICHARDSON,
Commanding Arctic Searching Expedition.

John Rae, Esq.

Two matters connected with these orders require special mention. The first is that Rae was not told to examine Wollaston and Victoria Lands in 1850 if for any reason he had been unable to reach them in 1849. This omission was in accordance with Richardson's original instructions, which specifically stated that his search (and by implication Rae's search) was not to be continued after the winter of 1849–50.[93]

The second matter which needs mention is that Rae was to abandon Fort Confidence on his return from Wollaston Land in 1849, and was to transfer all the stores, and the instruments left him by Richardson, to Fort Simpson, in preparation for the disposal of the stores and for the despatch of the instruments to England. But, as the sequel will show, Rae in 1850 received orders to continue the search, and in the end he returned to Fort Confidence during the autumn of 1850 after having abandoned the establishment in 1849.

On June 9, 1849, Rae left Fort Confidence for the sea and, as he hoped, Wollaston Land, and on the 21st reached a provision station which he had established in April on the Kendall River. The onset of summer was unusually retarded, and the ice on the Coppermine was late in breaking up. Rae, under great difficulties, at last succeeded in reaching Dolphin and Union Strait, but closely packed hummocky ice proved an insurmountable obstacle to crossing to Wollaston Land. On August 23, as winter seemed to be approaching, Rae decided to return to Fort Confidence, which he reached on September 1. He then abandoned Fort Confidence according to orders, took all the stores and instruments with him, and went to Fort Simpson, where he arrived on September 26. The 1849 journey therefore, as regards its principal purpose, was a failure.

As soon as he reached Fort Confidence, Rae wrote his report to the Admiralty.[94] His letter to Sir George Simpson, dated September 1, 1849, included in the present collection,[95] has not apparently been published before. It omits the latitudes and longitudes contained in the report to the Admiralty, but is in some respects more detailed. Rae's report, dated September 22, 1849, to the Hudson's Bay Company, also published for the first time in the present collection,[96] contains nothing of importance omitted from the official report to the Admiralty or from his letter to Sir George Simpson.

On Rae's arrival at Fort Simpson he was re-absorbed into the fur trade and took over the duties of Chief Factor in charge of the Mackenzie River District. On October 3 he was unexpectedly joined by Lieutenant (later Vice-Admiral) William John Samuel Pullen (1813–87), who had left H.M.S. *Plover* near Wainwright Inlet, north of Bering Strait, on July 25, 1849. He had travelled in boats along the north American coast to the estuary of the Mackenzie, and then by way of the Hudson's Bay Company's post on the Peel River, and Fort Good Hope. He and two of his men wintered with Rae at Fort Simpson. His second-in-command, William Hulme Hooper (1827–54), mate in the *Plover* (later lieutenant) and the remainder of the men, wintered at Great Bear Lake.[97]

7. *Rae's Third Expedition, 1851*

FRANKLIN RELIEF EXPEDITIONS, 1849–50

Rae and Pullen seem to have passed an uneventful winter at Fort Simpson. Rae was now installed at Fort Simpson as Chief Factor for the Mackenzie River District and presumably had no expectation of taking any further part in the Franklin search. Pullen believed that he himself would return to England during the summer. As will appear later, both Rae and Pullen received orders in June 1850 to resume the search, and the circumstances which gave rise to these orders must now be described.

Richardson, on his return journey from Fort Confidence, reached Lake Winnipeg in August 1849, where he read some Canadian or English newspapers. These contained statements which prompted him to write to Rae as follows:

Lake Winipeg, August 19. 1849.

My dear Rae,

As I learn from the newspapers which I have just read, and shall forward for your perusal, that Sir James C. Ross did not reach Barrow's Strait till after the 28th of August, and that it is probable that he may have been arrested short of his intended wintering quarters at Melville Island or Banks's Land, and could not consequently send off his proposed spring party to the Coppermine River this season, I consider it likely that he may determine on sending that party next spring; and if so, by the present arrangements they will, on their arrival at Great Bear Lake, find Fort Confidence deserted.

I therefore think it important that you should engage either the chief of some band, or two expert hunters, to pass the months of June and July, 1850, on the portage between Bear Lake and the Coppermine River, promising them a handsome reward if they render any assistance to the expected white party, and paying them such moderate sums, in addition to a full supply of ammunition, as may content them for spending the summer on such excellent hunting grounds.

You will have no difficulty in engaging either Martin Lake or Bear Lake Indians for this service; and there is abundance of time, after the arrival of the March packet, by which you will receive this letter, for them to reach Fort Confidence long before the snow begins to melt. I will thank you to furnish them with five or six memoranda in waterproof cases, with directions to plant them in conspicuous places at the mouth of the Kendall, Flett's Station, Fort Confidence, and elsewhere.

These precautions may prove to be unnecessary, as Ross's party will most likely, early in their march, discover some of your landmarks, and learn, by the notes you have left, your intention of quitting Fort Confidence this season, and thereupon turn back to the ship. But, at a small expense, if the Indians carry their instructions out fully, they will save the party, should it come on, from having to make the long journey round Bear Lake without assistance.

I remain, &c.

(Signed) JOHN RICHARDSON.

P.S. Mr. M'Pherson recommends Tecon-ne-betah for this service.[98]

The source of the information contained in the newspapers seen by Richardson was not mentioned in his letter to Rae, but was presumably a record which had been thrown overboard from H.M.S. *Investigator*. Sir James Ross sailed from England on May 12, 1848,[99] with H.M. Ships *Enterprise* and *Investigator*, and at first all went well. A Hull whaling ship, which returned home late in October, reported that Ross had arrived near the Devil's Thumb, on the west coast of Greenland, on July 25, and had in all probability crossed Baffin Bay to Lancaster Sound during the first week of August.

Early in November 1848 another Hull whaler brought home a record found in a cask picked up in Davis Strait on October 1. This record stated that on August 28, 1848, H.M.S. *Investigator*, with the *Enterprise* in company, was in latitude 73° 50' N., longitude 78° 6' 30" W.[100] The place thus indicated was in Baffin Bay near the entrance to Lancaster Sound, and the record therefore showed that Ross's passage across the bay had been so greatly retarded that he had little prospect of reaching Melville Island before the onset of winter. This led Richardson to write to Rae as he did.

Richardson's communication probably reached Rae in March or April 1850, and in any case before Rae left Fort Simpson on June 10. As soon as Rae received it, he made the necessary arrangements with Teconnebetah, who was at Fort Simpson, to carry out Richardson's orders.[101] Rae did not know that Ross had not only failed to reach Melville Island in 1848 (as Richardson had already surmised) but that he had also returned to England in the autumn of 1849.

Ross's proceedings, briefly stated, were as follows. It had originally been intended that one ship should winter near Cape Rennell and the other at Melville Island or Banks Land, but the state of the ice in Baffin Bay in 1848 was so unfavourable to navigation that Ross was unable to proceed westwards through Barrow Strait beyond Port Leopold, where he spent the winter. Numerous sledge parties left the ships at Port Leopold during the following spring. Ross himself travelled along the north coast of North Somerset, but found the ice in Peel Sound so rough that he could not cross it to Cape Walker, and travelled southwards instead along the west coast of North Somerset as far as Four Rivers Bay. He was then, on June 5, 1849, one hundred and eighty miles from the position of the *Erebus* and *Terror* when abandoned about thirteen months before, but was of course quite unaware of this. After his sledge-parties had returned to the ships, Ross left Port Leopold on August 28, and again tried to reach Melville Island, but his ships were beset in pack-ice in Barrow Strait. They drifted into Baffin Bay, and by the time they were free, it was so late in the summer that Ross was compelled to return home. He had found no traces of the Franklin expedition,[102] and apparently had even expected that Franklin would have returned home before him.[103]

Richardson arrived back in England in November 1849, very shortly after Ross. He found that the most serious apprehensions were now being entertained regarding the safety of the missing expedition, which, provisioned for three years, had been absent for more than four. No communications had been received from Franklin, and nothing was known of his proceedings since his ships had been seen in Baffin Bay at the end of July 1845. Very soon after Sir James Ross's return, the Admiralty decided to re-equip immediately the *Enterprise* and *Investigator*, and to appoint Captain (later Admiral Sir) Richard Collinson (1811–83) to the command. He sailed in the *Enterprise*, and his second in command, Commander (later Vice-Admiral Sir) Robert John Le Mesurier M'Clure (1807–73) in the *Investigator*. Collinson had orders to proceed round Cape Horn to Bering Strait, make certain arrangements with the commander of H.M.S. *Plover*, and then search to the eastward of Point Barrow. His course after he had reached Point Barrow was left to his discretion,[104] but Franklin was believed to be somewhere in the neighbourhood of Melville Island or Banks Land,[105] and Collinson was expected to search in that direction. He sailed from Plymouth on January 20, 1850. As the sequel will show, Collinson in the course of his explorations in 1852 and 1853 visited parts of Wollaston Land and Victoria Land, which had already been examined by Rae in 1851, and found on Victoria Land a record deposited there by Rae.

The Admiralty, apparently in November 1849, consulted the Hudson's Bay Company regarding the best method of continuing the search begun by Richardson and Rae in 1848. The Company, expecting that the Admiralty would take this step, had already written to Sir George Simpson in Canada and had asked him for his opinion. Neither the Admiralty, when it consulted the Company, nor Sir George Simpson, when he received the Company's letter of inquiry, knew that Rae had failed to reach Wollaston Land in 1849 and that Pullen had arrived at Fort Simpson from the *Plover* and was spending the winter there with Rae. Sir George Simpson was consequently quite unaware of what Pullen had accomplished, and made the following suggestion in a letter which reached the Company in London on December 19, 1849: "If another expedition be employed, it should be to search the coast to the westward of the Mackenzie, and that service had better be left entirely to the Company, under the management of Dr. Rae, who would do the work at a very moderate outlay. If you approve of this suggestion, and authorize me, in course, to set such an expedition on foot, I think there is still time to have the coast from the Mackenzie to Point Barrow examined next summer; but the loss of a single mail might delay it for another year".

The Secretary to the Hudson's Bay Company sent Sir George Simpson's suggestion to the Admiralty as soon as it reached London, and added: ". . . it will be perceived that Friday, the 28th of December (which is the next mail day for Canada), is the latest day at which instructions for continuing the search next year can be transmitted to Sir George Simpson. It is, therefore, desirable that the Committee should be apprised of their Lordships' intentions with as little delay as possible".[106]

The Admiralty lost no time in complying with this suggestion; and the Company on December 28 were able to forward the Admiralty's proposals, together with orders for their fulfilment, to Sir George Simpson. Simpson in his turn transmitted them as an express to Rae in the following letter:[107]

> Lachine, 21 January. [1850.]
>
> Dear Sir,
>
> Up to the present time no intelligence of any kind has been received respecting the Expedition under the command of Sir John Franklin, its fate exciting the most intense interest, not only on the part of the British Government and public, but of the whole civilized world. The maritime powers of Europe and the United States are now vieing with each other as to who shall be the first to discover some trace of the missing navigators, and, if they be still alive, to render them assistance. By the accompanying correspondence between the Governor and Committee and the Admiralty, and by the annexed copy of a letter addressed to me by Lady Franklin, and my reply, you will see that Her Majesty's Government are exceedingly anxious that further efforts should be made by the Hudson's Bay Company to explore the Arctic Sea from the Mackenzie River. I am in hopes that in the course of a few weeks hence we may be in possession of your report on your operations last summer, with,

I trust some intelligence respecting the Expedition. If they be still alive, I feel satisfied that every effort it may be in the power of man to make to succour them will be exerted by yourself and the Company's officers in Mackenzie River; but should your late search have unfortunately ended in disappointment, it is the desire of the Company that you renew your explorations next summer, if possible.

By the annexed correspondence you will observe that the opinion in England appears to be that our explorations ought to be more particularly directed to that portion of the Northern Sea lying between Cape Walker on the east, Melville Island and Banks' Land to the north, and the continental shore or the Victoria Islands to the south.

As these limits are believed to embrace the course that would have been pursued by Sir John Franklin, Cape Walker being one of the points he was particularly instructed to make for, you will therefore be pleased, immediately on the receipt of this letter, to fit out another exploring party to proceed in the direction above indicated, but varying the route that may have been followed last summer, which party, besides their own examination of the coast and islands, should be instructed to offer liberal rewards to the Esquimaux to search for some vestiges of the missing expedition, and similar rewards should be offered to the Indians inhabiting near the coast and Peel's River, and the half-bred hunters of Mackenzie River, the latter being, perhaps, more energetic than the former; assuring them that whoever may procure authentic intelligence will be largely rewarded.

Simultaneously with the Expedition to proceed towards Cape Walker, one or two small parties should be despatched to the westward of the Mackenzie, in the direction of Point Barrow, one of which might pass over to the Youcon River, and descending that stream to the sea, carry on their explorations in that quarter, while the other going down the Mackenzie might trace the coast thence towards the Youcon. And these parties must also be instructed to offer rewards to the natives to prosecute the search in all directions.

By these means there is reason to believe that in the course of one year so minute a search may be made of the coast and the islands, that in the event of the Expedition having passed in that direction, some trace of their progress would certainly be discovered.

From your experience in Arctic discovery and peculiar qualifications for such an undertaking, I am in hopes you may be enabled yourself to assume the command of the party to proceed to the northward; and, as leaders of the two parties to explore the coast to the westward of the Mackenzie, you will have to select such officers of the Company's service within the district as may appear best qualified for the duty: Mr. Murray, I think, would be a very fit man for one of the leaders, and if one party be sent by way of the Youcon, he might take charge of it. In the event of your going on this Expedition, you will be pleased to make over the charge of the district to Chief Trader Bell during your absence.

In case you may be short-handed, I have by this conveyance instructed Chief Factor Ballenden to engage in Red River 10 choice men, accustomed to boating, and well fitted for such duty as will be required of them; and if there be a chance of their reaching Mackenzie River, or even Athabasca, before the breaking up of the ice, to forward them immediately.

Should the season, however, be too far advanced to enable them to accomplish the journey by winter travelling, Mr. Ballenden is directed to increase the party to 14 men, with a guide, to be despatched from Red River immediately after the opening of the navigation, in two boats, laden with provisions and flour, and a few bales of clothing, in order to meet, in some degree, the heavy drain that will be occasioned on our resources in provisions and necessary supplies in Mackenzie River. The leader of this party from Red River may, perhaps, be qualified to act as the conductor of one of the parties to examine the coast to the westward.

You will notice that the Lords of the Admiralty are desirous that the depots of provisions left on the northern coast should be visited, and, if necessary, replenished. I fear, however, that our means will not allow of your carrying out this part of their plans to any great extent; but whatever may be possible in that way you will of course do. At all events, it is absolutely necessary to keep up the depot of clothing and provisions at Fort Good Hope, with an ample supply of ammunition and fishing tackle, and experienced fishermen should be stationed at the post. These precautions are required in case of any men of the missing Expedition finding their way, or being brought to that place, so that we may be enabled to relieve their wants in food and clothing until an opportunity offers to forward them toward the civilized world.

I am averse to giving too minute instructions on matters of detail, as I rely much on your good judgment, energy and experience in giving the fullest effect to the views of Her Majesty's Government and the Company; and you are to consider you have *carte blanche* to render available the Company's resources in carrying out this service; and should you not have a sufficient number of men to form the parties contemplated, you may abandon one of the posts in order to draught the men to this service. It is very much to be regretted that circumstances have prevented these instructions being given earlier, as I am apprehensive they may not reach you in time to do much towards the prosecution of this painfully interesting duty this season; but, in that case, you will have to consider whether the parties may not pass the winter near the scene of their future explorations. This, however, is a point which must be left to your own determination.

I remain, &c.,

(signed) *George Simpson.*

Mr. John Rae, Hon. Hudson's Bay Company, Mackenzie River District.

Rae did not receive the above letter until June 25, 1850, when near the Great Slave Lake on Company business.

About three weeks after the Company in London had sent its instructions to Sir George Simpson on December 28, 1849, despatches arrived at the Admiralty from Captain Kellett of H.M.S. *Herald* and from Commander Moore of H.M.S. *Plover*.[108] Kellett had co-operated during the previous summer with Moore, and the despatches reported the proceedings of the searching ships in Bering Strait up to September 29, 1849, on which day Kellett in the *Herald* had left the *Plover* in winter quarters in Kotzebue Sound, Bering Strait. The despatches showed that Pullen, after leaving the *Plover* on July 25, 1849, had passed Point Barrow and had sent a party back to the ship on August 4 from near Fatigue Point; and that no further intelligence of his proceedings had reached the *Plover*. The Admiralty, unaware that Pullen had joined Rae, consulted Richardson regarding Pullen's whereabouts. Richardson stated that Pullen could be assumed to have reached the Mackenzie and to have met Rae.[109] The Hudson's Bay Company offered to send a despatch to the Mackenzie; and the Admiralty at once availed itself of this opportunity to send further orders to Pullen. These orders necessarily gave Pullen wide discretionary powers, but suggested his searching for the missing expedition from Cape Bathurst in the direction of Banks Land. The Admiralty also told Pullen that the Hudson's Bay Company had been asked to instruct Rae to give advice and assistance, and that the Company would furnish the supplies required for Pullen's return journey overland from the Polar Sea.[110]

The Hudson's Bay Company sent these orders, together with copies of Kellett's and Moore's despatches and of Collinson's orders, and some correspondence, etc., to Sir George Simpson by the mail for Canada on January 25, 1850. He received them on February 13, and at once arranged for their transmission by express to Pullen and Rae. In his letter to Rae, Sir George Simpson stated, with reference to his previous letter of January 21, that he had instructed John Ballenden, if only ten men had been sent to Rae from Red River, to forward an extra boat, laden with provisions etc., to Portage la Loche during the summer. Sir

George Simpson drew Rae's attention also to the Company's orders, set out in a letter of which he enclosed a copy,[111] that these orders given to Rae were not to be superseded by those sent by the Admiralty to Pullen.

Very soon after these orders had been sent to Pullen from London, extensive preparations were made in Britain for resuming the Franklin search on an extensive scale from the Atlantic side. An Admiralty expedition, consisting of two sailing ships and two steam tenders, was manned by officers and men of the Royal Navy, and was commanded by Captain (later Admiral Sir) Horatio Thomas Austin (1800–65). A second expedition, acting under orders from the Admiralty, but commanded by a whaling captain, William Penny (1809–92), consisted of two sailing ships. The Hudson's Bay Company, aided by public subscription, also equipped two ships which sailed under the command of Sir John Ross; Lady Franklin herself organised an expedition in a ship named the *Prince Albert*, commanded by Commander Charles Codrington Forsyth; and the United States sent two ships under Lieutenant Edward Jesse de Haven. Copies of the orders given by the Admiralty to Pullen, Austin and Penny were forwarded to Rae, and reached him on November 13, 1850.[112]

EVENTS AT FORT SIMPSON, 1850

The ice broke at Fort Simpson on May 11, 1850. Rae, unaware of the orders that were on their way to him from Sir George Simpson, devoted himself to the business of the Company. He left his winter quarters at Fort Simpson on May 20 to superintend the loading and despatch of furs to be sent on to York Factory. On May 22 he reached Fort Norman, where Hooper had already arrived with his men.[113] Rae returned to Fort Simpson on June 10, where he found that Hooper and his men had already joined Pullen on June I. On June 20, Rae with four boats laden with furs (other boats had already departed) and Pullen with Hooper and his entire command, left Fort Simpson for the south. Pullen not unnaturally believed that he and his men were now on their way home to England, but when near Great Slave Lake on June 25, two Indians arrived in a canoe and handed to Rae and Pullen all the orders and despatches which, sent by Sir George Simpson from Lachine on January 21 and on or about February 13, have already been described.

Rae and Pullen had now to deal with a wholly unexpected situation. The provisions and stores available were sufficient for one party to return to the Arctic coast but insufficient for two parties. Since Pullen and his men were available then and there, Rae agreed with Pullen that the best solution of the difficulty was for Pullen, not Rae, to resume the search in 1850, and for Rae to postpone his further search until 1851.

In accordance with this decision, Pullen and Hooper separated from Rae on June 29.[114]

It suffices to say that Pullen and Hooper went down the Mackenzie and reached the sea on July 22, and Cape Bathurst on August 10. The ice conditions were such that they could not cross the sea in the direction of Banks Land, and Pullen and his party returned to Fort Simpson on October 5, 1850. Pullen, Hooper and two of their men wintered at Fort Simpson, the others at Great Slave Lake. Pullen and Hooper did not meet Rae during this particular winter. They left Fort Simpson in June 1851, and arrived in England about four months later.[115]

Rae continued to occupy himself during the summer of 1850 with the Company's affairs. He reached Portage la Loche (Methy Portage) on July 20 and later returned to Fort Simpson.

RAE'S EXPLORATIONS, 1851

In preparation for the 1851 expedition, Rae went to Fort Confidence, which he reached on October 10, 1850. The houses at Fort Confidence were still in good condition, and were soon made habitable. Two boats were built from wood collected locally, and provisions collected. A shortage of food occurred but this was temporary, and apart from this, the winter seems to have been passed by Rae in comparative comfort.

Rae's plans were to travel first on foot in the direction of Banks Land before the thaw, and then in boats during the summer. A depot of provisions was made at the Kendall River, and the boats were to be sent there as soon as the ice broke up on the Dease River. Rae intended to end his travels on foot on his return to the provision depot, and thence take the boats to the sea, and did not propose to return to Fort Confidence after the journey on foot. Before leaving, he handed written instructions regarding these matters to his second in command, Hector Æneas Mackenzie, and wrote an official despatch to Sir George Simpson as well as a long private letter. These instructions to Mackenzie and the official report were forwarded by Sir George Simpson to London, and published in a Parliamentary Paper.[116]

Rae left Fort Confidence on April 25, and continued his foot journey beyond the provision depot and landed on Wollaston Land on May 6. His original intention was to travel on from the Kendall River with two companions and to take one sledge with three dogs and thirty days' provisions counting from the date of leaving the mouth of the Coppermine. Later on the plan was modified and Rae decided to take two dog sledges and five days' additional provisions and a fatigue party of three men. The two parties separated on May 2, and Rae proceeded with two sledges, drawn by five dogs and his two picked men, Beads and Linklater.

After landing on Wollaston Land Rae travelled along the south coast eastwards as far as Welbank Bay, which lay at the western extremity of the coast seen by Dease and Simpson in 1839. Having ascertained that no strait existed between Wollaston Land and Victoria Land at this point, considered probable first by Thomas Simpson and then by Richardson,[117] Rae retraced his steps and marched westwards along the south coast and then up the west coast of Wollaston Land until he reached, on May 24, a point about seven and a half miles from Cape Back, on the south side of Prince Albert Sound. Rae was inclined to believe that this sound was a strait, but Collinson in 1852 found it to be a gulf.[118] Rae clearly saw land on the north side of the sound, though quite unaware that it had been reached only ten days previously by Lieutenant William Haswell of H.M.S. *Investigator*,[119] which had been wintering in Prince of Wales Strait. Rae then returned to the Kendall River, which he reached on June 10, and he at once sent a report to Sir George Simpson.[120] This long letter of Rae's is one of the liveliest and most interesting of the series.

The boats from Fort Confidence reached Rae at Kendall River on June 13; he returned to the sea, coasted eastwards along the south side of Coronation Gulf and Dease Strait, and on July 24 reached Cape Alexander. Open water lay along the shore to the eastward, and, as Rae stated in his official report to the Hudson's Bay Company,[121] "Had Geographical discovery been the object of the expedition, I would have followed the coast eastward to Simpson Strait, and then crossed over towards Cape Franklin. This course however, would have been a deviation from the route I had marked out for myself, and would have exposed me to the charge of having lost sight of the duty committed to me".

Rae carried out his orders, but if he had decided to sail eastwards and had succeeded in reaching Simpson Strait and in travelling northwards along the west coast of King William Land to Cape Franklin (seen to the south-west of Point Victory by James Clark Ross in 1830) he would not only have contributed to geographical knowledge but also have fulfilled the principal purpose of his journey, for he would unquestionably have ascertained the fate of the Franklin expedition.

Rae crossed Dease Strait, reached Cape Colbourne on August 1, and travelled along the coast of Victoria Land in his boats to the eastward. Anderson Bay, about sixteen miles to the east of Cape Colbourne, had not been seen by Dease and Simpson, so that Rae's charting of new coast began at Anderson Bay. He continued his voyage along the south coast and then up the east coast of Victoria Land, until on August 9 the boats were stopped by ice near Cape Alfred. Rae then left his boats temporarily and continued his journey northwards on foot; two of his men went a few miles further than he did, Point Pelly being the most distant headland which these men could see to the north when they turned back. Rae returned to his boats and left a record in a cairn which was found by Collinson, of H.M.S. *Enterprise*, on May 8, 1853. This record was as follows:

> A party of 10 men and 2 officers of the Hudson's Bay Company descended the Coppermine river in the latter end of June,

> in two boats. Found a channel of open water along shore on the 5th of July. Came along the coast eastward as far as Cape Alexander; were detained there some days as the ice in the strait was still unbroken. Then crossed over by the Finlayson islands to Victoria land, which was found to run nearly E. to long. 102° 40', when it turned up to the north. There is a deep and irregular shaped bay between lat. 69° 15' and 69° 40' N. in long. 102° 3'.[122] The boats were arrested by ice in lat. 69° 43' and 101° 24'(?) W. long. A walking party traced the coast 35 miles further nearly due N. The only particular worthy of notice was an island seen about 5 miles long, and 4 miles from the shore.[123] Much of the ice was still unbroken and was pressed close to the shore by a continuance of north-easterly winds, which will probably make our return difficult. As far as regards the object of the expedition, a search for Sir John Franklin and party, we were quite unsuccessful.
>
> JOHN RAE. Chief Factor. H.B.Co.,
> Commanding the Expedition.
>
> Lat. 70° 2' 30" N., long. 101° 18' (?) W. 13th August, 1851.
> NOTE.—To-morrow I return to the boats. J.R.[124]

On August 15 and 16 Rae wanted to cross to Cape Franklin on King William Land, forty miles to the east, but the state of the ice prevented his doing so. His map[125] shows that from some point on the east side of Victoria Land he saw land to the east of him in Victoria Strait. The day on which he saw this land clearly for the first time appears to have been August 20. Rae neither visited this land nor named it. It was explored for the first time in 1905 by Lieutenant Godfred Hansen, second-in-command of Roald Amundsen's expedition through the North-west Passage (1903–07). Hansen then discovered that the land seen by Rae consisted of some small islands forming part of a large group which he named the Royal Geographical Society's Islands; and he gave English names to their most prominent features because the islands had been first sighted by Rae.[126]

On his way back Rae found two pieces of wood, one of oak and one of pine wood, at Parker Bay on the south coast of Victoria Land on August 21. These are of special interest since they were probably relics of the Franklin expedition. Rae reached Fort Confidence on September 10, started on the 11th for Fort Simpson, which he reached on September 26, and next day wrote his official report to the Secretary of the Hudson's Bay Company. It is included in the present collection and was published in 1852.[127]

PIECES OF WOOD FOUND BY RAE AT PARKER BAY, AUGUST 21, 1851

The first of the two pieces was of pinewood, and appeared to be the butt end of a small flagstaff. It was stamped with the letters "S.C.", was five feet nine inches long, and was round except at the lower end, which had been cut square for a length of one foot. A looped white line containing a red thread, showing that the line was British Government property, had been attached to the wood by two copper tacks stamped with the broad arrow (another Government mark), so that there could be no reasonable doubt that the fragment had come from one of Her Majesty's ships.

The second piece of wood, found by Rae about half a mile from the first piece, was of oak, and was three feet eight inches long; it seemed to be a stanchion. The bottom end was square and a portion of this part had been removed, presumably for the purpose of enabling the piece of wood to be fixed in a clasp or socket of some kind, for it bore a mark that appeared to have been caused by a clasp. The upper part of the piece was round; a hole, apparently for the passage of a chain, had been bored through the top and the wood on one side of the hole had been torn away, presumably by pressure exerted on the chain. The lower part had been painted black.[128]

Both pieces of wood were "touching the beach" and had apparently been washed up by the flood tide only a short time before they were found. Since this flood tide came from the north along the east coast of Victoria Land, Rae believed that a strait must separate that land from North Somerset, a belief that was later found by M'Clintock to have been perfectly correct. Rae concluded that both pieces of wood had been carried through the strait in question "with the immense quantities of ice that a long continuance of Northerly and northerly easterly winds aided by the flood tide had driven southward".

Relics derived from the *Erebus* and *Terror*, when these were beset in the upper part of Victoria Strait, would have drifted towards Parker Bay from the north, the precise direction from which Rae concluded that the pieces of wood had come. That these pieces were derived from the Franklin expedition has not been proved, but that they were so derived is virtually beyond doubt.

What was almost certainly another fragment of either the *Erebus* or the *Terror* was found further westwards by Collinson in July 1853 on one of the Finlayson Islands in Dease Strait, about sixty geographical miles to the west of Parker Bay. Collinson believed that it had not been left by Eskimos, but had been washed ashore. This fragment was a piece of door-frame; it bore a hasp secured by screws stamped with the broad arrow, and had been painted. Both ends were broken and worn, apparently by having been struck against rocks by waves. Collinson brought the piece of door-frame back to England; and the foreman joiner at Woolwich Dockyard believed that it had formed part of either the *Erebus* or the *Terror*.[129]

Rae no doubt fully considered all likely sources of his pieces of wood. That the flagstaff had come from one of Her Majesty's ships was quite certain; the tacks used to fasten the line to the wood, and the line itself, bore British Government marks. There was no evidence that the stanchion, however, had come from one of Her Majesty's ships. Neither fragment presented any feature suggesting a particular ship.

Rae evidently came to the conclusion that he had no adequate grounds for suggesting the Franklin expedition as a possible source, for he stated in his report that he had obtained no information concerning that expedition; and he did not specifically mention that he had found possible traces of it. He confined himself to stating the facts, and he left the authorities to draw their own conclusions. He may well have had several reasons for adopting this course. He knew that relief expeditions by sea had been sent to Barrow Strait in 1850; he could reasonably assume that some of them had arrived there; but of the positions which they had finally reached he was entirely ignorant. One or more ships, for all that he knew to the contrary, might have penetrated far southwards through the strait which he believed to lie between Victoria Land and North Somerset, and have been the source of the pieces of wood.

Moreover, Rae had no reason to suppose that the Franklin expedition had reached Victoria Strait. No Eskimos tried to tell him, as they apparently tried to tell Collinson at Cambridge Bay in 1853, that ships were in the ice to the eastward,[130] and nothing, apart from the two pieces of wood, was seen by Rae during his journey which could have led him when he was on the west side of Victoria Strait to suspect his proximity to the site of the Franklin disaster. Indeed, he did not believe that the missing expedition was anywhere in the vicinity of King William Land. In a letter written at Fort Confidence to Richardson in April 1851, before he set out for Wollaston Land and Victoria Land, he commented as follows on some statements made in a letter to him from Lady Franklin:

> . . . Lady Franklin also says that a growing opinion prevails in England that the long-missing expedition is icebound somewhere in the direction of the magnetic pole, or towards Back's River, and to search in the neighbourhood of these places was the principal object of the small expedition under Captain Forsyth.[131] It is very proper that those parts should be examined, but I have very little expectation that any traces of those looked for will be found in that quarter. If not found in the space bounded on the west by the meridian of 118 deg. west longitude, and on the east by long. 104 deg., and between latitude 71 deg. and 74 deg. north, the most likely place for Sir John Franklin's party to be heard of will be at Melville Island, or in the neighbourhood of some other of the Parry group.[132]

The centre of the quadrilateral area indicated by these latitudes and longitudes lay approximately mid-way between Cape Walker to the east-north-east and Cape Bathurst to the west-south-west.

Lastly, it must have been evident to Rae when he found the two pieces of wood that a prolonged investigation might be required to determine the ship from which they had come and the whereabouts of that ship, and he himself was not in possession of the information needed for such an investigation. He consequently took with him the tacks, the line, and portions of the two pieces of wood, and apparently delivered them, together with some descriptive notes and a sketch of the stanchion,[133] to the Admiralty as soon as he reached England.

The Admiralty at once instituted an inquiry into possible sources of the fragments. Pullen stated that they had not come from the boats which he had used; Hooper expressed a similar opinion. James Clark Ross said that the stanchion had not formed part of H.M.S. *Enterprise* when under his command (1848–49), but declared that its appearance was so familiar to him that he thought it must have come from some ship in which he had sailed, and suggested H.M.S. *Fury*, abandoned by Parry in Prince Regent Inlet in 1825.[134] He stated, however, that if the stanchion had come from the *Fury*, it was difficult to understand why no other pieces had been found, and, furthermore, how the stanchion had reached Parker Bay from Prince Regent Inlet unless it had passed through a channel leading westwards from Brentford Bay. In point of fact, a channel in this situation does exist in the form of Bellot Strait; its presence had been suspected by James Clark Ross when serving in the *Victory* expedition,[135] but no proof of its existence had yet been obtained.[136] Ross himself, as commander of the Antarctic expedition, had sailed for about four years (1839–43) in H.M.S. *Erebus*, the ship afterwards commanded by Franklin; and it should be noticed that he did not suggest the *Erebus* as a possible source. Ross also declared that neither of the pieces of wood had formed part of the flagstaff erected by him at the North Magnetic Pole in June 1831; the flagstaff used there had been made from a boarding pike.

On the other hand, Captain Austin, who also had been a Lieutenant in H.M.S. *Fury* (1824–25) did not think that the stanchion had come from that ship; he suggested a whaling vessel as a possible source, and he doubted if the stanchion was of English workmanship.

The question whether the pieces could have come from one or other of the four ships (*Resolute*, *Assistance*, *Pioneer* and *Intrepid*) that had composed the Franklin relief expedition which Austin had commanded (1850–51) was fully investigated, and a signed report was presented by five officers and four warrant officers. All of these had served in one or other of the four ships; and two of the officers (F. L. M'Clintock and J. H. Allard) and three of the warrant officers (H. J. Osbourn, R. Hall and W. Dean) had served also under the command of James Clark Ross either in the *Enterprise* or in the *Investigator* (1848–49). Their conclusion was that all six ships could be eliminated.

The line attached to the flagstaff afforded no assistance. It was found to have been made at the Devonport Dockyard, but line of the same variety had been supplied by that yard to all other yards for some years, and the date of manufacture of the piece found by Rae could not be ascertained.

None of the authorities consulted by the Admiralty seems to have suggested either the *Erebus* or the *Terror* as a possible source, and strange to say no officer other than Ross who had served either in the *Erebus* or *Terror* during the Antarctic expedition or in the *Terror* in an unsuccessful attempt (1836–37) by Sir George Back to reach Wager River or Repulse Bay, appears to have been asked to express an opinion.[137] According to one periodical,[138] the *Fury* seemed to be the most likely source, but so far as can be judged only negative conclusions were reached; the actual source was never determined.

8. *Rae's Fourth Expedition, 1853–54*

RAE IN GREAT BRITAIN, 1852–53

Rae's application, made in his letter of November 2, 1850, to Sir George Simpson for leave of absence in order to go to England, appears to have been favourably received, and Rae, following his great journey in 1851, proceeded southwards during the autumn and winter.[139] He was in New York on March 8, 1852, and soon afterwards sailed for England.

On May 24, 1852, the Founder's Gold Medal of the Royal

Geographical Society was awarded to Rae "for his survey of Boothia under most severe privations in 1848,[140] and for his recent explorations on foot, and in boats, of the coasts of Wollaston and Victoria Lands, by which very important additions have been made to the geography of the Arctic regions". In his speech Sir Roderick Murchison referred to Rae's "boldness never surpassed" in deciding to winter at Repulse Bay. He also referred to Rae's 1851 expedition, when Rae had "shown equal judgment and perseverance. Dreading, from his former experience, that the sea might be frozen, he determined on a spring journey over the ice, and performed a most extraordinary one . . . he set out accompanied by two men only, and, trusting solely for shelter to snow-houses, which he taught his men to build, accomplished a distance of 1060 miles in 39 days, or 27 miles per day including stoppages—a feat which has never been equalled in Arctic travelling." Rae himself was not in London when the Medal was presented, being at that time in Stromness, and the Medal was accepted by Sir George Back, on behalf of "the honest and unassuming traveller who, in his severest trials, evinced a judgment always equal to the occasion".[141]

By the time Rae reached London in 1852 all the expeditions sent to search for Franklin in 1850 by way of Barrow Strait had returned. They had found definite proof that Franklin had passed the first winter (1845–46) at Beechey Island, but no indication of the direction in which he had afterwards sailed. Their extensive searches need not be described; it is enough to say that an Admiralty Committee, after careful consideration of all the available data, came to the conclusion that Franklin, after wintering at Beechey Island, had not found it possible to sail southwards and westwards from the neighbourhood of Cape Walker, and had probably sailed up Wellington Channel in 1846, and that therefore further search south and west of Cape Walker was unnecessary.[142]

In actual fact, Franklin had already sailed up Wellington Channel in 1845, and he had returned to Barrow Strait before wintering at Beechey Island, so that although the members of the Committee judged correctly with regard to his having sought a passage through Wellington Channel, they were mistaken about his course in 1846, and ignorant of what he had already done in Wellington Channel in 1845. In accordance with the Committee's recommendations, a fresh Admiralty expedition, one of the purposes of which was an examination of the upper part of Wellington Channel, was equipped; and it sailed under the command of Sir Edward Belcher on April 21, 1852.

On April 10, 1852, Rae had a long discussion with Dr. Robert M'Cormick (1800–90), surgeon to the *North Star*, one of the ships about to sail under Sir Edward Belcher. They met at the Admiralty, and Rae pointed out on a polar chart "a spot to the southward and westward of Cape Walker as, in his opinion, the most likely spot for discovering the fate of Franklin".[143] This opinion agrees substantially with that expressed by Rae to Richardson in April 1851, as has been mentioned on a previous page.

When Rae spoke to M'Cormick he must have been acquainted with the proceedings of the Franklin relief expeditions which had returned to England, and he can reasonably be presumed to have known that Captain Ommanney and Lieutenant Sherard Osborn had found such heavy ice pressing against the west coast of Prince of Wales Land that they concluded that Franklin could not have passed along that coast to the south-west of Cape Walker.[144] If Rae accepted Captain Ommanney's opinion, which was also held by Lieutenant Sherard Osborn, he presumably thought that Franklin either had gone down Peel Sound or had sailed westwards far beyond Prince of Wales Land before striking to the south-west. That Rae had Peel Sound in mind is suggested by the remarks in his official report of September 27, 1851, to the Secretary of the Hudson's Bay Company,[145] that he had no doubt that a channel separated Victoria Land from North Somerset.

Rae, in opposition to the general trend of opinion at the time, evidently believed that the Franklin expedition was to be sought somewhere to the south of Barrow Strait, but he thought that it had penetrated further to the westward than in fact it had done.

RAE'S PLANS FOR A FURTHER EXPEDITION

Soon after his return to London, Rae submitted to the Hudson's Bay Company, in a letter to Barclay, the secretary, dated May 1, 1852,[146] a plan for the completion, as he said, "of the survey of the northern shores of America, a small portion of which, along the west coast of Boothia is all that now remains unexamined". Several geographical problems connected with the "west coast of Boothia" still awaited solution.

Rae had ascertained in 1847, at least to his own satisfaction, that Boothia was part of the mainland. All the authorities did not agree that the possible existence of a strait extending westwards from the southern end of Pelly Bay had been definitely disproved, for Rae had not actually marched round that part of the bay. Rae himself was convinced that he was right and consequently that the west coast of Boothia was part of the continental coastline.

Two stretches of this coast, a northern and a southern, had not been examined.

As regards the northern stretch, North Somerset was believed to be attached to Boothia and was not known to be separated from it by Bellot Strait, discovered by Captain William Kennedy (1813–90) in April 1852.[147] Rae's original plan, which was based on this belief, provided for his travelling northwards as far as Four Rivers Bay, the furthest point reached to the southward on the west coast of North Somerset on June 5, 1849, by Sir James Clark Ross from Port Leopold. Ross had seen a headland which he named Cape Bird lying about fifty geographical miles to the south of Four Rivers Bay, and believed that the coast between these two points was continuous. When Captain Kennedy returned to England in October 1852, his discoveries showed that Cape Bird was situated on the north side of the west end of the newly discovered Bellot Strait, and that Boothia was bounded on the north by that Strait, and, consequently, that the coast between Four Rivers Bay and Cape Bird was not part of the continental coastline of North America.

Rae thereupon changed the original plan of continuing his survey as far north as Four Rivers Bay, and stated in his letter of November 19, 1852, to Sir George Simpson that his "furthest north point "would be the region reached by Kennedy before proceeding westwards.[148] By this "furthest north point" Rae undoubtedly meant Bellot Strait, since he himself stated in a letter dated November 26 to *The Times*[149] that he intended to examine the west coast of Boothia as far north as latitude 72°, which is the approximate latitude of Bellot Strait.

These considerations explain why Rae, in the plan which he submitted to the Hudson's Bay Company on May 1, 1852, before Kennedy had returned from the Arctic, suggested travelling as far northwards as Four Rivers Bay, whereas in the letter which he wrote to Sir George Simpson on November 19, 1852, after Kennedy had returned, he expressed his intention of proceeding no further than Bellot Strait.[150]

The unexplored northern stretch of the west coast of Boothia, the scene of part of Rae's proposed survey, was thus believed after Kennedy's return to extend from Bellot Strait southwards to Cape Nicolai.[151] This was the furthest point seen to the north on the west coast of Boothia by James Clark Ross in 1831,[152] and the unexplored coast from Bellot Strait to that cape was presumed to be about one hundred and fifty geographical miles in length. As the sequel will show, Rae never reached this part of the Boothian coast. It remained unexplored until Lieutenant W. R. Hobson, M'Clintock's second-in-command in the *Fox*, examined part of it near Bellot Strait when laying down a depot in October 1858, and until M'Clintock himself marched along the whole of it for the first time in February and March 1859.[153]

The officers of the *Victory* expedition had also examined the west coast of Boothia from near Cape Nicolai southwards to the Boothian Isthmus and a small part extending southwards from this isthmus to the Dundas Islands. James Clark Ross, on June 7, 1830, had seen from a place near those islands that the coast to the south of him stretched towards the south-west, the furthest headland visible in that direction being Cape Porter.[154] This continuous line of known coast from Cape Nicolai to Cape Porter intervened between the two unexplored stretches which Rae proposed to examine.

The first has been described; the second stretch, that is the southern, lay between Cape Porter on the north and Castor and Pollux River to the south.

Part of this unexplored stretch was believed to be occupied by an isthmus uniting the east side of what was then known as King William

Land with the west side of the land lying to the south of the Boothian Isthmus. The chart issued by John Ross with his narrative of the *Victory* expedition delineated James Ross Strait as a gulf by the insertion of a supposed coast, indicated by dotted lines, running from west to east from King William Land, near the south end of Matty Island, to near Cape Porter. This supposed coastline may have owed its origin to James Clark Ross, for in 1830 he crossed the strait bearing his name about fifteen miles to the north of the position assigned to the supposed coast, but it is possible that he was misled by what an Eskimo had told him.[155]

Dease and Simpson, during their boat voyage from the estuary of the Great Fish River to Castor and Pollux River, appear to have seen no land to the north except some islands within a few miles of the continental coastline, but their map[156] showed by means of a dotted line a supposed west to east line of coast extending from Point Booth, on the south coast of King William Land, to Boothia. Their map necessarily showed some of the discoveries made by the officers of the *Victory* as well as those which they themselves had made, and it consequently represented King William Land as a peninsula, joined to the land to the east of it by a supposed isthmus, having a width at its narrowest part of about twenty geographical miles.[157]

As will appear later, Rae discovered in 1854 that this supposed isthmus had no existence. This discovery may have accorded with his expectations, but Rae can be presumed to have been fully prepared to find that the isthmus did exist, that King William Land was a peninsula and therefore part of the American continent, and that an examination of the unexplored parts of that island or peninsula would be required for the fulfilment of his purpose,"the completion of the survey of the northern shores of America".

These unexplored parts consisted not only of the north and south sides of the isthmus (if it existed), but also of the west coast of King William Land between Point Victory (the furthest point reached to the southward on the north-west coast of that island by James Clark Ross in 1830)[158] and Cape Herschel (the most westerly point reached on the south coast by Dease and Simpson in 1839).[159] Ross had seen the coast stretching towards the south-west from Point Victory and had given the name Cape Franklin to the most distant headland which he could see in that direction; and Dease and Simpson had seen the land extending for some distance northwards from Cape Herschel towards Cape Franklin. The coastline between Cape Herschel and Cape Franklin had not been examined (so far as Rae was aware);[160] it was believed to run approximately from south to north and to be about sixty statute miles in length.

In the plan submitted to the Hudson's Bay Company, Rae proposed to travel in boats from York Factory to Chesterfield Inlet, cross overland to the Great Fish River, descend the river, and then proceed northwards. He believed that the unexplored part of the north American continental coastline was three or four hundred miles long,[161] and the wide difference between these two estimates was probably due in part to the impossibility of determining, without an actual examination, whether King William Land was or was not part of the continent. Rae had no expectation of finding any traces of the Franklin expedition, for he believed that the *Erebus* and *Terror* had gone south-west of Cape Walker. As he himself stated in his letter published in *The Times*, on November 27, 1852: "I do not mention the lost navigators, as there is not the slightest hope of finding any traces of them in the quarter to which I am going".

RAE'S EXPLORATIONS, 1853–54, AND FIRST NEWS OF FRANKLIN'S FATE

The Hudson's Bay Company accepted Rae's proposals, and Rae thereupon communicated with the authorities at York Factory and asked them to make all the arrangements needed for the projected expedition. Rae sailed from Great Britain for New York during the spring of 1853, and travelled overland to York Factory, which he reached on June 18.

Rae left York Factory on June 24, 1853, and Churchill on July 13, with two boats and thirteen men, including Munro, an Eskimo. On the way north he engaged another Eskimo interpreter, Ouligbuck the younger, who had served in Rae's first expedition. Rae was unable to carry out his original intention of travelling overland from Chesterfield Inlet to the Great Fish River, and this led him to send back one boat and seven men, including Munro. Rae himself decided to winter at Repulse Bay, where he arrived on August 15.

He found no Eskimos at Repulse Bay and none arrived during the winter. Rae and his men were content to live in snow-houses, and finally succeeded in procuring sufficient provisions for the winter. In March he made a depot at Cape Lady Pelly, and on March 31 set out, with three men and Ouligbuck, for Castor and Pollux River. He followed his route of 1847 to Colvile Bay, and then crossed Simpson Peninsula to Pelly Bay, where he met some Eskimos, the first since his arrival at Repulse Bay eight months previously.

On the following day, April 21, 1854, he met two other Eskimos, from one of whom, named In-nook-poo-zhee-jook,[162] he obtained the first intelligence, fully amplified later, of the deaths of white men. Rae ascertained subsequently from relics in the possession of the Eskimos that these white men must have been members of the Franklin expedition.

Rae's meeting with In-nook-poo-zhee-jook is of sufficient historical importance to be given here in detail. The original rough notes, written down on April 21 and 22, were as follows:

> Met a very communicative and apparently intelligent Esquimaux; had never met whites before, but said that a number of Kabloonans, at least 35 or 40, had starved to death west of a large river a long distance off. Perhaps about 10 or 12 days' journey? Could not tell the distance, never had been there, and could not accompany us so far. Dead bodies seen beyond two large rivers; did not know the place. Could not or would not explain it on chart. Had seen a pillar of stones that had been built by whites near a small river. Top of pillar had fallen down; Suppose Simpson and Dease cairn at Castor and Pollux River?

(The last remark was Rae's). To this note Rae added:

> This information too vague to act upon, particularly at this season, when everything is covered with snow.[163]

Another account, written by Rae about twenty years later, contained some additional information:

> When travelling westward on my spring journey, I met an Eskimo, to whom we put the usual question, 'Have you seen white men before?' He said, 'No, but he had heard of a number having died far to the west,' pointing in that direction. Noticing a gold cap-band round his head, I asked him where he obtained it, and he said it had been got where the dead white men were, but that he himself had never been there, that he did not know the place, and could not go so far, giving me the idea that it was a great way off. I bought the cap-band from him, and told him that if he or his companions had any other things, to bring them to our winter quarters at Repulse Bay, where they would receive good prices for them.[164]

Rae then travelled westwards to Castor and Pollux River, where he found a cairn which, although it contained no indication of its origin, was evidently that erected by Dease and Simpson in 1839. He turned northwards and found that the coast, though broken into numerous bays, was continuous to Cape Porter, and that the so-called "Committee Islands", charted by Dease and Simpson and believed by them to be in the Gulf of Boothia, were actually rocky elevations lying to the north of Murchison River. Rae by this journey completed the exploration of the southern unexplored stretch, and definitely showed that King William Land was not a peninsula but an island, and that the isthmus, supposed by some geographers to connect the east side of the island with the mainland, had no existence.

Fog and bad weather had caused so much loss of time that Rae found that he would be unable, without taking great risks, to complete his task, i.e., the examination of the northern stretch of the west coast of Boothia from Cape Nicolai to Bellot Strait and so decided to return to Repulse Bay. On the return journey he examined the head of Pelly Bay and discovered, as he had confidently expected when at Helen Island in 1847, that there was no opening extending to the westward from the head of the bay. This examination, together with the survey which he had just carried out on the coast north of Castor and Pollux River, demonstrated beyond all doubt that Boothia was a peninsula, and not an island.

Rae reached Repulse Bay on May 26 and met Eskimos, some of whom he had already seen at Pelly Bay during his outward journey.[165] Rae now learnt for the first time that the estuary near to which some of Franklin's men had died must be that of the Great Fish River.

It was then too late for Rae to go to the Great Fish River during that season. As he himself explained, the thaw would have prevented sledge travelling; he could not have crossed the Great Fish River or have reached King William Island without a boat or canoe, and neither was available; he and his men were dependent on their guns for food and could not have procured sufficient provisions for the winter if absent from Repulse Bay during the autumn, when the deer migrated southwards—a possibility with which he had been confronted during his first expedition. Alternatively, the sea-ice would in all probability have formed before he could have returned from the Great Fish River to Repulse Bay, and would have prevented him from travelling southwards by boat to Churchill before the onset of winter.

Rae also reasoned that he had no hope of rescuing any survivors of the Franklin expedition, for although he offered the Eskimos large rewards for information of a survivor or even of the bare possibility of one, the natives invariably stated that all the white men were dead and had been dead for four years. Rae therefore considered it his imperative duty to put the Admiralty in possession as soon as possible of the information which he had acquired about the Franklin expedition, so that the relief expedition commanded by Sir Edward Belcher, whose orders when he sailed in 1852 included a search of Wellington Channel and of the unexplored area to the west of Melville Island, might be informed that in Rae's opinion searches in those directions offered no prospects of success.[166]

Rae therefore left Repulse Bay for the south on August 4, 1854, and Chesterfield Inlet on August 9, and arrived at York Factory on August 31. Towards the end of September, 1854, he embarked on the Hudson's Bay Company's ship *Prince of Wales*, and sailed for England.

Rae's return at this time has always been a matter of regret, for a great chance had been lost. No less than five years were to elapse before M'Clintock reached King William Island, and had Rae gone at once to the places indicated by the Eskimos he would almost certainly have obtained more information than M'Clintock and possibly even have found written records.

Rae's proceedings during the period from June 24, 1853, the day of his departure northwards from York Factory, till August 9, when he left Chesterfield Inlet for Repulse Bay, do not seem to have been fully described in print before. The letters, which he wrote on July 1, 10, 13 and 15, and on August 9, 1853,[167] have not been published hitherto and possess considerable historical interest. They furnish, for example, the first description of the Quoich River. His official report, dated September 1, 1854, to the Secretary of the Hudson's Bay Company, describing his proceedings from the evening of August 9, 1853, to August 31, 1854, the day of his arrival at York Factory, has however been published several times.[168]

9. *Rae in London, 1854*

Rae landed at Deal on Sunday, October 22, 1854. He then learnt that Sir Edward Belcher, after abandoning four of his five ships, had brought back all his officers and men, together with those who had sailed with M'Clure in H.M.S. *Investigator*, which had been abandoned at Mercy Bay, in Banks Land.[169] Some of the officers and men had returned to England in Belcher's fifth ship, H.M.S. *North Star*, which had been stationed as a depot ship at Beechey Island, others in

H.M. Ships *Phoenix* and *Talbot*, which had been sent from England with stores and instructions for Belcher, and had reached Beechey Island on August 26, 1854. So far as was known in England when Rae returned, three Franklin relief expeditions were still actively engaged in the Arctic—Commander Rochfort Maguire in H.M.S. *Plover*, and Commander Henry Trollope in H.M.S. *Rattlesnake*, both in or near Bering Strait; and Captain Collinson in H.M.S. *Enterprise*. In point of fact, all three ships had already left the Arctic, but reports of their having done so had not yet reached the Admiralty.[170]

Rae immediately went to the Admiralty and presented a brief report[171] with lists of the relics and carefully drawn sketches of the crests on the pieces of table silver which he had recovered from the Eskimos. He also delivered to the Hudson's Bay Company his letter of October 22, 1854,[172] and the Secretary of the Company sent a copy to the Admiralty on the following day.[173] The Admiralty at once sent the report of July 29, 1854, which it had received from Rae, to *The Times* and it was published on October 23,[174] together with a few additional details and a letter which Rae had written to *The Times* on October 20, when he was still at sea on board the *Prince of Wales*. These communications gave the British public the first definite news of the Franklin disaster; two days earlier a letter from Rae to Simpson dated September 4, 1854, had given the news to the readers of the *Montreal Herald* for October 21, 1854.[175]

Rae's report of July 29, 1854, to the Admiralty dealt almost exclusively with the information which he had acquired about the Franklin expedition; it included only a very brief and incomplete account of his own journey. This brevity was unfortunate, for it exposed him to public criticism which would not have been made if the further particulars, which he said[176] would be included in his report to the Hudson's Bay Company, had been published simultaneously with or very shortly after his report to the Admiralty. His full report dated September 1, 1854, intended for the Company, was not finished at that time and, for a reason to be mentioned later,[177] its completion was further postponed.

The criticism to which reference has been made arose out of the following circumstances. Rae, in his report of July 29, 1854, to the Admiralty, stated: "... during my journey over the ice and snow this spring, with the view of completing the survey of the west shore of Boothia, I met with Esquimaux in Pelly Bay, from one of whom I learnt that a party of 'white men' (Kabloonans) had perished from want of food some distance to the westward, and not far beyond a large river containing many falls and rapids. Subsequently further particulars were received, and a number of articles purchased, which place the fate of a portion (if not of all) of the then survivors of Sir John Franklin's long-lost party beyond a doubt ...".[178] Rae then described what he had been told about the Franklin expedition, and all his statements were perfectly correct so far as they went, but he did not specifically state that he had been unable, until he had returned to Repulse Bay, to ascertain where the final tragedy had taken place. Moreover, he did not explain his reasons for his premature return to England. The consequence was that some people got the impression that Rae's information that some of Franklin's officers and men had died near the estuary of the Great Fish River had been obtained by him at Pelly Bay during his outward journey. This impression led in turn to Rae's being charged with having failed to execute the obvious duty of at once proceeding to the supposed site of the tragedy, and of prosecuting the search to a final conclusion. His report to the Hudson's Bay Company, dated September 1, 1854, contained a full and complete explanation of the circumstances, but, even after it had been published, criticisms of the kind which have been described were still levelled at him from time to time.[179]

The relics recovered by Rae from the Eskimos precluded any possible doubt concerning the identity of the white men who were said to have died near the estuary of the Great Fish River. In addition to Franklin's Guelphic Order of Hanover, and a small circular plate bearing his name, the relics included a number of forks and spoons, almost all of which were marked with the crests or initials of seven officers of the *Erebus* and five officers of the *Terror*. The seven officers of the *Erebus* were Sir John Franklin; Commander James Fitzjames; Lieutenants Graham Gore, Henry Thomas Dundas Le Vesconte, and

James Walter Fairholme; Robert Orme Sargent (Mate); and Harry D.S. Goodsir (Assistant Surgeon). The five officers of the *Terror* in question were Captain Francis Rawdon Moira Crozier; Robert Thomas (Mate); Gillies Alexander Macbean (Second Master); John Smart Peddie (Surgeon); and Alexander Macdonald (Assistant Surgeon).[180] M'Clintock later concluded, as a result of his discoveries regarding the Franklin expedition in 1859, that the officers must have distributed their plate amongst the men,[181] and Sir John Ross told Rae that this was what he himself had done before abandoning the *Victory*.[182]

Rae recovered several other articles of which the owners could be identified—a fragment of under-vest marked "F.D.V.6.1845" (Charles Frederick Des Voeux, Mate in the *Erebus*); part of a gold watch bearing the name "James Reid" (Ice-Master in the *Erebus*); a certificate case marked on the lid with the name "Fowler" (William Fowler, Paymaster and Purser's Clerk in the *Erebus*); a knife handle marked "C.H." on one side and "Hickey" on the other (Cornelius Hickey, Caulker's Mate in the *Terror*); a certificate case on which had been scratched the letters "WM" (presumably the initials of William Mark, Able Seaman in the *Erebus*). In addition Rae recovered a number of articles bearing no indication of the ownership—a small ebony box; two pieces of very thin gold watch chain; eight pieces of silver watch cases, one with initials which cannot be clearly deciphered;[183] a pocket compass box; a large surgeon's knife with wooden handle; two sovereigns and six silver coins; the case of a silver gilt pocket chronometer and the dial; a piece of silver tube, probably part of a surgical instrument; a small silver pencil case; a German silver spoon; a gold cap band (the first relic recovered by Rae); etc.[184]

The list of Franklin expedition relics appended to Rae's report of September 1, 1854, to the Secretary of the Company, is incomplete.[185] The reason probably is that Rae, after he had written out a list, obtained a *few* more relics from the Eskimos, such as a coin, part of a silver watch, a teaspoon which had belonged to Dr. Macdonald (Assistant Surgeon, H.M.S. *Terror*), etc.

Rae handed all these relics to the Hudson's Bay Company, which in turn gave them to the Admiralty.[186] They were exhibited to the public shortly afterwards in the Painted Hall of Greenwich Hospital.[187] Most of them are now in the National Maritime Museum at Greenwich. Rae was, however, permitted to keep a fork and a spoon of Franklin's, a fork said to have belonged to Fitzjames, and a few small articles of lesser interest. These form part of the Rae collection presented to the University of Edinburgh, and now exhibited in the Royal Scottish Museum.

Rae's Eskimo informants gave him no indication of the position of the *Erebus* and *Terror* when abandoned. He himself did not think that the Eskimos could have found either ship, partly because of the very small quantities of wood which he saw in the possession of the natives, partly because they always stated that the *Victory*, abandoned by John Ross on the east coast of Boothia in 1832, was the only ship from which they had taken wood.[188] That the natives at some time found one of the ships is, however, quite certain. They informed M'Clintock of this in 1859.[189] This ship finally sank somewhere near the west coast of Adelaide Peninsula, near O'Reilly Island, as Charles F. Hall was told in 1869,[190] or opposite Grant Point, as Schwatka was told in 1879.[191] There appears to be no reason to suppose that the natives would deliberately have misled Rae, and it may be assumed that no Eskimo who had seen or heard of the O'Reilly Island (or Grant Point) ship was among the Eskimos questioned by Rae in 1854.

The information collected by Rae shed no definite light either on the route taken by Franklin after his departure from Beechey Island in 1846 or on the course of events which had resulted in the arrival and death of some of the officers and men near the estuary of the Great Fish River. There is no need to enumerate the various opinions expressed about these matters; the mystery was solved by M'Clintock in 1859. It requires emphasis, however, that there can be no doubt that the Eskimos saw some of Franklin's officers and men marching along the coast of King William Island in 1848, not in 1850, as Rae had been told by the natives at Repulse Bay.

Very soon after his arrival in England, Rae had a long interview with Sir James Robert George Graham (1792–1861), the First Lord of the Admiralty,[192] and on October 26 he prepared, at the request of the

Hydrographer, Sir Francis Beaufort, plans for two overland expeditions to the north coast of America.[193] The first of these expeditions was to search by way of the Mackenzie River for Captain Collinson in H.M.S. *Enterprise*. The second was to proceed down the Great Fish River and search the places where Rae had been told that some of Franklin's men had died. The Admiralty on October 27 requested the Hudson's Bay Company to organise both these expeditions,[194] but a few days later, on November 8, a report of Collinson's safe arrival in August 1854 at Port Clarence, Bering Strait, reached London,[195] and therefore the proposed expedition down the Mackenzie River became unnecessary.[196]

The Hudson's Bay Company took immediate steps to comply with the Admiralty's request for the other expedition down the Great Fish River and appointed two of its officers, James Anderson and James Green Stewart, to lead it in 1855.[197] Rae was offered the command but declined.[198] He recommended several of his former men for employment for the new expedition,[199] and four of them—Thomas Mistagan, Murdoch McLennan, John Fidler, and Henry Fidler—were engaged.[200]

Almost as soon as he set foot in England, Rae became the recipient of so many letters from relations and friends of Franklin's officers and men that, with consent of the Hudson's Bay Company, he resolved to devote the whole of his time to this correspondence, and to postpone completion of his chart, and of his report of September 1, 1854, to the Company.[201] He also found himself involved in an extremely unpleasant controversy, for which he can hardly have been unprepared.

Most people had very reluctantly come to the conclusion, long before October 1854, that the Franklin expedition had met with disaster, and that no hope remained of there being any survivors. The Admiralty itself had in fact adopted the view that all Franklin's officers and men had died in Her Majesty's Service and the presumed date of death was fixed as March 31, 1854.[202] The definite evidence of their deaths consequently did not take the British nation completely by surprise,[203] but Rae's statement that the Eskimos had told him that some had been driven by starvation to resort to cannibalism shocked and horrified the public.[204] That Rae had acted in good faith was not disputed. As he himself stated, it was his duty to inform the Admiralty and the Hudson's Bay Company exactly what he had been told, and it rested with the authorities to release for publication as much or as little of the reports as they considered right.[205] Moreover, as Rae declared many years later, for him to have omitted any part of the information given to him by the Eskimos would have been futile, for the men who had accompanied him would in any case have made the whole of it known.[206] The criticism and indignation which arose were consequently directed principally against the Eskimos rather than against Rae.

The chief features of the attacks were these. Among the remains was the body apparently of an officer with his double-barrelled gun lying beneath him in a position which to some people suggested that he had been taken unawares and struck down from behind;[207] and therefore that in all probability the Eskimos had attacked and killed Franklin's men. There was reason to suspect treachery and violence. Wild beasts had mutilated the corpses. None of Rae's informants had actually seen the white men, and therefore all their statements were secondhand. The Eskimo interpreter Ouligbuck was probably imperfectly acquainted with the dialect spoken by the Repulse Bay natives and did not necessarily understand what they said; his knowledge of English may not even have been sufficient to enable him to explain correctly to Rae what the Eskimos told him; and he probably exaggerated. Furthermore, and more important still, the religion, courage, discipline, and sense of duty of Franklin's men would have prevented anything whatever of the kind described by the Eskimos. The moral improbability far outweighed in relative importance the "wild tales of a herd of savages". To these and other criticisms, Rae answered at length; he pointed out that some were based on imperfect knowledge; and he affirmed his entire belief in what the Eskimos had told him.[208]

10. *The Payment of the Reward*

The British Government in March 1850 had offered to any party or parties of any nationality, a reward of £20,000 for discovering and effectually relieving the missing officers and men; a reward of £10,000 for discovering and effectually relieving any of them or for conveying information resulting in the relief of any of them; and, lastly, a reward of £10,000 for ascertaining their fate.[209]

Strange as it may seem, Rae did not hear of this offer until more than four years had elapsed.[210] He did not know until he arrived in England in October 1854 that the Government in 1850 had offered these rewards in connection with the Franklin expedition, and that the reward of £10,000 was still on offer "to any party or parties who, in the judgment of the Board of Admiralty, should, by virtue of his or their efforts", first succeed in ascertaining the fate of Franklin's officers and men.

On November 13, 1854, Andrew Colvile, Governor of the Hudson's Bay Company, wrote to the Admiralty, at the request of Rae, and claimed on Rae's behalf that he was entitled to a reward of £10,000. The Admiralty answered that it could not reach any decision regarding this claim until it had received a report from Captain Collinson, of H.M.S. *Enterprise*,[211] then on his way home but not expected to reach England before the spring of 1855.

Colvile evidently told Rae what the Admiralty had said, for Rae, having waited for a month, which he thought was sufficient time for the Admiralty to study Collinson's report, which had already arrived, sent to the Hudson's Bay Company the letter of December 14, 1854.[212] Rae in this letter asked if the Company proposed to take any further steps in prosecution of his claim. Colvile stated in answer to this letter that the question affected Rae as a private individual rather than as a servant of the Company; he advised Rae to apply in person for the reward, and to leave the Company to support his claim in the way that it considered best. Rae thereupon wrote to the Admiralty and advanced his claim.[213] Colvile again wrote to the Admiralty on March 19, 1855, and intimated that he thought the time had arrived when a decision could be expected.[214] He evidently sent Rae a copy of his letter and a copy of the Admiralty's reply of November 15, for Rae wrote to the Secretary of the Company on March 27, 1855, and expressed his sincere thanks for the efforts made on his behalf by the Governor and

Committee with respect to his claim for the reward. This letter is the last in the present collection.[215] Rae was irritated even by the short delay, and in May 1855 was considering whether to take legal action by a Petition of Right.[216]

The remainder of the story can be briefly told. The Hudson's Bay Company wrote to the Admiralty on June 19, 1855, and stated that since Collinson had been for some time in England,[217] it hoped that Rae's claim would now be favourably considered. The Admiralty answered on June 29 that although it was of opinion that Rae would in any case be entitled to a portion of the reward, it could not come to a final decision until it had received a report on the proceedings of the expedition which, commanded by James Anderson, had been sent by the Hudson's Bay Company down the Great Fish River in 1855.[218]

Anderson's report reached the Admiralty in January 1856. He had left Fort Resolution in June 1855, and reached the estuary of the Great Fish River about a month later. He recovered several relics of the Franklin expedition, but no papers or journals, and he found no graves or human remains. He had no interpreter, but Eskimos led him to understand that all the relics had come from a boat, the property of white men, all of whom had starved to death. Anderson was compelled to return after searching at the estuary for only ten days.[219] He thus discovered no more than that some members of the Franklin expedition had apparently reached the estuary of the Great Fish River, had had a boat with them, and, according to the Eskimos, had died, so that his researches merely verified part of the information already gleaned by Rae.

The Admiralty, on receipt of Anderson's report, decided to undertake no further searches for the lost expedition. It gave notice on January 22, 1856, that Rae had claimed the reward offered for ascertaining the fate of the officers and men of the *Erebus* and *Terror*, and that his claim, and any other claims that might be submitted, would be adjudicated in three months' time.[220]

Lady Franklin protested against what she considered an untimely adjudication. She pointed out that the fate of the lost expedition had not been fully ascertained, and hence that the intended adjudication was premature. The reports given to Rae by Eskimos might refer only to a detachment; no search had been made for the ships; these might still be in existence not far from the Great Fish River. She supported these contentions for postponing payment with much argument,[221] her principal objection being that the fate of the Franklin expedition had not been fully ascertained.

Lady Franklin was by no means the only person who held the latter opinion. A petition signed by men eminent in every walk of life was presented to the Prime Minister (Viscount Palmerston) in June 1856. The petitioners raised no objection to payment of the reward to Rae; they did not mention the matter; but they appealed for a final Government expedition in search of the *Erebus* and *Terror*, to "clear up a mystery which has excited the sympathy of the civilised world", and they expressed the hope that this expedition would recover "records which will throw fresh light on Arctic geography, and dispel the obscurity in which the voyage and fate of our countrymen are still involved". In short, the petitioners denied that the fate of the Franklin expedition had been fully ascertained, and their advocacy of a final expedition was supported by all the principal British Arctic explorers.[222]

The correctness of the petitioners' opinion was demonstrated a few years later. The private search expedition organised by Lady Franklin and commanded by M'Clintock succeeded in 1859 in ascertaining more fully the proceedings and ultimate fate of the missing officers and men.[223] M'Clintock, not Rae, has ever since been acknowledged as the real discoverer of the fate of the Franklin expedition.

Lady Franklin's protest against premature adjudication fell on deaf ears. The Admiralty was in all probability not at all sorry to find itself possessed of an opportunity of liberating itself once and for all of obligations contracted in the Arctic, and possibly for that reason was not disposed to modify its views. Several other claims were made for the reward,[224] but the Admiralty, as was virtually a foregone conclusion, decided in favour of Rae.

Rae himself, before he was made aware of this decision, suggested to the Admiralty that if his claim were favourably entertained, a difficulty might arise in deciding the proportion of the total reward to be paid to the men who had accompanied him, and that if such a difficulty were to arise, it might be referred for settlement to the Hudson's Bay Company. On June 19, 1856, the Admiralty informed Rae and the Company that he and his companions were entitled to the reward, and requested the Company to distribute the money among Rae and the men.[225] On July 2 the Company advised the payment of £8,000 to Rae, and the division among the men of £2,000, in the following proportions suggested by Rae: John Beads, Jacob Beads, James Johnstone, John McDonald, Thomas Mistagan, Murdoch McLennan, £260 each; William Ouligbuck, £210; all these men had accompanied Rae to Repulse Bay. Rae suggested that the remaining men, who had returned to York Factory from Chesterfield Inlet in 1853, should be paid as follows: James Clouston (in charge of the boat) £60; Charles Harrison, Henry Fidler, Murdoch McDonald, George McDougald, Louis St. Michel, £30 each; Munro (Eskimo) £20. The Admiralty approved the Company's suggestions, and paid £10,000 to the Company for distribution among Rae and the men.[226]

11. *Rae's Achievement*

Rae's methods of travel are referred to, though only occasionally, in the letters describing his various expeditions, but many of his remarks clearly illustrate his ideas and principles. Rae on his travels, however, did no more than exploit to the utmost a method well known to the Hudson's Bay Company. There are frequent references to nets and methods of fishing in the letters received from Sir George Simpson and from the Company as well as in Rae's own letters. M'Clintock nevertheless said of Rae "I believe he and his party were the first white men who maintained themselves in the Arctic regions by their own unaided exertions".[227]

By these methods, and as a result of Rae's great strength and endurance, he was able to set up records of travel which can seldom have been surpassed.

Dependence on hunting (which to-day has come to be known as "living on the land") was the method employed also by Schwatka, who in 1878–80 travelled overland to King William Island and back from Camp Daly near Chesterfield Inlet, and covered 2,819 geographical, or 3,251 statute, miles in 11 months and 20 days.[228] One of the later exponents was David Hanbury, who travelled in 1901–02 from Chesterfield Inlet to Coronation Gulf, and whose travels have hardly received the credit which is their due.[229]

Rae has himself set out a complete statement of his achievements in a letter written to an unknown recipient in February 1856, which is given below. The origin of this letter is uncertain but a copy in printed form is in the Hudson's Bay Company's archives. The fact that Rae wrote this letter showed how much importance he himself attached to his own travel records, and he must have considered them as of no ordinary standard.

VOYAGES AND TRAVELS OF DR. RAE, IN THE ARCTIC REGIONS.

Copy of a Letter from Dr. Rae to ________
February, 1856.

London, February, 1856

My Dear Sir,
As my Arctic wanderings are now I believe at a close, I send you a brief account of them.

I entered the Hudson's Bay Company's service as a Surgeon in 1833, and spent ten years at and near Moose Factory, where I acquired some experience of the fatigue and privation attending on life in that country, and the best modes of providing against them. I gained a fair knowledge of the habits of wild animals, birds, and fish, and the most sure ways of killing them; in fact various *accomplishments* which are in most cases considered rather disadvantageous than otherwise to the possessor, but which, under the circumstances in which I was subsequently placed, were of very great value to me and to those under my command.

My first hard work in Arctic service or rather preparatory to it, was a journey on snow shoes from Red River Colony to Sault St. Mary's, in the winter of 1844–45 (a distance by the route followed of nearly twelve hundred statute miles), for the purpose of receiving instructions in Astronomy, &c. &c.

This journey occupied two months of constant travelling, and at the end of it, the only man who had accompanied me the whole distance was found to have lost 26 lbs. in weight (he was certainly rather fat when he started), whilst I had gained 2 lbs.

During my first visit to the Arctic Sea in 1846–47, I was absent from York Factory nearly fifteen months with a party of twelve men, and passed the winter in a stone house at Repulse Bay without fuel of any kind to warm ourselves, the temperature in-doors being often 25° below the freezing point (7° Fahrenheit) and sometimes considerably colder; but we picked up sufficient Andromeda* and moss for cooking.

The whole stock of provisions carried with us was only sufficient for four months consumption at full allowance, and we brought back with us one quarter of this quantity; so that by our own exertions we had procured food for twelve months.

Of the game which formed our winter stock, nearly one-half was shot by myself.

The result of this Expedition was the tracing of about six hundred and fifty-five statute miles of new land and coast, forming the shores of Committee Bay, lying between latitudes 66° 30' and 69° 30' N. and longitudes 85° and 91° W.

The distances travelled and the length of the boat voyages will be given at the end of this letter.

In 1848, I accompanied Sir John Richardson in a search for Sir John Franklin's party, along the coast from the M'Kenzie

* A plant used for fuel. [Note by John Rae.]

River to the Coppermine. We were compelled to abandon our boats two days march north of the mouth of the Coppermine, and had a very fatiguing walk of thirteen days to Fort Confidence on Great Bear Lake, where we wintered.

In 1849, I descended the Coppermine with one boat and crew of five men, but in consequence of the coldness of the season was prevented by ice from crossing the Union and Dolphin Strait to Wollaston Land, as my instructions directed me to do.

In consequence of timidity on the part of the steersman, we lost our boat and excellent interpreter in an attempt to ascend the Coppermine.

During the winter of 1849–50 I remained in charge of M'Kenzie River District, and in the summer of 1850 was appointed by the H.B.Co. at the desire of Government to lead an Expedition in search of Sir John Franklin; my only instructions being that I was to select any route I believed most advantageous. I chose the route by Great Bear Lake and the Coppermine.

Many difficulties presented themselves;—the Indians, on whom we had to rely for provisions, had not been informed of the intention of a party to winter at Fort Confidence,—we could not carry in our boats provisions enough for winter use, and had we been able to do so, the District had been drained of its supplies by the party of Commander Pullen—we had boats to build of the requisite size and lightness for transport overland to the Coppermine and the descent of that river, and the report of Simpson (see his narrative) was far from favourable to the hopes of obtaining wood at the north-east end of Great Bear Lake, of a sufficiently good quality for the purpose. Relying however upon my experience, and determined to make the best of everything, I without hesitation chose that route as the one I thought best for the purpose, and after superintending the dispatch of boats from Fort Simpson with supplies to the various trading ports [sic] of the District, I proceeded with a party by the M'Kenzie River and Bear Lake to Fort Confidence, where by great economy and with some privation (during part of the winter we were on little more than half allowance) we passed the cold season. Two excellent little boats were built,—a draft of which I was obliged to make for the guidance of the carpenter, who had not seen any craft of the build I wanted. The sails for these boats were cut out, and all the rigging, both standing and running gear, spliced, served, and fitted by myself, none other of the party being in any way acquainted with such work.

The results of the spring and summer operations of 1851, were a journey on ice and snow of 1080* statute miles, and a boat voyage along the Arctic Coast going and returning of 1390 statute miles; the tracing and laying down correctly (as was proved by Capt. Collinson's subsequent survey) six hundred and thirty miles of previously unexplored coast, along the Southern Shores of Victoria and Wollaston Lands, between longitudes 101° and 117° W., and the finding two pieces of wood, in probability parts of one of Sir John Franklin's vessels or boats. This is I believe the most quickly performed Arctic journey on record. The time occupied, exclusive of five days detention by bad weather, &c. was 39 days, which will give an average distance per day of 27⅔ statute miles. I hauled a sledge of about 100 lbs. weight for the greater part of the journey.

During the winter of 1851–52 I proceeded to England, having travelled in snow shoes from Athabasca to St. Paul's, a distance of 1730 statute miles, being aided by dogs for the last four hundred and fifty miles, which four hundred and fifty were accomplished in ten days.

In 1853 I proceeded to Repulse Bay for the purpose of completing the survey of coast on the west side of Boothia, and passed the winter of 1853–54 in snow houses at Repulse Bay with a party of seven men, without fuel except for cooking.

* This distance is greater than that mentioned in my original Report, because in it I omitted to include the distance between Bear Lake and the Coppermine. [Note by John Rae.]

We obtained food by shooting and fishing, sufficient for eleven of the thirteen months we were absent, and the skins of the animals shot were dressed and made by ourselves into winter clothing and warm bedding.

During this Expedition, a new river which falls into Chesterfield inlet, was traced in a boat to the extent of 210 miles; two hundred and seventy miles of previously unexplored land and coast line were added to the Charts. During the spring eleven hundred miles, including a preliminary journey, were travelled over, and information of the fate of a portion (I believe the last survivors) of Sir John Franklin's party was obtained.

It has been asked why I did not, when at the Castor and Pollux River of Simpson, travel westward when I knew from the report of the Esquimaux that a party of whites had starved some years before in that direction.

The information obtained on my outward journey was not sufficiently clear to enable me to fix with any degree of certainty on the position at which the party were starved, and to have travelled westward without sufficient knowledge on this point, when the land was covered a foot and a half or more deep with snow would, as I then thought, and still think, have been useless. It was after my return to Repulse Bay towards the end of May, that I received from the natives the particulars which enabled me to ascertain with accuracy the place where the bodies of our dead countrymen were found. Then it was too late to travel to the spot, as in the months of June and July it is all but impossible to travel across that country. In consequence of the melting of the snows, the low lands are perfectly flooded, and every little stream is converted into a torrent, shut in on each side by drift banks of snow, with perpendicular sides, so that there is no crossing them even with Halkett's admirable little boats. Therefore having gained what I thought conclusive information, I came home to stop farther expeditions rather than wait a year to visit the spot.

The difficulties of overland travelling in July are mentioned in Capt. M'Clintock's journal (we can have no better authority) see Arctic Blue Book for 1855, page 584—July 15. "Travelled overland 2¼ miles in 7½ hours,"—" Another such march would knock up the party."

The peculiarities of the expeditions on which I have been employed are these—I have, with the exception of one season, been always commander, and sole officer.* My party have twice wintered without fuel, except for cooking,—once in a stone house, and once in snow huts; having carried an inadequate supply of provisions, we obtained by our own exertions food for twenty-two months of the twenty-seven we were absent, fully two-fifths of which (as far as was requisite for our winter stock) was killed by myself. The above allusion to the quantity of game shot, is to show how advantageous it is for the leader of an Arctic expedition to be acquainted with the use of the gun. A party situated as mine were, but with a commanding officer who could not shoot, would in all probability have either perished, or have been unable to perform any lengthened spring journey.

You may think it strange that we could procure food enough to support ourselves, whilst some three hundred miles to the west Franklin's party starved, but Repulse Bay is most advantageously placed for obtaining venison during the spring and autumn migrations of the deer, whereas the neighbourhood of the mouth of the Great Fish River is one of the most unfavourable positions for procuring food, particularly during the spring. The Esquimaux never remain there at that season. Indeed, except Repulse Bay and its vicinity, there is only one other place on the Arctic Coast at which I would attempt wintering, unless I *carried with me* nearly a full supply of provisions.

By following the native custom of using snow houses (which I learnt and caused my men to learn how to build)

* In the boat voyage of 1851, I had a second in command [H.Æ. Mackenzie], but in consequence of his carelessness and inattention, he was put off duty before we reached the sea, and remained so until our return to Bear Lake. [Note by John Rae.]

to rest in during our spring journies, the weight we had to haul was considerably reduced. The bedding for myself and four men amounted to 24 lbs. weight, or about 5 lbs. for each man. The bedding, &c. including oil cloth for tent floor, of Captain S. Osborne's party of eight in spring, 1853, amounted to 156 [140] lbs. weight, or 19½ [17½] lbs. per man—add to this 58 lbs. for tent and tent poles, and we have a total of 214 [198] lbs. or very nearly 27 [25] lbs.[230] per man. The time required for building a snow house varies from 25 minutes to 1 hour 30 minutes, according to size and circumstances.

I will not enter into details of hardships endured, but it cannot be supposed that men could remain two winters on the Arctic Coast, without fire, except just sufficient for cooking; could pass along nearly 7000 miles of coast in open boats, and travel more than 6000 miles on foot, without often experiencing cold, hunger, and fatigue. Having very few men I could not, as was the case with the Naval expeditions, have auxiliary sledges and fatigue parties to accompany me a portion of the journey. In the journies of 1847, 1851–54, I either hauled a sledge or carried a load.

The distances travelled on foot and in boats, on and in connexion with these expeditions are as follow; the distances being given in English miles, and one-fifth allowed for turns and deviations in the route, as allowed by Arctic Naval Officers.

Journies on foot either with or without snow shoes.

		St. Miles	Miles
1844–5 Winter.	Red River Colony to St. Mary's	1180	
1851–2 Winter.	Athabasca to St. Paul's aided by dogs for 450 miles of it	1730	
	Total of journies, inland	____	2910
1847 Spring.	From Repulse Bay round Committee Bay	1200	
1848 Autumn.	From Coast near Coppermine River to Bear Lake	150	

1849 Autumn.	From Coppermine River to Bear Lake	115	
1851 Spring.	From Bear Lake and on Arctic Coast	1080	
1854 Spring.	From Repulse Bay to Castor and Pollux River, &c. including preliminary journey with provisions	1100	
	Total of journies on or near coast	——	3645
	Total of journies on foot		6555

Boat Voyages.

		St. Miles	Miles
1846	Voyage in open boats from York Factory to Repulse Bay	870	
"	Ditto in boats from Repulse Bay, portage, and in Committee Bay	155	
1847	Ditto from Repulse Bay to York Factory	870	
1848	Ditto from M'Kenzie River to Coppermine, with Sir J. Richardson	820	
1849	Ditto from Coppermine to Cape Kruseustern [sic] and back	135	
1851	Ditto from Coppermine to East end of Victoria Land and back	1390	
1853	Ditto from York Factory to Repulse Bay	870	
"	Ditto up and down Chesterfield Inlet	300	

"	Ditto up and down Quoich River	420	
1854	Ditto Repulse Bay to York Factory	870	
	Total of boat voyages		6700

Surveys

1847	New Land and Coast line previously unsurveyed	655	
1851	New Coast line ditto	630	
1853	" River (Quioch) ditto	210	
1854	" Land and coast line ditto	270	
	Total previously unexplored		1765

Expences of the Expeditions of 1846–7 and 1853–5[231] *including wages of men, my pay, &c. &c:—*

	£.	s.	d.
Expedition of 1846–7	1387	0	0
Ditto of 1853–4	1694	0	0
	£3081	0	0

Extent of Land, Coast Line, and River previously unexplored, added to the Charts during these two Expeditions, 1135 statute miles, at the expence of about £2 15s. per mile.

It is impossible to obtain a correct estimate of the expences of the Expeditions of 1849–50 and 1851, as these are mixed up with those under Sir John Richardson and Commander Pullen. The expences would be considerably heavier than those give above, in consequence of the great extent of inland transport.

I remain,
Very sincerely yours,
JOHN RAE.

By way of comparison with other arctic travellers at that period one must first mention Lieutenant G. F. Mecham, who made a sledge journey with man haulage of 1,157 geographical, or 1,336 statute, miles in 70 days.[232] On this journey Mecham had the advantage of four or five depots with provisions both on the outward and on the homeward journey.

It is difficult, of course, to make comparisons between one man's performance and another's. Much depends on supporting parties and on whether dogs, either large teams or two or three dogs only, were employed.

By common consent the most successful arctic journeys in the middle of the nineteenth century were those of Rae and M'Clintock. Rae and M'Clintock held different views about the type of sledge which should be used. Rae advocated what must have been a development of an Indian type with flat under surface and pulled by two or three dogs. M'Clintock employed a modified Greenland sledge, at first with man haulage, but later, in the 1857–59 expedition, with a team usually of six dogs. Rae's and M'Clintock's views on sledges are to be found in a discussion on a paper "On Arctic Sledge-travelling", read by M'Clintock to the Royal Geographical Society in June 1875.[233]

At this meeting remarks were also made about records. Mention was made of M'Clintock's own journey in 1851 of 900 [statute] miles, made in 80 days, and of the still longer journey in 1853, of 1,400 [statute] miles in 105 days. On the latter journey M'Clintock had the advantage of being able to kill musk-oxen and deer. M'Clintock and his second in command, Hobson, made some remarkable journeys with dog teams during the voyage of the *Fox* in 1857–59. M'Clintock himself on his 78 day journey to and from King William Island had one sledge pulled by 4 men, one sledge with 6 dogs driven by Petersen, and a small sledge, driven at first by M'Clintock, pulled by 5 puppies. The distance travelled was 920 miles.[234]

Rae must be given credit for the length, speed and variety of his journeys. It must also be borne in mind that he was not overweighted with equipment as he was not outfitted with the same lavishness as the naval expeditions at that time, and this must have been an advantage. Rae's record journeys were due to his personal strength and to his being accustomed to travel light.

The following passage from the Royal Society obituary notice of Rae may be of interest.[235] "It is easy to understand that Dr. Rae's views as to the equipment of expeditions in Arctic travel would differ in many respects, rightly or wrongly, from those who advocated the costly naval expeditions then in vogue. He could point to instances of his own superior success, and to the disasters that befel the survivors of the Franklin expedition, as they toiled homewards with a miscellaneous collection of heavy articles. Putting forward his views, as he did with point and insistence, his remarks were, as a rule, somewhat unwelcome to the naval authorities."

A word may be said about his use of dogs. Rae held that dogs were essential in sledging, but his dependence upon them was not as great as might have been expected. On the first expedition the party started out on April 5, 1847, with three men, an Eskimo and Ouligbuck's son as interpreter, with two sledges each drawn by four dogs, but ten days later the dogs were described as nearly useless and were left to recoup. On the second part of the journey, towards Fury and Hecla Strait, which began on May 13, the party consisted of four men and, for one day only, Ouligbuck, supported by "A fatigue party of 2 men and an Esquimaux, with a dog sled . . . for 3 days". Thereafter Rae carried about 40 lbs. of baggage, and his men about 70 lbs. each.[236]

The only other journey on foot on which Rae depended on dogs was that in the spring of 1851. On this occasion he left Fort Confidence on April 25 with 4 men, 3 sledges drawn by dogs, and a small sledge drawn by the men alternately. A fatigue party was sent back on May 2, and from then on Rae travelled with 2 men and 2 sledges drawn by 5 dogs. This was the journey of 39 days' duration during which the average rate of travel was as high as 27⅔ statute miles per day.[237]

Rae's outstanding characteristics on his travels were his dependence on hunting, his habit of travelling light, and of building snow houses, and the speed with which he was able to explore and survey his new discoveries. He speaks of his sleeping gear averaging about five pounds a man and compares this with a weight of nearly twenty-five pounds a man carried on Sherard Osborn's journey in 1853.

It must also be borne in mind that Rae was an expert on snow-shoes. Of still more value, however, to his exploratory work was his ability to design and to sail small boats. The boats for the 1851 expedition were built and fitted out at Fort Confidence from plans made by Rae. Kirkness, the carpenter, had not previously had much experience but Rae himself supplied this, no doubt from his boyhood days in Orkney, and it was in Kirkness' boats that he made the voyage of 1,390 miles to Victoria Land immediately following his long sledge journey to Wollaston Land.

12. *Rae's Later Life*

Sixty years have elapsed since Rae died, and very little information is available about his later life, which as he grew older appears to have been mainly spent in London.

It is known that he contemplated one more arctic expedition. Apart from the naval officers who had taken part in the Franklin search, Rae after 1854 was the leading British arctic explorer. He began to plan for his new expedition at about the time of the payment of the £10,000 reward. On receiving his portion he arranged for a small schooner costing £2,000 to be built in Canada, his object being to complete the survey of the American arctic coastline. The vessel was not ready in time for the 1855 season and in the interval before the 1856 season she was employed commercially on the Great Lakes in the autumn. She was unfortunately lost in a storm, and Rae's project of a further arctic expedition was apparently never renewed.

In Feburary 1857 Rae gave evidence before the Select Committee appointed by the House of Commons to enquire into the affairs of the Hudson's Bay Company, and in November 1858 he made a tour through the United States in company with Edward Ellice, junior. Rae was in Canada again in the following year, and that summer, 1859, he was one of a party which went across the prairies to Red River. At forty-five he was still very fit, and it is recorded that on this visit he walked, travelling on snow-shoes, from Hamilton to Toronto, a distance of about forty miles, in seven hours, and that he dined out that same evening without showing any signs of fatigue.[238]

In 1860 he undertook the land part of a survey for a contemplated telegraph line from England to America via the Faroes, Iceland and Greenland. There was at one time an idea of landing a sledge expedition under Rae's charge on the east coast of Greenland with the object of crossing the inland ice to the west. Rae, however, has stated emphatically that "there was not the slightest intention of its being attempted". The *Fox* reached the southern part of the east coast of Greenland about the middle of September and then went round to the west coast. At the end of October Rae made an attempt upon the inland ice near Julianehaab. He reached the glacier ice, probably the first time he had been on a glacier, but turned back at "a deep and wide crevasse that effectually stopped further progress".[239]

He also took part in a second telegraph survey made in 1864 from Winnipeg across the Rocky Mountains to the Pacific coast in 53° N. latitude. During the course of this expedition Rae travelled along several hundred miles of the Fraser River in small dug-out canoes without guides. There is no record of any further field activities after 1864.

In early middle life Rae is described as "remarkable for manly beauty in form and feature, combined with a temper that was quick and somewhat fiery".[240] Rae's marriage took place in 1860, to Catharine Jane Alicia, the third daughter of Major George Ash Thompson of Ardkill, Co. Londonderry, and Glenchiel Munechrane, Co. Tyrone. There were no children of the marriage, and Mrs. Rae survived her husband for nearly twenty-six years and died in April 1919 at Chislehurst in Kent.

In 1864 Rae was fifty years of age but his active days appear to have ended. He lived chiefly in London, but spent several summers in Orkney, where he had a small shooting on hill ground at Westhill in Rendall parish. He was a prominent member of the Royal Colonial Institute and one of the representatives of Ontario on the executive of the Imperial Institute.[241] He was also one of the first Directors of the Canada North West Land Company. He was a keen Volunteer, signing himself in 1883 as "Private J. Rae, M.D., F.R.S., London Scottish". He is said to have won a prize at Wimbledon for rifle shooting while serving in the Orkney Artillery Volunteers. Rae was also a regular attender at meetings of the Royal Geographical Society, and a member of the Council in 1862–63, and in 1870–73.

The list[242] of Rae's scientific papers is as follows:

1. Notice of the effect of solar heat in raising a balloon. *Silliman, Journ.*, XXXIII, 1838, pp. 196–198.[243]
2. Journey from Great Bear Lake to Wollaston Land. *Geogr. Soc. Journ.*, XXII, 1852, pp. 73–96.
3. Arctic Explorations, with information respecting Sir John Franklin's missing party. *Geogr. Soc. Journ.*, XXV, 1855, pp. 246–256.
4. Formation of icebergs and transportation of boulders by ice. *Canadian Journ.*, IV, 1859, pp. 180–183.
5. On the formation of icebergs and ice action, as observed in Hudson's Bay and Straits. *Brit. Assoc. Rep.*, 1860 (pt. 2), pp. 174–175.
6. Exploration of the Færöes and Iceland, &c. *Geogr. Soc. Proc*, V, 1861, pp. 80–89.
7. On some physical properties of ice; on the transposition of boulders from below to above the ice; and on mammoth-remains. [1874.] *London, Phys. Soc. Proc.*, 1, 1876, pp. 14–20; *Phil. Mag.*, 48, 1874, pp. 56–61.
8. Eskimo migrations. [1877.] *Anthropol. Instit. Journ.*, 7, 1878, pp. 125–131.
9. Eskimo skulls [1877.] *Anthropol. Instit. Journ.*, 7, 1878, pp. 142–143.
10. Arctic and sub-arctic life [1877.] *Roy. Instit. Proc.*, 8, 1879, pp. 378–389.
11. Anchor-ice. *Nature*, 21. 1880, p. 538; 22, 1880, p. 54.
12. Geological climates. *Nature*, 23, 1881, pp. 337–338.
13. Sound of the aurora. *Nature*, 23, 1881, p. 605.
14. Arctic research [1881.] *Nature*, 25, 1882, pp. 53–54, 102.
15. Unconscious bias in walking. *Nature*, 29, 1884, 310–311, 384.
16. Wind sand ripples. *Nature*, 29, 1884, 357.

17. Common domestic duck diving for food. *Nature*, 29, 1884, 428.
18. Right-sidedness. *Nature*, 29, 1884, 477.
19. Intelligence in animals. *Nature*, 30, 1884, 7.
20. Atlantic ice and mild winters. *Nature*, 30, 1884, 76.
21. Peculiar ice forms. [1884.] *Nature*, 31, 1885, 81–82.
22. Do flying-fish fly? [1884.] *Nature*, 31, 1885, 101–102.
23. On overland expeditions to the Arctic coast of America. *Brit. Ass. Rep.*, 1885, 1133–1136.
24. On the best and safest route by which to attain a high northern latitude. *Geogr. Soc. Proc.*, 7, 1885, 760–761.
25. Lieutenant Greely on ice. [1885–86.] *Nature*, 33, 1886, 126–127, 244–245.
26. Anchor frosts. *Nature*, 33, 1886, 269.
27. Proposed new route *via* Hudson's Bay and Strait to the Great Prairie-Lands of Canada. *Scott. Geogr. Mag.*, 2, 1886, 727–732.
28. Hudson's Bay and Hudson's Strait as a navigable channel. *Geogr. Soc. Proc*, 10, 1888, 653.
29. Hail formation in relation to descent of ice-pellets from a tree. *Nature*, 37, 1888, 344.
30. Notes on some of the birds and mammals of the Hudson's Bay Company's Territories and the Arctic coast [1888.] *Canad. Rec. Sci.*, 3, 1889, 125–136; *Linn. Soc. Jl.* (*Zool.*), 20, 1890, 136–145.

It will be seen that there is an interval between 1861 and 1874 when no papers have been recorded. This interval was followed in the late seventies and early eighties by a period of numerous papers. This gap in Rae's output remains unexplained, but it is interesting to see his return to prominence and to record the standing which he attained as he grew older and which led to his election to the Royal Society in 1880. He had received an Honorary Doctorate of Medicine from McGill University, Montreal, as early as 1853, and an Honorary Doctorate of Laws at Edinburgh in 1856. The latter was an honour which he very much valued.

Rae died on July 22, 1893, at 4 Addison Gardens, London. He had previously lived at No. 2, but this may have been the same house renumbered. The burial took place at Kirkwall in the churchyard of St. Magnus Cathedral.

Rae left no direct descendants but he had numerous nephews and nieces, the children of his brothers and of his sisters Mrs. Hamilton and Mrs. Munro. Many of them are mentioned in his Will and all were resident in Canada. Rae's wife was the principal beneficiary under his Will, but he suggested that his medals, the Franklin relics and his Eskimo implements and curiosities should ultimately go to Edinburgh University. This was arranged by his widow in 1893; in 1926 they were deposited in the Royal Scottish Museum, where they are described as (a) a series of ethnographical specimens from the Eskimo and the North American Indians; (b) personal relics (snow-shoes, moccasins, books, needlebook, gold medal of Royal Geographical Society, Arctic Medal,[244] gold watch and chain); and (c) relics of the Franklin Expedition, retained by special permission of the Hudson's Bay Company (silver spoon and forks, watch-case, coins, button, badge).

Soon after Rae's death a fund was raised in Orkney[245] to set up a memorial which was erected in 1895 in St. Magnus Cathedral. The memorial is a striking one, and one of the visitors most impressed at seeing it was Edward Wilson, Captain Scott's companion in the Antarctic. Wilson wrote: "'John Rae, M.D., LL.D., F.R.S., F.R.G.S., Arctic Explorer. Intrepid Discoverer of the fate of Sir John Franklin's last Expedition. Born 1813. Died 1893. Expeditions 1846–7; 1848–9; 1851–2; 1853–4.' . . . . That is the whole inscription—and the man is a life-size figure lying asleep wrapped in a buffalo sleeping bag, with moccassins on and a gun and a book open by his side."[246]

RAE'S ARCTIC CORRESPONDENCE 1844–55

Moose Factory 19*th August* 1844[1]

Sir George Simpson
&c &c &c

My Dear Sir
I have now the honor to acknowledge receipt of your much valued favor of 24th ulto.[2] which duly reached me by return of Misere, Garton, and the Indians. Having hourly expected for some days past to see the signal of the ships[3] arrival at our Commodore's mast head, I deferred writing until the eleventh hour but as I intend starting to morrow as proposed, it is now necessary to scribble all my epistles, having many adieus (some of them *tender ones* no doubt) to make.

Inclosed is a packing account of sundries forwarded from this to your address also a note of the sums paid for them. I am afraid that there are not so many Rogans[4] as you would have wished, but the *Ladies* employed to make them, said they could get no good Bark until late in the spring.

As the canoe brought down from Abitibi was rather small for my voyage to Red River, Mr. Miles[5] kindly allowed a man from Ruperts House named John Clouston[6] to build one, and he has made a very good job of it, rather deep in the bow and stern, but all the better on that account for Lake way.

John Corrigal[7] is the only man that goes along with me from this, the other Man (Merryman)[8] would wish to be of the party, but he appeared doubtful of being able to do his duty as well as his companions, so I did not press the matter. There is no lack of volunteers, some of whom are incapable, and the others cannot well be spared; but no doubt the North can produce as efficient men, if not more so, there being a larger *assortment* to choose from.

I do not think that there are any other instruments than those already requested, required for the expedition.

As I have no pocket case of surgical instruments and I find the want of it when travelling, I hope you will not be offended at my requesting you to send me one, to be forwarded with the sextant &c. I should wish it of the best quality to fold like a pocket book, the outside of Russia leather, the caustic holder to be of silver, not Ivory.[9] Inclosed is a Bill on the Honble. H B. Co. to pay for it, the amount being left blank.

Hoping that you have reached England in safety, and found all well there, I have the honor to remain with the greatest respect

My Dear Sir
Your most obt. & obliged servt.
John Rae

— DR. RAE, RECD. 16 OCTR., ANSD. 2 DECR.[10], ENCLOSING BLANK BILL IN PAYMENT OF CASE OF SURGICAL INSTRUMENTS —

[Addressed]

Private Sir George Simpson
&c &c. &c
Hudson's Bay House
Fenchurch Street[11]
London

[Endorsed]

1844
Moose Factory 19 August

[Enclosure to letter from John Rae to Sir George Simpson, dated Moose Factory, August 19, 1844]

1 A Case—10 Large flat Rogans wth. handles
7 basket Do. Do.
5 nests round Do. ea. 12
1 pair snow shoes
2 " Do. 3 nests Rogans 12/2, 13/1 & 1 quill wrought Basket
1 half size Canoe wth. 6 Paddles, poles, Gum, Bark &c &c.
1 pair Moose deer Antlers

—Sir George Simpson—			Dr.
To Mrs. Gladman for Rogans	1 nest round, 7 basket & 8 flat Rogans.		2 – –
Mrs. Vincent Do.	3 nests round ea 12	10/–	1 10 –
Mrs. Flett[12] Do.	1 nest & 2 flat Rogans superior make		– 15 –
Settled in Sale Shop Accts. Debited Sir Geo. Simpson			£.4 5 –

Moose Factory 19th August 1844

Mechipicoton *25th February* 1845[13]

My Dear Sir

You will be surprised to receive a letter from me dated at this place, but an unforeseen occurrence has rendered it necessary that I should see you early this spring.

I reached Red River last fall on the 9th October and found Mr. G. Taylor[14] very unwell with a severe attack of gout, accompanied by a broken down constitution. The deseases of his body had affected his mind considerably, so that up to the day of his death, (15th November) he was incapable of affording me any assistance in my *studies*. At first my intention was to endeavour to gain a knowledge of Astronomy &c. by my own unaided exertions, but a little reflection caused me to give up the idea of doing so, as altho' I might have become sufficiently *scientific*, yet there could not be that dependance placed on my observations, necessary in a matter of so much importance, without their being tested by a person of experience.

I proposed to accompany the winter express to Canada, but Mr. Christie[15] recommended me (Mr. C. F. Ross[16] agreed with him) to proceed no farther than St. Mary's, there to await the arrival of the canoes and receive your instructions. I am thus far on my way thither, where it is not my intention to remain idle, having taken a small sextant and some books with me from the colony, in case such articles are not to be procured at the Sault.

Between Long Lake and the Pic one day's journey from the latter place, I met the packet from England, and on opening it had the pleasure of finding your official of the 28th[17] and private letter of the 29th November.[18] The contents of the latter set my mind much at rest, as I was afraid you might feel displeased that the expedition could not set out this summer. Even had Mr. Taylor lived, and altho' Mr. Hargrave[19] would use every exertion to get things in readiness, the arrangements could not have been completed so perfectly as they can be by deferring proceedings until 1846. We would also have been obliged to make York Factory[20] our starting point.

Before leaving the Colony I made out a requisition for the provisions &c. supposed to be requisite for the Expedition. In it the articles snowshoes, Twine and Nets were not forgotten. I likewise wished a small seine to be made, which may be useful where fish are numerous.

It will be gratifying to learn that by Esquimaux report, there is a passage connecting Repulse Bay with the Arctic sea, converting Melville Peninsula into an island. Should this information prove correct (and there is little doubt of it) the distance to be gone over will be much shortened.[21]

Should no better plan be proposed, my mode of proceeding would be, on arriving at *new ground*, immediately to look out for winter quarters, and on finding a convenient place, leave a boat and boat's crew to make such preparations as may be thought necessary—i.e. building huts or a house if possible, catching fish, shooting deer, musk oxen &c. With the other boat proceed either towards the straits of the Fury and Hecla or towards Dease & Simpson's farthest,[22] as the state of the ice and weather may permit. Should we complete one half of the survey the first season, I would attempt the remaining portion on foot the same fall, if there was time enough before winter setting in—or at all events by ice the ensuing spring, so as to be able to return to Churchill in good time, summer 1847.

By information received from the northern Indians it is supposed that there is a large and well wooded River which falls into Boothia Gulf, and which cannot be very far distant from the strait joining Repulse Bay with the Polar sea. This will be a good situation for wintering.[23]

It will be much more agreeable for me to have a companion, to consult in any case of difficulty as well as for the safety of the party—but he will require for his own sake to be *pretty hardy* and ready to meet danger & undergo fatigue, and privations *cheerfully*—Neither of these he may exposed to, however it is as well to be prepared for them all.

If the Young Gentleman[24] you mention be either too delicate or averse to join the Expedition, you will not I hope be offended at my mentioning Mr. Erlandson[25] as a person apparently well fitted for such service. He is an able and *now* healthy man, accustomed to the country, acquainted with the habits of the Esquimaux, and has some knowledge of Astronomy—He expressed a wish when I was at the Pic to make one of the party—but I then said nothing to him on the subject—he was not aware that there was to be any person in charge but myself.

I saw neither McKay nor Sinclair[26] (steersmen with Messrs. Dease & Simpson) whilst at Red River—But from what I learn neither have any great wish to join the present party for the *Arctic Regions*—except at very high terms—Indeed McKay is so much in debt to the Company (£60 I believe) that the greater part of his wages would go to pay it—probably both those men think their services necessary, if so, they are not the men to be wished.

George Flett[27] (one of the late Expedition men) is at York Factory and will likely engage to be of the present party. A man named Lambert at Fort William and another called Richd. Turner[28] at New Brunswick are anxious to engage *without asking about* terms—Turner altho' short, is an active and strong fellow and would be a very efficient assistant to the Carpenter, in building the Boats at Churchill.

The packet being about to start I have not time to write more fully at present, but will take an opportunity of doing so from the Sault. Hoping to have the pleasure of seeing you in Spring I have the honor to remain

My Dear Sir George
Most respectfully yours
John Rae

Sault St. Mary's *4th March* 1845[29]

My Dear Sir
Having remained at Mechipicoton an entire day after the packet was sent off, I had no expectation of overtaking the men carrying it, they being reported smart fellows. After breakfast on the second morning from Mechipicoton I took a blanket, five days' provisions, a kettle, axe &c. on my back, left the men that were with me, and proceeded alone. I overtook the express men much to their surprise on the following day about noon, and reached this place yesterday in company with them.

It is difficult to determine what would be the best plan as regards the amount of Wages to be given to men for the Expedition—Low wages with a handsome gratuity if successful would be more likely to stimulate them to exertion. Were the amount of gratuity to be to some extent discretionary, it would act as a further inducement to conduct themselves well.

While at Red River I read in a newspaper an extract from a letter written on board a Davis straits whaler, which mentions that having proceed up Prince Regents' Inlet as far as Fury Beach; a boat landed there, and found as much preserved meats, vegetables, sugar &c. all in a good state of preservation as would maintain 50 persons for a winter and fuel enough for a whole year. The people left every thing as they found it, the Captn. not allowing any thing to be taken away.[30]

I am sorry to say that the large sextant at Red River is not in the best of order altho' well enough for taking observations of the Sun (for which purpose alone it was used by Mr. Finlayson).[31] The mercury has been removed from many places on the reflecting glasses, so that it is difficult to take either a lunar distance or the altitude of a star with it. However there will be no want of sextants as I have taken the liberty of requesting Mr. Miles to forward the one at Moose to Mechipicoton—and there is quite a new one, property of the deceased Mr. Taylor at the Colony.

Inclosed is a copy of a Requisition which I have taken the liberty of transmitting to Mr. Finlayson at Lachine requesting him to send it to the Hudson's Bay House London so that the articles requested may be forwarded to York Factory by the ship of the season. Should any of the articles appear superfluous, I have expressed a wish that they should be erased.

With much respect
I have the honor to be
My Dear Sir
very sincerely Yours
John Rae

P.S. You will I hope excuse the confused mode in which this letter is written—but a long winters journey is not the best mode of steadying either a mans *head* for composition nor his hand for writing.

J. Rae

JOHN RAE, RECD. 29 APL., NO ANSWR.

[Endorsed]

1845
Michipicoton 25 February

[Enclosure]

Sault St. Marys *4th March* 1845

Requisition of sundries for Arctic Expedition to be forwarded to York Factory pr. ship of 1845 viz.

4 bolts T. M. Canvas [No.] 7 for boats sails
12 sheets thinnest copper sheathing for boats bows
1 nautical Almanack 1847
2 Gns Alcohol for spirit lamp
1 case Pickles for scurvy
1 Oz Oil of Cinnamon
1 " Do. " Peppermint

A few tins preserved meats & soups, in case of sickness

John Rae

Toronto Club *9th July* 1845[32]

My Dear Sir George

I am extremely sorry that it is not in my power to be at Ste. Maries on the date (15th July) appointed.

Having erroneously supposed that Mr. Lefroy[33] had all the necessary instruments, I left the dip Circle at the Sault; but shortly after my arrival I learnt that it would be better to have it sent down here, so that the accuracy of the needles might be tested. I accordingly wrote Mr. Ballenden,[34] who forwarded it immediately, but by some mistake the person who received it at Detroit, sent it back to Mackinac consequently it has not yet made its appearance here.

My progress in the study of Astronomy has been slow, however I hope to acquire sufficient scientific knowledge for the purpose,—Lefroy has been very kind and attentive.

Being on a visit to Kingston the other day, I tried Massey's patent Log[35] both in going from and in returning to Toronto; the result was very satisfactory, the distance shewn being 138¼ Miles one way and 138⅜ Miles the other. The distance measured on a chart gives about 136 Miles.

By a letter the other day from Windsor I learn that a cassette or trunk from Lachine has been received by the Dugall's addressed to you.

I shall endeavour to be at Detroit when you pass, so as to receive any farther orders or instructions that you may deem necessary.

My brother Tom intends commencing a wholesale dry good and hardware business in Hamilton; he is supported by Mr. Wilson late cashier of the commercial Bank at Montreal.

All were well at Lachine a few days ago. With the greatest respect I remain My Dear Sir George

Your obliged & attached servt.
John Rae

Sir George Simpson
&c &c &c

— JOHN RAE, RECD. I AUG, ANSD. 12 DEC[36] —

[Endorsed]

priv 1845
Toronto 9. July

[in a different hand]

Recd. 1st August 1845

Mansion House Buffalo 20*th July* 1845[37]

My Dear Sir George
I was much annoyed to learn on arriving here this evening that you had started for Niagara by the forenoon trains. I felt the disappointment more, as from what the Captn. of the *Emerald* steamer told me I fully expected that you would not leave this until tomorrow morning.

I addressed you a few lines some time ago mentioning my reasons for not being at Ste. Marie's on the 15th July. The none receipt of the Dip Circle being one of the principal causes.

Lefroy has been very attentive and his labors have not been entirely thrown away, altho' they have not proved so successful as they would have done, if he had had a less stupid head to work upon.

As Lefroy purposes to visit Detroit in a few days I intend to stay there a short time, hoping to have an opportunity of testing the dip Circle for the Expedition with one which he will bring from the Observatory.

As I shall take the liberty of addressing you from Detroit I shall not trouble you farther at present.

Hoping most sincerely that you may find Lady Simpson and family well, I have the honor to remain

My Dear Sir George
Most faithfully yours
John Rae

P.S. I leave this tomorrow morning at ten Oclock for Detroit

J.R.

Sir George Simpson
&c &c &c

— JOHN RAE, RECD. 25 JULY, ANSD. 12 DEC —

[Addressed]

Sir George Simpson

[Endorsed]

1845
Buffalo 20 July

Sault de Ste. Marie 29*th July* 1845[38]

Sir George Simpson
&c &c &c

My Dear Sir
On arriving here yesterday evening by the steamer I had the pleasure of receiving your esteemed favor of the 11th inst.,[39] the contents of which I have carefully noted.

I am most happy to learn, that in the fitting out of the proposed Arctic Expedition, I am to have the advice and assistance of three such able gentlemen as Messrs. Christie, Ross, and Hargrave, as from my total want of experience in such matters I should feel much at a loss without some person to consult when in doubt on any subject.

Although my stock of scientific knowledge is small I hope to find it sufficient for all the necessary purposes of the survey. The winter's study at Churchill will no doubt improve me a little if I make good use of my leisure time.

I hope Mr. Hargrave has not yet got the boats built as I should like to see them put together, and have the advice of Mr. W. Sinclair,[40] who has got a good idea of the mould of a sailing boat. Many carpenters after being employed a few years building flat bottomed river Batteaux, become quite unable to build a good sea boat.

The high wages given to boatmen on former Expeditions will render it difficult to procure good men at lower terms; particularly as the servants in the Northern Department appear to have an idea that the dangers and privations to be encountered on the intended Expedition will be greater than usual; although this is not probable, still it will not be easy to change their opinion by reasoning; they will think that something more substantial is necessary.

When I passed this on my route to Toronto, being quite ignorant of the mode of using the dip circle, I could not tell what sort of instrument the one belonging to the Company was; since my return here I have examined it, and find that it is very inferior and that a very important part is wanting i.e. a needle to indicate the intensity of the magnetic attraction. All observations on the variation of the compass, dip of the needle, magnetic force &c are at present exciting great interest,[41] it would therefore be advantageous to have any observations that I may be able to make, done in the most complete manner that my time and the instruments with which I am provided will permit, I have consequently taken the liberty of requesting Lieut. Lefroy to get a needle made of the sort wanted and of a size to fit the dip Circle. It may easily reach me at Churchill next spring or perhaps sooner. The cost will only be a dollar or two.

I still think that two boats instead of one should be used for the Expedition; for many reasons. Should one boat only be taken and she gets among ice, springs a leak, or runs ashore on a rock (accidents likely to occur) we become almost helpless, whereas if there are two, the one will always be at hand to aid the other in any case of danger.

The men will for this reason feel more confident and proceed on the voyage more cheerfully than they otherwise would.

Lieut. Lefroy has given me for the use of the arctic Expedition a very fine Thermometer with exposed bulb, for shewing the decrease of temperature caused by evaporation. The bulb to be covered with a piece of silk kept moist with water. Before concluding permit me to express my sense of the attentions received from the above named gentleman whilst at Toronto, and if I have not benefited so much by his instruction as I ought to have done the fault lies entirely with myself.

With the utmost respect I have the honor to remain My Dear Sir

Very faithfully yours

John Rae

—— JOHN RAE, RECD. 22 AUG., ANSD. 12 DEC. ——

[Addressed]

Sir George Simpson

&c &c &c

Lachine

[Endorsed]

1845

Sault de S. Marie 29. July

Sault de Ste. Marie 30*th July* 1845.[42]

My Dear Sir George

When I landed at Buffalo and learnt that you had left that place only a few hours before by the trains, I felt much annoyed and would have returned to Toronto if I had had any hopes of overtaking you there. Whilst at Detroit I should have written, but a severe cold and headache prevented me doing so. The cold still remains but I expect that some exercise at the paddle or on the portages will put me all right.

My time passed pleasantly enough at Toronto, although I would rather have been in the Indian country.—At Moose for instance, so as to bother the parson and keep all the godly in hot water, but they will not require any assistance to do that if the parson's and Bourgeois' families live in the same house. War there will be ere long, or I am much mistaken.[43]

I take the liberty of inclosing the account of a few articles necessary for the Expedition, procured at Toronto. The azimuth compass also required repairs as it would not traverse at all until altered. My own expences for travelling and board were somewhere about £30. 0. 0 this with other items has I am afraid caused me to overdraw my account with the company. Next year however will I hope leave a balance in my favor, as I shall not probably have an opportunity of spending much cash for one or two years after this.

I leave here in two days by canoe unless the schooner arrives from Mechipicoton, when I shall take a passage in her.

Wishing you and Lady Simpson all happiness believe me to be

My Dear Sir
Most respectfully & truly yours
John Rae

P.S. Remember me to Mr. Finlayson—I should have written him, but there is nothing to write about.

J.R.

— JOHN RAE, RECD. 22 AUG, ANSD. 12 DEC, ENCLOSING ACCT. OF EXPENCES FOR ARCTIC EXPEDITION —

[Addressed]

private
Sir George Simpson
&c &c &c
Lachine

[Endorsed]

priv 1845
Sault de S. Marie 30. July

Fort William 18*th August* 1845[44]

Sir George Simpson

My Dear Sir
I left Ste. Maries on the 5th inst. and reached Mechipicoton on the 7th Pic Post on the 11th and Fort William on the 16th having had very fine weather altho' rather stormy occasionally in coming through the Lake. I remained a day and a half at Mechipicoton taking observations and otherwise engaged.

When writing you from the Sault I forgot to mention that neither the chart with Dease and Simpsons discoveries, Simpsons narrative nor a telescope requested for the Expedition has been received. Probably those articles may have been forwarded to Red River, if so they can be easily got; should this not be the case it will be necessary that they be forwarded so as to reach me at Churchill: as altho' none of them are absolutely necessary they will be very useful.

I leave this tomorrow, having remained so long getting a canoe put in order and taking observations.

There is a gun in the store here, addressed to Mr. W. Simpson[45] which I take on for him, intending however to use it on the road, not having any room for the clumsy case in which it was packed.

I have the honor to remain with much respect

My Dear Sir
very truly yours
John Rae

JOHN RAE, RECD. 12 OCTR., ANSD. 12 DEC.

[Endorsed]

1845
Ft. William 18 August

York Factory 29*th November* 1845[46]

Sir George Simpson
&c &c &c

Sir

I arrived here on the 8th ulto. and as soon as possible had the Boats for the Expedition, launched and every thing put in readiness for proceeding to Churchill, but the weather which at my arrival was very unfavorable, became still more so, and continued thus until ice began to form on the river. It was consequently found necessary to take the boats out of the water again. An opportunity was however afforded of testing their sailing qualities and I am happy to say the result was favorable—they were found to work well and to sail very nearly alike. Their respective lengths of keel are 21½ and 20 feet with 7 ft. 8 in and 7½ feet breadth of beam. Each is rigged with two lug sails, to which a jib of light sheeting is to be added, it being a useful sail in light winds.

During our progress towards Repulse Bay much time would be lost by landing to Cook. To obviate this a small sheet iron stove, is to be placed in each boat.

The party will probably consist of five Orkneymen one highlander, two canadians, one halfbreed and an active YFactory Indian to serve in the double capacity of boatman and deerhunter. Few able half-breeds or canadians have volunteered their services. They appear to dislike the idea of going along the coast, most of them being subject to seasickness in rough weather. The wages are the same as those given by Messrs. Dease & Simpson viz £40.

A strong canvas cover has been made according to directions for Halkett's air boat[47] to protect it from getting chafed or torn.

C. F. Hargrave affords every possible assistance in getting the party outfitted in the most efficient manner, and his advice (which from his long experience in this country is most valuable) is always very kindly and readily given.

Hoping to receive further instructions by the spring express I have the honor to be,

Sir
Your most Obedt. Servant
John Rae

[Endorsed]

1845
Yorkfactory 29. Novr.

Private

York Factory 29*th November* 1845[49]

My Dear Sir

I regret much to have to address you from this place instead of from Churchill. That it is so, I have unfortunately myself to blame, as I remained too long at Toronto waiting for a dip circle from Ste Maries; Mr. Lefroy being anxious to test its accuracy, so as to make the observations taken with it of more value.

An attempt would have been made to reach Churchill and every thing was got in readiness for any favorable change in the weather, but from the 8th ulto. (the day of my arrival) until the ice began to form on the river, there was one continued gale of wind from the northward.

I am told by those acquainted with this coast, that we are not likely to loose much time by making this our starting point instead of Churchill as we can advance as fast to the northward as the season. I hope it may prove so. The boats are remarkably well built, being strongly put together, without being heavy. The sails are rather small but another cloth is to be put to them, which will with a jib carry them through the water at the rate of 8 miles an hour.

I expect that with a head wind and smooth water we will be able to turn to windward 15 or 16 miles pr. day, when nothing could be done with oars, or in boats more flatly built.

All the necessary books and instruments have been provided except a telescope and Simpson's Narrative. The latter I will require only for a short time to take a few extracts from it, I have therefore requested the loan of Mr. Christie's copy from him. The former would be very useful, and I should wish to have one if possible.

There is a very steady and determined man here named Geo. Flett (one of Messrs. Dease & Simpson's men) who I intend to put in charge of one of the boats. The man (Corrigal) whom I took with me from Moose, will act as steersman of my own boat. He has been taught to assist in taking observations noting the time &c which he does very correctly.

It is rather cold work handling the sextant, with the Therr. 20° below Zero, but by practice it may readily be managed with a temperature of -40°.

The rate of the Chronometer had grown irregular from continual motion while travelling, but it has now become steady, being the same that it had when I left Toronto vizt. a daily gain of 3 seconds.

Anticipating the pleasure of hearing from you by the spring express I have the honor to remain

My Dear Sir
Most respectfully yours
John Rae

Sir George Simpson
&c &c &c

— JOHN RAE, RECD. 24 MARCH, ANSD. 15 DO [SIC] —

[Endorsed]

priv 1846
Yorkfactory 29. Novr.

York Factory 24*th February* 1846[50]

Sir George Simpson

Sir
I have the honor to inform you that all the preparations for the proposed Arctic Expedition are in a forward state, some things are intentionally left incomplete until the weather becomes warmer, as they cannot be so well done during winter.

The following men[51] are engaged vizt.

1	George Flett	Steersman	from	Orkney
2	John Corrigal	Do.	"	Do.

3	John Folster	Middleman	"	Do.
4	Willm. Clouston	Do.	"	Do.
5	Edwd. Hutchison	Do.	"	Do.
6	Willm. Adamson	Do.	"	Shetland
7	Richard Turner	Do.	"	Moose Hudson's Bay
8	Jacque St. Germaine	Do.	"	Canada
9	Hilard Minaux	Do.	"	Do.
10	Nibitabo	Do. and Deer Hunter		YF Indian

Their wages are each £40 p. annum. I mentioned in my letter of the 29th November last, the reasons for there being so large a proportion of Orkneymen nor do I think this any disadvantage, as altho' these men may not be quite so active as canadians and natives in river or lake voyaging, they are from their greater experience much better qualified for managing a boat in stormy weather and a rough sea. I have taught one or two of the men to assist me a little, by noting the time when taking observations,—This is not always necessary as the observer can do it for himself, but it is of some consequence in cold weather and in taking lunar distances.

Another has learnt to skin birds, fishes &c in short every necessary arrangement has been made to supply the place of a colleague or assistant.

The Esquimaux Oulibuck[52] with one of his sons is to join the party at Churchill. I prefer the younger lad, as in addition to his own language he can speak both Indian and English.

The winter having been unusually mild, I am in hopes of getting away from this, about the middle of June; for although the ice in the bay will not be broken up at that time, still there may be a passage for the boats found close in shore, when the tide is in.

With sentiments of the utmost respect and esteem

I remain
Sir
Your Most Obedt. Servant
John Rae

—— JOHN RAE, RECD. 6 JUNE, ANSD. 15 DO. ——

[Endorsed]

1846
Yorkfactory 24. Feby.

Private

York Factory *24th February* 1846[53]

My Dear Sir George
Having already addressed to you an official letter, or rather an apology for one, I have now little to communicate. The few duties to which I turn my attention are going on quietly and regularly. My time is principally occupied in taking observations, studying Natural History, Geology, Botany &c. With one branch of Natural History (Ornithology) and to me the most useful one, I am slightly acquainted, having read a little on the subject, but learnt more by observation during my many shooting excursions. If I can find time, I purpose employing myself during a part of the month of May, in making a collection of the birds to be found here, as I think there are some which have not yet been described among the birds migrating to Hudsons Bay. Of Geology and Mineralogy I know little or nothing—t'is [sic] true, I can tell a boulder stone from a brick-bat and a bank of alluvial deposite from a stratum of lime stone when I see them, and could form a pretty good guess of quartz, slate, granite and some other of the more common minerals, I might also venture a few remarks on the Geological features of a new country, if they were not very complicated, but this is all. I intend making a collection of plants whenever I have time and opportunity, but shall not attempt to name or class them; a much more intimate acquaintance with Botany than I possess would be requisite to do so correctly.

Having made arrangements to do without a colleague or assistant, I would now as soon be without one and I find by a few words that I heard one of the men say at Christmas, that they think as I do—and certainly the fewer there are to feed the better. I merely mention this, neither wishing nor expecting it to influence the opinions of others.

Being desirous of sending some buffalo tongues[54] to my mother,[55] I mentioned the subject here, and learnt that none were to be sent home on private account without your sanction. Would you have the kindness to permit me have a few dozen? If you grant me this favor, Mr. McTavish[56] will see that they are packed up and shipped.

With sincere good wishes

I remain with much respect
My Dear Sir
very faithfully yours
John Rae

Sir George Simpson }
Red River }

— JOHN RAE, RECD. 6 JUNE, ANSD. 15 DO —

[Endorsed]

priv 1846
Yorkfactory 24. Feb.

York Factory 12*th June* 1846[57]

My Dear Sir
Your much esteemed letter of the 12th December was brought me by the winter packet. The distressing news contained in it had reached me sometime before. I know not how to thank you for your warm Sympathy and continued kindness to my dear excellent Mother—little did I think that the good old lady was in need of money. I sent her a Bill for £30 when in Canada but I know not whether it has been received or not, as nothing has been said about it in any of my letters from home. I rather think Mr. Finlayson kept a duplicate of the Bill at Lachine.

I would have sent a Bill of Exchange for the sum you were so good as advance, but Mr. Hargrave signed no blank Bills of this description before leaving York. Would you be pleased to cause the sum of £30 with interest on the same to be placed to your credit, debiting my account with the amount. I have forwarded a Bill for £40 Stg. to my mother, and requested the Governor and Committee to pay her annually the sum of £70, during my absence. The first payment to be made in 1847.

I was aware that my brother Dick[58] intended offering his services to the H.B. Company. I believe I attempted to dissuade him from such a proceeding, but the poor fellow feels deeply for the difficulties which have been brought upon John Hamilton by his becoming security to John Barr for himself and Tom. Barr from what I can learn has acted very harshly in the business.

Tom his [sic] found a worthy friend in his brother-in-law Mr. Wilson who has got both the means and ability to aid him in carrying on large mercantile transactions. The same good friend has offered to supply Richard with goods on the same liberal terms as he has done to his brother. The kindness and friendship which you have always shewn to the family has induced me to write so much about the affairs of my relatives, and you will I hope pardon me for having done so.

Regarding the Expedition I remain of the same opinion as when I wrote you last season vizt. To proceed with all dispatch to Wager River, survey its northern shores closely—and if there is no opening to the arctic sea found there; the coast between that and Rupulse Bay and Repulse Bay itself should be minutely examined. If still no passage is discovered I shall try whether it is not practicable to make a portage, which would be preferable even should it occupy a week, to going round by the Fury and Hecla Straits. Once in the Arctic sea we could proceed either towards Dease and Simpson's farthest or along the west shore of Melville peninsula as the weather and ice may permit.

The fitting up of the boats and other arrangements are as complete as it is possible to make them. Messrs. Hargrave and McTavish (I beg the C.F.'s pardon for clubbing his name with a clerk's) have readily supplied all I required. From the former I have not received a single suggestion as far as I can remember of the least value. The few hints I did receive were either on subjects which had been attended to previously or were connected with my own comforts (a secondary consideration with me) which he thought a very important part of my duty, probably feeling that he would have done so in my place. Fortunately I am under no personal obligations to Mr. Hargrave, he being one of the last persons of my acquaintance from whom I would like to ask a favor. Yet notwithstanding his disagreeable manner he has a warm and kind heart when his selfishness will permit it.

That there are many gentlemen in the country as well at least if not better qualified for conducting the present Expedition than myself I am well aware and some of the Commissioned Gentlemen in this Department are very justly of the same opinion, but this I will say, that none could set out with a more firm determination to return successful, always trusting in the aid of providence without which our efforts would be vain, and the above resolution an empty boast.

The oldest residents at York Factory do not remember a spring so favorable as the present one. The ice which was forced up into immense heaps along the banks when the river was breaking up has almost entirely disappeared, and the thermometer has been as high as 70° or 75° for some days past. The men are all as anxious as myself to get away from this, as it is believed that the coast between this and Churchill is already clear of ice for some distance to the northward of North River.

One of the men going with me (Richard Turner a brother of the boat-carpenter at Moose) is a fine active lad and very ingenious. He built a boat at New Brunswick, and forged the nails for her himself, having previously made a blacksmiths bellows although he had never been employed either with carpenter or blacksmith. He is anxious to learn the trade of a Boat or ship-carpenter and I am certain that one or two years with a good tradesman would make him very efficient. If you would permit him to work with some man that knows his trade (supposing that he conducts himself properly whilst on the Expedition) you would oblige me much, and at the same time make a useful servant to the company. I probably may find time during the winter to give him some slight knowledge of draughting and arithmetic.

I shall leave this tomorrow forenoon between ten and eleven O'clock if the weather does not prevent us.

Having *stuck* to the house pretty closely during the winter, I found that I required some exercise, I have therefore moved about a good deal since the ice broke up and have amused myself making a collection of insects and birds' skins.

Should any opportunity occur of sending letters by Esquimaux along the coast to Churchill I shall avail myself of it. Believe me, My Dear Sir

Most respectfully & faithfully yours
John Rae.

Sir George Simpson }
&c &c &c }

— JOHN RAE, RECD. 26. FEB., ANSD. 30 JUNE/47[59] —

[Endorsed]

1846
Yorkfactory 12. June

[Enclosure to letter from John Rae to Sir George Simpson, dated York Factory, June 12, 1846.]

Names of men engaged for the Arctic Coast Expedition—Spring 1846.

				Native of
1	Adamson	William	Middleman	Shetland
2	Corrigal	John	Steersman	Orkney
3	Flett	George	Do.	Do.
4	Folster	John	Middleman	Do.
5	Hutchison	Edward	Do.	Do.
6	Matheson[60]	Peter	Do.	Western Isles
7	Menaux	Hilard	Do.	Canada
8	Nibitabo		Do.	York Factory
9	St. Germain	Jacques	Do.	Canada
10	Turner	Richard	Do.	Hudson's Bay

York Factory 12t*h June* 1846.

[Endorsed]

Names of men engaged[61]
for the arctic coast Expedition.

York Factory 12t*h June* 1846.[62]

Dear Sir

I have now to acknowledge the receipt of your valued favor of the 13th December[63] which reached me by the winter packet on the 23rd April. An excellent telescope for the use of the Expedition was brought by the same conveyance.

The spring here has been the mildest known for many years past. There have been some strong gales of wind which will materially aid the warm weather in clearing the coast of ice. The river at this place broke up on the 5th ulto. and cleared out to some distance below the Factory on the 9th of the same. North River was three days ago sufficiently clear of ice to be crossed by boats. I have therefore determined to start tomorrow forenoon. The men are all in good spirits and full of confidence. They are a cheerful good tempered set of fellows, with at the same time sufficient courage and coolness should those qualities be called into action. In fitting up the boats (which I have named the *North Pole* and *Magnet*) nothing has been left undone that could tend to make them sea worthy and work well under canvas. I tried the speed of the *North Pole* a few days ago, with Massey's patent Log and also with the Log line and glass, and found that with a very moderate breeze, she sailed at the rate of 5 miles an hour when close hauled to the wind.[64]

The only liquors I have taken are 4 Gns. Brandy and and 2 Gns. port Wine, besides my voyaging allowance—probably the greater part of the brandy will be used for fuel. Every possible assistance has been received from Mr. C. T. Hargrave and since his departure from Mr. McTavish, in making our various arrangements.

Inclosed is a note of my expences from the time I left the Sault Ste Marie to proceed to Toronto until my return there. I have only entered the expences which were absolutely necessary.

Should no express arrive before the Expedition leaves this, nor overtake it before reaching Churchill, I shall remain there until I receive further instructions.

Whilst at Churchill I shall again do myself the honor of addressing you. I remain

Dear Sir
Yours most obedient servant
John Rae.

Sir George Simpson }
&c &c &c }

— JOHN RAE, RECD. 26 FEB., ANSD. 30 JUNE 47 —

[Addressed]

Sir George Simpson

[Endorsed]

1846
Yorkfactory 12. June

Churchill, Hudson's Bay 6 oclock P.M. *4th July* 1846.[65]

Sir

The express from York Factory reached this place a few hours ago, and I have now to acknowledge the receipt of your letter dated at Red River Settlement 15th June,[66] containing instructions relative to the proper conducting of the Expedition placed under my charge. Those instructions I shall endeavour to follow out to the best of my ability. Simpson's narrative, a chart, and 2 static needles for the dip circle were also received. The latter fit the circle very well, and I have got them balanced to the *intensity* of this place.

The season has hitherto been remarkably favorable for the progress of the Expedition northward, the ice having become broken up or dissolved much earlier than usual, so that we were enabled to leave York Factory on the 13th Ulto. We met in with much ice as we sailed along the coast, which compelled us to beach the boats frequently or when practicable to run into a creek or river for shelter. After passing Cape Churchill we had a clear sea, and having a fresh and fair breeze, a few hours sailing brought us to Churchill at 6h. A.M. on the 27th ulto.

The boats are found to be excellent craft, going fast through the water when under sail and turning well to windward when necessary. The only fault to be found with them is that they are rather small for stowing the requisite cargo.

Our stock of provisions consists of 25 bags Flour, 20 bags pemican[67] and 2 bags Grease, with some Tea, sugar, and chocolate. Being aware of the injurious effects of spirits, particularly in cold climates, I have taken no more than 4 Gns Brandy and 2 Gns. Port Wine.

I am happy to say that the men under my charge have all hitherto behaved well, and appear much interested in the success of the Expedition nor does this appear to be a mere mercenary feeling.

Unless circumstances are very much against our returning via Churchill, I shall prefer that route to the one by great-fish River, as our boats are not well adapted for river navigation being too *sharp* and consiquently drawing much water. Their present draught is two feet, six inches.

The sheet iron stoves are found most useful. In them our food can be cooked when either sailing, rowing, or poling and with a very small expenditure of fuel.

We shall leave this tomorrow morning about 4 oclock, the tide being then in.

Should I meet any Esquimaux coming towards Churchill, I shall send a few lines by them

I have the honor to remain

Sir
Your most obedt. servant
John Rae.

P.S. I have received every assistance and some useful information from William Sinclair Esquire C.T. the gentleman in charge of this place
J. Rae.

—— JOHN RAE, RECD. 11. AUG, ANSD. 30 JUNE/47 ——

[Endorsed]

1846
Churchill 4, July

Churchill 3h. A.M. 5*th July* 1846[68]

My Dear Sir

I have only time to acknowledge the receipt of your valued favor of the 15th Ulto, which came to hand yesterday afternoon.

We have been waiting here ever since the 27th for the packet, at which I am not at all sorry, as it shows that we lost no time by wintering at York Factory.

You appear to think that I have got a head stuffed with all sorts of knowledge, if I may judge by my letter of instructions. The head is big enough certainly outside, but whether there is a large quantity of bone in it or not I have not yet tested. It is certainly a poor affair, but I shall endeavour to make the best use of it I can.

My Men (I mean the Expedition men) are all in fine spirits, some of them are famous fellows that appear to care about cold and hunger very little, or make it a subject of jest. An old voyager (George Flett) is always ready to jump into the water and be the first at any disagreeable duty when necessary—he is at the same time a careful and intelligent man.

With fervent thanks for your many acts of kindness and wishing you many happy years,

I have the honor to remain
with much respect
very faithfully yours
John Rae

P.S. I am just going down to the boats. The weather is moderate and wind fair.

J.R.

[Addressed]

private Sir George Simpson &c &c &c
near Montreal Lachine

[Endorsed]

priv 1846
Churchill 5. July

---

146 miles North of Churchill An Island, Knaps Bay
Latitude 61" 9" 42 N. 8*th July* 1846[69]

Sir

Having been compelled to take shelter here yesterday morning at 7 oclock, we were visited shortly after casting anchor by five Esquimaux who informed me that they were in the habit of visiting Churchill, and altho' they do not intend going there soon, they may see some of their neighbours passing, who may carry this note thither.

Since leaving Churchill we have had a fine leading breeze and have made as you will perceive considerable progress northward. During our first 24 hours run we made 94 miles northing.

On the 6th instant at 7 h. p.m. when at least 10 miles distant from the mainland, we found ourselves suddenly in shoal water and got aground notwithstanding our utmost endeavours to push out to sea. The ebb tide was too quick for us. We however had a soft bed of sand to lay the boats upon.

At 2h. A.M. on the 7th we got underweigh with double reefs in our sails and stood on our course, There was a very heavy sea running which with the wind continued to rise until we shipped some water over both lee and weather side. One sea came right over me and my bedding, giving us all something to laugh at. As remaining out any longer would have been rashness, I ran in for land and found a splendid little harbour formed by the point of an island and some ridges of stones. In this little bay there are 4 or 5 fathoms close in shore, when the tide is out, with a fine soft sandy bottom. A vessel drawing 10 or 12 feet might run in easily. The Latde. by meridian observation of sun is 61° 9' 42" N. Variation of Compass 7° 48' East. Longde. 94° 40' West. We have not yet seen any ice, and the heavy sea yesterday would lead me to suppose that there is none within many miles.

I consider it a fortunate circumstance that we got aground on the 6th as had we sailed during the night, we would probably have been compelled either to sail or ride out the gale on some exposed part of the coast, neither a very pleasant nor safe alternative.

The men have all behaved well and the boats realize our fullest expectations.

1 h. 30 m. p.m. The wind is becoming more moderate and the swell is going down. I intend getting underweigh again at 2 oclock p.m.

I am now in hopes of completing the survey this season, the weather is so favorable and the sea so free from ice.

I have the honor to remain
Sir
Your most obedient servant
John Rae

Sir George Simpson }
&c &c &c }

— JOHN RAE, RECD. 18 OCT. '47, NO ANSWER —

[Addressed]

Sir George Simpson
&c &c &c

[Endorsed]

1846
Knaps Bay 8. July

Knaps Bay Latde. 61" 9" 42 N 8*th July* 1846[70]

My Dear Sir

The accompanying letter is a miserable scrawl, but the motion of the boat is not favorable to penmanship—nor does handling ropes render the fingers more pliant.

I endeavour to follow up your instructions as near as possible—collecting plants, skins &c and taking observations whenever I have an opportunity. This gives me occupation enough.

With much respect

believe me My Dear Sir
very faithfully yours
John Rae

Sir George Simpson
&c &c &c

P.S. All the party are well and in good spirits

JR

—— JOHN RAE, RECD. 18 OCTR. '47, NO ANSWER ——

[Addressed]

private
Sir George Simpson
&c &c &c

[Endorsed]

1846
Knaps Bay 8. July

York Factory Hudson's Bay 10*th August* 1847[71]

Sir George Simpson
&c &c &c

Sir

I have now the honor to inform you that the Expedition under my charge which left Churchill on the 5th July 1846, for the purpose of exploring the northern shores of America between Dease & Simpson's furthest and the Straits of the Fury and Hecla returned in safety to this place on the 6th inst. having accomplished the object of the Expedition and traced all the coast, with the exception of 6 or 8 miles near the Strait of the Fury and Hecla.

After sailing from Churchill we lost no time on our outward route and saw no ice until between Cape Fullerton and Wager River when we were detained a few days by it. On the 25th of the month we reached Repulse Bay. It was completely clear of ice. Some Esquimaux whom we met here told me that the distance to the Arctic sea westward of Melvile Peninsula was 2 or 3 days journey or about 40 miles and that the greater part of the route was intersected by deep Lakes. The boats were immediately unloaded and one of them (the *North Pole*) put in order for hauling across land.

Leaving 1 man and Ouligbuck in charge of the baggage and provisions, we commenced ascending a narrow but rapid stream which flowed from one of the Lakes we had to pass through. After traversing 7 Lakes and passing over 6 portages in a N Westerly direction, we reached the sea on the 1st August. There was not a pool of open water to be seen, and I had learnt that this large Bay (called Ak-koo-lee by the natives) was always full of ice. I first directed our course to the N.W. and only gained a distance of 17 miles in 2 days, there was a bold, prominent point here which was honored with the name of Cape Lady Pelly.[72] A few miles beyond this our progress was completely impeded and we were detained a couple of days, during part of which a fresh breeze from off shore was blowing, but which had not the slightest effect upon the ice. With the first favorable opportunity, I retraced our route and ran across to Melvile Peninsula for the purpose of proceeding towards the Strait of the Fury and Hecla, but our success was even worse than on the other side. A gale of Easterly wind did remove the ice a short distance from shore, but it had hardly become calm, when the enemy returned and was in a very short time as closely packed as before. The boat being in danger, we had either to haul her up or run back to our starting point. I preferred the latter alternative; the ice followed close in our wake and we had not been an hour under shelter, when there was not a trace of open water to be seen. When we landed some Esquimaux informed me that the deer had commenced migrating southward and that the salmon were entering the mouths of the rivers. To ascertain the truth of this report I with 3 of the men crossed over to Repulse Bay. Here I found all well. Some deer had been shot and a few fish caught. The Esquimaux had already scattered themselves along the margins of the Lakes near the deer passes, so as to intercept these animals in their swift Kay-aks whilst swimming across. Finding that there was no probability of completing all that was required this season and fearing that should I attempt to accomplish a portion of the survey, I might be detained so long, that either the necessary preparations for wintering could not be made, and thence endanger the safety of the party or that we should be obliged to run back to Churchill with only a portion of our work finished. Under these circumstances I decided on collecting all the party together and making every arrangement in our power for the preservation of life and health during the long and cold winter we had to encounter. Remaining with one man at Repulse Bay, the others were sent across to bring over the boat. On the 16th she was brought within 5 miles of our Encampment and left there, as it might still be required on the Lake.

All hands except our deer hunters Nibitabo and Ouligbuck were set to work to collect stones for building a house, which was finished on the 2nd September and named Fort Hope.[73]

Its internal dimensions were 20 feet by 14, height in front 7½ feet sloping to 5½ feet at the back. As much moss as possible and a plant resembling heather were collected for fuel. Towards the end of the month deer became numerous and 17 were shot in one day, and before the latter part of November when the animals had all passed, 162 had been killed, so that our snow provision store, presented a very respectable appearance. During the open water some salmon were caught in the sea, but a small marine insect cut up our nets so much notwithstanding that they had been steeped in a strong decoction of tobacco, that there was no keeping them in repair. From some nets set under the ice a few trout and salmon were occasionally procured but in the beginning of January, the nets were taken up as they produced little or nothing.

The Thermometer first fell to Zero on the 16th October and the lowest temperature during the winter was 47° below Zero on the

8th of January. Gales and storms of wind were very frequent, usually from NNW.

On Christmas and New Years Day, our amusement was a game at foot ball, our fare some excellent venison steaks and plum pudding, and sufficient allowance of brandy to the men to make them all merry and *comfortable*.

The temperature of my *room* (a small space seperated from the rest of the house by a piece of oil cloth) was frequently 12 or 14° below Zero; the men's quarters were rather less cold. Our fire whilst cooking, as far as heating the house was concerned was worse than useless, as the chimney not being built on the most approved principles would not permit any smoke to pass through it unless the door was open. Our trifling discomforts were the subject of many a joke, and with one or two exceptions, only added to the hilarity of the party: thus a poor fellow who got his knee frozen (not dangerously) whilst in bed, was rallied on the subject for some time afterwards.

Before the end of March all the preparations for a journey on the ice along shore were completed; but an accident which happened to Ouligbuck detained me for some days. I started on the 5th April with 3 men,[74] an Esquimaux, and Ouligbuck's son as Interpreter two sleds each drawn by 4 dogs carried our Provisions and bedding. Our route for the two first days was the same as that followed by the boat last summer, but on the 7th we turned somewhat more to the westward and cut over land. Our snow hut was built on a small lake where we had our sled runners iced anew.

The coast as far as Keith Bay[75] had a North westerly trending—when at this place on the 11th I was told by our Esquimaux ally that by crossing over land we could considerably shorten our distance; this plan I adopted and we arrived at the sea again on the 15th at a large Bay called Ak-ku-li-gu-wiak by the natives, but which I named after Sir John H. Pelly[76] Governor of the Hudson's Bay Compy.

As there was some heather to be got on the Island where we encamped, I determined, as our dogs were now nearly useless, to leave them here to recruit, with one of the men the Interpreter, and

Esquimaux to take care of them. The latter was also to hunt seals if he could find any.

After a day's detention by stormy weather, I went forward with the remainder of the party[77] for the purpose of tracing the coast, to some part of Sir J. Ross's[78] furthest discoveries in a SE direction. We made rapid progress as the ice was smooth and our loads comparatively light. On the second day I was much annoyed to find that we had been tracing the shore of a deep Inlet. By Observation and Reckoning I found that we could not be far from Lord Mayors Bay of Sir John Ross. I therefore struck across land due North for some miles. A meridian observation of the sun placed us in Latitude 69° 26' 1" N. Walking a league beyond this we did not obtain a view of the coast. Ordering the men to stop and build our usual night's quarters (a snow hut) and *grub* among the snow for fuel, I proceeded alone and had travelled scarcely a mile, when I reached the sea which here formed a narrow Inlet running nearly E and W. I followed it up in the latter direction for 3 miles when I was again at fault—land was before me, and no opening in the desired direction. Some high rocks close at hand afforded the chance of a distant view, one of these I ascended and from its summit I thought I could discern some rough ice to the westward. Hurrying on among snow, stones, and masses of ice, in half an hour my utmost wishes were gratified. As far as the eye could reach lay the ice covered sea, its white surface marked with numerous Islands. The former was "Lord Mayor's Bay". The latter the "Sons of the Clergy of Scotland". The Isthmus joining the land to the Northward to the Continent is only 1 mile broad. Having taken possession of our discoveries in the name of our most gracious Sovereign, we turned our faces homewards but as I follow the coast Eastward, it was three days before we joined our companions at Pelly Bay. When 5 miles from the Island where we had left them and nearly the same distance ahead of my fellow travellers, I suddenly came upon 4 Esquimaux. After considerable pressing and promises of presents I made them consent to come to our snow hut. They wished me to enter their houses, but as I was completely unarmed, a common pocket knife excepted, I declined the invitation, and shaking hands with my new acquaintances who promised soon to follow me I soon reached our house, where preparations for cooking were instantly commenced, as I doubted not but my men would be as hungry and thirsty as I was.

Our meeting with the Esquimaux was a fortunate circumstance as we bought from them a quantity of blubber for our dogs, and some seal's flesh and blood for ourselves. Whilst making preparations for examining the bay more minutely I learnt from one of the Natives that in clear weather, I might see the whole Bay from the top of the Island[79] on which we were Encamped. This information I found to be correct and I was thus saved the fatigue of a pretty long walk.

Our stock of Provisions would with economy be sufficient to allow me follow the coast on our way home, instead of crossing the country. We started on the 24th and although we had fine weather, did not arrive at our snow hut in Keiths Bay until the 30th. I called the land which we had now travelled round Sir Geo. Simpson's Peninsula. Hence to Repulse Bay our route was very nearly the same as that followed as we came. Arriving at our winter quarters on the 5th May, we found all well. Since our departure we had travelled 560 Geographical miles.

Our journey towards the strait of the Fury and Hecla was commenced on the 13th May. My companions were 4[80] *picked* men and Ouligbuck. A fatigue party of 2 men and an Esquimaux, with a dog sled accompanied us for 3 days. With these I sent back Ouligbuck who was unable to walk so fast as was desirable. Each of the party was laden with 60 or 70 Lbs. My own load was only about 40 Lbs. but as I led the way this trifling weight was quite enough.

Time will not permit me to enter into details, suffice it to say that we traced the west shore of Melvile Peninsula to within 6 or 8 miles of the Fury and Hecla Strait, and if Arrowsmith's Chart be correct I joined my discoveries to those of Sir Edward Parry.[81] We reached Repulse Bay on the 9th June all in good health but very much reduced in flesh. Wading through deep snow, scrambling among rough ice and short *commons* all contributed to this. Although not very stout when I set out, I had to tighten my belt six inches before my return. Both on this and the former journey we suffered much from want of water, and used often to take a small kettle or two of snow to bed with us when we lay down to rest, so that it might thaw a little before we rose to resume our march.

The spring was very lingering but there was no want of provisions or fuel as soon as the snow began to disappear.

The Esquimaux who visited us frequently during the winter brought some venison for sale, but in no great quantities. They behaved with a few exceptions remarkably well. When about to leave, a large party encamped near us, and made many enquiries when we were to pay them another visit.

On the 11th August the ice cleared out of the bay, and on the 12th we embarked on our return to Churchill. When pushing off from shore many of the Esquimaux ran out in the water up to their knees to shake hands with me, and some of them appeared really sorry at our departure. Our progress was much impeded by foul winds, but we saw no ice after passing Southampton Island, and entered Churchill River on the 31st, with 8 Bags of Pemican and 4 Bags of Flour still on hand, thus our total expenditure of Provisions had been 12 Bags of the former and 21 of the latter. Mr. Sinclair the gentleman in charge of Churchill was absent at York Factory, but I was very kindly supplied with every thing required for myself and the rest of the party by Mrs. Sinclair.[82]

Stormy weather detained us 2 days here, On the 3rd of September it became more moderate, and we were able to put to sea. The nights being now dark we could only sail during the day, it was on this account late on the 6th before we arrived here—all alive and well—and so stout and healthy looking that our appearance quite surprised the good people of York Factory, many of whom had no expectation of seeing us so soon.

Before finishing this letter, I must bear testimony to the good conduct of the men under my charge; they were all obedient, and did whatever duties they were put to with alacrity.

Enclosed with this is a rough draft on tracing paper of my discoveries.[83] Want of time alone prevents me writing more fully, but I hope to have the honor of sending you a more detailed account of our proceedings when I reach England. With assurances of my utmost respect

I remain Sir
Your most obedient Servant
John Rae

—— JOHN RAE, RECD. 8. MARCH, NO ANSWER ——

[Endorsed]

1848
Yorkfactory 10. August

York Factory Hudson's Bay 20*th September* 1847[84]

Sir George Simpson

Sir

I have now the honor to acquaint you that the Expedition which left Churchill under my command on the 5th July 1846, for the purpose of completing the survey of the Northern Shores of America, reached this place in safety on the 6th Inst.

Having already written you by way of Red River and inclosed an outline of my discoveries, I shall merely mention here that I reached Repulse Bay on the 25th July last and immediately had a boat taken across land and through Lakes to the sea West of Melvile Peninsula. The ice here was too close packed for us to make any progress so that I determined on returning to Repulse Bay and making preparations for wintering. A stone house was built, measuring 20 feet by 14, and covered with Oilcloths as a roof. There being no wood some moss and a sort of heather were collected for fuel and 162 deer were shot before November was ended, when all these animals had passed southward. Our house was frequently cold enough, the Thermometer being sometimes 10° or 12° below Zero.

On the 5th of April I started with a party and traced the coast up to Lord Mayor's Bay of Sir John Ross[85] thus proving that veteran Discoverer to be correct in his statements—Boothia Felix is part of the American Continent. This journey occupied us until the 5th May, and we had travelled about 560 Geographical Miles.

I again set out with 4 chosen men on the 13th of the month and after undergoing much fatigue and suffering some privations, we traced the west shore of Melvile Peninsula to within 6 or 8 miles of the Fury and Hecla Strait. We arrived at Winter quarters on the 5th June all in good health and spirits but much reduced in flesh. From this time until the 11th August when the ice broke up, we were all busily occupied in procuring the means of existence and in making preparations for our homeward voyage. We took leave of our dreary home, and of our Esquimaux acquaintances on the 12th August. Our progress southward was much impeded by contrary winds so that we did not enter Churchill River until the 31st. We had still 8 bags of Pemican and 4 cwt of Flour on hand. Being detained here two days we did not arrive at York Factory until late in the evening of the 6th Septr. where my sudden appearance somewhat surprised my friends, who had not expected to see me so soon.

As I intend going to England by the ship, I shall do myself the honor of addressing you more fully from London.

With the utmost respect I remain Sir

Your most Obedient Servant
John Rae

— JOHN RAE, RECD. 14 NOV., ANSD. 25 DO[86] —

[Endorsed]

1847
Yorkfactory 20. September

Private

York Factory 20*th September* 1847[87]

Sir George Simpson

My Dear Sir
As the Chartered ship *Westminster*[88] is to proceed to one of the Ports in the Gulf of St. Lawrence after she has discharged her cargo here, I take the opportunity of sending you a few lines by her, expecting that you

will receive the intelligence of my return much sooner by this conveyance, than by any other. The objects of the Expedition have been as far as practicable attained, without the loss of or injury to any of the party, and at the comparatively trifling expense of £1,100 or £1,200 Stg. I have had some heavy walking among the snow during my stay in the Hudson's Bay Company's service but my journey to the Fury and Hecla Strait gave me harder work than any thing I had previously experienced. This may possibly have arisen from my having become somewhat stiffer in the joints than I had been some years ago, but as my companions were all able young fellows, and as they felt the exercise equally as severe as I did, the above surmise appears rather doubtful.

Much praise is due to the men under my charge for their steady conduct and cheerful obedience on all occasions and I hope the Honble. Company will with their wonted generosity give them something handsome as a gratuity.

Your valued favors along with my commission as C. Trader were duly handed me, and I have most sincerely to thank you for all your kindness.

As you left me at liberty to dispose of my time as I pleased until spring, I have decided upon visiting England by the ship. I however must be very economical whilst there, as my stock of cash is but very small. I have still much to do in the writing way my chart and memoranda being still in a very rough state. Hoping to have the pleasure of seeing you in London and with kind regards to Mr. Finlayson

Believe me, My Dear Sir
Most respectfully and truly yours
John Rae

— JOHN RAE, RECD. 14 NOVR., ANSD. 25 DO —

[Addressed]

Sir George Simpson

[Endorsed]

priv 1847
Yorkfactory 20. September

York Factory Hudsons Bay 21*st September* 1847[89]

To the Governor, Deputy Governor and Committee of the Honble. Hudson's Bay Company.

Honorable Sirs

I have now the honor to inform you that the Expedition under my charge which left Churchill on the 5th July 1846, for the purpose of tracing the coast of America between Dease and Simpson's furthest and the Strait of the Fury and Hecla returned in safety to this place on the 6th instant after having by travelling over the ice and snow in the Spring surveyed the coast from within eight or ten miles of the Fury and Hecla Strait, to Lord Mayor's Bay of Sir John Ross, thus proving that gentleman's statement to be correct as regards Boothia Felix being a portion of the American Continent.

After leaving Churchill the crews of the boats[90] were divided into *watches* so that we continued under sail day and night whenever the weather was sufficiently moderate—Having a stove and small quantity of fuel in each boat we cooked on board and seldom went on shore except to replenish our water casks.

On the 15th when about ten miles to the north of Cape Fullerton, we first met with ice, which was so heavy and close packed, that it was found necessary to seek shelter in a deep and narrow Inlet, that opportunely presented itself—We were detained here two days during which I found that our harbour formed the Estuary of a considerable stream, on the beach near the mouth of which a great number of seals were lying. The Latitude 64°–6'–45" North was observed Variation of the Compass 22° 10' West.

We reached the most southerly opening of Wager River on the 22nd and were detained all day by immense quantities of heavy ice driving in with the flood and out again with the ebb tide, which ran at the rate of seven or eight miles an hour, forcing up and grinding the ice against the rocks, causing a noise resembling thunder. By an excellent observation of the sun in quicksilver, the Latitude 65°–16'–8" North was obtained, which is about 4 leagues to the northward of the same place as laid down in the charts.

On the 23rd being wearied with delay, I determined on attempting the traverse as soon as the flood tide was nearly spent. With some trouble and risk we reached the north side of the channel a distance of four and a half miles. One of the boats got a severe squeeze, but received no material injury. The night was rather foggy as we advanced northward among a number of small Islands, and keeping a sharp look out for the north mouth of Wager River, but no appearance of a river could be seen. Not wishing to loose time and a fine breeze of fair wind in making a closer search, we held on our course towards Repulse Bay and at a few minutes after 7 p.m. on the 24th rounded Cape Hope and sailed up during the night to within eight miles of the head of the Bay, where we cast anchor for a few hours under shelter of a small Island near its south shore.

At 3h. p.m. on the 25th we entered Gibson's Cove, on the banks of which I was rejoiced to observe three Esquimaux tents, and four of the natives standing on the shore. They appeared much alarmed at our approach, but their fears were soon dispelled, on my landing with the Interpreter and explaining our friendly intentions towards them. They were all of low stature but stoutly built, and one of them, an elderly man named Ou-too-ou-niak had a formidable moustache and pair of whiskers. They had a lively and good natured expression of face and were more cleanly in their persons and deer skin dresses, than any Esquimaux I had previously seen. None of the party had ever visited Churchill, but one or two of the women had seen Captain Parry's ship's both at Igloo-lik and Winter Island, and they still wore beads round their wrists which they had obtained from on board those vessels. They had neither heard nor seen anything of Sir John Franklin.

From a chart drawn by one of the party I inferred that the Arctic sea (named Akkoolee) to the west of Melville Peninsula was not more than forty miles distant in a NNW direction, and that about thirty five miles of this distance was occupied by deep Lakes, so that we would have only five miles of land, to drag our boat over; a mode of proceeding which I had decided upon even had the distance been much greater, in preference to going round by the Fury and Hecla Strait. In the event of wintering, our present situation was a most favorable one; for although there was nothing but moss and a plant resembling heath to be procured for fuel, yet deer were said to pass in great numbers to the southward at the commencement of the cold weather, and salmon were to be caught in the Lakes, and at the mouths of some neighbouring streams.

Having unloaded the boats, and placed one of them and the greater part of the cargo in security, the other was hauled three miles up a rapid and narrow river, which flowed from one of the Lakes we were to pass through. This work occupied us the whole of the 26th as the current was very strong and the channel so full of large boulder stones, that the men were frequently to the waist in ice cold water whilst lifting or launching the boat over these impediments. Our landing place was found to be in Latitude 66°–32'–1" N. The rate of the Chronometer had become so irregular that it could not be depended upon for finding the Longitude and during the winter it stopped altogether.

On the 27th leaving one man[91] in charge of our property which was placed "in cache" on the rocks and covered with oilcloths, the remainder of the party assisted by three Esquimaux carried what baggage and provisions were necessary to the boat and as the remainder of the River (a distance of one and a half mile) was neither so rapid nor so shallow as that passed through yesterday we soon reached the Lake, which was 6 miles long and varied from half a mile to 200 yards in breadth, its depth being in some places upwards of thirty fathoms.

After traversing several Lakes and crossing over six portages we on the 1st August entered a shallow stream flowing to the Northward. Following this we arrived at the sea at 5h. p.m. in Latitude 67°–13'–00" N Longitude by account 87°–30' West. The tide being out the men had some rest which they much required after their hard labour. I expected to have got the boat floated during the night but was disappointed as the water did not rise by two feet so high as it had been the previous day, a difference which I could only account for by a change of wind from Northwest to south.

Early on the morning of the 2nd we carried the baggage a mile further down stream and afterwards with much trouble dragged our boat over some shoals. We were now afloat in a salt water Lake of a few miles diameter across which we steered towards the only apparent opening bearing north. On passing a point to our left, two Esquimaux tents came into view. As we had not yet breakfasted I went on shore, and whilst the men were cooking, visited them to ascertain if there were any inhabitants. After calling once or twice outside the door of one of the tents, an old woman popped out her head but although (as I afterwards learnt) she had never seen Europeans before, she showed no symtoms of fear, as she very coolly drew on her capacious boots. An aged man soon after appeared. From them I learnt that their two sons with their wives had gone a day's journey inland with the intention of hunting the muskox and that the sea before us was continually full of ice and could with difficulty be traversed in their Kayaks or small canoes. Appearances led me to suppose that this information was correct, but it was necessary to judge for myself and at least make an attempt to get forward although not a pool of open water could be seen to seaward.

After landing three of our men[92] who had assisted us across and who were to return to Repulse Bay, and giving some presents to our new friends, we pushed off and began a tedious progress to the northwestward among heavy and close packed ice. Ranges of low granite hills lined the coast, sometimes a few hundred yards distant from it, at other places projecting into the sea. After tracing the shore for eleven miles we passed a steep rocky point which was named after Chief Factor Hargrave, the gentleman in charge of York Factory, when the Expedition was fitted out. When a few miles past Point Hargrave, being completely stopped by ice, we put on shore and found a large wooden sledge, half of which we cut up for fuel, intending to pay the owner who I was pretty sure of finding on my return.

At 11h. A.M. on the 3rd we rounded a high bluff cape which was called after the Lady of Sir John Henry Pelly, Governor of the Hudson's Bay Company. It is situated in Latitude 67°–28'–00" North. Longitude by acct. 87°–40' West. With much exertion we advanced three miles beyond the Cape when we were inclosed by the ice so that we could neither advance nor retreat. The shore still kept its Northwest trending, and presented a succession of low muddy points and alternate bays.

Into each of the latter a deep ravine opened which during the melting of the snow in spring, must form the beds of considerable streams, although at present they were nearly dry. The tides here were very irregular in their height one tide flowing eight or ten feet and the next not above half as much. The depth of water within a hundred yards of the shore was from three to five fathom on a bottom of mud and sand.

There was a fresh breeze off shore on the 5th which had but little effect upon the ice, I therefore determined on returning and if possible crossing over to Melville Peninsula for the purpose of tracing its shores to the Fury and Hecla Strait. By chopping off some pieces of ice, and pushing aside others, after much exertion we succeeded in getting our boat among ice somewhat less closely packed. During our detention the weather had been so foggy that no observations of any value could be obtained, our clothes were all either wet or damp, our fuel was nearly expended and we had much difficulty in finding water that was drinkable. I had travelled five miles along the coast, but the walking was so fatiguing that I gave up all hopes of performing the survey on foot at this season.

Working our way among the ice until a mile or two past Point Hargrave, there now appeared to be sufficient open water to allow us to cross over to Melville Peninsula, the nearest point of which bore NE (true), distant ten miles We completed the traverse in five hours amidst torrents of rain, accompanied by thunder and lightning, the wind having shifted from south west to East. Having secured the boat to the rocks, the men although drenched to the skin went immediately to sleep in their wet clothes; eighteen hours hard work at the oars and ice poles having thoroughly tired them all.

There was a thick fog with rain all the night of the 6th but about six oclock on the morning of the 7th a fresh breeze from SE. dispersed the mist. As soon as the weather cleared up we started, but our progress was very slow; in four hours we gained as many miles and were again stopped by our constant enemy. Some deer were seen feeding among the rocks and I landed for the purpose of endeavouring to get some venison, but the animals were too shy to be approached. An hour's sun shine dried our clothes and bedding, and thus made us feel rather more comfortable than we had been for some days past. The breeze having driven the ice a short distance off shore, we ran a league to the northward. The wind having increased to a gale, it became dangerous to proceed among the ice, we therefore pushed for shore, which was only a quarter of a mile distant, but we had much trouble in reaching it although pulling six oars and ran much risk of being crushed by overhanging masses of ice, under which we were obliged to pass.

Early on the 8th it became calm, and so slight had been the effect of the late gale, that the ice had nearly surrounded us before we got our anchor up. The boat could not be placed in safety here, so I decided on running back to our starting point, and there await some favorable change. A light breeze aided our retreat, but the ice followed close in our rear and before we had been half an hour under shelter, every spot of open water was filled up.

I learnt from our Esquimaux acquaintances that the deer had already commenced migrating southward. This being the case I prepared to walk across to Repulse Bay to learn how the men left there, were getting forward with arrangements for wintering. Leaving three men[93] in charge of the boat I started on the 9th in company with the others, and reached our destination on the following day at 2 p.m. A few deer had been shot and some salmon caught but neither were yet abundant. The Esquimaux had gone to the Lakes and stationed themselves at the several deer passes where they watch for and intercept the animals with their swift canoes and spear them in the water.

After mature consideration I determined on giving up all hopes of prosecuting the survey at present. My reasons for arriving at this conclusion, I shall here briefly mention, as such a step may appear somewhat premature. I saw from the state of the ice and the prevalence of northerly winds that there was no likelihood of our completing the whole of the proposed survey this season, and although part of the coast either towards the Strait of the Fury and Hecla or towards Dease and Simpson's furthest might be traced, yet to accomplish even this might detain us so long, that there would be no time to make the necessary preparations for wintering, and would thus be under the necessity of returning to Churchill, without accomplishing the object of the Expedition or if we remained at Repulse Bay run the risk of starving, for I could obtain no promise of supplies from the natives and all the provisions that we carried with us, amounted to not more than four months expenditure which was all that our boats could carry. We would thus have to depend almost altogether on our own exertions for the means of existence as well of food as fuel.

On the 11th retaining one man with myself to gaurd our property and attend the nets, the remaining six were sent to assist in bringing over the boat. They returned on the 15th having been only two days crossing. Two Esquimaux had accompanied them to assist and also to act as guides, three of the portages were thus avoided and they had likewise the advantage of a fine fair breeze in the Lakes. The Esquimaux had wrought well and were liberally rewarded: one of them—a merry little fellow named Ivit-chuk,[94] (anglice seahorse) was engaged to accompany me on my *intended* spring journies over the snow and ice.

All hands were now busily occupied in making preparations for a long and cold winter. To build a house was our first object, and not having wood, stones were collected at a favorable spot in a hollow on the north side of the River, a quarter of a mile from the sea. Our hunters Nibitabo and Ouligbuck were continually on the look out for game, and whenever I had leisure, I shouldered my rifle, and had frequently some fine sport among the deer, shooting seven one day within a couple miles of our encampment.

On the 2nd September our house was finished. Its internal dimensions were twenty feet long by fourteen broad, height in front seven and a half feet sloping to five and a half at the back. The roof was formed of Oilcloths and moose skin coverings, the masts and oars of our boats serving as rafters. The door was made of parchment deer skin, stretched over a frame of wood. It was named Fort Hope and is situated in Latitude 66°–32'–16" North, Longitude (by a number of sets of Lunar Distances) 86°–55'–51" West. The Variation of the compass on the 30th August 1846 was 62°–50'–30" West. Dip of the needle

88°–14' and the mean time of a hundred vertical vibrations in the line of Declination 226 seconds.

During the open water salmon were caught in the Bay, but a marine insect somewhat resembling a shrimp in miniature, cut up our nets so much that it was impossible to keep them in repair, steeping the nets in a strong decoction of tobacco had no effect.

On the 16th of October the Thermometer first fell to zero and the greater part of the rein deer had passed. We had at this date shot a hundred and thirty of these animals, and during the remainder of the month and in November thirty two more were killed, so that with two hundred partridges and a few salmon our provision Store (built of snow) was pretty well stocked.

Sufficient fuel had been collected to last (if economically used) for cooking until spring and I had shot a couple of seals which produced oil enough for our lamps.

By nets set in the Lakes under the ice, some salmon were caught, but the numbers were latterly so few, that on the 4th January the nets were taken up Our house long ere the above date had become sufficiently cold, the temperature in my room (a small space seperated from the rest of the dwelling by a partition of oilcloth) was frequently from 10° to 12° below zero. The mens quarters on account of the number of them crowded together were rather less cold, nor did we receive any heat from our fire when cooking, as the chimney (not being built on the most approved principles) obstinately refused to allow any smoke pass through it, without the door being open. Fortunately the majority of the party had been accustomed to cold weather and being all in excellent health our trifling discomforts furnished the subject of many a joke, thus a poor fellow[95] who got his knee frozen (not severely) whilst in bed, afforded merriment for some time. In the early part of winter a school had been established, which I had hoped to continue until spring, but the coldness of our house prevented this.

On Christmas and new years day a double allowance of fuel and flour was supplied. Fat venison steaks and plum pudding, for which a spirited game at foot ball gave a keen appetite, were the order of the day. A small supply of brandy from our scanty stock (3 Gallons) made the men feel quite happy, and I will venture to say that few merrier parties could be seen any where than they presented.

The winter was extremely stormy, indeed so much so that frequently we could not move fifty yards from the house for several days together. On those occasions we took only one meal pr. day. The prevailing winds were from the Northwestward and the lowest temperature we experienced -47° degrees below zero—occurred on the 8th January.

Towards the end of February preparations for our spring journies were commenced. Two sleds resembling those used by the Esquimaux were made by nailing together some of the battens which formed the ceiling of our boats.

In the beginning of March, the Reindeer began to migrate northward but were very shy. One was shot by Nibitabo on the 11th.

I had intended setting out on my journey over the land and ice on the 1st April but an accident that happened to Ouligbuck detained me until the 5th on which date I left Fort Hope, in company with three men,[96] the Esquimaux Ivitchuk and Ouligbuck's son as Interpreter. Our bedding and provisions we placed on two sleds each drawn by four dogs. For two days our route was the same as that of the boat through the Lakes last Autumn. On the 7th when two miles from the sea we struck across land to the westward and built our snowhut on a small Lake four miles from Point Hargrave. This being the last fresh water Lake we were likely to see for some days our sled runners were re-iced and an Esquimaux who had assisted us this far with his sled and dogs returned to his home

A strong breeze of head wind with thick snow drift impeded our progress on the 8th but we nevertheless advanced seven miles beyond Cape Lady Pelly before encamping. The 9th proved fine and the ice was less rough than that passed over yesterday; but our dogs began to fail and one of them having become quite useless was shot. Our dwelling for the night was built on the bank of a small River (frozen to the bottom) about seventy yards wide, where we found enough of loose stones to secure a "cache" of provisions for our return journey.

About midday on the 10th we arrived opposite a rounded Point which was named Cape Weynton.[97] Our course now lay across a Bay about six miles deep and ten wide, which received the name of Colvile[98] in honor of the Deputy Governor of the Honble. Hudsons Bay Company. Not being able to reach the land on its north side, we built our house upon the ice. The north point of the Bay which we reached the following forenoon was called Beaufort[99] after the learned and scientific Hydrographer to the Admiralty.

The land which had hitherto been rocky and ran in a NNW direction, now turned to the north and became gradually more level, exhibiting every indication of a lime stone country. Our next encampment was in Keith Bay situated in Latitude 68°–17'–00" N Longitude 88°–22'–00" West.

The coast here took a sharp turn to the Eastward and our Esquimaux companion informed me that by crossing over land in a northwest direction to a large Bay which he had formerly visited, we would shorten our distance considerably. I decided on adopting the plan proposed and left the coast on the morning of the 12th. We found the snow much softer as we got inland and our dogs being now very weak felt the change severely. After travelling twelve miles we came to a small Lake that was not frozen to the bottom. Here we stopped so as to give our dogs some rest and to ice our sleds. We also enjoyed the *luxury* of an unlimited supply of water. The surrounding country presented a flat snow covered surface, with the exception of two elevations formed of mud, lime stone and shingle from a hundred to a hundred and fifty feet in height between which we had passed, an hour and a half before encamping. On the 15th which was very stormy with a temperature of 20° below zero, we arrived at the steep mud banks of the Bay spoken of by our guide and called by him Ak-ku-li-gu-wiak. Its surface was marked with a number of high rocky Islands, towards the highest of which—six or seven miles distant—we directed our course and were before sunset comfortably housed under a snow roof. We had the extreme good fortune to find some fuel by digging under the snow, and could thus afford to have our Pemican warmed and a kettle of tea made. A gale of north wind made this the coldest day we had been exposed to during the journey and not one of the party (not even the Esquimaux) escaped without being severely marked on the face.

As the dogs were now nearly useless, I determined on leaving them here with some of the party including the Esquimaux for the purpose of recruiting their strength and if possible to kill seals which were numerous, whilst I with two of the men proceeded to trace the remainder of the unexplored coast. The 16th was so stormy that we could not attempt to cross the Bay, but a search was made among the Islands for Esquimaux, the recent foot tracks of two of whom had been noticed the previous day. No natives were found although there were numerous signs of there having been in the neighbourhood a few days ago.

Early on the morning of the 17th I set out in company with two of the men,[100] for the purpose of following the coast to some point surveyed by Sir J. Ross as I now felt confident that that veteran Discoverer was correct in his opinion as to Boothia Felix being part of the American Continent. We directed our course to the farthest visible land which bore NW (true). The weather was beautiful but cold, and the ice being smooth, a brisk walk of seventeen miles brought us to the point towards which we had been proceeding, in time to obtain a meridian observation of the sun. Cape Berens[101] (so named after one of the Directors of the Hudson's Bay Company) is situated in Latitude 69°–4'–12" north and Longitude 90°–35' West. It is formed entirely of granite partially covered with moss. Thirteen miles beyond this we arrived at two narrow points in the small Bay between which we built our snow hut, which being made too small we passed a rather uncomfortable night. Bed and bedding for the party consisted of one blanket and a hairy deer skin—the latter being placed on the snow to prevent our clothes getting wet.

The shore still trended to the NW and we had not travelled more than four leagues on the 18th when the coast took a sharp turn to the Easward. We had been tracing the west side of a deep Inlet which was named Halkett[102] after one of the members of your Honorable Board.

As we were now near the Latitude and Longitude of Lord Mayor's

Bay of Sir John Ross, I struck across land nearly in a north direction and at noon when passing over a considerable Lake the Latitude 69°–26'–1" N was observed. Advancing three miles beyond this, we reached another Lake and as there was yet no appearance of the sea, I ordered my companions to build a snow hut and search for fuel whilst I went to look for the coast.

A walk of twenty minutes brought me to an Inlet not more than a quarter of a mile wide, this I traced to the westward for three miles, when my course was again obstructed by land. Ascending some high rocks from which a good view could be obtained I thought I could distinguish rough ice in the desired direction. With renewed hopes I set out at a rapid pace plunging among deep snow, scrambling over rocks, and through rough ice, until I gained some rising ground close to the beach. From the spot where I now stood as far as the eye could see to the Northwestward lay a large extent of ice-covered sea, studded with innumerable Islands. Lord Mayor's Bay was before me, and the Islands were the Sons of the Clergy of Scotland.

The Isthmus which connects the land to the Northward[103] with the Continent is only one mile broad and appears to be a favorite resort of the natives, to judge by the number of stone marks set up on it. Its Latitude is 69°–31' north, Longitude by Account 91°–29'–30" West. With a grateful heart to him who had thus brought our journey so far to a successful termination, I began to retrace my steps towards my companions and at a late hour reached the snow hut—an excellent *roomy* one—in which I enjoyed a pleasant night's rest after the fatigues of the day.

On the following morning, after taking possession of our Discoveries with the usual forms, we traced the Inlet Eastward. When we had gone four miles the land to our left turned up to the north leaving an opening[104] in that direction two miles wide, bounded on the east by one or more Islands. The strait separating this or these last from the mainland was in some places very narrow and ran about South.

Finding on the morning of the 20th that we were at the head of a deep Inlet, I was obliged to take the straightest route across land towards our snow hut of the 17th as our provisions were all but consumed. There were many steep hills and deep ravines to be climbed over and crossed before we reached Halkett Inlet. This we at last effected a little before midday the snow being very soft, made the distance—only ten miles—appear like twenty. We reached our old hut at 2h. p.m. One of the men suffered so much from fatigue and inflammation of the eyes that I went on alone during the following day, leaving Corrigal (a fine able young fellow) to come on at a slower pace with his lame companion. When five miles from the Island where the remainder of the party had been left I was met by four Esquimaux whom I had not seen before. After shaking hands with them they wished me to visit their houses which were close at hand, but as my men were not in sight, and as I was quite unarmed, I declined the invitation, but with some trouble prevailed on them to follow me to our encampment. This was a fortunate meeting for us, as we obtained a quantity of seals blubber for fuel and dogs food, and some of the flesh and blood of the same animal for our own use. A couple of fine large dogs were also bought. As we were all more or less affected with snowblindness and the dogs were still weak we remained on the Island[105] which I found to be situated in Latitude 68°–53'–44" north. Longitude by Account 89°–56'–00" West. It is formed almost entirely of granite and is upwards of 730 feet above the level of the sea. From the highest point of it I obtained a fine view of the Bay and was thus saved the trouble of tracing its shores. It extends sixteen or eighteen miles to the southward, and contains a number of rocky Islands, the highest of them being that on which we encamped. The Bay was named after Sir John H. Pelly Governor of the Hudson's Bay Company, and the group of Islands after Benjamin Harrison[106] Esquire one of the Directors.

Having now as much seals flesh and blood as would maintain us for six days at half allowance, I determined on tracing the shores of the land, over which we had travelled on our outward journey.

We set out on the morning of the 24th and directed our course to the Eastward of north, the coast preserved this trending for twenty five miles, it then ran eight miles due East, forming a Cape which was named Chapman.[107] We now turned S.E. and continued this course forty miles, and finally south thirty five, which brought us to Keith Bay on the 30th where on account of a strong gale of wind and thick drift we had much trouble in finding a small "cache" of provisions left here in passing. The whole of the land which we had traced during the last seven days, was low and flat, and very regular in its outline, there being few or no Bays and Points. It was called Simpson's Peninsula in honor of the Governor of the Hudson's Bay Company's Territories. During the remainder of our journey we followed as nearly as possible the same route as that by which we had come and arrived at Repulse Bay on the 5th May, all safe and well, but as black as negroes from the combined effects of frost bites and oil smoke.

At our winter Quarters every thing had gone on prosperously; enough of venison had been procured by the hunters and purchased from the Esquimaux to support the people without having recourse to pemican, of which useful article it was my object to save as much as possible for future contingencies.

Having still to trace the West shore of Melville Peninsula, I started for this purpose on the evening of the 13th May (intending to travel by night) with a chosen party of four men.[108] Our course to the sea was nearly due north through a chain of Lakes, and on the 16th we built our snow hut on Cape T. Simpson in Latitude 67°–19'–14" N Longitude 87°-00' West, a rocky point which I had visited last autumn in the boat. From this place I sent back a fatigue party of three men[109] and a sledge of dogs that had assisted us this far. As the dogs were of little use during the last journey, I took none with me now.

We left our snow hut on the evening of the 16th each of the men being laden with about 70 lbs. weight, whilst I carried my Instruments, Books &c. weighing altogether 40 lbs. Two blankets and as many hairy deer skins constituted the bedding of the party. Our progress was very slow as the ice was rough and the snow both soft and deep. We advanced only twelve miles the first night. On the 17th we crossed a Bay eighteen miles wide and encamped at its north point, opposite to which and within two miles of the shore there is a large Island which was honored with the name of His Royal Highness the Prince of Wales.[110] A small Island to the south of this was called Sabine.[111] The general trending of the coast was now NNE. Near the shore the banks were high and steep, and where visible through the snow formed of sand, shingle, mud, and granite boulder stones, whilst a range of rocky Hills of various but not great altitudes were to be seen a few miles inland.

On the 20th we were detained twenty four hours by stormy weather at Cape Lady Simpson, a long point in Latitude 68°–10'–N Longitude 85°–53' West. We rounded Selkirk Bay (called after the noble Earl[112] of that name) on the 21st and after passing a number of small points and Bays we encamped on what at first appeared to be a part of the mainland but which was afterwards found to be an Island. Our snow house on the 25th was built in Latitude 68°–48' north, Longde. 85°–4' W. near a small stream frozen (—like all others we had passed—) to the bottom. We had not yet obtained a drop of water of nature's thawing, and fuel being rather a scarce article, we sometimes took small kettles of snow under the blanket with us, to thaw it by the heat of our bodies.

Leaving two men to endeavour to fish and shoot I went forward with the others and crossed Garry Bay passing inside a number of Islets which by breaking the force of the ice from seaward, had given us much better walking than I could have anticipated. We passed the day on an Island near the north side of the Bay, some bear tracks and a flock of Long-tailed ducks were seen.

Our course on the following night lay to the westward of north, the coast being high and rocky, and indented with numerous Inlets. After accomplishing twenty miles in a straight line we encamped; as the weather looked fine we did not build our usual comfortable lodgings which I had afterwards cause to regret, as a heavy fall of snow soon came on. We were now in Latitude 69°–19'–39" N and Longitude 85°–4' W. The latter is evidently erroneous, as I had neither Chronometer nor watch that I could place dependance upon, and the Compasses were much affected by local attraction.

Our provisions being nearly done, I could only proceed half a days journey further Northward and return the same night to our present quarters. Leaving one of the men I set out with the other.[113] The snow fell fast and the walking was extremely tiresome. After advancing ten miles the land turned sharp to the Eastward, but as the weather was thick I could not see how far it trended in this direction. When we had waited here nearly an hour, the sky cleared up and I discovered that we were on the south shore of a considerable Bay, and could trace the coast to the northward, for about twelves miles beyond it.

To the most distant visible point (Latitude 69°–42' North Longitude 85°–8' West) I gave the name of Cape Ellice,[114] the land where we stood was called Cape Crozier[115] and the intervening Bay received the name of Parry.[116] Finding it hopeless to attempt reaching the Strait of the Fury and Hecla from which Cape Ellice could only be a few miles distant, we retraced our steps and after an absence of eleven hours, joined our companion,[117] who had built a snowhouse and was on our arrival very busy attempting to coax a little wet moss into sufficient flame to boil some chocolate, but to no purpose; we were consequently obliged to finish the process with Alcohol, a small quantity of which still remained.

Early on the morning of the 30th we arrived at our snowhut of the 25th. The men we had left here were well, but very *thin*, as they had neither caught nor shot anything eatable except two marmots—had we been absent twelve hours more, they were to have cooked a piece of parchment skin for supper.

Our journey hitherto had been the most fatiguing I have ever experienced, the severe exercise with a limited allowance of food had reduced the whole party very much. However we marched merrily on, tightening our belts (mine came in six inches) the men vowing that when they got on full allowance, they would make up for lost time.

Nothing of importance occurred during our journey homeward. Our several "caches" of provisions were found safe and some partridges that were shot aided our short commons. At 8h.20m. on the morning of the 9th June we arrived at Fort Hope all well, having been absent twenty seven days. During the whole of this trip our snow houses were built by one of the men named Corrigal, an able and active fellow who had also accompanied me when tracing the opposite shores of the large Bay; the survey of which I had now completed, and to which I gave the name of Committee.

Hutchins and Laughing geese[118] had been seen, and one of the latter shot, on the 1st June. Eider King, and Long-tailed Ducks made their appearance some days later.

During the remainder of our stay at Repulse Bay the whole party were occupied in procuring food, collecting fuel, and preparing our boats for sea.

In the latter part of July many natives visited us, with all of whom we were on the most friendly terms. Our spare nets, Knives, Files &c. were distributed among them, in portions according to the several merits of the recipients.

The ice in the Bay broke up on the 11th August On the following day after bidding farewell to our good humoured friends (—who were loud in their wishes that we would soon return to them) we left our dreary winter quarters. It had been my intention to proceed some distance up Wager River on the homeward voyage, and also to attempt tracing the shores of Southampton Island between Point Harding, and Cape Kendall, but to do the former at so late a season would have been imprudent, and I was prevented from crossing over to Southampton Island by a heavy stream of ice in mid channel.

Head winds and stormy weather retarded our progress much, so that we did not reach Churchill until the 31st August, when I found that we still had 8 Bags of Pemican and 4 cwt. of flour remaining. Our expenditure altogether having been 12 Bags of the former and 21 cwt. of the latter.

We were detained in Churchill River by a gale of wind until the 3rd September when the weather became more moderate, and we were able to continue our voyage towards York Factory, at which place we arrived late on the evening of the 6th.

I cannot close this without mentioning the excellent and praiseworthy conduct of the men under my charge. They were always willing and obedient, and although not ail equally able to do their duty, they did their utmost to accomplish it.

With the utmost respect I remain
Honorable Sirs
Your most Obedient Servant
John Rae

London 2*nd November* 1847[119]

Sir George Simpson

My Dear Sir

Before leaving York Factory I had the honor of addressing a letter to you giving a short account of my wanderings on the shores of the Arctic Sea, with a rough chart on tracing paper of the Discoveries made by the party. A few lines on the same subject were sent on board the chartered ship *Westminster* which vessel was to proceed round to Halifax after discharging her cargo at York Factory.

Availing myself of your kind permission to pass the winter in the way most agreeable to myself, I decided on coming to England, and landed at Plymouth from on board the *Prince Rupert*[120] on the 25th ultimo after a passage of thirty two days. On the 27th I arrived here, and presented to the Committee[121] a brief report of the proceedings of the Expedition—which after being slightly altered and somewhat curtailed by Mr. Barclay, the Secretary (to whom I gave full licence on the subject) was published in the *Times* paper of the 1st November.

Sir John Ross is quite delighted to find his assertions as regards Boothia Felix proved to be correct.[122] It is a portion of the American Continent.

My stay in London has not been very long I am however already quite tired of the great City and shall leave it as soon as possible.

I see my friend and old fellow traveller Weymss Simpson almost daily—he has not yet quite recovered his health. I have been endeavouring to persuade him to visit Orkney for a month or two. He shall receive a hearty welcome if we have little else to offer.

You will not I hope accuse me of carelessness or want of gratitude when you see this scrawl, although it bears the stamp of the former at least, as well in the writing as in the composition, but the fact is I have been endeavouring for some hours past to compose something like a letter, but to no purpose. I believe I could better express my feelings, had I but the pleasure of seeing you.

With the utmost respect believe me ever

Most truly and devotedly yours
John Rae

— JOHN RAE, RECD. 26 NOVR., ANSD. 8. DEC[123] —

[Endorsed]

priv 1847
London 2. November

London 9*th November* 1847[124]

Sir
With reference to the Hudson's Bay Company's recent Expedition to the Arctic Sea, permit me to mention that the men when engaged for that undertaking, were promised a gratuity, but no particular amount was specified. As the wages of the steersmen and middlemen were all alike (i.e. £40 pr. ann.) I would wish—if agreeable to the Honble. Committee—that the steersmen, George Flett and John Corrigal and also a man named John Folster (who had charge of Fort Hope during my absence) should receive a larger sum than the others.

I have the honor to remain
Sir
Your very obedient servant
John Rae

Archd. Barclay[125] Esquire
Secretary Honble. Hudson's Bay Co.

— C.T., JNO. RAE, NOV 9/47 —

Stromness Orkney 30*th November 1847.*[126]

Sir

I beg to acknowledge receipt of your letter of the 25th Inst.[127] conveying to me the gratifying intelligence that the Governor, Deputy Governor and Committee have seen proper to approve of my conduct and that of the party under my command in the late Expedition to the Arctic Sea.

I have to request that you will tender my sincere thanks to the Honble Gentlemen for the very handsome and flattering terms in which they have expressed their approval of our humble exertions, as well as for their extreme liberality in awarding us such a large pecuniary mark of their approbation and which I am sure will be appreciated as it ought by the whole party.

With reference to your letter of the same date[128] informing me that the Governor Deputy Governor and Committee have granted me permission to accept the offer made by Sir John Richardson[129] to accompany him in his proposed Expedition, I can only repeat my former thanks for their further kind consideration in this matter, and I shall leave it wholly in their Hands to settle with the Admiralty, in the event of my services being required; and I have written Sir John Richardson to that effect.

I am Sir

Your very obedt. Servant

John Rae

Archibald Barclay Esquire

&c &c &c

— CTR., JNO. RAE, NOV 30/47 —

Stromness Orkney 21*st January* 1848[130]

My Dear Sir

I have now to acknowledge the receipt of your most kind and obliging favours of the 25th November and 8th ultimo,[131] which reached me, the former on Christmas day, the latter on the 6th instant.

It is impossible for me adequately to express my grateful sense of your extreme kindness and consideration in sending me the letter of Credit on Messrs. Albert Pelly and Co.,[132] which I would most readily have availed myself of had there been any necessity, but as the Company have made me a present of £400 there was no occasion to make use of it, it is consiquently now returned.

I feel highly flattered by the terms in which you speak of the manner in which my report was drawn up, and as much do I regret that from want of attention on my part, you have had reason to imagine for a moment that I could ever have been so ungrateful as to have intentionally omitted any opportunity either public or private of expressing my obligations. On referring to the rough sketch of my letter to the Governor and Committee I find the following paragraph—"The whole of the land which we had traced during the past seven days was low and flat and was named Simpson's Peninsula after the able Governor of the Hudson's Bay Company's Territories". Whether I omitted this passage by some unaccountable oversight in the report[133] sent to the Hudson's Bay House or whether it was afterwards suppressed, I shall be unable to ascertain before my return to London.

In a meagre Newspaper report, I considered it best merely to mention your name, reserving for my intended publication to do every justice to your foresight and judgement in planning and projecting an Expedition which contrary to the opinion of most of the gentlemen of experience in the Indian Country terminated successfully and which could not be so effectually accomplished by any other route.

Ingratitude I hope is no ingredient in my composition, and it has occasioned me no slight uneasiness, that you should have such seeming good cause to think otherwise.

I have written Captn. Lefroy by this mail and have requested Mr. Arrowsmith[134] to forward him a copy of the chart of my wanderings, by which he will see that I did not forget him when in the north.[135]

Unfortunately before the receipt of your last letter, in which you express a wish that I should not be employed in the way of discovery unconnected with the Fur Trade, I had agreed to a proposal made me by Sir John Richardson to accompany him in search of Sir John Franklin the Company being willing to lend my services for this purpose, so that I cannot with consistency throw up the appointment—had it not been for this your slightest wish on the subject had been attended to.

I know not whether the Company intend proposing to Government to do any thing for me, as I have had no communication from them on the subject, and there is only one among them (the worthy Mr. Halkett) to whom my pride would permit me to say a word regarding personal matters. Most of the other great men at the House speak to a poor fellow from Hudsons Bay more as if he was a dog than a fellow creature indeed Governor Pelly said when I happened to mention that I was coming to Town in the latter part of January that he supposed it was "to be shown about like a wild beast" a compliment which I fully appreciated coming from so high a quarter.

It is Sir John Richardsons intention to leave England on the 3rd March if there is no steamer to sail about the middle of the same month. In either case I shall be happy to take charge of the articles of Jewelry &c from Mr. Smith which you wish me to carry out for you.

On my arrival here eight weeks ago I found all my friends in good health except my brother-in-law Hamilton[136] who was dangerously unwell with inflammation of the bowels from which he is only just now recovering. This and a slight attack of influenza that I experienced, has prevented me from making much progress with my intended narrative—which gives me more annoyance than the fatigues and privations to be indured during half a dozen Expeditions would do.

I passed a very pleasant evening at Mr. Simpson's[137] hospitable mansion when in London, and frequently saw my friend Wemyss, whose health I am sorry to say had not been much improved by the treatment of the Metropolitan Doctors.

It affords me much pleasure to learn that my brothers are doing well, if they get over the present depressed state of the markets they will I trust continue to prosper.

My mother and sister beg to be most kindly remembered and that you may enjoy every blessing is the sincere wish of yours

Most respectfully and devotedly
John Rae

Sir George Simpson
Hudson's Bay House Lachine }

—— JOHN RAE, RECD. 23 FEB., NO ANSWER ——

[Endorsed]

1848
Stromness 21. January

Exchange Hotel Detroit *24th April* 1848[138]

My Dear Sir George

I arrived here last night and found Sir J. Richardson at this Hotel waiting for the Detroit Steamer which is expected to reach this in the evening and to leave for St. Maries early tomorrow morning.

I am sorry to say that J. Bte. Poirier[139] did not make his appearance at the Coteau Landing a boy was sent to his house but he was from home.

I saw Captn. Lefroy for a few minutes at Toronto and gave him what I thought was a chart of my recent wanderings but since arriving here, I find that I had handed him (Lefroy) Arrowsmiths new chart of British North America instead. You would much oblige me if you could spare him one of the copies of my Chart sent to Lachine, and I shall leave one at St. Maries to replace it.

Hoping that you will excuse my thus troubling you and with kindest regards to Lady and Miss Simpson[140] and to Mr. and Mrs. Finlayson.[141]

Believe me
very respectfully & truly yours
John Rae

Sir George Simpson
&c &c &c }

Sir John Richardson begs to be remembered and joins with me in hoping that Lady Simpson is in better health

J. R.

— JOHN RAE, RECD. 27. JULY, NO ANSWER —

[Endorsed]

priv 1848
Detroit 24. April

Cumberland House 13*th June* 1848[142]

My Dear Sir George

Had any thing of importance occurred I would have written you ere now, but our progress so far has been as favorable as could be hoped for, and except a little irritation and fretting on the part of my worthy *chief* when detained by ice or high winds, which served to amuse me occasionally we have been on excellent terms and I trust we will continue so, although I do now and then require to put a *bridle* on my temper. By all I can learn from the several Gentlemen with whom I have conversed on the subject, neither the Expedition men nor boats are very well fitted for what they have to go through, and as Sir John does not intend to take any of the old winterers to the coast with him, we shall find some difficulty in getting up the Coppermine, should we be fortunate enough to reach that river. I mentioned this to him, but he said that we could leave the boats and travel over land. To this I could offer no objection, as it is probable that an old Northwester like myself shall be able to rough it as well as most of the party.

We take no hunters with us to the coast, much dependance being placed on the *quantities of game* to be killed by my double barrel (rather a poor dependance I am afraid) and the exertions of our Esquimaux Interpreter[143] who is a fine active lad, and will no doubt prove a good deer hunter.

Some of the sappers and miners and sailors[144] are making great complaints about being ill used by some of the men engaged in the country, who hit them over the back with a pole now and then (to make them be somewhat smart I suppose). Poor Mr. Bell[145] must have had his own troubles with them, although they appear to be a well disposed set of men. Possibly the women[146] may some way or other have been the cause of the quarrels—this however is merely surmise on my part.

In writing Mr. Barclay to send me out a copy of my letter to the Committee. I requested him to address it to me to your care, so that if any bulky looking letter so addressed comes to Lachine be so good as open it.

With kindest regards to Lady Simpson (who I hope has quite recovered long before this date) Mr. and Mrs. Finlayson and Miss Simpson

Believe me Dear Sir George
Most respectfully and truly yours
John Rae

P.S. I shall again do myself the honor of addressing you before the canoes leave us on their return to Canada

J. R.

JOHN RAE, RECD. 25. JUNE, ANSD. 21 NOVR.[147]

[Endorsed]

priv 1848
Cumberland 13. June

Portage La Loche 5*th July* 1848[148]

My Dear Sir George
We shall probably leave this tomorrow about noon, being three days earlier than Sir John expected having been eight days on the portage, which is pretty well considering that we had no assistance from any four footed animals except two or three indian dogs that carried some trifles, and lightened a few of the bags of pemican. If we are not much impeded by bad weather we expect to reach the mouth of the McKenzie on or about the 8th of next month, and although my worthy superior is

rather doubtful of getting along the coast as far as the Coppermine at so late a date, I have no fears on that account, if the season is at all favourable. There has been much stormy weather for the last 10 days, the wind being principally from the northward which I trust will have some effect in breaking up the ice in the arctic Sea, although it is rather early in the season yet. As the sappers and miners are only to have one suit of clothes a year (at least such is their agreement) they are at a present a set of the most ragged and dirty looking fellows I have ever seen (a party of d—d Orkney men being even more respectable looking) however the poor fellows do their utmost to keep up with their neighbours and many of them do so. The seamen are the worst carriers but they are very willing. I am at a loss how we are to get up the Coppermine, for we do not intend taking any of the *old hands* with us. Not having crossed to the west end of the portage until this morning, I was much struck with the splendid view down the valley of the Clear water River. The beautiful effect of light and shade on the variously colored foliage, the undulations of the sides of the valley and the pure water showing itself here and there over and between the branches of the trees, looking like sheets of polished silver produced a scene which I have seldom or never seen surpassed.

I find that Sir John has almost entirely forgot the mode of taking observations so that the greater part of that duty devolves on me—not but that by a very little practise he would become very possibly the better observer of the two, but his time is taken up with other duties and he is so very anxious to get forward that he cannot fix his attention sufficiently to study the subject. The sextants supplied by Government are neither of them good, and are not at all well suited for taking the most accurate observations, such as Lunar Distances.

The whole of our men in the canoes behaved remarkably well with the exception of Gros Thomas[149] against whom I have but little to say except that, he was sulky, *lazy*, and soft and would have been insolent had he dared.

We had three much better guides and more active men in the canoe than him viz: Thos. Petit, Lazard Tacanajaze, & Ignace Atawackou, all of whom are temperance men whilst Thomas Karahoton is one of the greatest sots I have ever seen.

I was somewhat amused and a little annoyed to hear of a story having got among the Expedition men that the Company were in debt to the Indians of the Athabasca district for the Furs of three years, nor can I account for any such rumour getting abroad, except by supposing that Mr. Ermatinger[150] who is rather fond it is said of "heaving the hatchet" spread it himself—for I am aware that he was boasting of the number of beaver skins he was in debt to his Indians, when on his way down.

The [men] under Mr. Bell engaged for the expedition appear to do their work very well, but they are not equal to the party I had with me to Repulse Bay—being principally halfbreeds and Canadians, they will eat much more provisions and be otherwise more extravagant.

Mr. Bell has left his daughter at Cumberland House, perhaps he feared that either Sir John or his second might prove a gallant gay deceiver.

I have had some tough arguments with my Bourgeois on the subject of his arrangements for the Expedition, and have proved to him that there might have been an improvement in some particulars for instance had he got his boats built at Fort Chipewyan[151] or somewhere on the McKenzie much time and trouble and also a great quantity of provisions would have been saved—for if they had had Cos. boats coming up from YF to Norway House last autumn they would have reached Cumberland before the navigation closed.

It was necessary to hawl up and unload the boats from England 29 or 30 times on the route to repair damages, this of it-self must have occupied altogether about two days or more.

Offer my kindest regards to Lady and Miss Simpson, and with sincere respect

believe me
most faithfully yours
John Rae

Sir George Simpson
&c &c &c

— JOHN RAE, RECD. 19 SEPTR., ANSD. 21 NOVR. —

[Endorsed]

priv 1848
Portage La Loche 5. July

Fort Confidence Gt. Bear Lake 16*th September* 1848[152]

Sir George Simpson
&c &c &c

My Dear Sir George
It is with much pleasure that I now address you, to mention that Sir J. Richardson myself, and the party under him arrived at this place yesterday all in good health.

We reached the most easterly mouth of the McKenzie on the 2nd August without meeting any Esquimaux, but we had no sooner put a few miles to sea on the following day than a great number (about 150) of men came off in their Kayaks and also above a dozen of their luggage boats pulled after us. The canoes were soon round us in all directions but the large boats could not overtake those in which Sir John Richardson and I were but the third boat being some distance astern and not having used their oars to join us, was boarded by an Oomiak on each quarter the people on board of which, taking advantage of some confusion among the crew, immediately commenced stealing all they could lay their hands on that was not too heavy to be removed. We immediately put about to the assistance of our *consort* but before we got near enough to her, some of the men fired a couple of musquets, when the Esquimaux pushed off in all haste, and altho' the Kayaks continued with us for an hour or so longer the womens boats kept aloof.

We met various other parties of Esquimaux but they were too few in numbers to be troublesome. We saw no ice until we rounded Cape

Bathurst. But even here it did not impede our progress as it was sufficiently open to permit us to sail or pull among it, and was of some use in keeping the water smooth. As we advanced towards the Dolphin and Union Strait the ice became more closely packed, and a strong gale of wind from the N.W. brought it close upon the shore on the 22nd. From this time our advance was very slow, but by much exertion and making frequent portages over the ice and rocks, and by moving aside small floes and chopping off projecting points of large ones we generally advanced a few miles each day.

On the 27th August we left one of the boats and 10 pieces of Pemican and the next day 8 pieces more were deposited under some steep rocks near Cape Krusenstern. Here we were stopped a whole day and it had snowed a good deal and new ice was forming on the salt water.

Between the 28th Augt. and 1st Septr. we got within 8 miles of Cape Kendall, but here our progress was completely arrested, All the old ice was firmly glued together by the new, the latter having cut the planking of Sir Johns boat fairly through. This arose however partly from the carelessness of the crew, as my boat which was usually foremost was still pretty sound We now decided on walking over land to this place and after having placed our spare pemican and some ammunition "en cache" we started on the 3rd Septr. with 13 days provisions which together with Halketts canoe and other necessary articles made a load of nearly 70 lbs. for each man. I carried nearly an equal weight.

We directed our course toward Backs Inlet, at the north shore of which we arrived the same evening. On the following morning we traced the Inlet to its head where we found a large river not before known (named after me by Sir John) on the opposite bank of which 10 Esquimaux Tents were pitched, Albert the Esquimaux Interpreter and myself had gone before the party, and no sooner did we reach the water edge, than 3 men came across to us. They were fine clean looking fellows, and one of them very tall and stout for an Esquimaux had a large tumour on his left temple, being the same person that Simpson mentions having seen at the mouth of the Coppermine.[153] These kind people readily got four of their canoes and having tied them two and two together, with the assistance of Halketts air boat soon ferried the party across, for which we paid them as well as we were able, yet for every article given they offered something in return, and I got a copper knife or dagger which I have brought on here. Before parting I bade Albert tell them to be at the bloody Fall next spring when we should probably be able to make them some presents. We encamped for the night on the banks of Richardson's River—a stream about 130 yards wide and much too deep to ford. On the following morning I went across the river with my load in Halketts air boat dragging a line with me. Two tin plates served for paddles.

One of the men in fastening some of the lines together made a slip knot, so that our Esquimaux was also obliged to paddle over so as to regain hold of the line He found the water so very cold on his hands when paddling that he had much difficulty in reaching the shore.

The boat was afterwards hauled backwards and forwards by the line and the remainder of the party got over with great ease. We came to the Coppermine the same day about 3 miles above the Bloody Fall.

The hills and rising ground were during this journey pretty thickly cover'd with snow and during the next five days in which we were occupied getting up to the Kendall River we require to use snowshoes frequently. The Kendall was so much swollen by the thawing of the snow that not being easily fordable, we having left the air boat made a raft which took over 3 persons at a time. Five days more brought us to this place having had the benefit of an Indian guide for the last half of the way. We found Mr. Bell and party quite well, with most of the houses completed. They were built on the site of the old Fort,[154] the whole of which except the mens house, two of the chimnies and the observatory had been destroyed by fire.

I have said nothing hitherto regarding the party forming the Expedition, but I may now mention that they were the most awkward, lazy, and careless set I ever had any thing to do with. I believe they would have been disobedient to me had they dared, one of them tried it once but did not venture to be so a second time. The only things they were good at, were eating, sleeping and smoking, and also taking care of themselves. I never had so many duties to perform before. My excellent superior officer was not of much use and latterly left the work or management a good deal in my hands. I acted as hunter for the party but only killed 4 deer on the coast, all of which were in beautiful condition. To a set of experienced men all we did or had to do was mere childs play, but to the party we had with us it appeared quite killing work.

I have already got a party of volunteers (picked men) among our own people for next summers work if it is necessary for me to go to the sea, all of whom are to receive extra wages, but I believe the fellows would have come without any increase of pay. James Hope[155] one of Dease & Simpsons men is to act as steersman of the boat. I forgot to mention that we found one of their (Dease & Simpsons) boats on the banks of the Coppermine at the place where she had been left 9 years before.[156]

If permitted to visit England after returning from the sea next summer I should like to proceed through Canada or the states, Government of course paying the expense. Two of the men (Neil McLeod & Halcro Humphrey[157]) who go to the coast with me are anxious to join some friends and relatives in Canada. They have both been good servants to the Company and would consider it a great favor if you would have the kindness to permit them to come down with me or if I do not go, by the canoes in 1850.

I know not whether you have yet received a copy of my original letter to the Company on the subject of the last Expedition on which I was engaged but the inclosed half sheet of paper which I found in my portfolio, before going down the McKenzie this summer and which appears to be portion of a letter which I intended addressing you when in London will show what my thoughts were, on the publication of the former in the *Times*.

We have every prospect of getting abundance of provisions for the winter; Deer are numerous, and the fisheries are as productive as we could expect. A fishery has also been established near Fort Franklin[158] which being only six or seven days journey from this can be easily reached should we fall short here.

Some Indians have been already spoken to about the Muskox

Robes, but I know not whether they will get them made or not.

Begging to be remembered to Lady Simpson (who I hope has now recovered,) to Miss Simpson and to Mr. and Mrs. Finlayson.

With much respect Believe me
Dear Sir George
very faithfully yours
John Rae

P.S. Should you see or write to Captn. Lefroy, would you be so kind as let him know that I am well

J. R.
turn over

P.S. You will I trust excuse this ill arranged scrawl as I have no time to copy it

J R.[159]

JOHN RAE, RECD. 6. JUNE, ANSD. 25 DO[160]

[Endorsed]

priv 1848
Ft. Confidence 16. September

[Enclosure to foregoing]
My Dear Sir
Before leaving York Factory I had the honor of addressing a letter to you, giving a short account of my wanderings on the shores of the Arctic Sea, with a rough chart on tracing paper of the Discoveries made by the party. A few lines on the same subject were sent on board the chartered ship *Westminster* which vessel was to proceed round to Halifax after discharging her cargo at York Factory.

Availing myself of your kind permission to pass the winter in the way most agreeable to myself, I decided on coming to England, and landed at Plymouth from on board the *Prince Rupert* on the 25th ultimo after a passage of thirty two days. As soon as I arrived here (on the 27th) I presented to the Committee a short report of the proceedings of the Expedition, which after being slightly altered and somewhat *curtailed* by Mr. Barclay the Secretary (to whom I gave a "Carte Blanche" on the subject) was published in the *Times* Newspaper of the 1st November. The press had made a number of errors and a passage which was in the original letter left out Thus when speaking of some land that had been traced—"It was named Simpson's Peninsula"—Should be, "it was named Simpson's Peninsula after Sir George Simpson Governor of the Hudson's Bay Cos. Territories".

Fort Confidence 20*th September* 1848[161]

Dear Sir George

Your much valued favor of the 12th June[162] and a note of the 2nd March last reached me this forenoon. Of the latter I say nothing as it is principally on subjects which I have already written about. Of the former I can only say that I feel highly honoured by the important charge you have placed in my hands viz. that of the largest or one of the largest Districts in the country and one in which the returns are yearly decreasing even in the hands of a gentleman of so much experience Mr. McPherson.[163]

Unacquainted is [sic] I am with the details of the business in this part of the country, I doubt much my ability to manage affairs properly however a man can but do his best, and that I shall be always anxious to do.

During this last summers operations, I have had work enough and suffered more petty annoyance (the most disagreeable of all) than I was ever subjected to before and I would not engage on another Expedition of the same kind for double the pay. However Sir John Richardson has spoken of me in his despatch in a most handsome manner, indeed far more *flatteringly* than I deserve[164] and has given my name to the only new object of any importance (a large river falling into Backs Inlet) that we met with.

The next summer I hope to get on more pleasantly as I shall have men who know and will do their duty, and moreover I shall be to a certain extent my own master.

As Mr. McPherson will probably be away before I arrive at Fort

Simpson[165] next Autumn I have requested him to leave me very full notes of the District affairs which I shall follow unless I find that I can improve or change them altogether for the better.

Should I be in charge of the District there are two things which I beg most respectfully to mention.

The first is that I trust you will give directions that the Indents for the District be not reduced at York Factory, particularly in the articles of ammunition, Twines and Tobacco, in all of which the lower Posts of the McKenzie were very deficient this summer or rather they had none at all and were considerably in debt to the Indians, indeed near Fort Hope[166] it was said that the Indians were nearly starving for want of powder and ball, there being plenty of animals in the neighbourhood and nothing to kill them with.

Secondly it appears to me very hard that the officers, clerks &c of the District should receive nothing in lieu of the wines and spirits of which they are deprived.

Some chocolate, some additional Sugar, Tea, Rice or Fruit, of an equal quantity though not of the same value as the liquids withheld would I have no doubt be very acceptable and would not cost the Company much.[167]

I hope you will not consider it impertinent in me to write on the above topics, in the first particular it is what I consider the interest of the Company that makes me do so, for no one ought to know so well what is required in a District or at a Post as him who is in charge of it. In the second instance I am actuated by the *interest* of *self*, and the gentlemen who serve with or after me in the District.

We are likely to be very comfortable here this winter. Deer are numerous and the fisheries are succeeding better than they appear to have done when Dease and Simpson were here.

With much respect
I have the honor to be
Dear Sir George
Very faithfully yours
John Rae

Sir George Simpson
&c &c &c

P.S. The boat arrived here this forenoon and leaves again early tomorrow morning

J R.

Mr. Bell is the slowest man I ever met with.

J R.

— JOHN RAE, RECD. 6. JUNE, ANSD. 24 DO —

[Endorsed]

1848
Fort Confidence 20. Septr.

Fort Confidence *4th Novemr.* 1848[168]

Sir George Simpson
&c &c &c

My Dear Sir George
As Sir John has decided upon sending an express from this in a few days to Fort Simpson, via Martin Lake I take the opportunity of again troubling you with a few lines.

We have now got very comfortably housed in our winter quarters, which are much on the same plan as those of Messrs. Dease and Simpson—the dwelling house only being a little smaller. There is an excellent kitchen behind the house, with an oven near it; but our attempts at bread making have hitherto been failures.

I take the liberty of inclosing a very rough sketch[169] of our establishment; the imperfections of which you will excuse as I have not the slightest pretensions to be a draughtsman and am very clumsy at this sort of work. From the quantity of dust in the room the paper has got much soiled.

Our fisheries have not been so productive as was anticipated. There are about 1500 whitefish and trout in store averaging 4 lbs. weight each, besides 500 that are only fit for the dogs. An Indian employed to fish for us at Kashah Lake a days journey to the north of this, has nearly 400 more white fish collected.

Deer were plentiful a week or two ago (they have now gone to a distance) and the Indians have a quantity of meat "en cache" which we are unable to send for, on account of the small quantity of snow on the ground. The sleds returned from their first trip yesterday morning, they were much cut and worn by the bare rocks.

The weather has been very mild until a few days since when the thermometer first fell below Zero and this morning it was at minus 21°.

My time is principally occupied making observations and for some days past in making lanterns, a winter *cap* of *Rat skins* and writing letters. Having a gun set for foxes &c about 2 miles from this, I usually visit it between 6 and 7 in the morning, the four miles being a comfortable hours walk before breakfast which we have at 8. As we take only two meals a day our dinner or supper hour is 4 or ½ past 4 with tea. Our fare consists principally of whitefish, trout, venison and occasionally partridges and hares, either roasted, boiled or fried, with the addition of a plum, currant or cranberry pudding on Sundays and Thursdays.

My worthy Superior has an excellent appetite and has *filled out* amazingly since the *fatigues* of his journey from the Coppermine. He had a habit of saying that every thing in this country was conducted on the *make shift* plan. He was tired enough of the word before our arrival here, for I made it pretty apparent that almost every thing connected with the Expedition was a *make shift* for such work—men included.

When I had the honour of conversing with you at Lachine you hinted what the Expedition would be, and what it has hitherto proved—i.e. very expensive, very troublesome and far from satisfactory.

I regret to say that some of the dogs sent from Athabasca are either so old or injured that one of them is quite useless and 2 others will be worn out long before the winter is over. As Mr. Ermatinger will doubtless charge full price for them, it was scarcely fair his sending such animals, as he must have known how very necessary good dogs are at a place like this. Those supplied by Mr. McPherson were excellent.

Permit me to remark that some of the charges made at Cumberland House last winter appear to be extremely high—that for the use of an ax (£30) for a few months, was particularly noticed by Sir John and must be remarked by any person.

Should the men who are to remain here all summer 1849, decline engaging for or not be required in the Company's service, what wages should be allowed them if they pass the Winter at Great Slave Lake or Athabasca, doing nothing but assisting to procure their own food? It would not do for them to have their present high rate of wages, for besides the expense to the Expedition, it would effectually prevent them engaging with the Company should their services be required. I have written Mr. Ross at Norway House, requesting to know the exact terms of the men's engagements.

Regarding the Government Stores that remain on hand after the close of this *establishment*, may I request to know what is to be done with them? Are those that will be serviceable to be transferred to McKenzie River District at a fair valuation and an Inventory of them forwarded to you?

If Mr. Mcpherson leaves Fort Simpson next season before I arrive there, I am at a loss to know how the fall business will be conducted. Not being acquainted with Mr. B. Ross[170] I cannot say whether or not he is able to distribute the Outfits and give the men their supplies.

Possibly Mr. Peers[171] from Peel River[172] might attend to this by coming up a few days sooner from his post and prolonging his stay at Fort Simpson a short time.

Having written my friend McTavish[173] at the Sault requesting him to send me a few things that will weigh 10 or 12 lbs. may I beg the favour of having them brought to Norway House by the canoes.

I hope it is not your intention to keep me *very long* in McKenzie River District, as I am becoming quite a grey headed old fellow and it is high time for me to be thinking of looking out for a *better half*. However pleasant charming and useful the native ladies are in some respects, I do not at all fancy buckling myself for life to one of them. The *womankind* of the family have done their part in supplying her

Majesty with subjects and I do not wish that the male portion should be so far *distanced* in this respect. My brother Tom has got only one *legitimate little* Rae, Dick none, and myself not one either on the right or wrong side of the blanket that I am *aware* of.

Mr. Bell leaves this with Sir John in the spring and I am making preparations for my voyage to the coast (of which you are already aware) which will be my second visit to the Arctic Sea unaccompanied by any other officer.

In a few days I purpose taking an 8 or 10 days journey with the object of discovering the head waters of the Richardson and another River named after me, both of which fall into Backs Inlet. I intend if possible to find out a nearer route to the Coppermine for the boat, than that followed by Dease and Simpson.

All the Indians have been spoken to about muskox skins for robes but they say they cannot get any till spring.

Remember me most kindly and respectfully to Lady and Miss Simpson and

With the utmost regard
I have the honour to subscribe myself
Very faithfully yours
John Rae

P.S. My omitting to write you when at Norway House, did not arise from forgetfulness nor altogether from want of time, but I sometimes find much difficulty in addressing my superiors and this was an occasion of the kind, there being little or nothing to write about. I remember saying something to Mr. Ross on the subject.

J. R.

JOHN RAE, RECD. 10 OCT '49, ANS 21 JUNE 50[174]

[Endorsed]

priv 1848
Fort Confidence 4 Novr.

Fort Confidence 9*th February* 1849.[175]

Sir George Simpson
&c &c &c

Dear Sir George
I have now little or nothing to mention worth troubling you with, but as we are sending people to Fort Simpson for the purpose of bringing the YF ship letters hither, I cannot permit the opportunity pass without addressing you a few lines. I had the pleasure some three months since by a packet that was sent from here on the 6th Novemr. with the expectation that it would reach Fort Simpson in time for the express of 1st December, but owing to the incapacity of the guide employed, we were disappointed, consequently the letters then sent, will only go out by the Athabasca boats as they were not of sufficient importance to warrant the expence of a special express.[176]

Every thing goes on well with us here; we have had an abundant supply of venison, whitefish and trout and at present there are about two months provisions in store. Our fishery has lately become less productive, but it still gives from 50 to 60 fish weekly besides feeding the three men that attend the nets. The two men left to fish at Fort Franklin have made a large "cache" which will serve as a dernier resort in the event of scarcity here.

To judge by Dease and Simpson's experience, the winter here has hitherto been unusually fine; December was calm but cold, the mean temperature being -35° and the lowest -59°, which as the thermometer registered, stood at 36° below Zero when mercury froze may be considered as -38° for the mean and for the lowest -62°. January was milder but more windy and February as far as it has gone, has been beautiful.

Most of my time is spent at the house making magnetic and other observations, I was however absent nine days in December and an equal time during last month for the purpose of endeavouring to find an easier and shorter route[177] by which to take the boat to the Kendall or Coppermine than that followed by Dease and Simpson. I believe I have succeeded but that can only be proved by trial. If what the Indians say is true, and from what I saw there is little cause to doubt their word *on this point*, it is a curious circumstance, that part of the water of a lake about two thirds of the distance from this to the Coppermine, falls into Great Bear Lake by Dease River, and part into one of the Dismal Lakes close to Flett's Station on the Kendall—so that there appears to be a water communication,—only in the spring however—all the way from Bear Lake to the Coppermine.

During these excursions a little was done in the hunting way; ten deer were shot during the first trip and 4 on the second. Only two were killed by me, as I found the mode of hunting here required too hard *running*; having become *too heavy* and stiff in the joints of late for such exercise.

I see by the last years minutes of council[178] that there are no more allowances of butter to be sent to McKenzie River District, this being the case I presume, it will be requisite to increase the stock of cattle both at Forts Simpson and Liard so as to supply those posts where no cattle are kept with the usual quantity, as it would be rather hard for the clerks and others in charge of these posts to have a *further* reduction made in their allowances.

The houses here are excellent and it is a pity that they should be left to go to ruin,[179] yet there is no advantage to be gained by having a post here as the surrounding country is very poorly stocked with fur bearing animals. Tis true a quantity of meat might be collected and a number of bags of pemican made, but were this an object I believe it could be much better effected on the N East side of Slave Lake where deer are said to be equally numerous and where the Indians are better hunters.

Sir John Richardson and Mr. Bell leave this early in May, and take with them all the men except eight, six of whom are to accompany me to the sea, and the other two to remain here to take care of the property.

May I beg to be remembered to Lady and Miss Simpson and with sentiments of the sincerest respect

Subscribe myself
very faithfully yours
John Rae

PS. This leaves here tomorrow

J. R.

[Endorsed]

1849
Fort Confidence 9. Feby.

Fort Confidence Great Bear Lake 5*th May* 1849[180]

Sir George Simpson

My Dear Sir George
Our winter party is now fast diminishing in numbers. Five men were sent across the Lake to Fort Franklin some days ago, and Sir John, Mr. Bell, with four others are to leave this on the 7th for the same place where all, but two who are to return here, are to wait until the arrival of a boat from Fort Simpson.[181]

There are eight to remain with me, two of whom are at present at the Kendall River in charge of the provisions, consisting of 2 bags Flour, 10 pieces Pemican, some ammunition &c for summer voyage, which were hauled there with sleds last month. Two others are to pass the summer at this place whilst the others accompany me to the coast. Should the season prove favourable I expect to leave this with the boat on the 7th or 8th proxo. as by that time Dease River will be sufficiently open to permit us to ascend it.

In a former letter I mentioned that it was my intention to select a different route from that followed by Dease & Simpson, which is supposed to be shorter and better, and of which I enclose a rough sketch, that has no pretensions to correctness, with regard either to relative distances or bearings, but it may give some idea of what it is designed to illustrate.

The crew engaged for the sea voyage is composed of 2 Cree Indians named Hope[182] (the elder of whom was with Dease and Simpson and is now to act as Steersman) Neil McLeod, a Stornaway man; Halcrow Humphray a Zetlander; Louis Dubrill,[183] a Canadian, and the Esquimaux interpreter Albert, who is a very fine lad, fit for any of the usual duties of a labourer, and whom I intend to engage in that capacity for McKenzie River District, should you have no objections. He would be useful in the event of it becoming desirable to have any *negotiations* with the Esquimaux at the mouth of the McKenzie.

The wages of the men are pretty high the steersman is to have £45, each of the others £42, except Albert who receives £35 only Pr. annum. There is no gratuity to be given.

My Instructions,[184] are to cross to Wollaston or Victoria Land and proceed to the northward through the strait between these, as far as practicable with due regard to the safety of the party. We are to examine the shores very closely for any traces of Franklins ships or any part of their crews, and to question all Esquimaux that we fall in with, whether they have seen or heard of any large vessels or white men in their neighbourhood. Sir James Ross[185] purposed detaching a party over the ice this spring towards the Coppermine, if he got so far as Winter Harbour last autumn. To meet, co-operate with or aid this party if necessary is one of our principal duties. Whilst attending to these primary objects, I hope, if moderately fortunate, by surveying some degrees of Latitude of the shores along which we pass, to simplify in a great measure the question of a northwest passage for should I get so far as the north coast of Banks land, and find deep enough water all the way for ships of some hundred tons burden, it is evident that there is nothing but ice to prevent a passage being effected, and should Sir John Franklin return by the way he went which is more than probable, if he return at all, I think it will yet fall to the lot of the Hudsons Bay Company to accomplish this long attempted undertaking if aided by some thousand pounds from Goverment, that has already spent millions in the cause. The plan that appears to me the most feasible would be to start from some of the Cos. Establishments on the north west coast in two strong square rigged vessels of from 70 to 100 tons burden, built so as to draw little water, with much rake in the stem so as not to strike hard on the ice, and with rounded sides so as to be raised up by the ice if squeezed.[186] To be manned with a crew of not more than 8 or 10 men each. Men chosen for their powers of indurance, engaged in England, Orkney or in any other place where they can be found, but a proportion of them to be persons accustomed to the Indian country fellows who would not only exist, but live well where men of less experience would starve. By sending these across the Rocky mountains their stamina would be tested to some extent. I believe the vessels could be built, 3 years provisions and fuel provided and the mens wages paid for nearly the same period at an expence of not more than £8,000 or £10,000.

In writing thus it may look as if I was on the alert for my own advantage by thinking that I might be employed were any such voyage attempted. This however cannot well be the case, as I am very little of seaman and not much of anything else—as far as I can yet find out.

I am to be back at the Coppermine between the 25th and 31st August, when I shall proceed without loss of time to Fort Simpson where Mr. McPherson says my presence will be required as soon as possible.

The men will be sent to Slave Lake or Athabasca to pass the Winter, and I am directed to forward to La Chine an Inventory of all the remaining stores of the Expedition that will be useful to the Company.

By some Indians who came yesterday from the provision station on the Kendall I learn that deer are numerous, and that 7 muskcattle had been killed so that I hope to get one if not two large robes, and I trust before spring is past to get as many skins of calves as will make another.

The weather continues unprecedentedly cold but otherwise very fine. Two nights since the temperature sank to 14° below zero, last night and tonight it is minus 6° or 7°, and it has not this year (49) been so high as the freezing point.

We have had an abundance of excellent provisions all winter and Mr. Bell will leave the store stocked with 7000 Lbs. of venison—principally half dried side ribs.

Our winter packet arrived here on the 11th ulto. whilst I was absent at the Kendall with the first load of our summer provisions, but I returned two days after and was annoyed at not finding a single letter either from Orkney or London if I except my account current from the latter place. I fancy that some letters must have been sent from Orkney at least, but that they have somehow got mislaid.

May I beg to be remembered to Lady Simpson.

With the utmost esteem
I remain
very respectfully & truly yours
John Rae

Sir George Simpson
&c &c &c

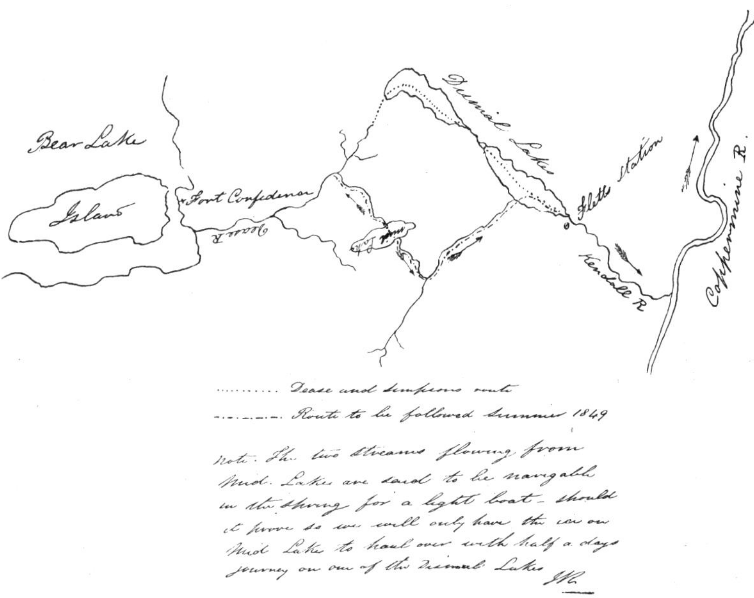

Sketch map of routes from Fort Confidence to Coppermine River, by John Rae

P.S. I am happy to say that Sir John and I have been on the most friendly terms since we came here, and I shall much regret parting with him.

J.R.

— JOHN RAE, RECD. 10TH OCT. '50, ANSD. 21 JUNE —

[Endorsed]

priv 1849
Fort Confidence 5. May

Fort Confidence 8*th June* 1849[187]

Sir George Simpson
&c &c &c

My Dear Sir George
Being all ready for an early start to-morrow morning to Dease River, en route to the Coppermine I shall leave those few lines here, in case it may be my fate not to return.

The season is an unusually late one, much more so than the worst of the two springs when Messrs. Dease & Simpson were here. Even in 1838 the ice in Dease River was broken up on the 1st June; at present the ice there is firm and strong but one days warm weather may set it in motion as there is plenty of snow in the mountains to cause the water to rise sufficiently. In 1839 the leaves of the willows were an inch long on the 6th inst.[188] Now there is not a leaf to be seen. There is tonight every appearance of a change in the weather, the sky is cloudy and the air much more mild than it has yet been.

Since the departure of Sir John and Mr. Bell my time has been principally occupied making observations and collecting specimens, and when time permitted following my favourite amusement of shooting.

Game is far from numerous here, but I have been pretty successful notwithstanding, and for the last fortnight have kept the *mess* in geese and ducks, besides giving a ration to the men.

The Indians in this neighbourhood are very poor shots, and the most careless, thoughtless and lazy set I ever met with. I must except those who bring their trade to Fort Simpson, who have evidently been much better drilled than those of Fort Norman,[189] and are quiet, well behaved characters. They are a lively race and many of the women, have a pleasing expression of countinance and would be rather good looking were they not so abominably dirty.

I mention'd in a former letter that I intended to follow a different route with the boat from that taken by Dease and Simpson, and as I will have only six people (4 men and 2 Indians) for my boat whilst they had 7 for each of theirs we will have a very fair trial which is best.

The property here will be left in charge of of [sic] a decent steady man named Olivier,[190] who I think will take very good care of it.

I have been able to procure only 4 musk ox skins (1 large & 3 small) yet, but hope to get some more small ones before the summer is over, and have given directions that as many as possible are to be collected whilst I am absent.

May I beg to offer my kind remembrance to Lady Simpson, and with sincere thanks for your many acts of friendship to myself personally and to other members of the family, for which I shall ever feel truly grateful. Believe me

With much respect
Very faithfully yours
John Rae

—— JOHN RAE, RECD. 22 APRIL 50, ANSD. 21 JUNE ——

[Endorsed]

priv 1849
Fort Confidence 8 June

Fort Confidence 1*st September* 1849[191]

My Dear Sir George
I beg to mention the return to this place of the Expedition which descended the Coppermine this summer to the Arctic Sea for the purpose of examining the shores of Wollaston and Victoria Lands in search of Sir John Franklin and Party.

I am sorry to say that we have been quite unsuccessful in the object of our voyage and I have to regret the loss of our excellent Esquimaux Interpreter Albert who was drowned at the Bloody Fall, the particulars of which unfortunate accident I shall mention in their proper place.

Having made every necessary arrangement at Fort Confidence and appointed a decent steady man named Olivier to take charge during the summer, we took our departure for Dease River at 1 h. A.M. on the 9th June. Our party consisted of 4 men and two Indians and 1 man who was to return to the Fort with the Dogs and sleds on which our baggage were hauled. The boat had been dragged over two days before and we had still to launch her two miles on the ice up the river before we reached open water. Our progress after this was extremely slow owing to the frequent obstructions (some of them 10 miles long) from ice over which we had to drag both boat and cargo. On the 15th we reached the forks of the river, having been two days and a half longer in coming that distance than Messers. Dease & Simpson, which may be easily accounted for by our having to haul our boat at least 30 miles over ice and points of land, besides being several times detained by driving masses. In short, the whole of the river was still covered with ice, except where the current was strong.

Our route here diverged from that of the former Expedition, we keeping the East branch whilst they followed the north one. In consiquence of the cold weather preventing the snow thawing on the hills, the water was very low and it was necessary to wade the boat up the greater part of this river (which is about 15 miles long) or haul it over the snow or ice still adhering to the banks.

On the 17th we hauled the boat over the lake from which the river flows, which is full of islands and 3½ miles broad where we crossed it in a south direction.

We now found that the Indian information as to their being water communication all the way to the Kendall R. incorrect, and that we had a portage of six geographical miles to make. I had examined this place in winter but as the ground was then covered with snow I could not perfectly ascertain whether the Indian report was correct or not. We were occupied the two next days on the portage and on the 20th we descended a stream of considerable size flowing to the N E until within 3 miles of its entrance into the most easterly of the Dismal Lakes not more than 5 miles from the provision station. This stream was also very shallow from the cause which I have already stated, and in many places the ice had not yet broken up. At the place where Sir John Richardson & party forded it last Autumn, it was at least 10 inches perpendicular less high now than at that time.

At half past 4 p.m. on the 21st we arrived at the provision station, where we found the men (Dubrill and Humphrey) quite well, with all the pemican in good condition, besides some bales of dry meat which the Indian hunters left with them for the purpose had procured.

In comparing the merits of the two routes,[192] I believe that which we followed to be preferable to the one taken by Dease & Simpson. We were 13 days in accomplishing what in ordinary seasons might have been easily effected in 9. They were likewise 13 days, during two of which no work was done in consiquence of bad weather. They had 7 men to each boat besides *camp* followers who assisted when required. We had only six men in all.

Notwithstanding that we avoided the whole length of the Dismal Lakes, 4 miles on the last one excepted I believe that the boat was hauled fully half the whole distance on the ice and land owing altogether to the lateness of the season and consiquent lowness of the water whereas in anything like a favourable season we would have had to launch it only 14 miles at the utmost.

We were occupied all next day descending the Kendall, having to make many portages and wade the boat down the rapids—in one of which it got broken. When we reached the Coppermine I was disappointed but not much surprised to find it still so firmly covered with ice that a person could have crossed from one side to the other a short distance above the mouth of the Kendall without being more than ankle deep in water.

On the 28th there was sufficient open water to allow us descend along with the driving ice as far as where Dease and Simpson left their boat where the river was again blocked up. Our advance was so often interrupted in this way that it was the 11th July before we reached the

Bloody Fall having ran all the rapids including the Escape[193] without shipping much water. Below the Fall down as far as the sea all was ice which did not clear away until the 13th, & which was sufficiently indicated by the numbers of fish that soon appeared in the eddies below the Fall.

A net was set with Halketts air boat (for which I had sent to the place where it was left last autumn six miles distant) out of which 7 fine salmon and 2 white fish were taken in a few minutes.

Next day we descended the stream and found a narrow and very shallow passage along the shore of Richardsons Bay until we came to its north side which being steep was full of ice to the very rocks.

During our stay here we were joined by 7 Esquimaux one of whom I readily recognised as the man who had afforded us such material assistance last season in ferrying the party across the river at the head of Backs Inlet, at which place they informed Albert, their tents were at present pitched. In the Winter these people had communicated directly or indirectly With the Esquimaux of Wollaston Land, none of whom had ever seen white people or large vessels.

During the time that we were making the portage from the Fort to the Kendall and whilst descending the Coppermine we obtained more venison than we could consume. I alone shot 10 deer, eight of which were large bucks (two of them killed by the same ball at 190 yds. distance). One of the men shot 3, and our two Indians 3 more. We might have easily killed double the number, but now they had become more scarce and shy owing to the proximity of the Esquimaux.

On the 16th by making several portages we doubled Point McKenzie and entered Backs Inlet which was in great measure clear of ice, and having a fair wind we soon ran to its head and entered Rae R. (so named last autumn by Sir J. Richardson) which it was my wish to examine for some distance to the westward. Here we found our Esquimaux friends who were so much alarmed at seeing the boat under sail that they were on the point of running away. They were well supplied with venison of which they gave us some not appearing to expect anything in exchange. Some presents were given them together with a supply of fish, the surplus produce of our nets whilst in Richardson Bay. The next two days were spent in examining the river, which is as large as the Dease with a very strong current and a fall of 10 feet, at the distance of 9½ miles from its mouth, which is a favourite station for spearing fish. On the west side of the Fall there is a sloping part a few yards wide where the salmon and white fish are able to ascend during the spring floods.

I traced the stream 30 miles in a due west direction when we met another party of natives, with whom we would not have been able to open a communication without the aid of our ferryman before mentioned who volunteered to accompany us, and seemed at once to accommodate himself to all our ways and habits, eating the same food we did, tracking the boat, assisting to take on shore and put on board the things that were required when landing to pass the night or embarking in the morning, in fact making himself generally useful.

The party whom we now met (10 in number besides women and children) said that the river maintained the same course and size as far as they had seen it which was 3 days journey or about 60 statute miles, how much farther it continued in the same direction they knew not as they had never been to its source.

Copy McDonell
10th Septr 1849[194] } On our return to the mouth of the river, we encamped for the night close to the tents of the natives who appeared to have recovered from much of their fear when they saw their countryman safe back again. The women even began to chat freely with Albert, and favoured me with one or two smiles (which they no doubt thought irresistible) in exchange for some trinkets. They were very cleanly in their persons and their tents were perfectly free from all filth or unpleasant smell.

On the 19th Augt. we took a friendly farewell of those simple and inoffensive people and directed our course towards Cape Kendall before reaching which a violent thunder storm came on and obliged us to land for shelter.

So slowly did we creep along shore, that it was the 24th before we arrived at the place where we had left the boats last season, only 13 miles distant from Cape Kendall.[195] The tents and some of the oil cloths were found entire but the boats were much broken up[196] by the natives to get at the iron work. A "cache" of six pieces pemican was also found untouched. After changing some of our pemican, and taking on board two tents and a few small oil cloths of which we stood in need, we continued our voyage and got to Cape Krusenstern on the 30th where our advance was arrested by the ice being driven forcibly against the shore by a NE breeze that had sprung up which obliged us to unload and haul our boat up on a drift bank of snow to save her from being ripped.

We pitched our tents on the top of the cliff to wait for open water as we were now at as convenient a point as any for crossing over to Wollaston Land Douglas Island being a sort of half way resting place.

Here for the first time this season we observed the ice broken up to seaward, caused evidently by the strong currents of the ebb and flood tides, whilst on looking back towards the Coppermine, all the surface of the ice was smooth, unbroken and as firm like as in winter, close along shore excepted.

During the long and tedious detention here, our situation was tantalizing in the extreme. Occasionally a pool of water would appear among the ice a mile or two in extent, and expecting it to increase all would be prepared for embarkation but our hopes were always disappointed. On the afternoon of the 19th August there being more open water than we had yet seen we with some difficulty pushed out among the driving floes, and when a mile from shore were able to use our oars. We now made rapid progress towards Douglas Island and had gone nearly 8 miles when a close packet stream of ice impeded our way over or through which we found it impracticable to pass. The current, too, was now driving us faster past the Island than we could have advanced in the direction of it, even had the ice been sufficiently smooth to allow us launch the boat on it. Under these circumstances I thought it advisable to return to the mainland which as well as Douglas Island was now completely hid by a thick fog.

After a long pull & by hauling the boat ½ a mile over the ice we reached the land a short distance south of our former bivouac at 2 h. a.m.

on the 20th having been 10 hours absent during which our craft was more than once nearly squeezed among the driving masses. A northwest breeze drove the ice a few yards out from shore before noon, and as our present situation under the cliffs was neither safe nor commodious, we went a few miles towards Point Lockyer and pitched our tents on the shore of a small bay where the boat was well protected. The wind which had cleared the shore of ice, had packed it more closely in the offing. We waited two days in hopes of still being able to make our way across the Union and Dolphin Strait, but a N E gale made this quite impossible, by jamming our cold and persevering opponent in large heaps along shore. Some open water now appeared to the South and S.E. but all in the direction we wished to go was as impervious as the solid rock.

On the 23rd thinking it useless to delay any longer, as there was every symtom of an early winter, I gave orders for our return to the Coppermine, and the men were at work early in the morning carrying the cargo, oars, mast &c to Point Lockyer, a distance of 3 miles. Having completed this work in the midst of a gale of N E wind with heavy rain, we had next to haul our little boat (now much shaken by the unavoidable hard usage it had undergone) to the same place, a duty of no little difficulty, over so rough a road as we had to pass, but this was accomplished in 6½ hours. The coast now turns to the west so that there was a passage along shore, along which we ran for some time under sail before the fast decreasing breeze, until it fell calm when we took to our oars.

From the long continuance of the N E gale and the great quantities of ice driven before it towards Basil Hall Bay and Cape Hearne I expected to find those places completely blocked up, but my anticipations were agreeably disappointed, on discovering that there were passages of open water through which we could make our way without being much stopped. I can only account for this by supposing that the gale had formed a curve to the south and S.E. and carried the ice along with it.

Late in the night our tents were pitched on Cape Hearne. Next morning 2 hours work brought us into open ice again, and between one and two p.m. we landed on Cape Kendall to take some dinner. An easterly wind now came on, to which sail was set. We crossed Backs Inlet and at a late hour entered the mouth of the Coppermine where we stopped for the night.

Next day we ascended to the Bloody Fall, at the foot of which there were still abundance of fish and 2 nets were set whilst some of the party were cooking. In an hour or two upwards of 30 fine herring salmon[197] and whitefish were caught—all of which were full of roe.

Being desirous of saving our boat the tear and wear of hauling over the portage, I was anxious to take her up by water after being launched over the rocks at the lower and steepest part of the Fall as had been done by Dease and Simpsons party, and this appeared quite easy of accomplishment to the steersman and others of the men, at all events they so expressed themselves to me. We had with ease surmounted the parts where there appeared any difficulty and had come to the upper end of the rapid where the current was strong but so perfectly smooth, that it was the general opinion that a loaded boat might be safely taken up it, so little indeed was thought of there being any danger, that the small line was given out to track with. When halfway up some unaccountible panic seized the steersman, he called on the trackers to slack the line, which was no sooner done sufficiently far, than he and the bowsman sprung on shore, and permitted the boat to sheer out into midstream the line snapped, and the boat driving broadside to the current was soon overset. Thinking that it would get caught in one of the eddies I ran down followed by Albert and stationed myself at a point of rock near which it was likely to pass, and directed Albert to stop at another point farther up the stream. The boat drove close in to where he was, and he hooked it by the keel with an oar, I ran round to assist him and snatching a pole out of the water fixed it in a broken plank; & called to my companion to hold on with me. He either not hearing what I said or thinking he would be of more service on the bottom of the boat, sprung to it, and ere I had time to think of his danger or call him ashore, a whirl of the current carried the boat towards the head of a little bay where I thought both were safe. However in less than a minute I observed them driving out again, the boat sinking more and more under water by some particular action of the eddy, and the last I saw of the brave lad was his attempting to leap to the rocks which he missed and instantly sank, nor did he rise again to the surface. This melancholy accident has distressed me more than I can well express. Albert was liked by every-one, for his good temper, lively disposition and great activity in doing anything that was required of him. I had become much attached to the poor fellow, and intended with your permission to have retained him at Fort Simpson as my servant, and ere long I had hoped to make him in every way a most useful man to the Company.

The sole blame of the loss of the boat and consequent drowning of Albert rests on the shoulders of the steersman James Hope who had readily expressed to me his opinion that there was no danger, when, from very fear (as I afterwards learnt from the other men) he was incapable of knowing what he was doing, nor would they have gone in the boat with him, had he not led them to believe by telling a falsehood that I had ordered the *boat* to be taken up by *water*.

The only reasons for my engaging Hope as a Steersman was that he had been employed in the capacity in McKenzie River for some years, and had been one of the bowsmen in Dease and Simpson's boats the last year of their Expedition. His character in other respects was very bad being a notorious thief and equally noted for falsehood, which with a most plausible tongue (which he had got oiled with a little learning at Mr. Jones[198] Red River School and when acting as cook to him) made him a most dangerous companion for men of not very fixed principles.

He had been dismissed the service by Mr. McPherson for very good reasons and was on his way to Red River when we met him in Slave River where it was all at once discovered that Mr. Bell required an Interpreter and he (although afterwards found very unfit) was engaged.

Having prepared everything yesterday for our journey on foot we started on the morning of the 26th, each of the men carrying about 90 lbs. including their own requisites and my bundle being little short of 50 lbs., which I find heavy enough now. Three days easy march brought us to that part of the river where we intended crossing land towards the Fort. Here we expected to find some Indians that were ordered to meet us, but we did not fall in with them until next evening 10 miles west of the Kendall.

Our loads were now much lightened and we easily reached Fort Confidence on the 1st September having been 7 days in coming from the Bloody Fall.

Next day we embarked all the party on board the bateau which was rather deeply laden for traversing the Lake.

I had commenced this hurried scrawl at Fort Confidence but was unable to finish it there. Since then we have been often detained by stormy weather but it has always been so cold that writing was not at all a pleasant occupation. We made an attempt yesterday (9th) to cross the traverse to the "scented grass Mountain"[199] but were obliged to bear up by a strong head breeze, when about midway between the two capes, and take shelter here again.

With kind regards to Lady Simpson I have the honour to remain

with much respect
very faithfully yours
John Rae

Sir George Simpson
&c &c &c

P.S. I fear that my time will not permit me to put this in any better form If so, I hope you will forgive so miserable a scrawl. My ink got frozen on the shores of the lake, even inside my tent.

J. R.

— JOHN RAE, RECD. 22 APRIL 50, ANSD. 21 JUNE —

[Endorsed]

1849
Fort Confidence 1. Septr.

McKenzie River, five days journey above Fort Norman
22nd Septemr. 1849[200]

Archibald Barclay Esquire
Secretary, Honble. Hudsons Bay Co.

Sir
I beg to mention for the information of the Honourable The Governor, Deputy Governor and Committee of the Hudsons Bay Company, that the Expedition under my command that descended the Coppermine this summer to the arctic sea for the purpose of tracing the shores of Wollaston and Victoria Lands to the northward in search of Sir John Franklin and party returned to Fort Confidence on the 1st instant, having been unsuccessful in its object, and with the loss of Albert the Esquimaux Interpreter, who was drowned at the Bloody Fall.

The spring at Bear Lake was so very late that we could not attempt to ascend the Dease River until the 9th June and even at that date we had to haul the boat and baggage two miles up its course on the ice before getting into open water. We met with so many interruptions from ice and shallow water whilst crossing, that we did not arrive at the provision station on the Kendall until the 21st having been thirteen days in accomplishing what, in ordinary seasons might have been easily effected in nine. Dease and Simpson were also thirteen days occupied bringing their boats over, during two of which bad weather prevented any work being done.

I followed a somewhat different route from what they took, having ascended the S.E. branch of the Dease instead of the north one, thereby avoiding the whole frozen extent of the Dismal Lakes four miles on the most easterly one excepted notwithstanding this we had to launch our boat more than half the whole distance over the ice and points of land, whereas had the season been an ordinary one the utmost distance we would have had to haul it, would be fourteen miles including the portage of six miles over the height of land.

We found the men at the provision station well, and having embarked our stores we descended the Kendall on the 22nd. This stream was 16 inches less deep than when Sir John Richardson and party crossed it on a raft last autumn we consiquently has [sic] some trouble in getting to the Coppermine, which was still firmly coated with ice. On the 28th it partially opened and we descended six miles among the driving masses when the stream was again obstructed.

So often and so long were we detained in this way that we did not arrive at the Bloody Fall until the 11th July, from which to the sea the river was still ice bound.

On the 13th numbers of fish appeared at Fall which was a sufficient indication that there was a clear channel to the salt water, had I not already been aware of it. A net was set which produced enough of fine salmon and white-fish for several days consumption.

On the 14th we descended to the sea, and found a narrow and very shallow channel along the shore of Richardson Bay until we came to its north side where the ice lay against the rocks. Here we were visited by seven Esquimaux, one of whom was the man who had afforded us such efficient assistance in crossing the river at the head of Backs Inlet last autumn. During the winter they had communicated either directly or indirectly with the natives of Wollaston Land none of whom had ever seen white men, large boats or ships. This information was confirmed by two Esquimaux that were afterwards met, who had been in company early in the spring with their countrymen of that quarter.

We found Backs Inlet partially clear of ice and ran under sail to its head on the 16th. Here I spent two days examining the Rae River (discovered and named by Sir John Richardson last autumn). It is about the size of the Dease, from 80 to 200 yards wide, with a very strong current and sufficient depth of water for a boat drawing 14 or 15 inches, as far as I traced which was not more than thirty geographical miles in a due west direction. Some natives whom we saw here stated that it continued of the same size and direction 3 days journey farther (say 50 or 60 miles), but beyond this they could not tell as they had never been to its source. Nine miles and a half from its mouth there is a perpendicular fall of 10 feet, extending across the stream, except for a few yards on its north side where the rocks slope so much that salmon and whitefish are able to ascend when the water is high.

Our progress along the coast was now so slow that we did not arrive at Cape Krusenstern until the 30th when a strong N E wind brought the ice in against the rocks with such force that to save our boat we had to unload as fast as possible and haul it up on a snow bank.

Being now at a very convenient point, from which to make the traverse to Wollaston Land should an opportunity occur we pitched our tents on the summit of the cliffs, to ascend which the snow bank already mention[ed] served as a ladder.

Here for the first time this summer we found the ice broken up to sea-ward, whilst all in the direction from which we had come was white, smooth and as firm looking as in winter. This difference was evidently caused by the strong currents that ran in the strait, whilst towards the Coppermine there was comparatively still water. We dared not venture out until the 19th August, at which date some lanes of open water appeared, and at the risk of having our boat squeezed we pushed off, with the hope of getting as far as Douglas Island which lay in our route—in this however I was disappointed for when eight miles from shore, we came to a stream of ice so close packed and rough that it baffled our efforts to pass either over or among it, we were consiquently obliged most reluctantly to return to the mainland.

I remained until the morning of the 23rd, expecting that a passage might still be effected, but the state of the ice was more unpromising than it had yet been, I therefore gave orders for our retreat towards the Coppermine, in the direction of which we had already come some miles, in search of a snug harbour for our boat.

A portage of three miles, with boat and cargo, brought us to point Lockyer on the south side of which there was some open water. We now made rapid progress to the west, and much to my surprise found a passage wide enough for the boat between the shore, and packed stream outside. This I could only account for by supposing that an East and E N E gale of wind that had been blowing for the last two days had shifted to the north and N W as it approached the land and carried the ice along with it.

By working sixteen or eighteen hours per day we entered the river late on the 24th, and arrived at the Bloody Fall next morning.

Dease and Simpsons party after launching their boats over the rocks at the lower and steepest part of the fall hauled them up the remainder—light—by water. I wished to do the same, both to save time and the tear and wear of the boat now much shaken. I was the more readily led to do this, as the steersman and crew appeared to think that it might be done without danger—indeed we accomplished all that was difficult without trouble and had only one place to ascend, which was so smooth that a loaded boat could have been hauled up it—here however the steersman was seized with a sudden panic, he called to the trackers to slack the line which was no sooner done sufficiently to permit him to get on shore than he leaped out of the boat followed by the bowsman, and allowed it sheer out into the stream, the line snapped, and the boat soon afterwards overset. It stopped in an eddy some distance below to which Albert and I ran and stationed ourselves at two points of rock near which it was likely to pass. It drove to where Albert was and he hooked it by the keel with an oar, I went round to him and fixing a pole firmly in a broken plank, called my companion to aid me. He either mistaking what I said or thinking he would be of more use on the bottom of the boat sprung to it, and before I had time to call him off or think of his danger, they were carried by a turn of the current into a small bay where I thought both were safe—but it proved not, for in a minute they were driven out again and the last I saw of our excellent Interpreter was his leaping towards the rocks, which he missed and disappeared under water, nor rose again to the surface. This melancholy accident has grieved me much. The brave lad, was universally liked for his activity, cheerful and friendly disposition and extreme good temper and for attention to his duty which made him a most valuable servant.

On the following day (26th) we commenced our journey on foot towards Bear Lake, each of the men carrying about 90 lbs. and myself a small bundle of nearly 50 lbs. After four days march we met with some Indians who materially lightened our loads, and we arrived easily at Fort Confidence on the 1st September having been seven days in coming from the Bloody Fall.

After supplying the Indians with some ammunition to enable them to procure provisions on their way to Fort Norman, we embarked on the 2nd. Whilst traversing the Lake we had much stormy and cold weather. The pools were covered with ice strong enough to bear a mans weight and the ink froze in my tent. On the 16th we began to descend Bear Lake River and at a late hour next night arrived at Fort Norman.

I write this whilst being towed up the river which will in a great measure account for its being in so rough a form.

I have the honour to be
Sir
your very obedient Servant
John Rae

Archibald Barclay Esqre.
&c &c &c

Fort Simpson *26th September* 1849

P.S. I arrived here yesterday afternoon and intend sending away the Expedition men tomorrow. Five of them are to pass the winter at Big Island in Slave Lake. The other two[201] have been permitted to carry the Admiralty Express to Sault Ste. Maries on their arrival at which place they are to be considered as out of the service of the Expedition.

J. R.

[Endorsed]

J Rae
Sept 22/49

Fort Resolution *30th June* 1850[202]

Sir George Simpson

Dear Sir

I have the honor to acknowledge the receipt of your favors of the 21st January (with instructions regarding the fitting out of searching Expeditions) and of 13th February,[203] dated at Lachine, brought by the Government Express which we met on the 25th Inst., one day's journey from Slave Lake. With every wish to obey your orders I found it impossible to do so by proceeding to the sea this Summer, for the following reasons. The stock of Provisions at Fort Simpson and the lower posts of the MacKenzie was so small as to allow only one party proceed to the coast properly supplied, and of course Commander Pullen[204] had the preference as he and his party were ready on the Spot. It was my intention to have taken Commander Pullen on as far as Fort Resolution for the purpose of obtaining an old Boat there, sufficiently good to take him and his men down to Fort Simpson; but being stopped by ice in hay river on the 28th, I thought it advisable next morning to send back one of our boats with him, reducing thereby our number to 7. He will clear our Stores of provisions (amounting to about 4500 lbs.) with the exception of a very small reserve at Fort Simpson absolutely requisite for the Summer and fall work, which must be attended to, unless we expose both Indians and men at the more distant posts to the chance of Starvation, a risk which I should not feel inclined to incur. Commander Pullen has got a carte blanche on all our other resources, which are more plentiful than could have been expected, and which the small trade will readily account for. He takes to the sea with him one of our large boats[205] (that has never yet been in the water) and one of his own small ones, with a crew of 13 men, and 2 Indians as hunters. Three of the men are Company's old Servants, engaged instead of two of the Seamen (John Senior and John Abernethy)[206] who return to England viâ Yorkfactory as unfit for active Service. The party proceeds to the eastward of the Mackenzie, as far as Cape Bathurst, and then strike out to sea in the direction of Banks land, the west side of which they expect to examine.

You will learn by a letter from Mr. Murray[207] that by information recently received from the Indians he is decidedly of opinion that the Colville and Youcon are not identical; but that the latter river falls into the Pacific, or at all events to the westward of Point Barrow, and that it was the intention of the Russians to build a fort at its mouth last Season: supposing that this report be true it appears to me needless to send any searching party in that direction as it is too far removed from the probable position of the missing party, who, if any of them find their way as far as Behring Strait, are pretty certain to fall in with some of the expeditions sent to that quarter. The coast between point Barrow and the MacKenzie has already been well examined by Pullen, and it is not likely that any traces of the lost navigators will be found there; as they would most assuredly make for the MacKenzie, could they get so far west as its mouth: under these circumstances it appears to me that the best plan I could adopt, would be to proceed this autumn, with two boats and the provisions & men sent from Red River, to Fort Confidence and winter there, during which two boats somewhat similar to those of Dease & Simpson could be built with which to descend the Coppermine next season if required. In the mean time, having first set all the work requisite to be done in a fair train, I would proceed on foot before winter Set in with two or three men to the mouth of the Coppermine, and to the north of Cape Kendall to examine Whether some Pemmican cached there in 1849[208] be still safe, of which I am very doubtful as the rocky nature of the ground prevented it being well concealed from the natives.

Should we be fortunate in procuring provisions during the winter, I shall endeavour to travel over the ice 12 or 15 days march to the Northward, along the Shore of Victoria or Wollaston Land; on my return, if unsuccessful I shall wait at the Kendall for the arrival of the Boats and descend the Coppermine as soon as it clears of ice, for the purpose of carrying on the search by some other route. To carry out this plan effectually it is requisite to have an assistant, so that I have taken the liberty of engaging Mr. Hector A. MacKenzie[209] to accompany me. He is very active and an excellent shot, and much liked by the men, whom he at the same time keeps in excellent order. He fixed on no terms but I have promised that he will receive £130 p. an: salary, and if he is as efficient as I expect him to be, he will earn that amount.

Expecting to receive additional instructions and information when I reach the Portage, I shall defer addressing you farther until then.

With much, respect, I remain
Dear Sir
Your most obt. Servant
John Rae

— JOHN RAE, RECD. 21. OCTR., ANSD. 10 DEC[210] —

[Endorsed]

1850
Fort Resolution 30. June

Portage La Loche 29*th July* 1850[211]

Sir George Simpson

Dear Sir
I arrived here with 3 boats on the 20th Inst.; but Mr. Bell did not make his appearance with the 4 others until the 23rd having been detained by heavy rain.

L'Esperance[212] reached the other end of the Portage on the 25th at which time your favors dated 15 ulto.,[213] and the duplicate of your instructions regarding the arctic Searching Expeditions that were to be set on foot were conveyed to me. The boats with the 14 men[214] and provisions for the Expedition came in company with L'Esperance's brigade; they must have been loitering by the way, as they should have been here about a week sooner, and I beg to mention that I do not feel particularly satisfied with the discription of men sent they are all, without a single exception Indians and half breeds, who, although good men enough for ordinary duties, are not so much to be depended upon in cases of difficulty as Europeans, and they are generally very extravigant and careless with provisions, a sad failing on such voyages or journeys as those contemplated. It appears to me that the amount of wages given was too small to enduce the best class of men to engage: however since these have come I must try and do the best I can with them, altho' I fear that will not be much.

In a former letter I mentioned the plan I intended to pursue, for the purpose of gaining some information or finding some traces of the missing party, and as the letters now received give me no further information or instructions it is my intention to follow it up. For this purpose I have engaged Mr. Hector A MacKenzie (who was on his way to Red River) at a salary of £130 p. an: to accompany me and have sent back two of the men[215] who wished to cancel their engagements, as I had more than I wanted, and thought it was better to lose a few pounds than feed and pay a man we did not require, for a whole year. One of the men who can act in the capacity of boat carpenter has been re-engaged for one year to take the place of the man now at Fort Simpson whom I shall endeavour to take to Fort Confidence with me to build the boats required.[216] An Interpreter[217] has also been engaged at £40 p. annum, for the time that his Services are required. Our party will thus amount to two officers and 14 men.[218] As an encouragement to those who accompany me to the sea, they have been promised a gratuity *of* £10 or £12 each in event of good conduct. This may be considered extravagant, but it is only fair, for they will then but be on an equal footing with the men who accompanied Captn. Pullen.

Of course we will have neither tea sugar nor soap as none has been sent in for the purpose and McKenzies River is so miserably supplied that we cannot sponge upon the people of that district, whose allowances have, for some years past, been so much less than they ought to be. In saying this I do not at all refer to the allowances of wines and spirits, but to curtailment made in the District. It is my intention to request Mr. Hargrave to procure me an Esquimaux interpreter from Churchill, also to forward the Halkett air boat, an azimuth Compass, Sextant, artificial horizon and chronometer as far as possible towards McKenzies River this fall so as to reach me at Fort Confidence before my departure in the Spring. The sextant, horizon, and chronometer which Sir John Richardson allowed me retain for a year were taken by Pullen. As the men will require some clothing &c. for winter 51/52 I shall send a small requisition to Yorkfactory for such articles as I may think requisite.

The quantity of dressed leather in the District has been so much reduced by the many additional people we have had to supply during the past two years, with this necessary article, that I shall be reluctantly compelled to take some bales from Athabasca, which were intended for New Caledonia: even with this aid unless the moose hunters be fortunate we will be unable to supply all demands fully.

Having said all that appears requisite on the subject of Expeditions, permit me to advert to District affairs which I regret to say are far from being in a flourishing state.

At the posts of the Youcon and Peels River[219] and at Forts Norman and Good Hope everything has gone on as favorably as we could readily expect. At the Youcon the returns on hand were very fair and there was so large a stock of provisions on hand that Mr. Murray hoped to do without any further supply of provisions from Fort Simpson: Lapierre's House under the charge of Mr. Hardisty[220] produced a large quantity of dried meat and grease; this post I have thought proper to place under the superintendance of the gentleman at Peels River, to which it is much nearer, than to the Youcon and the communication is far more easy and frequent. At Fort Good Hope a large quantity of provisions was collected during the winter and spring amounting in all to more than 60 pieces among which there were 15 bags Pemmican, upon this I had in a great measure depended for our fall business; but Captn. Pullen will have taken all or greater part to the sea with him. At Fort des Liards[221] the people were living from hand to mouth all winter and the Indians suffered much privation, a number of them being fed at the Fort; but although there were some deaths, none of them was from Starvation, but by a complaint resembling influenza. Mr. Pruden[222] whose management at Fort Halkett[223] appears to have been excellent, got over the winter with his one man, without any inconvenience. I learn that he (Mr. P) has improved his post so much in appearance principally with his own hands, that those who had seen the place a couple of years since would scarcely know it again.

By the arrival at Fort Simpson of Mr. J. Stewart[224] on the 8th June we learnt that the mismanagement of the west Branch business last fall has caused all the misfortunes at Pelly Banks that were likely to arise from so unfortunate an event.[225] On the 30th Novr. when Mr. Pambrun[226] and his 2 men were absent searching for food, the Fort caught fire and every thing in it was consumed with the exception of about 3 packs Furs and a little powder. Furs to the value of more than £800 were destroyed. During the winter great privations were suffered from want of food and clothing, until the 5th March when Dubois one of the men died, and his companion Foubister[227] shared the same fate on the 25th after eating all or greater part of his dead companion. Mr. Pambrun by great efforts managed to support life until joined by Mr. J. Stewart who came to Pelly Banks to obtain information and learn the cause that there was no communication from Fort Simpson, to which place he accompanied Mr. Stewart and is in charge there for the Summer.

Being absent at Fort Good Hope when Mr. Stewart arrived, I did not return until two days after when we immediately commenced preperations for sending off a half laden boat with the most necessary articles for Fort Selkirk[228] which Mr. Stewart thought he could get carried over the Portage (which is 4 long days journey) before the winter set in,—this I fear he may not be able to do, as the water in the Liards became very high some days after he started. But if any man in the country can get on in such a difficulty Mr. Stewart will, and he deserves much praise for having made so long and difficult a journey in coming down with but very little provisions for himself and companions. The Posts on the Lewes and Pelly have always been the most troublesome in the District, and the trouble and fatigue of the fall voyage to Frances Lake,[229] is a great cause that so many of the men leave the District as soon as their contracts expire.—and few will engage for a second unless they are exempt from this duty. It is my opinion that goods might be much more easily brought into that part of the country from the Pacific, and the returns taken out in the same direction.

As every effort will be required to procure a stock of provisions for the use of the District next year, I have made arrangements with the two Marten Lake Chiefs to bring their dry meat within six or eight days march of Fort Simpson early in the winter so that we might send sleds and dogs for it from thence as soon as there was sufficient snow on the ground; for this purpose they received a large supply of ammunition, and went away very well satisfied. By the old custom among the natives of that quarter (Marten Lake) they fire away all their ammunition before they think of bringing any meat in, and consequently they eat all the largest and fattest of the venison. A boat also will be sent to the North Side of Slave Lake with a careful man, before the winter sets in, to some place appointed by Mr. MacMurray[230] and the Copper Indians, by which means it is expected, if the deer be as numerous as usual, that a large stock of the best meat and fat will be procured which otherwise would not find its way into the store.

The accompanying abstract will show how miserably poor our returns for this year are, being about £2,300 less than last year: the principal defficiency is at the Post of the Peel River, Forts Good Hope and Liards. Fort Simpson itself is £700 or £800 better than it was the preceeding outfit. As the returns of Fort Halkett were not brought down except a few martens, upwards of 500 Beaver and a few other furs remain on hand there. This great falling off arises from various causes, from scarcity of martens and cats; but chiefly from the want of Rabbits which obliged the Indians to pass this winter at the fishing lakes instead of on their hunting grounds. I have now as far as appears necessary given a slight sketch of the affairs of the District, which I trust will improve in a year or two. As the men with L'esperance are engaged not to carry on this portage we are put to some inconvenience to provide horses for them, and the Company to much expense, as it has been found absolutely necessary to employ all the Indian horses at about 4 M Br.[231] ea: p. day, which were the lowest terms they would work at, and we had some trouble to get them to work for this pay without being promised to receive it all here from the McKenzie River goods.

Being extremely short of provisions at Athabasca, so much so indeed, that although we took less than was requisite, there only remained 7 Bags when we left that place. The cause of this scarcity is that only 16 pieces of provisions were brought down from Dunvegan[232] instead of about 40 as heretofore. Fortunately I brought up two nets with which we obtain enough fish to feed half our crew, and thus our pemmican may be sufficient to take us back to Athabasca.

In consequence of the late arrival of L'Esperance, the badness of the weather, the scarcity of horses and the great amount of work to be done, we will not be able to leave this for 6 days to come if so soon. With much respect

I have the honor to remain
Dear Sir
Your mo: obedt. Servant
John Rae

— RECD. 31., OCTR., ANSD. 10 DEC. —

[Endorsed]

1850
Portage La Loche 29. July
John Rae

Portge La Loche 1*st August* 1850[233]

To the Governor in Chief, Governor,[234]
Chief Factors & Chief Traders Northern Department.

Gentlemen

I beg leave to acquaint you that I arrived here with 3 Boats on the 20th ultimo, and Mr. Bell made his appearance three days after with the remaining 4 having been detained by heavy rain. Lesperance with his brigade and the two boats for the Expedition reached the other end of the Portage on the evening of the 25th and Bruce[235] arrived next day.

I shall now advert to the affairs of the MacKenzies River District, and I regret to say that my report will be far less favorable than I would wish.

In consequence of the late arrival of the Express from the Youcon, Peels River and the lower Posts on the MacKenzie I was unable to give you any information regarding the welfare of those places. I am now happy to mention that at the Youcon there were very fair returns of Furs, and so large a stock of provisions on hand, that Mr. Murray hoped to require no further supplies of pemican from Fort Simpson. The house is now perfectly completed and enclosed with very high and strong stockheads, and I believe it is as comfortable and snug an establishment as there is to be found in the country. Mr. Murray informs me that from news recently recently [sic] received from the Indians that the Russians are about to locate themselves at the mouth of the river, and it is also his impression that the Youcon and Colville are not identical: but that the latter falls into the sea southwestward of point Barrow. At Peels River the returns of Furs are miserably low; but both there and at Lapierres House there is a good stock of dried provisions, particularly at the latter place, which I am informed would, if abundantly supplied with ammunition, be as productive a provision station as there is in the country. Mr. MacBeath[236] was extremely fortunate at Fort Good Hope in procuring dried meat, of which he had 45 pieces and 15 Bags Pemmican ready for transport to Fort Simpson when I visited him in Spring.

By the failure of the boats to reach Frances Lake last Autumn some danger of starvation to those stationed at the posts on the Pelly and Lewes was anticipated. It is distressing to state that these anticipations have been more than realized, as far as regards Pelly Banks, at which place there appeared to be less danger than at Fort Halkett: as I had been informed that there had been a quantity of ammunition on hand at the former place, which was in part true.

Mr. Pambrun, finding that the boats did not arrive, sent his two men to fish, while he endeavoured to support himself by hunting. On the 30th Novr., when all parties were thus employed at a distance, the house caught fire and was completely consumed with about £800 worth of Furs and all the private property: three packs of Furs and a little powder being all that was saved. During the winter the party suffered much from hunger and want of sufficient clothing until the 5th March, when, having eaten all the skins one of the men (a Canadian named Dubois) died of starvation, and the other (an Orkneyman named Foubister) shared the same fate 20 days afterwards, having first eaten all or greater part of his dead Companion. Mr. Pambrun by hunting succeeded in keeping himself alive, until joined by Mr. J. Stewart and a man from Fort Selkirk with whom he came down to Fort Simpson, which place they reached on the 8th June during my absence at Fort Good Hope. Immediately on my return from whence, preparations were made for sending a boat with a light cargo of the most requisite goods as far as Frances Lake. This I deemed absolutely necessary as it was Mr. Campbells[237] intention to abandon his Post if no news was received from Fort Simpson by the 12 August, and it is very doubtful if Mr. Stewart will be now in time to prevent him putting his determination in force, as the water in the Liard was high. As the men had not yet arrived from Big Island, Mr. Stewart started on the 13th June with a very inferior Crew, expecting to meet Mr. Bell on his way down from Fort des Liards, from whom he was to take 4 of his best men; but unfortunately the boats passed each other without being seen. This circumstance obliged me to forward a Canoe manned by 4 good men and an Indian to overtake Mr. Stewart at or near Fort des Liards, when the surplus men and Indians were to be sent back as soon as possible to be in time for the Portage Boats; but as they did not make their appearance their services were lost for this trip and additional indians engaged. I beg to mention that much credit is due to Mr. Stewart for his energy and perseverance in coming down to Fort Simpson, from so great a distance with very little provisions of any kind, until he arrived at Fort Halkett. The affairs of that small post have been well managed by Mr. Pruden, and the returns were good when the circumstances are taken into consideration; but all the furs consisting of more than 500 Beaver and a few other skins remain at the Post, except about 60 martens and a few Foxes that were brought to Fort des Liards by the return of the sleds that took up goods there in the winter, at which time I requested Mr. Bell to forward an express to Pelly Banks, *if at all possible*. Had this been done much inconvenience would have been avoided, as Mr. Stewart would not have come down to Fort Simpson, but waited for the usual fall boats. Comparatively few furs and little provisions were obtained at Fort des Liards: the Indians were starving most of the winter, and a large party were dependant for subsistance upon fish supplied them by Mr. Bell.

At Fort Simpson little occurred worthy of notice, about the usual quantity of dry meat was received from the Marten Lake Indians, and the value of the furs obtained amounts to about £800 more than last season. Mr. MacMurray at his well arranged post of Fort Resolution had fewer furs than usual in consequence of 10 of his best Indians dying of a complaint resembling influenza. The valuation of the total returns of the District is £10,300 being £2,300 less than last year, and I fear that unless the rabbits increase the current outfit will show a still more unfavorable result.

Having had for the last two winters to supply so many additional men with leather our stock of this requisite article has been completely exhausted to recruit which may I beg that a quantity of not less than 6 or 8 Bales be supplied MacKenzies River from some of the other Districts next Summer, and I will this summer be under the disagreable necessity of taking 4 of the bales of Moose Skins now lying at Fort Chipweyan for the service of New Caledonia, trusting that Vermilion may be able to make up the deficiency.[238]

Our voyage from Fort Simpson hither occupied 31 days, and although the number of boats we started with was 8, they were reduced to 6 before getting to Athabasca, in the following manner. On the 25th June when one days journey below Slave Lake we were met by a government express by which orders were received by Commander Pullen for himself and party to return to the coast and resume his search for Sir John Franklin and party. It was requisite that he should have a boat to return to Fort Simpson, and we parted company at Hay River in Slave Lake on the 29th ulto. The supplying of Commander Pullen with the requisite quantity of provisions (amounting to about 4500 lbs.) will almost entirely empty our stores, owing to which I fear we shall have much difficulty in carrying on the fall business. The party now gone to the coast consists of 17 persons, vizt. 2 officers ten seamen, three company's servants and two Indians as hunters forming the crews of two boats, one a large Company's boat, the other one of the *Plovers* whale boats. In ascending the rapid at the Pelican portage, one of Mr. Bells brigade of Boats, having sheered out into the current and snapped the cable, was lost: as far as I can learn no blame can be attached to any one. The cable that broke had only been one season in use, and was supposed to have been strong enough. On arriving at Athabasca we found an old boat which by some repairs was made fit for service; but as only 16 Bags of Pemican were received this spring from Dunvegan, provisions were scarce, and when we left only 7½ Bags remained on hand although we took with us a less quantity than was necessary. Ever since our arrival here the weather has been most unfavorable for the transport of the pieces, not a day has passed without more or less rain, the Portage is on this account a complete mire in many places, and in worse order than it ever had been seen by the oldest tripper. This, the want of sufficient horses, the great number of pieces to be transported together with the Red River trippers being exempt by their engagement from carrying their cargoes to the middle station will detain us much longer than usual, and our provisions would have been finished in a couple of days hence had I not brought two nets with me, which being set in Mithy Lake supplied fish enough to feed half our party.

Seven boats being unable to carry the ladings of 10 an attempt was made to haul a boat over the Portage; but this it was found would occupy more time than I could spare, the plan was therefore abandoned, and one of the Athabasca will be taken, and another sent back thence time enough to be at the white earth Portage before the arrival of the Athabasca Brigade. I regret to be under the necessity of doing this but there is no other alternative.

Having received instructions to fit out another Expedition in search of the missing navigators, it is my intention to pass the winter at Fort Confidence and build two boats there with which to descend the Coppermine in the spring to endeavour to reach Wollaston land in attempting to do which I so signally failed last season. The men engaged to accompany me appear able, active, and willing; but instead of being all Indians and half breeds, I should have preferred a few Europeans among them, whom I think might have been readily procured by the promise of somewhat higher wages than were given.

Should LEsperances men be exempt next year from carrying pieces on this Portage, it is absolutely necessary that Desjarlais[239] be supplied from Edmonton with 25 additional horses, so that the transport may be effected without employing Indian horses, which causes considerable additional expense, as will be found the case this year, being compelled to employ them. Both the Carpenter and Blacksmith at Fort Simpson have given in notice of their intention to leave the service next year, others will necessarily be required to fill their places, as the services of neither of these tradesmen can be dispensed with. I beg to mention the excellent condition in which the cargoes of L'esperance and Bruce have been delivered, there is little breakage of any kind; but there has evidently much more care been taken of the packages in the boats under Bruce than in the others—indeed the bales, flour bags &c are so clean, that they appear as if they had just been handed out of the store.

I have the honor to remain
Gentlemen
Your mo: obt. Servant
John Rae

— J: RAE C F., TO GOVR., CHIEF FACT., & C. T'S, RECD. AT YF, 29TH AUGT. —

[Endorsed]

Circu.[240]
Portage La Loche 1st Augt. 1850

Portage La Loche 1*st August* 1850[241]

My Dear Sir George
Your private letters dated 16th April and 15th June[242] were duly received on the 25th ulto. from Lesperance and permit me to mention that with every desire to obey all your orders and wishes, I have been forced by circumstances to deviate from them as you will perceive by a letter which I have already forwarded to your address by Lesperance in which I enter rather fully upon the subject of Expeditions, it is therefore unnecessary to repeat here what I have already said. There appear to be difficulties and troubles to contend with in your extensive dominions this year, as

well as in other more civilized countries and McKenzies River has had its share of them, nor do I believe that these are yet at an end.

You will pardon me when I say that I do not think Mr. Bell a very fit person for the charge of such a District as McKenzie River, as the clerks or people with him do just as they please. Bilieve me I am actuated by no other motive than the good of the concern when I make this statement. Mr. Bell and I are excellent friends, and he is a worthy good man, but he has been all his life at outposts, where he could aquire no knowledge of businiss and it can scarcely be accounted a fault in him that he is ignorant in a great measure of accounts. My own knowledge on such subjects is shallow and meagre enough, and my playing the critic on the qualifications of another may appear very absurd, but I think the sooner Fort Simpson receives a new bourgeois the better for all parties. Mr. Ross know what duties are to be carried on there well enough, but he may not feel inclined to inform Mr. Bell on the subject, as he may rather prefer to have a joke at the old gentlman's expense.

Having last year requested leave of absence, I now beg leave to repeat the application, which I hope you will grant me. I will not pretend to be in bad health for I am not, but the continued anxiety which my various and ever changing duties has caused me has affected my mind, and memory so much, that even I feel a great change for the worse in myself, so that if you cannot grant my request, I fear I shall be obliged to leave the service. Should I take this latter step, I trust you will not suppose that there will be any ill feeling in my mind on account of your refusal, far from it Dear Sir George your kindness has been to me so constant and of such long continuance, that I feel certain that it will require years if not a life time to obliterate it from my my [sic] memory. My success in the country has been far beyond my utmost expectations and deserts, all of which I attribute to your kind interest. It is true that my means are not very great, and I cannot settle down as an *idle gentleman* to live on *my property*, but I have my profession and am not too lazy to attend sick people if I could find any foolish enough to trust me. If you can permit me leave of absence I would try to come out to Red River on snow shoes after returning from the coast next summer. I fear that I have given offence to Mr. Barclay the secretary as I have not had a line from him, in answer to my several letters. This I am sorry for, as he seemed very willing to oblige me when I was at home and offered to act as my agent in receiving and laying out my pay from Government for which purpose I gave him a power of attorney. The manuscript of my narrative has been lying for the last year with Sir Francis Beaufort into whose hands it was put by Mr. Barclay for what reason I know not. The latter said he did not like to ask for it and the latter forgot that he had it, so Sir John Richardson writes me.

My worthy friend Bell appears rather disappointed that nothing has been paid him for his trip to Bear Lake with the Government Expedition. He certainly had anxiety of mind enough in conducting the party from York Factory—but perhaps the each [sic] is still forthcoming. Should it not I think Goverment will have dealt rather shabbily in the matter.

By letters from my friends I learn that brother Tom has again failed in business but has settled with his creditors, who after a strict examination of his books, pronounced that his dealings had been all fair, the only entry that had been omitted being one of £2–10. or some such sum, in transactions of £37.000. Munro[243] has sold out of the Army and now resides in Hamilton having invested his money £2500 in such a way that it produces him 11 or 12 pr. cent a year. If he has learnt a little more prudence and economy this would give him income enough to live comfortably upon.

In a letter from Lady Franklin[244] she mentions having been in Orkney last summer and speaks in *raptures* (!!!) of our bleak rocks. She was frequently with my Dear Old Mother, and made herself a great favorite with every one by her kindness of manner and affability.

May I beg to offer my regards to Lady and Miss Simpson and with much respect believe me

My Dear Sir George
very faithfully yours
John Rae

Sir George Simpson
&c &c &c

P.S. I believe the goods were never received in such good order at Portage La Loche as they have been this year. The cargoes of Bruces boats are the best, the bales and bags Flour being as unsoiled as when they were taken out of the store.

J. R.

— JOHN RAE, RECD. 31. OCTR., ANSD. 10 DEC. —

[Addressed]

Private
Sir George Simpson
&c &c &c
Hudsons Bay House

[Endorsed]

priv. 1850
Portage la Loche 1. August

Portage La Loche *August* 1*st* 1850[245]

Dear Sir
As I am again ordered to visit the arctic Sea and as I intend following the same route I did last season, it would be very desirable to have an Esquimaux Interpreter if by any possibility one could be forwarded this winter from Churchill[246] to Fort Confidence. The MacIntosh air boat would also be very useful if it could be sent up. As Commander Pullen took with him the instruments left under my care by Sir John Richardson—A Sextant, artificial horizon, azimuth compass, and chronometer are very much required, indeed absolutely necessary if I get on new ground. I therefore beg of you if these Instruments are at York Factory to forward them with orders to be sent on by the winter express. If there are none of these at the Depot, would you have the kindness to cause to be opened any packages there may be to my address by the Ship, as I expect a sextant, azimuth compass, Telescope

and horizon out, which would answer the same purpose and suit me better.

Inclosed is a requisition for some Clothing &c. required for the men who are to accompany me to Bear Lake for their use winter 1851/52, to be sent into McKenzie River District next summer

I remain with much respect
Your most obedient Servant
John Rae

—— JOHN RAE, RECD. AT YF, 29 AUGT. 1850, ANSD. AT, 31 OCT.[247] 1850; MEMO. TO SEND A COPY OF THIS LETTER TO MR. C. F. ROSS, BY THE WINTER EXPRESS '50. ——

[Note added in pencil]
Memo all Mr. Raes property was forwd. to Nor Ho before the receipt of this Letter

YF 29 Augt. 1850
J H

[Endorsed]

Pub.
Portage La Loche 1 Augt. 1850

Rapid ½ way up Bear Lake River
River [sic] 30*th August* 1850[248]

Sir George Simpson
&c &c &c

Dear Sir George
Expecting that Captn. Pullen should he get safe back to the McKenzie, will send off an express for England as soon as he arrives at Fort Simpson, I take the liberty of addressing you a few lines to go by it.

We had a most prosperous voyage from the Portage to Fort Simpson, having been only 13 days "en route" notwithstanding the heavy lading of our boats and the large proportion of Indians forming the crews. We found Mr. Pambrun and all at the Fort well a good stock of hay boated home, and the crops both of Barley and potatoes looking beautiful although it was still early in the season (16th Augt.) no time was lost in getting the outfits ready for the west branch, and they were sent off on the 22nd in 3 boats under charge of Mr. Pambrun, who is to pass the winter at Frances Lake with 4 or 5 men. He will have 25 or 30 bags pemican for winter stock.

I am happy to inform you that Mr. Stewart and party arrived safely at Frances Lake with his small cargo on the 6th Augt. He had the goods carried a short distance over the portage and then put them "en cache" with 3 or 4 bags pemican as provisions for Mr. Campbell's men. The boat under Forcier[249] (as guide) arrived at Fort Simpson again on the 18th and formed one of the west Branch brigade.

Having a considerable quantity of iron work to get ready, we did not leave Fort Simpson until the 23rd having sent Marcellais[250] away with our boat the previous day, so as to get some birch for axe helves, sleds, boat timbers &c on the way down. Our party consists of 14 men vizt. 11 of those sent from Red River and 3 others (including the Carpenter and Interpreter) engaged in the District[251] with 2 women.

On the evening of the 24th we met Mr. Peers from whom I was sorry to learn that just as the men and Indians going from Fort Good Hope to Peel's River this spring, arrived at Point Separation, an affray took place between some Louchoux and a party of 7 or 9 Esquimaux[252] in which our people appear to have joined. Four of the Esquimaux were shot whilst none of their opponents (by far the most numerous) were injured. The Louchoux were as far as I can learn the aggressors. This is a most unfortunate occurrence, and will render it even less safe than formerly for a small party of whites to visit the sea in the neighborhood of the McKenzie.

The returns of the post at Peels River are miserably low, those of the Youcan now at Lapierres House are upwards of £1800 value. Mr. Murray is evidently an excellent manager and a very interested person, but unfortunately his men will not stay any length of time with him. This is a sad drawback at so distant a post, it being requisite to keep two or three additional men in the District for the purpose of changing.

On reaching Fort Norman we were informed that 10 of the more distant Indians of that place had perished last winter for want of food, part of them having been eaten by their relatives. This terrible occurrence was not caused by want of ammunition but by the scarcity of animals and partly I believe by previous sickness.

Having addressed you pretty fully on the subject of the Expedition from the portage, I have little now to add, as my plans have not undergone any change. Red River half breeds being of all classes in the country the worst adapted for forming a party to execute the work contemplated, being very extravagant and wasteful of provisions and not much enured to privations, I have little hope of doing much either for the credit of the company or myself unless circumstances are more than usually favorable—this however will not prevent me making every effort in the good cause and if the navigation is at all open on the coast in summer, we may be able to penetrate pretty far to the northward. 'Tis the spring journey over ice that I am doubtful of.

From others I learn that Commander Pullen intends doing wonders this summer. His object is to reach Melville Island, Banks Land and after that proceed to Port Leopold[253] where he expects to winter. If he does this, he will excel any expedition that has yet visited the Arctic Sea, at the same time I fear that if he attempts to push too far he will never be heard of again, although he has got two Fort Good Hope Indians as hunters, but should these become alarmed at their situation or distance from the coast, as they are very likely to be, little dependance can be placed upon them, even as chasseurs.

From the report of Messrs. Dease and Simpson[254] it might be thought difficult or impossible to build boats at Fort Confidence but I hope to get over this difficulty notwithstanding that our carpenter is not the most expert person possible at *making shifts*. The size of boat I contemplate having, is, 22 feet keel, 6 ft. 8 ins. beam and 2 feet depth from top of gunwale to upper part of keel. These dimensions are 2 feet shorter, and some inches broader than those of Dease and Simpson's boats.

As the men who arrived from Red River had little clothes except what was on their back it has been necessary to take more than half the clothing sent from Red River to supply their wants. The stock of provisions taken is 35 bags Pemican, 1 bag grease and 22 bags Flour including provisions for the voyage which is not I think more than we will require if we happen to meet with any strangers.

Our boats are now arriving with the remaining half of the cargoes, which they were unable to take up the Rapid last night owing to the lowness of the water.

With the hope of again having the honor to address you by the winter express, I shall now conclude and with sentiments of the utmost respect My Dear Sir George

I beg to subscribe myself
most faithfully yours
John Rae

P.S. Some pemican, Flour, Tea, Sugar, and Biscuit with a bale of clothing have been sent to Fort Good Hope for the use of Commander Pullens party or any strangers who may arrive there either alone or with him.

J. R.

P.S. I must apologize for writing on note paper but I have no other sort at present within reach.

J. R.

— JOHN RAE, RECD. 4. APRIL '51, ANSD.[255] 25 DO —

[Endorsed]

1850
Bear Lake River 30. August

Fort Confidence Great Bear Lake *28th October* 1850[256]

To The Governor, Chief Factors & Chief Traders of the Northern Department

Gentlemen

I beg to acquaint you that I arrived here safely on the morning of the

10th Ulto. after a tedious passage of 18 days from Fort Simpson, having been detained by head winds and stormy weather in this lake. We found the houses I am happy to say in excellent order requiring only windows, doors, and a coat of mud on the walls to make them comfortable winter quarters, and no time was lost in arranging the store, in which our Cargoes were housed and under lock and key before the evening. Next day a party was sent to Dease River with a boat to collect logs for boat wood, and preparations were made for establishing two fisheries at 6 or 7 miles distance. Having given directions to Mr. McKenzie, regarding the duties that were first to be attended to, I started on the 12th in company with two men for the Coppermine to see whether some pemican left at the Bloody Fall last autumn was still safe, and also to inform some Indians that were hunting in that direction of our intention of wintering at the "great Lake", a circumstance with which they had not before been made acquainted. On our third days journey we met with the natives (twelve men and their families) from whom I learnt that a part of their band had been down as far as the Bloody Fall during summer, and had eaten all the pemican left there viz. 3 tins[257] ea 80 lbs. although they were in no want of food. The Esquimaux had been there before them, and had removed a tent and many other articles but had not touched the pemican. As there was now no necessity for my proceeding farther (the pemican being so *satisfactorily* disposed of) we retraced our steps accompanied by the Indians and arrived here after an absence of seven days Some bands of deer were seen as we returned, out of which 8 or ten animals were shot. I found that the wood party had easily found logs, crooks, stem and stern posts and had procured enough of these in one day for all purposes required, but I was still in some anxiety whether the quality of the wood was suitable for building boats so light, as those I wished, required to be, it being mentioned in Simpson's narrative that the carpenter of the Expedition on which he was engaged, could find no boards sufficiently good even to repair their boats nearer than a days journey from the house.[258] We have fortunately found no difficulty in this respect; one of the boats is now completed, except a few of the interior fittings, and is a very fine looking craft doing her builder Kirkness great credit. Its dimensions are 22 ft. keel, 6 ft. 6 ins. broad, and 2 ft. 3 ins. high amidships, the boards being ½ or ⅜ in thick and the timbers bent birch 1 in × ⅝. The build is clinker and the rigging is to be two lug sails. The wood here although knotty is sound and so tough that not one of the boards split in bending notwithstanding that many of them were fitted in without being steamed.

The winter set in unusually early; the temperature on the 22nd ulto. having fallen to zero, the channel to the opposite island became covered with ice, and soon afterwards there was a foot of snow on the ground. Since then the weather has been mild for the season, which was for some time unfavorable for our fisheries, as the ice by continuing weak or breaking up and driving about prevented nets being set either in the open water or under the ice. As a number of the most active Indians had taken their departure for Smith's Bay before our arrival, we shall lose their services as hunters, but there are still as many here as we will require, if they exert themselves and deer are at all plentiful. So far we have been pretty successful and have at present more than two months stock of provisions (consisting of fresh and dry venison and fish) in store for all our party numbering 18 persons and 13 dogs.

Having one man more than is required I send François Savoyard[259] to Fort Simpson with directions that he is to accompany the packet bearers to Red River. It was expected that Savoyard would have been one of our best men, but he has been very dilatory in doing his duty, and when spoken to on the subject by Mr. McKenzie he was extremely insolent. As his book debts are already as much or more than his wages will amount to for the time that he is in the service of the Expedition, I hope that no advances will be made to him at any of the posts "en route", as he shall receive everything that is requisite either here or at Fort Simpson.

Two men and two Indians are to take our packet (which is to be sent off on the 3rd or 4th proxo.) to Fort Simpson; the latter are to return hither as soon as possible with some iron works that are required; of the former, one is to remain at Fort Simpson until the winter express from the southward arrives there, whilst the other is to proceed to Red River as above mentioned.

With much respect, I beg to subscribe myself, Gentlemen

Your most Obedt. Servant

John Rae

— C.F. JOHN RAE, RECD. AT YF, 14 MARCH '51 —

[Endorsed]

Circu.

Fort Confidence, Great

Bear Lake 28 Oct. 1850

Fort Confidence Great Bear Lake 1*st November* 1850[260]

Sir

For the purpose of relieving you from all further trouble on my account, may I beg of you to hand over to Sir George Simpson or any person whom he may appoint the Power of Attorney signed by me in March 1848, by which I empowered you to receive and invest my pay from Govt. &c. during my absence on the Expedition under command of Sir John Richardson.

I have the honor to be

Sir

Your most Obedt. Servant.

John Rae

Archibald Barclay Esq }
&c &c &c }

[Addressed]

Archibald Barclay Esquire

Secretary, Honble. Hudsons Bay Co.

4 Fenchurch Street

London

Fort Confidence Great Bear Lake 1*st November* 1850[261]

Sir George Simpson Govr.-in-Chief }
of Hudsons Bay Cos. Territories }

Sir

I have the honour to inform you that I arrived here accompanied by

Mr. H. A. McKenzie, fourteen men, two women and thirteen dogs in two boats, on the morning of the 10th ulto. after a tedious passage of 18 days from Fort Simpson, having been much detained by head winds and stormy weather in this lake before crossing to Cape McDonell, during which, we had several times to unload the boats and haul them up as a protection from the surf on the beach.

We found the houses here in very good condition, requiring nothing but windows, doors, and a coat of mud to make them habitable, and the store was arranged and the cargoes housed in it, under lock and key before the evening. As it was so late in the season not a moment [was] lost in setting about the requisite duties. Next day a party was sent with a boat to Dease River for logs, and crooked timber for boat building &c and nets were put in the water opposite the house, whilst preparations were being made for establishing two fisheries at six or seven miles distance. Having given directions regarding the work that was first to be attended to, I started on the 12th with two men for the Coppermine River with the intention of visiting the Bloody Fall to see if some pemican left there by me last autumn was still safe, and also to inform a band of Indians that were said to be hunting in that direction, of our purpose to winter at the "great lake" a circumstance with which they had not previously been made acquainted. On our third days journey when about twenty miles from the Coppermine, we arrived at the Indian camp, where we found 12 men and their families who set up a perfect yell of delight as they rushed out of their tents to shake hands with us. After giving and receiving the news and distributing a present of tobacco some peace was restored. I learnt that some of the party had during the summer been down to the Bloody Fall, and had placed a few notes[262] wrapped in oiled silk, (which had been supplied them for the purpose), on poles in conspicuous situations so as to be found by any parties of Europeans that might land in the neighbourhood. There being every appearance of an early winter, and no particular necessity for my proceeding farther northward, we retraced our steps accompanied by the Indians, and reached this after an absence of seven days.

As the best season for fishing had passed and many of the most active natives had left the neighbourhood to join their families at Smiths Bay before our arrival, I was at first in some apprehension that we would be unable to procure sufficient food for so large a party, having brought nothing from Fort Simpson but the Pemican & Flour required for voyaging: we have however been more fortunate than was expected and have now in store more than two months provisions (consisting of dry & fresh venison and fish) for the whole party.

From the description given of the wood in this neighbourhood by a former Expedition, it was very doubtful of [sic] any suitable for boat building could be procured close at hand. I am happy to say that no difficulty has been found in this respect, one of our boats being now nearly completed without a single plank having split or broken whilst being fitted in. She is a very fine looking clinker-built craft, of 22ft keel, 6 feet 6 ins beam, and 2 feet 3 inches high amidships. The planks are only ½ or ⅜ inch thick and the timbers are bent birch 1 × ⅝ inch.

Cold weather set in here rather sooner than usual. On the 22nd September the temperature fell to zero, the channel to the opposite island became frozen over, and in a few days after there was a foot of snow on the ground. Since this month began it has been more mild, which for some time was unfavorable for our fisheries as the ice by continuing weak or breaking up and driving about, prevented nets being set, either in the open water or under the ice. Both the people of the establishment and the natives are and have been in excellent health, only a few slight ailments among the latter and consequent application for medicines, which I need not say has always been supplied them when thought requisite.

The men have hitherto behaved well, with one exception whom I send to Red River in company with the winter Express bearers, as I have as many as are required without his services.

Expecting to have again the honour of addressing you before leaving this for the Coppermine next spring

I beg to subscribe myself with much respect

Sir

Your most obedt. servant

John Rae

— JOHN RAE, RECD. 11. SEPTR., ANSD. 15 DECR.[263] —

[Endorsed]

1850

Fort Confidence 1. November

PRIVATE

Fort Confidence Great Bear Lake *2nd November* 1850[264]

Sir George Simpson
&c &c &c

Dear Sir George
I have deferred writing as long as possible, in hopes that two Indians (that were left at Fort Franklin for the purpose of bringing any letters that might come in by the Athabasca boats,) might arrive before sending off our packet for the south but there is now little chance of that, and it will not do to delay any longer.

All the information worthy of notice, regarding our proceedings since arriving here, will be found in an official communication which accompanies this, so that there is little or nothing more to mention on this subject. My trip towards the Coppermine was a very pleasant one but it let me into a secret of which I had not previously been fully aware i.e. that a walk of 25 miles was quite as much for me now as 40 or 50 miles would have been some years since. Our reception by the Indians whom we met was one of the most joyous I have ever witnessed, but it had its disagreeables too, for I very narrowly escaped being clasped in the embraces of two or three elderly, wrinkled dames in dirty greasy leather garments, who were very affectionate indeed, and did not scruple to inspect closely the pockets of my companions extracting therefrom, doubtless unconsciously—plugs of tobacco and other little articles that suited their fancy; reminding me strongly of a somewhat similar scene, as described by a late celebrated Arctic traveller. How these poor people were to have passed the winter, had we not come here, I am at a loss to know unless they had betaken themselves to some good fishing station, for they had very little provisions and still less ammunition, although they had received a large supply at Fort Norman in the spring; but they are the most improvident creatures I have ever seen, frequently firing away 10 or 12 ball at a mark to test guns that they have been using for perhaps a year before. The whole party accompanied us to within a short distance of the Fort and killed 6 or 8 deer on the way.

Fearing that we would have some trouble in finding wood good enough for boat building here, I brought a few planks with me from Fort Simpson, but this precaution has been quite unnecessary, as we find the wood here better than that we carried with us from the McKenzie it being, although knotty much tougher. Yesterday the first of our boats was taken off the stocks, and it certainly does the carpenter "Kirkness" great credit. It is so light (notwithstanding that the wood is green) that two persons can lift it with ease, and 4 carry it without inconvenience. Being a sort of "Jack of all trades" (no recommendation I am sorry to say) I made the draught of it, as the carpenter had never before built a boat of the mould required. Of course there are none of my men that know anything about rigging a craft properly, but this I can easily manage, having practiced a little, some years since, at splicing ropes and roping sails.

Should I unfortunately receive no accounts next spring, of any of the vessels, that have been in search of Sir John Franklin during the past summer, having found traces of his ships or party, it is still my intention to travel over the ice northward between Victoria and Wollaston Lands in May next, for it would be extremely annoying to be stopped by the ice again as I was in 1849. My plan will be to leave this about the 1st of May, with the last load of our provisions for the summers voyage to be deposited at the Kendall and from thence proceed northward with two companions and a sled of three good dogs, taking another sled and dogs to be sent back from about the Bloody Fall, which I would consider our starting point and from which we will be provided with 30 days provisions &c consisting of

Bedding for 3 persons *large allce.*	24 lbs.		—Distribution—	
Shoes, Socks &c "	12 "		Sled with 3 dogs	325 lbs.
Tea & Sugar	14 "		Do. for 2 men turn about	70 "
Grease and *Brandy* for fuel	20 "		Do. " self to go in advance	40 "
Flour ½ lb. each pr. diem	45 "			435 Lbs.
Pemican 2 lb. each pr. diem	180 "			
Provisions for dogs (1 lb. ea pr d. dry meat)	90 "			
Instruments, Books &c.	24 "			
Presents to Esquimaux	4 "			
Ammunition	10 "			
Cooking kettle, axes, ice chisel &c	12 "			
	435 Lbs.			

To reach Cape Krusenstern or some of the Islands near it, from the Bloody Fall would take 3 days, then there would be still 12 days to travel outwards, in each of which, if there are no great obstacles in the way, we ought to get over at an average 20 geographical miles; this would bring us acquainted with 240 miles of new coast, and be a guide to my future movements with the boats, should the ice providentially clear away in the summer. If nothing serious happen, I can be back time enough to meet the boats at the Kendall, and descend the Coppermine with them. Could I accomplish this, it is to be hoped, that neither the great men at the Admiralty nor their Honors in Fenchurch Street, will think that I have been making a sinecure of my situation as person in charge of the Expedition.

It will be requisite during the winter to renew my acquaintance with snowhouse architecture, to accustom my teeth to munch and my stomach to digest frozen pemican and lastly to do with as little drink as possible.

The men have hitherto behaved well, with one exception (Savoyard) who having been in the Company's service formerly, I expected would have proved one of the best of the batch. He was found to be very dilatory in doing his duty, and on being spoken to by McKenzie on the subject was very insolent to him, and said something on going out of the hall which caused me to administer a *dose* of *manual chastisement*, but not to any great extent, as the fellow did not attempt to make any return. Savoyard is to accompany the winter express carriers from Fort Simpson to Red River, having enough of men without him. McKenzie makes himself useful and manages the Indians very well. Like most of his countrymen he is somewhat thoughtless and careless about provisions, but as a check I make him keep a regular account of receipts and expenditure.

As I cannot well swallow quietly the injustice that appears to have been done me at the Hydrographic office in leaving part of my discoveries in 1847 a blank on the charts, I take the liberty of inclosing another letter on the subject, which I would wish much to be sent to the Editor of one of the leading London periodicals (say the *Spectator* or *Athenæum*) if you think after perusing it, that there would be any use in doing so, for little confidence can be placed in my own judgement in such matters.[265] Another subject in which I would beg to trouble you is this. When last at home Mr. Secretary Barclay most kindly offered to transact some business affairs for me during my absence in this country, such as receiving the pay due me by Government for accompanying Sir J. Richardson, and investing it in some way so as to bear interest, for which purpose I left him a Power of Attorney. But as Mr. Barclays numerous and onerous duties, or some other cause have prevented him from honouring me with a single note or letter since I returned to America in answer to numerous communications from me, it is possible that the receiving of my salary from Government may have also been forgotten. Being wholly ignorant of how business affairs are conducted at home, I don't know if a Power of Attorney can be legally transferred from one party to another and still be valid. If it can, you would add another favor to the many for which I am already indebted to you, by making arrangements with Messrs. Pelly & Co., or any other whom you may think proper, to act as agent or agents for me. For this purpose I inclose one note to which an address may be added, and another addressed to Mr. Barclay both of which may be requisite. Even should you have the kindness to trouble yourself in this affair, all that I have said on the subject may be quite unnecessary for two reasons. In the first place Mr. Barclay may have already received the pay due to me, but in that case I think he would have mentioned it; again the transfer of the Power of Attorney may be a thing impossible or useless.

I am still desirous of coming out to Red River in winter 1851/2 and thence to England if you will grant me permission. It is quite evident that if I go the Arctic Sea next summer, it will be impossible for me to be back at Fort Simpson time enough to superintend the autumn business, which at that place is the most important of the year, as any mismanagement or needless delay at that time may derange the affairs of the whole District. In the event of its being required, I have taken the liberty of addressing Mr. Colville (Govr.), mentioning my application to you, in order that—should it prove successful—he may make arrangements to send some person to succeed me.

I fear that in addressing you about my private affairs and requesting your aid in settling them, I have taken an unwarrantable liberty; if so, I beg most humbly to apologize, and state that circumstances alone induce me to do so. I was unfortunate in the advice I received when in England last, (unless I had acted on that of Mr. Arrowsmith) by attending to it, I lost an excellent chance of obtaining one of the Geographical Society's medals, the plea urged being that if I sent a paper to the society the sale of *my book* would be injured—the book never appeared and likely never will now—you prophecied as much two years since.[266]

Requesting to be kindly remembered to Lady and Miss Simpson
With much respect believe me

Dear Sir George
very faithfully yours
John Rae

P.S. By the news in the latest papers I have seen, the money market appears glutted, if this is still the case, perhaps money invested in Canada would be more productive—will you be so good as act in this case as you may think best?.

J. Rae

I see that Mr. McPherson has sent in a package to McKenzie River from Canada addressed to me, but not *for* me, being for young Pambrun. I mention this, in case you might suppose that I had ordered anything in Canada which I wished sent by the canoes without requesting your leave.

J.R.

— JOHN RAE, RECD. 11. SEPTR., ANSD. 15 DECR. —

[Endorsed]

Priv. 1850

Fort Confidence 2. November

Fort Confidence *April* 17*th* 1851[267]

To the Governor-in-chief, Governor
Chief Factors and Chief Traders Ruperts Land

Gentlemen

Supposing that many if not all of you, take a deep interest in the fate of the long missing party under Sir John Franklin, and that the same interest in a less degree may extend to the Expeditions that are employed in searching for it, I beg to communicate for your information, a brief statement of our proceedings here.

When I had the pleasure of addressing you in the early part of November last, there was every prospect of our being abundantly supplied with provisions, but this expectation has been to some extent disappointed in consequence of the deer having moved off to a great distance in the early part of winter induced thereto, it is supposed, by the prevalence of easterly and S.E. winds which led the animals (as they generally travel head to wind) towards Marten & Slave Lakes.

This although injurious to us, has been very favorable for Fort Simpson where dry provisions were much wanted, and the Marten Lake Indians have collected a more than usual quantity.

During Novr. and December we received few or no supplies and our fisheries produced very little, so that in January our store was very empty indeed, notwithstanding that the men as a precautionary measure had been for some time put on reduced allowance. Fortunately our pemican was saved untouched by the opportune arrival of some Indian Couriers to report that there was a quantity of venison "en cache" for us six days journey hence, for which our sledges were immediately sent, and we have experienced no scarcity since: but the hard work in dragging meat so far over an uneven road has very much reduced our dogs and rendered them rather unfit for the spring business.

We have now enough of provisions in store to serve our party until the season for taking the boats across to the Coppermine arrives, unless we are very much burdened with starving Indians, of whom there are at present about 30, more or less dependant upon us. These according to the common custom in the country receive daily rations when unable to catch fish for themselves and I am determined that none are allowed to die of starvation as long as we have anything eatable in store, at the same time those that are able are made to exert themselves in setting hooks (for which they receive lines and baits) for trout, and spearing herrings. The latter mode of taking fish altho' very common near Fort Franklin, had never been attempted in this part of the Lake, until a short time since when learning from the fisherman that he had seen a number of small fish near the ice whilst setting a net, I made a small spear, and killed 70 herrings in a very short time. Yet this work easy and simple as it is (for a child might do it) does not suit the thoughtless natives here, and it is only by threatening to give them nothing to eat that they can be prevailed upon to attend to it at all.

The winter has generally speaking, been fine, few storms, abundance of snow, and some cold days. The coldest occurred in January when the temperature fell to 72° below Zero.

Our four sledges are at present employed hauling to the Kendall River the stores amounting to about 2,700 Libs required for the summer voyage to the coast. As soon as this duty is accomplished, which will be about the 21st Instant, I intend setting out with two Companions and 2 dog sledges on a foot journey to the northward. We shall take provisions with us for 35 days consumption, counting the mouth of the Coppermine as a starting point, and I hope if blessed with health and unopposed by any very great obstacles to examine about 300 miles of new coast or sea. Our fuel is to be grease at the rate of 1 Lib. pr. day. Bedding for all the party *one blanket* and one deer skin Robe, and our lodgings the snow-house, in building which I have refreshed my experience this winter, and have taught the men that are to accompany me to be very good snow masons.

As soon as the ice on Dease River breaks up, Mr. McKenzie with the remainder of the party and some Indians will transport the boats across to the Kendall where I shall await their arrival after my return from the coast.

It is my intention should I discover any extent of land or particularly if any traces of Europeans have been seen, to forward a couple of active Indians to Fort Simpson with dispatches, which I shall request all those in charge of posts "en route" to forward with the least possible delay, in hopes that it may reach Norway House time enough for the Fall canoe to Canada, or perhaps York Factory before the departure of the ship; at least there can be no difficulty in its getting to Canada, or to the States via Red River before the winter sets in.

All the men of my party that were engaged in Red River will be sent thither during the ensuing winter, unless I receive orders to the contrary and they may probably get as far as Athabasca by open water, if we have a favorable passage across this Lake, and the autumn fine.

Permit me to notice that Mr. Bell in his official letter of December last mentions that the "Arctic Expedition had cleared the Stores" at Fort Simpson, which was perfectly correct. But it should have been stated that it was the Government Expedition under Comr. Pullen that did so, as I took not an ounce of provisions (except a few dry fish for the dogs) from Fort Simpson with me: at the same time with great risk to ourselves I left at

Fort Simpson more than 2/5 of the Pemican and Flour brought from Red River last summer for Expedition purposes, as a reserve for Comr. Pullens Party this season or for any other service for which it might be required.

I have now only to mention that the health of the party has been excellent, not a man on the sick list all winter, and I hear of no deaths among the Indians, except those of two children who died of inflammation in the chest at some distance from this.

I have the honor to remain
Gentlemen
Your very obedient Servant
John Rae

— JOHN RAE, ESQ, RECD. 28TH AUGT. 51 YF —

[Endorsed]

Pub
Fort Confidence 17 Apl. '51

Fort Confidence *April* 18*th* 1851[268]

Sir George Simpson
Governor in Chief

Sir
I have now the honor to acquaint you with the proceedings of the Searching Expedition at this place, since my last communication in the beginning of November. At that date there was every prospect of our being abundantly supplied with food, but these hopes were not fully realized in consequence of the deer having migrated to a great distance Eastward, led thereto, it is supposed by a long continuance of winds from that quarter, which appears to have had an equally prejudicial effect on our fisheries, for the Nets so early as December produced scarcely sufficient fish to maintain the two men attending them. During two months we received scarcely a mouthful of food, which induced me to put the people on reduced rations, as a precautionary measure. Notwithstanding that every economy was used, our stock of provisions

in the beginning of January was very low, when most fortunately two Indian couriers arrived bringing the welcome intelligence that their party had a large quantity of venison "en cache" for us, six days journey distant. Our dogs and sleds were immediately sent for it, since then—having obtained supplies from other quarters,—we have experienced no scarcity, and have collected sufficient for our own consumption to last until the beginning of June, were it not that we are much burdened with starving Indians, about 30 of whom receive assistance from us, more or less, as they appear to require it. Twelve of these being women or old men who have no one to provide for them, are according to the usual custom at the H.B Co's. posts supplied with rations as regularly as our own people, not certainly in such large quantities, but enough to recruit their strength gradually.

These poor creatures are in a great measure indebted to their own obstinacy and want of forethought for the privations they are suffering. Some weeks since they received two or three days provisions to carry them to where their friends had been killing Musk Cattle, and some ammunition (gratis) to enable them to procure the means of subsistence for themselves. At the same time they were told where I knew by the experience of Messrs. Dease and Simpson and my own observation that deer were likly to be numerous. Instead of going there however, and living in abundance (which they would have done as our sledge drivers saw large herds of deer at the place pointed out) they went in the very opposite direction and killed little or nothing. The consequences were that they returned here so much reduced that some of them would scarcely have reach the house had not provisions been sent to meet them.

Nothing in my opinion can more clearly show the careless and unobservant habits of the natives of this quarter, than a circumstance that took place here some weeks since. Having learnt that our fisherman whilst setting a net had seen a number of small fish at no great depth under the ice, I had a spear made, and 70 herrings (equal to a weeks rations for one person) were killed in a few hours. The custom of spearing herrings is very common near old Fort Franklin, but had never been tried before at this end of the Lake and the Indians were surprised to hear of such a thing being done. Yet easy and simple as this mode of obtaining food is for a child—after a hole has been cut in the ice for him—can do it, we cannot prevail on the natives to practise it, altho' the weather has been so beautiful for some time past that it is a pleasure to be in the open air.

I am aware that it is foreign to the purpose in such a letter as this to enter into particulars regarding the condition and character of the aborigines, more especially to you, Sir, who know so well the customs at the Hudsons Bay Cos. posts and the general disposition of the natives, but my reason for doing so, is, the having noticed that of late years some credulous persons in England have been censuring in no measured terms, the conduct of the Honble. Cos. officers towards the Indians—a subject on which those would-be-philanthropists are personally in perfect ignorance and have little to found their arguments upon beyond the misstatements and exaggerations of parties known to be inimical to the Company, very generally for causes, which if fairly stated would tell not much in their own favor.

The winter has been unusually fine, with a great quantity of snow and but little stormy weather. January was the coldest month, on the 21st of which the temperature fell to 72° below Zero.

The health of the party has been excellent,—not a man on the sick list since we came here. We have heard of no deaths among the natives, except one or two children in the first of the winter at a distance from this, of inflammation of the chest. There are many of the Indians here much reduced by want, but whilst they remain near us, not a soul will be allowed to die of starvation as long as the store contains any provisions. Their own conduct forces us to give them less than I would wish to do, as were they to be supplied more abundantly they would make no exertions to obtain food for themselves by setting hooks for trout or hunting.

Our sledges are now employed hauling to the Kendall River the stores &c. requisite for the summer's boat voyage, amounting in all to about 2700 Libs weight to which some bales of dry meat are to be added. This duty will be completed about the 22nd inst. immediately after which I contemplate setting out with two companions on a foot journey over the ice and snow to the north. Our course will be in the direction of Banks Land through the supposed Strait dividing Victoria and Wollaston Lands. We shall be accompanied by 5 dogs and 2 sledges for the transport of our baggage. Our provisions will consist of Pemican and Flour sufficient for 35 days consumption counting from the date of leaving the mouth of the Coppermine. We will carry grease as fuel for the same time at the rate of one pound pr. day, which has been found sufficient to do our simple cooking. Bedding for the whole party will be one blanket, one deer skin Robe and two hairy deer skins to place between us and the snow. As tents at such a season would be mere useless lumber, I shall follow the same plan as when tracing the shores of Committee Bay, and make our lodgings of snow. For this purpose, I have during winter renewed my experience in snow-house building and the men who are to accompany me have become very tolerable snow masons. Our whole equipments including food for the dogs &c. will not exceed 560 Libs which is not a heavy lading for two sledges. In short, nothing that our few means would admit of, has been left undone, that can in the slightest degree tend to the advancement of the object of the Expedition, and it is hoped, that, if blessed with health, and if no very great obstacles oppose our progress, we may examine about 300 Miles of coast or ice covered sea, before the 7th or 8th of June, at which date I expect to be back at the Kendall, where, we will await the arrival of the boats which are to be brought across by Mr. McKenzie and the remainder of the party aided by Indians, as soon as the ice on Dease River breaks up.

Should I meet with any incidents of interest during the spring journey an express will be immediately sent off to Fort Simpson with orders that it be forwarded without loss of time to the southward in expectation of its reaching York factory before the ship sails, or Canada or the States before the closing of the navigation.

It has not yet been decided which direction will be taken with the boats during the summer. Much must depend upon the state of the ice and the observations made in the spring. The most probable route will be round either the east or west known extremity of Victoria Land and then to the N. Eastward in the direction of Cape Walker. I shall endeavour to be here again by the 10th Septr. so as to embark all the party, for Fort Simpson, unless instructions are received desiring that I should pass next winter at this place. To provide for such contingency I have forwarded a requisition to the Gentleman in charge of McKenzie River District for such goods as we may require, and which he will send hither if the services of the party are required for another season.

In the event of any accident preventing my return from the coast in spring, Mr. McKenzie has learnt to make the necessary observations for Time, Latitude, Longitude and variation, so that he may carry on the search during the summer in the boats without my aid, and a Memorandum has been given him for his guidance, copy of which I beg to enclose.

With the assurance that no effort, it may be in my power to make, in any way likely to lead to the discovery and assistance of the venerable Sir John Franklin and his gallant party, will be omitted.

I have the honor to be
Sir
Your most obedient humble Servant
John Rae C.F.

P.S. During the last three days we have had a great thaw which is remarkable here at this season. The temperature has ranged from 34° to 41° in the shade and much snow has disappeared. It will be unfavorable for our transport business.

J. Rae.

— JOHN RAE, RECD. 18. OCTR., ANSD. 15. DECR. —

[Endorsed]

1851
Fort Confidence 18. April

[Enclosure to letter from John Rae to Sir George Simpson, dated Fort Confidence, April 18, 1851.]

MEMORANDUM

Before taking my departure on a foot journey to the Arctic Coast I beg to hand you the following observations for your guidance during my absence.

It is almost unnecessary to say any thing on the subject of the common duties at this place, as they are to be carried on much in the same manner as during the winter, bearing in mind always that there should be no useless waste either of ammunition or provisions as our stock of both is far from large. You will also impress upon John Fabien[269] (the man to be left in charge during the summer) the necessity of care on these two particulars.

The most important duty you will have to attend to, is the transport of the boats across to the Kendall River. This work occupied Dease & Simpson's party 13 days, and mine, in 1849 a like time. However, by having favorable weather and following the route I took it may be easily accomplished in a less period. Two of the small streams through which you will have to pass are navigable only during the spring floods, which circumstance is the only cause for haste, so as to reach them before the the [sic] water subsides too much. But in no case allow even this consideration to induce you to hurry forward at the risk of damaging the boats, which ought to be particularly guarded against: and you will caution your men on this subject especially, and whenever there is any difficulty, let both crews unite and pass one boat at a time. Six or seven Indians will be engaged to assist you, to be paid a MBr. each, or more in the event of good conduct for every day they are employed. These with one of the men that is to summer here will make your party amount to thirteen or fourteen—a number large enough for any purpose required.

The ice on Dease River usually breaks up between the 1st & 10th June, possibly earlier, you will consequently about that time station there or send daily a trustworthy man (who may have nets set to obtain a supply of fish) to notice when the ice has ceased driving. After which no time should be lost before hauling the boats and baggage to the river and commencing the ascent of it. If there be symptoms of a speedy decay of the Lake ice, you might take the boats to the river, or as near it as danger from the driving ice will admit at an earlier date, but this you will be able to judge of for yourself.

It is difficult to specify the quantity of provisions that will be required for your party during the time you are crossing to the Kendall but I should consider 2 Bags of Pemican 1 Bale of dry meat, and ½ Bag of flour, amply sufficient, as in a few days after leaving this your Indians can in all probability kill deer enough for the maintainance of all. Should such be the case, venison is always to be used instead of Pemican or dry meat to save the two latter as much as possible.

In the event of my considering it requisite to send an Express to Fort Simpson, after my return to the Kendall from my foot journey, the Indian that has been engaged to carry it, will accompany you part of the way across, so as to meet the person I may send with despatches. On the receipt of these, they are, without a moments loss of time to be sent hither, where the Indian, and a companion are to be supplied with sufficient provisions (say 40 Libs dry meat each) and a quantity of ammunition, so as to start without delay by the shortest route to Fort Simpson. The guide will be paid 40 MBr. for the trip with 10 Skins additional if he performs the journey in less than 20 days. His companion is to receive 30 Skins.

As it is not improbable but an express may arrive here during my absence and before you leave this, you are hereby authorized to open any official letters or letters to my address that it may bring. If you learn by them that the party of Sir John Franklin has been found, or certain knowledge of their fate obtained, making it unnecessary to carry on the summers search with boats, you will as quickly as you can use every effort to get the stores &c now at the Kendall River transported to the forks of the Dease and "cached" there under the care of a man or two until the River is navigable when you will send one of the small boats for them. It would nevertheless be advantageous to leave a couple of men and Indians at the provision station on the Kendall to await my return.

Any packet that may be brought here after your departure should be sent after you by Fabien, and directions are to be given him to do so.

Should any unforeseen occurrence prevent my return from the coast to the Kendall in June, you are to endeavour to carry out the object of the Expedition in the same way as I would have done if present, with this exception, that you had better proceed in the direction as nearly as you can which I had previously taken, unless the men that accompanied me reach you in safety and report that there are no traces of the missing navigators in that quarter. In such a case, the route I would recommend is round either the east or west known extremity of Victoria Land and then towards Cape Walker if the land trends that way—but information from the Esquimaux may lead you to follow some other course.

With these harmless people you will carry on a friendly intercourse, and endeavour to gain their confidence which is not easy to do, as they are very shy and timid.

Whatever may be the distance that the ice permits you to advance you should commence your return, so as to reach the Coppermine by the 4th or 5th September at latest, unless the autumn is very fine and there is some advantage to be gained by a longer stay on the coast.

On your arrival here you will immediately embark all the Party and property of every description in the two large Boats, and proceed to Fort Simpson, thence,—if no orders to the contrary are received from Sir George Simpson, or Mr. Colville—on to Slave Lake or if possible Athabasca by open water, with the men that were engaged in the Red River Colony, who are to travel thither as soon as winter journeying is practicable.

At your earliest convenience you will forward to Sir George Simpson a brief statement of your proceedings from the time of my leaving this place to the date of your letter.

Having full reliance upon your solicitude to execute efficiently the duties assigned to you, I trust you may be successful in their performance and be blessed with health and favorable weather to carry them on satisfactorily.

Given under my hand at Fort Confidence
Bear Lake this 22nd day of April 1851

John Rae C.F.
Commanding A. S. Expedition

[Endorsed]

—Copy—
—Memorandum—
to Mr. H. A. McKenzie

Private

Fort Confidence Bear Lake 23*rd April* 1851[270]

Sir George Simpson

My Dear Sir George
It was my intention to have set out to-morrow for the coast, but we must defer doing so for at least one day as our dogs have not yet returned from the provision station, being three days later than expected, in consequence it is supposed of detention occasioned by a great thaw that occurred some short time ago. This will make Friday our starting time, an ill omened day—but I defy omens, at least such silly ones as this.

I have left this letter to the last, because being addressed to you, I consider it the most important. Regarding our affairs here I shall say little, as my official letter will give all particulars that are of interest.

You may readily imagine that this winter has from beginning to end, been to me a most anxious time and has added not a few grey hairs to my scanty wig. My health is however, excellent and spirits mounting daily in anticipation of my contemplated journey, which my two companions Beads and Linklater,[271] are equally as desirous as myself to commence; this shows that they have the right sort of spirit for the work. You may observe that our arrangements are somewhat different from what they were mentioned as likely to be, in a former letter The principal alteration being the carrying of five days additional provisions and taking two extra dogs. The latter change was made because I find the Indian dogs—tho' weaker—are much more hardy in every respect, and require less provisions than the common sledge dogs. What we require is great powers of endurance combined with moderate strength.

Had any uninterested person been witness of my numerous avocations for the past 3 or 4 months, it is very certain he would have enjoyed many a hearty laugh at my expence. Nothing from the securing of the buttons and seams of my travelling *breeks* to the splicing, fitting and serving of our boats' rigging but I had my hands at. Such duties and occupations for a C.F. may be thought infra dig. by my brother-*officers*, but I care little about that as long as the work is done to my mind. I cannot avoid saying a word in praise of our boats which please even *me* who am somewhat particular in such matters. They are really pretty looking craft, and what is better, they seem well suited for their purpose. The workmanship does great credit to Kirkness the builder who is to be paid wages at the rate of fifty pounds stg. pr. annum from the time of his engagement until the date of his embarkation at York Factory for England. This I hope you will not think high when I mention that one of the Cos. servants engaged to steer Pullens boat last summer had £58 pr. ann. If thought worthy of it by you, or their Honors in Fenchurch Street, I should be happy if Kirkness received a small gratuity but I have not hinted at nor intend to hint to him anything on the subject. The very rough sketch and draught[272] which accompanies this, will give some idea of the appearance of our sea craft—one or both of which *may* reach Leopold Harbour.[273] The good things there would be a great attraction particularly as one of the most likely routes for finding information of the missing party lies in that direction at least as far as Cape Walker. This is a mere fancy on my part, and not likely to be realized.

My men have improved wonderfully, the English half-breeds in particular who are, for any work about the place as good men as we could wish, but they may not be equally efficient on salt water. Of the Canadian half-breeds I can't speak so favorably, but I am weeding the *stock*. There were five here at first, of whom two (one of them Marcellais the guide) are sent to Red River. One of those remaining is son-in-law to Lesperance[274] (the guide to the Long portage) and is an active, strong fellow than can be bent any way, another has taken fright at the idea of going to the "great sea" and has changed places with one of the summer men, so there is only *one Camsteery*[275] youth, who being so much in the minority, can do no great harm even should he be mutinous, and I daresay there will be no occasion to use the "fortiter in re" to keep him in order, as I have generally noticed that most of his breed when not suported by numbers lost the little pluck they may have been possessed of, as soon as they got off their ain *middin tap*.

Should any of the many vessels that visited Barrows Straits last season winter among the ice, doubtless there will be a generous? rivalry among the several crews as to which can make the longest foot journies this spring in pursuance of their object. Were I less broken down and our dogs in better condition (they are thin as laths from continued hard work) I might venture to enter my little band as a competitor in the noble race, and perhaps might not be the last! but Alas!! "gone is my muscles brawny vaunt" that is to say comparatively, for there is still some work in me, but the amount is woefully diminished. Still it is likely we may do as much as some of the blue jackets who are not generally speaking famed as walkers.

We must do our best for our own credit, and that of the service, whatever the result may be. The arrangements made are perfect, considering our means—not an article from an awl to an ice chisel has been omitted that could in any way arrest our progress, whilst we carry not a pound weight uselessly. Our bedding *is* rather *luxurious* being 22 lbs. weight for all, but we can easily lighten it if not required. My whole toilet apparatus are a pocket comb, a tooth brush, towel and bit of coarsest yellow soap, with a wardrobe, which will boast of one flannel shirt (in addition to the shoes and socks absolutely requisite) besides my every day suit. We shall if spared to return look clean figures when we reach the Kendall River,—as grease is dirty fuel—but that is nothing as there is plenty of running water in June.

I am happy to learn by letter from Mr. Bell that affairs go on favorably with him at Fort Simpson and also at the other posts of the District from which news have been received.

Mr. McMurray at Slave Lake notwithstanding that his fall provision hunt failed and in consequence of the early setting in of cold weather and other adverse circumstances he was unable to send a boat to the northern shore of the Lake (by which he would have nearly doubled his stock of provisions) has enough grease and dry meat to make 50 bags of pemican. Mr. McMurray is a very efficient post manager and otherwise an intelligent man; I hope his claims, when his services have been of sufficiently long duration to entitle him to promotion, may meet with the attention they deserve. He is a half-breed it is true, but he is also a very interested servant for the Company. There is another clerk in this District whose claims appear to me to deserve *present* advancement. I allude to Mr. R. Campbell, who, altho' he has been—from many adverse circumstances—unfortunate, appears always to have exerted himself to the utmost for the Companys interest, under difficulties and against obstacles that would have daunted the courage or worn out the patience of most men. I do not know Campbell personally and can therefore have no object in interesting myself in his favour, except the firm belief I have in his merits. I am aware that latterly he was not held in high estimation by my worthy predecessor, for whose enmity to him I can discover no cause, unless it be that Campbell when corresponding with you, forwarded his letters *sealed*—A great offence under former management.

I know not what your opinion of Campbell may be and my using the little interest (if any) I possess for his benefit may appear impertinent and premature after so short a residence in the District, but in mentioning the subject, I consider that I am only doing my duty by one whom I believe to be a deserving man. Of another clerk in that quarter (West Branch) my opinion is equally opposed to that of Mr. McPherson but in the very reverse order of the former case. Mr. Pambrun was represented to me as one of the most efficient or the most efficient half-breed clerk in the District. I consider from the little I saw of him at Fort Simpson to be among the worst. McMurray, Hardisty and Pruden are all his superiors in every way. Pambrun is a powerful, active, and bustling fellow enough, but full of conceit, and quite deficient in management, a quality so very requisite at a bad provision Post. He wishes to leave the service and he will be no great loss to the District. I firmly believe that had Stewart been in charge at Frances Lake or Pelly Banks during the past two or three years, few or none of these melancholy occurrences that have distinguished that quarter would have taken place.

I regret to say that the health of Mr. Murray is in such a delicate state that a change of quarters will be very requisite for his recovery. He says he has addressed you on the subject and requests me to do so also, which is probably unnecessary, as Murrays abilities are such as to make him useful anywhere and he has got a very efficient person in Mr. Hardisty to take his place. Murrays irritability and harshness with men may probably arise from his bad state of health. This is the only failing he appears to have being in every other respect a most efficient officer.

I took the liberty of proposing to Mr. Bell that the removal from Peels River of Manuel[276] (who was implicated in the massacre of the Esquimaux last spring near Point Separation) might be desirable; this the man I now learn also wishes, so that most likely he will be forwarded to Canada, where he will be at hand, should any investigation into that unfortunate affair, be thought requisite.

The services of young Alexr. McKenzie P.M.[277] could well be dispensed with, as he has got nearly all the *bad* qualities of the *bad* among the halfbreed race, but perhaps if my friend Anderson[278] is placed in charge of the District, he may, as he is McKenzie's brother-in-law take him under his own special care and try to reclaim him. It would be a pity too for his worthy old father's sake, to use severe means until more mild measures had first been tried.

I believe Mr. Bell is rather tired of acting bourgeois on the *grand scale* (I speak comparatively) for he lately got into a small controversy with Murray of the Youcan, in which the latter had evidently the right on his side and Bell did not cut a great figure. He is certainly a strange person and very much afraid of taking responsibility on his own shoulders; to screen himself from which, I suppose, he has spread abroad an idea that I have still the superintendance of District affairs, a duty which I entirely disclaim, as far as regards dictating to the gentleman at present in charge, although I have gone so far as most humbly to recommend some changes which I thought would be beneficial, in the event of my being again required to take the management of affairs and the *arm chair* at Fort Simpson. It is very gratifying to find that all those in charge of Posts in the District whose opinions I consider of any value (and this leaves but two or three of the under strappers whose feelings are doubtful) wish me among them again as they dont seem to place much confidence in Mr. Bell. You may think me vain to mention this, but instead of vanity, I hope, it is a pardonable pride that I feel, to find that my efforts to act justly and impartially towards all classes, has been more highly appreciated than I could ever have expected by persons altogether strangers to me, the more particularly as I was a mere tyro in the District business. Our intercourse whether of a public or private nature has always been of the most friendly nature and I have almost invariably found the greatest alacrity and willingness to meet my views in every respect. But it is hoped that this consideration will not induce you to appoint me to my old charge, at all events for the next year, as Mr. Anderson is much better fitted for such a station than I am, being blessed with a clear judgment, and vigorous understanding.

I regret that Ballenden mentioned to you some particulars regarding the bargaining so common in this District, which I had written to him about in a private letter, for it was never my wish that they should figure in Council and be the cause of a resolution being passed, stopping all transfers between officers and men. I suspect that the prohibition of these will not stop the practise of bargaining as long as there are *gentlemen* mean enough to do it, for the sake of making a profit, particularly if such person be at the head of a District, as ways can be always found of settling accounts without having recourse to money transfers. This traffic was carried to a disgraceful length, particularly in the articles of tea and sugar for which a poor labouring man, would give any price, as he could only get 1 lb. Tea and 8 lbs. sugar to purchase from the shop, for a years stock. Whilst some parties ordered from YFactory 10 lbs. or more of Tea a part of which they retailed at an advance of 400 or 500 pr. ct. A Keg of sugar has been bought out of the Fort Simpson sale shop, and a quarter of it sold for as much or more than the whole keg cost, leaving the first purchaser ¾ keg for nothing. I mentioned circumstances such as these to friend Ballenden as mere matters of news, but said nothing about them to you, as I thought the past could not be remedied, and I was determined that if I could prevent them, such occurrences would not take place in future.

The failure of Pullens Expedition to the sea last summer has annoyed and disappointed him much. It won't help him to the other step up the ladder, which I believe—from some half muttered words he let drop—was the uppermost thought in his mind when he received instructions to turn back last June. The check he has met with has done him much good, and he now looks upon arctic voyaging in a very different light from what he did a year ago. *Then* "it was nothing, a mere bagatelle, an every day work," because he had found no difficulties—except those caused by the defects of their boats and other equipments. *Now* it is "*awful work*" the most severe and harassing duty he had ever experience "during his 22 years of a seamans life"; he had never been able to make a proper meal on our "*country fare*"; he was sick and tired of the work "and hoped to go to England *straight* this time"—and more to the same tune.[279]

Now let us compare his labours with those of the venerable Sir John Richardson in 1848, and the idea that Pullen has, of What *are* hardships, will not raise a very exalted opinion of his powers of endurance. Sir John had at least as much, perhaps double as much ice to fight against, whilst in addition there was a 13 days march over a most villainous country at that time all swamp and snow, whilst Pullen was not forced to walk a step.

Although all the dried meat that was supplied for Pullen's party to the coast, had not been long kept and in *our* estimation good, I am informed that much of it was thrown overboard as not eatable. I cannot vouch for the truth of this, but it is very probable.

Although both Pullen and Hooper[280] are *vastly* civil to me, yet for some cause or other which I cannot divine, and which they themselves would probably be at a loss to explain, they have an evident dislike to the Company or those connected with them, of which they make no secret this winter, as Bell is no check on them, and as they may publish some tales, that at least one of them has been most industriously picking up, from the playful fabricators of all classes in the District I think it right to mention to you some of the stories circulated in this quarter by the seaman.

Whilst the "*Plover*" wintered on the Asiatic coast Moore[281] the commander kept an Esquimaux girl in his cabin for purposes that were but too evident, thus giving a fine precedent of morality to his officers and men, who were no way loath to follow so laudable an example when they had the opportunity. When the captain and fair lady took an airing in a dog sledge or cariole, they had a *running* accompanyment of officers, at least, one before and another behind who did all the duties of labouring men in this country when during the winter a person travels *en bourgeois*, a luxury by the way that I have not yet enjoyed, having never had my foot in a cariole except when it was standing still with no *animals* tackled to it.

The prices paid to the Tchukchi for provisions appear to have been less than we give in McKenzie River to the Indians if we are to judge by what Moore says in his report[282] to the Admiralty, where he mentions having given to a *chief*—as a great favor,—a musket for the carcases of 12 deer whereas we have traded a number of guns here this winter for 8 deer each. But Moore says nothing of their selling spirits to the natives, and cheating them as much or more than the most rascally fur trader ever heard of. The plan was this, the trader pro. tem, gradually diluted the spirits very much, but this the poor Tchukchis had no means of finding out until the seamen (who were probably parties interested) put them "up to" a plan of discovering the imposition by holding a little of the liquid to a light, if it took fire all was right, if not the "brown skin" went back to have his "drap o' drink" strengthened. But the acute trader was still too knowing for the native, as on future occasions he reduced the strength of the grog as before or rather more, and then poured carefully on the top a little strong rum or alcohol, which being of less specific gravity remained on the surface.

When the boats were in the neighbourhood of Point Barrow on their way hither,—the *Nancy Dawson* Yacht being still in company—Pullen went on board that vessel. During his absence Hooper and nearly all the men scattered themselves among the Esquimaux women on the floes, when an opportune rupture of the ice took place, and caused a number of very ludicrous exposes. This circumstance I suspect Pullen is not aware of, as he is himself strictly guarded in his moral conduct. Hooper appears to be slightly the reverse of this, and is much dispised and disliked by his men, not one of whom he could induce to washes [sic] his clothes, or *cook and* clean his fish when he wintered at Fort Franklin so he was *obliged to* do these *duties* himself. We seldom here of such a case as this, even in Hudsons Bay.

I would not trouble you with these trifles were it not for the reasons previously assigned. These selfsufficient donkies come into this country see the Indians sometimes miserably clad and half starved, the causes of which they never think of inquiring into, but place it all to the credit of the Company quite forgetting that 10 times as much misery occurred in Ireland during the last few years, at the very door of the most civilized countries in the world, than has happened in the Hudsons Bay Cos. Territories during the last ¼ of century.

I had written a few remarks on Fitzgeralds[283] book (*Vancouver Island*) pointing out the exaggeration and utter falsehood he had brought forward as facts either for the support or foundation of his arguments, and intended to have forwarded them to you, but scarcity of paper, and other considerations caused me to change my mind. I had in it rather a lengthy notice of Parson Barnley[284] and the would-be saints at Moose.

Murray of the Youcan says in his letter to me, "The Northern Indians that were here in the fall, say that a large ship remained over last winter amongst the ice *straight out to sea* to the north of this. It must have been some vessel in search for the missing explorers, for the Esquimaux who had frequently been at the ship mentioned that, the white people had plenty to eat and that there were animals (I suppose pigs) on board".

What vessel can this be,? The *Plover*, the *Herald*, or a Yankee Whaler. I suspect it cannot be Sir J. Franklin, he would have no pigs on board.[285]

Peers writes thus "By the bye I suspect there are more *Britishers* not far off. My men on a recent visit to the Rat Indians saw a bell in their possession, larger than a common House Bell said they got it from their neighbours the Esquimaux who had during summer been visited by a party of white men in 3 boats[286] who gave them beads and shirts, said they were coming to build a fort near them and also they say there was a ship[287] far out to sea & they describe her as being internally like a house".

The 3 boats spoken of must I think be Pullens. He had beads and shirts with him but I cant say anything about the bell.

I shall now take the liberty of inflicting upon you some thing of my own private affairs.

For a wonder I received from Mr. Barclay a long letter, accompanied by a copy of my long looked fo [sic] book.[288] In the letter there is a detailed account of my trifling money affairs, by which I find that Mr. B. has been most attentive to them, but I suppose, because he had no opportunity of investing it, nearly 7 months of the salary due me by Government remained undrawn at the date of his letter. Should this sum be still available after the receipt of this letter, I should wish it, with any other sums that may fall due to me, until the total amounts to £700 or £800 laid out in Canada on mortgage or otherwise as may be thought fit by Mr. Finlayson who most kindly offered some time ago to transact any business I might require to be done in that quarter. For the purpose of enabling him to do this I inclose herewith a document on unstamped paper (which may be valueless) empowering him to act as my Attorney in Canada, whilst at the same time I have requested Mr. Barclay to pay to you or any-one you may appoint such sums (not to exceed altogether the amount above specified) as Mr. Finlayson may find a good investment for.

I do not wish to have *much* of my *little* in Hudsons Bay Stock[289] as I believe better interest with equally good security may be obtained in Canada.

It may be thought strange that having brothers in Canada I should request any one else to transact business for me, but I dont think either of them guarded enough and Tom is decidedly too fond of speculation without sufficient foresight and caution.

At the same time let me mention that by accts. received from them they are not now at all in my debt except for a small sum, which I alway considered as a gift not a loan.

In requesting your powerful interest in the matter about which I am now to speak I fear I may be trespassing too far on your kindness but I shall do so nevertheless craving pardon if I appear too forward.

I have a niece in Orkney (a natural daughter of my late brother James) who was brought up with every care by my *good* Mother and was admitted into all the little society of the village. She got married some years since to young fellow named Jobson (son of a Lieut. Jobson R.N) who had little to recommend him in a pecuniary point of view, but being possessed of a fine face, powerful and well built figure and a winning tongue he won the lassey's heart and they have lived most happily together since, although he occupies no higher station than boatman in the coast gaurd boat, the humble duties of which he performs I believe with every care and attention. He has a very fair education and writes a decent hand, is sober and good tempered so that I think he might fill some higher situation very creditably altho neither he nor any one has ever spoken to me on the subject. Under these circumstances I have taken the very great liberty of desiring him to write to you, should any situation he is compitent to fill be vacant, acquainting you with the circumstance, at the same time he has been told not to be too sanguine of success, for that instead of my having any claims on your kindness, I already owed you a larger debt of gratitude than I ever could repay.

I have spun this letter out to such an unreasonable length and entered into so many different details, that you will be heartily wearied before it is half perused. The style is also more free than I have been in the habit of using when addressing you, but I hope you will excuse it for this time as I happen to be in one of my buoyant humours brought on, likely by the prospect of the long walk before me.

I had a most friendly letter from Sir John Richardson by the York Ship, and so many *apparently* sincere good wishes from every quarter by the last Express, that, if good wishes are of any avail, I should be successful this spring and summer. Even Pullen notwithstanding our many little tiffs (and we had enough of them whilst together, tho' now very good friends) wishes me all success and thinks we are likely to do more than any of the ship Expeditions, which opinion, however complimentary to the little band here, shows that he estimates the travelling capabilities of his brother officers at no very high figure.

Begging to be respectfully remembered to Lady & Miss Simpson

I remain Dear Sir George
With high regard
Yours most faithfully
John Rae

P.S. Our people came in late this evening, the mild weather killed 3 of them, and the others became very weak.

J R

— JOHN RAE, RECD. 18. OCTR., ANSD. 15 DECR. —

[Endorsed]

priv 1851
Fort Confidence 23. April

Provision Station, Kendall River 10*th June* 1851.[290]

Sir George Simpson
Governor-in-chief, Hudson's Bay Cos. Territories

Sir

I have the honour to acquaint you that I with my two men arrived at this place today a few minutes after noon from the arctic coast having been absent 42 days during which the shore of Wollaston Land was examined to the eastward of Longitude 110° and westward as far as Longde. 117° 17, without finding any strait or passage leading to the north or without seeing any traces of Sir John Franklins party or obtaining any tidings of them from the Esquimaux we met.

I left Fort Confidence on the 25th April accompanied by four men, with three sledges drawn by dogs and a small sledge drawn by the men alternately on which our provisions and baggage were stowed. We reached this station on the 27th and were detained two days by stormy weather. This time was profitably employed in arranging our baggage and stores, repairing and strengthening our sledges, and in recruiting the dogs.

On the 30th everything being in readiness and the weather fine I started for the coast with two men (Beads and Linklater) and two sledges drawn by five dogs. A fatigue party of 3 men and two dogs accompanying us to within half a days march of the coast. In consequence of a great thaw that had occurred the previous week which cleared much of the ground of snow the travelling was extremely bad and although long detours were made to find a good road for the sledges they got much injured by the stones.

On the 1st May, we put en cache for our return journey a little pemican and Flour, and next day when 10 miles from the coast the fatigue party was sent back. After having much difficulty in crossing some deep ravines we reached the shore of Richardson Bay about 5 miles west of the mouth of the Coppermine near midday when I was most happy to find that as far as visible the ice to seaward was not unfavorable for travelling.

Being desirous of walking during the night to prevent the glare of of the sun on the snow inflaming the eyes we commenced our journey at 10 p.m. on the 2nd. The weather was unpleasant with a strong breeze of cold north wind as we directed our course as straight as possible for Point Lockyer. The ice being smooth and the snow hard we advanced rapidly until 8 A.M on the 3rd when we stopped for the day in Latitude by observation 68° 8' 44" N. The building of an excellent snowhouse occupied us 1¾ hour, during which our simple cooking was going on so that no time might be lost.

On the 4th we encamped on the beach five miles north of Point Lockyer where we found some wood for cooking, and as the weather was fine, no snow hut was required; the wind was however still sharp and a temperature of +10° made a shelter in the form of a semicircular wall of snow agreeable.

At 9 h. 15 m. p.m. we were again on foot our course being directed towards the N W end of Douglas Island, on which we landed at 3 h. 5 m. a.m. on the 5th when we cooked a kettle of pemican and flour with some wood picked up and put "en cache" a quantity of provisions for our return.

After 2 h. hours stay we resumed our march in a nearly N E. direction, when we built our usual comfortable snow dwelling on the ice.

At the same hour as on the previous evening we commenced our nights march and a walk of 1¾ miles brought us to a low point covered with debris of sandstone and limestone and a few boulders of granite.[291] The land was so low that from our snow house it appeared much more distant. We now turned eastward but had much difficulty in keeping along shore as there were several small bays and islets among which in the hazy weather we had some trouble to find our way. Under these circumstances rather than lose time uselessly I determined to travel over land due east leaving the coast to be traced when returning, at which time the thawing of the snow would have laid bare a greater extent of the shore and make it more easy to define.

On our second days march over an uninteresting track of low ground swamp and Lakes we arrived at the coast at 6 a m on the 7th nearly opposite to some large rocky Islands, and at a place where the shore presented a high sloping front. After two hours walk to the E by N along shore, we built our snowhut in Latde. 68° 31' 42" N Long 111° 30' W under a steep bank surmounted by some whitish limestone and reddish brown sandstone in situ. Here during the interval between taking the observations for time and Latitude I shot 10 hares. These fine animals were very large and tame, and several more might have been killed, also a number of partridges had it been requisite to waste time or ammunition in following them.

7th & 8th May. Our course for the first five miles of this nights march was nearly E S E. until we rounded a long point and crossed a deep bay in an East direction, some large Islands lying outside at a couple of miles distance from shore at first, but gradually approaching to within ½ mile as we advanced westward. These Islands I named after the distinguished Naturalist and traveller Sir John Richardson. They as well as the adjacent coast were high, rocky, and in many places precipitous. Specimens of the rocks have been preserved.

The land now turned imperceptibly northward to N 40° E, in which direction we proceeded 4 miles to the entrance of a narrow Inlet on the west side of which in Latde. 68° 38' 5" Longde. 110° 50' we stopped at 8 h. 30 m. A.M. but built no snowhut as the weather was not bad.

Previous to taking the noon observation and whilst supper was cooking I examined the Inlet hoping to find it a passage leading to the northward, but a walk of 2½ miles undeceived me. Several deer were seen but as we had abundance of provisions no attempt was made to approach them.

On the night of the 8th the weather was so stormy with thick snow that we could not travel, we therefore built a snowhouse and made ourselves comfortable, occupying our time repairing shoes, making up calculations &c.

Next night the weather having become better we resumed our march and travelled nearly three miles rather to the southward of East then east one and a half mile after which we crossed a point two miles broad in the same direction. We now traversed a considerable bay with low shores, our course being E by N. To this bay I gave the name of Welbank[292] after one of the Directors of the Hudson's Bay Co.

As we travelled onwards the land still continued low and had an easterly trending during the remainder of our nights walk, which was not continued so long as usual, the weather being extremely cold for the season. The Thermometer showed a temperature of 22° below zero which made the shelter of our snowhut more than usually acceptable. One of the men got rather deeply frost bitten in the face and the taking a set of Lunar Distances was rather unpleasant work. I have generally found that a temperature which in winter would be pleasant is in the latter part of spring almost unsupportably cold. The Latitude of our position was 68° 37' 48" N by observation Longitude by acct. 110° 2'.

The furthest point of land about six miles distant bore E S E, so that it appeared unnecessary to travel farther in this direction as my survey and that of Messrs. Dease & Simpson must have met here, although our Latitudes do not agree, mine being some distance south of theirs.

There were now two modes of proceeding open to me, the one being to strike over land to the north in search of the sea coast, the other to return along the coast and travel westward in hopes that some of the spaces of Wollaston Land left blank in the charts might prove to be the desired strait. I chose the latter of these plans because to travel over land in a north direction would be very difficult and fatiguing, and would always be getting worse, as the ridges of land (most of which were already clear of snow) lay *across* our line of route, so that a few days of warm weather would have made travelling with sledges and dogs very difficult, if not wholly impracticable.

The night of the 10th was very stormy with thick snow drift, but the wind being on our backs we commenced our return to our previous days resting place. After walking some time we fell upon our old track, which saved me much trouble in taking bearings, as they would have been often requisite the snow being so thick that we could not see to the distance of twenty yards. After a very cold but smart walk of rather more than 7 hours duration, we were very glad to find ourselves snug under cover of our old quarters, our clothes being penetrated in every direction with the finely powdered snow.

The weather on the night of the 11th continued so bad that we were obliged to remain *indoors*; but the following night was fine enough to allow us to proceed westward by our former track.

Our journey to Douglas Island was favourable. The coast from Latde. 68° 31' 40" N and Long 111° 30' W up to Cape Lady Franklin in Lat 68° 29' Long. 113° 5' was, with the exception of one high rocky point, low and indented with many bays of small extent, the general direction being nearly West. The weather continued good so that we arrived at the N W extremity of Douglas Island at a few minutes to 8 A.M on the 15th when we found abundance of drift wood to cook with.

As to return by Douglas Island would lead us out out of the straight road homewards, when we started on the 16th for Wollaston Land we carried with us the provisions we had previously put in cache. We directed our course to the most distant visible point bearing about N N W. and found that it was 9 miles distant; but in reaching it we were much delayed by rough [ice] in rounding which we increased the length of our walk very much, and a very heavy fall of snow stopped our farther advance.

Our next nights journey was rather long to make up for the time lost by the bad weather. For 13 miles our course was about N N W along a series of bays and points, the coast then ran north for some distance, and afterwards slightly to the eastward until we encamped on a small peninsula near the head of a bay in Lat 69° 1' 00 Long 113° 25' both by account.

17th & 18th May. We walked for 2¾ miles N 28° W. which brought us to a point on which we deposited some pemican &c having made another cache about seven miles from our former days sleeping place. We also left here a small sledge on which I had hauled from 35 to 50 Lbs. since leaving Richardsons Bay—two days excepted. We now traversed a deep and wide bay in a direction N 40° W. towards some high hills which appeared to be not very far off, but finding that we could not reach the coast there, I turned more to the northward and ended our nights walk on the west point of a small bay in Latde. 69° 17' 30" Long 114° 7' W.

Being anxious to discover how the land looked to the northward, and as a high hill about thirteen miles inland afford the opportunity of obtaining a very distant view, our next days journey along shore was only five and a half miles—the course being West.

Here I left the dogs and baggage under the care of one of the men whilst I with the other set out for the hill already mentioned but unfortunately the walking was so bad, that although we were quite unencumbered we could get no further than ten miles, when we returned rather fatigued to our sleeping place. Many partridges (Tetrao Mutus) were seen, but they were so shy that only 11 were shot. These birds are large and fine eating.

To the large bay we had just traced, and to a range of hills, of which the most prominent is the one I attempted to reach I gave the names of Simpson and Colvile in honour of the Governor-in chief and Governor of the Hudsons Bay Cos Territories.

During the journey of the 19th & 20th the trending of the coast was still to the West as far as our sleeping place, on a point with high limestone cliffs Lat 69° 15' 54" N Long 115° 24' 54" W.

The next night our course was to the north of west until within a mile or two of the end of our nights walk which was in nearly a north direction to the head of a small bay where we took up our quarters, in Lat 69° 24' 47" Longde. 116° 23' 34".

On the 21st 22nd we travelled nearly N W. for five miles which brought us to a cape with limestone cliff, at least 170 feet high. This cape was named after Captn. Hamilton R N. secretary to the Admiralty.

A couple of miles to seaward there were 13 Esquimaux lodges and we had an amicable interview with the good harmless inhabitants who were rather timid at first but soon gained confidence. It was difficult to make them understand that no return was expected for some presents I made them. None of the women showed themselves but all the men were well and cleanly dressed in deerskin and being all very fat, having evidently abundance of seals flesh and fat, large quantities of which were carefully deposited in sealskin bags under the snow. We purchased a quantity of this for our dogs, and some boots, shoes, and seal skin for our own use. After a most friendly interchange of signs and words few of which could be understood on either side we parted after six of them had walked some distance with us, both parties apparently equally well pleased with the meeting.

Our course was now N 36° W across a bay 11 miles wide, the north side of which was bounded by a curiously shaped point which I called

Pullen after the commander in the navy of that name who successfully performed the voyage from the westward of Pt. Barrow to the McKenzie River in 1849. To the bay the name of Lady Richardson was given. Three miles farther in the same direction brought us to an Island which was the terminus of our nights journey. This Island is high but not rocky, and about 3½ miles long. It received the name of Bell after a chief trader in the HB Cos. service. Near it to the east there is a small islet covered with large pieces of rugged limestone.

Next night our course for 7½ miles was N 33° E. to a point with limestone precipice 70 or 80 feet high the coast then rounded up to the northward until it attained a true north direction, and for a mile before we ended our nights walk a NNE course into a small bay where we rested for the day in Latitude 70° 00' 23" N Long 117° 16' 35" W.

The period I had allowed for our outward journey having now arrived I left our dogs and one of the men here whilst I travelled half a days journey farther as soon as we had obtained some rest.

At 8 h. 30 m. on the 23rd the night was beautiful as we started with no other incumbrarance except a gun telescope and compass so that we travelled fast over the hard snow and ice. After walking two miles to the NW we turned a Cape which received the name of Baring[293] in honour of the First Lord of the Admiralty beyond which the coast took a sudden bend to E by N for 8 miles, and then became more northerly for 6½ miles which was the farthest point reached. A high cape which was called after after Sir George Back[294] bore N 73 E about 7½ miles distant and bounded our view of the coast in that direction.

Near the place from which I turned back the land was fully 300 feet high, from which objects could be seen at a great distance and some land 15 or 20 miles off was observed the most westerly point bearing N 25° W, the view of its more distant eastern extremity being obstructed by Cape Back.

It is difficult to determine whether the water dividing these two shores is a bay or a strait, but from the little information I could obtain from the Esquimaux I suspect it to be the latter. Unfortunately want of time (as the interests of the summer voyage with the boats required my presence at this place) would not allow me to dicide this question.

Our return was effected at the same quick pace as our outward journey and we arrived at our bivouak after an absence of 10 h. with excellent appetites for supper to which we as usual did ample justice.

On the 24th May at 8 h. 25 m. p.m. we commenced our homeward route the details of which I shall not mention, except that the bearings and distances were carefully checked and several observations for Lat Variation and time obtained which the cloudy state of the weather prevented being taken previously. Where the depth of the bays were at all doubtful I made a circuit round them whilst the men and dogs followed the straight route.

We had several more interviews with the Esquimaux all equally friendly as the first. At one of the tents two of the women made their appearance and were not in the slightest degree timid.

All the land near the coast from Cape Lady Franklin to Cape Baring is so extremely barren, that although many deer cross from the main shore to it, they do not remain along shore but make their way directly inland too far for persons travelling as we were and abundantly supplied with food to follow them.

On the 30th May we reached our cache of the 16th and found it as well as two others perfectly safe, notwithstanding that one or perhaps all of them had been seen by the Esquimaux.

On the night of the 30th we crossed over, in as direct a line as the rough ice would permit, to the high rocky point north of Cape Krusenstern traversing a portion of Lambert Island on the way. Next night we reached the south side of Point Lockyer where a laughing goose (Anser albifrons) was shot and water was obtained without thawing snow.

On the 2nd June the extremity of Cape Hearne formed our head quarters at which place 11 geese, all in fine condition were killed.

Being anxious to know if a deposit of provisions left in Icy cove by Sir John Richardson in 1848 and examined by me in 1849 was still safe I deviated half a days journey from our direct route so as to visit it, but a deep snow drift prevented my attaining my object. As the Esquimaux appear to have a great respect for "caches" of any kind I believe it is still quite safe unless destroyed by wet or the barren ground bear.

Our next sleeping place was seven miles NW of Cape Kendall. Here 10 geese were shot, and double that number might have been got had we required them.

At 7h. 50 m. a m. on the 4th June we encamped on the south shore of Richardson Bay two miles east of where we stopped on the 2nd May. During the last two days there was much water on the ice and it was evidently high time that our journey should be approaching a conclusion. As the consumption of provisions for the coast journey began here it may not be out of place to mention that the quantity used in 33 days was 54 lbs Flour and 128 lbs. Pemican or nearly 2 lbs for each person per diem, with 1¼ lb. Tea, 2 lbs. chocolate and 10 lbs sugar for all the party during the same time.

We stayed a day here to arrange loads for ourselves and dogs and to make a cache among the rocks of, 30 lbs. Pemican, 20 lbs. grease (Fuel remaining) and several other things which we did not require to carry with us.

On the 5th June between 9 h. and 10 h. p m. we started for the Kendall lightly laden and came on to within four miles of our cache of provisions made on the first of May, and one of the men was sent to examine it, but found that every-thing except an axe had been either eaten or destroyed by a barren ground bear. We saw a very large one next day, probably the very fellow that robbed us, but he was too wary to allow us get within shot of him—possibly he may be less successful in avoiding us in the summer.

On the 9th when nine miles from this, a large musk bull was shot, and his flesh was found excellent—the skeleton will be preserved.

A short time after midday on the 10th we arrived here having been five days coming from the coast, during some of which we were 14 hours on foot and continually wading through ice cold water or wet snow which was too deep to allow our Esquimaux boots be of any use.

The latter part of our journey if not the most fatiguing was by far the most disagreeable. Through every hollow and valley a stream more or less large flowed, some of them so deep and rapid that we had often to walk three or four miles out of our course to find a ford and even then it was so difficult to keep on our feet that one of the men fell and lost all our cooking utensils, plates, pans and spoons, so that for two days we were compelled to use stones as substitutes.

Our principal food was geese, partridges, and lemmings, the latter being very fat and large were very fine when roasted before the fire or between two stones. These little animals were migrating northward and were so numerous that our dogs as they trotted on, killed as many as supported them, without any other food.

The dogs did their work well considering their leanness when we set out: had they been in better condition I have no hesitation in saying that our our daily journies would have been three or four miles longer. We were frequently delayed by rough ice but when this happened, we made up for lost time by additional exertion either on the same or subsequent days.

I subjoin a note of the daily and total distances travelled, counting this place as our starting point.

I beg to inclose a very rough tracing[295] of the coast examined. It has been done in great haste and without much pretentions to great accuracy, as I have many of my calculations to revise and several sets of Lunar Distances to work out. Some Islands are also omitted and the positions of others may require alteration.

In conclusion permit me to observe that the conduct of the two men who accompanied me has been excellent, and they as well as myself are in a much better state for commencing another such journey than when we left Fort Confidence.

Apologizing for the hurried manner in which this is written, my only excuse being the anxiety I feel that it should be sent off with the least possible delay,

I have the honour to remain
Sir
Your most obedt. servant
John Rae

Distances travelled

Kendall R. to coast				64	miles
2nd	&	3rd	May	25	"
3	"	4	"	27.5	"
4	"	5	"	23.0	
5	"	6	"	20.5	
6	"	7	"	19.75	
7	"	8	"	19.5	
8	"	9	"	—	stormy
9	"	10		21.5	
10	"	11		21.5	
11	"	12		—	stormy
12	"	13		19.5	
13	"	14		20.25	
14	"	15		21.	
15	"	16		10½	thick snow
16	"	17	"	26.75	
17	"	18		25.5	
18	"	19		5.	{ along coast
				20.	inland
19	"	20		23	
				413.75	

20th	and	21st	May	22.25	miles
21	"	22		19.75	
22	"	23		23.50	
23	"	24		31.	
24	"	25		23	
25	"	26		18.75	
26	"	27		23.25	
27	"	28		23	
28	"	29		24.5	
29	"	30		21.	
30		31.		16.5	

31st	&	1	June	21	
1st	&	2	"	25.5	
2	"	3		23.0	
3	"	4		19.5	
4	&	5		—	did not travel
5	to	10		75.0	
				410.50	
				413.75	
				824.25	Geographical miles
			or	942.	English miles

[Endorsed]

Jno. Rae
June 10/51

Private

Provision Station Kendall River 10*th June* 1851[296]

Sir George Simpson

My Dear Sir George
The very ill written official despatch that I have addressed to you will inform you that I have returned once more from the arctic coast safe and well, with a prodigious appetite which we have fortunately abundance of provisions here to satisfy, the musk ox which I shot being alone equal to 4 or 5 deer.

I regret much that my journey although a long one (perhaps the longest ever made on the arctic coast over the ice) has been so unsatisfactory. It will however be the means of saving me some trouble with the boats in summer should I be fortunate in getting into open water with them. I believe the route I shall follow will be to the eastward, going round by Cape Krusenstern and hauling the boats across to Wollaston Land on the ice should it still be fast in mid channel, as I feel convinced a passage will be found along shore there sooner than among the numerous islands near mainland.

The spring appears to be more favourable than in 1849 and I learn from an Indian that McKenzie has got the boats nearly half way across to this place.

We have a large supply of Pemican and dry meat for the voyage—upwards of 30 pieces—and we intend to add to this quantity whilst descending the Coppermine, as its banks at this season generally abound with deer and musk cattle and one or two of the party are very fair shots although I find that notwithstanding that my eyes are failing I can keep pace with the best of them in killing game of any kind.

While writing this I am so sleepy that I hardly know what I am about. The same was the case with my public letter which may to some extent account for the many blunders in it. If it is considered of sufficient interest to be printed I hope you will have the kindness to get any mistakes corrected as I am certain there are many of them.

I would also desire much that a copy of it be sent in the first place to the Geographical Society as I should like to try to obtain the *medal*, which I can scarcely expect to receive unless my summer boat voyage is very fortunate and besides there will be so many competitors from the arctic coast and from other quarters that my chance is but a poor one.

I trust this may still be in time for the York ship or the Canada fall canoe. If no time is lost on the route there is no doubt about it.

I hope you have granted me leave of absence this fall as I would like much to travel to Red River in winter, and to facilitate our progress this autumn whilst the navigation is open, I shall attempt to take one of our small sea boats across to Fort Confidence if any of them are brought back in safety hither.

It was my intention to address a few lines to Sir John Richardson and Lady Franklin but I find that my time will [not] allow me to do so—perhaps you would have the kindness to apologise for my remissness.

Begging to be kindly remembered to Lady and Miss Simpson I remain most faithfully and respectfully yours

John Rae

P.S. I stood the journey much better than I anticipated. The heart did its work well, and the legs also did not fail me—although when passing among rough ice I had a twitch or two in one of knees that had been formerly sprained.

J R

[Written on back]
Whilst writing in this leather tent, the dust and ashes are flying about so much that my paper gets soiled all over. The Indians too have been a great pest, there is no keeping the rogues quiet.

J R

— JOHN RAE, RECD. 27. NOVR., ANSD. 15 DECR. —

[Endorsed]

priv 1851
Kendall River 10. June

Fort Simpson 27*th September* 1851[297]

Sir
Having in my report, dated at the Kendall River on the 11th June, & addressed to Sir George Simpson, communicated the details and result of my spring journey over the ice and snow along the Arctic Shores, I have now the honor to acquaint you that, the boat expedition under my command which visited the polar sea this summer, arrived here yesterday in safety, but I regret to say, without having gained any information of the missing explorers.

On the 13th June, exactly three days after my return from the coast, the boats from Fort Confidence joined me at the Kendall River, having made a most expeditious trip across, of only six and a half days.

On the 15th, we ran down to the confluence of the Kendall and Coppermine Rivers, the water being so high in the former, that although we had on board full cargoes we did not touch a stone. The latter stream was still covered with ice, which did not break up until the 18th.

About noon on the 20th, there being a clear passage, we commenced the descent of the river, more for the purpose of getting to better hunting grounds than for any other object, as the season was still too early for the ice on the coast to be broken up. In the evening we encamped at the great bend of the river, about seven miles above the first rapid. Here we remained two days, during which six deer and four musk cattle were shot, the greater part of their flesh was partially dried over a fire for future use.

23rd June. In the evening we ran down to the Rapid which looked so formidable, owing to the great height of the water, that the steersmen, although daring almost to recklessness, would not venture to run the boats down, even without their cargoes.

Next day a portage was made, and the boats launched over a point of rocks. Finding some of the rapids a few miles farther down so very rough, that notwithstanding the excellent qualities of our boats they shipped much water, we encamped again to allow the river to subside a little, before passing through the more dangerous portions of the stream.

During our stay of four days the water fell but little, and my patience being exhausted, we continued our voyage.

At every rapid, notwithstanding the care and coolness of the steersmen, much water was shipped and when we came to the Escape Rapid, we found the rock that had endangered the safety of Simpson's boat in 1838 was completely hid from view shewing thereby that the height of water was considerably greater now, than at that period: we passed down in safety but the boats were nearly half filled.

In the evening we encamped at the Bloody Fall, and had not been there more than 15 minutes, when 40 salmon were taken in a net set in the eddy below the fall.

Having deposited a bag of pemican and a bale of dry meat, "en cache", in a small Island, we proceeded to the mouth of the river, near which we remained for some time, killing deer, fish, and geese enough to support the party. The weather was extremely beautiful, and the ice along shore wasted fast under the influence of the sun's rays.

On the 5th July, a slight breeze from the south opened a narrow channel along shore to the eastward, of which immediate advantage was taken, and we gained twenty two miles before evening, when we came again to the fixed ice.

It had been my intention, to follow the coast to Cape Krusenstern, and from thence cross over to Wollaston Land, but as the ice except in Back's inlet, was still strong and solid to the beach in that direction, I deemed it best to take advantage of the first open water.

Our passage along shore was slow and difficult. In many places the ice lay against the rocks, and compelled us to make portages, which although arduous duty to those unaccustomed to it, gave my men comparatively little annoyance.

On the morning of the 16th July we rounded Cape Barrow whilst torrents of rain were falling. From the high rocks, as soon as the weather cleared, a good view to the eastward across Coronation Gulf was obtained, The prospect was far from promising, the whole sea, as far as it was visible, being covered with an unbroken sheet of ice, on which a great many seals were seen. Our days voyage terminated within 3 miles of Detention Harbour, which is separated from Inman Harbour on the west side of the Cape by an Isthmus not more than 200 yards wide.

The passage across the Gulf was very slow. We had to make the complete circuit of Moore Bay, and it was not until the 20th that we reached Walker Bay, having found a narrow, but very crooked lane of open water, among the Wilmot Group north of Mareet Island.

On the 22nd, a fresh breeze from S.E. opened a channel across Riley Bay to Cape Flinders, of which we immediately availed ourselves. When near the Cape, we had an interview with 3 Esquimaux, and others were seen on a neighbouring Island. These people appeared to have been poorly fed, as they were much leaner than Esquimaux generally are. They had never been in communication with whites before, and were at first much alarmed, but we very soon gained their complete confidence.

We arrived at Cape Alexander on the 24th, being two days earlier than Dease and Simpson in 1839.

The ice in the strait was still unbroken, but along shore eastward, as far as visible, there was an open passage of a mile or more in width. This, however, was of little advantage, as my intention was to cross from our present position to Victoria Land, as the strait was here narrower than at any other point.

Had Geographical discovery been the object of the expedition, I would have followed the coast eastward to Simpson Strait, and then crossed over towards Cape Franklin. This course however, would have been a deviation from the route I had marked out for myself, and would have exposed me to the charge of having lost sight of the duty committed to me.

The ice having broken up on the 27th we pushed our way among the loose pieces, to the nearest of the Finlayson Islands, and had afterwards little difficulty in reaching the one nearest to Victoria Land, on which we passed the night, as the ice was again in our way. A gale of NW wind having during the next night and morning dispersed the ice, we made our way to a point, equidistant from our resting place, and the head of Cambridge Bay. Here we found shelter in a creek, the entrance to which swarmed with salmon, and 90 were caught by running a net across the stream. Few of these were large the average weight being about 5 lbs; and the greater number of them having spawned, were in poor condition.

Late on the night of the 29th, we arrived at the N. Eastern extremity of the bay as laid down in the Charts by Dease & Simpson, but I found, that it extended several miles further, taking a bend to the westward, and forming an excellent harbour, with a sufficient depth of water for vessels drawing upwards of 24 feet, and having good holding ground of sand or mud. Into the west side of this harbour a rapid river about 50 yards broad of beautifully clear water empties itself. This stream flows from a lake of considerable extent some miles inland, and appears to be a favorite resort of the natives, judging by the numerous stone marks, and several "caches" of provisions, clothing &c. deposited on its banks. Doubtless, this is an excellent fishing station immediately after the breaking up of the ice, as many salmon were still seen sporting in the transparent waters in the vicinity.[298]

During the next two days, a gale from West and W N W made so much havoc among the ice, that there was a clear passage opened to the East point of the bay:—and on the 1st Aug. 11h.a.m. the wind being still fair and more moderate, we started; but had not been off more than ten minutes, when it chopped round directly in our teeth and blew a gale, against which, having lowered the masts and sails, we had great trouble in making way with the oars. At length we reached a small island in the bay; from thence by plying to windward under close reefed sails, at about 4P.M. we doubled the point.

Our course being now east, the wind was fair, & aided by the flood tide, an hours sailing brought us to Cape Colbourne, where the examination of untraced coast commenced.

The shores at Cape Colborne are high and steep, but became gradually lower as we sailed eastward: when seven miles east of the Cape we landed to cook supper;—after 45 minutes stay, we were again under sail, and very soon came to the west point of a bay running up to the northward. This bay was found to be 8 miles wide, and apparently about 6 miles deep. Its eastern shore is low, and could not have been seen by Dease & Simpson from any point in their route; no doubt some high ground I saw inland, was mistaken by them for the boundary of the coast. I have therefore, in the rough chart[299] which accompanies this report, taken the liberty of transferring the name of Point Back to the west point of the Bay, whilst the bay itself is called Anderson Bay in honor of the Right Rev. The Bishop of Ruperts Land.[300]

The weather remaining fine and the wind fair, we continued under sail all night, our course being slightly to the southward of east. The shore was low, indented with small bays and having several Islets lying near it.

After advancing nearly 16 miles, we arrived at a bay of considerable extent across which, as the breeze freshened, we ran rapidly. The farthest visible point bore East (true), and the bay being eleven miles wide, we were about two hours in crossing. Here I was surprised to find the flood tide coming from the eastward, as hitherto it had flowed from the opposite direction. To this bay the name of Parker[301] was given:

its west point I named Sturt[302] after the celebrated Australian traveller, and its eastern boundary received the appellation of Macready[303] in honour of the distinguished tragedian. When we had sailed nearly three miles farther, we put on shore for breakfast: During our stay, high land, having the appearance of a large island, was observed through the haze, bearing E by S, and apparently about 18 miles distant. Fuel being extremely scarce, we were detained an hour and a half here.

Immediately after getting under weigh again, we commenced the examination of a curiously shaped bay, having an Island two miles in extent near its middle, and being divided into two narrow inlets near its head, by a long projecting point. The most northerly of these inlets was admirably sheltered, but I cannot speak with confidence of the depth of water, as I did not examine it closely. The name of Stromness was bestowed on this bay.

Some time having been spent in examining the shore and taking bearings, it was 10h 45m A.M. when we passed the east boundary of the bay—a low stony point, fronted with limestone rocks a few feet in height, which was named Kean[304] Point.

The coast now turned to the NE, and having a single-reef-breeze right aft with smooth water, the little boats ran along swiftly.

About noon, we passed among a cluster of small Islands, in the channels between which, the flood ran strong against us. I landed on one of these islands, and observed the latitude to be 68° 52' 21" N, the variation 68° 30' E.

The island, already mentioned as having been seen from Point Macready, was now not more than 10 miles distant. It appeared to be more than 15 miles in extent—high towards either end, but low in the middle. It was called *Lind*,[305] in honour of one, whose sweetness of voice and noble generosity, have been the theme of every tongue.

The general trending of the shore was still N.E., but its outline was irregular, being broken into strangely shaped bays and points. Having advanced 13 miles, we came to a point where the coast turned abruptly to the north. Tracing it for eight miles, we found ourselves near to what looked like the head of a bay, but on closer examination, a very narrow channel leading northward was discovered. It was so completely blocked up with ice, as to be unnavigable.

Altering our course to S.S.E. we ran round the south end of Taylor[306] Island, so named, as a tribute of respect, to the memory of the late much regretted President of the United States. We here got among very heavy and closely packed ice, which we anticipated, from having some hours before seen several very large floes aground in 5 fathoms water. The ebb tide being strong in our favour we made good progress to the N. Eastward, running some risk occasionally, of being nipped between the floating and grounded masses.

About 8P.M. we landed for a short time and then pushed on again, and at 11h. 40m. on the 2nd Augt. put on shore for the night under shelter of the most easterly point of the Island, on the outer extremity of which, the ice was forced up so as to form an insurmountable barrier to farther advance. The place at which we landed and its neighbourhood were barren in the extreme. Scarcely a vestige of vegetation, and not a bit of drift wood, were to be seen:—nothing but a level tract of light grey coloured limestone, which had been forced up in immense blocks, close to the shore, by the pressure of the ice. The stone was in many places covered with minute brown coloured crystals.

Next day our position was ascertained by observation to be in latitude 69° 12' 20" N, Longde. by Chronr. 101° 58' 15" W. The variation of the compass was found to be 58° 58' East, but as the needle was extremely sluggish, and evidently acted upon by local attraction, little reliance could be placed upon it.

It will be observed that, we had been extremely fortunate, and had made an excellent run of more than one hundred miles, without a single stoppage, except the detention requisite for cooking.

During the whole of the 3rd August, there was a gale from North with heavy squalls, and showers of sleet and snow. In the intervals between the showers, land could be seen to the N W by N, and N E (true), apparently twelve to fifteen miles distant, but the horizon was never sufficiently clear, to permit a distinct view of it.

The weather on the 4th continued much the same, but about

11h. A.M. the wind fell a little, and having shifted a point or two to the westward, a lane of water along shore was opened, up which we pulled to the N W, until we doubled some reefs which stretched out a few miles to seaward. Having rounded these we got into open water, set close reefed sails and stood towards land close hauled on the starboard tack, steering W.S.W. There was an ugly chopping sea running, but the boats behaved admirably, and a run of little more than five miles, brought us to the shore. The wind again set in from the north, increasing to a perfect gale, and although we could gain ground pretty fast by plying to windward, our slight built craft strained so much in the heavy seas that frequently washed over us, (in fact one of the boats had a plank split,) that we lowered sails on gaining a partial shelter from the land, and after a tough pull of 2 miles, during which we were sometimes barely able to hold our ground, we entered a snug cove, where we secured our boats.

5th August. The weather was still stormy, and finding that we could make no headway with the oars, our sails were again set, and we turned up to windward until the gale became too violent for our most reduced canvas; there was consequently no help for it but to put ashore, which we did on the north side of a long narrow bay; having gained about six miles. Satisfactory observations were here obtained giving Latitude 69° 20' 53" N Longde. by Chronr. 102° 30' 2" W and variation 63° 56' E.

On the 6th we could not start until the evening, and then advanced only eight miles, at first to the N by E, and afterwards to the W N W, passing some limestone cliffs of considerable altitude faced with deep snow banks.

A very thick and cold fog coming on, which encrusted every article with ice, we landed and were soon snug in our tents. Here a quantity of drift wood was found, being the first we had seen of any size since leaving Cape Alexander. The wood was poplar and must have grown on the banks of the McKenzie or some of the rivers near it.

The well marked Cape on which we now were, was named in honor of the Princess Royal.[307] It presents a precipitous front to the East & N.E.

Next day being clear and fine, observations were obtained, which gave the Latitude 69° 27' 6" N, Longde. by Chronr. 102° 27' 12" W and Variation 72° 30' E. The bearings of several islands and points in sight having been taken, we pulled out from shore due north, towards the highest visible land, passing between two islets near the shore. We were seven hours crossing, the distance being fully twenty miles, and the current during the greater part of the time against us. Soundings were taken regularly, the greatest depth being 22 fathoms on a bottom of mud.

Our landing place was a small point in a bay, on the shore of which, about a mile inland, were a cliff and some high ground, from which I had a good view of surrounding objects. To the S.E. there was a small peninsula a few miles in extent, connected with the shore by a very narrow ridge. Off the point west of us, there was a number of low stony Islands or reefs extending to the southward 4 or 5 miles: beyond this in the same direction was an opening in which no land was visible. Directing our course, under sail, towards this apparent passage, we passed between the most northerly of the reefs above mentioned, and the shore, through a narrow channel having barely sufficient depth of water for our boats, and continued advancing in the same direction, until it fell calm at 2h.30m. A.M. on the 8th when we landed on a small island at the entrance of a narrow inlet running north. Here we passed the remainder of the night.

It was past 7 next morning before we were under weigh again, and as there was no wind, we pulled up the inlet with the hope that it might prove to be a passage northward, but in this we were mistaken. When half a league from the head of the inlet, we landed, and ascertained our position by very excellent observations to be in Latitude 69° 50' 2" N, Longde. by Chronr. 102° 30' 46" W. After this, we pulled down to the southward and put ashore on the west point of the inlet, to pick up a piece of pine, the dimensions of which were 18 feet long by 10 inches diameter. As the wood was straight grained and free from knots, it had doubtless been carried to the sea by some stream far to the west of the Coppermine. The wood, being perfectly dry and not at all decayed, furnished us with sufficient firewood for several days consumption.

From some elevated ground in the vicinity, land was seen from

West to S.S.W., and as there were no indications of Esquimaux having recently visited the several points we touched at, and no signs whatever of Europeans having ever been on this coast, I considered that it would be a useless waste of time to examine the bay more closely. Having pushed off, we took a direct course towards the small peninsula, mentioned as having been seen the day before.

Here we landed at 9h.25m. P.M. Several snow Owls (Stryx nictea) were seen, and I may add that these beautiful birds were to be found all along the shore of Victoria Land, wherever there were any elevated spots of ground or large stones for them to perch upon.

A light breeze of north wind, that had been blowing for some time having increased in force, we again started and stood to the eastward under sail across a deep bay, with the ebb tide strong in our favour, until we passed between two small Islands, where we were met by the flood. In two hours, having run between seven and eight miles, we were abreast of the east point of the bay. As we advanced, turning slightly to the northward of East, we passed two more bays of small size. On the farthest point of the most easterly one, the ice lay fast aground and too closely packed to permit a passage: we consequently landed under the lee of the point at half past three A.M. of the 9th.

9th August. There was a gale of wind from N N E during the greater part of the day with a temperature of +30°. The weather was cloudy, but at noon a glimpse of the sun allowed me to obtain the Latitude 69° 41' 2" N. The weather in the evening being finer, we pushed off, and by pulling and poling, forced our way upwards of a league northward, when all further efforts to proceed, proved fruitless.

The prevalence of north easterly winds, during the remainder of our stay here, kept the ice close to the shore, and in the offing to the eastward, nothing but large pieces of very heavy ice, thrown up in great confusion, was to be seen.[308] By observation our Latitude was 69° 42' 45" N, Longde. by Chronr. 101° 23' 42" W. The compass was here perfectly useless, being acted upon, I suspect, by the large quantities of pyrites that were strewn along the beach.

On the 12th, finding that there was little or no prospect of change in the wind, preparations were made for a foot journey of a weeks duration to the northward. Leaving directions that one of the boats should follow us along shore if the ice cleared away, I started a short time before noon, in company with three men. As we trusted to killing both deer and geese on our way, we carried with us provisions for only four days.

Hoping to avoid the sharp and rugged limestone debris with which the coast was lined, we at first kept some miles inland, without however gaining much advantage, as the country was intersected with lakes, to get round which, we had to make long detours. Nor was the ground much more favorable for travelling, than that nearer the beach: in fact, it was as bad as it well could be, in proof of which I may mention that, in two hours, a pair of new mocassins with thick undressed Buffalo skin soles, and stout duffle socks were completely worn out, and before the day's journey was half done every step I took was marked with blood.

We gained a direct distance of 17 miles after a walk of 24 and bivouacked near the shore. Although we had passed a good many fine pieces of drift wood some time before, here we had difficulty in getting enough to boil the kettle.

Opposite our resting place, and not far from shore, was an Island some miles in extent, to which I gave the name of Halkett.

Next morning when we had travelled three miles northward, a large piece of wood was found, very opportunely about breakfast time. As the travelling continued as bad as ever, and as the whole party, were more or less foot sore, I resolved to remain here to obtain observations whilst two of my men travelled ten miles to the north, and the other went to kill deer.

The results of my observations were Latitude 70° 2' 36" N, Longde. 101° 24' 47" W and Variation 89° 30' E. The compass traversed here much more freely than it had done for some time past, which may possibly be accounted for, by there being no appearance of iron in the vicinity.

In the evening, the men returned rather lame, having walked 10 miles, as nearly as I could estimate by the time they had been absent. Their view northward was limited to 7 miles, and the whole shore presented the same dreary, uninteresting aspect, being low, flat, and stony. To the farthest point seen, I gave the name of Pelly, in honor of Sir J. H. Pelly, the Governor of the Hudsons Bay Company.

Next morning, we commenced our return, and reached the boats in eight and a half hours. During this short journey many deer were seen, and at least half a dozen might have been shot, had it been necessary, but we killed only two. These were in high condition.

The people left with the boats had, according to my orders, erected a couple of stone monuments. Near the summit of one of them a short note of the object and proceedings of the expedition was deposited.[309]

On the 15th the wind continued to blow most obstinately from the N.N.E. and as our boats were now in a dangerous position should the wind shift more to the eastward, I determined to run back a few miles to a safer harbour, where we could wait any favorable change in the wind and ice, and also if an opportunity offered, make an attempt, by getting under the lee of Admiralty Island, to cross over towards Sir James Ross's Point Franklin only forty miles distant.

This Island had been observed and bearings taken of it on the 8th August, but I omitted to notice it in the proper place. Having taken possession of our discoveries in the name of her Majesty Queen Victoria, we started, but a little before noon the breeze increased to a gale and shifted two points more easterly, and there being a great accumulation of ice between us and the Admiralty Island, I sought shelter under the lee of a point in Latitude 69° 40'. Here our stock of provisions being low, three deer were shot.

Large flocks of geese were migrating to the S.S.W. Golden Plover and other small birds appeared to take a S.E. Course possibly to visit the shores of Hudsons Bay, in their passage southward.

On the morning of the 16th it blew hard from N until 9h. A.M., when the wind subsiding a little we made another attempt to push across to Admiralty Island but with as little success as before, there being even more ice in our way than on the preceding day.

Being unable to advance either to the northward or eastward, I occupied the time in examining more closely the bay in which we now were, and which I named after His Royal Highness the Prince of Wales.

We steered nearly S W by W (true) as soon as the ice would allow, and as the ebb tide was carrying us somewhat to the northward, we made about a W S W course, and after advancing 21 miles we landed at 9h. 45m. PM near some limestone cliffs, on the south shore of a long point that projects into the bay in Lat. 69° 32' N Long. 103° 10' W.

During the early part of the 17th there was a thick fog, so that whilst coasting to the W by N, we had to hug the shore.

At 9h.30m. when on shore for breakfast, the weather cleared up and excellent observations were obtained, giving Latitude 69° 33' N Longde. 103° 33' 49" W.

We afterwards pulled seven miles W by N (true) obliquely across a strait to a point on which I landed to take bearings and obtain a view of the coast. Land was seen all round forming a wide bay. Near us, to the east, was a deep narrow inlet running south which was examined. After leaving the inlet we steered S E 5½ miles to a small island on which we landed to pass the night.

Our course the following morning was extremely devious, as there was so thick a fog that it was necessary to follow closely all the winding of the shore. In the forenoon and at noon our Longde. was 103° 7' 2" W, Lat. 69° 24' 51 N Variation of Compass 77° 30' East.

The general direction of the coast afterwards for 10 miles was N E by N, it then turned to E.S.E., until we arrived at the most westerly of the two Islets near our position on the 7th August. We landed on the small island in a short time and being again afloat at 9h.40m. P M pulled E by S to another island 9½ miles off, at which we arrived a little after midnight. Here the fresh track of a large white bear was seen.

On the morning of the 19th another attempt was made to force a passage eastward, but after an advance of 5½ miles we reached the close pack and there was no alternative but to pull back.

Having landed on one of the islands a round of bearings was taken, after which the wind being still from the N E we commenced our voyage homewards. Seeing that the ice lay close on the east side of Taylor Island, I steered between it and Victoria Land and found the channel dividing them open, It is about 50 yards wide and eight feet deep at its narrowest part.

In the evening we were much annoyed by both the old and new formed ice. The latter would have speedily cut our boats through had we persevered in pushing through it.

The morning of the 20th August being very fine and clear, land was seen in one or two directions in which it had not previously been noticed, and bearings were taken of it. The young ice did not thaw until 10h. AM, after which by great perseverance, we made very tolerable progress. Working all night and sometimes aided by the sails, at 7h. 15m. AM on the 21st we landed on the west shore of Stromness Bay and after staying two hours again pushed on, but the ice being lighter and consequently more closely packed on the shore, we had more difficulty in making headway, and were at last obliged to wait the rise of the tide at a point in Parker Bay.

Having remained here 3 hours and had an interview with a party of Esquimaux,[310] at 3h. 30m. P M we again commenced creeping along shore, and had proceeded but a short distance when a piece of pine wood was picked up which excited much interest. In appearance it resembles the butt end of a small flagstaff, was 5ft 9ins in length, and round except 12 inches at the lower end which was a square of 2¾ inches. It had a curious mark resembling this (S C) apparently stamped on one side and at 2½ feet distance from the step there was a bit of white line in the form of a loop nailed on it with two copper tacks. Both the line and the tacks bore the Government mark. The broad arrow being stamped on the latter, and the former having a red worsted thread running through it.

We had not advanced half a mile when another piece of wood was discovered lying in the water, but touching the beach. This was a piece of oak 3ft 8ins long. The lower part to the height of a foot and a half was a square of 3½ inches. Half of the square to the extent of six inches at the end was cut off, apparently to fit into a clasp or band of iron, as there was a mark three inches broad across it. The remaining part of the stancheon, (as I suppose it to have been) had been turned in a turning lathe and was 3 inches in diameter.

As there may be some difference of opinion regarding the direction from which these pieces of wood came, it may not be out of place to express here my own opinion on the subject.

From the circumstance of the flood tide coming from the northward along the east shore of Victoria Land, there can be no doubt but there is a water channel dividing Victoria Land from North Somerset, and through this channel I believe these pieces of wood have been carried along with the immense quantities of ice that a long continuance of Northerly and northerly easterly winds aided by the flood tide had driven southward. The ebb tide not having power enough to carry it back again against the wind, the large bay immediately south of Victoria Strait[311] became perfectly filled with ice, even up to the south shore of Victoria Land. Both pieces of wood appear to have come to shore about the same time, and they must have been carried in by the flood tide that was at the time flowing on during the previous ebb, for the simple reason that although they were touching the beach they did not rest upon it. The spot where they were found was in Latde. 68° 52' N, Longde. 103° 20' W.

All the night of the 21st we continued our course, sometimes having to cut a passage for the boats, at other times finding a channel wide enough to allow us to use the oars. On the afternoon of the 22nd when within four miles of the east point of Anderson Bay, we entered open water, and there being a fine breeze of North wind, sail was set. At 7h.45m. P M we landed on Point Back to pass the night, as the wind had fallen and the tide was against us.

The morning of the 23rd was very foggy, but a light breeze from S.S.E. sprang up at 4h.25m. AM and we sailed and pulled along shore to the east point of Cambridge Bay, near which we landed at 9h.45m. Here we repaired some injury one of the boats had received, and were off again at 1h. P M. The flood tide being against us most part of the distance we did not pass the most westerly of the Finlayson Islands until 8h.10m. P M, and a few miles farther on we landed on a rocky point to cook. After an hour's detention the breeze being favourable, we continued our course and during the night rounded Wellington

Bay which does not run nearly so far to the northward, as is represented by Simpson. The nature of the ground which is low near the sea, and high some miles inland may have easily led to an error on Simpson's part as he merely ran across the mouth of the bay without entering it.

As the morning of the 24th dawned the wind which had been blowing fresh from S.E by E gradually increased to a gale. Reef after reef was taken in, until we were under our smallest canvas. A very heavy sea was running which washed over us now and then from stem to stern and bent and twisted our slight built but fine little craft in every direction. At last the weather became so bad that I was reluctantly obliged to look out a harbour. This was dangerous work as we had to run almost among the breakers before it was possible to see whether the place we made for would afford a shelter. In this we were fortunate, and at 9h.30m. A M when 8 miles N E of Cape Peel we were snugly moored in a small land locked bay, the entrance into which was not 20 yards wide.

During the whole of the 25th there was a storm from the eastward, but at night the wind shifted to N N W, with an ugly cross sea. A little after 7 A M on the 26th we stood out under close reefed foresail and at 9 doubled Cape Peel. At 5 P M the wind fell and shifted round to S W, and half an hour afterwards we landed about 4 miles west of Byron Bay. After three hours rest here, we rowed onwards until 10h. P M, when the wind again favoured us, and we sailed on until the darkness of the night and the heavy sea caused us to beach the boats. Our present position was 16 miles west of Byron Bay.

Next day the wind being again in our favour, we made a good run and landed for the night on the SW shore of one of the largest of the Richardson group in Lat. 68° 32' N, Longde. 111° W.

On the 28th when we landed for breakfast at Pt. Ross, some observations were obtained which verified the position of that place laid down by me in the spring journey. From this place our run to the Coppermine was a splendid one. Stopping only once to cook, we sailed all night; at 3h.30m. A M on the 29th we passed by the south end of Douglas Island, at 5h. abreast of Cape Krusenstern, at noon opposite

Cape Kendall,and between 7 and 8 reached the Bloody Fall, not having seen a bit of ice since leaving Point Back.

Our consumption of provisions from the 20th June until this date was

4	bags Pemican 90 lbs ea.[312]
4½	bags Flour
150	lbs dry meat (principally given to our dogs)
70	" Fat

about 11 pieces

Twenty one deer had been shot on the coast, and many more could have been killed had I permitted it.

The water being very high in the river I remained a day to allow it to subside, and our time was occupied in strengthening one of the boats for the ascent of the stream. The other boat was to be left behind.

On the 31st although the water had fallen 12 inches, it was still much above its usual level, but as I had every confidence in the skill and coolness of my men, we commenced our upward course.

I believe that the Coppermine was never ascended in so dangerous a state. The ledges of rock along the base of the cliffs, which in the worst part of the river had afforded footing to Dease and Simpson's party in 1838 and 1839 were covered by water in consequence of which the men had to walk with the tracking line along the top of the cliffs. In doing this, although the line was a strong one it snapped four miles [sic], and other means were resorted to. After five days most arduous and dangerous duty during which the conduct of the party was most praiseworthy, we entered the Kendall River and encamped on its banks.

Simpson says somewhere in his narrative that it is impracticable to take a boat across from the Kendall to Bear Lake or vice versa, at any season except during the floods in Spring.[313] I was desirous of making the attempt, as by getting one of our light sea boats into the McKenzie much time would be saved on the portages "en route" to Athabasca.

Now that the high water would have been an advantage we had the misfortune to find that it had fallen to its usual summer level: nevertheless I determined to make the attempt.

On the 5th and 6th we ascended the Kendall and traversed the Dismal Lakes, at the Northwestern extremity of which we arrived about 3 P M on the last mentioned day. The guide was immediately sent to find the best route to the north branch of the Dease whilst the remainder of the crew carried the baggage a portion of the way over the portage.

To give a detailed account of the difficulties we met with and overcame would occupy too much space in a report like this. It is sufficient to say that on the afternoon of the 10th Septr., we arrived at Fort Confidence where I found everything in good order and more than 3000 lbs of dried provisions in store.

Having given my assistant Mr. MKenzie instructions regarding the payments to be made and the gratuities to be given to the Indians, I started at 10 PM on the 11th in the small boat with four men and an Indian for Fort Simpson, and arrived there on the 26th having been impeded in the river by continued head wind.

Late the next evening the large boat came up and the party were again united.

In concluding this report I have to express my satisfaction at the good conduct of most of my men. Two of the party, my assistant and a Canadian half breed did not behave well, but the others fully made up for any defects in these. Had there been a few steady European Servants in the expedition, it would have been one of the most efficient that ever visited the Arctic Sea. For voyaging, either during winter or summer no men could be better than those I had, but for several other duties they were not so well adapted as the men engaged by the Company in the Orkneys or Hebrides.

I have the honor to remain
Sir
Your most obedient Servant
(Signed) John Rae[314]

Archibald Barclay Esq
Secretary to the
Hudsons Bay Company
London

U.S. Biddle House Detroit 28*th March* [February] 1852[315]

Sir

I beg to acquaint you that I arrived here today, and that my search for Sir John Franklin has been fruitless.

The farthest point reached during the summers voyage on the Arctic Sea was Latitude 70° 30' N Longde. 101° W on Victoria Land, about 80 miles West of the Magnetic Pole. Here we were arrested by ice for nearly a fortnight and despairing of being able to push on farther we commenced our return on the 19th August. On our way to the Coppermine River 2 pieces of wood—the one oak the other pine—were picked up. The former, appeared to be a stancheon, in the upper end of which there had been a hole, through which a chain had evidently passed. The wood on one side of the hole had been torn away, as if by pressure against the chain.

The piece of pine looked like the butt end of a small flag staff, and had certainly belonged to one of H.B. Majesty's vessels, as there was a piece of line and two copper tacks attached to it, all of which bore the Govt. mark. The thread in the line is red. The line, tacks, and portions of the wood are preserved, and shall be delivered to the Admiralty or the Hudson's Bay Co. on my reaching England.

We had a quick but rough passage of 11 days to the Coppermine. Left one of the boats and a quantity of pemican at the Bloody Fall, ascended the stream with the other boat, transported it from the Kendall River to Bear Lake in six days and took it on as far as Athabasca Lake and two days journey up Athabasca River, when we were stopped by ice and obliged to return to Fort Chipewyan on foot.

On the 17th November (after a detention of three weeks) the ice having become sufficiently strong for travelling I started in company with 8 persons for Red River Colony and arrived there on the 10th

January, having walked all the distance on snowshoes in forty four days, exclusive of detentions at the trading posts.

Having several arrangements to make, I did not leave Red River until the 31st January and in ten days afterwards arrived at Crow Island, being the quickest journey ever made to that place—from the Colony. There being little snow farther south, my men and dogs were sent back from Crow Island, whilst I came on hither by Stage and Railroad.

I shall leave New York for England by the Steamer of the 10th March and expect to be in London on or about the 22nd, when I shall have the honor of handing you a more detailed report of last summers operations and also a rough chart of the new coast examined—about 500 miles in all—including the shores traced on the over-ice spring journey.

I am happy to say that with two exceptions the conduct of the party under my command was excellent.

I have the honor to be
Sir
Your most obedt. Servt.
John Rae C.F.
Commandr. A.S. Expn.

Archd. Barclay Esqre.
Hudson's Bay House London }

— RECD. MARCH 20/52 —

[Endorsed]

John Rae
March 28/52

[Note, undated, written in pencil on a small envelope][316]

My Dear Sir George
I have just this morning received your kind note and had I but known a little sooner that you were still in Canada I would have passed by Lachine. To know this I sent two telegraphic messages—one from Chicago the

other from Hamilton to neither of which I received a reply. I now forward some letters I carried down from the North. Some of them are from Campbell and will give some interesting details of McKenzie River affairs, which I am happy to say were in a prosperous state.

As the mail leaves in a short time I cannot write any more just now but shall address you fully by tomorrows mail.

With every good wish and kindest regards to Lady Simpson

I remain ever faithfully yours

J Rae

New York. Irving House *9th March* 1852[317]

My Dear Sir George

On my arrival here yesterday afternoon I was gratified by the receipt of your valued note of the 4th Inst.[318]

I regret exceedingly that I was not previously aware of your still being in Canada as I should most undoubtedly have passed by Montreal but it is too late now, as I sent a letter to Mr. Barclay by last steamer stating my intention of being in England on or about the 22nd of this month, and as even the little information I have to give, may affect the movements of the Expedition[319] about to leave England this spring in search of Sir J. Franklin, I consider it my duty to hurry home, without permitting my own feelings (which would certainly induce me to visit Lachine) to have any voice in the matter.

I have now to ask your pardon for doing one of the most silly and thoughtless things that ever man was guilty of.

The letters (some 7 or 8 in number) to your address which I brought down from the north with me being wrapped in a paper addressed to Sir George Simpson Lachine I posted them last night without looking at the particular address of each, and it was not until this morning that I thought that several of them must have been addressed to you in London.

On calling at the post office this morning I learnt that it was impossible to have them returned or searched for. The only excuse that I can offer for my stupidity is that I was suffering severely from a very bad cold, which for some days has annoyed me very much, but it is better today.

My short letter to Mr. Finlayson would acquaint you with the result of my visits to the arctic sea and I have now no time to give many further particulars.

I am happy to say that McKenzie River was when I passed through it in Septr. last in a very flourishing condition.

At Fort Simpson the crops were good and including 3000 lbs. of dry meat brought by me from Bear Lake there were about 7000 Lbs. besides pemican in store.

The fall business had been very efficiently managed by Barney Ross, whose whole arrangements had been judicious.

Campbell descended the Youcan to Murrays post from his own in 70 hours. The River is a fine one, with a strong current but not a single rapid of consequence. Campbell crossed to Peels River, visited Fort Simpson got his outfit, returned to Peels River again, was to transport some articles that were absolutely requisite over the portage on mens backs, and expected to reach his post on the Pelly & Lewis easily before the setting in of winter.

You may remember that I thought the route by Peels River would not answer for the transport of goods to Campbells post. I was led into this belief, by the report that there was little or no wood on the portage from the Peel to the Porcupine River. This information I have since learnt was erroneous.

In coming up the McKenzie Anderson and I passed each other most unaccountably. He had learnt from one of the fish boats that I was on the way up, and he then stated that he would not drive at night so the only way it could have occurred, is by his guide having led him to the wrong side of some of the islands in the River

On reaching Slave Lake I found the post there in its usual prosperous state under the careful management of McMurray.

According to an arrangement made the previous year, a boat had been sent to the NE end of the Lake and had just returned from thence with 65 pieces of dry meat and grease on board. This was all excellent provisions the best and greater part of which would have been consumed had it been left in the Indians possession until winter.

I regret to say that the prospects of provisions were not so favorable at Athabasca but as no news had been heard from Fond du Lac[320] up to the date of my departure (17th Novr.) it is possible they may have a good stock on hand there.

Isle a La Crosse is I fear also ill provided with grub and the very slow way they have of hauling provisions from Carlton thither, will scarcely supply the requisite quantity for next summers transport business unless some additional means are adopted.—of 9 horses that came from Green Lake to Carlton only 2 were able to return with loads.[321]

The oxen that were sent from Fort Pitt[322] for the Portage La Loche transport business, ran away in the woods before reaching Green Lake, and will not be available for this summer.

I omitted to say that Boucher[323] remains at Fort Chipewyan, Dechambault[324] being at Vermilion. The latter if left in charge of the District will I think soon spoil the men there as he is by far too easy.

Neither Mr. Finlayson nor Boucher sent any letters for you if my memory serves me correctly.

At Carlton buffalo were rather distant, about 5 days journey off, but Pruden[325] had enough dry meat and pemican on hand to supply all demands on him from Isle a la Crosse.

Everything at Fort Pelly was prospering under Buchanans[326] management, and to judge by appearances there was much need of an active, enterprising man there.

Fisher[327] a[t] Beaver Creek was up to his eyes in opposition both he and Buchanan are likely to make very fair returns.

At Red River everything goes on quietly. Provisions seem plentiful and the halfbreeds satisfied, altho' Black[328] does not appear to be such a great favorite as Ballenden was. Poor B.s wife has been very unwell but was recovering. I did not see her.

The clergy are the only people that seem at war with each other. As for Corkran[329] I believe he is mad his last freek was an attempt to persuade his neighbors to burn to death two silly women named

Cook[330] who had been found guilty of infanticide, having exposed a young child to the cold until it was frozen as stiff as an icicle.

During the 18 days that I passed at Red River my time was most pleasantly spent; having nothing to do with the *slight coolnesses* that exist among parties there I mixed with everyone and heard all that could be said on the late Pelly and Foss case[331]

Thom[332] was very friendly and is a pleasant fellow, but I think he gets far too much pay for all he does.—£725 pr. ann. for acting as Clerk of the Council is rather too much, particularly as it is paid by the *Fur trade*.

Mr. Colvile came as far as Pembina with me. He is a very pleasant companion—"Laugh and get fat" should be his motto. Neither Mrs. Colvile[333] nor Mrs. Black show any symptoms yet, of having a family.

My journey through the states was far more disagreeable to me than snowshoe travelling. At St. Paul's I saw Govr. Ramsey[334] of Minnesota Territory, by whom I was most kindly received, having a letter of introduction to him from Colvile.

Between St. Pauls and Galena our sled broke through the ice on the Chipewa river.

The driver had a very narrow escape, having been dragged out of the water, by another passenger and myself just as the current was sweeping him under the ice. One of the horses was drowned and my portmanteau got full of water—fortunately there was not much in it to spoil.

Before arriving at Chicago it was my intention to take the southern road to this place, but I learnt that by staging it from Windsor to Niagara I could get on equally fast. By this means I was enabled to pass 2 days with my brothers in Hamilton. They are very busy curing pork, and I am happy to see are enabled to obtain as much credit at the banks as they wish. They live in a very quiet, homely manner but seem on friendly terms with some of the most respectable people of the town.

Tom is still a pushing, active little fellow, but I think less fond of *speculation* than he was.

The Count De Laguiche[335] has been my travelling companion since I overtook him at Prairie du Chien. He is a very agreeable, fine fellow, but he does not come up to my ideas of a great sportsman or traveller, being rather too fond of taking it *easy*.

The report of my summers voyage on the coast is not yet written out, if it was I would send you a copy of it. Unfortunately I have little of interest to communicate.

During my detention at Athabasca I was occupied revising calculations making chart &c and at Red River I had still something to do at the latter. It is in but a so, so, state of finish yet, but I shall do no more to it. I mention this in case you may think that I have become a lazy idle fellow.

When I next have the pleasure of seeing you, I shall expect a good scolding about my stupidity regarding the letters. I hope it will be soon for the quicker those things are over the better.

The disappointment it will cause you in not receiving the letters alluded to, will I suspect prevent my sleeping very soundly tonight; I know that after the thought first struck me on waking about 2 this morning I did not close an eye.

With sincere respect and regard, and kindest remembrances to Lady Simpson whose health I trust will soon be sufficiently good, to allow her cross the Atlantic.

I remain
ever most faithfully
Yours
John Rae

P.S. I must apologize for this scrawl, but my hand is shaky (not *from grog or wine* for I have tasted not a drop for the last 48 hours) and I feel feverish,—the effects of a cold which I expect the sea voyage will remove.

I shall write Mr. Finlayson either by tonight or tomorrow's mail.

J R

People that wish to flatter, say that I look younger and better than I did four years ago.

Grey hairs and the want of a front tooth dont generally improve a mans face

J R

— JOHN RAE, RECD. 13 MARCH, ANSD. 13 DO[336] —

[Endorsed]

1852

New York 9. March

1 St. Alban's Place Haymarket 1*st May* 1852[337]

Sir

I beg to communicate to you, for the consideration of the Governor, Deputy Governor, and Committee of the Hudson's Bay Company, a plan for the completion of the survey of the northern shores of America, a small portion of which, along the west coast of Boothia is all that now remains unexamined.

The scheme I propose is to equip a party at York Factory, consisting of one officer, two Esquimaux, and ten men, part Orkneymen and Zetlanders, and part English halfbreeds. Two boats would be required for this service. The one strongly built and well suited for sailing in all weathers, resembing in form the boats I had with me at Repulse Bay in 1846, but somewhat larger. The other boat to be as light as possible, about 24 feet length of keel and of the same form and construction (minus the sledge runners) as the light boats built for Sir Edward Belchers[338] searching squadron. The former of these boats could be built at York Factory. The light boat would be better built in England, and there is still sufficient time for one to be got ready before the departure of the ship for York Factory in June.

Every arrangement having been made the Expedition would leave York Factory next spring as soon as the navigation opened, coast northward to Chesterfield Inlet, proceed up it as far as practicable, then leave the large boat in charge of two men and an Esquimaux.

The remainder of the party would then transport the small boat and the requisite stores and provisions across to Backs River. Two men would then return to rejoin those left at Chesterfield Inlet, whilst the officer with a crew of seven persons would descend the river and use his best efforts to complete the required survey.

Should the season prove moderately favorable the following may be considered an approximation to the dates of arrival at and departure from certain points—

> Leave York Factory on the 15th June.
>
> Arrive at the West extremity of Chesterfield Inlet on the 15th July.
>
> Commence descent of Backs River by the 1st August—perhaps earlier.
>
> Arrive on or about the 16th August at the most southerly point of Sir Jas. Ross' discoveries (spring 1849) on the west coast of North Somerset.[339]
>
> On the 31st August the party might be re-united at Chesterfield Inlet.
>
> On the 15th September arrive at York Factory.

The expense of such an expedition as the one proposed would be small as the men would not be on high pay longer than six or seven months, and not more than four months provisions would be required.

Should the Company consider my proposal worthy of attention, more minute details can be given, but permit me to say that if there is any *probability* of their carrying into effect such an Expedition, no time should be lost in ordering the few articles mentioned in the accompanying list, so that they be sent to York Factory this season.

In conclusion let me add that there are many young and enterprising officers in the Company's service, well qualified for the command of an exploring party, and who I have no doubt would gladly volunteer for such duty. Should there, however, be any difficulty in this respect, I,—although much less efficient than I was some years ago—would have no objections to take charge of it myself.

I have the honor to be
Sir
Your Most Obedt. Servant
John Rae

Archibald Barclay Esqre.
Secretary H H B Co.

[Endorsed]

John Rae
May 1/52
Fresh Arctic Expedn.

[Enclosure]
List of Articles required to be forwarded to York Factory this Summer, for the service of a contemplated Expedition to the Arctic Sea.
vizt.

1 light Boat 24 feet keel, planks thin and lined inside with water-proof cloth, like those built for Sir E. Belcher's Expedition. The keel and bilge pieces to be *shod* with iron, no sledge runners required.
1 Halkett's Air Boat large enough to carry 3 persons
1 Cwt. preserved Meat and Soups
1 " Edward's preserved Potato.

1 St. Albans Place Haymarket 1*st May* 1852.
John Rae

By application to the Admiralty, the name of the builder of the boats for the Govt. Expedition may be easily ascertained. Searle built one, but his charges are very high I learn.[340]

J Rae

[Endorsed]

List of Sundries

Hudsons Bay House 16*th June* 1852[341]

Dear Sir
As there is likely to be a great want of fuel on the contemplated

Expedition, particularly on the west shores of Boothia, I beg to request that 4 Gallons Alcohol be ordered from the Apothecaries Co. and forwarded to York Factory by the vessel that leaves this on Saturday.

I have the honor to be
Sir
Your most obedt. servant
John Rae[342]

Archibald Barclay Esq
&c &c &c

[Addressed]

Archd. Barclay Esqre.
&c &c &c
Hudson's Bay House

[Endorsed]

John Rae
June 16th 1852

Stromness Orkney 20*th July* 1852[343]

Sir Geo Simpson

My Dear Sir George
On my arrival here yesterday from England your much valued favor of the 26th ulto. was handed me and by it I was much surprised to learn that you had returned to Lachine at so early a date. I regret much that owing to my dilatoriness in writing there was no letter from me in reference to the contemplated Arctic Expedition awaiting you at Lachine and unfortunately I have no good excuse to offer for my remissness. In a letter addressed to you some weeks ago, I believe I gave full details of my own plans, but feeling as usual not very much confidence in them, I shall be most happy to receive and adopt any suggestions and modifications that your greater experience and judgement may think advisable.

It is my desire to remain in this country until the end of Feby. or beginning of March next, then come out to Boston or New York, thence to Montreal &c &c. By this means I will have some time to see my friends in Canada before the opening of the river and lake navigation.

I should prefer going as far as St. Marys by steamboat and then by canoe to Norway House or York Factory. Any of the party of 10 men that I will require for the Expedition, (exclusive of 2 Esquimaux or persons who speak Esquimaux) who may be engaged at Red River would require to be at Fort Alexr.[344] or Norway House, so as to accompany me to York Factory.

I am happy to say that the Govt, paid me most handsomely for my late services. I was only 20 months occupied with their affairs but I received pay for two years at the rate of £600 pr. ann. minus income tax.

Sir F. Beaufort has lately been most kind, and offers to provide me with compasses and several other useful instruments for next years service.

In a month or two hence I intend taking advantage of very kind invitations from Lord Selkirk and Mr. Ellice to pass a portion of the shooting season with them. The former is to give me a lesson at deer stalking after the Scotch fashion and the latter promises both deer and blackcock shooting.

There is keen contest going on at present for the election of the county member; Fk. Dundas and Mr. Inglis the Lord Advocate of Scotland are the candidates. The former a whig, the latter conservative. It is impossible to say how affairs will go, but Inglis appears to be the favorite with all the influential men of the place. As to ability there can be no comparison between the parties, Dundas being a slow, very slow coach and extremely prosy with all, Inglis being the very reverse. The speach of the latter on the nomination day was one of the best things I ever heard, and cut up the Dundas party most awfully. I never saw people look more foolish.

It grieves me much to learn that your health is in a worse state than usual, for I was in great hopes that a trip to the north would be rather beneficial than otherwise, particularly as you would be exposed to few of the discomforts of canoe travelling.

I am happy to say all my friends here are well, and that I feel no bad effects from change of climate, unless a tendency to get fat may be considered so—but this I can keep down by exercise.

My Sister Mrs. Hamilton has now got nine bairns and there is another underweigh so there is no saying when the little body is to be done adding to Her Majesty's subjects.

This mail leaves in a short time, and I am unable to write more at present, being desirous that this should go by the steamer of Saturday.

With kindest regards to Lady Simpson and Miss Simpson

Believe me, Yours,
Most respectfully and faithfully
John Rae

— JOHN RAE, RECD. AUG, ANSD. I. OCTR.[345] —

[Endorsed]

1852
Stromness 20. July

.....

Birsay Orkney 18*th August* 1852[346]

My Dear Sir George
When your very kind letter of the 24th ulto.[347] reached me I was a few miles from this place, where I am at present *located* enjoying one of my old favorite amusements—grouse shooting—but as I have at present but one dog and that not a very tough one my success has not been great, having shot only 45 brace as yet. The birds are however large and fine. I feel much indebted for your advice about paying a visit to the Earl of Selkirk and Mr. Ellice, and it is my intention to see both gentlemen sometime in September.

Wandering over the moors will be a good preparation for my next summers trip I find my *legs* can carry me through a pretty fair days work still, and as I have neither aches nor pains of any kind, I hope there is still some work in me.

Regarding the wages to be given to the men for the expedition, I believe, that good hands cannot be got for less than £40 stg. pr. annum with the promise of a bonus of £10 or £15 in event of good conduct.

Perhaps it would be rather hard to make the bonus dependant on the success of the Expedition, as the poor fellows are likely to have harder work if not successful, than if we were so. Several of my old hands such as Beads, Foster and Corrigal[348] would require to have about £50 pr. annum wages, being about the sum they had formerly, but perhaps they should be engaged so as to have pay for only the time they are employed as it may probably be considerably less than a year.

I do not think that the Expedition would be in any way advanced by the arrangements being made at Churchill, for in 1846 I got along the coast from York Factory quite as fast as the navigation opened.

It is probable that men, quite as good as any that can be obtained here, may be engaged in the Red River or at the Cos. posts, at least I have never had any difficulty in procuring the best hands, particularly when there is no likelihood of wintering, and not much portage work on the route.

Very many thanks for your very interesting news regarding H B affairs—Buchannan will be a most able successor to Black but I daresay his appointment to the chief charge will give Pelly[349] some annoyance; fortunately they are great friends and are most likely to pull well together if both at the same place. I regret to learn that poor Cloustons[350] health requires a change of climate, I suspect he does not take sufficient exercise, a very common fault in the service.

May the porpoise fishing succeed, something of the kind is required to increase the profits, now that furs are getting scarce.

I know not how the Cos. acct. with the Admiralty on expedition matters has been settled. As regards myself the admiralty have paid me liberally as I believe I mentioned before—£600 pr. ann. The Company have done their part I fancy, by letting my salary run on without any abatement.

The cash sent to my brothers is invested for me in Hamilton with good security, and most of it is at present paying 15 pr. ct. which is very fair considering all things.

The *McNab*[351] from Canada is here at present accompanied by a niece who is a *ward in chancery*. She is rather a queer looking lass.

The chief is desirous of shooting grouse but I am not sure if he has yet got leave from any of the proprietors to shoot over their ground. He is dressed in green silk and is very grand with his piper &c. He creates quite a sensation in Stromness, and his every movement is noted with as much care as if he were a Duke at least.

Our election here has just terminated and Mr. Dundas has much to the annoyance of many been returned instead of the Lord Advocate. The latter had with one or two exceptions all the respectable portion of the community on his side—but the freekirk and methodist parsons carried the day despite every effort, being most unscrupulous in the means they used.

All my friends in this quarter are well. My Mother holds out remarkably but is quite unhappy unless she can get me to eat and drink something at least 5 times pr. day. My little sister is in a fair way to have the tenth addition to her family—and as they are all at home but one, there is a pretty house full of bairns.

My hand is rather shaky after todays walk in the moors, during which I got a complete drenching as there was a complete down pour of rain nearly all the time I was out; I managed however to pick up 7 brace of grouse and would, I believe, have shot double that number had the day been fine.

May I beg to offer my kindest regards to Lady and Miss Simpson and

Believe me ever
Most respectfully & faithfully yours
John Rae

JOHN RAE, RECD. SEPTR., ANSD. OCTR. 1

[Addressed]

Sir George Simpson
Lachine
Care of Archibald Barclay Esquire
Hudsons Bay House
4 Fenchurch Street
London.

[Endorsed]

1852

Orkeney 18. August

Tavistock Hotel Covent Garden 19*th Novr.* 1852[352]

Sir George Simpson

My Dear Sir George

I regret that, owing to the detention of my letters at the Hudsons Bay House until my arrival in London I have not had an opportunity of answering your valued favor of the 1st October until now. Why Mr. Barclay did not forward my letters to Orkney as usual I cannot learn, probably he thought that I would hasten to town as soon as I heard of the arrival of the ships.

With reference to the contemplated expedition and the men required for it, I am still of opinion that people qualified for the service may be better obtained at R. River and at some of the Cos. posts, than in this country. I may probably bring out one man with me, if I can find a suitable person ready, willing and able to go through the fag he may have to encounter.

Regarding the wages to be paid I am of opinion that old and tried men, should have something more either in the form of regular wages or gratuity, than persons unaccustomed to arctic travelling. For instance such a man as Beads would scarcely engage for the same terms as those who would have to act as middlemen. I am particularly desirous of this man's services as he is a most cool, able steersman in rapids—fully equal I suspect if not superior to either Sinclair or McKay so highly spoken of by Back, Dease and Simpson. I am sorry that I cannot at present obey your instructions about sending you copies of my letters and requisition on the subject of the Expedition forwarded by the ship to York Factory to Mr. Mactavish. These documents are among my papers at Stromness, and shall be forwarded to you as soon as I can lay my hands on them.

From the delay of the Company in sanctioning the expedition, it was only a few days before the sailing of the Bay ships that I could commence any arrangements, and of course everything was done in a very hurried manner.

You mention that I ought to take a passage up to the north in the spring canoes. Will it not be better and quicker for me to go by steam as far as St. Maries and thence on by Canoe? If I hope to complete the survey in one season, not a moment must be lost "en route". If the season is at all favorable I hope to be at Lake Winnipeg by the end of May and at York Factory about the 12 or 15 June. In 1846 I left York Factory for Repulse Bay on the 13th June, and was then quite early enough for the ice, but we were detained two days at Churchill waiting for my instructions.

As far as I can *calculate* the dates of my arrival at the various stages of my journey or voyage will be as follows—

Lake Winnipeg	May 30
York Factory	June 13
Churchill	" 22
Chesterfield Inlet	July 12
Backs River (over Land)	July 24
The Sea	July 30
Furthest North Point	Augt. 22
Back to York Factory	Septr. 26

These calculations are based on the the supposition that everything goes on prosperously should we meet with unexpected difficulty I shall be provided for wintering or for walking back to Churchill as the case may be. One thing is certain I shant feel inclined to return without completing the job, unless like some of my contemporaries I get cooled down by a short stay beyond the arctic circle. The way to get into credit here is to plan some impossible scheme, no consequence how absurd, to assert most positively that you will do more than anyone else ever did or could do, and after having signally failed, return with a lot of paltry reasons—sufficiently good to gull John Bull—for your failure.

It is perhaps unnecessary for me to mention that Kennedy[353] has done little, he and his party made a long journey greater part of it over land, and traced only a few miles of new coast. Like a *good fellow* he just touched my (*to be*) furthest north point and then struck off west, instead of doing what I would have done—divided my party and sent one portion of it southwards to the Magnetic pole.

In the three primary objects of the Expedition which he firmly asserted were easy of accomplishment by *him* (Kennedy) he signally failed vizt.—The reaching Brentford Bay with his vessel, the examination of the coast on the west of Boothia as far south as the magnetic pole, and the finding of *Franklin*. All which appeared to the sanguine gentleman mere childs-play. It appears now, by report of everyone employed on the Expedition that M. Bellot (the frenchman) was the main-spring of the party he alone being capable of taking the requisite astronomical observations.

I shall be prepared to answer any questions put me at the Admiralty regarding the charges made by the H.B.Co, against the Government—but altho' I will not say so to any of the officers of the Admiralty, I cannot help being of the opinion that many of the charges do seem *rather high*, and unfortunately some of the officers of the H.B. service on the route from McKenzie River to York Factory gave Pullen priced accounts of his supplies, which prices I suspect will not agree with those entered at Lachine. All I can say on this head is that the persons who gave Pullen such priced accounts had no authority for doing so.

I passed a most pleasant three weeks of the shooting season with Mr. Ellice at Glenquoich and received every kindness from him Mrs. Ellice and old Mr. Ellice.[354] Altho' not in good shooting condition whilst there, I believe, I supported the credit of the *concern* as a *pedestrian*, beating all the nobs there to sticks, and keeping pace with the smartest of the gillies on level ground or going up hill, and distancing them all hollow at running down a steep place—the most trying work of all for the legs. I shot only one deer but a good many ptarmigan and grouse.

I stayed so long at Mr. Ellice's that Lord Selkirk had left his shooting Box in Ross-shire before I took my departure, consequently I did not visit his Lordship.

Yesterday was the funeral of the great Duke,[355] and I through the kindness of a friend had a fine view of the procession. It was a very splendid sight. I was particularly fortunate in having offers of seats. Mr. Ellice as soon as he heard I was in town sent me a ticket of admission to St. Pauls, and I had the offer of another seat in St. James' Street. In the evening I dined at the hospitable mansion at Stamford Hill, and passed a few hours most pleasantly. Mrs. Simpson,[356] I am sorry to say, although able to sit at table, appears in very delicate health.

All my friends in Orkney were well when I left them about a week ago. I return there to pass the christmas, after paying a short visit to Paris, which I have not yet seen.

I forgot to mention that by a letter received from McTavish from York Factory I learn that he can make all the required arrangements for my next summers operations but he says, there are no men at Y.F. that he could recommend to form a portion of my party. My requisition for goods, provisions &c was not very full, but I referred him to the list of my supplies in 1846 as a guide.

By a letter from my brother Tom I learn that his wife and child received much benefit from the sea bathing Helen in particular was in better health than she has been for 10 years past. Both write in the warmest terms of their kind reception at Lachine.

The cash I sent for investment has been lent out on excellent security at rates of interest varying from 10% to 15% per cent I have been thinking of selling out my puget sound shares (23 in number)[357] and my mite of H.B. stock[358] and investing the proceeds in Canada—I can clear about £100 by the sale.

I shall have the pleasure of again addressing you next week, and shall enclose copy of a letter I propose writing to McTavish at York Factory.

With kindest regards to Lady and Miss Simpson

Believe me Dear Sir George
most respectfully & faithfully yours
John Rae

—— JOHN RAE, RECD. 11 DECR., ANSD. 20 DO[359] ——

[Endorsed]

1852
London 19 November

Tavistock Hotel Covent Gn. 25*th Novr.* 52[360]

[Archibald Barclay]

My Dear Sir
I have now ordered both the chronometers for the Cos. next Expedition. The one from Dent, of Charing Cross &c. which is to cost, *not more* than 45 guineas. The other at the recommendation of Sir Francis Beaufort has been ordered from Mr. Losely 44 Gerard Street Islington. The cost of the latter will be from *£63 to £65 Stg.* a pretty strong price, which if you think too much, the order may still be *countermanded.*

I shall be busy during the greater part of tomorrow in writing Sir Geo. Simpson and Mr. McTavish on Expedition affairs.

Believe me
My Dear Sir
very truly yours
John Rae

P.S. I have of course referred the Chronometer makers to you for further particulars if they have any questions to ask

J.R.

[Endorsed]

J Rae
Nov 25/52

London, Hudsons Bay House 26*th Novr.* 1852[361]

Sir George Simpson
&c. &c. &c.

My Dear Sir George
I inclose you copy of a letter I have addressed today to Mr. McTavish at York Factory on the subject of the Expedition to the Arctic coast next year. It contains but little worthy of notice as I had in my communications by the Bay Ship, said everything that I deemed necessary on this important subject.

My stay here will be about a week longer by which time I hope to have all done, that I had to do in town. I should like however to be on the spot when Kennedy's book[362] appears as I have no doubt he will lug the Companys name into it, in some form or other, not very favourable to them.

I spent a very pleasant evening some days ago at Stamford Hill and met for the first time Mr. and Mrs Scott and 2 of their fine family. The Finlaysons had gone to Scotland sometime before so I did not see them.

The new Govr. (Colvile)[363] has a small party tonight for which I have the honor of an invitation I fancy there will be a great meeting of the big folks of Fenchurch Street.

I have frequently seen Mr. Lewis,[364] who looks remarkably well, and still in London with his family. He is living quietly and *inexpensively* at a small cottage near Regents Park. Keeps no servants, but makes his family do everything, one cooks, another goes to market, a third acts as waiter, and so forth—Madam looks immensly broad and dark.

By last news from Orkney all were well there
With Kindest regards to Lady Simpson

Believe me
Very faithfully & respectfully yrs
John Rae

— JOHN RAE, RECD. 13 DECR., ANSD. 20 DO —

[Endorsed]

1852
London 26 November

[Enclosure]

Tavistock Hotel London 26*th November* 1852

(Copy)
Willm. McTavish Esquire
&c. &c. &c.

My Dear Sir
As Kennedy has returned from the Arctic Sea without completing any part of the survey that I had marked out for myself, nothing now prevents the arrangements for next summers expedition being carried out tō the fullest extent. Having addressed you pretty fully on this subject by the Bay Ships and having at the same time sent a note of all the stores &c. considered requisite for the service of the party, I have now little to add, well knowing that your foresight and attention will supply anything essential that you may notice as having been omitted. This you may the more readily do, having doubtless a detailed account of the stores &c. supplied to my party in 1846.

The following articles were probably omitted in my former requisition, I beg that they may now be prepared vizt.

4 good well turned dog sledges—lightly made 2 of them with runners 2 inches broad and ½ in thick lined with iron hoop.
13 pairs good snowshoes
12 good rein deer or buffalo Robes
8 *dog* Harnesses the collars to be left unstuffed.

I shall probably take with me from England not more than one man—perhaps none—it will therefore be requisite to provide the whole number in Hudsons Bay.

If any other Interpreters could be obtained instead of Oulibuck and his son I should prefer them. To Oulibuck I have no particular objection but the boy (his son) that I had with me formerly is one of the greatest rascals unhung—and by his falsehood and misconduct made his father sulky and discontented. I should prefer Oulibucks son Donald, who, altho' he spoke but little English was a good tempered hard working fellow.

Are there none of Dunnings[365] family at Churchill that would suit our purpose?

Should next spring be a fine one, I hope to be at York Factory on or about the 13th June and to leave it again on the 15th or 16th—if the ice along the coast has broken up.

Having nothing further to add at present I beg to subscribe myself

very faithfully yours

(Signed) John Rae

[Endorsed]

Copy of Letter to Wm. McTavish Esqr.

Stromness Orkney 17 *January* 1853[366]

Sir George Simpson

My Dear Sir George

I received your kind favor of the 20th ulto a few days ago but was unable to answer it immediately in consequence of ill health an attack of lumbago together with an affection of the Kidnies having kept me to my room I may say to my bed for the last fortnight. I am now better however and hope soon to be quite on my legs again.

I believe I have been rather sanguine in my expectations of an early arrival at York Factory but I calculated my time by Sir John Richardsons journey in 1848 when he and I arrived in Lake Winipeg in May—but that was I believe an early season.

I never thought or expected to make a quicker trip to the north than you do,[367] not even so quick—but was desirous of being at St. Maries in good time to be ready for an early season should we fortunately have one—and my wish to proceed as far as Ste. Maries by steam merely arose from the desire to avoid as far as possible the tedium of the canoe voyage thither from Canada, as I shall have enough of boating and canoing before the end of the summer.

The proceeding by steam would also allow me time to spend a few days with my friends in Hamilton before starting on this the last (I hope) and most difficult of my visits to the arctic sea.

It was my intention even had you not directed me to do so, to visit Lachine on my way north so as to receive instructions for my further guidance and I shall probably be in Canada about the beginning of April instead of towards the end of the month. A short stay at New York and perhaps at Toronto will be requisite so as to re-rate the Chronometers.

It is probable as you suggested take out one steady man with me who will be capable of acting as steersman of the large boat.

Several young gentlemen have volunteered to accompany me (two of them officers in the army) and to pay all their own expenses but I have courteously declined their offers. One of these volunteers is a Mr. Sayer who writes me from Toronto.

A fortnight hence I intend leaving this for London, where it is my intention to put myself under the instruction of Colonel Sabine who has got a very delicate little magnetic Instrument made specially for this survey—the proper use of which I will require to learn.[368]

In 1846 when I coasted along Hudsons Bay, the express with your instructions reached me at Churchill on the 5th July and it is my hope to be so far on my way this season at the same date, but to do so not a chance of any kind is to be lost.

Few are the advantages that I expect to myself from my contemplated visit to the arctic sea however successful it may be, but should I return safe and complete the survey intended I shall have the satisfaction of feeling that I traced more new coast in the Arctic Sea that any other *single* individual living.

I have again to apologize for not forwarding to you copies of my letter to Mr. McTavish at YF actory on the subject of the Expeditions. *Copies* I certainly had but they have been mislaid.

On my way hither from London I spent a few days in Edinr. with Dugald McTavish[369] at his fathers. The old gentleman is to pass the winter in Auld Reekie[370] and he and Madam are two of the Most Kind hospitable people I have ever met. Dugald promises to visit Orkney about the end of the month; he appears to keep his health well, but speaks of the climate as horrible as compared with the Sandwich Islands, which from his description a person would fancy a sort of heaven on earth.

Black and his wife and Miss Christie are staying in Edinr. during part of the winter. The two ladies are under the care of the famous Dr. Simpson[371] for whom it seems all the women of got a sort of craze.

All my friends here are tolerably well, my mother altho' her memory is failing holds out remarkably.

My back aches with sitting up so long so that I must draw a close

With Kindest regards to Lady Simpson and family

Believe me
Most respectfully & faithfully yrs
John Rae

— JOHN RAE, RECD. 15 FEBY., ANSD. 19 DO[372] —

[Endorsed]

1853
Stromness 17 January

Liverpool 25*th March* 1853[373]

Archd. Barclay Esqr.
&c. &c. &c.

Sir

Would you have the goodness to cause the sum of £65 Stg. instead of £70 Stg. to be paid to my Mother Mrs. J. Rae, at the usual time for the present year—say 1853 and charge the same in my Acct. with the Company.

I am Sir
your very obedt. Sert.
John Rae

[Endorsed]

John Rae
March 25/53

Steamer "*Europa*" at sea 8*th April* 1853.[374]

My Dear Sir George

As we expect to arrive at New York early tomorrow forenoon, I drop you a few lines to mention the fact our passage has been a very tedious one in consequence of almost constant head winds and stormy weather.

I shall spend 2 or 3 nights in N. York to have the Chronometers which I find have be going rather wild re-rated.

I have no packages or letters for either you or Lady Simpson; probably none of the former were sent owing to Mr. Finlayson's coming out so soon after me.

All my friends at home were well when I left.

With kindest regards to Lady Simpson whose health I hope is wholly restored,

Believe me
Most respectfully & faithfully yours
John Rae

Should you have anything to communicate before I leave New York would you address to the care of the British Consul

J.R.

— JOHN RAE, RECD. 13 APRIL, ANSD. PERSONALLY —

[Endorsed]

1853
Str. *Europa* 8 April

Delimonico's New York 11*th April* 1853[375]

Archd. Barclay Esqr.

Sir

I have the honor to acquaint you for the information of the Governor, Deputy Govr. and Committee that I arrived here on the 9th instant and intend starting for Lachine tomorrow morning.

I have had the pleasure of making Mr. Grinnells[376] acquaintance here, and have received much gratifying attention from that nobly generous gentleman.

With much respect I have the honor to be

Your very obedte. servant
John Rae

[Endorsed]

John Rae
Apl. 11/53

Hamilton Canada W. 29*th April* 1853[377]

My Dear Sir George
I am in receipt of your two notes the one accompanying a letter for Mr. Buchanan and the other (which came to hand today) with letters for Hargrave and Black which I shall carry with me. I am happy to learn that Black is to be my companion as far as Fort Alexander as, it will make the time pass more pleasantly.

I leave this for St. Marys via Buffalo and Detroit on the 2nd proxo. and hope to be at Lake Superior one or two days before my canoe.

Enquiries have been made for Mrs. Ballentyne,[378] at the Gore Bank and elsewhere but not a trace can be found of her.

An advertisement will be put into tomorrows or Mondays paper regarding her.

With kindest respects to Miss Simpson,[379] and the other members of your family

Believe me
very respectfully & faithfully Yours
John Rae

— JOHN RAE, RECD. 4 MAY, NO ANSWER —

[Endorsed]

1853
Hamilton 29 April

Sault St. Maries 10*th May* 1853[380]

Sir George Simpson

My Dear Sir George
For the last four days I have been here, *fretting a little* at not having the means of getting forward on my journey. Lake Superior has been perfectly navigable since the first of the month, for a canoe passed between Fort William and Michipicoton prior to that date, so that should the spring to the northward be comparatively as early as it has been here, I shall lose some eight or ten days at least by not having at this place the means of proceeding.

To me every hour is of importance and much shorter detention than this is likely to prove, may cause either the failure of the Expedition in its object or force me to winter in the north, neither of which are very pleasant prospects to look forward to—some years since I would not have cared much about being forced into the latter alternative, but now much exposure of any kind injures me, and more care will be requisite to keep me in a fit state of health to carry out the work I have to do.

It appears that my calculations published in the *Times*[381] have been so far correct, and as it was necessary that my friends in England should be made aware that they were so, I have mentioned to them that the navigation of Lake Superior was open at the time I supposed it would be, but that circumstances over which I had not the control, prevented my proceeding on my journey until a much later date.

By having my friend Black with me as far as Bas de la Riviere I shall pass any time much more agreeably than I would have done if alone, but I doubt whether his being in the canoe will tend anything to the quickness of our march.

As a stimulant to the guide when the canoe does *come*, I shall promise him *out of my own pocket* a pretty handsome gratuity, provided he can reach York Factory by a certain date, which we cannot decide upon until the day of leaving this.

I have forwarded to Mr. Lockhart[382] an account of my expences from London to Lachine, also a note of cash paid by me for freight of Halkett boat and for wads and Guncaps for Expedition.

The expences of journey from Lachine hither I have of course no claim to, as I came by way of the Lakes for my own pleasure.

I shall have the honor of adding a line or two before starting

With much respect
Believe me
very truly yours
John Rae

JOHN RAE, RECD. 21 MAY, ANSD. 16 JUNE[383]

[Endorsed]

1853
Sault Ste. Marie 10 May

Sault Ste. Maries 3 P.M. 12*th May* 1853[384]

My Dear Sir George

The Canoe arrived a few hours since, but as there is a strong gale of head wind I have deferred starting until tomorrow morning.

The cargo and agres[385] are correct as per Bill of Lading, but I feel a little surprised to find among the packages, 2 cases for Red River.

These I shall take the liberty of leaving here whatever may be the consequences as were the canoe lumbered more than it will be by Blacks luggage and my own, it is perfectly impossible that I can make up by quick marching the time that has already been uselessly lost. By this date instead of being at Ste. Maries, I should have been in Rainy Lake; and now there is every chance of detention in Lake Superior by stormy weather.

One of the winterers that came up in the canoe is very unwell and quite incapable of work, I shall however take him on as far as Fort William or Michipicoton.

Mr. Black is in rather a nervous state in consequence of not having had any letters from his Wife or other relatives, by the "*Koloolar*" Steamer which arrived at the same time as the Canoe. He does not appear to be a believer in the old proverb that "No news is good News".

Since being here I have rated the Chronometers and find that one of them (McCabe's) goes very well the other (Dent) is very irregular in its rate.

An Aneroid Barometer that I had the lend of from the Admiralty has been broken by a jerk or fall of the case in which it was packed, and I shall send it to England by the Moose Ship. It is not an indispensable instrument.

It is still possible, should no very great obstacles stop our progress to be at York Factory about the 15th June, if so, something may done this summer on the Arctic Coast.

With much respect
I have the honor to remain
very faithfully Yours
John Rae

—— JOHN RAE, RECD. 21 MAY, ANSD. 16 JUNE ——

[Endorsed]

1853
Sault Ste. Marie 12 May

Fort William 21*st May* 1853[386]

My Dear Sir George
Black and I arrived here this afternoon having had rather a long passage (9 days) across the lake. The winds were almost constantly ahead and during one whole day we were unable to move, which will account for our slowness.

No ice has been seen here since the 6th or 7th of the Month and the season altogether has been an unusually fine one, I trust it may prove equally so in the Arctic Sea—but I fear that I shall not be able to take so good advantage of it as I at one time had hoped, for I cannot now reach York Factory much earlier than the 15th June.

I leave here the man Collins, who besides being in rather delicate health, has got a sore foot which wholly unfits him for work—possibly a day or two's rest here may enable him to do his duty in one of the Canoes that follow us.

The water being very low I take from this a half sized Canoe so as to lighten us over the shallow water on this side the dog portage.[387]

Having no instructions by which to direct my proceedings after arriving at York Factory I am led to infer that the plan I proposed for the Expedition is to be carried out as far as practicable without modification or alteration, unless something should present itself "en route" to cause me to alter my views.

It may be as well to mention that I purpose retiring from the service, as soon as I return from the present *tour*, for altho' far from having a competence, I may manage to live by some exertion on the means I have saved, small as they are. Next spring I shall have been four years a C.F. which I suppose will entitle me to the retired allowance[388] and I suppose their *honors* will give me something extra (as usual on such occasions) whilst employed on the present service altho' I must say I don't expect much from them—in fact I had a strong idea of making a *bargain* with them before leaving England, but was dissuaded from doing so;—Regard and respect for one of the directors (Mr. Ellice) whose kindness I hope never to forget being a strong enducement to follow the advice given instead of my previous determination.

With the utmost respect
Believe me
very faithfully Yours
John Rae

P.S. The wine put into the case sent from Lachine appears to have been the dregs of all the casks or bottles emptied there during the year for neither the port nor Madeira were palatable—fortunately Hargrave had the power and the will to supply us with some better stuff at the Sault. Ermatinger has been most kind and liberal in supplying us with all we required.

J. R.

— JOHN RAE, RECD. 27 MAY, ANSD. 16 JUNE —

[Endorsed]

1853
Fort William 21. May

Norway House 12*th June* 1853[389]

My Dear Sir George
I arrived here this morning but as there were some arrangements to make I shall not leave this until tomorrow at an early hour however.

The men[390] that have been engaged for me appear to be a fine set of fellows, young active and civil, and I have no doubt well fitted for the work they have to do; they will give me hard work to keep pace with them, should we be obliged to have recourse to snowshoes.

Permit me to mention to you the case of Mr. Murray formerly of the Youcan, who altho' in the opinion of every one acquainted with him, well fitted for almost any station in the country, was last season placed at Pembina under George Setter,[391] who is an excellent fellow but only a postmaster in rank. Perhaps you may think it worth while to remedy this in some way.

The men in the canoe have wrought well, although a little slow in some respects and I hope to be at York Factory by the 17th. Hoping to have this pleasure again both from York Factory and Churchill with many and sincere thanks for all your kindness—Believe me

My Dear Sir George
very respectfully & faithfully yours
John Rae

P.S. I find by an acct. just handed to me that I am charged with freight of 4 Pces. from Red River to York Factory of 2½ Pces. from Norway House to the Colony. The first is for transport of Skeletons for benefit of science that I was requested to get. The latter was probably for some property that I had be obliged to leave in consequence of my late wanderings. Are these charges fair?

J. R.

— JOHN RAE, RECD. 13 JUNE, ANSD. 16 DO —

[Endorsed]

1853

Norway House 12 June

York Factory *24th June* 1853[392]

Archd. Barclay Esquire

Sir

I beg to acquaint you for the information of the Governor, Deputy Governor and Committee that I arrived here on the 18th instant, and found every preparation that could be effected, made for the farther advance of the Expedition.

A detention of several days here was requisite for the purpose of rating the chronometers, so that there was no attempt made to leave this until the 22nd on which day the boats were loaded, but a gale of wind from North East prevented our moving; Yesterday the weather was still worse there being heavy snow all day, which now covers the ground to the depth of several inches. Today the wind is ahead but being moderate, I shall get underweigh about 9h. A.M. but do not expect to get farther than across North river as the recent easterly winds must have forced the ice against the coast in great quantities which it will require a breeze from the opposite direction to remove.

Before closing this permit me to express my gratification at the great care and attention that has been paid by Mr. McTavish the gentleman in charge here, to the efficient equipment of the Expedition. Nothing that he had the mean of providing has been omitted.

I have the honor to be

Sir

Your Most Obedt. Servant

John Rae C.F.

Commanding Arctic Expn.

[Endorsed]

John Rae
June 24th 1853

Coast 37 Miles North of York Factory 1*st July* 1853[393]

Sir George Simpson
&c. &c. &c.

Sir

Seeing some Indians in the neighborhood I take the opportunity of acquainting you by them that we have been detained here for the last four days by ice, which a constant succession of NE and East winds has driven on the beach in great quantities. Two nights ago the large boat narrowly escaped being crushed as the flood tide made. She was only saved by slipping the anchor and chain and being allowed to drive in shore as the water flowed. The anchor and chain were found next day at low water.

The ice is very much wasted and broken up, too much so indeed, as it floats in less water than the boats draw, and thus endangers them on every turn of the tide, which runs with great rapidity, the shore being very level and drying to the distance of 6 or 8 miles from the bank at low water. All we require is a breeze off shore to give us a clear passage and there is some hopes of it today as the weather is very warm and agreeble, and very different from what it has been since leaving York.

With much respect
I have the honor to be
Sir
Your very obedt. Servant
John Rae

JOHN RAE, RECD. 4 OCTR., ANSD. 1 DECR.[394]

[Addressed]

On Service
Sir George Simpson
Hudsons Bay House
Lachine
Canada East

[Endorsed]

1853
35 Miles fm. York—1 July

Coast Six Miles West of Cape Churchill 10*th July* 1853[395]

My Dear Sir George

Having at last doubled Cape Churchill and arrived within a few hours pull or sail of Churchill R. if the ice would make a little room for us, I take advantage of our being stopped by a ridge of stones and ice (past which we cant get until the tide flows) to write you a brief account of our *trip* along the coast, which has been far from a pleasure one.

We left York Factory on the 24th ulto. but did not get across north river until the following day, when we immediately encountered the ice and have been battling with it ever since. Until yesterday the boats could not be kept afloat for a single tide, and the only way we could save them from being nipped, was by attaching them to the largest grounded pieces we could find, and then with poles keeping the floating masses as well off as we could, notwithstanding every effort, the large boat got two planks stove in, fortunately above the water line, and on three other occasions both boats very narrowly escaped being crushed.

To save ourselves the boats were at one time laid on shore at high water, and got neaped, as there was a slight opening in the ice, at low water next day the cargo was carried out some distance seaward and placed on a large floe, with the flood tide came an easterly breeze which soon raised a short breaking sea that speedily reduced the size of our floe and it was only by the greatest exertion, and wading about waist deep in the water that the baggage was saved from being completely soaked. The whole was bundled into the small boat and carried out to a safer landing place. Now getting wet in a river or lake or any other place the banks of which are lined with wood is no great hardship but where there is no fire to be had the case is different and some of the poor fellows looked particularly blue until they got their clothes changed.

The men are active, willing, good tempered and obedient, and all we want is a little more open water to work in. Our large boat draws too much water to be handy among ice, but it will be admirably fitted for rough fall weather, and will carry the whole party quite easily. She sails remarkably fast, both by and with the wind, and should I be fortunate enough to get my work done (of which I am now doubtful) I expect to be at York Ft. or Churchill by the last of September.

From the 24th ulto. up to this date, we have had only a few hours of off shore winds, all the other winds have tended to bring the ice closer to the beach.

Altho' our hunters have been out frequently for a short time no deer have been killed but one that I shot when taking a walk one day. It was a *nursing doe*, and of course poor.

I shall leave this open, so as to add a few lines at Churchill.

With Kindest regards to Miss Simpson, Augusta and Baby and my little friend "*Moses*"[396]

Believe me
Dear Sir George
very respectfully & faithfully yours
John Rae

12th July Churchill—I arrived here yesterday morning and would have been off again this forenoon, had not the wind been directly in our teeth, and forced me very much against my will to remain idle; I say idle because I might be employed making magnetic observations were it not for the clouds of Musquitoes that attack a person as soon as he puts his nose out of doors. Anderson[397] has this place in excellent order, but his whole hunt has been very unproductive only one small fish having yet been caught.

Ever
very respectfully Yours
John Rae

— JOHN RAE, RECD. 27 OCTR., ANSD. 1 DECR. —

[Addressed]

Sir George Simpson
Hudsons Bay House
Lachine
Canada East

[Endorsed]

1853
Cape Churchill 10 July

Coast about 50 Miles North of Churchill 13*th July* 1853[398]

My Dear Sir George

We have just met a number of Esquimaux and among them young Ouligbuck who has agreed to accompany me.[399] We have had a good run since we left Churchill at half an hour after midnight last night. About 50 miles and altho the wind is easterly we shall be underweigh again in a short time.

I cannot write more as the boat is jumping about so that writing is almost impossible, nor indeed have I anything more to say, except that I fear you will have much trouble in making out what I have already written.

Believe me ever
gratefully & faithfully yours
John Rae

P.S. There is no ice to the north so we only want a fair wind.

J.R.

— JOHN RAE, RECD. 27 OCTR., ANSD. 1 DECR. —

[Addressed]

Sir George Simpson

Per
Esquimaux } H.B.House
Lachine

[Endorsed]

1853
Arctic Coast 13 July

Knaps Bay 9h. A.M. 15 *July* 1853[400]

My Dear Sir George

As there are some Esquimaux coming off to us, I write these few lines to leave with them hoping that some one may be going to Churchill during the summer.

It is now 56 hours since leaving Churchill River, and we are nearly half way from thence to the entrance of Chesterfield Inlet, so that our run has been a prosperous one; if equally so for the next 150 miles, I may still reach the head of the Inlet by the 20th inst. The wind is from S.E. and fair although on the land. We shall put to shore in a few moments on the south point of Knaps Bay to fill our water kegs and immediately push off again.

Not a bit of ice has been seen since we left Churchill and we might have easily made way along this coast ten days sooner. Indeed I believe we would have made a quicker passage from York to Churchill earlier in the season, as the ice then would not have been so much wasted and consequently would not have floated so close in to the beach.

With the utmost respect
Believe me very faithfully Yours
John Rae

— JOHN RAE, RECD. 27 OCTR., ANSWD. 1 DECR. —

[Addressed]

Sir George Simpson
Hudsons Bay House
Lachine
Canada East

[Endorsed]

1853

Knaps Bay 15 July

Near Mouth of Chesterfield Inlet West of it *9th August* 1853[401]
William McTavish Esqre.

Dear Sir
Having failed to reach Backs River via Chesterfield Inlet, I intend now to proceed to Repule [sic] Bay, winter there if possible, and in the spring complete the survey on foot previous to the opening of the navigation.

As it would difficult under any circumstances to maintain so large a party, I send back half the men in the small boat under the charge of Clouston whom I have found steady and attentive. The following are the men who return[402]

James Clouston in charge	£30
Charles Harrison	" 22
Murdoch McDonald	" 23
Louis Michel	" 23
John Geo. McDougald	" 25
Henry Fidler	" 25

These men have all behaved very well with the exception of M.McDonald whom I found had told Clouston a falsehood, I therefore give him £2 less than the other men engaged at Red River. To those engaged at the Colony (McDonald excepted) I think it but right to give a little more than to the others as they will be some time longer employed on this service and have farther to go.

Have the goodness when explaining to them their accts. to let the men know what amount they would be entitled to by their engagements and if there is the least grumbling pay them only their due. It was only in the event of success that I promised them anything extra.

Charles Harrison seems to know well how to manage a boat and I believe would make a very fair slooper, perhaps on his new engagement (if he does engage) he might be worth sloopers wages.

The three men from Red River and the Canadian from Norway House[403] may get a passage thither in some of the fall boats, being supplied with provisions, and obliged to work in the rivers and lakes but to carry only their own baggage and provisions over the portages—Louis Michel is not to receive wages in the Cos. regular service until he reaches Norway House unless of course retained at York or Oxford.

Let the men have the usual regale on acct. of Expedition and a little grog to purchase on their own account if not against rules.

I would wish the small boat repaired and with the agres kept in order as I may possibly require it this autumn or next season.

May I beg of you to send to Churchill by the Schooner next summer

1	Ham	
15	lbs fine Biscuit	
1	" Hyson Tea	
1	" Souchong Do.	
2	" Chocolate	On acct. of Expedition
20	" Sugar	
1	Keg Brandy 2 Gns	
½	Bag Flour	
1	Do. Pemican	

I inclose with this a note of Articles received for the use of the Expedition from some of the men sent back, which I request you will cause to be returned to them or the values credited to their accounts.

I have to apologize for the rough way in which this is written, but the boat is very unsteady and as there is a strong breeze the spray flies over us occasionally.

With much regard
Believe me
Dear Sir
Your very obedt. Servant
John Rae

P.S. If the men wish to purchase the guns they have had the use of they may get them at prime Cost.

J. Rae

—— JOHN RAE, ESQUIRE, RECD. 30 AUGT. 1853 ——

[Endorsed]

Chesterfield Inlet 9th Augt. 1853

Chesterfield Inlet South point of entrance 7pm *9th August* 1853[404]
Dear Sir George
It is with much regret that I have now to report the failure of the attempt to reach the Arctic Sea by Chesterfield Inlet and Backs River, a failure that I am the more annoyed at, as it may have arisen from my having deviated from my original plan as I shall mention farther on.

Having addressed you from Churchill and since leaving there by an Esquimaux, I have now to mention that our run hither was a remarkably fine one, having met with not a single detention until we arrived within a few miles of this. Either with sails or oars we were travelling day and night sometimes under close reefs and again with full sail, the wind being the greater part of the time on shore, there was often a heavy sea that washed over the small boat some times.

We entered the Inlet on the 17th or 4½ days after our departure from Churchill and on the 20th (it being rather foggy in the morning) the steersman whilst I was asleep, ran into the mouth of a deep river[405] about half way up the Chesterfield on its north side, and being there I examined it, and finding that as far as I could see it flowed from the direction in which I wished to proceed and being a stream equal to the Coppermine in size I determined to ascend it thinking that after running north some distance it would turn to the West, as I could not believe that the drainage of the Country north and East of it, could supply so large a stream. In this I was deceived for the river flowed from the N W. for about half its tortuous course and then turned to the N E, a direction that it maintained until it diminished so as not to be navigable for the boat, the extreme point reached with it being in Latitude 65° 51' N Long. 93° 46' W. Still fully 70 miles from the Back. On examining the country to the westward it was found so rugged that although impracticable for the transport of a boat, the difficulties were so many that we could not reach the sea until too late a date for me to complete the survey I wished.

I now send back half my men, and with the remainder I start in an hour for Repulse Bay as it is much too late in the season now to attempt to carry out the original plan via the head of the Inlet down which we have had a beautiful run of 23 hours since leaving the Quoich River.

Should animals be as abundant at Repulse Bay as when I wintered there will be no difficulty in maintaining the party, and living snugly in snow houses If there is any danger of being starved I shall return to York Factory late this Autumn.

The men[406] with me are

John Beads	Halfbreed	Guide
Jacob Beads	Do.	Bowsman
James Johnston	Do.	Fisherman
Murdoch McLean[407]	Highlander	Middleman
John McDonald	Halfbreed	Do.
Thomas Mistegan	Cree Indian	Hunter
William Ouligbuck	Esquimaux	Interpreter

I omitted to mention that at the place in the newly traced river where I left the large boat and six of the party game of all kinds was very scarce, towards the head waters of the stream however muskox and deer were abundant, 5 of the former and 4 of the latter were shot all in very poor condition being so tormented by the Musquitoes (exceeding in numbers and pertinacity anything I had ever before seen) that they had no leisure to feed.

My men are all volunteers, smart fellows everyone of them but rather wastefull, so that I must keep a sharp look out on the expenditure.

I have no leisure to make a tracing of the Quoich (so I have named the river) to send you for indeed I have not been idle, acting in all sorts of duties particularly as hunter, at which although a poor shot I am very successful, having killed as many animals as all the others put together.

I hope you will excuse my writing you in this semi-official form, for I cannot write a private letter besides this, as we would lose the tide and with it some hours time.

Offer my regards to Miss Simpson, and my little friends all of whom have got Islands or something else named after them in the Quoich.

With much respect
Believe me Dear Sir George
Most faithfully Yours
John Rae

P.S. I expect to be at Repulse Bay in 4 days say on the 13th inst.

J.R.

—— JOHN RAE, RECD. 21 OCB., ANSD. 1 DECR. ——

[Endorsed]

1853
Chesterfield Inlet 9 August

South Point of Entrance Chesterfield Inlet 6 P M *9th August* 1853[408]
Archibald Barclay Esquire
&c. &c. &c.

Sir
I have the honor to acquaint you for the information of the Governor, Deputy Govr. and Committee that having failed in reaching Backs River from Chesterfield Inlet, I am now on my way to Repulse Bay for the purpose of wintering there, can we obtain the means of subsistence and endeavouring next spring to complete the survey on foot, which I have been unable to effect by the route I had at first intended.

I left Churchill on the 13th Ulto. and after an excellent passage of 4½ days passed this point and entered the Inlet on the afternoon of the 17th. On the morning of the 20th July whilst I was asleep the guide during hazy weather entered a deep river that falls into the Inlet on its north side about half way up it. This stream is marked in Arrowsmiths chart as having

35 fathoms depth in fresh water at its mouth. Being at the place I examined the river and finding it about as large as the Coppermine and flowing from the very direction I wished to proceed in I decided on ascending it, as I could not suppose that the drainage of the country to the North and North east of the Inlet could supply so large a stream of water.

Having secured the baggage and large boat, and obtained observations which placed us in Latitude 64° 12 45" N Longde. 93° 51' 21" W Variation of Compass 6° 20' E, I commenced the ascent of the river on the 22nd (the 21st being too stormy to allow us move) with the small boat and 8 of the party, the other six being left in charge of the baggage and at the same time being instructed to collect fuel and food.

A mile above our resting place there is a steep Fall about 25 feet high, (which I named the Ellice) which caused us to make a portage of about 200 yds. For the three following days the trending of the river was most favorable with a very strong current but after passing Latitude 64° 54' N Longde. 94° 50' W, it altered its course to the North eastward, and maintained the same direction with innumerable windings as far as it was practicable to take the boat, the extreme point reached with it being in Latitude 65° 50' N Long 94° 06' W and we were still fully 70 miles in a direct line from the nearest point of the Back.

On the following day (3rd August) after reaching this point two parties were sent out to examine the Country, but their report after travelling over 15 miles of it, was as unfavorable as I had been led to expect by a view I had from the summit of an adjoining hill. The whole Country was a bed of rocks and stones thrown together in the most confused manner, and though not impracticable to take a boat over, yet the difficulties to be overcome would have been so great that we could not have arrived at the sea earlier than the 20th or 25th August which would not allow time to complete the survey previous to the closing of the navigation.

This being the case I immediately commenced the descent of the stream the water in which had fallen several feet. Many of the rapids were difficult and dangerous. In running one the boat got filled with water to the thwarts, fortunately it was smooth immediately below, and we had leisure to bail.

Late on the evening of the 7th we reached our encampment having been 4 days coming down stream which it occupied us 11 to ascend, but the current had become much less swift, and the rapids more shallow requiring us to make more portages.

It was now much too late in the season to attempt carrying out the original plan, which I now regret much having deviated from, although we might have been equally unfortunate had I attempted it at first.

The most favorable starting point for a spring journey is my old quarters at Repulse Bay, and if the resources are as abundant as they were when I wintered there formerly I do not despair of passing the winter in snowhouses without suffering much privation.

The following named men are to accompany me

John Beads	Guide	halfbreed
Jacob Beads	Bowsman	Do.
Murdoch McLellan		Highlander
Thomas Mistegan	Hunter	Cree Indian
James Johnstone	Fishern.	halfbreed
John McDonald		Do.

If I find on arriving at Repulse Bay that the deer have taken another route by which to Migrate, and that the Esquimaux have left that quarter, (a sure sine of a scarcity of animals) I shall return late this autumn to York Factory.

Having writing this partly in the boat and part in my tent, in great haste so as to lose as little as possible of a fine fair wind which has carried us down the Inlet in 23 hours will I trust be sufficient excuse for the rough way in which it is done. The same cause prevents me from sending a tracing of the river I have surveyed and which I have called the Quoich After the highland glen of that name.

I have the honor to be
Sir
Your most obedt. Servant
John Rae C.F.
Commanding Expedn.

[Endorsed]

John Rae
August 9th 1853

Yorkfactory Hudson's Bay 1*st September* 1854[409]

Archibald Barclay Esquire
Secretary
Hudson's Bay House
London

Sir,
I have the honor to report for the information of the Governor, Deputy Governor and Committee, that I arrived here yesterday with my party all in good health, but from causes which will be explained in their proper place, without having effected the object of the Expedition. At the same time information has been obtained, and articles purchased from the Natives which prove, beyond a doubt, that a portion, if not all, of the then survivors of the long lost and unfortunate party under Sir John Franklin, had met with a fate as melancholy and dreadful as it is possible to imagine.[410]

By a Letter dated Chesterfield Inlet, 9th August 1853, you are in possession of my proceedings up to that time. Late on the evening of that day we parted company with our small consort, she steering down to the southward, whilst we took the opposite direction towards Repulse Bay.

Light and variable winds sadly retarded our advance northward, but by anchoring during the flood, and sailing or rowing with the tide, we gained some ground daily; On the 11th, we met with upwards of three hundred Walrus, lying on a rock a few miles off shore. They were not at all shy, and several were mortally wounded, but one only, (an immensely large fellow) was shot dead by myself. The greater part of the fat was cut off and taken on board, which supplied us abundantly with Oil for our Lamps all Winter.

On the forenoon of the 14th having a fair wind, we rounded Cape

Horn [Hope], and ran up Repulse Bay, but as the weather was very foggy, completely hiding every object, at the distance of a quarter of a mile; we made the Land about seven miles east of my old winter quarters: next day, midst heavy rain, we ran down to North Pole River, moored the boat, and pitched the tents.

The weather being still dark and gloomy the surrounding Country presented a most dreary aspect. Thick masses of ice clung to the shore, whilst immense drifts of snow filled each ravine, and lined every steep bank that had a southerly exposure. No Esquimaux were to be seen, nor any recent traces of them: appearances could not be less promising for wintering safely, yet I determined to remain until the 1st September, by which date, some opinion could be formed as to the practicability of procuring sufficient food and fuel for our support during the winter, all the provisions on hand at that time being equal to only three months consumption.

The weather fortunately improved, and not a moment was lost. Nets were set: Hunters were sent out to procure Venison; and the majority of the party was constantly employed collecting fuel. By the end of August a supply of the latter essential article, (Andromeda Tetragona,) for fourteen weeks was laid up, thirteen deer and one musk bull had been shot, and one hundred and thirty six salmon caught. Some of the favourite haunts of the Esquimaux had been visited, but no indications were seen, to lead us to suppose, that they had been lately in the neighbourhood.

The absence of the Natives caused me some anxiety, not that I expected any aid from them, but because I could attribute their having abandoned so favourable a locality, to no other cause than a scarcity of food, arising from the deer having taken another route in their migrations to and from the north.

On the 1st September, I explained our position to the Men; the quantity of provisions we had, and the prospects, which were far from flattering, of getting more. They all most readily volunteered to remain, and our preparations for a nine months winter were continued with unabated energy. The weather, generally speaking, was favorable, and our exertions were so successful, that by the end of the month, we had a quantity of provisions and fuel collected, adequate to our wants up to the period of the spring migrations of the deer.

One hundred and nine deer, one musk ox, (including those killed in August,) fifty three brace of Ptarmigan, and one Seal had been shot; and the nets produced fifty four Salmon: Of the larger Animals above enumerated, forty nine deer and the musk ox were shot by myself, twenty one deer by Mistegan the deer hunter, fourteen by another of the Men, nine by William Ouligbuck, and sixteen by the remaining four Men.

The cold weather set in very early and with great severity. On the 20th, all the smaller and some of the larger Lakes were covered with ice four to six inches thick. This was far from advantageous for deer shooting, as these animals were enabled to cross the Country in all directions, instead of following their accustomed passes.

October was very stormy and cold. About the 15th the migrations of the deer terminated, and twenty five more were added to our Stock. Forty two Salmon and twenty Trout were caught with nets and hooks set in lakes under the ice, On the 28th, the snow was packed hard enough for building, and we were glad to exchange the cold and dismal tents (in which the temperature had latterly been 36° or 37° below the freezing point,) for the more comfortable shelter of snowhouses, which were built on the S.S.E. side of Beacon Hill, by which they were well protected from the prevailing N.W. Gales. The houses were nearly half a mile south of my winter quarters of 1846/7.

The weather in November was comparatively fine but cold, the highest, lowest and mean temperature uncorrected for error of thermometer being respectively 38° and 18° 3° below Zero. Some deer were occasionally seen, but only four were shot, some wolves, several foxes and one wolverine were killed and from the nets 59 Salmon, and 22 Trout were obtained.

Our most productive Fishery was in a Lake about three miles distant, bearing East, (magnetic) from Beacon Hill or the mouth of North Pole River.

The whole of December a very few days excepted was one continued gale with snow and drift. When practicable the men were occupied scraping under snow for fuel, by which means our stock of that very essential article was kept up. The mean temperature of the month was 23° below zero. The produce of our nets and guns was extremely small, amounting to one partridge, one wolf, and twenty seven fish.

1854 On the first of January the temperature rose to the very unusual height of 18° above zero, the wind at the time being S E with snow. Our nets after being set in different lakes without success, were finally taken up on the 12th, only five small fish having been caught. The thermometer was tested by freezing mercury and found to be in error the temperature indicated by it being 4°5 too high.

The cold during February was steady and severe, but there were fewer storms than usual. Deer were more numerous and generally were travelling northward. One or two were wounded but none killed. On two occasions, (1st and 27th) that beautiful but rare appearance of the Clouds near the Sun,with three fringes of pink and green following the outline of the Cloud, was seen, and I may add that the same splendid phenomenon was frequently observed during the Spring, and was generally followed by a day or two of fine weather.

During the latter part of the Month, preparations were being made for our Spring journies. A Carpenters work shop was built of snow, and our sledges were taken to pieces, reduced to as light a weight as possible, and then re-united more securely than before. The mean temperature of February, corrected for error of thermometer was 39° below zero. The highest and lowest being -20° and -53°.

On the 1st of March a female deer in fine Condition was shot, and on the 9th and 10th two more were killed. Three men were absent some days during this month in search of Esquimaux from whom we wished to obtain dogs. They went far as the head of Ross Bay but found no traces of these people.

On the 14th I started with three men hauling sledges with provisions, to be placed in "cache" for the long spring Journey. Owing to the stormy state of the weather, we got no farther than Cape Lady Pelly, on the most northerly point of which our stores were placed under a heap of large stones, secure from any Animal except Man or the bear. We returned on the 24th, the distance walked together being 170 miles.

On the 31st March leaving three men in charge of the boat and stores, I set out with the other four including the Interpreter, with the view of tracing the west coast of Boothia from the Castor and Pollux River to Bellot Strait. The weight of our provisions &c. with those deposited on the way amounted to 865 lbs, an ample supply for 65 days.

The route followed for part of the Journey being exactly the same as that of Spring 1847, it is unnecessary to describe it. During the two first days, although we did not travel more than fifteen miles per day, the men found the work extremely hard, and as I perceived that one of them (a fine active young fellow but a light weight,) would be unable to keep pace with the others, he was sent back and replaced by Mistegan, a very able man and an experienced sledge hauler. More than a day was lost in making this exchange, but there was still abundance of time to complete our work if not opposed by more than common obstacles.

On the 6th April, we arrived at our provision "caches" and found it all safe. Having placed the additional stores on the sledges, which made those of the men weigh more than 160 lbs each, and my own about 110 lbs, we travelled seven miles further, then built a snow house on the ice two miles from shore. We had passed among much rough ice, but hitherto the drift banks of snow, by lying in the same direction in which we were travelling, made the walking tolerably good. As we advanced to the northward however, these crossed our track, (shewing that the prevailing winter gales had been from the westward,) and together with stormy weather, impeded us so much that we did not reach Colville Bay until the 10th. The position of our snowhouse was in Latitude 68° 13' 5" N, Longde. by Chronometer 88° 14" 51 W., the variation of the Compass being 26° 20" W. From this place it was my intention to strike across Land as straight as possible for the Castor and Pollux River.

The 11th was so stormy that we could not move, and the next day after placing "en cache" two days provisions, we had walked only six miles, in a westerly direction, when a gale of wind compelled us to get under shelter. The weather improved in the Evening, and having the benefit of the full moon, we started again at a few minutes to 8 p m. Our course at first was the same as it had been in the morning, but the snow soon became so soft and deep, that I turned more to the northward in search of firmer footing. The walking was excessively fatiguing, and would have been so even to persons travelling unencumbered, as we sank at every step nearly ankle deep in snow. Eight and a half miles were accomplished in six and a half hours, at the end of which, as we required some rest, a small snow house was built, and we had some tea and frozen pemican.

After resting three hours, we resumed our march, and by making long detours, found the snow occasionally hard enough to support our weight. At 30 minutes to noon on the 13th, our days journey terminated in Latde. 68° 23' 30" N, Longde. 89° 3' 53" W, variation of Compass 83° 30' W. At a mile and a half from our bivouac, we had crossed the arm of a lake of considerable extent, but the Country around was so flat, and so completely covered with snow, that its limits could not be easily defined and our snowhut was on the borders of another lake apparently somewhat smaller.

A snow storm of great violence raged during the whole of the 14th, which did not prevent us from making an attempt to get forward; after persevering two and a half hours, and gaining a mile and a half distance, we were again forced to take shelter.

The 15th was very beautiful with a temperature of only 8° below zero. The heavy fall of snow had made the walking and sledge hauling worse than before. It was impossible to keep a straight course, and we had to turn much out of our way, so as to select the hardest drift banks. After advancing several miles, we fortunately reached a large Lake containing a number of Islands, on one of which I noticed an old Esquimaux tent site. The fresh footmarks of a partridge (Tetrao Rupestris) were also seen, being the only signs of living thing, (a few tracks of foxes excepted,) that we had observed since commencing the traverse of this dreary waste of snow clad country. To the lake above mentioned, and to those seen previously, the name of Barrow was given, as a mark of respect to John Barrow[411] Esquire, of the Admiralty, whose zeal in promoting and liberality in supporting many of the Expeditions to the Arctic Sea are too well known to require any comment; further, than that he presented a very valuable Halketts Boat for the Service of my party, which unfortunately by some irregularity in the Railway baggage trains between London and Liverpool did not reach the latter place in time for the Steamer although sent from London some days before. Our snow hut was built on the edge of a small lake in Late. 68° 31' 38 N, Longde. 89° 11. 55 W, Variation of Compass 83° 3° W.

The difficulties of walking were somewhat diminished on the 16th, by a fresh breeze of wind which drifted the snow off the higher ground, and we were enabled to make a fair day's Journey. Early on the 17th we reached the shore of Pelly Bay, but had barely got a view of its rugged ice covering, before a dense fog came on: we had to *steer* by compass for a large rocky Island, some miles to the westward, and we stopped on an islet near to its east shore until the fog cleared away. This luckily happened some time before noon, and afforded an opportunity of obtaining observations, the results of which were Latde. 68° 44' 53" N, Longde. by chron 89° 34' 47 W, and variation 84° 20 W. Even on the ice we found the snow soft and deep, a most unusual circumstance. The many detentions I had met with caused me now, instead of making for the Castor and Pollux River, to attempt a direct course towards the magnetic Pole, should the land west of the bay be smooth enough for travelling over. The large island west of us was so rugged and steep, that there was no crossing it with sledges we therefore travelled along its shore to the northward, and stopped for the night, within a few miles of its northern extremity. The track of an Esquimaux sledge drawn by dogs was observed to day, but was of old date.

The morning of the 18th was very foggy, but after rounding the north point of the Island, it became clear and we travelled due west or very nearly so, until within three miles of the west shore of the bay, which presented an appearance so rocky and mountainous, that it was evident we could not traverse it, without loss of time. As the Country towards the head of the bay looked more level I turned to the southward, and after a most circuitous walk of more than sixteen miles, we built our snow house on the ice, five miles from shore. Many old traces of Esquimaux were seen on the ice to day.

On the 19th we continued travelling southward, and our day's journey (about equal to that of yesterday) terminated near the head of the bay.

20th April. The fresh footmarks of Esquimaux, with a sledge having been seen yesterday on the ice within a short distance of our resting place, the interpreter and one man were sent to look for them, the other two being employed in hunting and collecting fuel, whilst I obtained excellent Observations, the results of which were Latde. 68° 28' 29" N Longde. by Chronr. 90° 18' 32" W, Variation of Compass 98° 30 W. The latter is apparently erroneous, probably caused by much local attraction.

After an absence of eleven hours the Men sent in search of Esquimaux returned in company with seventeen natives, (five of whom were Women,) and several of them had been at Repulse Bay when I was there in 1847. Most of the others had never before seen "Whites", and were extremely forward and troublesome, they would give us no information on which any reliance could be placed, and none of them would consent to accompany us for a day or two, although I promised to reward them liberally. Apparently there was a great objection to our travelling across the Country in a westerly direction.[412] Finding that it was their object to puzzle the Interpreter and mislead us, I declined purchasing more than a small piece of Seal from them, and sent them away, not however, without some difficulty, as they lingered about with the hope of stealing something, and notwithstanding our vigilance, succeeded in abstracting from one of the sledges a few pounds of Biscuit and Grease.

The morning of the 21st was extremely fine, and at 3 a m we started across land towards a very conspicuous hill, bearing west of us. On a rocky eminence some miles inland, we made a "cache" of the Seals flesh we had purchased. Whilst doing this our Interpreter made an attempt to join his Countrymen, fortunately his absence was observed before he had gone back very far, and he was overtaken after a sharp race of four or five miles. He was in a great fright when we came up to him, and was crying like a child, but expressed his readiness to return, and pleaded sickness as an excuse for his conduct. I believe he was really unwell, probably from having eaten too much boiled Seals flesh, with which he had been regaled in the snowhuts of the Natives.

Having taken some of the lading off Ouligbuck's sledge, we had barely resumed our Journey when we were met by a very intelligent Esquimaux, driving a dog's sledge laden with musk ox beef. This man at once consented to accompany us two days Journey, and in a few minutes had deposited his load on the snow, and was ready to join us. Having explained my object to him, he said that the road by which he had come was the best for us, and having lightened the men's sledges we travelled with more facility. We were now joined by another of the Natives who had been absent Seal hunting yesterday, but being anxious to see us, had visited our snow house early this morning, and then followed up our track. This man was very communicative, and on putting to him the usual questions as to his having seen "white men" before, or any ships or boats—he replied in the negative; but said, that a party of "Kabloonans", had died of starvation, a long distance to the west of where we then were, and beyond a large River;—He stated that, he did not know the exact place; that he had never been there; and that he could not accompany us so far.

The substance of the information then and subsequently obtained from various sources, was to the following effect:

In the Spring, four winters past, (1850) whilst some Esquimaux families were killing Seals near the north shore of a large Island named in Arrowsmith's Charts, King William's Land, about forty white men were seen travelling in company southward over the ice, and dragging a boat and sledges with them.[413] They were passing along the west shore of the above named Island. None of the party could speak the Esquimaux language so well as to be understood, but by signs the Natives were led to believe that the Ship or Ships had been crushed by ice, and that they were then going to where they expected to find deer to shoot. From the appearance of the Men (all of whom with the exception of one Officer, were hauling on the drag ropes of the sledge and were looking thin)—they were then supposed to be getting short of provisions, and they purchased a small Seal or piece of Seal from the natives. The Officer was described as being a tall, stout, middle aged man: When their days journey terminated, they pitched Tents to rest in.

At a later date the same Season but previous to the disruption of the ice, the corpses of some thirty persons and some Graves were discovered on the Continent,[414] and five dead bodies on an Island near it, about a long day's journey to the north west of the mouth of a large stream, which can be no other than Backs Great Fish River, (named by the Esquimaux Ool-koo-i-hi-ca-lik,) as its description, and that of the low shore in the neighbourhood of Point Ogle and Montreal Island agree exactly with that of Sir George Back. Some of the bodies were in a tent or tents; others were under the boat which had been turned over to form a shelter, and some lay scattered about in different directions. Of those seen on the Island,[415] it was supposed that one was that of an Officer, (chief) as he had a telescope strapped over his shoulders, and his double barrelled gun lay underneath him.

From the mutilated state of many of the bodies and the contents of the kettles, it is evident that our wretched Countrymen had been driven to the last dread alternative, as a means of sustaining life. A few of the unfortunate Men must have survived until the arrival of the wild fowl, (say until the end of May,) as shots were heard, and fresh bones and feathers of geese were noticed near the scene of the sad event.

There appears to have been an abundant store of ammunition, as the Gunpowder was emptied by the Natives in a heap on the ground out of the kegs or cases containing it and a quantity of shot and ball was found below high water mark, having probably been left on the ice close to the beach before the spring thaw commenced. There must have been a number of telescopes, guns, (several of them double barrelled,) watches, compasses &c. all of which seem to have been broken up, as I saw pieces of these different articles with the Natives, and I purchased as many as possible, together with some silver spoons and forks, an order of merit in the form of a Star, and a small silver plate engraved Sir John Franklin K.O.H.

Inclosed is a list of the principal articles bought, with a note of the initials and a rough pen and ink sketch of the crests on the forks and spoons. The articles themselves I shall have the honor of handing over to you, on my arrival in London.

None of the Esquimaux with whom I had communication saw the "white men" either when living or after death, nor had they ever been at the place where the Corpses were found, but had their information from Natives who had been there, and who had seen the party when travelling over the ice. From what I could learn, there is no reason to suspect that any violence had been offered to the sufferers by the Natives.

As the dogs in the sledge were fatigued before they joined us, our days journey was a short one. Our snow house was built in Latde. 68° 29' N & Londe. 90 42. 42. W on the bed of a river having high mud banks, and which falls into the west side of Pelly Bay about Latde. 68° 47' N, and Longde. 90° 25' W.

On the 22nd, we travelled along the north bank of the River, (which I named after Capt. Beecher of the Admiralty) in a westerly direction for seven or eight miles (until abreast of the lofty and peculiarly shaped hill already alluded to, and which I named Ellice Mountain,) when we turned more to the northward. We soon arrived at a long narrow lake on which we encamped a few miles from its east end, our days march being little more than thirteen miles. Our Esquimaux auxiliaries were now anxious to return, being in dread or professing to be so, that the wolves or wolverines would find their "cache" of meat and destroy it. Having paid them liberally for their aid and information, and having bade them a most friendly farewell, they set out for home, as we were preparing to go to bed.

Next morning provisions for six days were secured under a heap of ponderous stones, and we resumed our march along the Lake. Thick weather, snow storms and heavy walking sadly retarded our advance. The Esquimaux had recommended me, after reaching the end of the chain of lakes, (which ran in a N' Westerly direction for nearly twenty miles, and then turned sharply to the southward,) to follow the windings of a brook that flowed from them. This I attempted to do, until finding that we would be led thereby far to the South, we struck across land to the west among a series of hills and valleys. Tracks of deer now became numerous, and a few traces of musk cattle were observed.

At 2 a m on the 26th we fell upon a River with banks of mud and gravel 20 to 40 feet high, and about a quarter of a mile in width. After a most laborious walk of more than 18 miles, we found an old snow hut, which after a few repairs was made habitable, and we were snugly housed at 6h.40m. a m. Our position was in Latde. 68° 25' 27" N, Longde. 92° 53' 14" W.

One of my men who from carelessness some weeks before, had severely frozen two of his toes, was now scarcely able to walk; and as by Esquimaux report, we could not be very far from the Sea, I prepared to start in the evening with two men and four days provisions for the Castor and Pollux River, leaving the lame man and another to follow at their leisure a few miles on our track, to some rocks that lay in our route, where they were more likely to find both fuel and game, than on the bare flat ground where we then were.

The morning of the 26th was very fine as we commenced tracing the course of the River seaward, sometimes following its course, at other times travelling on its left or right bank to cut off points. At 4 a m on the 27th, we reached the mouth of the river, which by subsequent observation I found to be situate in Lat 68° 32 N, Longde. 93. 20 W. It was rather difficult to discover when we had reached the Sea, until a mass of rough ice settled the question beyond a doubt. After leaving the river we walked rapidly due west for six miles, then built our usual snug habitation on the ice, three miles from shore, and had some partridges, (Tetrao mutas,) for supper, at the unseasonable hour of 8 a m. We had seen great numbers of these birds during the night. Our latitude was 68° 32 1 N, Longde. 93° 33' 48" West, being 3' 38" N and about 40' East of Simpsons position of the mouth of the Castor and Pollux River.

The weather was overcast with snow, when we resumed our journey at 8h. 30m. P.M. on the 27th; we directed our course directly for the shore, which we reached after a sharp walk of one and a half hours, in doing which we crossed a long stony island of some miles in extent.[416] As by this time it was snowing heavily, I made my men travel on the ice, the walking being better there, whilst I followed the winding of the shore, closely examining every object along the beach.

After passing several heaps of stones, which had evidently formed Esquimaux "Caches", I came to a collection larger than any I had yet seen, and clearly not intended for the protection of property of any kind. The stones generally speaking were small, and had been built in the form of a pillar, but the top had fallen down, as the Esquimaux had previously given me to understand was the case.

Calling my men to land, I sent one to trace what looked like the bed of a small river immediately west of us, whilst I and the other man cleared away the pile of stones in search of a document. Although no document was found there could be no doubt in my own mind, and in that of my companion, that its construction was not that of the natives: My belief that we had arrived at the Castor and Pollux River was confirmed, when the person who had been sent to trace the apparent stream bed, returned with the information that it was clearly a River.

My Latitude of the Castor and Pollux is 68° 28' 37" N, agreeing within a quarter of a mile, with that of Simpson, but our longitudes differ considerably, his being 94. 14 West whilst mine was 93° 42' W. My Longitude is nearly intermediate between that of Simpson and Sir George Back, supposing the latter to have carried on his survey eastward from Montreal Island.

[Note in manuscript] A number of rocky elevations to the north of the River, were mistaken by Simpson for Islands, and named by him the Committee.[417]

Having spent upwards of an hour in fruitless search for a memorandum of some kind, we began to retrace our steps, and after a most fatiguing march of fifteen hours during which we walked at least thirty miles, we arrived at the snow hut of the men left behind. They had shot nothing, and had not collected sufficient andromeda for cooking, but had been compelled to use some grease. The frost bitten man could scarcely move.

Early on the morning of the 29th during a heavy fall of snow, we set out for the mouth of the River, which was named in honor of Sir Roderick Murchison[418] the Late President of the Royal Geographical Society, and after losing our way occasionally in attempting to make short cuts, we arrived at Cache Island, (so named from an Esquimaux cache that was on it) within two miles of the Sea at 8 a m and stopped there, as it blew a gale with drift.

As soon as we got shelter and had supped, preparations were made for starting in the Evening for Bellot Strait. An ample stock of provisions and fuel for twenty two days were placed on two of our best sledges, and I hauled on my own small sledge, my instruments, books bedding &c. as usual.

On the Evening of the 29th the weather was so stormy, that although we were prepared to start at 8 O'Clock we could not get away until past 2 on the following morning, when after travelling little more than five miles, a heavy fall of snow and strong wind caused us again to take shelter.

Our advance was so much impeded by thick weather and soft snow that we did not arrive within a few miles of Cape Porter of Sir John Ross until the 6th May. In doing this we had traversed a bay the head of which was afterwards found to extend as far north as Latde. 68° 54' N. Point Sir H. Dryden, its western boundary, is in Latde, 68° 44 N, Longde. 94 W. To this bay the name of Shepherd[419] was given, in honor of The Deputy Governor of the Honble. Hudsons Bay Company, and an Island near its head, was called Bence Jones,[420] after the distinguished medical man and Analytical Chemist of that name, to whose kindness I and my party were much indebted, for having proposed the use, and prepared some extract, of tea for the expedition. This Article we found extremely portable, and as the tea could be made without boiling water, we often enjoyed a cup of that refreshing beverage, when otherwise from want of fuel, we must have been satisfied with cold water.

From Point Dryden the Coast which is low and stony runs in a succession of small points and bays about ten miles nearly due west, then turns sharply up to the North in Lat. 68° 45 N. Longde. 94° 27' 50" W which was ascertained by Observations obtained on an Island near the Shore. The point was called Cape Colvile, after the Governor of the Company, and the Island, Stanley. To the west, at the distance of seven or eight miles, land was seen, which received the appellation of Matheson Island,[421] as a mark of respect to one of the Directors[422] of the Company.

Our snow hut on the 6th May situate on Pointe de la Guiche was by good Observations found to be in Latde. 68° 57' 52" N, Longde. 94° 22' 58" W. One of my men Mistegan, an Indian of great intelligence and activity, was sent six miles farther along the Coast northwards: by ascending some rough ice at its extreme point, he could see about five miles farther; the land was still trending northward, whilst to the north west, at a considerable distance, perhaps 12 or 14 miles, there was an appearance of land, the channel between which and the point where he stood, being full of rough ice. This land, if it was such, is probably part of Matty Island, or King Williams Land, which latter is also clearly an Island.

I am happy to say that on the present, as on a former, occasion, where my Survey met that of Sir James C. Ross, a very singular agreement exists, considering the circumstances under which our Surveys have been taken.

The foggy and snowy weather which continued upwards of four days, had occasioned the loss of so much time, that although I could easily have completed a part, (perhaps the half,) of the survey of the Coast, between the Magnetic Pole and Bellot Strait or Brentford Bay, I could not do the whole without great risk to my party, and I therefore decided upon returning.

Having taken possession of our Discoveries in the usual form, and built a cairn, we commenced our return on the night of the 6th. Having fine clear weather, we made long marches, and at Shepherd Bay, having got rid of the sledge which I had hitherto hauled, I detached myself from the party, and examined the bay within a mile or two of the shore, whilst my men took a straighter route.

Thick weather again came on as we entered the bay, (named in honor of Sir Robert H. Inglis,[423]) into which the Murchison River falls, and we had much trouble in finding the mouth of the River. Here the services of my cree hunter were of much value, as custom had caused him to notice indications and marks, which would have escaped the observation of a person less acute and experienced.

On the 11th May at 3 a m, we reached the place where our two men had been left. Both were as well as I could hope for, the one whose great toe had been frozen, and which was about to slough off at the first joint (thereby rendering the foot very tender and painful when walking in deep snow,) had too much spirit to allow himself to be hauled. One deer, and eighteen partridges had been shot; but notwithstanding I found a greater reduction in our Stock of provisions than I had anticipated, and I felt confirmed in the course I had taken.

The day became very fine, and Observations were taken which gave the position of Cache Island where our snowhut was, Latde. 68° 32' 2" N, Longde. 93° 13' 18 W.

Having completed my observations, and filled in rough tracings of the Coast line, which I generally did from day to day, we started for home at 8.30 p m. The weather being now fine, and the snow harder than when outward bound, we advanced more rapidly and in a straighter direction, until we came to the lakes about midway in the Isthmus, after which, as far as Pelly Bay, our outward and homeward route were exactly alike. We reached Pelly Bay at 1 a m on the 17th, and built a snow house about 2½ miles south, and the same distance west, of my observations of the 20th April.

Observing traces of Esquimaux, two men were sent after supper to look for them. After 8 hours absence they returned with 10 or 12 native men, women, and children. From these people I bought a silver spoon and fork. The initials F.R.M.C[424] not engraved, but scratched with a sharp instrument, on the spoon, puzzled me much, as I knew not at the time, the Christian names of the Officers of Sir John Franklins Expedition; and thought possibly that the letters above named might be the initials of Captn. McClure, the small c between the M C being omitted.

Two of the Esquimaux, (one of them I had seen in 1847) offered for a consideration to accompany us a day or two's march with a sledge and dogs. We were detained some time by the slow preparations of our new Allies, but we soon made up for lost time, and after a journey of 16 geographical or about 18½ statute miles, we arrived at the east side of the bay, in Latitude by reduction to the meridian 68° 23' 10" N, Longde. 89° 58' 39" W.

It may be remembered, that in the Spring of 1847 I did not trace the shore of Pelly Bay, but saw it from the summit of one of the lofty islands in the bay. Desirous of being always within, rather than of exceeding the limits of truth, I that year placed the head of the bay about 10 miles north of what it ought to have been, a mistake which will be easily accounted for, by those who know the difficulties of estimating distances in a snow clad country, where the height of the Land is unknown.

The width of the Isthmus separating Pelly and Shepherds Bays is fully sixty geographical miles.

In the evening before parting with our Esquimaux Assistants, we bought a dog from them, and after a most friendly farewell, resumed our journey eastward, and found on a long lake some old snow house in which we took up our lodgings. Here a set of good Observations placed us in Latde. 68° 12' 18" N Longde. 89° 24' 51" W Variation 81°W.

On the morning of the 21st we arrived at Committee Bay, from thence our route to Repulse Bay was almost the same as before, and I shall not therefore advert to it further than to mention that we arrived at our winter home at 5 a m on the 26th May, having from the better walking travelled in 20 days, the distance (less 40 or 50 miles) which had taken us 36 days to accomplish on our outward journey.

I found the three men who had been left in charge of the property quite well, living in abundance, and on the most friendly terms with a number of Esquimaux families, who had pitched their tents near them.

The Natives had behaved in the most exemplary manner, and many of them who were short of food, in compliance with my orders to that effect, had been supplied with venison from our stores.

It was from this time until August, that I had opportunities of questioning the Esquimaux regarding the information which I had already obtained of the party of whites who had perished of starvation, and of eliciting the particulars connected with that sad event, the substance of which I have already stated.

In the early part of July the Salmon came from the Sea to the mouths of the Rivers and brooks which were at that date open, and we caught numbers of them, so that occasionally, we could afford to supply our native friends with fifty or one hundred in a night. As is the usual custom at the Hudson's Bay Companys inland trading posts, all provisions were given gratis, and they were much more gratefully received by the Esquimaux than by the more southerly and more favoured red man.

We had still on hand half of our three months stock of pemican, and a sufficiency of Ammunition to provide for the wants of another Winter. We were all in excellent health and could get as many dogs as we required: so that (D V) there was little doubt that a second attempt to complete the survey, would be successful, but I now thought that I had a higher duty to attend to; that duty being to communicate with as little loss of time as possible the melancholy tidings which I had heard, and thereby save the risk of more valuable lives being jeopardized in a fruitless search in a direction there was not the slightest prospect of obtaining any information.[425] I trust this will be deemed a sufficiently good reason for my return.

The Summer was extremely cold and backward; we could not leave Repulse Bay until the 4th August and on the 6th had much difficulty in rounding Cape Hope. From thence, as far as Cape Fullerton, the Strait between Southampton Island and the main shore, was fully packed with ice, which gave us great trouble. South of Cape Fullerton, we got into open water. On the evening of the 19th calms and head winds much retarded us, so that we did not enter Churchill river, until the morning of the 28th August. There we were detained all day by a storm of wind. My good interpreter Wm. Ouligbuck was landed, and before bidding him farewell, I presented him with a very handsomely mounted hunting knife, intrusted to me by Captain Sir George Back, for his former travelling Companion Ouligbuck; but as the old man was dead, I took the liberty of giving it to his Son, as an inducement to future good conduct should his Services be again required.

A three days run brought us to York factory, at which place we landed all well on the forenoon of the 31 August. I am happy to say that the conduct of my men under circumstances often very trying, was generally speaking, extremely good and praiseworthy, and although their wages were higher than those of any party who have hitherto been employed on Boat Expeditions, I thought it advisable after consulting with Chief Factor William Mactavish to give each a small gratuity, varying the amount according to merit.

In conclusion, I have to express my regret that, I was unable on this occasion, to bring to a successful termination, an Expedition which I had myself planned and projected; but in extenuation of my failure, I may mention, that I was met by an accumulation of obstacles, beyond the usual ones of storms and rough ice which my former experience in Arctic travelling, had not led me to anticipate.

I have the honor to be,
Sir,
Your very obedt. Servant,
John Rae C.F.

[Endorsed]

Dr. Rae

Report 1st. Septr./54

[Enclosure][426]
List of Articles purchased at Repulse and Pelly Bays said to have been found with the party of men that starved to the West of Back's River in the Spring of

1850

1	Silver table Fork			Crest No 1	
4	" "	Do.		" "	2
			Motto		
1	" "	Do.	Spero Meliora	" "	4
2	" "	Do.		" "	5

1	Silver dessert Fork		Crest No 5
1	" table Do. with initials		H.D.S.G.
1	" " Do.	"	A.McD.
1	" " Do.	"	G.A.M.
1	" " Do.	"	J.T.
1	" " Spoon		Crest No 3
		Motto	
1	" " Do.	Spero Meliora	" 4
1	" " Do.		" 5
1	" tea Do.		" 5
1	" " Do.	initials	J.S.P.
1	" dessert Do.	"	J.S.P.
1	" " Do.	"	G.G.
1	round silver Plate Sir John Franklin K.C.H.		
1	Star or Order		
2	Pieces Gold Watch Case		
1	Case silver gilt pocket Chronometer & dial		
7	pieces Cases of Silver Watches		
1	small silver pencil Case		
1	piece of Silver Tube		
1	piece of an Optical Instrument		
1	old cold [gold] Cap Band		
2	pieces (about 2 inches) gold Watch Chain		
2	Sovereigns		
1	Half crown		
4	Shillings		
2	Leaves of the Students Manual		
1	surgeons Knife		
1	Scalpel		
2	Knives		
1	Do. Womens or Shoemakers		
1	pocket Compass Box		
1	Ivory Handle of a table Knife Marked "Hickey"		

1 narrow tin case Marked Fowler
1 " " Do. no cover W.M.
Sundry other articles of little consequence.

Tavistock Hotel Covent Garden London *22nd October* 1854[427]

The Secretary
of the Honble. Hudsons Bay Co.

Sir

I have the honour to aquaint you for the information of the Governor, Deputy Governor and Committee that I arrived here today at 3 p.m. having landed from the Honble. Company's Ship *Prince of Wales*[428] (32 days from York Factory) this morning off Deal.

I regret to say that my expedition has been unsuccessful in its object as regards the completion of the survey of the west Coast of Boothia, on the other hand information has been obtained and articles purchased from the Esquimaux by me, which clearly prove that a portion if not the whole of the *then* survivors of Sir John Franklin's long lost party died of Starvation in spring 1850, at no great distance to the north west of the mouth of Backs Fish River.

Among the Articles purchased from the natives (all of which accompanied by a list of them will be found in the YF packet box) are, a small silver plate with "Sir John Franklin K.C.B."[429] engraved thereon, a star of the Hanoverian order of Knighthood, and a number of Silver spoons and forks, on which are marked the initials of several of the officers of *both* ships—viz. Captn. Crozier, Lieut. G. Gore, Surgeons and Asst. Surgeons Goodsir, Peddie, and McDonald &c.

We passed last winter at the head of Repulse Bay in snowhouses without suffering much privation having by great exertion in the Autumn collected a sufficient stock of fuel, venison and fish to place us beyond the reach of want for the cold season.

I beg to apologize for not having a detailed report of the Expedition and chart of my discoveries (amounting to about two hundred miles) prepared for the perusal and inspection of the Honble. Committee, but my duties were so various and required such constant attention from the time of my leaving Repulse Bay on the 4th of August until my arrival at York Factory on the 30th of the same month, and the voyage across the Atlantic has been so stormy that I have not been able to complete these documents, but hope to place them in your hands in a day or two.

In conclusion I may remark that the conduct of my men was generally speaking excellent, and the whole party enjoyed perfect health

I have the honor to be
Sir
Your most obedt. Servant
John Rae

[Addressed]

The Secretary
of the Honble H.B.Co.
4 Fenchurch Street London.

[Endorsed]

John Rae
22nd October 1854

---

13 Salisbury Street Strand 14*th December* 1854[430]

Sir

As my Lords Commissioners of the Admiralty must by this time, have had ample leisure to take into consideration the contents of Captain Collinson's[431] report, would you do me the favor to inquire if it is the intention of the Governor and Directors of the Honble. Company to take any further measures in prosecution of my claim to the reward[432] offered by Government for discovering the fate of Sir John Franklins party?

I would not venture to trouble their Honors on this subject, but as they have taken the first step in the matter, I have thought it proper to address this communication to you previous to applying elsewhere.

As I leave London for the North on the 16th or 17th inst., should no answer be vouchsafed me before either of these dates, have the Kindness to address to, Stromness, Orkney.

I have the honor to be
Sir
Your very obedt. Servant
John Rae

To The Secretary
of the Hudson's Bay Company

[Endorsed]

John Rae
December 14th 1854

---

13 Salisbury Street Strand 16*th Decr.* 1854[433]

Sir
I had this morning the honor of receiving your note of yesterdays date, on the subject of the reward offered by Government for tracing the fate of Franklin.

I am exceedingly sorry that the Company should have been put to the trouble of taking the first steps towards the settlement of any business in which I was *alone* interested—and I certainly never would have applied to them, had I not thought that as I was one of their servants, such was the proper course.

I must now endeavour to do the best I can for myself regreting only that much time has been lost in requesting others to do, what it now appears I should have done personally.

Permit me one remark and I make it in a purely business spirit. How does it happen that I am looked upon as a private individual when applying for the above named reward and as only affecting myself personally, at the same time that the amount of my salary from the Hudson's Bay Company, is made dependant upon the receipt or non receipt of such reward with which neither I nor one or two friends I have consulted on the subject can trace its having any connexion?

I have the honor to be
Sir
With much respect
Your most obedt. Servant
John Rae

Andrew Colvile Esqre.
Governor
&c. &c. &c.

[Endorsed]

John Rae
December 16th 1854

Aberdeen 20*th December* 1854[434]

Honorable Sirs

I sometime ago addressed a letter to one of the Members of your Committee (Eden [sic] Colvile Esquire) on the subject of my salary during my employment on the recent Arctic Expedition—I took this liberty from a belief that the many important duties which must occupy your time, might have prevented you from taking any notice of a matter comparatively so trivial.

The reply to my communication was to the following effect "It is the opinion of the Members of the Committee that the question of your salary should remain in abeyance, until it is decided whether you were to receive the Government Reward for discovering the fate of Sir John Franklin and Party".

Had your Honors declined to give me the usual additional pay awarded to persons employed as I have been, I should have at once supposed that my conduct had not met with your approval, and have requested to know in what particular I had committed an error; but to make the amount of my Salary as a servant of the Company dependant upon my receipt of a Reward from Government with which it can have no connexion is a proceeding perfectly beyond my comprehension.

Having little faith in the correctness of my own views on this subject, I referred the point to the consideration of a few friends on whose judgement I could rely. Their opinion fully coincided with mine. The only conclusion which they and I could arrive at, was, that should I receive the reward alluded to (with which as I have already said, the amount of my salary ought to have no connexion) Your Honors would consider yourselves absolved from giving me that amount of pay, to which I am, although perhaps not in law, yet in honor and common fairness entitled.

If this view of the case be an erronious one, I beg in the most humble manner to apologize for having formed it.

Permit me to call attention to several former Expeditions to the Arctic Sea, and first of all to that under Dease and Simpson. On that Expedition two of the most intelligent and experienced of the Company's Officers were employed. They were three summers and two winters engaged in completing the very extensive survey they accomplished. During that time these gentlemen and the men with them received additional pay, or a gratuity equivalent to it, and after their return a pension of £100 per annum for life was given by Government to each of the two Leaders. I have been eight summers and four winters employed on Arctic Survey and research, and in all these years (one excepted) was commanding and sole Officer of the Expeditions with which I was connected (a circumstance almost unprecedented in Arctic voyages and journies) and thus saved the expense of a second Officer. I have seen more of the Arctic Coast of America than any man living and have individually traced as much new coast as Dease and Simpson did jointly; the only difference being that the greater part of my survey was performed on foot,—the most fatiguing of all modes of travelling when the supplies have to be carried or hauled—whilst theirs, with a very trifling exception was performed in boats, and was of course comparatively easy work.

I have done more than this, for when I twice wintered at Repulse

Bay relying on my own experience as a sportsman, I carried with me, not above a third part of the provisions that the generality of persons would have taken, and thus not only saved to the company the cost of extra Stores, but also the price of the boats, and the pay of the men required to transport them. On both these occasions I did all the duties of Commanding Officer unaided, and in addition shot more than one third of the game killed by the whole party.

In 1847 there was no demur about giving me additional salary. When employed under Government in the Years 1848, '49, '50 and '51 my pay was liberal but when I returned this Autumn from the Arctic Coast, at nearly the same time as several hundred others[435] who had been employed on a somewhat similar service as myself—I was the only one of all the number, with whom any difficulty was made in deciding the amount of pay. They each and all received double salary; the amount of mine was left in abeyance.

It is very humiliating and extremely disagreeable to be forced thus to bring before the notice of Your Honors, these few particulars regarding my services in the Polar Regions, but no other course was open to me, except one, to which I would be most sorry and reluctant to resort.

Hoping that you will give my case your favorable consideration.

I have the honor to be
with much respect
Your most obedient Servant
John Rae

To The Governor
Deputy Govr. & Committee
of the Honble. Hudsons Bay Co.

[Endorsed]

John Rae
December 20th 1854.

Stromness Orkney 27*th January* 1855[436]

The Secretary
of the Hudson's Bay Co.

Sir
I have the honor to acknowledge the receipt of your letter of the 22nd instant[437] having reference to the subject of my Salary during the period I was employed on the recent Expedition.

Without noticing the nice distinction made in your letter, between the funds of the Hudson's Bay Company and those of the "Fur Trade Concern" about which something might be said, I thought (it seems erroneously) that the gratuity or extra remuneration given by the Company to the Leader or Leaders of their Arctic Expeditions (although of course a voluntary award on their part) was bestowed for the purpose of placing these Officers on a somewhat equal footing with others who were or had been similarly employed and with the men who acted under them, and not as a pecuniary mark of the Governor and Committees approbation and favor.

Had this latter view of the case occurred to me I should not for a moment have thought of making any application on my own account, as it might very justly be considered that I was asking a favor.

Fortunately the men who accompanied me did not require any such application made on their part and I rejoice that it was so. They by written agreement were entitled to more than double the usual amount of wages given to those employed in the ordinary service of the Company, with the *promise* of a gratuity in the event of good conduct, whether the Expedition were successful or not. Both wages and gratuity have been paid to them; but this, I believe, would be no bar to their receiving a portion of the Reward offered by Government for discovering the fate of Sir John Franklin and his people, if the Lords Commissioners of the Admiralty consider the party entitled to it.

I am perfectly aware that I entered into no agreement nor received any promise as to the amount of my pay and consequently have no legal claim to an increase of salary, which I fear, I have been absurd enough to expect without having either promise or document to produce in my favor. The legality of the Governor and Committee's proceedings no one would venture to question.

That my return to England with information regarding the fate of the long missing navigators prevented my carrying into effect the object of the Expedition is problematical—I should certainly at every risk have made another attempt to complete the service I had undertaken to perform, and which I would have performed had I not been met by difficulties which my former experience had not led me to anticipate, and which no foresight could have provided against, but equal if not similar difficulties might have again opposed themselves, and I might have been equally unsuccessful.

Were the amount of pay of persons employed on Arctic Service to depend upon success, few indeed would have received any remuneration beyond the salary generally given for the performance of any routine duties, unless special agreements were entered into, a precaution which I did not consider requisite before leaving England in 1853: but even had I been successful in completing the desired survey I should have been quite as much at the mercy of the Governor and Committee on this point as I am at present.

It is hinted in the last paragraph of your letter, that I was actuated by selfish motives in returning to England with the information I had so unexpectedly obtained regarding Sir John Franklin and party. I feel neither surprise nor annoyance at the insinuation, for I may most truly affirm that a desire to do what was just and proper for the interests of my employers and the satisfaction of the public alone influenced me, nor did I know until I reached London in October last, that a reward had been offered by Government for discovering the fate of the lost navigators. That I was not influenced by any selfish feeling when I proposed and planned the Expedition is equally true, for it was no desire of mine to take command of it. I had hoped that one or two of the very able officers of whom there are not a few in the "Fur Trade"—men who were not, like myself, comparatively or in a great measure broken down by previous hardships and privations on Arctic service—would have been placed in charge. In this expectation I was disappointed, and circumstances which it is unnecessary to mention, left me no alternative by which I could honorably decline the command, when tendered to me. I may add that My Lords Commissioners of the Admiralty have been in possession of Captain Collinson's Report for upwards of two months, and as the Captain was in Behring Strait on his way homeward when his despatch was dated, there is not much probability that he would subsequently obtain any news of Sir John Franklin his ships or their crews.

Trusting that the Governor and Committee will have no objections to my publishing this correspondence should I think proper.

I have the honor to be, Sir
Your Most obedt. Servant
John Rae

[Endorsed]

John Rae
Jany. 27th 1855

---

13 Salisbury Street Strand 27*th March* 1855[438]

Dear Sir
I beg to acknowledge the receipt of your note[439] of yesterdays date, accompanied by a copy of a letter from the Admiralty on the subject of my claim to the reward[440] for ascertaining the fate of Sir John Franklin and his party. Would you have the kindness to express to the Governor and Committee my sincere thanks for the efforts they have made to obtain from the Lords Commissioners of the Admiralty a *direct* reply regarding the decision of the question above referred to.

I am
Dear Sir
Your obedt. Servant
John Rae

W.G. Smith Esqre.[441]
Secretary &c.

[Endorsed]

Dr. John Rae
March 27th 1855

APPENDIXES

APPENDIX A

SUPPLEMENTARY DOCUMENTS

Sir G. Simpson to J. Rae (Extract), May 11, 1844
Sir G. Simpson to J. Rae, July 17, 1844
Sir G. Simpson to J. Rae, November 28, 1844
Arctic Land Expedition, Outfit 1845
Sir G. Simpson to J. Rae, July 11, 1845
Sir G. Simpson to J. Rae, December 13, 1845
Sir G. Simpson to J. Rae, June 15, 1846
Sir G. Simpson to J. Rae, June 30, 1847
A. Barclay to J. Rae, November 25, 1847
A. Barclay to J. Rae, November 25, 1847
Sir G. Simpson to J. Rae, June 12, 1848
Sir G. Simpson to Sir J. Richardson, June 12, 1848
Sir G. Simpson to J. Rae, November 21, 1848
Sir G. Simpson to J. Rae, June 15, 1850
Sir G. Simpson to J. Rae (Extract), December 10, 1850
Articles required for Arctic Expedition Summer 1853, June 16, 1852
Sir G. Simpson to J. Rae (Extract), October 1, 1852
Sir G. Simpson to J. Rae, December 20, 1852
Sir G. Simpson to J. Rae, June 17, 1853
Sir G. Simpson to J. Rae, December 1, 1853
Sir G. Simpson to J. Rae, June 13, 1854
Sir G. Simpson to E. Ellice (Jnr.), October 23, 1854
W. G. Smith to J. Rae, January 22, 1855

Encampment near Michipicoton 11 *May* 1844[1]

Dr. John Rae
Moose Factory.

Private (Extract from private letter)
By another letter you will find that your services are required to relieve Mr. Cowie at Ruperts River, which I trust may be an agreeable appointment to you; & I hope business there will enable you to come on to meet me at Moose from the 15th to 20th July, when I expect to be there on my way to Canada. Besides my desire of having the pleasure of seeing you, I am anxious to confer with you personally on the business of the District, & of talking to you on another subject, which I shall now merely mention, in order that you may direct your attention to it, but it is not to be spoken of until after we meet. An idea has entered my mind that you are one of the fittest men in the country to conduct an Expedition for the purpose of completing the Survey of the Northern Coast that remains untraced, say between the Straits of the Fury & Hecla & the Gulf of Boothia, from whence Dease & Simpson returned. As regards the management of the people & endurance of toil, either in walking, boating or starving, I think you are better adapted for this work than most of the gentn. with whom I am acquainted in the country, & with a little practise in taking observations, which might very soon be acquired, I think you would be quite equal to the scientific part of the duty. My plan would be for you to start from Churchill in the Spring of the year with a Junior or second & a party of 10 men & 2 Esquimaux, in two light boats, & if good use were made of the season, I think it would be sufficient to enable you to go round to the Gulf of Boothia & back to Churchill, or if not, you should pass a winter with Esquimaux, & finish the Survey the following season, either by boat or on foot. The honor of completing this survey I think is reserved for you, & then the world will see that Orkney has produced at all events one good man. Turn this matter in your mind, & if you think favorably of it, you shall have every facility & support that can be required.

(sd.) Geo. Simpson.

Moose Factory 17 *July* 1844[2]

Dr. Rae

Dear Sir,

The Govr. & Com: you are aware, are very anxious that the discovery of the Northern Shores of this continent (from the Straits of the Fury & Hecla to Dease & Simpsons farthest point) should be completed by the Hudsons Bay Company, and I see no one better qualified for that service than yourself, especially so, as you appear to enter upon it as a Volunteer with a determination of using your best endeavours to accomplish this arduous & interesting survey.

In order to its being entered upon next season (1845) you will proceed as early as possible to Red River Settlement in a half sized canoe to be provided from hence, with crews from post to post, & with a view to qualifying yourself to conduct the scientific branches of the Expedition, it would be well that you occupied the greater part of the ensuing winter in the study of Astronomy, filling up any spare time you may have, in making yourself conversant with Geology, Botany & such other sciences as you may have an opportunity of giving attention to.

The party I think, should consist of 10 persons in all; say, yourself as sole leader, a steady active man (such as James McKay) as your assistant in conducting the people, 6 resolute, active European, Canadian & half-breed servants to act as Boatmen, & two Esquimaux to serve as guides & interpreters, forming the crews of two boats. The two boats ought to be sufficiently large, to take together about 80 pieces of provisions & goods, but so light as to be moved about by the two crews united, & to be properly rigged, so as to be used as row or sail boats as might be required. Mr. C. F. Hargrave will get the boats built agreeably to any suggestions you may forward him from Red River, & will forward to Churchill such provisions, goods &c. as you & Mr. Christie may consider necessary for the service, which you ought to calculate as likely to occupy two years. You cannot, however, to take with you sufficient provisions for the maintenance of the party for so long a time,

& must count on taking up your quarters for the winter with any bands of Esquimaux you may fall in with, being satisfied with such rude fare & accommodation as they can provide.

James McKay, already named & now at Red River, who accompanied Messrs. Dease & Simpson, I think would make a very efficient assistant, and he may be paid after the rate of £50 pr. annm. while employed on the Expedition, & £25 @ £30 pr. annm. may be given to the other people according to their qualifications, with the prospect of further pecuniary reward should their conduct be satisfactory to you & the Expedition ultimately successful.

I have already written to Mr. Harding, directing that an Esquimaux Interpreter should be provided at Churchill this summer, & you will have an opportunity of engaging another there next year.

It is desirable you should be in readiness to leave Churchill at the opening of the navigation, or as soon as there may be water enough along shore for floating the boats; & the necessary instruments &c, as per list, will be provided from England by the Spring Express from Canada, when you will receive formal instructions for your guidance. Meantime,

Believe me
Dear Sir, Very sincerely Yours
(sd.) Geo Simpson.

Hudsons Bay House London 28 *November* 1844[3]

Dr. John Rae

My Dear Sir

I have had great pleasure in communicating to the Govr. & Com: the readiness with which you last summer embraced my proposition to attempt the completion of the discovery of the Northern Coast of America, from the Straits of the Fury & Hecla to Dease & Simpson's farthest—They think favorably of the plan of starting from Churchill with one boat & a party of 8 in all, or with two smaller boats & a party of 12, as you, after a full examination of the nature of the service may determine upon. If you can procure Esquimaux guides and interpreters, &

that there be time to build the craft & make the necessary preparations, it is considered very desirable the Expedition should be put in operation immediately, so as to take your departure from Churchill at the opening of the navigation in June or July 1845. If you think there is a possibility of getting away next season, I would recommend your proceeding to York & Churchill without loss of time, for the purpose of completing your arrangements, and Mr. Christie & Mr. Hargrave will assist you in securing the services of such men as you may consider well adapted for the arduous duties of the Expedition. But instead of giving extravagant wages, as was done in the Expedition under Dease & Simpson, I think it would be better to keep them within moderate limits, say not exceeding £30–£35 to one or two principal men, such as Mr. Kay & Sinclair (if not considered too old) & £20–£30 to the others, with the prospect of a Gratuity in the event of success. But, in this, we must be regulated by the popularity or unpopularity of the service in the estimation of the men.

I learn from Mr. Finlayson, that there are two Sextants in good order at Red River & you may take either one or both. The Dipping Needle used by Mr. Thos. Simpson has been repaired & I shall take it out with me via Canada.

In making your arrangements, I think it may be well to count on the Expedition occupying two years & on its being necessary to winter with the Esquimaux, in which case, I think you will have to complete the greater part of the Survey on foot. It will, therefore, be well to provide Snowshoes, & as you may have to depend on fish for subsistence, you should have ample supplies of Nett Thread, & all the people should be able to make and set netts, both under the ice & in open water.

Agreeably to my instructions to Mr. Harding last summer, the services of Ooligbuck the Esquimaux guide & interpreter have been secured: but, I think, another able bodied Esquimaux, who has been in the habit of visiting Churchill, ought also to be engaged, & as a considerable band of those people will be at Seal River at the latter end of June, you will have an opportunity of making a selection.

When I saw you at Moose, you seemed rather averse to a *gentleman* assistant, principally because we saw no one well adapted for the service, within reach, who would be likely to volunteer. There is a feeling, however, on the minds of the Govr. & Com: that the presence of an assistant is highly proper, in case of sickness or accident occurring to you,—There is a young man now in Canada (lately engaged as an App. Clerk) who if hardy enough for the service & of sufficient experience, would be very useful, on account of his scientific attainments. Nothing, however, will be said to him or any other person, until either I have seen or heard from you on this subject.

The plan of operations cannot be finally determined upon, until I meet the Council at Red River, from whence you will receive formal instructions, this being merely a private communication, for the purpose of putting you in possession of the views, wishes & intentions of the Govr. & Com: in reference to the Expedition, in the success of which they feel every confidence, from what I have stated to them of your zeal, energy & judgment.

I shall write to Messrs. Christie, Ross & Hargrave by this conveyance, requesting their assistance & co-operation, upon which you may fully depend, & with best wishes,

Believe me, My Dr. Sir, Very truly Yours

(sd.) Geo Simpson.

P.S. Have the goodness to exhibit this letter to Messrs. Christie Ross & Hargrave, if you determine on starting next season.

Arctic Land Expedition Cr.[4]

By Norway House Out. 1845

2	Gro Indian Awls	4/8	–	9	4
8	round head half Axes	1/6	–	12	–
15	Square " large Do.	4/7	3	8	9
32	" " half Do.	3/2	5	1	4
15	" " small Do.	2/–	1	10	–
12	lbs. Com round Beads	1/3	–	15	–

12	Broad Scarlet Belts 6 in	3/4	2	–	–
12	Nar: Com " D. 2 in	1/1	–	13	–
10	Plain Blankets 3½ pts.	9/–	4	10	–
30	" Do. 3 "	7/6	11	5	–
10	" Do. 2½ "	6/2	3	1	8
5	" Do. 2 "	4/2	1	–	10
5	" Do. 1½ "	3/3	–	16	3
2	doz plain Japnd. Tobco. Boxes	4/8	–	9	4
2	gro metal Coat Buttons	5/8	–	11	4
1	doz Grey milled Caps	14/8	–	14	8
1	" Scarlet " Do.	15/4	–	15	4
10	Blanket Capots 4 ells	18/11	9	9	2
7	Grey Illinois Do. 3½ "	14/9	5	3	3
5	Indian Do. 1½ "	5/–	1	5	–
5	" Do. 2 "	6/4	1	11	8
3	" Do. 3½ "	13/1	1	19	3
20	" Do. 4 "	15/9	15	15	–
⅙	doz Firmers Chisels	10/2	–	1	8
6	Broad Ice Do.	8½	–	4	3
18	Narrow " Do.	8½	–	12	9
2	Boat Oil Cloths	46/–	4	12	–
2	doz large Horn Combs	2/8	–	5	4
1	pr. Carpenters Compasses	3½d	–	–	4
60	pieces Net Cork	5d	1	5	–
1	lb. Cotton wick	2/8	–	2	8
1	doz Hand Dags 7 in	16/–	–	16	–
1	" " Do. 9 "	20/–	1	–	–
3	" flat Bastard Files 8 in	5/8	–	17	–
3	" " " Do. 10	8/9	1	6	3
¼	" Rattail Do. 4	2/10	–	–	9
¼	" " Do. 8	5/8	–	1	5
½	" x Cut Saw Do.	6/2	–	3	1
1	" Hand " Do.	3/5	–	3	5

2	" Pit " Do.	6/2	–	12	4
½	" Tenon " Do.	2/10	–	1	5
1	Gro Army Lace Garters	5/9	–	5	9
1	" High " Do.	8/4	–	8	4
6	yds Green Silk Gauze	3/4	1	–	–
1	doz assd. Gimlets	1/4	–	1	4
1	Grindstone	4/8	–	4	8
5	Bags mixed Gunflints	2/3	–	11	3
2	Gro wire Gunworms	2/–	–	4	–
2	Carpenters large Claw Hammers	1/11	–	3	10
1	Carpenters Clenching Hammer	10d	–	–	10
6	doz 4/4 Cotton Handkfs	5/11	1	15	6
3	Cents Cod Hooks	5/10	–	17	6
1	" Mackerel Do.	2/1	–	2	1
24	Powder Horns	2/4	2	16	–
½	Cwt flat Bar Iron	18/8	–	9	4
1	dble Jack plane Do.	1/6	–	1	6
1	" Hand " Do.	1/6	–	1	6
1	" Trying " Do.	1/10	–	1	10
2	doz Com Clasp knives	7/–	–	14	–
18	doz Scalping knives	5/7	5	–	6
10	dble Cod lines 24thd.	5/4	2	13	4
2	doz Small fishing Lines	1/–	–	8	–
2	" mackerel Do.	9/4	–	18	8
⅙	" Pad Locks 3 in	9/4	–	1	7
⅙	" wooden stock Do. 8 in	52/–	–	8	8
⅙	" " Do. 10 "	57/4	–	9	7
⅙	doz. Cupboard Padlocks	10/–	–	1	8
2½	m 10d. Clench Nails	5/9	–	14	5
1⅗	" 16d. " Do.	8/1	–	12	11
½	" 4d. fine drawn Do.	2/11	–	1	6
1	" 8d. " " Do.	4/–	–	4	–
½	" 14d. " " Do.	5/8	–	2	10

1	" 20d. " " Do.	7/7	–	7	7
1/10	" 6 Sharps Do.	3/5	–	–	4
3	Cents Brown thd. Needles	4d	–	1	–
1	" Darning Do.	9d	–	–	9
1	" Glovers Do.	1/–	–	1	–
4	Galls prepd. oil	4/1	–	16	4
1	pr. Carpenters Pincers	9d	–	–	9
1	dble. Sash plane	5/6	–	5	6
2	gro brass finger Rings	4/–	–	8	–
1	Carpenters 2 feet 2 fold Rule	1/9	–	1	9
1	doz Tailors Scissors 9 in	36/4	1	16	4
2½	gro wood screws	11d		2	4
94	yds Brown Russia Sheeting	1/4½	6	9	3
30	mens Com blue strpd. Cotton Shirts	2/4	3	10	–
10	mens fine blue strpd. Cotton Shirts	3/5	1	14	2
20	mens Com whit flannel Shirts	6/5	6	8	4
2	unhandled Garden spades	2/8	–	5	4
4	pieces Com. sponge	3/–	–	12	
4	doz Oval polished fire steels			14	8
4	pieces H.B. plain blue strouds	137/4	27	9	4
2	" " " Red Do.	137/–	13	14	–
4	" " " White Do.	116/4	23	5	4
1½	Gall. Tar	1/–	–	1	6
5	lbs Cobl. Thread	1/11	–	9	7
10	pr. Com. blue Cloth Trousers	9/4	4	13	4
10	" Corduroy Do.	8/5	4	4	2
100	Skiens Twine No. 1	11d	4	11	8
20	" Do. 5	2/2	2	3	4
30	" Do. 9	2/11	4	7	6
2	lbs Vermilion	5/–	"	10	–
10	Swansdown Vests	5/–	2	10	–

6	whitefish Net	31/9	£9	10	6			
1	Set Irons p. Grindstone	10/–	–	10	–			
1	Sounding Lead	5/–	–	5	–			
41	Cents Iron Rivets	m 2/5		9	11			
			———			10	15	5
Stores &c.								
5	Galls Brandy	8/3	2	1	3			
1–2	" Keg Currants	7/10	–	7	10			
12¾	lbs Cheese (useless)	"	–	–	–			
6	Squares Mustard	2/5	–	14	6			
6½	lbs Black Pepper	8d	–	4	4			
2	" Pimento	7d	–	1	2			
2⅞	Gall Shrub	4/8	–	13	5			
60	lbs Loaf sugar	5d	1	5	–			
32	" Hyson Tea	3/4	5	6	8			
16	lbs souchong Tea	2/8	2	2	8			
1	2 Gall Keg Raisins	7/10	–	7	10			
2	2 " " Rice	5/9	–	11	6			
4	Galls Madeira wine	13/4	2	13	4			
¾	" Port Do.	9/5	–	7	1			
			———			16	16	7
Stationary								
6	Bazil bod. memo. Books	1/7	–	9	6			
20	quires plain 4to. Post paper	11d	–	18	4			
3	doz fine Black lead Pencils	7/4	1	2	–			
1	lb. Red Sealing Wax	5/4	–	5	4			
			———			2	15	2
Medicines								
½	doz Turlinglons Balsam	21/4	–	10	8			
1/6	Gro Vial Corks	11d	–	–	2			
½	doz Essce. of Pepperment	14/–	–	7	–			
1	Lancet	3/4	–	3	4			

½	lb. Soap Liniment	5/7	–	2	10	
¼	" white Lint	6/8	–	1	8	
¼	" Gum arabic	4/11	–	1	3	
½	" Castor Oil	2/–	–	1	–	
2	Jars Baz. Ointment	10d	–	1	8	
2	" Cal. Do.	10d	–	1	8	
2	yds Spread Plaster	2/–	–	4	–	
½	lb. Blister Do.	6/3	–	3	2	
2	Doz Purges	1/4	–	2	8	
4	lb. Epsoms Salts	3d	–	1	–	
1	doz Vials 1 oz.	1/4	–	1	4	
1	doz Vomits	1/4	–	1	4	
2	jars Sat. Ointment	1/–	–	2	–	
						2 6 9
Whole Pieces						
1	Bag B B Shot	25/5	1	5	5	
½	Basket Covd. Copper Kettles	9K^{5} 203/8	5	1	10	
½	" Open " Do.	15 209/–	5	4	6	
1	Case Com. Guns	309/8	15	9	8	
1	" 5 " Do. } P^{2} Cost	22/–	5	10	–	
	5 fine Do. } Damaged Do.	56/–	14	–	–	
5	Kegs Gunpowder	43/7	10	17	11	
2	" Loaf Sugar	40/11	4	1	10	
4	" mixed Do.	34/6	6	18	–	68 9 2
						£319 18 –

[Endorsed]
Arctic Land Expedn. Cr.
By Norway House

Michipicoton 11 *July* 1845[7]

Dr. Rae

My Dear Sir,

In case we may miss each other while you are on your way up from Toronto to the interior, and I proceeding from thence to Canada, which I should very much regret, I now hand for your information a copy of the 113. Resolution of the Northern Council of this season, by which you will observe that, it has been determined to put the contemplated boat discovery expedition into operation next spring, under your charge. By that Resolution you will see that, Messrs. Chief Factors Christie, Ross & Hargrave are directed to engage men & make other necessary arrangements for promoting the object in view, you will, therefore, have to communicate with those gentn., & point out whatever you may consider necessary towards the proper equipment of the party, so as to render it as efficient as possible.

I presume you have by this time qualified yourself, under the instructions of Mr. Lefroy, for the scientific part of the survey, & that you are provided with the necessary instruments for carrying on your observations. Should any, however, be wanting, I think that, either at Red River, among those in the possession of the late Capt. Taylor, or at York, you will find all that may be required;—and at the Sault de Ste. Marie there has been left for the use of the expedition, an India Rubber boat, the invention of Lieut. Halkett R.N.; and at Red River you will find some India rubber paste for repairing it.

The route of the expedition having been already determined upon, it will be unnecessary to say anything upon the subject here, further than, that, the object in view is to trace the Coast from Churchill round to "Dease & Simpson's furthest". I am decidedly of opinion that, the survey cannot be completed in the course of one season, & that, it will be necessary to pass either one or two winters on the voyage. It would be quite impossible to take a sufficient quantity of provisions for the maintenance of the people for so long a time, you must, therefore, be prepared to winter with the Esquimaux, & fare as they do, & as, in all probability, it may be very difficult to maintain so large a party as contemplated by the Minute of Council, say 12 besides yourself, I am still of opinion that, it is a matter worthy of grave consideration whether the party should not be confined to the crew of one boat. Upon this reduced scale, the party ought to consist of 8 or 9 in all, say yourself, an Esquimaux Interpreter and 6 or 7 Servants; but you will consider this merely as a suggestion, to be acted upon or not as you may hereafter determine.

Should you, in the course of your journey to the interior, fall in with any good men willing to volunteer for the service, you may engage them, and I think the wages should not exceed £35 per. ann. for the time they are employed, say from the date of departure from Churchill until their return thither, with the prospect of a gratuity if the expedition be successful.

I shall await a communication from you at Lachine after receipt of this, before addressing you a formal letter of instructions, which I shall do from thence in the course of the autumn, to be forwarded to York in time to reach you before your departure from Churchill. In the meantime, you will understand that, you have a carte blanche on the Company's resources to render the Expedition efficient in every point of view, & under your management we consider the failure of the objects thereof next to impossible.

Believe me &c. &c.
(sd.) G. Simpson.

Hudsons Bay House Lachine 13 *Dec.* 1845[8]

Dr. Rae

Dear Sir,

Your different letters of 9. 20. 29. & 30 July & 18. August, have reached me, & I shall now notice such points therein as require observation.

With regard to the Dip Circle, respecting which you say you have addressed Mr. Lefroy, requesting him to get some spare Needles made, in order to guard against any disappointment on the subject, I have requested Mr. Sec. Barclay to apply to the maker to have the deficiency supplied, & hope the spare needles will be sent out with the Spring dispatches in which case they will be taken on by the Light Canoe. The Telescope applied for will likewise be provided: and I shall request Mr. Barclay to send by the Spring Express a copy of Dease & Simpson's Narrative & a Chart shewing their discoveries.

I observe that, you consider it better to have two boats than to trust to one only for the Expedition—and I hope you have reached Churchill in time to superintend their construction.—Messrs. Christie Ross & Hargrave wrote me respectively on the subject of men, & think they will get the number required: & you will understand that, you have a carte blanche to avail yourself of the Company's resources in order to put the Expedition on an efficient footing.

The outlay you incurred at Toronto for repairs to instruments & books for observations, amounting to £4. 15/–, has been placed to your credit here: and I have to beg you will forward to me a statement of your travelling expences &c. from the Sault to Toronto & back, the accts. to comprehend all expences which may fairly be considered as connected with the public service, with a view to your being credited with the same.

I have communicated with you so fully & frequently, both verbally & in writing, on the subject of the Expedition, that nothing further occurs to me to be said thereon at present. I shall, however, have occasion to communicate with you further either from Bas de la Rivière or Red River in the early part of June, & my letters will be forwarded direct, so as to reach Churchill previous to your departure.

I regret very much not having met with you last summer, arising from your being unable to keep your appointment at the Sault de Ste. Marie.

I remain &c. &c.

(sd.) G. Simpson.

Red River Settlement 15. *June* 1846[9]

Sir,

You are aware that the grand object of the Expedition which has been placed under your direction, is to complete the geography of the Northern shore of America, by surveying the only section of the same that has not yet been traced, namely, the deep bay, as it is supposed to be, stretching from the Western extremity of the Straits of the Fury and Hecla to the Eastern limit of the discoveries of Messrs. Dease & Simpson.

2. For this purpose, you will proceed from Churchill with the two boats and twelve men that have been selected for this arduous and important service, losing not a moment, at least on your outward voyage, in examining such part of the coast as has already been visited and explored. In a word, you will reach, with as little loss of time as possible, the interesting scene of your exclusive labors.

3. In prosecuting the Survey in question, you will, as a matter of course, endeavour to ascertain as accurately as circumstances may permit, without occasioning any serious delay, the latitudes and longitudes of all the most remarkable points within the range of your operations, and also the general bearing and extent of all the intermediate portions of coast, embodying the whole, at the same time, in the form of a Chart, or rather of the draft of a Chart, from day to day.

4. But, in addition to this your principal and essential task, you will devote as much of your attention as possible to various subordinate and incidental duties. You will do your utmost, consistently with the success of your main object, to attend to Botany & Geology; to Zoology in all its departments; to the temperature both of the air and of the water; to the condition of the atmosphere and the state of the ice; to winds and currents; to the soundings as well with respect to bottom as with respect to depth; to the magnetic dip and the variation of the compass; to the aurora borealis and the refraction of light. You will also, to the best of your opportunities, observe the ethnographical peculiarities of the Exquimaux of the country; and, in the event of your wintering within the Arctic Circle, you will be careful to notice any characteristic features or influences of the long night of the high latitudes in question. These particulars, and such others as may suggest themselves to you on the spot, you will record fully and precisely in a journal to be kept, as far as practicable, from day to day, collecting, at the same time, any new, curious or interesting specimens in illustration of any of the foregoing heads.

5. In order to provide against the probable necessity of requiring

two seasons for your operations, you will take with you all the provisions that your boats can carry, with such shooting, hunting and fishing tackle as may enable you to husband your supplies. I need hardly mention medicines and warm clothing among the necessaries of your voyage, for, in full reliance on your professional zeal and ability, I place the health of your people, under providence, entirely in your hands.

6. In the event of wintering in the country, you will cultivate the most friendly relations with the natives, taking care, however, to guard against surprise. For this purpose, you will repeatedly and constantly inculcate on your men collectively & individually the absolute necessity of mildness and firmness, of frankness and circumspection.

7. If, in the event of your being unable to accomplish the whole of your task in one season, you see ground for doubting, whether the resources of the country are competent to maintain the whole of your people, you will, in that case, send back a part of them to Churchill with one of the boats. For the remaining part of your men you cannot fail to find subsistence, animated as you and they are by a determination to fulfil your mission at the cost of danger, fatigue and privation. Wherever the natives can live, I can have no fears with respect to you, more particularly as you will have the advantage of the Esquimaux not merely in your actual supplies but also in the means of recruiting and renewing them.

8. During the winter, you will pursue the various objects of the expedition, by making excursions, with a due regard, of course, to safety, on the snow or on the ice; and at the close of your second season, after having accomplished the whole of your task, you will return, according to your own discretion, either by your original course or by Back's Great Fish River, keeping constantly in view, till you reach Churchill or Great Slave Lake, the general spirit of these your instructions.

9. In conclusion, let me assure you that we look confidently to you for the solution of what may be deemed the final problem in the Geography of the northern hemisphere. The eyes of all, who take an interest in the subject, are fixed on the Hudsons Bay Company, from us the world expects the final settlement of the question that has occupied

the attention of our country for two hundred years; and your safe and triumphant return, which may God in his mercy grant, will, I trust, speedily compensate the Hudsons Bay Company for its repeated sacrifices and its protracted anxieties.

I remain
Sir
Yours very faithfully
G. Simpson

John Rae Esq.
Churchill Hudsons Bay

[Endorsed in pencil]

Instructions
Arctic Boat Expedition

Received at Churchill
—4th July 1846.

Norway House 30. *June* 1847[10]

John Rae Esq.

My Dear Sir
Your various communications, both public & private, of 12 June, 4 & 5. July, reached me at different periods of the season. I need scarcely say that we are very anxious about you & indulge in a hope that we may, in the course of the season, hear of the welfare of yourself & party, & of your having accomplished the arduous duties you have on hand; but being uncertain when or where you may cast up, I do not write officially, having nothing to communicate beyond what has been already said to you in the letters of instruction handed you from time to time. If you get back this fall to Churchill in time to report the result of your operations you will of course communicate with the Board direct, transmitting a copy of that communication addressed to me in Canada, & saying whatever else connected with your proceedings

you may consider to be either useful or interesting. In the event either of success or failure, if you get back to York before the close of the navigation, you will give their freedom to any of the men employed upon the expedition who may be disposed to go to Red River, whereby we may be relieved from the charge of their wages & maintenance: those under engagement to be retained & placed at the disposal of the gentleman in charge of Yorkfactory, who will employ them to the best advantage, or should they arrive sufficiently early, some of them might be attached to the party under the charge of Mr. Bell, with a view of being employed on the Admiralty expedition about to be fitted out under the command of Sir John Richardson, for the purpose of going in search of Sir John Franklin's expedition; & should you arrive before the departure of the ship, any of your people, Europeans, whose engagements have expired, are to be discharged & allowed passages to England, should they not feel disposed to renew their engagements for the term of 2 or 3 years. The British public is getting anxious for the safety of Sir John Franklin's expedition, nothing having been heard of it since the summer of 1845: that anxiety has led to the formation of the expedition under Sir John Richardson above referred to. Perhaps you have learnt something respecting it in the course of your northern travels: any information you may be able to give on this subject will be exceedingly interesting.

By the official communication conveying your commission as a Chief Trader, you will see that you have not been entirely forgotten during your absence, & I hope we may both live long enough to see you a "two-share man".

You will no doubt hear from Orkney: I had a letter from your mother in the cource of the spring, when I have the pleasure to say she was in her usual health. It is curious enough that your private letter of 12 June 1846 did not reach me until the month of April last, when it was handed to me in London; I cannot conceive where it could have been wandering in the interim. Should you happily get to York before the departure of the last canoe of the season for Canada, let me have the pleasure of hearing from you by that conveyance, & as time will hang heavily on your hands during the winter without any appointment, you may go when & where you please, either on business or pleasure, until about the middle of June next, when it is desirable you should be at this place, to attend a Council intended to be here about that time.

With kindest & best wishes,
Believe me &c. &c.
(sd.) G. Simpson.

London *Novr. 25th* 1847[11]

John Rae Esq

Sir
I am directed by the Governor, Depy. Governor and Committee to acquaint you that they were much gratified by the perusal of your interesting Dispatch dated the 21st September.

The report, contained in that communication, of the proceedings of the expedition under your command, whereby you have succeeded in connecting the surveys of Sir John Ross on the north side of the Gulf of Boothia with those of Captn. Parry on the south side of that Gulf, thus proving that Boothia Felix is united to the Continent of America is most highly satisfactory to them.

The great ability and judgment manifested in this arduous service reflect upon you much honour and entitle you to their warmest commendations: and in order to mark their approbation of the conduct of the Expedition, they have voted from the funds of the stock-holders of the Company the sum of £630 as a gratuity, to be divided as follows vizt. £400 to you—£200 to be equally distributed among the ten men who accompanied you on the expedition, and £30—to be divided in equal portions among three of the men, namely, George Flett John Corrigal and John Folster, as an additional gratuity, in consideration of their extra services and responsibility.

An abstract of your dispatch has been forwarded to the Lords Commissioners of the Admiralty and to the Royal Geographical

Society, who notice the important services rendered by the expedition in very complimentary terms.

I am Sir
Your obedt. Servt.
A[rchibald] B[arclay] Secy.

London *Novr. 25th* 1847[12]

(from YF 1847) John Rae Esq.

Sir John Richardson's letter to you of the 12th inst. has been submitted to the Governor, Depy. Governor & Committee and I am directed to acquaint you that if you are disposed to accept the offer made you by Sir John Richardson they do not object to your doing so, and will comply with the wishes of the Admiralty should they desire your services.

I am
Sir Your obedt. Servt.
A[rchibald] B[arclay] Scy.

Norway House 12 *June* 1848[13]

John Rae Esqr.
McKenzie River

My Dear Sir
I was disappointed at not hearing from you on my arrival here, but having addressed Sir John Richardson very fully on the affairs of the expedition, I have little to trouble you with at present, further than to say that, as soon as Sir John Richardson considers that he can dispense with your services, I have requested him to give you written intimation to that effect, and from that date you will consider yourself attached to the district of McKenzie River, in the charge of which you will relieve Chief Factor McPherson. You will, therefore, proceed to Fort Simpson as soon as you are relieved from your present duty, and Mr. McPherson will make over his charge to you on his departure.

I shall be happy to hear from you whenever an oppertunity may offer for writing, & with best wishes,

Believe me
Yrs. &c.
(signed) G. Simpson.

Norway House 12 *June* 1848.[14]

Sir John Richardson
McKenzie River.

My Dear Sir,

Your valued favours of 2nd May written at the Sault, of 28 May at Fort Alexander, and 6 June at this place, have all duly come to hand, and I think I can with truth say that you cannot feel more disappointment and regret than myself at the derangement of your plans arising from the misfortunes which befell the party under Mr. Bell from the Factory last autumn. These misfortunes are attributable to a combination of adverse circumstances which could not possibly have been foreseen or guarded against by us, vizt. the unusually low state of the rivers, the early setting in of winter, the unfitness of the English boats for carrying large cargoes, and the inexperience and consequent inefficiency for this particular service of the seamen and sappers and miners sent from England. The consumption of the English pemican on the voyage and after arrival at winter quarters is very much to be regretted, although I presume it was necessary under the circumstances in which the party were placed after being set fast below Cumberland. You must have observed, however, that I endeavoured to guard against such a contingency, as in my instructions to Mr. Bell last summer, copy of which I forwarded to you, I directed him, if possible, to render the *whole* of his cargo provisions untouched at McKenzie River, maintaining his people on the voyage on country produce, and in winter quarters principally on fish. The necessity for leaving part of the provisions at this place is said to have arisen from an apprehension that it would be unsafe to take the boats with their full ladings across the lake at the late period of the season at which they left here. Mr. Ross informs me that you expressed some disappointment that two or more boats were not sent in company with Mr. Bell, when it was found that the English boats were inadequate to convey all the goods and provisions. Not having all my papers with me here, I am unable to speak positively, but as far as my memory serves, you never expressed any desire last year that the Company should provide craft for conveying your stores inland, and that the addition of a boat to the brigade last autumn was my own suggestion, as on examining the indents &c. I foresaw that the English boats alone would be unable to take in sufficient freight for the wants of the expedition; but I certainly thought that, with the assistance of a large inland boat an ample provision had been made in the way of transport.

The requisition which you handed me at Lachine and which I transmitted to Mr. Ross, will be complied with this summer and forwarded, part by a boat to accompany the Portage la Loche brigade to start today and part by the Athabasca brigade in July, together with the pieces left here by Mr. Bell and some of the goods lying at York. As regards guns, I have reason to believe that a case was sent in by the boats last autumn, as I find them in Mr. Bell's requisition on York Factory last summer, & the impression on the minds of Mr. Ross & Mr. McTavish is that they were supplied; but in order to guard against the possibility of their not having been forwarded, I have, by this conveyance, given instructions to Mr. McPherson to furnish the expedition with a case of trading guns out of his outfit.

As regards provisions, it appears that 40 bags of pemican were ordered across from Carlton last winter, to be stored at Isle a la Crosse this spring, in time to be available for the use of your boats, but as the Saskatchewan brigade has not yet arrived, I am not sure that this arrangement was carried out. Every endeavour will be used to forward pemican to McKenzie River this summer by way of Peace River, which will be placed at your disposal, either for the return voyage or for the maintenance of your post on Great Bear Lake; and as you will be absent on the coast when this arrives, I have, agreeably to your desire, directed Mr. McPherson to have 8 bags of pemican deposited at Fort Good Hope for the use of any boat parties touching at that place, to be furnished out of the stock of provision on hand in the district intended for the use of our own trade. The English pemican will be retained at York Factory as you requested & assumed by the Company.

With reference to Mr. Bell's letters, you express an apprehension that the desponding tone which pervades them will lead to a feeling in England that the expedition will prove a failure. No copies of these letters, however, have been transmitted to the Company by me, nor do I intend to forward any, indeed I have had no opportunity hitherto to do so, as immediately after their receipt at Lachine I sent them on under cover to you at the Sault without having had time to take a copy.

The melancholy report respecting the loss of four of your sappers & miners last winter below the Pas, I very much fear is too true, but as yet we have received no confirmation of it.[15]

By next conveyance I shall hand you copy of Minute of Council of this season in reference to your expedition, which I trust will prove our sincere desire to render the resources of the country subservient to the purposes of your mission; but the circular with which I furnished you at Lachine, addressed to all the officers in the Company's service, will secure their ready cooperation, & you may rely on them affording you every assistance which the means at their disposal may admit. In the remote Northern Districts we may not be enabled to comply with your demands to the letter, but whatever the resources of the country can supply will be forthcoming.

I have to beg that, as soon as you may consider the services of Messrs. Bell & Rae are no longer required on the expedition, you will intimate the same in writing to those gentlemen, when Mr. Rae will be attached to the McKenzie River District, and Mr. Bell will accompany your return craft to Norway House.

In a letter from Fort Alexander Mr. Rae applied for two men, Peter Matthieson & Hilard Monceaux, to be engaged for the expedition, they were accordingly sent here from Red River, but after arrival positively refused to engage for that service. I understood that no desire was expressed that, in the event of their refusal, substitutes should be provided, on the contrary it was clearly understood that these particular men only were wanted. Should two men, however, be necessary, they may be procured in

McKenzie River, and I have given instructions to Mr. McPherson to make over to you two of the Company's servants, should you require them.

Since writing the foregoing I have succeeded, after much difficulty, in making an arrangement to forward to Portage La Loche from Cumberland by the brigade about to start from hence 35 pieces of pemican, to be delivered to Mr. McPherson for the use of your expedition. I have made this arrangement, as there is always a degree of uncertainty attending the transport of pemican from the Saskatchewan to Peace River. This will be over and above the 8 bags pemican to be deposited at Fort Good Hope. I have, moreover, instructed Mr. McPherson to make over to you, if you require it, a portion of the provisions, say at least one third, of all he may receive for the purposes of our own trade.

With best wishes for your success & a happy return

Believe me
My dear Sir
Very truly yours
(signed) G. Simpson

P.S. Herewith are forwarded two letters & some news papers received at Lachine to your address after your departure thence, which reached Norway House by one of the light canoes the day after you left for the Grand Portage. A hat case was delivered to me at Lachine which you had left on board the steamer in which you went up to Kingston. Had I any idea I should have overtaken you, or been in time to have forwarded the hat case by the Portage La Loche Brigade (having only taken my departure from Lachine on the 7 May) I should have brought it up with me.

G. S.

Lachine 21 *November* 1848[16]

John Rae Esq.

My Dear Sir,

I have the pleasure to ack: your letters of 13 June & 5 July, by which

I was truly glad to learn that both the canoe & boat parties had got as far as Portage la Loche, all well, & I sincerely hope that the remainder of the voyage may be accomplished in safety; altho' I cannot help feeling some degree of alarm & apprehension from the intention of Sir John not to take any of the old hands to the coast, which I think is injudicious, & I trust you may have succeeded in persuading him to relinquish that determination and, tho' you & your Esquimaux guide will no doubt do every thing in your power to provide for the mess, I think it is almost too much to expect that two guns, however well handled, can accomplish so much in a country where preserves are unknown: had some of the old hands been with you, they might have assisted in that necessary duty.

I notice the difficulties you have to contend with, arising from the irritability of your chief: but he is fortunate in having for his second a man of great buoyancy of spirits & equable temper; and as you know his sterling worth, I am quite sure you will make every allowance for any little testiness he may shew, & ascribe it to his great anxiety to accomplish the object of his mission creditably—and to the nature of the service which cannot fail to harrass a man of his time of life—& recent habits of personal ease & comfort.

From the exertions that have been made to meet all the demands of the expedition in provisions & supplies of every description, which, from your experience, you must be aware has been a matter of much difficulty, I trust the expedition will be exempt from everything like privation in the way of food & clothing. I have not the least expectation of success in the ultimate object of the Expedition, notwithstanding the reports conveyed by Mr. McPherson of the Esquimaux having seen "two large canoes" with whites to the Eastward of McKenzie River, the impression on my own mind being that Sir John Franklin & his party will never again be heard of; but I entertain confident hopes, in a great measure arising from your own good judgment, activity, & untiring perseverance, that your expedition will accomplish that part of the duty assigned to it, & get through the winter "as well as might be expected".

Sir John Richardson when here, told me that it was not his intention to remain out longer than one winter, & that he would return next season. Under those circumstances, I presume he will not require your assistance after this winter, which I hope may be the case, as your services are highly necessary in McKenzie River to relieve Mr. McPherson in charge of that, our most valuable district, his health, he says, being such as to render it necessary for him to withdraw next summer. When I saw you here, I think we spoke of the probability of this appointment being made, & gave it as one of the reasons of any regret that you had joined the expedition, & as I do not recollect that you made any observation thereon, manifesting a disinclination to enter on that charge, I hope it may be entirely to your satisfaction. From your habits of business, zeal & activity, I am exceedingly anxious that this important district should fall under your management, as there appears to me to be still a wide field for the extension of trade, & that under your management it would have a fair chance of being cultivated to the advantage of the Company & your own individual interest.

You will learn that Mr. Murray has been pushing to the Westward of Peel's River & established a post on the Youcon. It is very desirable we should know the precise situation of that post, both as regards latitude & longitude, I should, therefore, be glad if you could instruct Mr. Murray, or some one else, in the use of the sextant, so as to remove any doubt on that point & that if your own instrument be out of repair, you will endeavor to get from Sir John one of the Admiralty instruments, to be returned or paid for by the Company as he may desire. Both Mr. McPherson & Mr. Robt. Campbell speak of the extending the discovery of the Pelly down to the sea, this we are not anxious about, it may, therefore, be deferred until we are more firmly established where, I presume, Campbell now is, say at the Forks of the Pelly & Lewes.

You will have heard of poor Ballenden's illness, & have more recent accounts of him from Red River than I can give, I am very apprehensive his constitution has got a shock from which there is no prospect of entire recovery. My "better-half", whose health is greatly improved, writes with me in kindest & best wishes & with much regard.

Believe me &c. &c. &c. (sd.) G. Simpson

P.S. Mr. & Mrs. Finlayson went to England in September. The Company's ships reached London & the Transports Cork in safety, early in October.

Norway House 15 *June* 1850[17]

John Rae Esq.

My Dear Sir,

Since I last wrote from Lachine I have received your public & private letters under dates 8 June, 1, 22, 26 & 27 September 9 October, 28 & 29 (three) November, but as I only arrived here last night & L'Esperance leaves to day, I have not time to do more than briefly acknowledge them, reserving to another occasion any remarks that may be necessary on their contents. I regret the disappointment you experienced on your expedition last season, but your report clearly shews that you did all that a man of energy, experience & courage could prudently attempt to surmount the difficulties you encountered. You will find you are not yet to be released from this arduous service, & I hope you may have better luck as regards the character of the season this year than last. The expresses which conveyed the instructions for yourself & Capt. Pulleen, despatched from Lachine last winter, got on well enough to Red River, but I find have since been somewhat unfortunate between Cumberland & Carlton, the bearers having fallen sick, lost their way &c. but they will no doubt reach you before you receive this, & in that case you will no doubt have turned your face northwards immediately, so that this will only meet you on your return from the Arctic sea.

I shall by the next conveyance have the pleasure of forwarding your commission as Chief Factor, accompanied by the usual covenant, which you will please to sign before two witnesses & return to me by first opportunity.

From Robert Clouston (who went to England last Autumn in ill health, returned to Lachine this Spring quite recovered) I was truly happy to receive the most satisfactory accounts of your Mother and other friends in Orkney, whom he saw only a fortnight or three weeks before leaving for America. Your brothers at Hamilton I believe are well, but I can give no information in reference to their present position or future prospects.

There is no news of importance from the civilised world; all over Europe there is a vast deal of talking about new constitutions & parliamentary representation, but conducted in a more orderly and peaceable manner than during the two preceding seasons. In England there is nothing new.

Wishing you every success in your further explorations, as regards your own comfort and safety—for the time I fear is past to hope for it in the realizing of the object for which the expedition is to be undertaken and with best wishes,

Believe me. &c. &c. &c. (sig) G. Simpson

Lachine 10 *Decr.* 1850[18]

John Rae Esq.

My Dear Sir,

As it is not my present intention to visit the Northern Department next season, unless unforeseen circumstances should render it necessary, the principal management of that Department will, therefore, devolve on my friend Mr. Colvile, who is in possession of your official communication of 1 August, & I shall now confine myself to a few observations under private cover, in replying to your valued favors of 8 & 20 February, 30 June, 27 & 29 July & 1 August.

The result of the past Outfit appears to have been less favorable than for several preceding years, but you seem to have been surrounded by many difficulties, arising from the misconduct of one of your officers (O'Brien) & a seeming want of cordial cooperation on the part of others, combined with a scarcity of furs & the means of subsistence for the natives. You seem to apprehend an unfavorable result to the current Outfit also, but I have great hopes a change for the better may occur.

I notice your application for one or two stores, which you think will be productive of a great saving in labor at Fort Simpson in supplying firewood, but the introduction of stores at inland Posts is contrary to the usage of the service, I shall nevertheless address Mr. Ross on the subject, with a view to his meeting your application.

I last winter ordered out a Corn mill to York, to be sent to McKenzie River, but subsequently learnt there was one already provided, which was sent in last summer from Norway House.

The Russian note enclosed in yours of 20 February, which was handed to Mr. Murray by an Indian at the Youcon, I could not get translated here, I have been, therefore, under the necessity of sending it to London, but have not yet received the translation. I have recd, a letter from Mr. Murray, who gives a great deal of interesting information & states his reasons for believing the Pelly and Youcon to be identical but that the Colvile is another stream altogether: from his correspondence & the activity with which he conducts the affairs of that section of the business, I should judge him to be a very efficient & intelligent officer. I shall write him a few lines privately by this conveyance.

I was very much pleased to learn that the two expresses sent from hence last Winter with instructions to yourself & Captain Pullen to continue the search of the Arctic Seas reached you in time to enable you to make arrangements for Captain Pullen to proceed to the Coast last summer. Those dispatches were very unfortunate, meeting with detention from Post to Post, being sent by the wrong route, & the bearers losing their way above Cumberland, & I almost feared you would get to Portage la Loche before them. I agree with you in opinion that there is but little probability of any traces of the missing expedition being found to the Eastward of the McKenzie, & as it seems to be the prevailing opinion that the Youcon empties itself into the Northern Pacific & not the Arctic Ocean, it would be useless to send an exploring party down that river, as was at one time contemplated.

It is satisfactory to find you were enabled to fit out Captain Pullen & his party in a complete manner, with an abundant stock of provisions, clothing &c. & I hope he may have been successful in his attempt to reach Bank's land last summer. I highly approve of the scheme you have laid down for your own operations this winter & next season, which, however, includes a good deal of active service to be performed by yourself. The salary allowed Mr. H. Æ. McKenzie is high, but as you required an assistant & his time was out, he had it in his power to dictate terms, which under the circumstances of the case and considering the nature of the service, I do not think unreasonable. I am sorry to find you are likely to be deficient in tea, sugar & soap on your expedition; under the circumstances, a fair division of the stock on hand could not have been found fault with by those who remained in the district but the nature of the service precludes the possibility of providing the men with all the comforts they would be enabled to procure if stationed at the Company's posts, & the additional pay allowed them is a compensation for such privations.

Ballenden sent with the Red River boats a supply of clothing, & stores for yourself and Capt. Pullen which would no doubt have proved very acceptable. I presume Mr. Hargrave will do his best to comply with your request to procure an Esqx. interpreter for you from Churchill & to send in the Halkett air boat, compass sextant &c, but it is no use my writing to him now on the subject, as it would be too late to take any steps in the matter after my letter reached him. From the anxiety which the Governor & Committee & the Council have manifested to promote these expeditions at every sacrifice of their own pecuniary interests, I should think every officer in the Country would feel himself bound to render his best assistance without special instructions. I was sorry to notice that in a letter you addressed Sir John Richardson this past summer, which was published in *The Times*, you complained of the description of men sent from Red River for the Expedition, which mortified Ballenden not a little, as he did his utmost to procure the best men that could be got—sparing neither wages nor fair promises. When fault must be found (& we know that the best laid arrangements are faulty in some particular)—it is better that should be done under private cover to the competent authority in the Country rather than to a stranger, who gives it publicity in the newspapers, without any explanation or modification & without affording us the opportunity of giving the requisite explanation. I daresay a mixture of races would have been better than all Canadians & Halfbreeds on such service, but you know we have little choice in the matter & that all our best voyageurs & most generally useful men are of the former class, at Red River & elsewhere in the Northern Department.

I perused your letter to Sir Frances Beaufort with attention & thought it was written in a very proper spirit, I forwarded it accordingly and hope that justice may be done you in the matter of your discoveries in the direction of the Straits of the Fury & Hecla.

Your official report on the affairs of the district under date 1 August is full of valuable information, but I shall not here enter upon a reply as it will be submitted to the Council & receive due attention from them. As regards our Post on the Youcon, we should carry on our operations there without reference to the movements of the Russians, until we ascertain to a certainty that we are upon their territory and are warned off by them, which will of course be done by the authorities in St. Petersburg; in the meantime we must make the most of our opportunities in that new & valuable country, working our way inland rather than towards the Coast, where there is a chance of meeting the Russians. The consequences of O'Brien's mismanagement last season are most disastrous & we shall be anxious about Campbell until we hear from him, but I have every confidence in his perseverance & experience I am sure he will hold his ground as long as possible. Stewarts exertions in this emergency are beyond all praise and have secured him a character for zeal, activity & perseverance, which will bring him prominently into notice. It is to be regretted Mr. Bell did not follow your instructions to forward an express to Pelly Banks, which might have saved Stewart much toil. I am glad to find you speak in favorable terms of the management of Pruden & McMurray. The scarcity of leather consequent on the extensive demand for that article by the exploring expeditions, must be attended with great inconvenience &

I have no doubt the Council will do their utmost to forward a supply to the district although the demands for leather from New Caledonia & elsewhere are very pressing. You seem to have had many difficulties to contend with on your way to Portage la Loche & on the portage, but you got well over them; your forethought in bringing nets saved you from very serious evils which wd. have ensued had you run short of provisions. I spoke to Mr. Ballenden about the exemption of the Red River trippers from carrying to the middle of the portage, but he says no condition to that effect was ever made with them, although they expect to have as much benefit from the horse transport as the McKenzie River Servants which is reasonable & if horses are used on the portage at all, they must assist trippers & our Servants alike. Oxen & Carts, I think, would answer much better than horses, & prove less expensive, keeping them during winter at Isle à la Crosse, driving them to the portage on the last ice & back to the Wintering grounds on the first ice in the fall. The route to the Pelly River viâ the West Branch is a great drawback to the developement of that country, & if another could be opened less difficult & tedious, it would be most desirable; the respective merits of the routes viâ the Youcon & the Pacific Coast, should be carefully investigated & reported to the Council, who will act upon the information they may receive on the subject.

With reference to your letter of 1 August, I notice your desire to visit the civilised world & hope arrangements may be made to enable you to quit McKenzie River, as soon as you have accomplished your present exploration service. I do not consider Bell well qualified for the superintendence of the district & as he is exceedingly anxious to come across Portage la Loche he will be directed to proceed to Norway House next summer, but his ultimate destination is uncertain. It appears to me that James Anderson is the fittest man within reach to succeed you in charge of McKenzie River & I have written to Mr. Colvile recommending that he be appointed to that charge, proceeding thither next fall, Barnston relieving him at Athabasca. I trust your visit to the civilized world may set you all to rights again & enable you to resume your duties in the interior at the end of your furlough with renewed energy "like a giant refreshed by sleep". I have it in view to cross the Atlantic with my family next summer & shall hope to have the pleasure of seeing much of you in the course of the winter of 1851/52.

(sd.) G. Simpson

P.S. As you and Captain Pullen will no doubt be anxious to hear what has been done by the various exploring vessels in the Arctic seas this year, I enclose a cutting from the *Morning Chronicle Times* & *Herald* which contain all the intelligence which has been received from those expeditions,—say the reports of Captains Austin, Ommaney, Penny & Forsyth & Sir John Ross.

Articles required for Arctic Expedition Summer 1853.[19]

1 Boat 28 feet keel 10 or 11 feet beam, built and rigged like the boats used in the Expedition to Repulse Bay in 1846, but larger, bows to be lined with thin sheet iron or copper at the water line, anchor and cable &c complete.

1 light boat for river navigation, wood nails &c sent from England, built as per draught now sent but 2 feet longer in keel that is 24 feet, to pull 6 oars and rigged with two lugs. A steering ring in stern post. A steering sweep and 7 oars. Bows near water line, defended by copper sheathing. Timbers bent ¾ × ⅝ or ½ in. Planks not more than half inch thick. Keel lined with iron.

Bilge pieces " Do.

12 setting poles with irons for the two boats

12 pairs snowshoes.

4 small sleds—say about 9 feet long ready turned

60 pairs good moose skin shoes.

6 good nets 30 fms. 4 inch mesh

8 comn. Indian Guns

4 ct. Gunflints

1 Keg Gunpowder

1 bag Ball No. 28
½ " Shot No. 1
½ " Do. " 3
½ " Do. " 5
6 Doz Scalping Knives
2 doz hand Dags small size
2 " " Do. large
6 lbs. common colord Beads
1 nest tin round Pans No. 1 to 8
1 " " " Kettles 1 to 8
2 Doz Files flat bastd. 6 in
2 " Do. " " 8 "
1 " Do. " cross cut saw
1 " Do. " hand saw
½ Do. pit Do.
½ Doz. grafting Saws
1 ct. Cod Hooks
2 ct. white ch needles
2 " glovers " Do.
1 " darning Do.
2 small sheet iron Stoves for boats
2 small tool chests
2 water Kegs ⅛ and 1/12 gns
1 spade with handle
4 large sqre headed axes & handles
4 half " " Do. " "
4 small " " Do. " "
4 ice chisels wth. handles
1 pick axe—
Anchors & cables for boats
2 double cod Lines 24 thds
60 fathom deep sea lead Line.

Provisions &c

2	cwt preserved meat
2	" " Potatoes
15	bags Pemican.
15	" Flour
4	Gns. Salt.
1	cwt. Biscuit fine/½ second/½
30	lbs. congou Tea
10	lbs. hyson Do.
10	" Souchong Do.
4	Kegs Sugar ea 8 Gns.
1	" port Wine 2 Gns
1	" Madeira Do. 2 "
2	" Brandy ea. 2 "
3	lbs. Pepper
3	" Mustard
30	" Chocolate
1	Keg Raisins 2 Gns
1	" Rice 2 "

Medicines &c.

1	oz. Tinct Opium
¼	" Croton Oil
2	lbs. Castor Do.
1	" Olive Do.
2	" Epsom Salts
2	ozs Calomel
¼	" powdered opium
2	" compd. colocynth Pills *in pills*
¼	yd Adhesive Plaster
1	box Basilcon ointment
1	box Calamine ointment ¼ lb.
1	" Saturnine Do.
1	" Spermaceti Do.
¼	lb. white Lint.
1	tooth key & scarificator.

Stationery

1	russia bound Memo. Book
2	fcp. bound Books 1½ Quire
2	M.C. Do. ¾ "
2	small mema. Books
1	tin case Ink Stand
1	Quire ruled qto Paper
2	" " foolscap Do.
2	" Cartridge " Do.
1	quire blotting " Do.
1	piece India Rubber
1	paper blk Inkpowder
2	doz steel Pens
½	" best blacklead Pencils
2	sticks red sealing Wax
1	" black " Do.

Hudsons Bay House London 16*th June* 1852

[Endorsed]

John Rae
June 16/52

Lachine 1 *October* 1852[20]

John Rae Esqre. (H. B. House London)

—Extracts from private letter—

With reference to the men required for your party next season, you suggest £40 wages with a gratuity of £10 or £15 to new hands & £50 to Beads, Foster & Corrigal, old hands, being about what they had on a former occasion. I think, however, we must fix a scale for all hands, whether new or old. You seem to prefer relying on the interior (Red River, Norway House & York) for procuring your men, I shall, therefore, instruct Mr. Buchanan by the winter packet to commence engaging 6 or 8 in the Settlement (particularly the three you mention, say Beads, Foster & Corrigal) giving him a latitude as to wages of from £40 @ £50 p. annum, for the time they may be employed upon the expedition, counting from their departure from Yorkfactory until their return to that place. If Buchanan engages 7 or 8 men, I think you might count on obtaining 4 or 5 at York or some other posts in the interior.

There will be ample time to hear from Red River the number of men that may have been engaged there before you can take your departure from hence for the interior by the Spring canoes. I believe you have already addressed Mr. W. Mactavish fully respecting the boat you require built, provisions, agrits &c.—but to prevent any misunderstanding it would be advisable you should send me copies of your letters to that gentleman & of your requisition on York. I presume the light boat, India rubber canoe, preserved meat &c. noticed in your letter to the Secretary of 1 May last, as being required for the Expedition, were forwarded to York by the Ship of this season.

When you go up to London, you will probably be called upon by some of the officials at the Admiralty to give information relative to our charges for supplies, labor &c. furnished the Arctic Searching Expeditions. I have had frequent occasion to address the Secretary, Sir John Richardson & Captain Lefroy in explanation of the principle on which we frame our prices & charges in reference to Government Expeditions—& in order that you may be prepared to enter on the subject if necessary, I have to beg you will request Mr. Barclay to afford you the perusal of my letters to Sir J. Richardson & Capt. Lefroy (to be found in the copy of my official correspondence at the HB House), also of my letters to him of 26 April 1848, 13 & 27 Octr. 1849, 21 Decr. 1850, 20 Decr. 1851, 27 March, 19 July & 18 Septr. 1852.

(sd.) G. Simpson

Lachine 20 *December* 1852[21]

John Rae Esq.
Hudsons Bay House London

My Dear Sir,
I have not much to say at present on the subject of your expedition next summer. I have written to Messrs. Buchanan, Barnston & W. McTavish

on the arrangements, particularly as to engaging men. I have directed Buchanan to secure 6 or 8 (including Beads, Corrigal & Foster—at all events the first), to be forwarded to Norway House at the opening of the navigation to meet you there; Mr. Barnston I have requested to have in view 4 men, willing to join the party, but not to engage them till you arrive, & I have given similar instructions to Mr. Mactavish at York. I hardly expect you will get 8 men from Red River, probably not above half the number, in which case you must make up the party at Norway House & York, by selecting at each place the best men willing to engage.

I think you are over-sanguine in expecting to reach Yorkfactory by the 13 June, if the Spring be a very early one, you might possibly do so, but certainly not in an average season.—& of course, if a backward one, you might be very much later in arrival there. The fall in this Country has been very fine, & open & even now, winter has hardly fairly set in—from which circumstance I am led to anticipate a late spring—but it is possible the season in the interior may differ from that in Canada. You seem to fancy that by going on to the Sault St. Marie by steam & thence by Canoe, you may gain time, but in this you are mistaken, as our Canoes reach Lake Superior quite as early as the navigation is practicable, being generally detained by ice in some part of the communication. I have frequently been ice bound in Lake Superior—in 1849 we were 3 days lying at the Tonnerre Point unable to cross the last traverse on account of ice, reaching Ft. William on the last day of May—some 4 or 5 years before we remained nearly 2 days at the Dog Portage unable to cross the Dog Lake for ice on the 27 & 28 May; & I have been ice bound in Knee Lake on the 2 July. It must be a very favorable season indeed that Lake Winipeg is clear before the first week in June. It will occasion very little delay for you to come round by Lachine on your way out from England en route to the Sault—perhaps half a day only—as we have railroads that shorten the distances very materially—(you may go from Lachine to Ogdensburg in 6 hours—formerly you may remember it took 20 hours p. steamboat). I shall, therefore, expect the pleasure of seeing you here about the end of April or early in May: you may reckon the voyage from England to Montreal @ 13 or 14 days, & regulate the date of departure from Liverpool accordingly. I purpose visiting the Northern Department next season & shall leave this as usual about the 10 @ 12 May, which by experience I have found to be sufficiently early for joining the Canoes at the Sault & for making a good march inland—& nobody ever makes earlier arrivals at Red River & Norway House than I do.

There is no news stirring here at present, My family continue in tolerable health. I write in haste in order to overtake the mail which closes this morning—& with kind regards,

Believe me &c. &c. &c. (sd.) G. Simpson

Norway House 17 *June* 1853[22]

John Rae Esq.
Private

My Dear Sir,
On my way inland I had the pleasure to receive your favors of 10, 12, 21 May and 12 inst.—Owing to a stormy passage through Lake Huron, we did not reach the Sault till the 21st May, and left Gros Cap next morning nine days after you: I was very anxious to come up with you, and pushed on steadily, at Fort Alexander we were two days behind you, and on arriving here on the morning of the 13th inst. I was disappointed to find you had not left not more than 4 hours before.

I am pleased to learn that you are likely to reach York so near the time you had calculated on, and trust nothing may occur to delay your preparations there & that the navigation of the Bay may be open early this season as has been the case inxland. This letter is not likely to overtake you, and as it will only get to hand on your return, it is useless to offer any suggestions as to Equipment, & other arrangements connected with the Expedition, I shall not therefore enter upon them further. In your letter of 21 May you mention having recd. no instructions relative to your proceedings after arrival at York, from which you infer that the plan you proposed is to be carried out; I was not at all aware that you expected any instructions from me, more especially so as you never asked for any while you were staying at Lachine, in fact I took it for granted that every thing had been fully arranged by you with the Committee in London, & that all that devolved on me was to give the requisite instructions for carrying out the arrangements relative to men, boats and provisions, in the interior, which I did at various dates, & I trust you found everything in readiness & your equipment as complete as our means admit.

With reference to your remarks on the date of your departure from the Sault Ste. Marie, I do not think you had any cause for dissatisfaction, as you left that place unusually early, earlier than it would have been possible in ordinary seasons, to effect the passage of Lake Superior. We did our best at Lachine to expedite your movements, dispatching your canoe very light and strongly manned, at the earliest date on record there—the 25 April, being the second time only in 20 years that the canoes have left so soon. It appears that the canoe made a rather lengthy passage to the Sault. I daresay had you stuck by them from Lachine, you might have gained 2 or 3 days going up the Ottawa. When they left no Steamers were running on the St. Laurence, the canals being still fast, so that we could not have sent your crew, canoe, agrets &c. up by Steam, even had such a scheme ever been suggested—as to the two small Boxes for Red River sent by your canoe it was not expected Mr. Black would accompany you when the canoe was dispatched, & when it was arranged you should take him, it was by mere oversight you were not requested to take out the two boxes in question, to be left for the canoes following you, at the same time Mr. Black was instructed to leave his luggage to come on after him if necessary. The two winterers sent in your canoe were the best Mr. McKenzie could select, out of 17 he had engaged; that one of them, Collins, fell sick was an unfortunate event that could not be foreseen. You did right in leaving him at Ft. William, as he was when lame only an incumbrance to your canoe. And now I come to your last complaint which is respecting the quality of the wine put in your case, which you state, on your judgment as a connoiseur, must "have been the dregs of all the casks or bottles emptied at Lachine during the year, for neither the port nor Madeira were palatable". This wine which you condemn so harshly on the voyage, was the same as that you and others at Lachine praised so highly when dining there a day or two before you left—actually out of the very same bin—rare old port that had been bottled in Mr. Keith's time, 10 or 12 years ago—and Madeira of the same stamp! I am in the habit of looking after the cellar myself, & with my own hands took out the bottles to fill your case, I recollect well giving them out to Mr. Hopkins, who placed them in a cool room, where Mr. Lockhart carefully decanted them into your flagons, taking special pains not to break the crust. The secret of the matter is this—the stoppers of the decanters are tinned at bottom & after a little time, discolor the wine & make it look muddy, but I have never found the flavor injured, although my wine is regularly injured *in appearance* every season from that cause. I hope your Esquimaux friends may furnish you with better drink.

I do not wish to say anything on your intention to withdraw from us after you return from this Expedition: it is a step everybody in the service would regret, & you may be sure, none more so than myself. I trust, therefore, you will think better of it and share the fortunes of the Fur Trade for a few years longer, at all events.

The case of Murray, to which you refer, has been arranged; he was sent to Pembina last year as a supernumerary, and George Setter being in charge and having great experience there, which Murray had not, it was not considered advisable to supersede him. I will enquire into the freight charge against you; I certainly think you ought not to be saddled with it.

I have now only, in conclusion, to wish you God speed, and to say that none of your friends will more warmly congratulate you on the safe and successful accomplishment of your present enterprise than myself.

Believe me
My Dear Sir
Yours very truly (sd.) G. Simpson

Lachine 1 *December* 1853[23]

John Rae Esqr. (Artic Coast)

My Dear Sir,

I have had the pleasure to receive in the course of the autumn your letters dated 1, 10, 13, & 15 July & 9 August. You appear to have encountered a great many vexatious detentions on your way up the Coast, concluding by the unfortunate loss of time in exploring a river in Chesterfield Inlet which led you out of your proper course. I much regret these untoward circumstances, but chiefly because they have rendered it necessary for you to endure the discomforts of another winter on that desolate Coast; & this is the more vexatious as after all your toil & privations, the result of your expedition will now be of little interest either to the public at large or the scientific coteries which have so long watched with attention all discoveries which tended to solve the question of a North West passage. The practical settlement of that "problem of three centuries" by Capt. McClure in H.M.S. *Investigator*, has of course wrought a great change & for the future nobody will trouble themselves about this useless passage which for all the purposes of commerce exists in vain. The public seem at length to have given up Sir John Franklin's case too, as hopeless, & as soon as the Expeditions now out can be extricated, I believe we shall hear no more of Artic expeditions. After all your exertions & the expenses incurred by the Company, I cannot but regret that it was not reserved to you & them to have the honour & credit of completing this discovery.

You will not of course attempt to stay out a second winter, so that we shall count on your arrival at York next autumn: but as you have requested leave of absence again on your return from this Expedition you will not be appointed to any charge for next Outfit, although we can but ill spare so active and useful an officer. You will I presume take a passage home in the ship from York, so that I am not likely to see you here after your return.

I purpose visiting the interior again next year, to hold a council at Norway House, and hope to have tidings of you at that place.

It is so uncertain where & when this letter may reach you that it is useless for me to enter into the news of the day, which may be old and insipid by the time you read it. I had a letter not long ago from Mrs. Hamilton, in which she reports that your mother was well. I am thankful to say we are all in good condition here, my own health benefitted considerably by my journey last summer. Wishing you a safe & speedy return & as much comfort this winter as can reasonably be expected in a snow hut,

Believe me &c. &c. &c. (sd.) G. Simpson

Norway House 13*th June* 1854[24]

John Rae Esq.
York Factory

Dear Sir,
As no tidings have reached us of your movements since August last & we are left in doubt as to the probable date of your return to York Factory, we have been at a loss in what manner to enter you on the Minutes of Council this year. You are, therefore, nominally re-appointed to the "Arctic Expedition" but a discretion is left you as to the manner of disposing of yourself next winter. From a remark in one of your letters last year, to the effect that your services must not be counted upon after your return from this Expedition, I presume it was then your desire to go upon leave of absence next winter, in which case you are at liberty so to do. Should you, however, in the meantime have changed your plans and decided on remaining on duty in the interior (which would be very satisfactory to us) I have, in that case, to request you will pass the winter at York Factory, so as to gain a knowledge of the business of that Depot, with a view to relieving Mr. Mactavish of his charge next spring, that gentleman having applied for leave of absence in 1855.

Should information reach you at York to the effect that Mr. Ballenden's health has so far failed him (which I am apprehensive may be the case) as to incapacitate him for his arduous charge at Red River you are hereby requested to leave York (for the charge whereof Outfit 1855 other arrangements would be made) and proceed to the Settlement and should it turn out that Mr. Ballenden was unable to continue his charge, this letter would be your authority for relieving him of it. Should it happen, however that his health had improved so that the change was unnecessary after you got to Red River, your services there in these troublous times may be turned to very good account.

I shall look with much anxiety for intelligence of your return to York, your expedition I trust, crowned with entire success.

If you remain at York you will please shew this letter to Mr. Mactavish who is hereby requested to consider these instructions as equally addressed to you & himself.

Believe me &c. &c. (signd.) G. Simpson

P.S. If you proceed to Red River to relieve Mr. Ballenden of his charge, you will please exhibit this letter to him.

Hudsons Bay House
Lachine 23 *October* 1854[25]

Confidential

My Dear Sir,
I am aware you and your excellent father feel a warm interest in Dr. Rae, and I am sure it will be to you, as to all persons connected with the Hudsons Bay Coy., a source of satisfaction that to him was reserved the honor of discovering Franklin's fate. His long & arduous labors in the Arctic regions & this important service with which they have been closed, seem to me to entitle him to some mark of distinction at the hands of his Sovereign and I should think the public would consider a knighthood well earned & worthily bestowed. Nobody could arrange this matter so well as your father, and if you agree in opinion with me, perhaps you will be kind enough to bring the subject under his notice.

Believe me
My dear Sir
Yours very truly
G. Simpson

Edward Ellice Esq. M.P.

Hudson's Bay House
London, *Januy*. 22. 1855[26]

John Rae Esq. M.D.

Sir
I have to acknowledge your letter dated Aberdeen, 20th December 1854, which came under the consideration of the Committee on the 15th Instant.

The Governor and Committee regret to observe that you appear to have misapprehended your position in respect to the late Expedition, by which it was intended to complete the survey of the Northern Coast of America.

It was at your own suggestion, and upon your undertaking to conduct the survey that the Governor & Committee recommended the Council of the Fur Trade to furnish the men and equipment that might be found necessary, and to sanction your employment in that way, the Fur Trade having a right to your services as a Chief Factor; but in no similar case was any salary paid to the Gentlemen conducting the Expeditions, nor in your case was there even any mention of salary or remuneration independent of what might come to you as Chief Factor.

In the case of the previous Expedition conducted by you the extra remuneration given to you was awarded by a voluntary and special vote of the Governor and Committee out of the funds of the Hudson's Bay Company distinct from the Fur Trade concern.

In the course pursued by the Governor and Committee it is not intended to shew any disapprobation of your conduct in the late Expedition; but as the object for which the expense of the Expedition was incurred has not been attained in consequence of your returning to this country with the information which you had received from the Esquimaux of the melancholy fate of Sir John Franklin, the Governor and Committee feel it incumbent upon them to exercise a sound discretion in this matter. They consider that you have a just claim to the reward offered by Government to any person who might ascertain the fate of Sir John Franklin, and have expressed that opinion to the Lords Commissioners of the Admiralty, and submitted your claim to their Lordships accordingly.

The Governor and Committee will take your case, and that of the men employed in the Expedition into consideration when their Lordships' decision upon your claim for the reward shall be given. This decision their Lordships have postponed until they shall receive from Captain Collinson of H.M.S. *Enterprize* a report of his proceedings in the Arctic Seas, and as he is now on his way to England from China this decision cannot be much longer delayed.

The Governor & Committee trust you are sensible that in the event of the Lords Commissioners of the Admiralty granting to you the reward, or any considerable portion of it, your claim upon the Hudson's Bay Company for a pecuniary mark of their approbation would be very materially affected, more particularly, as your return to this country with the intelligence was the cause of your failing to complete the survey, whilst it secured to you the reward granted by the Government.

I am, Sir,
Your obedt. Servant
W[illiam]. G[regory]. S[mith] Asst. Secy.

APPENDIX B

BIOGRAPHICAL

B[1] LISTS

I

1846–47 *Expedition commanded by Dr. John Rae*

The Northern Department District Statements[1] and Rae[2] list the following men as attached to the "H.B. Discovery Expedition" during outfit 1846–47:

Adamson, William	Middleman
Corrigall [Corrigal], John	Steersman
Flett, George (e)	"
Folster, John	Middleman
Hutchison, Edward	"
Matheson, Peter	"
Menaux, Hilard	"
Nepitabo	Middleman and Hunter
Oulibuck [Ouligbuck]	Interpreter
Ouligbuck, William	"
St. Germain, Jacques	Middleman
Turner [Tumor], Richard	"

II

1848–49 Admiralty Expedition commanded by Sir John Richardson assisted by Dr. John Rae

(a)

Men of the Royal Sappers and Miners.[3]

Rank.	Name.	Trade.	Age. Years.	Age. Months.	Service. Years.	Service. Months.	Character.
2d Corporal	James McHaren[4]	carpenter	28	1	6	11	very good.
"	David Brodie	carpenter	21	3	1	—	good.
"	Robert Graham	carpenter	25	5	7	5	good.
"	Henry J. Ralph	carpenter	26	7	6	9	very bad.[5]
"	Robert Mackie[6]	carpenter	26	4	6	6	very good.
"	Donald Fraser	carpenter	25	1	1	4	good.
"	Edward Dodd	(wood and iron-turner)	20	6	1	4	good.
"	Hugh Geddes	painter	19	5	1	5	good.
Privates	Richard Webber	millwright	24	4	1	4	good.
"	James Mitchell[6]	smith	25	4	7	—	very good.
"	Jacob Hobbs	smith	23	9	1	2	good.
"	Thomas Bugbee	smith	25	5	1	5	good.
"	John Salter	smith	29	10	6	10	good.
"	James Waddell	miner	20	9	1	9	good.
"	Robert Dall	miner	23	9	1	5	good.

II

1848–49 *Admiralty Expedition* (cont.)

(b)

Seamen[7]

Daniel Clarke, A.B.	from *St. Vincent*
Thomas Selley, A.B.	" " "
William Done, A.B.	" *Excellent*
George Stares, A.B.	" "
Thomas Cousins, A.B.	" *Victory*

(c)

Hudson's Bay Company Officers and Men[8]

Rae, John	Chief Trader
Bell, John	" "
Bruce, Baptiste	Guide
Chartier, Joseph	Steersman
Emelin or Hamlin, Baptiste	Bowsman and Fisherman
Frederique, Baptiste	"
Hope, James	Steersman
Hope, Thomas	Middleman
Laplante, Xavier or Plante, Antoine	Middleman
Laronde, Louison	Bowsman
Lebrule (Dubrill), Louis	Boatman
McLeod, Neil (b)	Fisherman
Misteagun [Mistagan], Thomas	Steersman
Morrison, Hector	Fisherman
Olivier, Louis	Steersman
One Eye, Albert	Interpreter
Sabiston, William	Bowsman and Fisherman
Smith, Henry (a)	"

Stevenson, Edmund	Steersman
Trembly, Narcisse	Middleman
Umphray [Humphrey], Halcrow	"
Wilson, Daniel	"

III
1850–51 *Expedition* *commanded by Dr. John Rae* *assisted by Hector Æneas McKenzie*[9]

Beads, John	Steersman
Dumas, Michel	Middleman
Fidler, John	"
Hebert, John, dit Fabien	Interpreter
Johnstone, James	Middleman
Kennedy, Charles	"
Kirkness, George (a)	Boatbuilder
Laliberté, Alexandre, dit Lachouette	Middleman
Linklater, Peter	Middleman
Marcellais, Baptiste	Steersman etc.
Peltier, Baptiste	Middleman
Roy, Joseph (d)	Steersman
Sinclair, Samuel	Middleman

IV
1853–54 *Expedition* *commanded by Dr. John Rae*[10]

Beads, Jacob	Middleman
Beads, John, Jnr.	Guide, etc.
* Clouston, James	Steersman
* Fidler, Henry	Middleman
* Harrison, Charles	"

* These men returned from Chesterfield Inlet in August, 1853.

Johnstone, James	"
McDonald, John (g)	"
* McDonald, Murdoch	"
* McDougall, George	"
[McDougald, John George]	
McLellan [McLennan], Murdoch	"
* St. Michel, Louis	Middleman and Carpenter
Misteagan [Mistagan], Thomas	Middleman

In addition to the men listed above there were two Eskimo interpreters attached to this expedition, viz, William Ouligbuck and Munro.

* These men returned from Chesterfield Inlet in August, 1853.

B[2] BIOGRAPHIES

Adamson, William

William Adamson of the parish of Tingwall in the Shetland Islands entered the service of the Hudson's Bay Company as a labourer on June 25, 1842. His wages were £16 per annum. He sailed in the Company's ship *Prince Rupert* to York Factory in the summer of that year and shortly after his arrival was sent inland to Norway House, where he spent the winter of 1842–43. The Norway House journal for October, 1842, records that he and a fellow labourer built the foundation of the Wesleyan Church at the Indian village of Rossville, near Norway House. On May 27, 1843, he left for the Red River District and it appears from transactions in the District account books that he continued to be employed as a labourer both at Fort Garry and Lower Fort Garry until the summer of 1845. Adamson spent the winter of 1845–46 at York Factory preparatory to accompanying Dr. John Rae as a middleman on the expedition of 1846–47. Whilst on the expedition his wages were at the rate of £40 per annum. On his return he worked as a slooper at York Factory for £20 per annum and he returned to Europe by the Company's ship in the autumn of 1850.

Beads, Jacob

Jacob Beads was a native of Rupert's Land and was first employed by the Hudson's Bay Company in outfit 1846–47 as a middleman in the Swan River District. He apparently left the service after five years, but on January 31, 1853, at Red River, he entered into a contract to accompany Dr. Rae's Arctic expedition of 1853–54 as a middleman and labourer. At the end of the expedition Rae reported Beads as "A very handy man and active when he chooses but extremely careless". Beads received £260 as his part of the reward given by H.M. Government to Dr. Rae for ascertaining the first news of the fate of Sir John Franklin's expedition, and apparently went back to the Red River Settlement for a year before re-engaging in the Company's service as a steersman in 1855. He served in the Swan River District until 1857, when he again retired to the Red River Settlement.

Beads, John (junior)

John Beads, junior, was a native of Rupert's Land and lived in the Red River Settlement. He joined Dr. Rae's expedition of 1850–51 as a guide, steersman and labourer and wintered at Fort Confidence. Beads was one of the two men chosen by Rae to accompany him on foot from Fort Confidence to the Arctic coast (see p. 257 et seq.) in the spring of 1851, and his conduct during the journey was reported as being excellent. He returned to the Settlement at the close of the expedition. Beads joined Rae's expedition of 1853–54 as a steersman at £50 per annum, plus £3 gratuity, and wintered with him at Repulse Bay. Rae afterwards reported him as having a "very indifferent" character, being very careless, and "his veracity [not] to be much relied upon". Beads retired to the Red River Settlement at the close of the expedition. His share of H.M. Government's reward to Dr. Rae for being the first to ascertain news of the fate of Sir John Franklin's party amounted to £260. This John Beads was presumably identical with the one who married Catherine Robelair at the Grand Rapids Church on February 6, 1845, whose daughter Mary was baptised on August 23, 1846, and whose son John was baptised on November 12, 1850, in the Red River Settlement.

Bell, John

See *H.B.S.*, III, 427–8.

Bruce, Baptiste

Baptiste Bruce, according to J. P. Turner in *The Beaver*, December, 1943, p. 33, "boasted Highland, French and Indian blood". In the Company's books he was listed as a native of Rupert's Land, and the Red River Land Register B recorded him as being a son of Pierre Bruce. In his first contract with the Company, Baptiste was described as of the English River District. By this contract, entered into on June 1, 1828, he agreed to serve as a middleman for two years at £8. 10s. 0d. for the first year and £17 for the second. He renewed his engagement in 1830 and continued to serve in the English River District until about the summer of 1836, when he retired to the Red River Settlement. In November, 1836, he entered into a contract "to proceed forthwith with Mr. Thomas Simpson to Isle à la Crosse or Athabasca as may be required—thereafter to return to or remain employed at Isle à la Crosse, to steer out to Yorkfactory one of the boats of the latter District, and in likemanner back to Norway House . . . to Red River . . . all in consideration of Twenty four pounds Sterling . . .". The Red River Census Papers for March, 1840, showed Bruce as a "Native Catholic", married, with no children, one female servant, and as living with his father. In the summer of 1840 he agreed to become a Mackenzie River guide at £29 per annum, and he was presumably one of the "distinguished voyageurs . . . dressed in sky blue capots scarlet sashes & high scarlet night caps & mocassins" mentioned in a letter dated York Factory, September 2, 1840, from Letitia Hargrave to her father, Dugald Mactavish (MacLeod, *Letters of Letitia Hargrave*, p. 78). When Bruce retired to the Red River Settlement in the summer of 1843, John Lee Lewes reported to the Council of the Northern Department that the district was being left "without a single person who has the least knowledge of either repairing or making a boat" as "Bte. Bruce the Guide . . . has done the needful . . . for the last two or three years . . .". Two years later Bruce re-engaged as guide for the Lac la Pluie District at £25 per annum, and during outfit 1848–49 he was attached to Sir John Richardson's Admiralty Arctic Expedition. Bruce wintered with Richardson and Rae at Fort Confidence, and in his *Arctic Searching Expedition*, I, 336; II, 66, 79, Richardson mentioned "Bruce, the guide, who superintended the [rebuilding] operations, and indeed did two men's work himself . . ."; "Bruce, the guide, [who] acted as general architect, and was able and willing to execute any kind of joiner's work that was needed"; and Bruce, "with that aptness which the half-breeds show to learn any thing that comes under their observation, had made his own fiddle, and taught himself to play upon it". Bruce again retired to Red River Settlement in 1849. About this time the Portage la Loche brigade was divided, Alexis l'Esperance (see p. 479, n. 212) having command of one half, and Baptiste Bruce having charge of the other. J J. Hargrave in his *Red River* (Montreal, 1871), pp. 236–7 mentioned Bruce leaving the Red River Settlement for Portage la Loche in June,

1862, and the following account from Isaac Cowie's *The Company of Adventurers* (Toronto, 1913), p. 127, shows that Bruce was still active in 1867: "On the 17th of September [1867] we made a portage past Trout Falls . . . Very soon the Portage la Loche brigade of four boats flashed past, and taking the cascade at full speed, disappeared one after the other over the brink, with a final flourish of the steering oar. The boats were under the veteran Red River guide, Baptiste Bruçe, and manned by Metis, all gaily decorated in fancy shirts and feathers, just as they had embarked that morning at Oxford, after a ball, attended by the beauty and fashion of that vicinity, which had been kept up till daylight . . .".

Chartier, Joseph

Joseph Chartier was born about 1817 and came from Saint Jacques, Quebec. He joined the service of the Hudson's Bay Company as a middleman in 1836 and was stationed in the Athabaska District until he retired to the Red River Settlement in 1846. In 1847 he joined the advance party of the Admiralty Arctic expedition commanded by Sir John Richardson as a steersman, but he was only attached to it for a little more than one season as he and Louis Laronde left Fort Confidence on September 18, 1848, to carry dispatches as far as Ile-à-la-Crosse. Both men wintered there during 1848–49. From outfit 1849–50 to the end of outfit 1852–53 Chartier was again employed in the Athabaska District as a bowsman and steersman, and then for two seasons was listed as a freeman in the Company's books. He again entered the Company's service as a steersman in 1855, receiving £25 per annum until he retired to the Red River Settlement in 1858.

Clouston, James

James Clouston came from Stromness in the Orkney Islands and entered the Company's service as a labourer for five years at £16 per annum in 1842. He sailed to York Factory in the summer of that year in the Company's ship *Prince Rupert* and was employed in the York Factory District. He renewed his contract in 1847 for a further three years at £17 per annum, and in 1850 he again renewed it for three years at £20 per annum. He was attached to Dr. Rae's expedition of 1853–54 to West Boothia, but was one of the men who returned to York Fort from Chesterfield Inlet when Rae had to arrange to winter at Repulse Bay. Rae reported Clouston as being "steady and attentive". Clouston spent seasons 1853–54 and 1854–55 in the York Factory District and returned to Europe in the Company's ship *Prince of Wales* in the autumn of 1855. His share of H.M. Government's reward to Dr. John Rae for first ascertaining news of the fate of Sir John Franklin's expedition amounted to £60.

Corrigal, John

John Corrigal of Orphir, in the Orkney Islands, entered into a contract on April 25, 1837, to serve the Hudson's Bay Company as a labourer for five years at £16 per annum. He sailed to Hudson Bay in the summer of 1837 and was stationed in the Moose Factory District. On the expiration of his contract in 1843 Corrigal was re-engaged as a slooper for two years. When Dr. John Rae left Moose for the Red River Settlement on August 20, 1844, he was accompanied by Corrigal, whose services were transferred from the Southern to the Northern Department of Rupert's Land. Corrigal was attached to Rae's expedition of 1846–47 as a steersman and is mentioned several times in Rae's *Narrative* of that journey. Against the sentence on p. 168 of the *Narrative* reading: "We made some bread in an oven which we had built of stones cemented with clay of an excellent quality" Rae has written in pencil in one copy in the Hudson's Bay Company's library: "This is a mistake of Dr. Barclays of which he had made several . . . The oven had only a stone foundation, the rest being built of clay mixed with grass in a very ingenious manner by J. Corrigal". On his return from the expedition in 1847 Corrigal was apparently transferred to the Red River District and in 1848 he left the Company's service to live in the Settlement. He was married to Eliza Firth in the Rapids Church by Robert James, missionary priest, on May 25,1848, and their daughter Eliza was baptised on July 15, 1849. A son, William Charles, was baptised on December 29, 1850.

Dubrill (Dubreuil), Louis
See Lebrule, Louis.

Dumas, Michel
Michel Dumas was engaged in the Red River Settlement as a middleman for Dr. Rae's expedition of 1850–51, and his name appears in the accounts showing advances made to him at Fort Confidence during that outfit. He was presumably identical with the Michel Dumas, a native of Red River, born about 1826, who joined the Company's service as a bowsman in 1853 and served for a year in the Upper Red River District before being dismissed. He returned to the Red River Settlement.

Emelin (Emliri) or Hamlin, Baptiste
Baptiste Emelin, or Hamlin, was a native of Rupert's Land who was apparently employed as a middleman in the Swan River District during outfit 1846–47. During outfits 1847–48 and 1848–49 he was attached to Sir John Richardson's Admiralty Arctic Expedition as a bowsman and fisherman. He was one of the two men mentioned by Richardson (*Arctic Searching Expedition*, II, 69–70) as leaving Fort Confidence on October 31, 1848, accompanied by an Indian, to carry a packet of letters to Fort Simpson. They arrived at Fort Simpson early in December and, after a few days, Emelin and the Indian returned to Fort Confidence. After helping to conduct Richardson's "eighteen European servants" to York Factory in the summer of 1849, Emelin retired to the Red River Settlement.

Fidler, Henry
Henry Fidler was a half-breed and apparently lived in the Red River Settlement. On February 19, 1853, he agreed to join Dr. Rae's Arctic expedition of 1853–54 as a middleman and labourer. He accompanied Rae as far as Chesterfield Inlet and when arrangements had to be made to winter at Repulse Bay he was one of the men sent back to York Factory. His share of H.M. Government's reward made to Dr. Rae for first ascertaining news of the fate of Sir John Franklin's expedition amounted to £30. Fidler also accompanied James Anderson (a) and James Green

Stewart as a middleman on their expedition down Back (Great Fish) River in 1855. He retired to the Red River Settlement.

Fidler, John

John Fidler was a native of the Red River Settlement. He does not appear to have been regularly employed by the Hudson's Bay Company except as a middleman attached to Dr. Rae's Arctic expedition of 1850–51, and as a steersman for James Anderson (a) and James Green Stewart on their journey down Back (Great Fish) River in 1855. Fidler was married at the time he was engaged to accompany Dr. Rae.

Flett, George (e)

George Flett, entered in the Company's books as George Flett (e) to distinguish him from contemporaries of that name, came from Birsay in the Orkney Islands and was born about 1803. On May 13, 1833, he entered into a contract to serve the Hudson's Bay Company for five years as a sailor at £23 per annum, and in the following June sailed in the *Prince Rupert* for York Factory. He reached York on September 7 and was apparently sent to the Red River District. Flett was attached as a middleman to the Company's Arctic Discovery Expedition of 1836–39 led by Peter Warren Dease and Thomas Simpson and on his return remained in the Northern Department of Rupert's Land. He returned to Europe in the Company's ship *Prince Albert* in 1841, but two years later he entered into a new agreement to serve the Company for five years as a slooper at £20 per annum. He sailed for York Factory in the *Prince Rupert* and was stationed in that district until 1846, when he was attached to Dr. Rae's expedition as a steersman. Rae wrote of him as "An old voyager . . . always ready to jump into the water and be the first at any disagreeable duty when necessary . . . at the same time a careful and intelligent man", and as "a very steady and determined man". Flett was stationed in the York Factory District as a schooner's mate after his return from the expedition in 1847. On October 15, 1849, he and Samuel Grey were sent from York Factory "to establish a fishery at six mile Island. They were sent off in the schooners boat, but in the course of the forenoon Grey returned in it to the Factory and reported that Flett had while handing one of the sails, stumbled overboard, and was drowned". His body was not recovered. Flett was survived by his wife, Elizabeth, and three children, who lived in Birsay.

Folster, John

John Folster of Firth in the Orkney Islands entered into a contract on March 19, 1838, to serve the Hudson's Bay Company as a labourer for five years at £20 per annum. He sailed in the *Prince Rupert* to York Factory in the summer of that year and was sent to the Red River District, where he served until the expiration of his contract in 1843. He settled in the Red River Colony and on February 22, 1844, he was married to Flora McDonald. Their son John was baptised on December 18, 1844, and six days later Flora, aged twenty years, was buried. John Folster joined Dr. Rae's 1846–47 expedition as a middleman and on his return in 1847 he was again stationed in the Red River District. Folster once more retired to the Red River Settlement in 1848 and on March 8, 1849, he was married to Isabella Brown. Their daughter Margaret was baptised on March 3, 1850.

Frederique, Baptiste (dit Paul)

Baptiste Frederique, dit Paul, was a native of Rupert's Land who joined the service of the Hudson's Bay Company as a middleman in May, 1843. He spent the first few years at Trout Lake post in the Severn District and in 1846 he was transferred to the Saskatchewan District. In the following year Frederique's services were transferred to the advance party of the Admiralty Expedition commanded by Sir John Richardson, who mentioned in his *Arctic Searching Expedition*, II, 115, that Baptiste Paul was left with "Louis Dubrill" in charge of Fort Confidence during the summer of 1849. His companion was, however, Louis Olivier. Frederique spent the winter of 1849–50 at Big Island, Great Slave Lake, and then returned to the Saskatchewan District, where he served as a bowsman at £23 per annum until his retirement in 1854.

Harrison, Charles

Charles Harrison was a native of Northmavine in the Shetland Islands. He joined the service of the Hudson's Bay Company as a labourer at £17 per annum on March 12, 1852, and in the summer of that year sailed for York Factory in the Company's ship *Prince of Wales*. He was stationed at York Factory during outfit 1852–53 and in the following season he was attached to Dr. John Rae's expedition to West Boothia. When Rae found that he was unable to reach Back River by way of Chesterfield Inlet he made arrangements to winter at Repulse Bay and sent seven of his men back to York Factory. Among these was Charles Harrison, whom Rae reported as seeming "to know well how to manage a boat", and who, he suggested, might be "worth sloopers wages". Harrison re-engaged as a slooper in September, 1853, his wages being £20 per annum, and until he returned to England in the *Prince of Wales* in 1856 he served in the York Factory District. The Government reward for first ascertaining news of the fate of Sir John Franklin was paid to Dr. John Rae and the members of his expedition, including Charles Harrison, whose share amounted to £30.

Hebert, John (dit Fabien)

John Hebert, dit Fabien, was a native of Rupert's Land and was born about 1828. He entered the service of the Hudson's Bay Company in 1846 as an apprentice interpreter at £10 per annum, and during outfit 1846–47 he was stationed at Fort Simpson, the headquarters of the Mackenzie River District. During the following season (1847–48) he was listed as a middleman at £12 per annum and appears to have wintered at Fort des Liards. He renewed his contract in 1848, obtaining £19 per annum. He wintered at Fort Simpson in 1848–49, and at Fort des Liards in 1849–50. In the summer of 1850 Fabien joined Dr. Rae's expedition as interpreter at £40 per annum, and he spent the winter of 1850–51 at Fort Confidence. At the close of the expedition Fabien remained in the Mackenzie River District, apparently being stationed at Fort Resolution during season 1851–52. William McMurray, who was in charge of that post, reported Fabien as being "an active industrious and interested man".

Fabien continued to serve in the Mackenzie River District and during 1852–53 was listed as a labourer and bowsman at Fort Simpson at £22 per annum, plus a gratuity of £3. The entry in the Fort Simpson journal for July 9, 1856, records that Fabien was drowned that day whilst bathing. His body, found about two leagues below the post on August 18, 1856, was buried at Fort Simpson on the following day.

Hepburn(e), William

William Hepburn or Hepburne was a native of Orphir in the Orkney Islands. He entered the service of the Hudson's Bay Company as a labourer in 1845 and sailed to York Factory in the Company's ship *Prince Rupert* in the summer of that year. He apparently spent trading season 1845–46 in the York Factory District and at the beginning of outfit 1846–47 he was transferred to Fort Simpson, headquarters of the Mackenzie River District. During the next three outfits Hepburn was listed as a middleman at Peel River post and as receiving £16 per annum. In the summer of 1850 Hepburn was engaged by Commander Pullen to accompany the party under orders from the Admiralty to proceed to Banks Land in search of Sir John Franklin. The party did not get beyond Cape Bathurst. Whilst employed by the Admiralty Hepburn was rated as an able seaman at £4. 10s. 0*d.* per month from July 1, 1850, until he embarked for home at York Factory in the autumn of 1851. He returned to Europe in the Company's ship *Prince of Wales* and appears to have died very soon after his arrival in London.

Hope, James

The Red River Register of Baptisms records that on July 21, 1822, the Reverend John West baptised "*James Hope* an Indian Boy abt. 9 yrs. of age taught in the Missionary School & now capable of reading the New Testament with [sic] repeating the Church of England Catechism correctly". According to the Bishop of Rupert's Land's *The Net in the Bay*, p. 135, James Hope was a son of Withewekahpo. The father, a Cree, was baptised on October 1, 1834, taking the name of William Hope, and his burial record of December 15, 1836, in the Red River

Registers identifies him as "Weethaweecapo". On December 20, 1832, when aged twenty, James Hope entered into a contract at the Red River Settlement to serve the Hudson's Bay Company as a middleman or labourer for five years at £17 per annum. He also undertook "to give his mother (Withery-capot's wife) an annual allowance out of his wages of Two Pounds Sterling". Hope was employed in the Mackenzie River District and when he re-engaged as a bowsman for two years as from June 1, 1838, his wages were raised to £22 per annum. During the early part of the second outfit (1839–40) he was attached to the Hudson's Bay Company's Arctic Discovery Expedition commanded by Peter Warren Dease and Thomas Simpson and he is referred to in Simpson's *Narrative*, p. 343, as a bowsman. Hope remained in the Mackenzie River District, renewing his contract in 1840 for a year at £22 and in 1841 for two years at £24 per annum. His contract was again renewed in 1843 and during outfit 1847–48 he was recorded as being stationed at Fort Simpson and having with him his wife, a son and a daughter. According to Dr. Rae, James Hope was "a notorious thief and equally noted for falsehood", and "for very good reasons" was dismissed from the Company's service in 1848. He was on his way to Red River when Sir John Richardson's party met him in Slave River and, again according to Rae, Hope "although afterwards found very unfit", was engaged as an interpreter for Chief Trader John Bell, who was responsible for the advance party of the expedition. Sir John Richardson in his *Arctic Searching Expedition*, II, 66, mentioned the brothers James and Thomas Hope who were regular attendants at Sunday service at Fort Confidence during the winter of 1848–49. Richardson also mentioned James Hope's eldest son, a boy of about seven years of age, "who had already begun to read the Scriptures". James Hope was also a member of Dr. Rae's boat crew of the summer of 1849. It was during this journey to the mouth of the Coppermine River that Albert One-Eye, the Eskimo interpreter, was accidentally drowned; Dr. Rae placed the blame for the accident on James Hope. He appears to have retired with his family to the Red River Settlement after spending the winter of 1849–50 at Big Island, Great Slave Lake.

Hope, Thomas

Thomas Hope, a Cree Indian, was a son of William and Catherine Hope who lived at the Indian Settlement at Red River. He was baptised on September 11, 1834. He was a younger brother of James Hope, and apparently had other brothers and sisters in the Settlement. Their father, Weethaweecapo, was baptised as William Hope on October 1, 1834, and was married to Catherine, an Indian woman on October 22 following. Thomas Hope joined the Hudson's Bay Company as an apprentice labourer in 1844, his term of service being for five years at £12, £15, £16, £16 and £17 respectively. He was sent to the Mackenzie River District and spent at least two seasons, those of 1846–47 and 1847–48, at Fort des Liards. He was attached to Sir John Richardson's expedition in 1848–49, and on April 2, 1849, when at Fort Confidence, he entered into a contract to accompany Dr. Rae down the Coppermine River in the following summer. On his return he wintered (1849–50) at Big Island, Great Slave Lake, and was then employed in the Mackenzie River District as a bowsman at £25 per annum until he retired to the Red River Settlement in 1851.

Humphrey (Umphray), Halcrow

Halcrow Humphrey or Umphray, as his name often appears in the Company's books, came from Burra Isle in the Shetland Islands. He joined the service of the Hudson's Bay Company as a labourer in 1842 and sailed for York Factory in the summer of that year in the Company's ship *Prince Rupert*. From outfit 1843–44 until the end of outfit 1846–47 he was employed in the Cumberland House District and his services as a middleman were then transferred to the advance party of the Admiralty Searching Expedition commanded by Sir John Richardson. Humphrey wintered at Fort Confidence during 1848–49 and was a member of Dr. Rae's boat crew down the Coppermine River in the summer of 1849. Humphrey and Louis Lebrule (Dubrill) carried the Admiralty Express from Fort Simpson to Sault Ste. Marie, where they arrived in March, 1850, and both men retired to Canada.

Hutchison (Hutchinson), Edward

Edward Hutchison came from the parish of Papa Westray, Scotland, and on December 4, 1843, at Stromness, entered into an engagement to serve the Hudson's Bay Company as a labourer for five years at £16 per annum as from June 1, 1844. On June 24, 1844, he embarked at Stromness in the Company's ship *Prince Rupert* and landed at York Factory during the second week of the following August. Hutchison was apparently employed at York Factory until the summer of 1846, when he accompanied Dr. John Rae on his expedition of 1846–47. On September 23, 1847, Hutchison shipped from York Factory "as one of the crew for the Homeward passage" in the *Prince Rupert* and returned to Scotland. He received £40 per annum whilst on the expedition and after his return to Scotland he was awarded a gratuity of £20 for good conduct.

Johnstone, James

James Johnstone was a native of Rupert's Land. He joined Dr. Rae's Arctic expedition of 1850–51 at the Red River Settlement, and after wintering at Fort Confidence returned to Red River. On January 31, 1853, he entered into a contract to accompany Rae's 1853–54 expedition as a middleman, labourer and fisherman at £45 per annum. At the end of the expedition Johnstone returned to Red River Settlement and Rae reported him as being "An able hardworking fellow, but rather inattentive as a fisherman". Johnstone's share of H.M. Government's reward to Dr. Rae for being the first to obtain news of the fate of Sir John Franklin's party amounted to £260.

Kennedy, Charles

Charles Kennedy was engaged at the Red River Settlement for Dr. Rae's expedition of 1850–51. Nothing is known about him except that he wintered at Fort Confidence during 1850–51 and that he had a wife in the Red River Settlement. He was presumably one of the "English half-breeds" Rae reported as being "good men as we could wish" for "any work about the place" (p. 246).

Kirkness, George (a)

George Kirkness, listed as George Kirkness (a) in the Company's books to distinguish him from contemporaries of the same name, came from Sandwick in the Shetland Islands. He joined the service of the Hudson's Bay Company in 1845 as a boatbuilder and sailed to York Factory in the Company's ship *Prince Rupert* in the summer of that year. He appears to have been stationed at York Factory until the autumn of 1848, when he was sent inland to Oxford House "to put the freight craft in a state of thorough repair", and afterwards to have been transferred to the Mackenzie River District. When Augustin Patnaude, one of the men engaged in the Red River Settlement to accompany Dr. Rae's expedition of 1850–51, was left at Fort Simpson, Kirkness took his place. He spent the winter of 1850–51 at Fort Confidence building boats for the use of the expedition and afterwards retired from the Company's service, sailing from York Factory to England in the Company's ship *Prince of Wales* in September, 1851.

Laliberté, Alexis (*dit Lachouette*)

Alexis Laliberté (dit Lachouette) was a Canadian half-breed who enlisted at the Red River Settlement as a bowsman for Dr. Rae's Arctic expedition of 1850–51. He apparently left a family in the Settlement. Laliberte spent the winter of 1850–51 at Fort Confidence and at the close of the expedition remained in the Mackenzie River District. He appears to have spent the winter of 1851–52 at Fort Resolution and to have returned to the Red River Settlement in the autumn of 1852. In the following year Laliberté joined the Company's service, and he appears to have been employed first as a bowsman and later as a labourer in the Athabaska and Red River Districts until he again returned to the Red River Settlement in 1865.

Laplante, Xavier (*or Plante, Antoine*)

Xavier Laplante (or Antoine Plante), as he was listed in the Company's books, appears to have been a native of Rupert's Land and to have entered the service in 1844 as a middleman. He was listed as a middleman at £17 per annum in the Saskatchewan District during outfit 1846–47, and in the two following seasons he was attached to Sir John Richardson's Admiralty Arctic Expedition. He was one of the men who wintered at the fishery on Big Island, Great Slave Lake, during the winter of 1848–49, and in the summer of 1849 he retired to the Red River Settlement.

Laronde, Louison

According to the Northern Department Engagement Register, Louison Laronde came from Montreal and entered into a contract at Fort Garry on June 1,1846, by which he agreed to serve the Hudson's Bay Company as a middleman for three years at £17 per annum. He was sent to the English River District and in the following year was attached to the advance party of the Admiralty Arctic Expedition commanded by Sir John Richardson. In the autumn of 1848 Laronde and a fellow-member of the Expedition, Joseph Chartier, carried Sir John Richardson's dispatches from Fort Confidence to Ile-à-la-Crosse, where they both wintered during 1848–49. According to Richardson (*Arctic Searching Expedition*, I, 337), Laronde's wife lived at Ile-à-la-Crosse. Whilst there Laronde entered into a new engagement to serve the Company for two years as a steersman at £22 per annum, but this was altered when he was at York Factory in the summer of 1850. Then his wages were raised to £25 per annum and his term of service extended to 1853. At the time of this agreement he was described as a native of Rupert's Land and as being twenty-eight years of age. He continued to serve at Ile-à-la-Crosse in the English River District until the end of outfit 1853–54, when he came out so that he could pass the winter of 1854–5 5 with his father in the Red River Settlement. On June 29, 1854, Chief Factor George Barnston, who was in charge of Norway House, requested Chief Factor John Ballenden at Upper Fort Garry to "engage De La Ronde [when convenient] at the usual Terms as Guide & Interpreter and send him here [Norway House] to meet the Brigades in spring [1855]. As it may be well to keep him out of harms way for the time he is free it might be advisable to find him employment in Red River for the Company, should he be disposed to look out for work. Good Guides are much needed by us, and

I am anxious to secure this man, who I think will fill the situation creditably. He is a Nephew of Mr. [Chief Trader George] Deschambeaults" (see *H.B.S.*, III, 436). Laronde entered into a new contract at Fort Garry on September 15, 1854, when he agreed to serve as an interpreter and guide for three years at £40 for the first year and £50 for each of the two following years. He was stationed in the Lower Red River District and retired to the Red River Settlement at the end of outfit 1856–57.

Lebrule, Louis

Louis Lebrule (or Dubrill, as Dr. Rae called him) was born about 1817 and came from Ste. Anne, Quebec. He entered the service of the Hudson's Bay Company as a middleman in 1838 and until 1844 was stationed in the Athabaska District. For outfit 1844–45 he was transferred to the Mackenzie River District and was listed in the account books of that district as a middleman at £19 per annum. He appears to have spent outfit 1846–47 in the Athabaska District and to have gone to Canada in the summer of 1847. If he indeed returned to Canada he must have rejoined the service almost immediately as he was listed as a bowsman under "General charges" for Outfit 1847–48. During the following two trading seasons Lebrule (or Dubrill) was attached to the Admiralty Arctic Expedition commanded by Sir John Richardson, and he was one of the men chosen to accompany Dr. Rae down the Coppermine River in the summer of 1849. Richardson, however, in his *Arctic Searching Expedition*, II, 115, mentions Dubrill (Lebrule) as one of the men left in charge of Fort Confidence during the summer of 1849. Lebrule and Halcrow Humphrey carried the Admiralty Express from Fort Simpson to Sault Ste. Marie, where they arrived in March, 1850, and then both men retired to Canada.

Linklater, Peter

Peter Linklater, a native of Rupert's Land from the Red River Settlement, was born about 1830. He joined Dr. Rae's Arctic expedition of 1850–51 and, after wintering at Fort Confidence, accompanied Rae on foot to the Arctic coast. Rae reported his conduct during the journey as being excellent. When at Ile-à-la-Crosse in December, 1851, Linklater entered into a contract to serve the Company as a labourer for two years at £20 per annum, and he was recorded as serving in the English River District. His contract was renewed at intervals and he was employed variously as bowsman, steersman and guide in the English River and Cumberland House Districts until he became a freeman in 1880. He died about 1882. He had a brother, Hugh Linklater, living in the Red River Settlement in 1851.

McDonald, John (g)

All that is known at present about John McDonald, listed in the Company's books as John McDonald (g) to distinguish him from several contemporaries of the same name, is that he came from the Red River Settlement. He entered into a contract there on January 31, 1853, to accompany Dr. Rae's Arctic expedition as a middleman and labourer at £45 per annum, plus a gratuity of £7 10s. 0*d*. McDonald was one of the men who wintered at Repulse Bay during 1853–54 and at the close of the expedition Rae reported of him: "A very good man and I believe perfectly trustworthy". McDonald returned to the Red River Settlement. His share of the reward given by H.M. Government to Dr. Rae for being the first to obtain news of the fate of Sir John Franklin and his party amounted to £260.

McDonald (McDonnell), Murdoch

Murdoch McDonald (or McDonnell) was engaged at the Red River Settlement in February, 1853, as a middleman and labourer for Dr. Rae's Arctic expedition of 1853–54. He was one of the men who returned from Chesterfield Inlet to York Factory when Rae had to arrange to winter during 1853–54 at Repulse Bay. McDonald returned to the Settlement and later received £30 as his share of H.M. Government's reward for first ascertaining news of the fate of Sir John Franklin.

McDougald (McDougall), John George

John George McDougald (or McDougall) came from the Red River Settlement where, on February 19, 1853, he entered into a contract to accompany Dr. Rae's forthcoming expedition as a middleman and labourer. When Rae found it necessary to spend the winter of 1853–54 at Repulse Bay, McDougald was one of the men who returned from Chesterfield Inlet to York Factory. He returned to the Red River Settlement. His share of H.M. Government's reward to Dr. Rae for being the first to ascertain news of the fate of Sir John Franklin and his party amounted to £30.

Mackenzie, Hector Æneas

Hector Æneas Mackenzie was the son of Charles Mackenzie (1774?—1855) of Ross-shire, Scotland, and his wife, Mary Mackay Mackenzie. Charles Mackenzie entered the service of the North West Company in 1803 and at the coalition of that Company with the Hudson's Bay Company in 1821 was retained as a clerk in the Southern Department. Hector Mackenzie appears to have entered the service of the Hudson's Bay Company as an apprentice postmaster at least as early as the summer of 1839, and to have been sent to the Mackenzie River District. He spent the winter of 1839–40 at Fort Good Hope and had charge of that post during the summer of 1840. Mackenzie, who seems to have spent the summer of 1842 at the post on Peel River, was apparently delayed in his intention to retire to Red River, and consequently spent the winter of 1842–43 in charge of the Big Island fishery at the western end of Great Slave Lake. He retired at the end of the outfit and was en route from Norway House to Red River Settlement in October, 1843. Mackenzie re-entered the service in the following summer as a postmaster and was again sent to the Mackenzie River District. He was listed as the postmaster in charge of Fort Norman at £40 per annum during the summer of 1849, and during the following trading season (1849–50) he received £50. Lieut. W. H. Hooper in *Tents of the Tuski* (p. 283), mentioned being received at Fort Norman by Mackenzie in October, 1849, when on his way up Mackenzie River from the Arctic coast. Hooper spent a month at Fort Norman and recorded that there was "little . . . to amuse or enliven" his party unless created by themselves, but "a great treasure was . . . in the amusement afforded by a very good violin belonging to

Mr. Mac Kenzie". Hooper also mentioned that he heard many tales "as narrated by the Salteaux tribe of Indians, in communication with whom Mr. Mac Kenzie passed much of his early life" (pp. 285–6). Mackenzie's contract expired at the end of outfit 1849–50 and he was about to retire to the Red River Settlement when Dr. Rae engaged him to accompany his forthcoming Arctic expedition as assistant at £130 per annum. Rae reported Mackenzie as "very active and an excellent shot . . . much liked by the men, whom he at the same time keeps in excellent order". The expedition party, consisting of Rae, Mackenzie and fourteen men arrived at Fort Confidence, Great Bear Lake, on October 10, 1850, and later Rae reported that "McKenzie makes himself useful and manages the Indians very well", adding "Like most of his countrymen [natives of Rupert's Land] he is somewhat thoughtless and careless about provisions, but as a check I make him keep a regular account of receipts and expenditure". During the winter of 1850–51 Mackenzie "learnt to make the necessary observations for Time, Latitude, Longitude and variation" and when Rae left Fort Confidence for the Arctic coast on April 25, 1851, he was left in charge of Fort Confidence and to arrange for the transport of the boats across Kendall River. Rae's instructions to him are on pp. 242–45. On his return to Fort Simpson Rae, without going into details, mentioned that his assistant had not behaved well (see p. 93, n. *). Mackenzie apparently retired from the Company's service at the close of the expedition and went to the Red River Settlement. David Anderson, Bishop of Rupert's Land, mentioned in his *The Net in the Bay* . . . (London, 1854), p. 7, that he left Red River Settlement on June 29, 1852, to visit Moose and Albany and that he was accompanied by Hector Mackenzie who wished to see his father, who was then the clerk in charge of the Company's post at Lac Seul. Charles Mackenzie was absent when the Bishop's party arrived there on July 14, 1852, but Hector Mackenzie once again met his mother after an absence of thirteen years. Hector apparently returned to the Red River Settlement and his father, who retired in 1854, died there in the following year. The beneficiaries under the will of Charles Mackenzie were his wife, his son Hector, and his daughters Catherine Mackenzie and Margaret

Mackenzie MacDonald. According to L. R. Masson, *Le Bourgeois de la Campaignie du Nord-Ouest* (Quebec, 1889), I, 321, Hector Mackenzie was still living in Winnipeg in 1889.

McLennan (*McLellan*), *Murdoch*

Murdoch McLennan's name sometimes appears in the Company's books as Murdoch McLellan. He was born about 1826 and came from Stornoway, Lewis Island in the Outer Hebrides. He entered the service of the Hudson's Bay Company as a labourer in 1847 and sailed to York Factory in the chartered ship *Westminster*. During season 1847–48 he was appointed to Island Lake post, and until he joined Dr. John Rae's expedition of 1853–54, he continued to be stationed in the Norway House District. When McLennan volunteered to accompany Dr. Rae, he was recommended by Chief Factor George Barnston "as an active steady honest servant", and at the end of the expedition to West Boothia Rae reported him as an "excellent servant and a good *hand* in a boat either at sea or in a river". It was during this expedition that news was first heard of Sir John Franklin, and when H.M. Government's reward for first ascertaining news of his fate was made to Dr. Rae, McLennan's share amounted to £260. But before he knew of this reward, McLennan had volunteered to join the Arctic expedition under James Anderson (a) and James Green Stewart, and on February 11, 1855, accompanied by Thomas Mistagan, he left Norway House for that purpose. This expedition travelled down Great Fish (Back) River to make further search for traces of Sir John Franklin's party. McLennan left the Company's service in 1856 and retired to the Red River Settlement.

McLeod, Neil (b)

Neil McLeod of Steenish, Stornoway, county Ross, Scotland, entered into a contract on June 15, 1840, to serve the Hudson's Bay Company as a labourer for five years at £16 per annum. He was entered in the Company's books as Neil McLeod (b) to distinguish him from contemporaries of the same name. He sailed to York Factory and his service was spent in the Island Lake District. He renewed his contract as a middleman at £17 per annum and was apparently employed at York Factory during outfit 1845–46. When he was transferred to the English River District in July, 1846, James Hargrave spoke of him as being one of "the best hands belonging to the Establishment". During outfits 1847–48 and 1848–49 McLeod was attached to the Admiralty Arctic Expedition led by Sir John Richardson, and in the summer of 1849 he was a member of Dr. Rae's boat crew down the Coppermine River. McLeod spent the winter of 1849–50 at Big Island, Great Slave Lake, and in the summer of 1850 he was engaged by Commander Pullen to accompany the party under orders from the Admiralty to proceed to Banks Land in search of Sir John Franklin. McLeod was rated as a steersman and fisherman at £4 10s. 0*d.* per month. Pullen recorded McLeod as being an intelligent man. McLeod left Mackenzie River District in 1851 at the end of his contract with the Admiralty and retired to the Red River Settlement.

Marcellais (Marsellois), Baptiste

Baptiste Marcellais (or Marsellois), born about 1818, was a Canadian half-breed from the Red River Settlement. He entered the service of the Hudson's Bay Company in 1835 as a middleman for five years at £15 per annum for the first two years and for £17 per annum for the following three years. He was stationed in the Mackenzie River District and in 1840 he re-engaged for two years as a bowsman at £22 per annum. He retired to the Red River Settlement in 1843, but two years later he rejoined the service as a guide at £29 per annum. Marcellais was listed in the Company's books as wintering at Fort Selkirk during 1846–47, and his wife and daughter were also living at the post at that time. Marcellais apparently wintered at Fort des Liards during 1847–48 and then retired to the Red River Setdement. In 1850 he joined Dr. Rae's Arctic expedition as a guide and wintered at Fort Confidence. In the summer of 1851 he retired once again to the Red River Settlement.

Matheson, Peter

Peter Matheson of the parish of Barvas, Ross-shire, Scotland, entered the service of the Hudson's Bay Company as a labourer on June 15, 1840.

He engaged to serve for five years at £16 per annum and less than two weeks later embarked at Stornoway for York Factory. Shortly after his arrival there he was sent to the Saskatchewan District and he appears to have spent the winter of 1840–41 at Edmonton House. He was then transferred to the Columbia District and, until his contract expired in June, 1845, he was employed at the Fort Vancouver Depot, first as a labourer and later, during outfit 1844–45, as a middleman. During that outfit his wages were at the rate of £17 per annum. Matheson recrossed the Rocky Mountains and on August 23, 1845, when at York Factory, entered into a new contract to serve as a labourer or slooper for three years at £17 per annum. During outfit 1845–46 he was employed in the Lower Red River District and in the following outfit he was attached to Dr. John Rae's expedition as a middleman at £40 per annum. In his *Narrative* (pp. 156–7) Rae, when describing Matheson's attempts to build a snow-house, remarked: "Matheson was one of the best men I ever had under my command. Always ready, willing, and obedient, he did his duty in every respect; and whilst he possessed spirit enough for anything, he had a stock of good humour which never failed him in any situation, however difficult and trying. Were the walking difficult or easy, the loads heavy or light, provisions abundant or reduced to less than half allowance, it was all one to Peter Matheson; he had a joke ready for every occasion". On his return from the expedition Matheson was employed in the Red River District, and at the end of his contract in 1848 he returned to Europe in the Company's ship *Prince Rupert*.

Menaux (*Mitiaux*), *Hilard*

Hilard Menaux, a French-Canadian from Rivière du Loup, was born about 1822 and entered the service of the Hudson's Bay Company as a middleman in 1844. His services were apparently disposable during outfit 1844–45 and during the following trading season he was stationed at Norway House. Menaux was attached to Dr. John Rae's expedition of 1846–47 as a middleman and on his return he served in the Red River District for one outfit. He retired to Canada in 1848.

Mistagan (Misteaguti), Thomas

Thomas Mistagan or Misteagun was described by Dr. Rae as "an Indian of great intelligence and activity", and as "a very able man and an experienced sledge hauler". It is not known exactly when he was first employed by the Company, but, after acting as steersman during 1847–49 for the Admiralty expedition, he entered into his first formal contract at Norway House on October 8, 1849, when he agreed to serve as a steersman at £25 per annum. Frequent references to him are to be found in the Norway House journals. Mistagan was attached to Dr. Rae's expedition of 1853–54 as a middleman and hunter, receiving £40 per annum plus a gratuity of £10 for his services. His wife, who was at Norway House, received 5 lbs. flour and 3 lbs. pemmican weekly during his absence. Rae also mentioned that Mistagan was very useful during the spring journey over the ice. Mistagan was paid £260 as his share of the reward paid to Dr. Rae by H.M. Government for bringing back the first news of the fate of Sir John Franklin and his party. At the end of the expedition Mistagan returned to Norway House, where he was employed until February, 1855, when he left to join James Anderson's expedition as a steersman down Back (Great Fish) River in the summer of that year. He was employed as a steersman at Norway House during outfits 1856–57, 1857–58 and 1858–59. Mistagan retired to the Red River Settlement in 1859 and was still living about 1890, when Dr. J. B. Tyrrell obtained from him a statement regarding two other members of the Anderson-Stewart party who saw one of Franklin's ships "northward beyond Montreal Island" but kept the information from their leaders. Mistagan was well known to Dr. Tyrrell as the Chief of the band of Ojibway Indians which had its headquarters at Norway House, and "though rather old at the time was a splendid type of physical manhood, besides having a good reputation as an honest, industrious man" (*Transactions of The Canadian Institute* (Toronto, 1910), Vol. VIII, J. B. Tyrrell, "A Story of a Franklin Search Expedition").

Morrison (Morison), Hector

According to his tombstone in the graveyard opposite the present post of Norway House, Hector Morrison, or Morison, was born at Sandwick

Hill, Stornoway, Lewis, in September, 1814. He joined the Hudson's Bay Company as a labourer at £16 per annum in 1832 and sailed to York Factory in the Company's ship *Prince Rupert* in the summer of that year. He presumably spent outfit 1832–33 at York Factory before leaving for the Athabaska District, where he was stationed during the next three trading seasons. In 1836 Morrison was attached to the Company's Arctic expedition of 1836–39 commanded by Peter Warren Dease and Thomas Simpson, and was one of the five men who, in the early days of August, 1839, accompanied Simpson when exploring the coast on foot from Boat Extreme to Point Barrow. On his return from the expedition Morrison was apparently transferred to the Red River District, where he was employed as a slooper at £20 per annum. In outfit 1842–43 he was stationed in the Norway House District as a fisherman and he remained there until 1847, when he was transferred to the advance party of the Admiralty Arctic Expedition commanded by Sir John Richardson. Morrison returned to the Norway House District in 1849 and spent the remainder of his life there. He left the Company's service in 1886 and died on June 28, 1902.

Munro (*Eskimo*)

Munro, an Eskimo from Churchill, was attached to Dr. Rae's expedition of 1853–54 as an interpreter. When Dr. Rae found that he could not reach Back River by way of Chesterfield Inlet he decided to winter at Repulse Bay and to send some of his men back to York Factory. As he had William Ouligbuck, the Eskimo, with him, Munro was one of the men chosen to be sent back to York Factory. Munro received £20 as his share of H.M. Government's reward to Dr. Rae for first ascertaining news of the fate of Sir John Franklin's expedition.

Nepitabo (*Nepetabo, Nibitabo*)

Nepitabo was an Indian, presumably a Cree, belonging to the York Factory District. He was referred to in the York Factory journals at least as early as October, 1829, and his first contract with the Hudson's Bay Company as a labourer and hunter began on June 1, 1832. He engaged to serve in the York Factory District for three years at £15 per annum. At the expiration of his contract in 1835 he became a freeman until June 1, 1841, when he again engaged as a labourer and hunter for three years at £15 per annum. He again became a freeman in 1844 when his contract expired, and he did not have another formal contract until he joined Dr. Rae's expedition of 1846–47 as a middleman. Nepitabo remained in the Company's service on his return from the expedition and in the books he was listed as a middleman, first at £17 per annum and later at £20 and £22 per annum. He was always stationed in the York Factory District. He "went free" in 1874 and died some time in 1886 or 1887.

Olivier, Louis

Louis Olivier, considered by Dr. Rae to be "a decent steady man", was born about 1819 and came from the parish of Varennes, Montreal. He joined the service of the Hudson's Bay Company as a middleman at £17 per annum on March 30, 1838, and was sent to the Athabaska District. He renewed his engagement in 1840 and his wages were increased to £22 per annum. During outfit 1847–48 he was attached to the advance party of the Admiralty Arctic Expedition commanded by Sir John Richardson and he wintered at Fort Confidence during 1848–49. Olivier took care of the property at Fort Confidence during Dr. Rae's absence on the journey down the Coppermine River in the summer of 1849 in furtherance of the search for traces of Sir John Franklin's missing party, and after spending the winter of 1849–50 at Big Island, Great Slave Lake, he was apparently transferred to Norway House District. He died at Berens River sometime during outfit 1850–51, leaving a family.

One-Eye, Albert

Albert One-Eye, or Albert as he was generally known, was an Eskimo from the east coast of James Bay, born about 1824. He was apparently at Rupert House in the summer of 1842 when Chief Trader Thomas Corcoran reached that place en route to Moose Factory. Corcoran thought it advisable that the "Esquimeaux Boy" should see Moose Factory and he accordingly sailed in the *Speedwell* sloop on August 2.

Whilst at Moose Albert entered into a contract to serve the Company as an apprentice labourer for seven years at a salary of £8 per annum for two years, rising to £10 in 1844, £12 in 1846, and £15 in 1848. Albert was brought back to Rupert House in the winter of 1842 by an Eastmain Indian and he then went on to Fort George where, with Moses another Eskimo, he acted as interpreter. Albert remained in the Rupert River District until early in 1848 when, his services being required for the Admiralty Land Arctic Expedition commanded by Sir John Richardson, he left Fort George for Moose Factory. John Spencer, the officer in charge of Fort George, was "exceedingly sorry to part with him" and noted that Albert "was a nice steady lad, and a favourite with his Tribe". Albert reached Moose Factory on March 12, 1848, and a few days later left for Cumberland House via Michipicoten escorted by Roderick McKenzie and George Miles. Richardson, in his *Arctic Searching Expedition*, I, 243, mentioned that although Albert had been born on the Eastmain he had no difficulty in making himself understood by the Eskimos of the Mackenzie estuary. On April 2, 1849, when at Fort Confidence, Albert agreed to accompany Dr. Rae down the Coppermine River as boatman and interpreter in the summer of that year. It was during the course of this journey (on August 24) that he was accidentally drowned at the Bloody Fall. Dr. Rae laid the blame for the accident on James Hope, the Indian steersman, and his report on the subject is to be found on pp. 196–97, 202, of the text of this volume. Of Albert, Rae remarked: "Albert was liked by every-one, for his good temper, lively disposition and great activity . . . I had become much attached to the poor fellow . . .".

Ouligbuck (*Ooligbuck, Oulybuck, Ullebuck*)
In the summer of 1824 the officer in charge of the Hudson's Bay Company's post at Churchill engaged two Eskimos to accompany Captain John Franklin's expedition which was preparing to explore the coast westwards from the Coppermine River to Icy Cape. One of these was Augustus, who had accompanied a previous Franklin expedition; the other, who had "never been employed by Europeans before", was

Ouligbuck. His pay was to be at the rate of 50 Made Beaver per annum, exclusive of equipment. On August 16, 1824, the Eskimos left for York Factory en route to Cumberland House and the north. In his *Narrative of a Second Expedition to the Shores of The Polar Sea in the Years 1825, 1826 and 1827* (London, 1828), Franklin recorded that he and Dr. Richardson arrived in Methy River on June 29, 1825, where they were welcomed by the other members of the expedition "and by none more warmly than our excellent friend and former interpreter Augustus the Esquimaux, and Ooligbuck, whom he had brought from Churchill, as his companion". Ouligbuck wintered at Fort Franklin during 1825–26 and in the following June he was attached to Dr. Richardson's party, which surveyed the coast between the Mackenzie and Coppermine Rivers. Richardson said of him "Ooligbuck was not of much use as an interpreter, in our intercourse with these people, for he spoke no English; but his presence answered the important purpose of showing that the white people were on terms of friendship with the distant tribes of Esquimaux. As a boatman he was of the greatest service, being strongly attached to us, possessing an excellent temper, and labouring cheerfully at his oar" (Franklin, *Narrative of a Second Expedition . . .*, p. 204). Richardson added that Ouligbuck's "attachment . . . was never doubtful, even when we were surrounded by a tribe of his own nation" (ibid., p. 283). Ouligbuck reached York Factory on his return from the expedition in September, 1827, and then apparently went on to Churchill. Robert Harding's Churchill report for outfit 1827 recorded: "Ullebuck . . . is a smart active obedient Man and ever ready for any duty required of him . . . would be a serviceable hand . . . if willing to engage" . Ouligbuck does not appear to have become an engaged servant until after the end of outfit 1828–29. The Churchill journal for the summer of 1829 contains frequent references to the duties he carried out, which varied from killing whales, making paddles and repairing nets to weeding turnips in the fort garden. In response to instructions from Governor George Simpson to supply an Eskimo interpreter for the Ungava expedition, Augustus not being available, Robert Harding sent Ouligbuck with an elderly companion, Moses, to York Factory on

October 18, 1829. They were escorted by two Indians and the party reached York on November 2. In the journal for November 22, Robert Miles, the officer in charge remarked: ". . . As I intend sending off the Southn. Express tomorrow morning, I had the two Esquimeaux & the two Indians from Moose brought into the Hall, and with Mr. Charles explained to the Indians the care which they are expected to take of the Esquimeaux, both in regard to feeding them the same as themselves and not to distress them by marching more expeditious than they find convenient, one of the Indians who appears to be a Halfbreed named Sutherland & understands English, assured me that I need be under no apprehensions, as he would pay every attention, indeed they already appear to be on very friendly terms . . .". On the following day Ouligbuck and his companions left for Albany Factory, where they left the two Indians and continued their journey to Moose Factory in the care of two Company servants. The entries for the first six months in the 1830 Moose Factory journal contain many references to Ouligbuck, and again he carried out a variety of duties. During these months preparations had been made for the Company's Ungava expedition, the object of which was to open up trade with the Eskimos in any marketable commodity which their country produced. On June 10, 1830, Nicol Finlayson, clerk and leader of the expedition, with a party of servants, including Ouligbuck and Moses, sailed from Moose Factory to Eastmain, where they arrived thirteen days later. Within three days the party, which now consisted of Finlayson, Erland Erlandson, clerk, eight Company servants, two Eskimos and four Indian guides, was on the way to Ungava Bay via Richmond Gulf. Fort Chimo was built about twenty-five miles below the mouth of the Koksoak River in September, 1830, and here Ouligbuck proved useful in opening trade with the Eskimos. He was stationed at Fort Chimo for the next six and half years. His wages at this period were £17 per annum. Nicol Finlayson always reported favourably on his work and conduct, but Erland Erlandson in his report dated June, 1837, referred to Ouligbuck and Moses as being "perfectly useless men, who by being too much indulged considers themselves independent". In 1836 Peter Warren Dease and Thomas Simpson needed an interpreter to accompany their expedition, which was sent by the Hudson's Bay Company to survey the Arctic coastline from Franklin's furthest points to Point Barrow and Repulse Bay. As it was not possible to obtain one from Churchill Ouligbuck was recalled from Ungava. Accompanied by his wife and children (additional to a wife, now dead, and a son left at Churchill in 1829), Ouligbuck eventually reached Albany on December 26, 1837. As he was then unfit for further travel, besides being encumbered with his family, he wintered at Albany, and in July, 1838, set out for Mackenzie River District via Red River. He eventually reached Dease and Simpson, who called him a "valuable and unhoped for acquisition", on April 13, 1839. By the autumn of 1843 Ouligbuck was back at York Factory with his family, and Letitia Hargrave, wife of the officer in charge there, wrote to her sister in Scotland on September 10, 1843. "There is a Huskie man here with his wife son & daughter. They have just returned from MacKenzies river & have saved £100—Imagine a genuine Huskie with such a sum. The boy is about 12 & speaks ten languages. He is otherwise a little scamp, but very smart & hideously fat & husky like, tho very well dressed. The girl looks better & the father told Hargve. the wife was pretty pretty" (MacLeod, *Letters of Letitia Hargrave*, p. 164). Ouligbuck and his family returned to Churchill and on January 20, 1845, James Hargrave wrote to Robert Harding there: "From your report of the usefulness of Oulybucks son I think that he is entitled to such remuneration for his services as you may consider them worthy of,—and which you will accordingly pay to him out of your Outfit . . . Oulybuck has been retained in the service solely with a view towards this object [going with Dr. Rae] and for the purpose of his being attached to the party—for his services in which capacity he will of course be liberally paid. As his son appears to be such a useful Lad he will likewise be included in the party,—an opportunity which must be gratifying to his father; and in order that he may be able to act as the second interpreter—you will be pleased to take measures for getting him instructed in the English Tongue. His father's partiality towards him will no doubt readily second you in this, and to aid still further, all the people at the Fort should be directed to address him in the English language only. His hopes of future benefit from the whites, after he is capable of speaking their tongue, will also no doubt have their weight on his own mind. Should Oulybuck appear to have any difficulties on the score of leaving the rest of his family behind, you can assure him they will be carefully provided for, by the Coy,—during his absence . . .". Ouligbuck and his son William accompanied Dr. Rae on the expedition of 1846–47 and afterwards returned to their family at Churchill. When Rae was making preparations for his 1853–54 expedition he expressed a wish to have other interpreters than Ouligbuck and his son William. Rae had no particular objection to the father, but he said he would prefer the "son Donald, who, altho' he spoke but little English was a good tempered hard working fellow". Donald was presumably the son left behind at Churchill in 1829 and, therefore, half-brother to William. Ouligbuck senior died in the autumn of 1852.

Ouligbuck, William

William Ouligbuck was a son of Ouligbuck, the Eskimo, who accompanied Captain John Franklin's expedition of 1825–27 and later joined the service of the Hudson's Bay Company. William was presumably the younger son mentioned by Dr. Rae in 1846 (p. 122) and described by Letitia Hargrave in 1843 as being a little scamp of about twelve years of age and speaking ten languages. With his father he was attached to Dr. John Rae's expedition of 1846–47, but his behaviour caused Rae to report that he was an "incorrigible thief . . . who . . . was twice caught with the old man's bale open, eating sugar; some tobacco was also taken, and the trousers of most of the men . . . completely cleared of buttons by the same hands". In 1850 William J. Christie, the officer in charge of Churchill, reported that he had tried to engage William Ouligbuck as interpreter, but the Eskimo, "now married . . . declined engaging, being also led away by the Father it was impossible to persuade him to remain". When Rae was preparing for his expedition of 1853–54 he said he would prefer other interpreters than Ouligbuck and his son William, who were with him formerly; he considered the son "one of the greatest rascals unhung". Ouligbuck senior died in the autumn of 1852 and as no other interpreters were available Rae was obliged to depend on William. It was during this expedition of 1853–54 that the Eskimos gave Rae news of the long overdue party under Sir John Franklin. In his lengthy dispatch of September 1, 1854, Rae remarked that his "good interpreter Wm. Ouligbuck" was landed at Churchill on August 28. Elsewhere he reported that Ouligbuck was a good interpreter but subject to fits of sulkiness, that he lied to suit his purpose, and that he was not too honest. On parting, William had been presented with "a very handsomely mounted hunting knife" which Sir George Back had sent for old Ouligbuck (now dead), his companion on the Franklin expedition of 1825–27. William was paid at the rate of £20 per annum whilst with the expedition of 1853–54, and his share of the Government reward as a member of the party which first ascertained news of the fate of Sir John Franklin's expedition amounted to £210. Ouligbuck wintered at Churchill during 1854–55, but when his services were needed for James Anderson's expedition of 1855 down Back (Great Fish) River, they could not be obtained as he was away sealing. As he was considered a good deer hunter and general worker and as he was able to interpret for the Chipewyans as well as the Crees, his services were in demand at Churchill, and on July 19, 1856, William Ouligbuck entered into a contract to serve the Company as a middleman and interpreter for three years at £17 per annum. References to the duties carried out by him at Churchill during this period were frequently made in the correspondence between that post and York Factory. On February 4, 1859, James Hackland wrote from Churchill to the officer in charge at York Factory: "William Ouligbuck is yet uncertain about engaging he wants to go with the Esquimaux again, he is very handy while he is in a good humour but is very unsteady". A few days later, whilst at York Factory, William agreed to re-engage as from June 1, 1859, for two years at £20 per annum and at the end of that period he went away with the Eskimo seal hunters. He visited Churchill at intervals during the next few years and from January 21, 1872, to September 15, 1874, he was employed by the Company as an interpreter and harpooner for £24 per annum. He again left the service in 1874, but returned in August, 1882, for three years as interpreter and harpooner at $116.80 per annum. He renewed his contract on slightly different terms in 1885, 1888 and 1891, and on June 1, 1894, he finally retired. He died during the winter of 1895–96.

Peltier, Baptiste

Baptiste Peltier was a native of Red River and was engaged there as a middleman for Dr. Rae's Arctic expedition of 1850–51. Peltier wintered at Fort Confidence and on returning spent a season in the Mackenzie River District, wintering during 1851–52 at Fort Resolution. Arrangements were made for his return to Red River, but on reaching the Saskatchewan District he entered into a contract to serve the Company as a steersman for five years. He retired in 1857, but was again employed as a steersman during outfits 1861–62 and 1862–63. He retired to the Red River Settlement in 1863.

Rae, John

See Introduction.

Roy (*Roi*), *Joseph* (d)

Joseph Roy or Roi, listed in the Company's books as Joseph Roy or Roi (d) to distinguish him from contemporaries of the same name, was born about 1807 and came from Vaudreuil, Quebec. He entered the service of the Hudson's Bay Company as a middleman in 1835 and was stationed in the Athabaska District until 1844, when he was transferred to the Mackenzie River District. At that time his wages were £19 per annum. During outfit 1846–47 he was stationed at Fort Resolution, where he served as a bowsman at £22. In August, 1847, he entered into a new contract for three years at £24 per annum and remained at Fort Resolution until he joined Dr. Rae's Arctic expedition of 1850–51. Reference to Roy's wife is to be found in the Mackenzie River account books for outfit 1849–50. During 1850–51 Roy wintered at Fort Confidence and his name appears in the accounts as being concerned with expedition business until June, 1852. His contract as a fisherman and bowsman at £25 per annum was renewed that year, and during season 1852–53 he was stationed at Fort Rae. Roy retired to Red River Settlement from the Mackenzie River District in the summer of 1855.

Sabiston, William

William Sabiston, a native of the Saskatchewan District of Rupert's Land, appears to have entered the service of the Hudson's Bay Company in 1820, when he was about seventeen years of age, and to have been employed in the Swan River District. In 1823 he entered into a new agreement to serve as a labourer for two years at £15 per annum, and at the expiry of that contract he re-engaged for one year at £17. He appears to have been employed in the Athabaska District during outfit 1824–25 and in the Winnipeg District during trading season 1825–26. During the following outfit (1826–27) he was transferred to the Southern Department and was employed in the Fort Coulonge area and at Timiskaming as an interpreter until the end of outfit 1836–37, when he returned to the Northern Department. From outfit 1837–38 until the end of outfit 1846–47 Sabiston was employed as boute, interpreter or middleman in the Lac la Pluie and Saskatchewan Districts. During the last trading season, that of 1846–47, he was listed in the Company's books as an interpreter at £25 per annum. He was attached to the advance party of Sir John Richardson's Admiralty Arctic expedition as a labourer during 1847–48 and retired to the Red River Settlement in the autumn of 1848.

St. George, Jerome (dit Laporte)

Jerome St. George (dit Laporte) was a Canadian, born about 1820. He joined the service of the Hudson's Bay Company as a labourer in 1841 and was stationed in the Lake Superior District for three years. On May 16, 1844, when at the Pic, he entered into a new agreement with the Company and his services were transferred to the Northern Department of Rupert's Land. Laporte was listed as a middleman at Peel River post in the Mackenzie River District accounts during 1846–47 and at that time his wages were £19 per annum. During the two following outfits he served as a fisherman at Fort Yukon, his wages being £22 per annum, and during trading season 1849–50 he was fisherman at Fort Good Hope. In the summer of 1850 he was engaged by Commander Pullen at £4 10*s.* 0*d.* per month to accompany his party, which the Admiralty had ordered to go to Bank's Land to continue the search for Sir John Franklin. On returning from the expedition, which was unable to get any further east than Cape Bathurst, Laporte again joined the Hudson's Bay Company and became fisherman at For Simpson, the headquarters of the Mackenzie River District. His wages were £25 per annum at this time. He spent the remainder of his working life in the Mackenzie River District, his last years being spent at Fort Good Hope. He ceased work as from June 1, 1890, and died shortly afterwards at Fort Good Hope. Jerome St. George "b", who was also employed at Fort Good Hope and had a wife and two children, was presumably the son of Laporte who, during later years, was often referred to in the Company's books as Jerome St. George (a).

St. Germain, Jacques

Jacques St. Germain came from Montreal and was born about 1819. He entered the service of the Hudson's Bay Company as a middleman in June, 1841, and his wages were at the rate of £17 per annum for three years. He appears to have been stationed at Norway House until he was attached to Dr. John Rae's expedition of 1846–47. On his return he was listed as a fisherman in the Norway House District at £20 per annum, and in 1848–49 he was employed as a steersman at £22 per annum. During outfits 1849–50 and 1850–51 St. Germain received £25 per annum and at the close of the last outfit, which was spent in the Lower Red River District, he was discharged.

St. Michel, Louis

Louis St. Michel, a Canadian from St. Timothée, Quebec, was born about 1829 and entered the service of the Hudson's Bay Company as a middleman and carpenter in 1849. He was employed in the Norway House District and was considered by Chief Factor George Barnston as "an excellent man . . . who gets through work rapidly". St. Michel renewed his engagement in 1852 for three years at £23 per annum as a carpenter and shingle maker, but in 1853 he joined Dr. Rae's expedition bound for West Boothia. St. Michel was one of the men who returned from Chesterfield Inlet to York Factory when Rae had to arrange to winter during 1853–54 at Repulse Bay. St. Michel completed his contract with the Company and was apparently stationed in the Swan River District during outfit 1854–55. He retired to Canada in 1855. His share of H.M. Government's award to Dr. Rae for first ascertaining news of the fate of Sir John Franklin amounted to £30.

Sinclair, Samuel
Nothing is known about Samuel Sinclair except that he enlisted at Red River Settlement for Dr. Rae's Arctic Expedition of 1850–51 and wintered at Fort Confidence. His wife, Elizabeth, remained in the Settlement.

Smith, Henry (a)
Henry Smith, known as Henry Smith (a) to distinguish him from contemporaries of the same name, was born about 1822. He came from Sorel, Quebec, and joined the Company's service as a middleman in 1843. He was apparently stationed in the Athabaska District and in 1847 joined the advance party of Sir John Richardson's Admiralty Arctic Expedition as a bowsman and fisherman. According to Richardson's *Arctic Searching Expedition*, I, 337, Smith wintered during 1848–49 with several companions at the fishery on Big Island, Great Slave Lake. He retired to Canada in 1849.

Stevenson, Edmund
Edmund Stevenson, a native of Rupert's Land, joined the advance party of Sir John Richardson's Admiralty Arctic Expedition as a steersman in 1847. At the end of the expedition Stevenson's services were apparently retained by the Company in the Norway House District until 1853 when he became a "Freeman".

Trembly, Narcisse
Narcisse Trembly of St. Isidore, Quebec, was born about 1825 and

entered the service of the Hudson's Bay Company as a middleman in 1842. He appears to have spent at least two trading seasons in the Columbia District, probably at Fort Vancouver Depot, before returning east of the Rocky Mountains. During outfits 1845–46 and 1846–47 he was employed as a middleman in the York Factory District, and during outfits 1847–48 and 1848–49 he was attached to Sir John Richardson's Arctic expedition. He retired to Canada in 1849.

Turnor (Turner), Richard

Richard Turnor was a native of Rupert's Land and a member of the numerous Turnor family living at Moose Factory. In the Moose Factory journal for the autumn of 1834 he was referred to as the "Boy Richard Turnor", and during the winter of 1834–35 he was employed as a cowherd. He must have been known to Dr. John Rae who was at this time stationed at Moose. Turnor was frequently mentioned in the succeeding Moose Factory journals as a cattle-keeper and it was not until March 19, 1839, that he was given a change of occupation. On that day he set off with an experienced companion carrying the spring express to Abitibi, but two days later he returned as he could not keep pace with the guide and resumed his work as assistant cattle-keeper. During outfit 1839–40 Turnor appears to have been transferred to the New Brunswick post, where he was employed as a labourer until 1845, when Rae described him as "altho' short . . . an active and strong fellow". Turnor volunteered to accompany Rae on the 1846–47 expedition and consequently his services were transferred from the Southern to the Northern Department of Rupert's Land. He wintered at York Factory during 1845–46. In his letter dated June 12, 1846, Rae mentioned to Sir George Simpson that Turnor was "a fine active lad and very ingenious", adding that he had "built a boat at New Brunswick, and forged the nails for her himself, having previously made a blacksmiths bellows although he had never been employed either with carpenter or blacksmith . . .". On his return from the 1846–47 expedition, Turnor remained at York Factory, where he served for three years as a boatbuilder at £25 per annum. In July, 1850, Rae requested Turnor's services as a carpenter in the Mackenzie River District, but as he had "fallen into delicate Health" he remained at York Fort and in the following October renewed his engagement with the Company as a carpenter for three years at £30 per annum. On the expiry of his contract in the summer of 1853 he retired to the Red River Settlement.

Wilson, Daniel

Daniel Wilson was born about 1823 and came from Stennes in the Shetland Islands. He joined the service of the Hudson's Bay Company in 1842 as a labourer at £16 per annum and sailed to York Factory in the Company's ship *Prince Rupert* in the summer of that year. Until 1847, when he volunteered for service as a middleman in the Arctic Searching Expedition to be commanded by Sir John Richardson, Wilson was employed in the Saskatchewan District. He was one of the men who left Fort Confidence on September 18, 1848, to winter at the fishery at Big Island, Great Slave Lake. In 1849 Wilson re-engaged with the Company as a labourer at £20 per annum and was stationed in the Cumberland House District. In the summer of 1852 he again renewed his contract with the Company, this time as a bowsman at £22 per annum. He apparently spent outfits 1852–53 and 1853–54 in the Cumberland House District and was then transferred to the Norway House District, where he remained until he retired to the Red River Settlement in 1857.

THE HUDSON'S BAY RECORD SOCIETY

LIST OF MEMBERS

Ainley, Dr. Wm. E., Vancouver, B.C.
Alanbrooke, Field Marshal The Rt. Hon. The Viscount, K.G., G.C.B., O.M., G.C.V.O., D.S.O., Hartley Wintney, Hants, England
Alexander of Tunis, Field Marshal The Rt. Hon. The Earl, K.G., G.C.B., G.C.M.G., C.S.I., D.S.O., M.C.
Allen, Sir George, K.C.V.O., London, England
Allen, D.A., London, England
Allenby, R.J., Highland Park, Illinois
Alligood, Sylvester, Washington, N. Carolina
Alton, F.H., Mapperley Park, Nottingham, England
Alton, J.A., M.D., Lamont, Alberta
Anderson, George, Winnipeg, Manitoba
Anderson, H.H.C., Vancouver, B.C.
Arbuckle, W.A., Montreal, P.Q.
Archibald, Dr. E.S., Ottawa
Arkin, N., Winnipeg, Manitoba
Ashton, Henry R., New York
Backus, Dr. P.L., London, England
Bain, J. Watson, Toronto, Ontario
Baker, Dr. J.O., Edmonton, Alberta
Ballantyne, M.G., Montreal, P.Q.
Bamber, Mrs. Gwynnedd M., Lymington, Hants, England
Banbury, P., Winnipeg, Manitoba
Barker, Dr. Burt Brown, Portland, Oregon
Barnum, C.R., Eureka, California
Bates, D.H., Portland, Oregon
Batt, F. Raleigh, LL.M., Manchester, England
Baxter, A. Beverley, M.P., London, England
Baylis, F.S., Purley, Surrey, England
Beatty, J.C, Junior, Portland, Oregon
Bender, Dr. Webster, Ebenezer, New York
Benjamin, G.H., Vancouver, Washington
Benn, Sir Ion Hamilton, London, England
Benson, H.A., C.B.E., F.C.A., London, England
Berliner, Harold B., London, England
Bignall, L.C., West Bridgford, Notts, England
Binford, P.A., Portland, Oregon
Birch, J.P., London, England
Bird, Prof. J. Brian, Montreal, P.Q.
Birks, Henry G., Montreal, P.Q.
Bishop, Col. A.L., Toronto, Ontario
Bishop, Clarence M., Portland, Oregon
Black, Leslie W., Toronto, Ontario
Blackhall, John, Aberdeen, Scotland
Blake, Anson S., Richmond, California
Blodgett, G.R., Portland, Oregon
Bond, Major-General J.A.M., London, England
Boulton, P.M., Montreal, P.Q.
Bourne, Mrs. E.N., Surbiton, England
Bowater, Sir Eric V., London, England
Bowlen, The Hon. J.J., Edmonton, Alberta
Bowman, Mrs. Arthur, Portland, Oregon
Boyd, Dr. Mark F., Tallahassee, Florida
Brackenbury, J.C., Williams Lake, B.C.
Brett, R.P., London, England
Breyfogle, R.J., London, England
Bromley, Rear-Admiral Sir Arthur, London, England
Bronson, Frederic E., Ottawa, Ontario
Brooks, V.P., London, England
Brown, Sir S.H., London, England
Buckham, A.F., Cumberland, B.C.
Burford, W.T., Ottawa, Ontario
Burger, O.R., New York, N.Y.
Burgesse, J.A., Isle Maligne, Quebec
Burnham, Howard J., Vancouver, Washington
Burns, Thomas H., Dingwall, Scotland
Burt, A.L., Minneapolis, Minnesota
Burton, Edgar, C.B.E., Toronto, Ontario
Butler, J. Dean, Oregon City, Oregon
Cabeldu, A.E., London, England
Cabell, The Hon. Henry F., Portland, Oregon
Caldwell, William C., Baltimore, Maryland
Cameron, J. Lyle, M.D., F.R.C.S., F.A.C.S., F.R.C.O.G., London, England
Campbell, K.C., London, England
Camrose, The Viscount, London, England
Camsell, Dr. Charles, C.M.G., LL.D., Ottawa, Ontario
Carter, D.C., Orillia, Ontario
Caufield, Raymond P., Oregon City, Oregon
Chessire, R.H., Winnipeg, Manitoba
Chester, P. A., Winnipeg, Manitoba
Chorley, Kenneth, New York, N.Y.
Christ, J.H., Portland, Oregon
Church, W.E., Portland, Oregon
Clapham, Sidney C., Burgh, Suffolk, England
Clarke, Mrs. Henrietta F., Bromley Kent, England
Clement, S.B., Sarnia, Ontario
Coe, W.R., New York, N.Y.
Colbert, Miss Mildred, Portland, Oregon
Coleman, D'A.C, LL.D., D.C.L., Montreal, P.Q.
Colthurst, R. St. John Bowen, Wakes Colne, Essex, England
Congdon, C.C., Palmeira, N.Y.
Congdon, Mrs. Dorothy H., Duluth, Minnesota
Congleton, Edith, Lady, Lyndhurst, Hants, England
Conn, Hugh, Limavady, Co. Derry, Northern Ireland
Constable, Guy, Creston, B.C.
Conway, D.J., Portland, Oregon
Coombs, F.J., Toronto, Ontario
Coonan, Clarence, San Francisco
Cooper, Sir Patrick Ashley, Hexton, England
Cornwall, G. Mackie, Portland, Oregon
Cosens, G.G., Toronto, Ontario
Cosier, S.M., Sorrento, B.C.
Coulthard, J.T., Maryport, Cumberland, England

Cowley, C.B., London, England
Coyne, J.B., Winnipeg, Manitoba
Coyne, J.E., Ottawa, Ontario
Crossley, Julian S., London, England
Cruickshank, Robert, Winnipeg, Manitoba
Daetwyler, A.R., Berne, Switzerland
Danson, J.R., Liverpool, England
Davidson, Marshall B., New York, N.Y.
Davies, David L., Portland, Oregon
Davis, Carl Henry, M.D., Miami, Florida
Davis, The Rev. W. L., S.J., Spokane, Washington
Dawson, Glen, Los Angeles, California
Decker, P., New York, N.Y.
Dederer, Michael, Seattle, Washington
De Long, Merton R., Portland, Oregon
Denne, M., London, England
Diggle, P.G.W., Capetown, S. Africa
Dixon, John, Meota, Saskatchewan
Doel, F.P., London, England
Douglas, G.M., Lakefield, Ontario
Douglas, The Hon. T.C., M.A., Regina, Saskatchewan
Douglas, William, Winnipeg, Manitoba
Downes, P.G., Concord, Massachusetts
Draper, Arthur S., Malton, Yorks, England
Dunlap, D.M., Toronto, Ontario
Dunn, Sir James, Bt., Montreal, P.Q.
Dwinelle, Mrs. J.K., Bozeman, Montana
Dyde, Mrs. D.R., Edmonton, Alberta
Eberstadt, Charles, Plainfield, New Jersey
Eccles, The Rt. Hon. Sir David, K.C.V.O., M.P., London, England
Eccles, John, Liverpool, England
Edwards, Ashley, London, England
Edwardson, Miss Lida S., Tacoma, Washington
Egilson, Konrad, Vancouver, B.C.
Esbenshade, J.H., Pasadena, California
Ethridge, F.M., Rossland, B.C.
Ewart, W.H.L., Belmont, Jersey, Channel Islands
Falkner, J.W., Toronto, Ontario
Farrell, Judge A. Gray, Toronto, Ontario
Faulkner, E.O., M.B.E., Wrotham, Kent, England
Fay, C. Ryle, M.A., D.Sc, Belfast, N. Ireland
Ferguson, Mrs. J., Walhachin, B.C.
Fetherston, R. J., London, England
Field, H., Wolverhampton, England
Flegel, Austin F., Jr., Portland, Oregon
Fleming, J. Stuart, Niagara Falls, N. Y.
Flint, Alfred T., Madison, Wisconsin
Forrest, John, Armstrong, Ontario
Frayling, A.F., London, England
Freeman, Miller, Seattle, Washington
Fuller, Harold E., Welland, Ontario.
Furniss, O.C., Alberni, B.C.
Fyfe, Sir William H., LL.D., F.R.S.C., D.Litt., London, England
Gardner, B.C, M.C., Montreal, P.Q.
Gardner, Dr. G., Montreal, P.Q.
Gary, G.L., Oakland, California
German, Gordon T., Rossland, B.C.
Gilbert, G., Victoria, B.C.
Glassey, J.R., Winnipeg, Manitoba
Glennie, William, Edmonton, Alberta
Glover, Dr. Richard G., Winnipeg, Manitoba
Goodrich, A.C., Bend, Oregon
Goodwin, J.C., M.A., M.D., Toronto, Ontario
Gordon, D., Montreal, P.Q.
Gordon, R.K., Penticton, B.C.
Gourley, R.J., Winnipeg, Manitoba
Governor-General of Canada, H. E., The, Ottawa, Ontario
Grafe, Paul, Los Angeles, California
Graff, E.D., Winnetka, Illinois
Grasett, Lt.-Gen. Sir Edward, K.B.E. C.B., D.S.O., M.C., Jersey, Channel Islands
Gravel, C.E., Montreal, P.Q.
Graves, L.O., Seattle, Washington
Gray, J.M., Toronto, Ontario
Greene, V.G., Toronto, Ontario
Greenly, A.H., Hoboken, N.J.
Grey, The Earl, Alnwick, Northumberland, England
Griswold, Charles H., Houston, Texas
Groulx, Abbé Lionel, Outremont, P.Q.
Haines, Francis, Monmouth, Oregon
Hardinge, The Viscount, Montreal, P.Q.
Harkes, A., Winnipeg, Manitoba
Harper, A.D., London, England
Harris, E. Vincent, R.A., London, England
Harris, Joseph, Winnipeg, Manitoba
Harris, Mortimer, London, England
Hartley, Brig-Gen. Sir Harold, K.C.V.O., C.B.E., M.C., High Wycombe, Bucks, England
Haslam, Greville, B.S., M.A., F.R.G.S., Philadelphia, Pennsylvania
Haycox, Mrs. Ernest, Portland, Oregon
Hayes, Edmund, Portland, Oregon
Henderson, Commander R.R. Gore-Brown, R.N., Wick, Caithness, Scotland
Hennessy, Sir Partick, Stondon Massey, Essex, England
Hewett, F., Toronto, Ontario
Hidden, Robert A., Vancouver, Washington
High Commissioner for Canada, London, England
High Commissioner for the United Kingdom in Canada, Ottawa, Ontario
Hildebrand, August, Astoria, Oregon
Hinchliff, W., Wirral, Cheshire, England
Hitchman, G.C., London, England
Hitchman, Robert, Seattle, Washington
Holbrook, Dr. J.H., Ancaster, Ontario
Holt, Major A.P., London, England
Holt, Major H.P., London, England
Hood, Mrs. Dora, Toronto, Ontario
Hoop, Colonel O.W., Laguna Beach, California
Howard, Archbishop E.D., Portland, Oregon
Howell, R.E., Winnipeg, Manitoba
Hubachek, F.B., Glencoe, Illinois
Hubbell, C.S., Seattle, Washington
Huffman, Percival, London, England
Hume, H.N., C.B.E., M.C., London, England

Hunter, Fenley, Flushing, New York
Hurley, C.T.L., Bristol, England
Iliffe, The Lord, G.B.E., J.P., London, England
Inch, Mrs. Una B., Medford, Oregon
Ingram, Charles H., Tacoma, Washington
Ireland, Willard E., Victoria, B.C.
Jackson, P.L., Portland, Oregon
James, Dr. E.S., Winnipeg, Manitoba
Jeffcott, P.R., Ferndale, Washington
Jeffries, Herbert, Knowle, Warwickshire, England
Jenkins, Alan C., Trail, B.C.
Jenkins, Hopkin, Portland, Oregon
Jennings, Major D.C., D.S.O., London, England
Jensen, George K., Sacramento, California
Johnson, F., Yateley, Surrey, England
Johnson, G.R., Calgary, Alberta
Johnston, J L., Winnipeg, Manitoba
Johnston, Norman M., London, England
Johnston, W.P., Edmonton, Alberta
Jolliffe, A.W., Kingston, Ontario
Jones, A.G.E., Bristol, England
Jones, George W., London, England
Jones, O.N., Cleveland, Ohio
Jones, Dr. Thomas, C.H., Aberystwyth, Cardigan, Wales
Joslyn, C.E., Winnipeg, Manitoba
Jukes, H.P., Bellingham, Washington
Karslake, Mrs. Leonora A., Silchester, Berks, England
Kashnor, L., London, England
Kelly, David, Hudson, Wisconsin
Kelly, The Most Rev. E.J., Boise, Idaho
Kemsley, The Viscount, LL.D., J.P., London, England
Kerry, L.L., Kelowna, B.C.
Keswick, W.J., London, England
Kibbe, L.A., Bellingham, Washington
Kidd, K.E., Toronto, Ontario
Kilpatrick, S., Thames Ditton, Surrey, England
Kindersley, The Hon. H.K.M., C.B.E., M.C., London, England
King, Ralph H., Portland, Oregon
Kingsford, The Rev. M.R., Nuneham Courtenay, Oxford, England
Kinnes, Walter, Killin, Perthshire, Scotland
Knox, H.C, Winnipeg, Manitoba
Knox, Colonel T.M., Victoria, B.C.
Konantz, Mrs. Margaret, O.B.E., Winnipeg, Manitoba
Krause, Herbert, Sioux Falls, S. Dakota
Krauss, E.L., Detroit, Michigan
Lamb, E.A., St. Briavels, Glos., England
Lamb, Dr. W. Kaye, Ottawa, Ontario
Lambert, Francis, Portland, Oregon
Langford, Dr. Geo. B., Toronto, Ontario
Larsell, Dr. Olof, Portland, Oregon
Lash, P.J.B., Toronto, Ontario
Lash, Z.R.B., Toronto, Ontario
Laughlin, K.E., Moscow, Idaho
Lavoie, P.E., M.D., Ile à la Crosse, Saskatchewan
Leach, C.H., Harrow, Middlesex, England
Lee, A.J., Bristol, England
Lee, Wallace, Halifax, Yorks, England
Lennox-Boyd, The Rt. Hon. A. T., M.P., London, England
Lent, Miss D.G., Calgary, Alberta
Leslie, Gary Anderson, Alexandra, Virginia
Links, J.G., O.B.E., London, England
Lips, Mrs. Eva, Leipzig, Germany
Lisenby, Albert S., Panama City, Florida
Little, A. Ross, Winnipeg, Manitoba
Livingston, Harold A., Toronto Ontario
Loeb, Alfred A., Portland, Oregon
Loening, Mrs. Sarah L., Long Island, New York
Long, Mrs. Ernest E., Outremont, Quebec
Long, F.S., London, England
Lotbinière, A. J. de, Leclercville, P.Q.
Love, J.P., London, England
Lowson, Sir Denys, Bart., London, England
Luxton, N.K., Banff, Alberta
MacCallum, F.O., M.D., Reading, Berks, England
McClelland, J.M., Jnr., Loneview, Washington
McClintock, F.S., Pittsburg, Pennsylvania
McCloy, T.R., Ottawa, Ontario
McConnell, J.W., Montreal, P.Q.
McCook, James, Ottawa, Ontario
McDonald, Dr. Ellice, Newark, Delaware
McEwan, Thomas, Winnipeg, Manitoba
MacFarlane, Dr. R.O., Winnipeg, Manitoba
Macgillivray, H. Darroch, St. Johns, Newfoundland
MacGregor, John M., New York, N.Y
McIlwraith, W.N., London, England
McInerney, E. Blake, London, England
McKelvie, B.A., Cobble Hill, B.C.
McKinnon, W.G., Edmonton, Alberta
McLaughlin, H.J., Toronto, Ontario
MacLehose, H.A., Maybole, Ayrshire, Scotland
McLeod, Fred, Winnipeg, Manitoba
MacLeod, J.E.A., Calgary, Alberta
MacLeod, Mrs. M.A., Winnipeg, Manitoba
McMillan, Fred O., Corvallis, Oregon
MacMillan, H.R., C.B.E., D.Sc., Vancouver, B.C.
McMurtry, R.O., Montreal, P.Q.
Macnabb, Hugh, Isle of Arran, Scotland
MacNaughton, E.B., Portland, Oregon
McNichols, A. Stewart, Montreal, P.Q.
McPhee, John M., Fairbanks, Alaska
McPherson, W.B., Q.C., Toronto, Ontario
McWilliams, The Hon. R. F., Winnipeg, Manitoba
Maggs, F.B., London, England
Mann, Henry J., Fortsmith, Alberta
Manning, T.H., Ottawa, Ontario
Mardell, H.G., Redhill, Surrey, England
Marks, Sir Simon, London, England
Marler, G.C, Montreal, P.Q.
Marshall, Geo. A., Toronto, Ontario
Martin, Brother David, C.S.C., Portland, Oregon
Martin, David J., Vancouver, B.C.
Martin, F.F., Winnipeg, Manitoba
Martin, Lt. John H., Plainfield, N.J.
Martin, R.C., Horsham, Sussex, England

Martin, W.H., London, England
Massey, The Rt. Hon. Vincent, C.H., Port Hope, Ontario
Mather, W.A., Montreal, P.Q.
Matthews, W.D., Toronto, Ontario
Meaden, J.T., Toronto, Ontario
Medler, J.V., Brooklyn, N.Y.
Mehmel, Paul C., Vancouver, B.C.
Mellen, Wilson, Montreal, Quebec
Mench, John, New York City, N.Y.
Miller, Winlock V., Seattle, Washington
Milner, H.R., Edmonton, Alberta
Mitchell, F.J., Sioux Lookout, Ontario
Mitchell, Ross, M.D., Winnipeg, Manitoba
Mitchell, Mrs. W.F., London, England
Mollins, Miss M., Berkeley, California
Monckton, The Rt. Hon. Sir Walter, K.C.M.G., K.C.V.O., London, England
Montgomery, A.H., London, England
Moore, L., Winslow, Arizona
Morgan, Dale L., Salt Lake City, Utah
Morris, J.R., Leamington, Ontario
Morris, Robert, Huntington, New York
Morton, W.L., Winnipeg, Manitoba
Moss, A.H., Cobalt, Ontario
Muir, E.F., Haslemere, Surrey, England
Munro, Donald R., Portland, Oregon
Munro, Sir Gordon, K.C.M.G., M.C., Storrington, Sussex, England
Munro, W.D., Salmon Arm, B.C.
Munroe, David, M.A., Ormstown, P.Q.
Murdoch, A.S., Glasgow, Scotland
Murphy, E.W., Boise, Idaho
Murray, Sir Alexander R., K.C.I.E., C.B.E., Hughenden, Bucks, England
Murray, Major Gladstone, Toronto, Ontario
Murray, Miss Jean E., Saskatoon, Saskatchewan
Nadeau, Gabriel, Rutland, Massachusetts
Napier, Mrs. F.M., Bristol, England
Napier, I.P.R., M.C., London, England
Neelands, A.R., M.C., Doncaster, Yorks, England
Nelson, Sir George, M.I.E.E., London, England
Niven, Lt.-Col. H.W., D.S.O., M.C., Glasgow, Scotland
Nix, Edwin C., St. James, Manitoba
Norton, Frank, Worthing, Sussex, England
Oberholtzer, Ernest C., Ranier, Minnesota
O'Brien, Robert A., London, England
O'Kieffe, de Witt, Kenilworth, Illinois
Oliphant, J. Orin, Lewisburg, Pennsylvania
Olrich, E. L., Minneapolis, Minnesota
O'Meara, Walter, New York, N.Y.
Ontario, Agent-General for, London, England
Osler, Miss Barbara, Toronto, Ontario
Osler, Mrs. Britton, Toronto, Ontario
Osler, B.B., Toronto, Ontario
Osler, P.S., Toronto, Ontario
Outerbridge, Col. the Hon. Sir L. C., C.B.E., D.S.O., LL.D., St. John's Newfoundland
Owen, Capt. L.T., O.B.E., Llanfair P.G., Anglesey, Wales
Palmer, Loyd, Duluth, Minnesota
Parsons, Ralph, St. John's, Newfoundland
Partoll, A.J., Missoula, Montana
Patteson, J.C., C.M.G., London, England
Peacock, Sir Edward R., G.C.V.O., D.C.L., London, England
Pearce, W.M., Toronto, Ontario
Peat, Sir Harry W., G.B.E., London, England
Peltier, Jerome A., Spokane, Washington
Penson, Dame Lillian M., D.B.E., LL.D., D.Litt., Ph.D., London, England
Perrine, Fred S., Cloverdale, Oregon
Perry, Roy A., Portland, Oregon
Perth, The Earl of, London, England
Peterson, Mrs. Elmer F., Portland, Oregon
Pierce, Lorne, Toronto, Ontario
Piper, Carson F., Fort William, Ontario
Powers, Alfred, Portland, Oregon
Preisig, Dr. A., Zurich, Switzerland
Price, Sir Keith W., London, England
Pritchett, Dr. John Perry, Flushing, New York
Rae, Robert, Toronto, Ontario
Rae, Lt.-Col. William, East Horsley, Surrey, England
Raisty, L.B., Atlanta, Georgia
Rand, Mrs. R.H., Victoria, B.C.
Rawlinson, H.E., M.D., Edmonton, Alberta
Rees, T.I., Bowstreet, Cards, Wales
Reincke, H.A., London, England
Reynolds, R.A., T.D., M.A., Purley, Surrey, England
Rich, Professor E.E., M.A., Cambridge, England
Richmond, Volney, Seattle, Washington
Riley, C.S., Winnipeg, Manitoba
Rinfret, The Rt. Hon. T., Ottawa, Ontario
Rogers, Dr. A.L., Portland, Oregon
Rose, W.A., Winnipeg, Manitoba
Ross, Norman, Winnipeg, Manitoba
Ross, R.W., Winnipeg, Manitoba
Rousseau, Jacques, Montreal, P.Q.
Russell, B.H., London, England
Russell, Gerald, London, England
Sage, D., Calgary, Alberta
Sage, Professor W.N., Vancouver, B.C.
St. Laurent, The Rt. Hon. L., Q.C., Ottawa, Ontario
Sale, G.S., London, England
Sanderson, J.F., Montreal, P.Q.
Sandilands, A., St. James, Manitoba
Sankey, Charles A., St. Catharine's, Ontario
Sawyer, Robert W., Bend, Oregon
Schnackenberg, W.C., Jr., Parkland, Washington
Scott, A.W., Madsen, Ontario
Scott, Osborne, Sydney, Vancouver Island, B.C.
Scrimgeour, H.C., London, England
Searle, S.A., Winnipeg, Manitoba
Selling, Mrs. Lawrence, Portland, Oregon
Shaw, J.N., Edinburgh, Scotland
Shaw, L.L., Klamath Falls, Oregon
Shiels, Archie W., Bellingham, Washington
Sibbald, Mrs. F.A., Fort William, Ontario

Simpson, Guy, Castleford, Yorks, England
Simpson, L.B., Winnipeg, Manitoba
Skelton, Mrs. O.D., Montreal, P.Q.
Skinner, T. Gordon, London, England
Smith, Colin Hugh, London, England
Smith, Preston W., Portland, Oregon
Smith, T. Brenton, Liverpool, Nova Scotia
Smith, Wm., Jr., Dundee, Scotland
Soliday, George W., Seattle, Washington
Somerville, James, London, England
Spencer, Horace, Carnforth, England
Spencer, O.C., Portland, Oregon
Spencer, O.L., Ganges, Salt Spring Island, B.C.
Spry, Graham, London, England
Stanley, George F.G., D.Phil., Kingston, Ontario
Starr, C.L., Portland, Oregon
Starr, Mrs. F.N.G., Toronto, Ontario
Steer, George H., Q.C., Edmonton, Alberta
Stefansson, Mrs. E., Hanover, New Hampshire
Stefansson, Dr. V., New York, N.Y.
Stevenson, C.D., Williams Lake, B.C.
Stevenson, H.A., Montreal, P.Q.
Stewart, Donald, Vancouver, Washington
Stewart, E.I., Cheney, Washington
Stewart, J. McG., Q.C., Halifax, Nova Scotia
Stewart, Leo W., Seattle, Washington
Stott, H.B., Shipley, England
Strange, H.G.L., Winnipeg, Manitoba
Strath, B., London, England
Stuart, Sir Campbell, G.C.M.G., K.B.E., LL.D., London, England
Stuart, R.R., San Leandro, California
Sullivan, Arthur, Q.C., Winnipeg, Manitoba
Sursham, E.A., J.P., St. Albans, Herts, England
Sutherland, The Duke of, K.T., P.C., Guildford, Surrey, England
Swannell, Frank, D.L.S., Victoria, B.C.
Taintor, C.M., Southport, Connecticut
Taylor, C.E. Page, London, England
Taylor, E.P., York Mills, Ontario
Teakle, Thomas, Spokane, Washington
Tessier, The Rev. Albert, Trois-Rivières, Quebec
Thayer, C.S., Vancouver, Washington
Thom, James B., M.C., London, England
Thompson, Mrs. G., York, England
Thomson, A., Toronto, Ontario
Thorman, Geo. E., St. Thomas, Ontario
Thornton, Mrs. R.B., Montreal, P.Q.
Tiemann, Louis, New York, N.Y.
Titus, O.W., Toronto, Ontario
Tomlinson, Roy E., New York, N.Y.
Traylen, C.W., Guildford, Surrey, England
Trueman, A.W., Fredericton, New Brunswick
Turnbull, Mrs. A.D., Trail, B.C.
Tweed, T.W., Toronto, Ontario
Tweedsmuir, The Lord, O.B.E., London, England
Tweedy, W.R., Vancouver, B.C.
Tyrrell, J.B., M.A., LL.D., Toronto, Ontario
Ulman, J.J., New York, N.Y.
Vail, Herman L., Cleveland, Ohio
Vaught, L.O., Jacksonville, Illinois
Veitch, Major-General W.L.D., C.B.E., Newcastle, Staffs, England
Vogt, Ernest A., San Francisco, California
Vogt, Hans, Salisbury, S. Rhodesia
Waldie, J. Kemp, Toronto, Ontario
Wallace, Col. The Hon. C., Victoria, B.C.
Wallace, J.M., London, England
Wallick, K.A., Winnipeg, Manitoba
Walsh, N.J., Chateauguay, Quebec
Walton, G., M.B., Regina, Saskatchewan
Warwick, W.C., London, England
Washburn, Dr. A.L., Wilmette, Illinois
Watson, C.S., Toronto, Ontario
Watson, George, Montreal, P.Q.
Watson, Sir Norman J., Bt., Haslemere, Surrey, England
Watts, E.H., London, England
Waverley, The Rt. Hon. Viscount, G.C.B., G.C.S.I., G.C.I.E., F.R.S., London, England
Weems, F.C., New York City, N.Y.
Wentjar, Miss Agnes, Tacoma, Washington
Weston, W. Garfield, London, England
Whittaker, D.A., Montreal, P.Q.
Wilkinson, R.J., Woodbridge, Suffolk, England
Williams, L.F., Fort Frances, Ontario
Wilson, J.E.J., Winnipeg, Manitoba
Wilson, Col. J.T., Toronto, Ontario
Winch, Mrs. S.R., Portland, Oregon
Windell, D.H., Whitstable, Kent, England
Wishart ,D.E.S., B.A., M.B., Toronto, Ontario
Wonnall, M.H., M.B.E., T.D., Brighton, Sussex, England
Woods, C.A., Portland, Oregon
Woods, J. Elmer, Winnipeg, Manitoba
Woods, L.C., Jr., Pittsburg, Pennsylvania
Woodward, A., Altadena, California
Wordie, James, Cambridge, England
Wright, P., Toronto, Ontario
Wulsin, Lucien, Jr., Cincinnati, Ohio
Wulsin, Lucien, Sr., Cincinnati, Ohio
Wynn, A., Birmingham, England
Zilka, Henry J., Portland, Oregon
Zillmer, Raymond T., Milwaukee, Wisconsin
Zimmerman, A.H., Niagara Falls, New York
Zimmerman, Edward A., Vista, California

ENDNOTES

INTRODUCTION

1 The eldest son was James, born May 19, 1805. The second was William Glen Rae, Hudson's Bay Company man, born in 1809, who died in 1845. The third son was Richard Bempede Johnstone Honeyman Rae, born September 17, 1811. The fifth son, Thomas, born October 23, 1815, seems to have died young, and there was a sixth son, also Thomas, born on May 24, 1817. When the latter died in 1868 at Hamilton, Ontario, he was described in a local newspaper as "brother of the explorer and of Mr Richard H. Rae, Emigration Agent at this port". The sisters were Janet, born October 18, 1806, Marion, born April 5, 1808, and a still younger sister, Jessie. Marion married Dr. John Macaulay Hamilton, and Jessie became the wife of Hector Munro. Both apparently figure in *The Pirate,* and Sir Walter Scott is said to have acknowledged them as the originals for the characters of Brenda and Minna.

2 Sir Walter Scott, in a diary giving particulars of his visit to Orkney in August 1814, mentions breakfasting and dining with Mr. Rae at Clestrain and remarks on his success as a farmer and in breeding horses of the Galloway breed from Lanarkshire "of which county he is a native" (J.G. Lockhart, *The Life of Sir Walter Scott* (Edinburgh, 1902), IV, 232, 234).

3 These incidents in his early life were the subject of a letter from Dr. Rae to D. Murray Smith, which is published in the latter's *Arctic Expeditions from British and Foreign Shores from the earliest to the Expedition of* 1875–76 (Edinburgh, 1877). Rae corresponded at some length with Murray Smith and this information forms the basis of Smith's chapters on Rae's explorations.

4 [Hudson's Bay Company Archives], A.5/10, p. 127. Subsequent classification numbers refer to Hudson's Bay Company Archives.

5 D.5/4.

6 D.4/20, fo. 4.

7 Ibid., fo. 6d.

8 D.4/127, fo. 26.

9 Simpson had been knighted in 1841.

10 Cowie, on learning of this, wrote to Simpson on June 20, 1844, stating ". . . If Mr. Rae takes charge of the District, a little lecture on economy will not be lost on him. I have no doubt he would be very popular with Indians as well as the officers & Servants, but am aware he is over liberal in all payments to Indians on his private account & might be disposed to go a little beyond the mark in Companys dealings . . ." (D.5/11)

11 See p. 365.

12 See p. 88.

13 M.A. MacLeod (ed.), *The Letters of Letitia Hargrave* (Toronto, The Champlain Society, 1947), p. 211.

14 R.M. Ballantyne, *Hudson's Bay* . . .(2nd edition, Edinburgh and London, 1848), pp. 225–6. Ballantyne, who had joined the Company's service as an apprentice clerk in 1841, was travelling from York Factory to Norway House.

15 The state of knowledge at this time is well shown by the maps in the following books: J. Barrow, *A Chronological History of Voyages into the Arctic Regions; undertaken chiefly for the purpose of Discovering a North-East, North-West, or Polar Passage between the Atlantic and the Pacific* . . . (London, 1818); D. Barrington, *The Possibility of Approaching the North Pole Asserted . . . with an Appendix . . . by Colonel Beaufoy, F.R.S.* (London, 1818).

16 J. Ross, *A Voyage of Discovery, made under the orders of the Admiralty, in His Majesty's Ships Isabella and Alexander, for the purpose of exploring Baffin's Bay, and inquiring into the probability of a North-West Passage* (London, 1819).

17 A. Basil Lubbock, *The Arctic Whalers* (Glasgow, 1937) p. 204.

18 W.E. Parry, *Journal of a Voyage for the Discovery of a North-West Passage . . . performed in the years* 1819–20, *in His Majesty's Ships Hecla and Griper . . .* (London, 1821).

19 W.E. Parry, *Journal of a Second Voyage for the Discovery of a North- West Passage . . . performed in the years* 1821–22–23, *in His Majesty's Ships Fury and Hecla . . .* (London, 1824).

20 W.E. Parry, *Journal of a Third Voyage for the Discovery of a North-West Passage. . . performed in the years* 1824–25, *in His Majesty's Ships Hecla and Fury . . .* (London, 1826).

21 This was Franklin's second visit to the Arctic. He had served as second-in-command to Captain David Buchan in an abortive attempt to reach the North Pole in 1818 in H.M. Ships *Dorothea* and *Trent* (F.W. Beechey, *A Voyage of Discovery towards the North Pole, performed in His Majesty's Ships Dorothea and Trent, under the command of Capt. David Buchan, R.N.* 1818 . . . (London, 1843).

22 J. Franklin, *Narrative of a Journey to the shores of The Polar Sea in the years* 1819, 20, 21, *and* 22 (London, 1823).

23 J. Franklin, *Narrative of a Second Expedition to the Shores of the Polar Sea, in the years* 1825, 1826 *and* 1827 (London, 1828).

24 F. W. Beechey, *Narrative of a Voyage to the Pacific and Beering's Strait to co-operate with the Polar Expeditions: performed in His Majesty's Ship Blossom . . . in the years* 1825, 26, 27, 28 (London, 1831).

25 James Clark Ross had served in the *Isabella* under his uncle in 1818, in the *Hecla* in 1819–20, in the *Fury* in 1821–23, again in the *Fury* in 1824–25, and in the *Hecla* in 1827, the last four under Parry's command.

26 *The Polar Record* (Cambridge, Scott Polar Research Institute), July, 1952, pp. 496–507, R. J. Cyriax, "The Position of Victory Point, King William Island".

27 J. Ross, *Narrative of a Second Voyage in Search of a North-West Passage . . . during the years* 1829, 1830, 1831, 1832, 1833 (London, 1835) and *Appendix to the Narrative of a Second Voyage in Search of a North-West Passage . . .* (London, 1835).

28 G. Back, *Narrative of the Arctic Land Expedition to the Mouth of the Great Fish River, and Along the Shores of the Arctic Ocean, in the Years* 1833, 1834, *and* 1835 (London, 1836); R. King, *Narrative of a journey to the Shores of the Arctic Ocean, in* 1833, 1834 *and* 1835, *under the Command of Capt. Back, R.N.* (London, 1836).

29 T. Simpson, *Narrative of the Discoveries on the North Coast of America . . . during the years* 1836–39 (London, 1843); A. Simpson, *The Life and Travels of Thomas Simpson the Arctic Discoverer* (London, 1845).

30 Simpson, *Narrative,* pp. xiii–xviii; A. Simpson, *Life and Travels of Thomas Simpson,* pp. 340–44.

31 J. Rae, *Narrative of an Expedition to the Shores of the Arctic Sea in* 1846 *and* 1847 (London, 1850), pp. 1–2, 14–17.

32 Parry, *Journal of a Second Voyage . . .* 1821–22–23, pp. 88, 95, 197–99, maps opposite pp. 198, 252; and general chart at the end.

33 Ross, *Narrative of a Second Voyage . . .* 1829, 1830, 1831, 1832, 1833, pp. 254, 255, 259, 260 and map opposite p. 258.

34 Ibid., map at the end.

35 Parliamentary Paper, 1834, Vol. XVIII, "Report from Select Committee on the Expedition to the Arctic Seas commanded by Captain John Ross, R.N.", Paper 250, pp. 17, 27. Further references to Parliamentary Papers will be given as P.P.

36 Bellot Strait, which separates North Somerset from Boothia, had not been discovered; but James Ross suspected its existence. F.L. M'Clintock, *The Voyage of the Fox in the Arctic Seas. A Narrative of the Discovery of the Fate of Sir John Franklin and His Companions* (5th edition, London, 1881), p. 153n.

[37] Simpson, *Narrative,* pp. 376–7, and map; A. Simpson, *Life and Travels of Thomas Simpson,* pp. 321–2; J. Barrow, *Voyages of Discovery and Research within the Arctic Regions, from . . .* 1818 *to the present time . . .* (London, 1846), map opposite p. 529.

[38] Rae ultimately found, though not till 1854, that Dease and Simpson's "Committee Islands" were rocky elevations on the north side of Murchison River, and Rae then named them "Committee Mounds". He gave the name "Sir John Ross's Hills" to some hills on the shore of Shepherd Bay, presumably because he believed that they were the so-called "Cape Sir John Ross", seen in the distance by Dease and Simpson (P.P., 1855, Vol. XXXV, "Further papers relative to the recent Arctic Expeditions . . .", Paper [1898], map opposite p. 830).

[39] See pp. 377–80.

[40] Extract of a letter from James Clark Ross. It is printed on the map accompanying Rae's *Narrative.*

[41] See, for instance, J. Brown, *The North-West Passage, and the Plans for the Search for Sir John Franklin* (London, 1858) p. 360n.

[42] Called Cape Parry on modern charts.

[43] See p. 143.

[44] See p. 89.

[45] These, and some other details, have been taken from Rae's *Narrative* and not from his letters.

[46] See p. 470, n. 89.

[47] J.E. Nourse, *Narrative of the Second Arctic Expedition made by Charles F. Hall* (U.S.A. *Senate Documents,* 45th Congress, 3rd Session, Vol. 3, Washington, 1879), p. 597. See also pp. 339–40, 350–1.

[48] Probably a mistake for Koo-loo-a.

[49] Nourse, *Second Arctic Expedition of C.F. Hall,* pp. 604–5.

[50] "Parry Bay" is called Franklin Bay on modern maps, but is used here to prevent confusion, as it was employed both by Rae and by Hall.

[51] Nourse, *Second Arctic Expedition of C.F. Hall,* pp. xxii, 331–4, 339–41, 344–8, 350, 351, 415, 596, 597, 604, 605.

[52] Op. cit.

[53] Published July 4, 1880.

[54] *Journal of the American Geographical Society,* (New York, 1880), XII, 284–8.

[55] Nourse, *Second Arctic Expedition of C. F. Hall,* p. 345.

[56] For a more detailed account of Hall's researches in connection with possible survivors of the Franklin expedition on Melville Peninsula, see *Polar Record,* July, 1944, pp. 170–77, R. J. Cyriax, "Captain Hall and the so-called survivors of the Franklin expedition". R. J. Cyriax concluded that there were no adequate grounds for connecting the cairn and tent-places with the Franklin expedition, but he did not become aware until some years after the article had been published that Rae had definitely stated in the *Journal of the American Geographical Society,* XII, 284–8, that he had built a cairn some miles to the east of Cape Crozier.

[57] For a more detailed account of the Franklin expedition see R. J. Cyriax, *Sir John Franklin's Last Arctic Expedition . . . A chapter in the history of the Royal Navy* (London, 1939).

[58] *The Geographical Journal* (London, The Royal Geographical Society, 1945), CVI, 169–97, R. J. Cyriax and J. M. Wordie, "Centenary of the Sailing of Sir John Franklin with the *Erebus* and *Terror*".

[59] P.P., 1847–48, Vol. XLI, "Copies of instructions to Captain Sir John Franklin . . .", Paper 264, pp. 3–7.

[60] Ibid., p. 36.

[61] Five men were invalided home on the voyage to Greenland.

62 When Rae on April 18, 1847, reached Lord Mayor's Bay on the east side of Boothia, he was only about one hundred and fifty geographical miles, measured in a straight line, from the ice-locked *Erebus* and *Terror,* on the west side of Boothia.

63 M'Clintock, *Voyage of the Fox,* 5th edition, p. 246.

64 There are several North-west Passages. At one time priority of discovery was believed to belong to Sir Robert M'Clure on his reaching the north end of Prince of Wales Strait on October 26, 1850. M'Clintock's discoveries in 1859 showed that the honour of priority of discovery of a North-west Passage belongs to the Franklin expedition which had found a Passage, at least two, and probably three, years before M'Clure's journey in 1850.

65 P.P., 1847–48, Vol. XLI, Paper 264, pp. 21, 22.

66 Richardson himself (in 1826) had already explored this coast when serving in Franklin's second overland expedition.

67 P.P., 1847–48, Vol. XLI, Paper 264, p. 33.

68 Ibid., pp. 24–26.

69 Ibid., pp. 28, 36, 37.

70 Ibid., pp. 56, 57, 58, 59–70, 71, 72, 73, 75, 76, 80, 81; J. Richardson, *Arctic Searching Expedition* (London, 1851), I, 36–46.

71 P.P., 1847–48, Vol. XLI, Paper 264, pp. 40, 73, 75; Richardson, *Arctic Searching Expedition,* I, 45–7.

72 P.P., 1847–48, Vol. XLI, Paper 264, pp. 77, 78, 82; Richardson, *Arctic Searching Expedition,* I, 48, 49.

73 P.P., 1847–48, Vol. XLI, Paper 264, pp. 26, 27, 29, 30, 33, 34. See also *Polar Record,* July, 1942, pp. 528–40, R. J. Cyriax, "Sir James Clark Ross and the Franklin Expedition".

74 Emma Harbour appears to be the present day Port Providence, or Providence Bay.

75 For full particulars of the movements of the *Herald* and *Plover* in 1848 and 1849, see P.P., 1847–48, Vol. XLI, Paper 264, pp. 7–9, 16–18; P.P., 1849, Vol. XXXII, "Extracts of any proceedings or correspondence of the Admiralty, in reference to the Arctic Expeditions", Paper 188, pp. 11–21; P.P., 1850, Vol. XXXV; "Copies of any reports or statements from the Officers employed in the Arctic expeditions . . .", Paper 107, pp. 9–44; B. Seemann, *Narrative of the Voyage of H.M.S. Herald during the years* 1845–51, *under the command of Captain Henry Kellett* . . . (London, 1853), II, Chapters 1, 5–8.

76 P.P., 1847–48, Vol. XLI, "A copy of the orders from the Lords Commissioners of the Admiralty under which Captain Sir James Clark Ross, R.N., has proceeded on an expedition in search of Sir John Franklin, R.N.", Paper 386.

77 P.P., 1847–48, Vol. XLI, Paper 264, p. 30 and footnote.

78 Ibid., p. 38.

79 Richardson, *Arctic Searching Expedition . . . ,* I, 26–31. The version given above is identical, except for a few unimportant verbal changes, with that contained in P.P., 1847–48, Vol. XLI, Paper 264, pp. 19–21.

80 Richardson, *Arctic Searching Expedition,* I, 49 et seq.

81 P.P., 1850, Vol. XXXV, Paper 107, p. 3.

82 *Arctic Searching Expedition.*

83 P.P., 1849, Vol. XXXII, Paper 188, pp. 8–10; P.P., 1849, Vol. XXXII, "Copy of a report from Sir John Richardson dated Fort Confidence, Great Bear Lake, 16th September 1848 . . .", Paper 497; and P.P., 1850, Vol. XXXV, Paper 107, pp. 1–7.

84 See p. 173.

85 Rae (born September 30, 1813) was now 35 years of age and 26 years younger than Richardson (born November 5, 1787), who was now 61.

86 Richardson, in a letter to the Admiralty, explained in detail how this saving was effected, P.P., 1850, Vol. XXXV, Paper 107, pp. 5–7.

87 Richardson, *Arctic Searching Expedition,* II, 114.

88 Ibid., 134–6.

89 P.P., 1850, Vol. XXXV, Paper 107, pp. 7–8; Richardson, *Arctic Searching Expedition,* II, 115–18. The version given in the text is taken from Richardson's book. Except for a few quite unimportant verbal changes, and the addition of a footnote, it is identical with the version published in the Parliamentary Paper.

90 Rae found in 1851 that no such strait exists. See p. 60.

91 Richardson evidently refers to Simpson, *Narrative,* pp. 385–6.

92 The "Winter Harbour" referred to by Richardson is on the south coast of Melville Island.

93 P.P., 1847–48, Vol. XLI, Paper 264, p. 21.

94 P.P., 1851, Vol. XXXIII, "Copy or extracts from any correspondence or proceedings of the Board of Admiralty, in relation to the Arctic expeditions . . .", Paper 97, pp. 44–50; also in Richardson, *Arctic Searching Expedition,* II, 118–31.

95 See p. 189.

96 See p. 199.

97 P.P., 1852, Vol. L, "Arctic Expeditions. Report of the Committee . . .", Paper [1435], pp. 127–30; P.P., 1852, Vol. L, "Further correspondence and proceedings connected with the Arctic expedition", Paper [1449], pp. 23–33, 148–79; W. H. Hooper, *Ten Months among the Tents of the Tuski* (London, 1853), p. 212 et seq.; Smith, *Arctic Expeditions,* pp. 435–59 (details from Pullen's private journal).

98 P.P., 1850, Vol. XXV, Paper 107, p. 8; Richardson, *Arctic Searching Expedition,* II, 132–3. The version given above is Richardson's. The version published in the Parliamentary Paper omits the postscript, but in other respects, except for a few verbal changes, is the same as Richardson's.

99 Several authors have stated that he sailed on June 12. The correct date is May 12.

100 P.P., 1849, Vol. XXXII, Paper 188, pp. 6–7.

101 Richardson, *Arctic Searching Expedition,* II, 133–4.

102 P.P., 1850, Vol. XXXV, Paper 107, pp. 58–64; *The Nautical Magazine* (London, 1850), J. D. Gilpin, "Arctic Expedition of 1848–9. Outline of the Voyage of H.M.S. Enterprize and Investigator to Barrow Strait in search of Sir John Franklin", pp. 8–19, 82–90, 160–70, 230.

103 C. R. Markham, *Life of Admiral Sir Leopold M'Clintock, K.C.B . . . ,* (London, 1909), pp. 66–7.

104 P.P., 1850, Vol. XXXV, Paper 107, pp. 82–5.

105 Ibid., pp. 74–82, 103.

106 Ibid., p. 45.

107 Ibid., pp. 46, 52–4. It also appeared in *The Times* for February 20, 1850.

108 P.P., 1850, Vol. XXXV, Paper 107, pp. 9–44. The despatches were published in *The Times* as soon as they arrived (January 24 and 25, 1850).

109 P.P., 1850, Vol. XXXV, Paper 107, pp. 48–50.

110 Ibid., pp. 47–8.

111 Ibid., pp. 47, 51, 55–7.

112 P.P., 1852, Vol. L, Paper [1449], p. 15. For the orders given to Austin and Penny, see P.P., 1852, Vol. L, Paper [1435], pp. 149–52.

113 See p. 48.

114 Hooper, *Tents of the Tuski,* pp. 326, 337–8; Smith, *Arctic Expeditions,* pp. 460, 463.

115 P.P., 1852, Vol. L, Paper [1449], pp. 34–63; P.P., 1852, Vol. L, Paper [1435], pp. 130–1.

116 See pp. 237–45, and P.P., 1852, Vol. L, Paper [1449], pp. 15–18.

[117] See p. 45, and Simpson, *Narrative,* pp. 385–6; P.P., 1850, Vol. XXXV, Paper 107, pp. 6, 7.

[118] R. Collinson, *Journal of H.M.S. Enterprise on the expedition in search of Sir John Franklin's ships by Behring Strait* 1850–55 (London, 1889), pp. 230, 231.

[119] S. Osborn (ed.), *The Discovery of the North-west Passage by H.M.S. "Investigator". . . from the Logs and Journals of Capt. Robert Le M. M'Clure* (London, 1856), p. 185; A. Armstrong, *A Personal Narrative of the Discovery of the North-West Passage . . .* (London, 1857), p. 334.

[120] See p. 256. See also P.P., 1852, Vol. L, Paper [1449], pp. 18–23; *Journal of the Royal Geographical Society of London,* XXII, 73–82.

[121] See p. 273. See also P.P., 1852, Vol. L, Paper 248, pp. 2–3.

[122] Albert Edward Bay.

[123] Halkett Island.

[124] Collinson, *Journal of H.M.S. Enterprise . . . ,* pp. 267–8; P.P., 1855, Vol. XXXV, "Further papers relative to the recent Arctic expeditions . . .' Paper [1898], pp. 947, 951.

[125] P.P., 1852, Vol. L, "Copy of the report of Dr. Rae . . .", Paper 248, map opposite p. 10.

[126] Roald Amundsen, *"The North-West Passage"; being the record of a voyage of exploration of the ship "Gjoa"* 1903–1907 . . . (London, 1908), II, 85–6, 360.

[127] See pp. 270–88. The report is headed "Fort Simpson, 27th September, 1851". Whether it was written on that day is, however, very doubtful, for Rae in his letter of March 9, 1852, to Sir George Simpson mentioned that his report of his summer voyage had not yet been written out. P.P., 1852, Vol. I, Paper 248. Also in the *Journal of the Royal Geographical Society,* XXII, 82–96.

[128] For a more complete description of the pieces of wood, see pp. 283–4, 288. See also London, Public Record Office, Admiralty Records, "Arctic Expeditions, 1852" (Rae's sketch and notes).

[129] P.P., 1855, Vol. XXXV, Paper [1898], p. 947, and picture of the piece of wood opposite p. 949; P.P., 1856, Vol. XLI, "Further papers relative to the recent Arctic expeditions in search of Sir John Franklin . . .", Paper [2124], p. 45; R. Collinson, *Journal of H.M.S. Enterprise . . .,* pp. 260, 278.

[130] Collinson had no interpreter with him; the interpreter appointed to the expedition was with his second in command in H.M.S. *Investigator.* The Eskimos drew a chart of the coast to the east of Cambridge Bay; this chart proved to be erroneous, and the story of the ships was therefore discredited. (R. Collinson, *Journal of H.M.S. Enterprise . . .,* pp. 261, 286, 339.)

[131] A private expedition financed by Lady Franklin and public subscriptions. The state of the ice in Prince Regent Inlet prevented Forsyth from carrying out his intention of searching in the direction of James Ross Strait and Boothia. He left England in the *Prince Albert* in June, 1850, and returned home the following October (W. P. Snow, *Voyage of the Prince Albert in search of Sir John Franklin* (London, 1851)).

[132] Published in *The Times,* October 13, 1851.

[133] The original notes and the sketch are preserved among the P.R.O. Admiralty Records, "Arctic Expeditions, 1852". The present whereabouts of the fragments is uncertain.

[134] James Clark Ross had served as a Lieutenant in H.M.S. *Fury,* 1824–25.

[135] M'Clintock, *Voyage of the Fox,* 5th edition, p. 153n.

[136] It was discovered in April, 1852. See p. 70.

[137] P.R.O., Admiralty Records, "Arctic Expeditions, 1852".

[138] *The Athenæum,* London, April 3, 1852.

[139] D.5/31, Eden Colvile to Sir George Simpson, dated Lower Fort Garry, January 28, 1851 [1852] ". . . Dr. Rae arrived here on II inst. having walked from Athabasca, and will proceed across the plains to St. Paul's, as soon as he has got his dog harness &c arranged. He proposes to proceed direct to England to make his report in person, so that it is not probable that you will see him at Lachine—but I shall direct him to write you an account of his proceedings from New York, as I dare say he will be able to give you a more lucid account thereof than I can do . . .".

[140] The correct dates are 1846 and 1847, *not* 1848.

[141] *Journal of the Royal Geographical Society,* XXII, lvii–viii.

[142] P.P., 1852, Vol. L, Paper [1435], pp. iii–vii.

[143] R. M'Cormick, *Voyages of Discovery in the Arctic and Antarctic Seas and Round the World. . .* (London, 1884), II, 326.

[144] P.P., 1852, Vol. L, Paper [1435], pp. 58, 99; P.P., 1852, Vol. L, "Additional papers relative to the Arctic expedition under the orders of Captain Austin and Mr. William Penny", Paper [1436], pp. 27, 102; see also S. Osborn, *Stray Leaves from an Arctic Journal; or, eighteen months in the Polar Regions, in search of Sir J. Franklin's Expedition in the years* 1850–51 (London, 1852), p. 213.

[145] See p. 284.

[146] See p. 295.

[147] P.P., 1852, Vol. LX, "Arctic expeditions. Copies of any correspondence received at the Admiralty from Sir Edward Belcher's Squadron . . .", Paper [82], pp. 25–32, and map opposite p. 32; W. Kennedy, *A Short Narrative of the Second Voyage of the Prince Albert, in search of Sir John Franklin* (London, pp. 131–2 and map; *Memoirs of Lieutenant Joseph René Bellot. . . With his Journal of a Voyage in the Polar Seas in search of Sir John Franklin,* (London, 1855), II, 269–70.

[148] See p. 305.

[149] Published November 27, 1852. See also the map in Kennedy, *Narrative of the Second Voyage of the Prince Albert,* opposite p. 27.

[150] Pp. 295–6, 304–5.

[151] Cape Nicolai is called Cape Nicholas on modern maps.

[152] Ross, *Narrative of a Second Voyage . . .* 1829, 1830, 1831, 1832, 1833, map at end and p. 560; P.P., 1850, Vol. XXXV, Paper 107, pp. 61–2.

[153] M'Clintock, *Voyage of the Fox,* 5th edition, pp. 174, 177, 200–03.

[154] James Clark Ross, in his account of his explorations, named the islands "Catherine Islands", and Cape Porter "Point Scott" (Ross, *Narrative of a Second Voyage. . .* 1829, 1830, 1831, 1832, 1833, p 424), and these names were used on the Admiralty charts for some years (e.g. No. 264, "Arctic America. Sheet II", published April 13, 1848). But John Ross, on the map published in his narrative of the *Victory* expedition (ibid.,) used the names Dundas Islands and Cape Porter; these names were finally adopted by the Admiralty, and are those in use today. In consequence of these changes and differences, the early Admiralty charts as regards names illustrate clearly James Clark Ross's statements about "Point Scott" and the "Catherine Islands", whereas John Ross's map does not.

[155] Ross, *Narrative of a Second Voyage . . .* 1829, 1830, 1831, 1832, 1833, pp. 316, 422–5, and map at the end.

[156] Simpson, *Narrative,* pp. 371–8 and map.

[157] Ibid., inset map on map at the beginning.

[158] Ross, *Narrative of a Second Voyage. . .* 1829, 1830, 1831, 1832, 1833, p. 418.

[159] Simpson, *Narrative,* pp. 379–80, and map.

[160] Part, if not all, of this coast may have been examined by Lieutenant Gore, of H.M.S. *Erebus,* in 1847. The whole of it was traversed by the officers and men of the Franklin expedition when trying to reach the Great Fish River in 1848, but this fact was not known until M'Clintock reached King William Island in 1859.

[161] P. 296, and *The Times,* November 27, 1852.

[162] In 1869 this same Eskimo spent several weeks with the American explorer, Charles Francis Hall. Both Rae and Hall considered In-nook-poo-zhee-jook to be an intelligent man. (J. E. Nourse, *Second Arctic Expedition of C. F. Hall,* pp. 397–421, 608–11.)

[163] P.P., 1856, Vol. XLI, Paper [2124], p. 55.

[164] Communicated by Rae to D. M. Smith, and published by Smith in *Arctic Expeditions,* p. 644.

[165] Letter from Rae, *The Times,* November 7, 1854.

[166] Smith, *Arctic Expeditions,* pp. 651–2; P.P., 1856, Vol. XLI, Paper [2124], p. 55.

[167] See pp. 321–33.

[168] See pp. 333–51, P.P., 1855, Vol. XXXV, Paper [1898], pp. 835–58; Charles Dickens (ed.), *Household Words,* (London, February 3, 1855), pp. 12–20; *Journal of the Royal Geographical Society,* XXV, 246–56.

[169] Two of M'Clure's officers had returned to England in H.M.S. *Phoenix* in 1853; the others returned in 1854.

[170] The *Rattlesnake* sailed from Port Clarence, Bering Strait, on August 23, 1854, the *Enterprise* and *Plover on* September 16, 1854.

[171] The original report, written on July 29, 1854, and signed by Rae, is preserved among the P.R.O., Admiralty Records, Arctic Expeditions, 1853–55.

[172] See p. 353.

[173] P.P., 1855, Vol. XXXV, Paper [1898], pp. 833–4.

[174] It seems to have appeared very soon afterwards in innumerable newspapers. Copies of the crests were published in *The Illustrated London News,* October 28, 1854 (Supplement), and the report itself was included in P.P., 1855, Vol. XXXV, Paper [1898], pp. 831–2.

[175] A.12/7, fo. 259. See p. 488, n. 410.

[176] Rae's letter of October 20, 1854, to *The Times.* It was published on October 23.

[177] See p. 82.

[178] P.P., 1855, Vol. XXXV, Paper [1898], p. 831.

[179] See, for instance, P.P., 1856, Vol. XLI, Paper [2124], pp. 32, 83, 84; Bedford Pim, *An Earnest Appeal to the British Public on behalf of the missing Arctic Expedition* (London, 1857), p. 14.

[180] Several of these officers were promoted after they had sailed; the ranks given were those held at the time of departure from England.

[181] M'Clintock, *Voyage of the Fox,* 5th edition, p. 253.

[182] Letter from Rae, *The Times,* November 7, 1854.

[183] The last letter seems to be "E". The markings preceding it may be the letter "H" or possibly two letters such as "I.T". Only one member of the Franklin expedition had a surname beginning with the letter "E"—Thomas Evans, Boy in the *Terror.*

[184] One of the writers (R. J. Cyriax) has personally examined all these relics and the list is in some respects more detailed than previous ones.

[185] See p. 351. For the complete list see P.P., 1856, Vol. XLI, Paper [2124], pp. 832–3.

[186] P.P., 1855, Vol. XXXV, Paper [1898], p. 833.

[187] Ibid., p. 845.

[188] Smith, *Arctic Expeditions,* p. 645 (Rae's own statement).

[189] He was told also that one ship had sunk and that nothing had been obtained from her. (M'Clintock, *Voyage of the Fox,* 5th edition, pp. 206, 219, 220, 227).

[190] Nourse, *Second Arctic Expedition of C. F. Hall,* pp. 400, 404, 405, 418.

[191] W. H. Gilder, *Schwatka's Search, sledging in the Arctic in quest of the Franklin Records . . .* (London, 1882), pp. 78, 79, 85, 130. H. W. Klutschak, *Als Eskimo unter den Eskimos. Eine Schilderung der Erlebnisse de Schwatka'schen, Franklin-Aufsuchungs-Expedition in den Jahren* 1878–80 (Vienna, Pest, Leipzig, 1881), pp. 70–1, 144.

[192] *The Illustrated London News,* October 28, 1854.

[193] *The Times,* October 27, 1854. For a previous suggestion by Rae, in June, 1852, regarding an expedition to get in touch with Collinson and M'Clure, see P.P., 1852, Vol. LX, Paper 82, pp. 72–4.

[194] P.P., 1855, Vol. XXXV, Paper [1898], pp. 846–7.

[195] *The Times,* November 8, 1854.

[196] P.P., 1855, Vol. XXXV, Paper [1898], p. 849.

[197] Ibid., p. 847 et seq.

[198] P.P., 1856, Vol. XLI, Paper [2124], p. 61.

[199] P.P., 1855, Vol. XXXV, Paper [1898], p. 849.

[200] P.P., 1856, Vol. XLI, Paper [2124], p. 26.

[201] Letter from Rae, *The Times,* October 31, 1854.

[202] Notice was given by the Admiralty on January 20, 1854, (*The London Gazette,* No. 21513, of that date) that Franklin's officers and men would be deemed to have lost their lives in Her Majesty's Service unless news of their safety arrived before the end of March, 1854.

[203] See the leading articles in *The Times,* October 24, 1854; *The Morning Chronicle,* October 25, 1854; *The Morning Herald,* October 25, 1854.

[204] The report of July 29, 1854, which was given by him to the Admiralty and was published in *The Times* on October 23, 1854, contained virtually the same information about the Franklin expedition as his later report dated September 1 to the Hudson's Bay Company, but omitted a few details.

[205] Letter from Rae, *The Times,* November 3, 1854.

[206] Gilder, *Scwatka's Search,* p. ix (letter from Rae to Gilder).

[207] P.P., 1855, Vol. XXXV, Paper [1898], p. 831.

[208] Correspondence in *The Times,* October 30 and 31, November 1, 3 and 7, 1854; *Household Words,* December 2, 9, 23, and 30, 1854.

[209] *The London Gazette,* No. 21075, March 8, 1850.

[210] Rae's own statement, P.P., 1856, Vol. XLI, Paper [2124], p. 55.

[211] P.P., 1856, Vol. XLI, Paper [2124], pp. 47–8.

[212] See p. 354.

[213] P.P., 1856, Vol. XLI, Paper [2124], p. 48.

[214] Ibid., pp. 51–2.

[215] See p. 361.

[216] Original letter in Royal Geographical Society Library.

[217] He arrived in H.M.S. *Enterprise in* May, 1855.

[218] P.P., 1856, Vol. XLI, Paper [2124], p. 54.

[219] Ibid., pp. 19–29; *Journal of the Royal Geographical Society,* XXVI, 18–25; ibid., Vol. XXVII, pp. 321–38; *Transactions of The Canadian Institute* (Toronto, 1910), VIII, 393–402, J.B. Tyrrell, "A Story of a Franklin Search Expedition".

[220] *The London Gazette,* No. 21841, January 22, 1856.

[221] P.P., 1856, Vol. XLI, Paper [2124], pp. 58–63. For other objections to Rae's being given a reward see Anonymous, *Arctic Rewards and their claimants* (London, 1856) *Φιλοι Συμβουλευομενοι, The Great Arctic Mystery* (London, 1856).

[222] F. L. M'Clintock, *The Voyage of the Fox in the Arctic Seas. A Narrative of the Discovery of the Fate of Sir John Franklin and His Companions,* 1st edition, (London, 1859), PP. 361–5. The list of petitioners is omitted from all the editions after the second (1860).

[223] M'Clintock, *Voyage of the Fox,* 1st edition. Many later editions.

[224] P.P., 1856, Vol. XLI, Paper [2124], pp. 65–79, 82–87.

[225] Ibid., pp. 57–8, 88; *The London Gazette,* No. 21895, June 24, 1856.

[226] P.P., 1856, Vol. XLI, Paper [2124], pp. 57, 89–91. The spellings of the names listed above are those most frequently found in the Hudson's Bay Company's records.

[227] M'Clintock, *Voyage of the Fox,* 5th edition, p. [74].

[228] Gilder, *Schwatka's Search,* pp. xi, 238–9.

[229] D. T. Hanbury, *Sport and Travel in the Northland of Canada* (London, 1904).

[230] The figures in square brackets are amendments made in ink, presumably by Rae, in the original.

[231] Corrected in ink in the original to 1853–4.

[232] P.P., 1855, Vol. XXXV, Paper [1898], pp. 689–706.

[233] *Proceedings of the Royal Geographical Society,* XIX, 464–79.

[234] Markham, *Life of Admiral Sir Leopold M'Clintock,* p. 235.

[235] *Proceedings of the Royal Society of London* (London, 1897), LX, v–vii.

[236] See p. 139.

[237] See pp. 257, 267–8.

[238] *Dictionary of National Biography,* and *Report from the Select Committee on the Hudson's Bay Company . . .* (London, 1857).

[239] *Proceedings of the Royal Geographical Society,* August, 1889; F. Nansen, *The First Crossing of Greenland. . . Translated from the Norwegian by H. M. Gepp* (London, 1890), I, 471; and T. H. Zeilau, *Fox-Expeditionen i Aaret* 1860 *over Fæøerne, Island og Grønland, med Oplysninger om Muligheden af et Nordatlantisk Telegraf-Anlaeg* (Copenhagen, 1861), pp. 155–71.

[240] *Proceedings of the Royal Society,* LX, v–vii.

[241] *Canadian Gazette* (London), July 27, August 3, 1893.

[242] *Catalogue of Scientific Papers.* Compiled and published by the Royal Society of London (London, 1871), V, 74; (London, 1896), XI, 93; (Cambridge, 1923), XVIII, 24.

[243] The authorship of this "Notice", dated Hamilton, Upper Canada, April 17, 1837, is attributed to Rae by the *Dict. Nat. Biog.,* but it is unlikely that it was his as he was at Moose Factory during outfit 1836–37. The author was probably John Rae (1796–1872), "economist, man of letters and science", who was headmaster of the Gore District Grammar School, Hamilton, Upper Canada, in 1837. He was interested in nautical and aeronautical devices. (*Dictionary of American Biography*).

[244] Rae's Arctic Medal has five "clasps", not apparently official, with the dates 1846–47, 1848, 1849, 1850–51, 1853–54, added no doubt by Rae himself.

[245] *Orkney Herald,* August 2, 9, September 13, 1893.

[246] G. F. Seaver, *Edward Wilson of the Antarctic, Naturalist and Friend* (London, 1933), pp. 188–9.

RAE'S ARCTIC CORRESPONDENCE

[1] [Hudson's Bay Company Archives], E.15/3. Subsequent classification numbers refer to Hudson's Bay Company Archives. Unless otherwise stated the letters were written in his own hand and signed by John Rae.

[2] Neither the original nor a copy of this letter has been found in the Company's archives, and only the bearer, François Misère, has been identified. He was "a tripper from the Sault Ste. Maries" (B.135/a/149, August 20, 1844). For Simpson's letters to Rae dated May 11 and July 17, 1844, see Appendix A, pp. 365–7.

[3] The Company's ship *Prince Albert* (Captain Robert Royal) did not arrive at Moose Factory until August 28 owing to the ice conditions prevailing from Cape Digges to James Bay.

[4] See p. 107, and *The Beaver* (Hudson's Bay Company, Winnipeg), September, 1941, H.M.S. Cotter, "A Fur Trade Glossary", "*Rogan*—a birch-bark container".

[5] Chief Factor Robert Seaborn Miles, then in charge at Moose Factory. For a biography see H[udson's] B[ay Company] S[eries], Vol. I, p. 459.

6 John Clouston (a), an Orkneyman, aged forty-five, who had served the Company for thirty years. He was listed in the Company's books as a guide and interpreter.

7 For a biography see Appendix B, p. 419.

8 Presumably Magnus Merryman, an Orkneyman, who had served for six years as a labourer in the Moose District.

9 Owing to the extreme dryness of the atmosphere during the winter, articles of English manufacture made of ivory, kept in warm rooms, became bent and broken. See Sir John Richardson, *Arctic Searching Expedition* . . . (London, 1851), II, 101.

10 Simpson had arranged to spend the winter of 1844–45 in London, where he arrived on November 1. The Company's London premises at this time were on the south side of Fenchurch Street, at Nos. 3 and 4. An illustration (circa 1840) is in C. Knight, *London* (London, 1851), VI, 49.

11 Neither the original nor the copy of this letter has been traced in the Company's archives. For Simpson's letter to Rae of November 28, 1844, see Appendix A, pp. 367–9.

12 Mrs. Flett has not been identified. Mrs. Vincent was described in George Gladman's will dated February 15, 1841, as "my Wife's Mother Jane Renton (or Vincent)" (A.36/7). In Thomas Vincent's will dated January 13, 1826, Jane Renton was named as the mother of his children John, Harriet, Elizabeth, James, Jane and Thomas, and in a later will dated May 24, 1832, she was described as Jane Renton of Moose Factory, and their daughter Harriet was referred to as the wife of George Gladman (A. 36/14). Both Jane Renton (or Vincent) and Harriet Gladman were living at Moose Factory in 1833 (ibid.), but by 1844 Harriet Gladman was presumably with her husband at Oxford House. Several references to Harriet Gladman will be found in M. A. MacLeod, *The Letters of Letitia Hargrave* (Toronto, The Champlain Society, 1947). Chief Trader George Gladman's elder brother Joseph was, in 1844, clerk in charge at Rupert River and the Mrs. Gladman referred to in the text may have been his wife. The Moose Factory Abstracts of Servants' Accounts for outfits 1844–45 and 1845–46 list a Mary Gladman under the heading of "Freemen & Petty Accounts" (B.135/g/28 and 29).

13 E.15/3.

14 George Taylor, surveyor to the Red River Settlement. For a biography see H[udson's] B[ay Company] S[eries], Vol. III, p. 459.

15 Chief Factor Alexander Christie, Governor of Assiniboia. For a biographical note see MacLeod, *Letters of Letitia Hargrave,* p. 38*n*.

16 Chief Factor Donald Ross. For a biography see *H.B.S.,* III, 453.

17 See Appendix A, pp. 367–9.

18 Neither the original nor copy of this letter has been found in the Company's archives.

19 Chief Factor James Hargrave, then in charge at York Factory. For details of his career and family see MacLeod, *Letters of Letitia Hargrave,* passim.

20 For a description of York Factory and life there in 1841 and 1843 see R.M. Ballantyne, *Hudson Bay; or, Everyday Life in the Wilds of North America* (4th edition), (London), pp. 47–49, 167–200. See also MacLeod, *Letters of Letitia Hargrave,* pp. xxxviii et seq.

21 It is not easy to understand why Rae had little doubt that this statement was true. That no such strait existed had been shown by Parry in 1821 (W. E. Parry, *Journal of a Second Voyage for the Discovery of a North West Passage . . . performed in the Years* 1821–22–23, *in His Majesty's Ships Fury and Hecla* (London, 1824), pp. 28, 29, 50–55, and Chart No. 3, at end).

22 I.e., Castor and Pollux River. See Introduction, pp. 16–7. For biographies of Chief Factor Peter Warren Dease and Thomas Simpson see *H.B.S.,* III, 434–6. 455–6.

23 See n. 21 above.

24 This man has not been identified.

25 Erland Erlandson, then in charge of the Pic post. For a biography see *H.B.S.,* III, 437–8.

26 James McKay, a Highlander, was described by Captain Back as "a powerful fellow, and one of the best steersmen in the country". He was one of Back's crew in the expedition of 1833–35 and was

also employed as a steersman by Dease and Simpson from 1836–39. George Sinclair, a native of Rupert's Land, was also employed as a steersman by Back and Dease and Simpson. (G. Back, *Narrative of the Arctic Land Expedition to the Mouth of the Great Fish River* . . . 1833, 1834, *and* 1835 (London, 1836), pp. 53–6, and T. Simpson, *Narrative of the Discoveries on the North Coast of America* . . . 1836–39 (London, 1843), pp. 97, 354).

27 See Appendix B, p. 421.

28 Presumably Michel Lambert, a labourer, aged twenty-four, who was stationed in the Lake Superior district (B.135/g/28, fo. 9). For a biography of Richard Turner see Appendix B, p. 450.

29 E.15/3. This letter was sent with the preceding one.

30 These stores had been deposited by Parry after the wreck of H.M.S. *Fury* in 1825. Some had been used by Sir John Ross, who wintered at Fury Beach (1832–33) after abandoning the *Victory,* but large quantities were left intact (W. E. Parry, *Journal of a Third Voyage for the Discovery of a North West Passage . . . performed in the Years* 1824–25, *in His Majesty's Ships Hecla and Fury* (London, 1826), p. 119 et seq. See also Sir A. H. Markham, *A Whaling Cruise to Baffin's Bay* . . . (London, 1874), pp. 243–52; Markham, *Life of Sir John Franklin* . . . (London, 1891), p. 238, and footnote on same page).

31 Chief Factor Duncan Finlayson. For a biography see *H.B.S.,* I, 437–8.

32 E.15/3.

33 Lieutenant, later General, Sir John Henry Lefroy (1817–90). In 1842 he was attached to the Observatory at Toronto and his 1843–44 journey undertaken for magnetic research through the north-west, partly by canoe and partly on snow-shoes, established his reputation as a geographer. See n. 41 below, and *Dictionary of National Biography.*

34 Chief Trader John Ballenden in charge of the Sault Ste. Marie and the Lake Huron districts. For a biography see *H.B.S.,* III, 426–7.

35 The screw or rotatory log of Edward Massey, invented in 1802, came into general use in 1836 and continued until 1861 (*Encyclopaedia Britannica*).

36 See Appendix A, p. 376, letter dated December 13, 1845. No letter dated December 12, 1845, has been traced in the Company's archives.

37 E.15/3.

38 E.15/3.

39 See Appendix A, p. 375.

40 Chief Trader William Sinclair. For a biography see *H.B.S.,* III, 456–8.

41 Rae was no doubt referring to the observations made by Lieut. Lefroy during his Magnetic Survey of 1843–44 (see n. 33 above). The results were published in Edward Sabine's "Contributions to Terrestrial Magnetism, No. VII", in *Philosophical Transactions,* 1846, Part III. Lefroy also published his observations in his *Diary of a Magnetic Survey of a Portion of the Dominion of Canada . . . executed in the years* 1842–1844 (London, 1883).

42 E.15/3.

43 This is a reference to the housing of the family of Chief Factor R.S. Miles and the family of the Rev. George Barnley, Wesleyan Missionary, under one roof. Rae was not mistaken. "Bourgeois", referring to a partner or senior officer, was a term surviving from the days of the North West Company.

44 E.15/3.

45 Wemyss McKenzie Simpson, brother of Lady Frances Simpson. For a biographical note see MacLeod, *Letters of Letitta Hargrave,* p. 205.

46 E.15/3.

47 John Rae, *Narrative of an Expedition to the Shores of the Arctic Sea in* 1846 *and* 1847 (London, 1850), pp. 116, 176, ". . . John Halkett, Esq., one of the Directors of the Hudson's Bay Company, whose son (Lieut. P. A. Halkett, R.N.,) is the ingenious inventor of the portable air-boat, which ought to be the travelling companion of every explorer . . . During the whole of our spring [1847]

fishing Halkett's air-boat was used for setting and examining the nets, and was preferred by the fishermen to the large canvas canoe, as it was much lighter, and passed over and round the nets with more facility. Notwithstanding its continued use on a rocky shore, it never required the slightest repair. It is altogether a most useful little vessel, and, as I have said before, ought to form part of the equipment of all surveying parties, whether by land or sea."

48 See Appendix A, p. 377, for Simpson's letter of instructions of this date. A letter also dated June 15, 1846, acknowledging the above letter of Rae's and the three following ones, has not been traced in the Company's archives.

49 E.15/3.

50 E.15/3.

51 For biographies of these men, except William Clouston, see Appendix B. William Clouston (b), an Orkneyman, was stationed in the Red River District during outfit 1845–46, but no record of his ever being attached to Rae's expedition, other than the inclusion of his name in the list on pp. 121–2, has been traced. See the list on p. 127 where Peter Matheson's name is substituted for that of William Clouston.

52 For a biography see Appendix B, p. 440.

53 E.15/3.

54 MacLeod, *Letters of Letitia Hargrave,* p. 149, Letitia Hargrave to Dugald Mactavish, York Factory, September 9, 1843, "Hargrave wd. explain why there are only 25 tongues—I did not say any thing about it as I think & so I daresay every one else does, that it is very unfair that we should not get a few. The Govr. wrote Hargrave to check the purchase of tongues on private account or there would be a minute of Council forbidding their use in the country or even one being sent out of it from or to an individual—always I suppose excepting the Directors." Ibid., pp. 199–200, same to same, York Factory, September 1, 1845, "Hargrave has already written & I suppose wd. tell you that the private sale of buffalo tongues has been put a complete stop to. I think he will be able to get some next year from the Free Settlers at Red River."

55 Margaret Glen Rae, widow of John Rae, senior, who had been the Company's agent in Stromness. See Introduction, p. 6, and MacLeod, *Letters of Letitia Hargrave,* xxxiii and 51.

56 William Mactavish, then a clerk at York Factory, and in later life Governor of Rupert's Land. He was a brother of Letitia, wife of Chief Factor James Hargrave in charge at York Factory, and is mentioned frequently in MacLeod, *Letters of Letitia Hargrave.*

57 E.15/3.

58 Richard Rae, who had previously been employed by the Company. He was described by Governor Simpson in 1832 as "An Orkneyman about 20 years of Age—2 Years in the Service. A very fine mild tempered promising young man of good appearance and address . . .". His service was spent in the King's Posts area and he retired in 1837. See MacLeod, *Letters of Letitia Hargrave,* p. 51, and G. P. de T. Glazebrook (ed.), *The Hargrave Correspondence* 1021–43 (The Champlain Society, 1938), pp. 78–9.

59 See Appendix A, p. 380.

60 Cf. list on pp. 121–2. Peter Matheson's name is substituted for that of William Clouston. For a biography of Matheson see Appendix B, p. 435–6.

61 Two Eskimos, Ouligbuck and his son William, had also been engaged and were to join the expedition at Churchill. See Rae, *Narrative,* p. 19.

62 E.15/3.

63 See Appendix A, p. 376.

64 See p. 468, n. 35.

65 E.15/3.

66 See Appendix A, p. 377.

67 See p. 286. A "bag" of pemmican contained 90 lbs. The actual bag was made of undressed hide with the hairy side outwards. (Richardson, *Arctic Searching Expedition,* I, 39–40).

[68] E.15/3.

[69] E.15/3.

[70] E.15/3.

[71] E.15/3. A fuller report on the expedition than the one contained in the letter of August 10 will be found in Rae's letter of September 21, 1847, to the Governor and Committee (see pp. 144–61). An even more detailed account is in Rae's *Narrative.*

[72] After the wife of Sir John Henry Pelly, Governor of the Hudson's Bay Company.

[73] The ruins of Fort Hope are still to be seen at Repulse Bay. For a photograph see *The Beaver,* September, 1936, Ross Mitchell, "Physician, Fur Trader and Explorer", p. 20. Major L. T. Burwash found in 1926 that the stone foundations of Rae's winter quarters were still intact. Rae wintered twice at Repulse Bay—from 1846–47 at Fort Hope, and from 1853–54 at a place about half a mile south of Fort Hope. The stone foundations seen by Burwash must have been those of the first Fort Hope (L. T. Burwash, *Canada's Western Arctic. Report on Investigations in* 1925–26, 1928–29, *and* 1930, (Ottawa, Department of the Interior, 1931), p. 48).

[74] Rae, *Narrative,* p. 98, "The party, consisting, besides myself, of George Flett, John Corrigal, William Adamson, Ouligbuck's son, and Ivitchuk, started early on the morning of the 5th." Rae had met the Eskimo Ivitchuk after he had landed at Repulse Bay (see p. 150).

[75] Rae, *Narrative . . .,* p. 107, ". . . the bay was called after my much respected friend, George Keith, Esq., Chief-Factor." Reference will also be found in the *Narrative* to many other places named by Rae which are not mentioned in this letter or in that dated September 21 (p. 144).

[76] For biographies see H[udson's] B[ay Company] S[eries], Vol. VI, pp. 399–401, and *The British Columbia Historical Quarterly,* XIII, R. Saw, Sir John H. Pelly, Bart. Governor, Hudson's Bay Company, 1822–1852", pp. 23–32.

[77] Rae, *Narrative,* p. 113, names Flett and Corrigal.

[78] Sir John Ross. Cf. Introduction, p. 15, and see Rae, *Narrative,* p. 117, April, 1847, ". . . From the spot on which I now stood, as far as the eye could reach to the north-westward, lay a large extent of ice-covered sea, studded with innumerable islands. Lord Mayor's Bay was before me, and the islands were those named by Sir John Ross the Sons of the Clergy of the Church of Scotland."

[79] Helen Island.

[80] Rae, *Narrative,* pp. 137–8, names ". . . Corrigal (our snow-house builder), Folster, Matheson, and Mineau, with Ouligbuck as deer-hunter and interpreter".

[81] See Introduction, p. 22. According to Rae, *Narrative,* p. 156, May, 1847, the most distant visible point he saw was Cape Ellice (now Cape Parry), which he reckoned to be not more than ten miles distant from Parry's Fury and Hecla Strait.

[82] Mary McKay, daughter of Marguerite Wadin McKay, wife of Dr. John McLoughlin. She married Sinclair in 1823. See MacLeod, *Letters of Letitia Hargrave,* p. 206*n*, and *H.B.S.,* III, 457.

[83] This tracing in ink and pencil is a draft of that part of the map accompanying Rae's *Narrative* which lies between longitude 85° and 91° W. and is marked in red.

[84] E.15/3.

[85] Cf. Introduction, pp. 19 and 21.

[86] Neither the original nor the copy of Simpson's reply of November 25, 1847, has been found in the Company's archives.

[87] E.15/3.

[88] The *Westminster* 513 tons, Old Measurement, (Captain Forbes Michie).

[89] E.15/3. This letter was published in *The Times* for November 1, 1847, "after being slightly altered and somewhat curtailed by Mr. Barclay, the Secretary . . .". The letter bears Barclay's alterations in ink and pencil, but the version printed here is as originally submitted by Rae. A condensed report also appeared in *The Illustrated London News* for November 6, 1847.

90 Rae, *Narrative* . . . , p. 6, "The crews of the boats were divided as follows:-

NORTH POLE.	MAGNET.
John Rae.	George Flett, Orkneyman, Steersman.
John Corrigal, Orkneyman, Steersman.	John Folster, ditto, Middleman.
Richard Turner, half-breed, Middleman.	William Adamson, Zetlander, ditto.
Edward Hutchison, Orkneyman, ditto.	Jacques St. Germain, Canadian, ditto.
Hilard Mineau, Canadian, ditto.	Peter Matheson, Highlander, ditto.
Nibitabo, Cree Indian, ditto and hunter.	

. . . The lading of each of the boats, including the men's luggage, amounted to about seventy pieces; and with this cargo they were quite deep enough in the water and very much lumbered—so much so that, to allow room for pulling, a quantity of the cargo had to be displaced."

91 Ibid., p. 42, ". . . I sent back John Folster and Ouligbuck to take care of the property left behind".

92 Ibid., p. 50, Adamson, Mineau and Nibitabo (Nepitabo).

93 Ibid., p. 59, "Leaving three men and Ouligbuck's son in charge of the boat, I started at 6.30 A.M. on the 9th, in company with Corrigal, N. Germain, and Matheson . . .".

94 Ibid., pp. 135–6, May 1847, "I may now say a few words about our travelling companion Ivitchuk, who had behaved well throughout the journey. We found him always willing and obedient, and generally lively and cheerful except when very tired, which was frequently the case, as he had not been accustomed to travel so many days consecutively. He accommodated himself easily to our manners and customs in every respect, living as we did, though he would swallow a piece of seal's blubber now and then as a delicacy. What surprised me most was, that he was by no means a very great eater, being often satisfied with as little as any of the party. Tea and chocolate were favorite beverages with him, and he had learned to smoke his pipe as regularly as if he had been accustomed to it all his life. He picked up a few words of English, which he made use of whenever he thought they were applicable, and was very anxious to be taught to read and write. As he, like the rest of the party, was much thinner than when he commenced the journey, he had made up his mind to do nothing during the remainder of the spring but eat, drink, and sleep, a determination to which I believe he most strictly adhered. It was with no small pride that he received a gun and some ammunition, as a reward for his services; and a few presents to his wife, one of the best looking of the fair sex of Repulse Bay, made the pair quite happy, although it was said that the lady had not behaved very well to her liege lord during his absence, having taken unto herself another husband named Ou-plik; but probably the good man knew nothing, or cared little, about it."

95 Ibid., p. 89 ". . . Hutchison . . . (who by-the-bye was the softest of the party) . . .".

96 Ibid., p. 98, "The party, consisting, besides myself, of George Flett, John Corrigal, William Adamson, Ouligbuck's son, and Ivitchuk, started early on the morning of the 5th . . . Our stores consisted of three bags of pemmican, seventy reindeer tongues, one half–hundred weight of flour, some tea, chocolate, and sugar, and a little alcohol and oil for fuel."

97 Presumably after Captain Alexander Weynton, who was elected to the Committee of the Hudson's Bay Company "in the room of Richard Wilson Pelly Esq. disqualified" (A. 2/3, fo. 51d.), at the General Court held on January 22, 1845.

98 Andrew Colvile. For a biographical note see *H.B.S.,* I, 435.

99 Sir Francis Beaufort (1774–1857), Rear-Admiral and Hydrographer to the Navy. See *Dict. Nat. Biog.*

100 Rae, *Narrative* . . ., p. 113, Flett and Corrigal.

101 Henry Hulse Berens, the fourth in line of the Berens family to serve on the Committee of the Hudson's Bay Company.

102 John Halkett. For a biography see *H.B.S.,* I, 441.

103 Rae named the isthmus after Sir James Clark Ross, and the land to the northward after Sir John Ross (Rae, *Narrative,* p. 117). That the isthmus reached by Rae had previously been reached by James Clark Ross is rendered certain by James Ross's statement, printed on Rae's chart in his *Narrative.*

104 The "Franklin Inlet" of Rae's chart.

[105] The "Helen Island" of Rae's chart.

[106] For a biography see H[udson's] B[ay Company] S[eries], Vol. X, pp. 252–3.

[107] Aaron Chapman, Esq., M.P., elected to the Committee of the Hudson's Bay Company in 1835.

[108] Rae, *Narrative* . . . , pp. 137–8, ". . . The party was to consist of Corrigal (our snow-house builder), Folster, Matheson, and Mineau, with Ouligbuck as deer-hunter and interpreter . . . Our provisions for the journey were two bags of pemmican, each 90 lbs., 70 reindeer tongues weighing nearly 30 lbs., 36 lbs. flour, and a little tea, chocolate, and sugar. We took also a gallon and a half of alcohol and a small quantity of oil. Leaving George Flett in charge at Fort Hope, we started at 10 P.M. on the 13th of May . . .".

[109] Ibid., p. 141, ". . . the sledge was to be sent back to Repulse Bay . . . and with it Ouligbuck, who from his inability to walk would have been an incumbrance to us . . .".

[110] Afterwards H.M. King Edward VII.

[111] After Lt. Col. Edward Sabine, then Foreign Secretary of the Royal Society. See p. 468, n. 41, and for details of his career see *Dict. Nat. Biog.,* (Sabine, Sir Edward (1788–1883), General Royal Artillery, and President of the Royal Society).

[112] Presumably after Dunbar James, sixth Earl of Selkirk, son of the founder of the Red River Settlement and a member of the Hudson's Bay Company's Committee from 1839–62.

[113] Corrigal accompanied Rae; Matheson stayed behind (Rae, *Narrative,* pp. 152–6).

[114] Rae, *Narrative* . . . , p. 156, "To the most distant visible point . . . I gave the name of Cape Ellice, after Edward Ellice, Esq., M.P., one of the Directors of the Company . . .". Edward Ellice, junior, was elected to the Committee of the Hudson's Bay Company in 1837. He was the only son of Edward Ellice, senior (see p. 234), and his first wife.

[115] After Francis Rawdon Moira Crozier (1796–1848) second-in-command of the Franklin expedition. See *Diet. Nat. Biog.*

[116] Parry Bay, the name given by Rae, was for some reason called "Franklin Bay" on Admiralty Chart 264, with corrections to 1847, printed April 13, 1848. The name "Parry" was apparently transferred to Cape "Ellice" (see n. 114 above). The names "Parry Bay" and "Cape Ellice" appeared on Rae's chart and on several later maps, so that all four names seem to have been in use for some time. The original names given by Rae seem now to have been entirely abandoned.

[117] Rae, *Narrative* . . . , p. 156, ". . . we found that Matheson, the man left behind, had built a snow-house after a fashion of his own, the walls being like those of a stone building, and the roof covered in the same way with slabs of snow placed on the opposite walls in a slanting position, so as to rest on one another in the centre. Seven hours had been spent in building this edifice, which was not a very handsome one; but being sufficiently wide, and, when our legs were doubled up a little, long enough for us all when lying down, we found it pretty comfortable."

[118] W. Swainson and J. Richardson, *Fauna Boreali-Americana . . . Part Second, The Birds,* p. 470, *Anser Hutchinsii* (Richards.), Hutchins's Barnacle Goose, ". . . They are well known in Hudson's Bay by the Cree name of *Apistiskeesh,* and are generally thought by the residents to be merely a small kind of the Canada Goose, as they have the white kidney-shaped patch on the throat, which is deemed peculiar to that species. Their habits, however, are dissimilar . . . the *Apistiskeesh* . . . more nearly resembles the Brent, than the Canada Goose . . .". Ibid., p. 466, *Anser albifrons* (Bechst.), Laughing Goose, ". . . its breeding places . . . are in the woody districts skirting the Mackenzie to the north of the sixty-seventh parallel, and also the islands of the Arctic Sea. It is not common on the coast of Hudson's Bay. The Indians imitate its call by patting the mouth with their hand, while they repeat the syllable *wah.* The resemblance of this note to the laugh of a man has given the trivial name to the species". See also H[udson's] B[ay Company] S[eries], Vol. XIV, p. 191.

[119] E.15/3.

[120] This was at least the fifth vessel named *Prince Rupert* to be owned by the Company. She was barque rigged and was built by Messrs. Green, Wigrams & Green of Blackwall, who also built the *Prince Albert* at the same time. Both ships were launched in March, 1841. The *Prince Rupert* was sold in 1853.

[121] H.B.C. Arch. A.1/65, October 27, 1847, "At a Committee

Present	Sir J. H. Pelly Bart. Govr.	H. H. Berens Esq.
	B. Harrison Esq.	John Halkett Esq.
	R. W. Pelly Esq.	

. . . Chief Trader John Rae was also introduced to the board and received their congratulations on having accomplished the objects of the Arctic Expedition, the result of which the Secy, was directed to communicate to the Lords Commissioners of the Admiralty and to the Royal Geographical Society."

[122] Cf. Introduction, p. 19.

[123] This letter has not been traced in the Company's archives.

[124] E.15/3.

[125] For a biography see *H.B.S.,* VI, 386–7.

[126] A.10/23.

[127] See Appendix A, p. 382.

[128] See Appendix A, p. 383. The Lords Commissioners of the Admiralty applied for John Rae to act as "second officer" in Sir John Richardson's expedition on December 16, 1847. Archibald Barclay's reply dated December 28, 1847, is printed in Parliamentary] P[apers], 1847–48, Vol. XLI, Paper 264, p. 77.

[129] Sir John Richardson (1787–1865), who had been surgeon and naturalist to Franklin's arctic expeditions of 1819–22 and 1825–27. See *Dic. Nat. Biog.*

[130] E.15/5.

[131] These two letters have not been traced in the Company's archives.

[132] Albert Pelly, fourth son of Sir John Henry Pelly (see p. 470, n. 76), was head of the firm of Albert Pelly & Co., merchants, of No. 1 Winchester Buildings, Great Winchester Street, in the City of London. This firm appears to have had considerable dealings with the Hudson's Bay Company, and to have acted as agents for the Russian American Company.

[133] The statement published in *The Times,* London, November 1, 1847, was: "The whole of the land which we had traced during the last seven days was low and flat, and very regular in its outline, there being few or no bays and points. It was named Simpson's Peninsula". In his report of September 21, 1847, to the Company (p. 144), Rae said: "It was called Simpson's Peninsula in honor of the Governor of the Hudson's Bay Company's Territories". Rae dedicated his book about the expedition to Sir George Simpson, and paid him the following tributes: "It was named Simpson's Peninsula after Sir George Simpson, the able and enterprising Governor of the Hudson's Bay Company's territories, who projected and planned the expedition, and to whose zeal in the cause of discovery Arctic travellers have been so often and so much indebted".

[134] John Arrowsmith (1790–1873), geographer, nephew of the elder Aaron Arrowsmith (1750–1823). With his cousins Aaron and Samuel he assisted his uncle from 1810 until he set up in business on his own account in 1823. On the death of Samuel Arrowsmith, John succeeded to the family business. See *Dict. Nat. Biog.*

[135] A reference to Lefroy Bay on the west side of Melville Peninsula.

[136] Dr. J. M. Hamilton who, with his wife, later joined Richard and Thomas Rae in Hamilton, Upper Canada. The *Erebus* and the *Terror* called at Stromness on their way to the Arctic in 1845, and Dr. Hamilton's house was the last one visited there by Sir John Franklin (P.P. 1850, Vol. XXXV, Paper 107, pp. 100, 101, 102).

[137] Sir George Simpson's father-in-law, Geddes McKenzie Simpson. By this time the Simpson family had moved from New Grove House, Bow, to Stamford Hill, Middlesex, where Geddes McKenzie Simpson died on December 27, 1848.

[138] E.15/5. For Richardson's and Rae's route from Liverpool to Fort Confidence see Introduction, pp. 41–2.

[139] This man has not been identified.

[140] Frances Webster Simpson, Simpson's elder daughter, who was fourteen years of age at this time.

[141] Chief Factor Duncan Finlayson was married to Lady Simpson's elder sister Isobel Graham Simpson.

[142] E.15/5.

[143] Albert One-Eye. See p. 172. For a biography see Appendix B, p. 439.

[144] For lists of the sappers, miners and sailors see Appendix B, pp. 411–3, and P.P. 1847–48, Vol. XLI, Paper 264, p. 65.

[145] Chief Trader John Bell. For a biography see *H.B.S.,* III, 427–8. Bell was directed to go to York Factory to meet the sappers and miners and stores expected out by the ships of 1847 and then, if practicable, to proceed to Ile-à-la-Crosse, where the party was to winter.

[146] P.P. 1847–48, Vol. XLI, Paper 264, p. 13, Simpson to Bell, Norway House, June 28, 1847, "Three of the men attached to the expedition will be accompanied by their wives, as the services of females may be useful in washing, making and mending the people's clothes and mocassins, netting snow-shoes, making and repairing nets, and other necessary work; these women, of course, will have to be maintained as a charge on the expedition, to be moderately remunerated for any public services they may render, but to be paid by the people themselves for washing, &c.". Richardson, *Arctic Searching Expedition,* I, 46, notes that there were also two children in the party, besides two children of John Bell.

[147] See Appendix A, pp. 387–90.

[148] E.15/5. *H.B.S.,* I, 37, "Portage la Loche [or Methy Portage] is the height of land that divides the waters which discharge themselves into Hudson's Bay from those that run into the Frozen Ocean, and is considered the N.W. boundary of the Honble. Hudsons Bay Coys. Territories . . .".

[149] Thomas Karahonton (dit Gros Thomas), an Iroquois guide. For the list of the men in the two canoes see Richardson, *Arctic Searching Expedition,* I, 52.

[150] Chief Trader Francis Ermatinger. For a biography, see H[udson's] B[ay Company] S[eries], Vol. II, pp. 212–13. According to Richardson, *Arctic Searching Expedition,* I, 97, the expedition party met "Chief Trader Armitinger" in Serpent Lake on June 22, 1848.

[151] Fort Chipewyan, on Lake Athabaska, was the headquarters of the Athabaska District. For a short account of the early history of this post see *H.B.S.,* I, 414–15. The boats mentioned by Rae were doubtless the four made in "Portsmouth Dock-yard, and by Camper, in Gosport". A fifth boat was provided by the Hudson's Bay Company at York Factory (P.P. 1847–48, Vol. XLI, Paper 264, pp. 12, 59). See also P.P. 1849, Vol. XXXII, Paper 188, p. 9, Simpson to the Governor and Committee, Norway House, June 24, 1848, "The boats made a very unfavourable voyage from York last autumn, getting no further than the end of Lac Bourbon, about half way between Lake Winipeg and Cumberland, where they were set fast by ice; and being badly adapted for river navigation, both as regards stowage of cargo and draft of water, a smaller quantity of goods and provisions was brought up from York than Sir John Richardson counted upon; and, being unable to reach Cumberland, Mr. Bell was compelled to use a considerable quantity of provisions which were intended to have been taken in as cargo to Mackenzie River, for the coast voyage. The Europeans, moreover, who were attached to the expedition, say the sappers and miners and sailors, being inexperienced in such labour, were found exceedingly inefficient." For Richardson's description of the boats see *Arctic Searching Expedition,* I, 40–2.

[152] E.15/5. Cf. Richardson's report dated Fort Confidence, September 16, 1848, in P.P. 1849, Vol. XXXII, Paper 497; P.P. 1850, Vol. XXXV, Paper 107; and Richardson, *Arctic Searching Expedition,* I, 236 et seq.

[153] T. Simpson, *Narrative of the Discoveries . . . ,* pp. 345–6, June 24, 1839, ". . . perceived at some distance three tents of Esquimaux . . . three [Eskimos] in number: an elderly man, named Awallook, who went on crutches from a dislocated joint; a fine young lad, his son; and a very stout man, about six feet high, with brown beard, and a countenance that would have been noble, were it not disfigured by a hideous wen on the temple."

[154] Richardson, *Arctic Searching Expedition . . . ,* I, 336–7, "All the houses erected by Dease and Simpson had been burnt down, except part of the men's dwelling. Mr. Bell reached the site on the

17th of August, and immediately set to work. Since that time he had built an ample storehouse, two houses for the men, and a dwelling house for the officers, consisting of a hall, three sleeping apartments, and store-closet. This building was roofed in when we arrived, but the flooring and ceiling of the rooms were not yet laid, though planks had been sawn for that purpose; the kitchen was still to be built, and tables, chairs, and other articles of furniture, to be made." See also ibid., II, 61–6. For a reproduction of John Rae's sketch of Fort Confidence see p. iv.

[155] See Appendix B, p. 424.

[156] Dease and Simpson left this boat at the Bloody Fall on September 16, 1839 (Simpson, *Narrative* . . . , pp. 389, 390).

[157] See Appendix B, pp. 434, 426.

[158] J. Franklin, *Narrative of a Second Expedition to the Shores of the Polar Sea, in the Years* 1825, 1826 *and* 1827 (London, 1828), pp. 51–2, 53, September, 1825,". . . Mr. [P. W.] Dease [of the Hudson's Bay Company] was determined in the selection of the spot on which our residence was to be erected, by its proximity to that part of the [Great Bear] lake where the fish had usually been most abundant. The place decided upon was the site of an old fort belonging to the North-West Company, which had been abandoned many years . . . We found . . . on our arrival, all the buildings in a habitable state, but wanting many internal arrangements to fit them for a comfortable winter residence . . .". W. H. Hooper described Fort Franklin in 1849 as "a shapeless mass of rubbish . . . a few stones still remaining of some of the chimneys, were all to be seen of his [Franklin's] resting place . . ." (*Ten Months among the Tents of the Tuski* . . . (London, 1853), p. 304).

[159] Despite the haste to dispatch the letters considerable delay occurred. See Richardson, *Arctic Searching Expedition,* II, 67–9, ". . . Our schemes for sending and receiving letters were, however, failures, and productive of much subsequent disappointment.

The packet of Admiralty despatches and private letters sent off on the 18th of September, 1848, on the third morning after our arrival from the coast, was placed in charge of François Chartier and Louis la Ronde, with directions for them to proceed with all speed to Isle à la Crosse, at which place Chartier's wife was residing. . . Chartier and his companion reached Fort Chepewyan by open water, and were despatched to Isle à la Crosse as soon as the ice was strong enough for travelling over. At Isle à la Crosse the letters were put *en route* again after a fortnight's detention, and at Carlton House they were kept two months. This last delay was unaccountable. When they did reach Red River they were sent on; but instead of reaching England in April or May, as we had a right to expect, and when a knowledge of our proceedings was much desired by the Admiralty previous to the sailing of the "North Star", they did not arrive till the middle of July . . .".

[160] This should be June 24, 1849. A copy is in D.4/70, fos. 234–5. It deals with the affairs of Mackenzie River District.

[161] E.15/5.

[162] Neither the original nor a copy of the note of March 2, 1848, has been traced in the Company's archives. The letter of June 12, 1848, together with a letter of the same date addressed by Simpson to Sir John Richardson is in Appendix A, pp. 383–7.

[163] Rae was appointed in charge of the Mackenzie River District to succeed Chief Factor Murdoch McPherson (1796–1863), a Scotsman, who entered the service of the North West Company in 1816. He had been stationed in the Mackenzie River District for about twenty-four years. For a biography see W. S. Wallace (ed.), *Documents Relating to the North West Company* (Toronto, The Champlain Society, 1934), p. 483, and for McPherson's correspondence with James Hargrave see Glazebrook, *The Hargrave Correspondence,* passim.

[164] Richardson, in his preliminary report to the Admiralty, wrote of the journey from Cape Cockburn to Icy Cove: "These laborious operations were conducted by Mr. Rae, to whose sound judgment, experience, and personal exertions we were indebted, under Providence, for the progress we were enabled to make". At the conclusion of his preliminary report he wrote: "I beg that you will be pleased to express to their Lordships the high sense I entertain of Mr. Rae's valuable services during the whole progress of the party, both on the coast and in leading the men overland . . ." (P.P. 1849, Vol. XXXII, Paper 497). Richardson again spoke in the highest terms of Rae in his

final report, but this was written after his return to England in 1849, and cannot be the despatch referred to by Rae (P.P. 1850, Vol. XXXV, Paper 107, pp. 1–7).

[165] The headquarters of the Mackenzie River District. Richardson, *Arctic Searching Expedition,* I, 166–7, "The fort stands on an island at the junction of the River of the Mountains (*Riviere aux Liards*) with the Mackenzie . . .".

[166] Fort Good Hope which was, at that time, the lowest post on Mackenzie River, and was in charge of Adam McBeath. Richardson, *Arctic Searching Expedition,* I, 213–14, July 28, 1848, ". . . Fort Good Hope, which now stands near its earliest site, a short way below the defile. At the time of Sir John Franklin's descent of the river in 1825 and 1826, the post stood about one hundred miles further down; but it was removed to its present position in 1836, after the destruction of the former establishment by an overflow of the river . . . Mr. Bell . . . was resident officer at the time . . .".

[167] *H.B.S.,* III, Minutes of a Council held at York Factory, June, 1826, pp. 168–9, "In order gradually to wean the Indians all over the country from the use of Spirituous Liquors to which they are so much addicted [Resolved] 130. That none of that article, either for Trade, Sales or gratuitous Indulgences to Servants or allowances to Officers be imported into English River, Athabasca or MacKenzie's River Districts for the current Outfit, and that such deficiency be made up by a proportionate increase in the Supplies of ammunition and Tobacco". D.4/70, fos. 234d.–235, Simpson to Rae, Norway House, June 24, 1849, "I Notice your remarks on the subject of the Officers allowances. . . I shall bring the matter under the Notice of Council". B.239/k/2, Minutes of Council, Northern Department, held at Norway House, June 21–26, 1849, fo. 227: "Whereas by the Standing Rules prohibiting the introduction of Wines and Spirits to the country lying north of Cumberland, Officers Stationed in the Districts of McKenzie River, Athabasca and English River are deprived of a portion of their wintering Allowances it is Resolve[d] 19th, That in lieu of the wine to which the above Specified Officers are entitled, tea chocolate and sugar to substituted on the following Scale:

	Tea	*Chocolate*	*Sugar*
Commissioned Officers	12 Libs	12 Libs	1 Keg
Clerk	6 "	6 "	½ "
Postmaster	3 "	3 "	¼ "

and that as the money value of the foregoing allowance does not amount to that of the wine &c as pr. the Scale, the difference be made up by giving permission to Officers in the districts to take from the store goods on public account to the extent of 20/- to a commissioned Officer, 10/- to a Clerk, & 5/- to a Postmaster, to be valued at the district prices".

[168] E.15/5. Richardson, *Arctic Searching Expedition,* II, 69–70, ". . . On the 31st of October, two men and an Indian guide were sent with a second packet of letters to Fort Simpson, hoping that they would be in time for an express which leaves that post annually for the south on the 1st of December. The Indian lost himself, or rather, I believe, went wilfully astray, for the purpose of falling in with some hunters that he expected to find. In this he failed; and the party, after suffering some privations, were saved from starvation by killing a deer. They did not reach Fort Simpson till some time after the winter express had left; and as the letters were not of public importance they remained there until the spring, when they were forwarded along with some others that we subsequently sent to Fort Chepewyan, that they might go down with the first boats. On my way out in the summer, finding part of these letters at one of the posts, I took them on with me; the others reached England by the same mail packet that I crossed the Atlantic in, and were delivered on the day after my arrival at home."

[169] For a reproduction see p. iv.

[170] Bernard Rogan Ross of Londonderry, Ireland, who entered the Company's service as an apprentice clerk in 1843.

[171] Augustus Richard Peers, clerk, who entered the Company's service in 1842. He married Christina, the eldest daughter of Chief Trader John Bell, and died on March 15, 1853, at Peel River post. See *The Beaver,* September, 1939, "Statement of Roderick MacFarlane", pp. 12–15, for the account of the removal of Peers' body from Peel River to Fort Simpson.

[172] Peel River Post, also known as Fort McPherson, was established by John Bell in the summer of 1840 on the east bank of Peel River, about ten miles above the mouth of Rat River. Because "it was yearly inundated", the post was removed some two miles higher up about the summer of 1849.

[173] William Mactavish (see p. 124), now a Chief Trader, had been transferred from York Factory to the charge of the combined districts of Sault Ste. Marie and Lake Huron at Sault Ste. Marie.

[174] A copy of this reply is in D.4/71, fos. 134d.–37. It deals with the business of Mackenzie River District.

[175] E.15/5.

[176] See p. 476, n. 168.

[177] See p. 190–1.

[178] B.239/k/2, Minutes of Council, Northern Department, held at Norway House, June, 1848, fo. 223d., "With a view of saving freight to Portage La Loche it is Resolve[d] 104 That from & after the close of Outfit 1848 no Butter be forwarded to Athabasca or McKenzie River, there being a sufficient stock of Cattle in those Districts to provide the necessary supply of that Article."

[179] As will be seen, Rae abandoned Fort Confidence in September 1849, but re-occupied it in October 1850, and spent the following winter there.

[180] E.15/5.

[181] The five men in the advance party have not been identified, but according to P.P. 1850, Vol. XXXV, Paper 107, p. 5, "all the Europeans of the party . . . remaining at the fort [Confidence], and such of the Canadians as were not to be employed with Mr. Rae on his summer expedition . . ." went to Fort Simpson. Richardson, *Arctic Searching Expedition,* II, 134, stated that "Bruce, Mitchell, Brodie M'Leod and Mastegan" left with himself and Bell on May 7. For their later movements see ibid., II, 135 et seq., and P.P. 1850, Vol. XXXV,Paper 107, p. 5.

[182] James Hope (see p. 174) and Thomas Hope.

[183] For biographies of Dubriel (Louis Lebrule) and the other Expedition servants attached to the Admiralty Expedition during summer 1849, see Appendix B.

[184] Cf. Introduction, pp. 44–7.

[185] Sir James Clark Ross (1800–62), nephew of Sir John Ross. See Introduction, pp. 49–51.

[186] This description seems to suggest a ship on the lines of Fridtjof Nansen's from. F. Nansen, *Farthest North . . .* (New York, 1897), I, 57–73.

[187] E.15/5.

[188] See T. Simpson, *Narrative of the Discoveries on the North Coast of America . . .* 1836–39 (London, 1843), p. 245.

[189] In 1825 Franklin's observations placed this post in latitude 64° 40' 30" N., and longitude 124° 53' 22" W., and it is shown on the left bank of the Mackenzie River on his map of the "Route of the Land Arctic Expedition" (see Franklin, *Second Expedition to the Polar Sea,* p. 18). Thomas Simpson (*Narrative,* p. 397) was at Fort Norman on October 6–7, 1838, and mentioned that Mr. McBeath had been unusually successful with his garden and was able to supply "some tolerable potatoes".

[190] Louis Olivier. See Appendix B, p. 439.

[191] E.15/5. For a copy of Rae's letter of the same date addressed to the Secretary of the Admiralty see Richardson, *Arctic Searching Expedition,* II, 118–30, or P.P. 1851, Vol. XXXIII, Paper 97, pp. 45–50.

[192] See p. 199.

[193] South of the Bloody Fall, Coppermine River. See p. 271.

[194] This remark in Rae's writing is unexplained.

[195] Richardson, *Arctic Searching Expedition,* I, 299, stated that the boats were left eight miles from Cape Kendall, and Rae gave the same distance in his letter to Sir George Simpson dated September 16, 1848 (see p. 172).

[196] Rae expected to find that the boats had been broken up. Cf. Richardson, *Arctic Searching Expedition,* I, 300.

[197] Salmo (Coregonus) Lucidus, the herring salmon. Richardson (*Fauna Boreali-Americana . . . Part Third. The Fish,* p. 207), says he had only found this fish in Great Bear Lake, and calls it "Bear Lake Herring Salmon". But it can also be found in the Coppermine River, especially when going up river to spawn.

[198] The Rev. David T. Jones. He came to the Red River Settlement in 1823 as successor to the Rev. John West, who started the Church Missionary Society's School for Indian boys and girls. See S. Tucker, *The Rainbow in the North . . .* (London, 1851), and *The Missionary Register.*

[199] *Canada, Department of Mines,* No. 92, Geological Series, Memoir 108 (Ottawa, 1919), C. Camsell and W. Malcolm, "The Mackenzie River Basin", pp. 21–2, "Scented Grass hills, on the north shore of the same lake [Great Bear], form the peninsula between Smith bay and the northern indentation of Keith bay known as Richardson bay. They are a round-topped ridge similar to Grizzly Bear mountain in general character and height and terminating to the east in a prominent point known as Gros Cap." Cf. Franklin, *Second Expedition to the Polar Sea,* Appendix I, vi.

[200] E.15/5.

[201] The five men who remained in the Mackenzie River District were: Baptiste Frederique dit Paul, James Hope, Thomas Hope, Neil McLeod (b), and Louis Olivier. Louis Lebrule (Dubrill) and Halcrow Humphrey, who intended to retire to Canada, carried the packet.

[202] E.15/8. This letter appears to be in a clerk's hand, but it was signed by John Rae. Describing Fort Resolution in 1851 Hooper (*Tents of the Tuski . . .* pp. 391, 393), said of it: "This was the neatest and cleanest establishment we had yet seen; much care was evident in every department. The houses were built of well split and squared logs placed edge to edge, and closely fitting, and the buildings were enclosed by pickets of regular height and make . . . We remained eight days at Fort Resolution, and were much indebted to Mr. W. M'Murray for his considerate attention to our comfort, which was, notwithstanding, sadly marred by the unfailing attacks of myriads of mosquitoes . . .".

[203] For the letter of January 21 and reference to that of February 13, see Introduction, pp. 53–8.

[204] Commander W. J. S. Pullen (1813–87). See Introduction, p. 48–9, and *The Beaver,* March and June, 1947, W. J. S. Pullen, "Pullen in Search of Franklin".

[205] Hooper, *Tents of the Tuski,* pp. 338–9, "The boats which we had brought from the 'Plover' were so much damaged that only one, the 'Logan,' (repaired from the other) could be made available, and we were furnished by the company with a large new boat, whose dimensions were in strong contrast to our own diminutive craft; she measured thirty feet on the keel, forty 'over all,' and was nine feet broad. She was christened 'Try Again,' in reference to our new attempt, in preparations for which we were busy enough for several days."

[206] The Fort Simpson account books (B.200/d/97a. and 104) contain transactions involving the following men apparently belonging to Pullen's party:

W. H. Hooper	William McCarthy	Thomas Mellish
John Herd	James Wabby	Robert Sullock
William Salmon	James Tulloch	John Senior
William Seymour	John Robertson	William Craigie

John or Robert Hemmett or Emmett
John Abernethy ("Gunner's Mate; served in the Greenland Fisheries seven years" (P.P. 1850, Vol. XXXV, Paper 107, p. 43)).
Neil McLeod (b) (steersman)
Jerome St. George dit Laporte (middleman)
William Hepburne (middleman)
B.239/I/31, fo. 32, names the last three as Company servants. For biographies see Appendix B. See also P.P. 1851, Vol. XXXIII, Paper 97, pp. 53–4.

[207] Alexander Hunter Murray, who had previously been employed by the American Fur Company. He entered the service of the Hudson's Bay Company as a clerk in 1845. For his illustrated "Journal

of the Yukon 1847–48" edited by L. J. Burpee, see *Publications of the Canadian Archives*—No. 4 (Ottawa, 1910). See also *The Beaver,* June, 1934, M. M. Black, "Alexander Hunter Murray", pp. 29–32, and June, 1947, C. Wilson, "Founding Fort Yukon", pp. 38–43.

[208] See p. 194.

[209] See Appendix B, p. 432.

[210] See Appendix A, p. 391.

[211] E.15/8. This letter appears to be in a clerk's hand, but it was signed by John Rae.

[212] Alexis L'Esperance, "an agile, dexterous man of good Quebec lineage and huge stature", who had had command of the Portage la Loche brigade since 1834 (*The Beaver,* December, 1943, J. P. Turner, "The La Loche Brigade", p. 33). MacLeod, *Letters of Letitia Hargrave,* Letitia Hargrave to Dugald Mactavish, senior, dated York Factory, September 2, 1840, p. 78, ". . . I have seen 2 of the most distinguished voyageurs. They were dressed in sky blue capots scarlet sashes & high scarlet night caps & mocassins—L'Esperance was a Canadian the other a half cast but there was little difference in their colour they have been so much exposed."

[213] See Appendix A, p. 390.

[214] The men engaged in the Red River Settlement for the expedition were, according to B.235/d/121, p. 54:

John Beads	steersman	François Laroque	bowsman
François Deschamps	middleman	Peter Linklater	middleman
Michael Dumas	"	Baptiste Marcellais	steersman etc.
John Fidler	"	Augustin Patnaude	middleman
James Johnstone	"	Baptiste Peltier	"
Charles Kennedy	"	François Savoyard	bowsman
Alexis Laliberté	"	Samuel Sinclair	middleman
dit Lachouette		Laurent Cadotte	guide to Portage la Loche

For a list of the men who actually wintered at Fort Confidence, 1850–51, see Appendix B, p. 413.

[215] B.235/d/121, p. 69, shows that François Deschamps, one of the men, returned to Red River. The other man, François Larocque, remained in the Mackenzie River District as a freeman.

[216] B.200/d/101, p. 152, and B.200/d/105, p. 181, show that Augustin Patnaude was transferred to the Mackenzie River District. George Kirkness (a) was the carpenter who took his place. See p. 224, and Appendix B, p. 428.

[217] According to B.239/1/31, fo. 32, the interpreter was John Hebert dit Fabien, a Mackenzie River servant. See p. 242, and Appendix B, p. 423.

[218] Rae had omitted to mention that another Mackenzie River District servant had been attached to the expedition to make the number up to fourteen. He was Joseph Roy (d), steersman (B.239/1/31, fo. 32). For a biography see Appendix B, p. 446. See also p. 221.

[219] See p. 477, n. 172. Fort Yukon, built in 1847, by Alexander Hunter Murray at the confluence of the Yukon and Porcupine Rivers in what is now Alaska. It was the most westerly fur trading post ever occupied by the Hudson's Bay Company. See p. 478–9, n. 207.

[220] William Lucas Hardisty, clerk, was a son of Chief Trader Richard Hardisty. For a photograph of W. L. Hardisty and a reproduction of Alexander Hunter Murray's sketch of La Pierre's House in 1847 see *The Beaver,* September, 1943, pp. 30–1. See also Burpee, "Journal of the Yukon", p. 28.

[221] Fort des Liards (Fort Liard) on the right bank of Liard River, just below the mouth of Petitot River.

[222] James Peter Pruden, a son of retired Chief Factor John Peter Pruden (see *H.B.S.,* 1, 461).

[223] Fort Halkett was situated on the north bank of the Liard River at its junction with Smith River. See *H.B.S.,* III, 235.

[224] James Green Stewart, clerk, who, in the spring of 1848, accompanied Robert Campbell to the Forks of the "Lewes and Pelly" to establish the post later known as Fort Selkirk. In 1855 Stewart accompanied Chief Trader James Anderson (a) down Back (Great Fish) River to the sea to obtain further evidence of the fate of Sir John Franklin. See Introduction, p. 85.

[225] John O'Brien, clerk, was re-appointed to the charge of Frances Lake and Pelly Banks Posts for outfit 1849–50 but, according to his own statement, he became so ill in body and mind whilst on the way there, and met with so many troubles, that he returned to Fort Simpson without delivering the outfits (see p. 212 and *H.B.S.*, VI, 399). Fort Selkirk was also affected by the non–arrival of supplies and in the spring of 1850 J. G. Stewart, accompanied by one man, made the journey of 1,100 miles to Fort Simpson to get help.

[226] Pierre Chrysologue Pambrun, junior, son of Chief Trader P. C. Pambrun (see *H.B.S.*, IV, 351–2), in charge of the post at Pelly Banks.

[227] Hyacinth Dubois, a Canadian, was entered in the Company's books as a middleman. He joined the service in 1844, when about twenty-two years of age. William Foubister, from St. Ola in the Orkneys, also joined the service in 1844 as a labourer. Hooper, *Tents of the Tuski*, pp. 329–36, gives an account of this sorry occurrence.

[228] See p. 479, n. 224. It was situated "on the very point of confluence" of Lewes and Pelly Rivers (B.200/b/28, p. 102).

[229] This post was established in 1842 on the point between the two arms of Frances Lake, where Robert Campbell's party built a hut in the spring of 1840 during their exploration of the "north branch" [Frances River] of the Liard River to its source. Frances Lake post was abandoned in the summer of 1851.

[230] William McMurray, clerk, in charge of Fort Resolution. He entered the service as an apprentice postmaster in 1838 and attained the rank of Inspecting Chief Factor in 1875.

[231] Made Beaver. For definitions see *H.B.S.*, I, 311*n*., and *H.B.S.*, XIV, xx*n*.

[232] Dunvegan, on the north bank of Peace River, was a provision post, originally established by the North West Company about 1805. D. W. Harmon in 1810 described the local situation as pleasant and referred to "the surrounding plains, over which are scattered buffaloes, moose, red deers, antelopes, black and grey bears, &c." (*Journal of Voyages and Travels in the Interiour of North America* (Andover, 1820), p. 184). See also *H.B.S.*, I, 415.

[233] E.15/8.

[234] Sir George Simpson had been Governor-in-Chief since 1839. Eden Colvile (1819–93), second son of Andrew Colvile, Deputy Governor of the Company, was appointed Governor of Rupert's Land in 1849, and in the absence of Sir George Simpson held all the powers and privileges of Governor-in-Chief.

[235] Baptiste Bruce. See Appendix B, p. 416.

[236] Adam McBeath, a native of Rupert's Land. He retired in 1887 after fifty-eight years' service in the Company.

[237] Robert Campbell who, in 1840, discovered the Pelly River and later explored it to its junction with the Lewes, where he built Fort Selkirk in 1848. See *The Beaver*, June, September and December, 1942, C. Parnell and J. P. Kirk, "Campbell of the Yukon".

[238] Fort Vermilion, on the right bank of Peace River. See *H.B.S.*, I, 425. Leather, i.e., dressed moose and deer skins were scarce on the west side of the Rocky Mountains, consequently New Caledonia, i.e., the region of the Stuart and Upper Fraser Rivers (*H.B.S.*, I, 420–1), had to be supplied from the east side where it was abundant.

[239] Joseph Desjarlais, horsekeeper, Athabaska District.

[240] I.e., to be circulated.

[241] E.15/8.

[242] Neither the original nor a copy of the letter dated April 16 has been traced. For a letter dated June 15, 1850, from Simpson to Rae see Appendix A, p. 390.

[243] Possibly Rae's brother-in-law, Hector Munro.

[244] Jane, Lady Franklin (1792–1875), second wife of Sir John Franklin.

[245] E.15/8. The letter appears to be in a clerk's hand, but it was signed by John Rae.

[246] James Hargrave made the following note in pencil on this letter: "Mr. Christie is to send one *if possible* to YF by the return of the schooner from P [code for Churchill] fall '50—to go in by the winter Express 50/51 J H." It was not possible to get an interpreter from Churchill as that post was without one for its own use.

[247] No copy of this letter has been traced.

[248] E.15/8.

[249] In outfit 1850–51 Jean Baptiste Forcier, a native of Rupert's Land, was listed as a steersman in the Mackenzie River District. He had nine years' service to his credit (B.239/g/30).

[250] Baptiste Marcellais. See Appendix B, p. 435.

[251] See pp. 206–7.

[252] See p. 249, and Hooper, *Tents of the Tuski,* pp. 367–72.

[253] James Clark Ross wintered at Port Leopold on the north coast of Somerset Island with H.M. ships *Enterprise* and *Investigator,* 1848–49. On August 28, 1849, he left there one of his steam launches, a house, and one year's provisions and fuel (P.P. 1850, Vol. XXXV, Paper 107, p. 63). A copy of Ross's report was no doubt included in the papers sent to Pullen with his orders in January, 1850. These orders stated that "copies of every paper that, in the opinion of their Lordships, might be of use to you are herewith enclosed" (ibid., p. 48).

[254] See n. 258 below.

[255] No copy of this letter has been traced.

[256] E.15/8.

[257] The Company's pemmican was packed in bags of 90 lbs. each (see p. 469, n. 67). The pemmican Rae referred to must have been part of the supply of "English Pemican", packed in "tin cases" and belonging to the 1847–49 Admiralty Expedition commanded by Sir John Richardson (B.239/b/99, J. Hargrave to J. Bell, May 20, 1848; Hargrave to Sir J. Richardson, July 12, 1848; and B.154/b/4, D. Ross to Richardson, July 15, 1848). Richardson to Simpson, Fort Alexander, May 29, 1848, "pemican put up in hide soon spoils when exposed to damp, is unfit to be put 'en cache' on the coast in the manner proposed" (D.5/22). See also Richardson, *Arctic Searching Expedition,* I, 37–40.

[258] Simpson, *Narrative . . .*, p. 225, "Ritch was sent in quest of wood for new oars, and for planks to repair the sea-boats; but, after a search resumed several days in different directions, he found only a few pieces fit for the former purpose, none for the latter. I subsequently fell in with some straight tall trees on the south branch of Dease River. The wood around Fort Confidence is stunted, knotty, and twisted into all manner of shapes—the deformed growth of frozen ages. From the eastern side of M'Tavish Bay, a distance of seventy miles, a quantity of dwarf birch was procured, for additional boat-timbers, snow-shoe frames, and axe handles."

[259] Rae's complement was thus reduced to one assistant, ten men from Red River Settlement, and three men from Mackenzie River District.

[260] E.15/8.

[261] E.15/8. For Rae's letter to Sir John Richardson dated October 8–31, 1850, see *The Times,* October 13, 1851.

[262] These notes were evidently those handed by Rae at Fort Simpson to the Marten Lake Chief Tecon-ne-betah in accordance with the orders sent to Rae by Richardson from Lake Winnipeg on August 19, 1849. See Introduction, p. 50.

[263] No copy of this letter has been traced.

[264] E.15/8.

[265] This appears to be a reference to Pelly Bay as delineated on the Admiralty charts. These indicated, by a dotted line, the position of the south part of that Bay, no doubt because Rae had not actually travelled round the coastline although he had seen this from Helen Island (Admiralty Charts, "Arctic America", Sheet II, 1836, with additions to 1847; ibid., with additions to 1849). See also Rae's letter of October 8–31, 1850, to Richardson published in *The Times,* October 13, 1851.

[266] When prophesying Sir George Simpson may have been thinking of his *Journey Round the World* which Barclay prepared for publication for him. See *H.B.S.*, VI, 387.

[267] E.15/8. This letter was signed by Rae, but it appears to be in a clerk's writing.

[268] E.15/8. This letter was signed by Rae, but it appears to be in a clerk's writing. For Rae's letter to Richardson dated April 18–21, 1851, see *The Times,* October 13, 1851.

[269] John Hebert, dit Fabien. See Appendix B, p. 423.

[270] E.15/8.

[271] John Beads and Peter Linklater. See Appendix B, pp. 416, 430.

[272] This sketch has not been found.

[273] Port Leopold. See p. 481, n. 253.

[274] This man has not been definitely identified, but evidence in B.235/d/130, p. 73, suggests that he was probably Michel Dumas.

[275] Camstairy, obstinately perverse, unruly, or wilful (*Oxford English Dictionary*).

[276] See p. 221. B.239/g/30, fo. 33, outfit 1850–51, lists Jean Hebert dit Manuel as a steersman in the Mackenzie River District. He came from Three Rivers, Quebec, was thirty-seven years of age and had served the Company for twenty-one years.

[277] Alexander McKenzie, Post Master, who entered the Company's service in 1846. He married the widow of Augustus Richard Peers (see p. 476, n. 171) at Fort Simpson in 1855.

[278] Chief Trader James Anderson (a), who served the Company from 1839–64. See p. 479, n. 224.

[279] No copies of letters from Pullen to Rae from which the extracts on p. 251 might have been taken have been found in the Company's archives.

[280] William Hulme Hooper (1827–54), mate of the *Plover* under the command of Commander T. E. L. Moore and author of *Ten Months Among the Tents of the Tuski* (London, 1853). He received the news of his conditional promotion to the rank of lieutenant by the Government express which arrived near Great Slave Lake in June, 1850 (see p. 204). He accompanied Pullen on his search for news of Franklin in 1849 and 1850.

[281] Commander Moore, in H.M.S. *Plover,* spent the winter 1848–49 at Emma Harbour, near Cape Chukotski, Bering Strait, and came in contact with many natives, the Tchukchis. These are fully described in Hooper, *Tents of the Tuski.*

[282] T. E. L. Moore to the Secretary of the Admiralty dated Her Majesty's Discovery Ship *Plover,* Choris Peninsula, Kotzebue Sound, September 25, 1849 (P.P. 1850, Vol. XXXV, Paper 107, p. 37).

[283] A reference to James Edward Fitzgerald's *An Examination of the Charter and Proceedings of the Hudson's Bay Company with reference to the Grant of Vancouver's Island* (London, 1849). See also *The British Columbia Historical Quarterly,* XIII, 1–21, Paul Knaplund, "Letters from James Edward Fitzgerald to W. E. Gladstone concerning Vancouver Island and the Hudson's Bay Company, 1848–1850".

[284] The Rev. George Barnley. See p. 116–7.

[285] It is difficult to determine which ship this was. No Franklin relief ship wintered on or near the north coast of Alaska from 1849 to 1850. The probability is that the ship was H.M.S. *Investigator.* She had on board one bullock and twelve sheep when she left Honolulu on July 4, 1850; whether any of these animals were still unslaughtered when Eskimos visited her for the first time on August 8, 1850, near Point Drew, does not seem to have been recorded, but that a few were still on board appears to be possible (A Armstrong, *A Personal Narrative of the Discovery of the North-West Passage* . . . (London, 1857), pp. 61, 62, 97–99).

[286] The boats were presumably Pullen's. He travelled along the coast from Fatigue Point to the Mackenzie River with three boats, one of which was an Eskimo "oomiak" purchased from the natives at Point Barrow. He came into contact with numerous Eskimos during this voyage, August 4–27, 1849 (Hooper, *Tents of the Tuski,* pp. 226, 232–66).

[287] This ship was presumably H.M.S. *Investigator.* She rounded Point Barrow on August 6, 1850, sailed along the north American coastline, and left this at Cape Parry on September 6, when she sailed

north-eastwards towards Banks Land. (S. Osborn (ed.), *The Discovery of the North-west Passage by H.M.S. "Investigator"... from the Logs and Journals of Capt. Le M. M'Clure* (London, 1856), pp. 59–101). She was visited by large numbers of Eskimos. H.M.S. *Enterprise* sailed along the same coast in 1851, but did not reach the north American coastline anywhere to the east of Point Barrow in 1850 (R. Collinson, *Journal of H.M.S. Enterprise, on the expedition in search of Sir John Franklin's ships by Behring Strait* 1850–55 (London, 1889), track-chart opposite p. 61).

288 Rae's *Narrative of an Expedition to the Shores of the Arctic Sea in* 1846 *and* 1847 (London, 1850).

289 Up to this time (April, 1851) Rae's holding of Hudson's Bay Company stock amounted to £160. He first bought £100 stock on May 26, 1849, paying £195 for it. This holding was made up to £110 by the ten per cent increase of capital in 1850. On March 30, 1850, Rae acquired a further £50 stock for which he paid £100. See also p. 486, n. 358.

290 E.15/8. This letter was written and signed by John Rae. The alterations made by Archibald Barclay when editing it for publication have not been shown. It was published in P.P. 1852, Vol. L, Paper [1449]; *The Journal of the Royal Geographical Society of London* (London, 1852), XXII, 73–82, "Journey from Great Bear Lake to Wollaston Land. By Dr. John Rae"; and in *The Times,* November 11, 1851.

291 On this day Rae crossed Dolphin and Union Strait. The first explorer to take a ship through this strait, and also through Dease Strait, was Collinson, who did so in H.M.S. *Enterprise* in 1852 during his voyage to Cambridge Bay from the westward, and again in 1853 during his return voyage. He did not know when he entered Dolphin and Union Strait in September 1852 that the land on the north side of it had been examined by Rae, and was unaware until he found Rae's record on May 8, 1853, that Rae had explored parts of the south and east coasts of Victoria Land in 1851. R. Collinson, *Journal of H.M.S. Enterprise* . . ., pp. 234–40, 267, 268, 291–6.

292 Robert Welbank, elected to the Committee of the Hudson's Bay Company in November, 1848.

293 Sir Francis Thornhill Baring (1796–1866), First Lord of the Admiralty from 1849–52, and created Baron Northbrook in 1866. See *Dict. Nat. Biog.*

294 Sir George Back (1796–1878), admiral and arctic navigator. See *Dict. Nat. Biog.*

295 The chart has not been found

296 E.15/8.

297 E.15/8. This is a copy and appears to have been made in London. It also appears to have been edited by Archibald Barclay for publication in *Journal of the Royal Geographical Society,* Vol. XXII, "Recent Explorations along the South and East Coast of Victoria Land. By Dr. John Rae", pp. 82–96.

298 Collinson who wintered in Cambridge Bay 1852–53, caught large numbers of fish here (Collinson, *Journal of H.M.S. Enterprise*. . . , pp. 240–91).

299 This has not been traced.

300 David Anderson (1814–1904), who was consecrated Bishop in Canterbury Cathedral in 1849 and in the same year went to the newly-established Diocese of Rupert's Land. See W. S. Wallace, *The Dictionary of Canadian Biography* (Toronto, 1945), I, 12; E. H. Oliver, *The Canadian North-West, Its Early Development and Legislative Records* (Ottawa, 1914), I, 65; *and Report from the Select Committee on the Hudson's Bay Company* . . . (London, 1857), pp. 231–47.

301 Possibly after Sir William Parker (1781–1866) Admiral of the Fleet. See *Dic. Nat. Biog.*

302 Charles Sturt (1795–1869), whose *Narrative of an Expedition into Central Australia*, 1844–1846 . . . was published in 1849. See *Dict. Nat. Biog.*

303 William Charles Macready (1793–1873). See *Dict. Nat. Biog.*

304 Presumably Charles John Kean (1811?–1868), actor. See *Dict. Nat. Biog.*

305 Jenny Lind (1820–87), the famous Swedish singer.

306 Zachary Taylor (1784–1850), inaugurated twelfth President of the United States on March 5, 1849.

[307] Victoria Adelaide Mary Louise (1840–1901), Princess Royal of Great Britain, eldest child of Queen Victoria, and later German Empress.

[308] The *Erebus* and *Terror* were beset by probably similar ice for eighteen months before being abandoned in April, 1848. Collinson (*Journal of H.M.S. Enterprise*, p. 268) found this ice so rough when he reached Gateshead Island, on the west side of Victoria Strait, on May 10, 1853, that he considered it impassable, even with lightly loaded sledges. See also F.L. M'Clintock, *The Voyage of the Fox in the Arctic Seas. A Narrative of the Discovery of the Fate of Sir John Franklin and His Companions* (London, 1881), pp. 265, 299–300.

[309] The record so deposited in this cairn was found by Collinson in 1853. See Introduction, p. 61.

[310] It is clear from Rae's brief record of this meeting that he saw no articles of European manufacture in the possession of the natives, and received no hint of ships in the ice on the other side of Victoria Strait. This implies that the difficulty of crossing Victoria Strait had kept the Eskimos of Victoria Land in ignorance of Franklin's fate. The heavy pack ice in the strait alone prevented Rae from crossing the strait (and ascertaining the fate of Franklin) on this occasion.

[311] The name "Victoria Strait" was apparently given by Rae. It appears on his chart in *Journal of the Royal Geographical Society*, XXII (1852), opposite p. 73, but not on previous charts.

[312] See p. 469, n. 67.

[313] Rae, who was writing from memory, seems to have been under the impression that Thomas Simpson had stated that the route was impracticable, except during the floods in spring. Simpson stated: ". . . my repeated winter journeys had entirely satisfied me of the practicability of the route in the spring, and they were the means of ensuring our success". (Simpson, *Narrative* . . . , p. 255).

[314] "(Signed) John Rae" was inserted by Archibald Barclay.

[315] E.15/8.

[316] E.15/8.

[317] E.15/8.

[318] No copy of this letter has been traced.

[319] This was Sir Edward Belcher's Expedition. See Introduction, pp. 69, 76, 77.

[320] Near the eastern end of Lake Athabaska.

[321] Ile-à-la-Crosse was an important stage on the journey to Athabaska. See H.B.S., I, 417. For notes on Carlton House and Green Lake post see ibid., pp. 414 and 416.

[322] On the North Saskatchewan River.

[323] Francis Butcher, clerk, who entered the Company's service in 1832. He was promoted to the rank of Chief Trader on June 1, 1852.

[324] Chief Trader George Deschambeault. For a biography see H.B.S., III, 436.

[325] Arthur Pruden, brother of James Peter Pruden (see p. 479, n. 222).

[326] Chief Trader Alexander Wilson Buchanan, who entered the Company's service in 1839, was stationed at Fort Pelly in charge of the Swan River District.

[327] Chief Trader Henry Fisher who was in charge of the Red River District. For a biography see H.B.S., III, 441.

[328] Chief Trader John Black, who entered the Company's service in 1839. He married Margaret, daughter of Governor Alexander Christie, at the Red River Settlement on July 3, 1845.

[329] The Rev. William Cockran (1798–1865), chaplain at Red River. For biographical notes see MacLeod, *Letters of Letitia Hargrove*, p. 69*n*, and Oliver, *Canadian North-West*, I, 60.

[330] In his evidence given before the Select Committee of 1857, Lt. Col. William Caldwell, who had been Governor of Assiniboia, referred to ". . . one instance in which infanticide was brought before me . . . it was the grandmother who had made away with the child; that is to say, she took out her daughter in the open air, while the snow was on the ground, and she took no care of the progeny after it was brought forth, and the child died, and she was brought up for infanticide, and was found guilty, and she was sentenced to be hung. From the recommendation of the jury,

and from circumstances which were recorded, I commuted the punishment of death to two years' imprisonment" (1857 Parliamentary Report, p. 305).

[331] Captain C. V. Foss, who conducted the second party of Pensioners to Red River, brought an action for defamation of character against Chief Trader Augustus Edward Pelly and his wife. See MacLeod, *Letters of Letitia Hargrave*, pp. 246–7; 255.

[332] Adam Thorn (1802–90), Recorder of Rupert's Land (1838–49). See Wallace, *Dictionary of Canadian Biography*, 11, 661. His name is given in error as "Thorn" in the 1857 Parliamentary Report.

[333] Anne, daughter of Colonel John Maxwell, late of the Fifteenth Regiment of Foot.

[334] Alexander Ramsey (1815–1903) was made Governor of the newly organised territory of Minnesota on June 1, 1849. See *Dictionary of American Biography*.

[335] Count Charles de la Guiche, a Frenchman, who was on a hunting expedition.

[336] No copy of this letter has been traced.

[337] E.15/9.

[338] Sir Edward Belcher (1799–1877). See *Dict. Nat. Biog.* See p. 216, and Introduction, pp. 69, 76, 77.

[339] Four Rivers Bay. Ross left a record on Cape Coulman, the northern entrance point of the bay (Sir Allen Young, *The Two Voyages of the Pandora* in 1875 and 1876 (London, 1879), p. 52).

[340] Searle built four ice-boats for the expedition commanded by Sir Edward Belcher. Their shape was suggested by a model of a flat Norway yawl, lent to Belcher by Captain Hamilton, Secretary to the Admiralty. They were made of very thin wood and canvas "cemented" together but were not all alike, as improvements were introduced while they were under construction. Two were of sixteen feet, two of twenty feet. The last one that was made was used by Belcher himself, and named by him the *Hamilton. The heaviest one weighed* 300 *lbs., and they seem to have proved very satisfactory* (*E. Belcher, The Last of the Arctic Voyages; being a narrative of the Expedition in H.M.S. Assistance under the command of Captain Sir Edward Belcher, C.B., in search of Sir John Franklin, during the Tears* 1852–53–54 (London, 1855), I, pp. 13, 14, 93, 94, and picture opposite p. 119).

[341] E.15/9.

[342] For the "Articles required for Arctic Expedition Summer 1853" see Appendix A, pp. 396–9.

[343] E.15/9.

[344] Fort Alexander (Bas de la Rivière), at the mouth of Winnipeg River.

[345] See Appendix A, p. 399.

[346] E.15/9.

[347] No copy of this letter has been traced.

[348] John Beads, John Folster and John Corrigal.

[349] Chief Trader Augustus Edward Pelly, who entered the Company's service in 1838. His father, William Pelly, was a first cousin of Sir John Henry Pelly. See n. 331 above.

[350] Either Chief Trader Robert Clouston or his brother James Stewart Clouston, clerk.

[351] Presumably a reference to Archibald Macnab, thirteenth Laird (1781?–1860), who was granted a township (named after him) on the Ottawa River, on which he settled a number of his clansmen. He had returned from Canada after an absence of more than twenty years to live on a small estate at Rendall in the Orkneys. See Wallace, *Dictionary of Canadian Biography*, II, 428, and R. Wild, *Macnab The Last Laird* (London, 1938).

[352] E.15/9.

[353] William Kennedy (1814–90), son of Chief Factor Alexander Kennedy of the Hudson's Bay Company and Aggathas (or Mary), an Indian woman. William Kennedy was employed by the Company as a clerk from 1831–45. Accompanied by Lieutenant J.R. Bellot of the French Navy he went out on behalf of Lady Franklin to search Boothia in the *Prince Albert*. See p. 486, n. 362.

[354] Edward ("Bear") Ellice, senior (1781–1880), who was active in bringing about the coalition of the Hudson's Bay and North West Companies in 1821. For a biography see *H.B.S.,* II, 210–11. Mrs. Ellice, his daughter-in-law, was Katherine Jane (died 1864), second daughter of Lieut.-General Robert Balfour, and first wife of Edward Ellice, junior.

[355] Arthur Wellesley, First Duke of Wellington (1769–1852). He died on September 14 and was buried "with unexampled magnificence" at Saint Paul's Cathedral on November 18, 1852. See *Dict. Nat. Biog.*

[356] Frances Hume Hawkins, widow of Geddes McKenzie Simpson, and mother of Lady Frances Simpson and Mrs. Duncan Finlayson. See p. 473, n. 137.

[357] Rae first acquired three £10 shares in the Puget's Sound Agricultural Company (see *H.B.S.,* VI, 15*n.*) in November, 1839. This amount was increased in November, 1850, by 5 shares; in March, July and September, 1851, by 3, 5 and 7 shares respectively, making a total of 23, all purchased at par. Rae sold his holding for £230 in September, 1867.

[358] Rae changed his mind about selling his Hudson's Bay Company stock at this time. Since April, 1851 (see p. 483, n. 289) his holding of £16o had become £168 by a five per cent increase of capital made in January, 1852. A further increase of capital in July, 1853, added £13 16*s.* 4*d.* to Rae's holding, making a total of £181 16*s.* 4*d.* He sold this amount on May 23, 1855.

[359] See Appendix A, p. 400.

[360] E.15/9.

[361] E.15/9.

[362] A reference to W. Kennedy, *A Short Narrative of the Second Voyage of the Prince Albert, in search of Sir John Franklin . . .* (London, 1853). Kennedy did not mention the Hudson's Bay Company in his book.

[363] Andrew Colvile succeeded Sir John Henry Pelly (died August 15, 1852) as Governor of the Company.

[364] Chief Factor John Lee Lewes, who was then on furlough prior to his retirement. See *H.B.S.,* I, 446–7, and MacLeod, *Letters of Letitia Hargrove,* pp. 138, 181.

[365] A reference to James Dunning, a Chipewyan halfbreed, who had spent nearly forty years in the Company's service. He acted as interpreter and harpooner at Churchill.

[366] E.15/9.

[367] See Appendix A, p. 401.

[368] See p. 468, n. 41.

[369] A brother of William Mactavish and Mrs. Letitia Hargrave. For a biography see *H.B.S.,* VI, 397–8.

[370] I.e., Edinburgh.

[371] Presumably Professor (later Sir) James Young Simpson, M.D., F.R.C.P. Edinb. (1811–70), an early advocate of the anaesthetic properties of chloroform; Professor of Midwifery and Diseases of Women and Children, Edinburgh University.

[372] No copy of this letter has been traced.

[373] E.15/9.

[374] E.15/9.

[375] E.15/9.

[376] Henry Grinnell (1799–1874), American shipping magnate. He was extremely interested in Arctic exploration, and gave financial help to several Arctic expeditions. He provided the ships for the United States Search Expedition carried out in 1850–51 by Lieut. E. J. de Haven under orders from the Secretary of the United States Navy.

[377] E.15/9.

[378] I.e., Mrs. Ballenden.

[379] Lady Simpson died in March, 1853.

[380] E.15/9.

[381] Rae's letter was published in the London *Times,* November 27, 1852.

[382] Presumably Andrew Lockhart, clerk at the Lachine Depot (B.134/g/28).

[383] June 17, 1853. See Appendix A, p. 402.

[384] E.15/9.

[385] The voyageur word for outfits. It was also applied to the equipment of canoes. *The Beaver,* September, 1941, H.M.S. Cotter, "A Fur Trade Glossary", "Agrets—The travelling equipment of a York Boat; i.e., cooking utensils, portage straps, tarpaulins, tents, tools, etc.".

[386] E.15/9.

[387] Portage du Chien is number seventeen in the list of "Portages and Decharges from Fort William to the Bas de la Rivière" in *Transactions of the] R[oyal] S[ociety of] C[anada],* 1900, "Diary of Nicholas Garry . . . 1821", Appendix B, p. 183. Garry reached Dog Portage (leading to Dog Lake) on his second day westward from Fort William and recorded: ". . . Portage de Chien—fine Waterfall. This Portage is over a very high Mountain on the Top of which is a most wild romantic View. The whole Country is undulating, covered with low Pines, Hill rising above Hill, in the Middle a narrow winding Stream with a strong Current, beautifully contrasted with the dark Shades of the Pine. Great Quantity of Strawberries. This Portage is two miles" (p. 119).

[388] Rae's salary ceased when, as from June, 1847, he was appointed a Chief Trader under the Deed Poll of 1834. Thereafter he was entitled to a share of the profits (amounting to one eighty-fifth) of the forty shares allocated by the Governor and Committee to a limited number of Chief Factors and Chief Traders. When he was promoted to the rank of Chief Factor as from June 1, 1850, Rae's share was doubled. Under article 23 of the Deed Poll a Chief Factor, entitled to two eighty-fifth shares, was permitted to retire after having held his commission four years. On retirement he was allowed to hold his shares for one year, and half of his shares for the next succeeding six years.

[389] E.15/9.

[390] See Appendix B, p. 413–4.

[391] George Setter (1782?–1862), an Orkneyman, entered the Company's service as a labourer in 1805. In 1832 Governor Simpson described him as "one of the most active attached and faithful servants" who, "by his great address, indefatigable labours & exertions and determined hostility to the North West Company in the Days of opposition, distinguished himself in an eminent degree . . ." (A.34/2, fo. 55d.). He retired on June 1, 1853.

[392] E.15/9.

[393] E.15/9. This letter travelled from York Factory to Lachine by the route indicated by the following Post Office markings:

"U'States 6 c.
Saint Paul Min Ter. Sep 24
Montreal L C Oc 3 1853
Lachine C E Oc 4 1853"

[394] See Appendix A, p. 405.

[395] E. 15/9.

[396] Augusta d'Este (born 1841), the second daughter of Sir George and Lady Simpson. Their third daughter, Margaret McKenzie, was called "Baby" (MacLeod, *Letters of Letitia Hargrave,* p. 255). Mrs. G. Haddon, great-grand-daughter of Sir George and Lady Simpson, has heard from other members of her family that Sir George's son, John Henry Pelly Simpson (born 1850), was nicknamed "Moses" as a child.

[397] William Anderson, who entered the Company's service as a labourer in 1833.

[398] E.15/9.

[399] Munro, another Eskimo, had joined the expedition at Churchill. See Appendix B, pp. 414, 438.

[400] E.15/9.

[401] E.15/9.

[402] For biographies see Appendix B.

[403] Henry Fidler, Murdoch McDonald (or McDonnell), and John George McDougald were from Red River. Louis St. Michel was the Canadian from Norway House.

[404] E.15/9.

[405] I.e., Quoich River. See p. 332.

[406] For biographies see Appendix B.

[407] This is an error for Murdoch McLennan (or McLellan). See Appendix B, p. 434.

[408] E. 15/9.

[409] E.15/9. This letter is in a clerk's writing, but it was signed by John Rae. Although dated September 1, it was not completed until later. It was read at the Committee meeting held on November 13, 1854 (A.1/69, p. 165), and was passed to the Admiralty on December 1. See Introduction, p. 82. This letter was printed in P.P. 1855, Vol. XXXV, Paper [1898], pp. 835–44, and it was also published in *Journal of the Royal Geographical Society,* XXV, 246–56. It was also published, with a few verbal changes, in *Household Words* (ed. Charles Dickens), London, February 3, 1855.

[410] Rae also wrote to the Secretary of the Admiralty from Repulse Bay, July 29, 1854, outlining the information obtained. (See P.P. 1855, Vol. XXXV, Paper [1898], pp. 831–2, and the London *Times,* October 23, 1854.) He also wrote to Simpson on August [should be September] 4, 1854. This letter was printed in the *Montreal Herald* for October 21, 1854 (A.12/7, fo. 259), but is not in the Company's archives. Cf. Introduction, p. 78.

[411] John Barrow, editor of *The Geography of Hudson's Bay: being the Remarks of Captain W. Coats, in many voyages to that Locality, between the years* 1727 *and* 1751 (London, The Hakluyt Society, 1852), was a son of Sir John Barrow (1764–1848) Second Secretary of the Admiralty.

[412] Rae discovered later that the favourite hunting grounds of the Eskimos lay to the westward, and that caches of provisions had been made there. He believed that for these reasons the natives wished to deter him from going in that direction (D. M. Smith, *Arctic Expeditions from British and foreign shores from the earliest to the Expedition of* 1875–76 (Edinburgh, 1877), p. 641*n*). It deserves mention, however, that C. F. Hall was told that the natives had acted in good faith; they had tried to persuade Rae to go to Prince of Wales Island, discovered but not visited by Rae in 1847, in Committee Bay, near the west coast of Melville Peninsula. The Eskimos believed that the spars, rigging, and possibly the hulk of a ship, to be found on this island, were the things which Rae was seeking (J. E. Nourse, *Narrative of the Second Arctic Expedition made by C. F. Hall* (U.S.A., *Senate Documents,* 45th Congress, 3rd Session, Vol. 3, Washington, 1879), p. 114). When Rae later on became acquainted with this statement, he said that it was baseless, and that the Eskimos had said nothing about wreckage (letter from Rae, *The New York Herald* (New York, July 4, 1880)).

[413] This meeting was probably the one that seems to have taken place on the east side of Washington Bay close to Cape Herschel. Hall and Schwatka were told much the same story (Nourse, *Second Arctic Expedition made by C. F. Hall,* pp. 405–16; W. H. Gilder, *Schwatka's Search, sledging in the Arctic in quest of the Franklin Records . . .* (London, 1882), pp. 89–92, and map, p. 16). More than one meeting may, however, have taken place.

[414] The place where thirty dead men and a boat were found by the Eskimos seems to have been at the south end of the bay lying to the west of Point Richardson, on the American continent. Schwatka named it "Starvation Cove", and numerous traces have been found there at different times (Nourse, *Second Arctic Expedition of C. F. Hall,* pp. 398, 407, 416, 607, 608; Gilder, *Schwatka's Search,* pp. 164, 202, 210, 288; K. Rasmussen, *Across Arctic America. Narrative of the Fifth Thule Expedition* (London, 1933), pp. 240, 241; *Arctic* (Ottawa, 1948), I, 122, 123, L. A. Learmonth, "Notes on Franklin relics"; *The Geographical Journal,* June, 1951, R. J. Cyriax, "Recently discovered traces of the Franklin expedition".

[415] The island on which five dead men were found was probably, but not necessarily, one of the Todd Islands, near the south coast of King William Island (Nourse, *Second Arctic Expedition made by C. F. Hall,* pp. 398, 416, 417, 606, 607, 608; *The Geographical Journal* (London, 1932),

Vol. 79, pp. 402–08, W. Gibson, "Some Further Traces of the Franklin Retreat"). See also *The Beaver,* June, 1937, W. Gibson,"Sir John Franklin's Last Voyage", pp. 44–75.

[416] Presumably Aberdeen Island, seen but not visited by Dease and Simpson (Simpson, *Narrative . . . ,* map).

[417] Cf. Introduction, pp. 20, 75.

[418] Sir Roderick Impey Murchison (1792–1871), geologist. See *Dict. Nat. Biog.*

[419] John Shepherd was elected to the Committee of the Hudson's Bay Company in 1850 and became Deputy Governor in 1852.

[420] Henry Bence Jones (1814–73), physician and chemist. See *Dict. Nat. Biog.*

[421] M'Clintock found that this was a flat-topped hill on the eastern extremity of King William Island; he named it Mount Matheson (M'Clintock, *Voyage of the Fox,* 5th edition, p. 229).

[422] Alexander Matheson (created a baronet in 1882) served on the Committee of the Hudson's Bay Company from 1852–62. He had been a partner in Jardine, Matheson & Co. of Hongkong from 1835–52, and was a partner in Matheson & Co. of No. 3, Lombard Street, founded in 1848.

[423] Sir Robert Harry Inglis (1786–1855), politician. See *Dict. Nat. Biog.*

[424] The initials "F.R.M.C." are those of Captain Francis Rawdon Moira Crozier (H.M.S. *Terror*). Rae's list of relics (p. 351–3) and his sketches show that he recovered only one spoon—a tablespoon—of this kind, and that this spoon bore not only Crozier's crest but also the initials "F.R.M.C." (picture of the crest, etc., in *The Illustrated London News,* London, October 28, 1854, Supplement). One tablespoon bearing this crest and initials is preserved in the National Maritime Museum; the initials are very clearly and neatly cut on the handle of the spoon near the bowl, not immediately under the crest, as Rae's sketch suggests. They present the appearance of having been the work of a trained silversmith. It is difficult to reconcile such a spoon with the description given by Rae in his letter.

[425] A reference to the five ships commanded by Sir Edward Belcher which had sailed from the Thames on April 21, 1852. Two were to proceed to the upper part of Wellington Channel, two to Melville Island, and one was to remain as a depot ship at Beechey Island (Belcher, *Last of the Arctic Voyages,* I, 1–6). This was evidently the expedition which Rae had in mind (Smith, *Arctic Expeditions,* pp. 651, 652, statement by Rae).

[426] The enclosure is in Rae's writing. Cf. Introduction, p. 79–80. This list, as already mentioned, is not quite complete. The crests, referred to by numbers, were those of the following officers: (1) Robert Orme Sargent, Mate, H.M.S. *Erebus;* (2) Lieutenant Henry Thomas Dundas Le Vesconte, H.M.S. *Erebus;* (3) Captain Francis Rawdon Moira Crozier, H.M.S. *Terror;* (4) Lieutenant James Walter Fairholme, H.M.S. *Erebus;* (5) Captain Sir John Franklin.

[427] E.15/9. This letter is printed in P.P. 1855, Vol. XXXV, Paper [1898], pp. 833–4. Barclay was ill and W. G. Smith was acting Secretary. See *H.B.S.,* VI. 387.

[428] The barque *Prince of Wales* was the second ship of that name owned by the Company. She was 524 tons burden and was built by Messrs. M. & D. L. Wigram. She was built and launched at Southampton in March, 1850, and continued in the Company's service until 1885. She was sold in 1886 to Messrs. Nelson Bros. Ltd.

[429] An error for K. C. H. Sir John Franklin received the Hanoverian Guelphic Order in 1836. The Royal Guelphic Order, instituted in 1815 by the Prince Regent (afterwards King George IV), was more British than Hanoverian. It has not been conferred since the death of King William IV in 1837.

[430] E.15/9.

[431] Captain Richard Collinson (1811–83) in the *Enterprise* commanded the 1850–55 Admiralty expedition in search of Franklin. See *Dict. Nat. Biog.;* P.P. 1855, Vol. XXXV, Paper [1898], pp. 943–52; and Collinson, *Journal of H.M.S. Enterprise.*

[432] See Introduction, p. 83–4.

[433] E.15/9.

[434] E.15/9.

[435] I.e., officers and men of the Admiralty relief expeditions.

[436] E.15/9.

[437] See Appendix A, pp. 408–9.

[438] E.15/9.

[439] There is a copy of this letter in A.5/19, pp. 139–40. The letter from the Admiralty dated March 23, 1855, stated that a further report from Captain Collinson was awaited.

[440] See Introduction, pp. 85–7.

[441] William Gregory Smith succeeded Archibald Barclay as Secretary to the Company in London in 1855.

APPENDIX A

[1] D. 4/64, fo. 99–99d. 301

[2] D. 4/65, fos. 63d.–65.

[3] D. 4/66, fos. 69d.–71.

[4] E. 15/3.

[5] K was the code letter used for the Lac la Pluie District.

[6] P was the code letter used for Churchill.

[7] D. 4/67, fos. 115–116.

[8] D. 4/67, fos. 250–1.

[9] E. 15/3. This letter is also printed in Rae's *Narrative,* pp. 14–17.

[10] D. 4/68, fos. 329d.–331.

[11] A. 6/27, fo. 117d.

[12] Ibid.

[13] D. 4/69. p. 745.

[14] D. 4/69, pp. 741–3.

[15] The report was untrue. For a list of Richardson's men see Appendix B, pp. 411–3. C.1/958, Log of the Prince Rupert, fo. 3, lists all Richardson's men (except the invalids McLaren and Graham) as passengers returning to England in the autumn of 1849.

[16] D. 4/70, fos. 100d.–102.

[17] D. 4/71, fo. 120–120d.

[18] D. 4/71, fos. 252–55.

[19] E. 15/9.

[20] D. 4/73, fos. 153d.–154.

[21] D 4/73. fo. 195–195d.

[22] D. 4/73, fos. 285d.–287.

[23] D. 4/74, pp. 66–7.

[24] D. 4/74. pp. 386–7.

[25] D. 4/83, fo. 146.

[26] A. 5/19, pp. 119–121.

APPENDIX B

[1] B. 239/1/17, fo. 29.

[2] See p. 116–7, and Rae, *Narrative,* pp. 6, 19.

3 P.P. 1847–48, Vol. XLI, Paper 264, p. 65.

4 "The Invalids McLaren [sic] & Graham, who were sent home last Autumn paid in ready money for such supplies as they received at this place during Summer . . ." (B. 239/b/100, p. 3, James Hargrave to Sir J. Richardson, York Factory, November 15, 1848).

5 P.P. 1847–48, Vol. XLI, Paper 264, p. 69, Sir J. Richardson to W. A. B. Hamilton, Haslar Hospital, June 2, 1847, "I was aware of the bad character of Henry Ralph, the Sapper and Miner; but having ascertained that his crime was repeated drunkenness, and that he was otherwise an obedient, hard-working man, I yielded to his request to be allowed an opportunity to reform, by employing him where no drink was to be had. The only hazard is his committing some excess before the ship leaves England, and he is physically well qualified for severe labour". Ralph went with the expedition (*Arctic Searching Expedition,* I, 338).

6 A further column headed "Remarks" records Mackie and Mitchell as being lance corporals.

7 P.P. 1847–48, Vol. XLI, Paper 264, p. 65.

8 This list includes all the men listed in the Northern Department District Statements for outfits 1847–48, 1848–49, and 1849–50 as being attached to the Admiralty Arctic Expedition (B. 239/1/18, 19 and 20). Each man's biography in Appendix B, gives the actual outfits during which he was employed on expedition work.

9 Compiled from B. 235/d/121, p. 54, and B. 239/1/21, fo. 32.

10 B. 239/1/24, fo. 29.

ABOUT JOHN RAE

JOHN RAE was a Scottish doctor and explorer born September 30, 1813, in Orkney. As a child, he enjoyed sailing, climbing, hunting, and fishing—skills that would serve him well in his future exploits. In 1833, shortly after graduating from medical school, Rae was appointed surgeon of the *Prince of Wales*, a Hudson's Bay Company ship bound for Moose Factory, Ontario, where he remained for the next ten years.

Rae had great respect for the peoples native to northern Canada and adopted many of their survival skills. He learned to hunt caribou, store meat, construct shelter, and walk using snowshoes. He was particularly known for this last skill, once walking 1,200 miles (1,900 km) in snowshoes through winter forest in order to learn how to survey.

Rae embarked on his first expedition in 1846. Over the next decade, he explored much of northern Canada's coastline and, in fact, discovered the final link in the Northwest Passage. However, his achievements have gone largely unrecognized due to the discovery he made in 1854 regarding the fate of the Franklin expedition and the subsequent criticism he received upon his return to England.

John Rae retired from the Hudson's Bay Company in 1856 but retained his love of exploration. In 1860, he was hired to explore Iceland and Greenland in an effort to establish a telegraph line to America. And in 1884, at the age of seventy-one, he was hired by the HBC to survey another telegraph route, in the west of Canada, from Red River to Victoria.

John Rae died in London on July 22, 1893. He was the only major explorer of his time not to receive a knighthood.

ABOUT KEN McGOOGAN

The award-winning author of eleven books, KEN McGOOGAN is best known for *Fatal Passage: The Untold Story of John Rae, the Arctic Adventurer Who Discovered the Fate of Franklin*. That work won the Drainie-Taylor Biography Prize, the CAA History Award, and an American Christopher Award for "a work of artistic excellence that affirms the highest values of the human spirit." With his related book, *Lady Franklin's Revenge*, Ken added the UBC Medal for Canadian Biography and the Pierre Berton Award for History. With degrees in journalism and creative writing, Ken worked for two decades as a journalist before turning mainly to books. His most recent works are the best-selling *How the Scots Invented Canada* and *50 Canadians Who Changed the World*. Please visit kenmcgoogan.blogspot.ca.